TEACHER'S EDITION

General Mathematics

SKILLS

PROBLEM SOLVING

APPLICATIONS

William J. Gerardi　　**Wilmer L. Jones**　　**Thomas R. Foster**

 HBJ　Harcourt Brace Jovanovich, Publishers

New York　Chicago　San Francisco　Atlanta　Dallas　*and*　London

We do not include a Teacher's Edition automatically with each shipment of a classroom set of textbooks. We prefer to send a Teacher's Edition only when it is requested by the teacher or administrator concerned or by one of our representatives. A Teacher's Edition can easily be mislaid when it arrives as part of a shipment delivered to a school stockroom and since it contains answer materials, we want to be sure that it is sent directly to the person who will use it or to someone concerned with the use or selection of textbooks.

If your class assignment changes and you no longer are using or examining this Teacher's Edition, you may wish to pass it on to a teacher who has use for it.

A "Teacher's Resource Book" is available for "General Mathematics: Skills/Problem Solving/Applications." For information, please call your sales representative.

CONTENTS

INTRODUCTION	M-1
THE CHAPTER OPENER/SKILLS LESSONS	M-2
PROBLEM SOLVING AND APPLICATIONS LESSONS	M-3
REVIEW AND TESTING	M-4
OPTIONAL FEATURES	M-6
TEACHER'S RESOURCE BOOK	M-7
TEACHER'S RESOURCE BOOK	M-8
LESSON PLAN GUIDE	M-8
TEACHING SUGGESTIONS	M-9
ANNOTATED STUDENT TEXTBOOK	Following M-46

Printed in the United States of America
ISBN 0-15-353601-2

INTRODUCTION

Overview

This textbook consists of twenty chapters. These chapters, as shown in the Table of Contents, are grouped into six units. Since the program is designed to meet the wide range of abilities and interests usually found in a class of general mathematics students, the content is structured around three levels of ability (see page M-9).

Level 1: Chapters 1-13   Level 2: Chapters 1-16   Level 3: Chapters 1-20

In addition to the three ability levels, each chapter also contains optional content with respect to these levels. The optional content is indicated in each of the *Suggested Timetable of Assignments* charts (see page M-9).

Most chapters of this text contain the following components:

1. Review of Related Skills for the chapter
2. Skills lessons
*3. Problem Solving and Applications lessons
4. Careers
5. Calculator Exercises
6. Chapter Review
7. Chapter Tests
8. Additional Practice

Philosophy

In the title of this text, the words "Skills/Problem Solving/Applications" focus on the three aspects of mathematical literacy which are essential tools in coping with real-life situations. Each Problem Solving and Applications lesson immediately applies the skill(s) that was taught in the preceding skills lesson. It is intended that this *integration* of the problem solving and applications topics with skills lessons will help not only to illustrate the need for achieving proficiency with computational skills but also to improve competency with these skills. Each Problem Solving and Applications lesson focuses on a technique for solving word problems. The Exercises for these lessons, are, in general, of two types: (a) those that apply the given problem-solving technique in a non-verbal setting, and (b) word problems.

The Career lessons focus on those career areas that present realistic career goals for general mathematics students. Each Career applies the skills taught in the chapter to real-life problems related to the given career.

Description

Pages M-2 through M-7 describe the structure of the program both verbally and pictorially.

*Chapters 4, 15, 17, and 19 do not contain separate "Problem Solving and Applications" lessons. In these chapters, the applications are an integral part of each skills lesson.

The Chapter Opener

Each chapter opens with a **Review of Related Skills.** These exercises review prior-taught skills that will be used in the chapter. Each set of exercises is referenced to those pages in the text where the skill was presented.

Skills Lessons

Each skills lesson follows this structure.

Procedure
This outlines the steps.

Examples
These illustrate the Procedures.

REVIEW OF RELATED SKILLS FOR CHAPTER 6

Multiply. (Pages 32–33, 36–37)

| 1. 27 ×31 | 2. 46 ×59 | 3. 802 × 21 | 4. 405 × 57 | 5. 753 ×402 | 6. 889 ×508 |

Divide. (Pages 50–51, 54–55)

7. 7⟌238 8. 6⟌156 9. 57⟌3876 10. 29⟌1073 11. 151⟌52548
12. 437⟌99636 13. 23⟌1518 14. 56⟌4984 15. 9⟌4716 16. 8⟌5928

Multiply each number by 10. (Pages 102–103)

17. 0.3 18. 0.9 19. 2.19 20. 6.21 21. 0.013 22. 0.286
23. 3.1 24. 8.7 25. 0.017 26. 0.574 27. 4.89 28. 6.38

Multiply each number by 100. (Pages 102–103)

29. 0.34 30. 7.72 31. 3.76 32. 0.489 33. 4.3 34. 0.8

EXERCISES

Divide. Check your answers. (Example 1)

1. 6⟌20.88 2. 3⟌7.23 3. 5⟌3.580 4. 7⟌43.96 5. 26⟌35.88
6. 17⟌59.67 7. 31⟌25.637 8. 93⟌191.58 9. 42⟌49.56 10. 86⟌474.72
11. 49⟌165.13 12. 23⟌8.28 13. 44⟌40.656 14. 82⟌33.62 15. 986⟌5324.4
16. 705⟌380.70 17. 677⟌798.86 18. 215⟌451.5 19. 624⟌4804.8 20. 885⟌5221.5
21. 411⟌2301.6 22. 191⟌349.53 23. 182⟌43.68 24. 348⟌87.348 25. 306⟌96.696

(Example 2)

26. 8⟌0.4544 27. 6⟌0.5886 28. 4⟌0.232 29. 9⟌0.585 30. 65⟌3.185
31. 43⟌2.236 32. 37⟌3.182 33. 21⟌0.462 34. 83⟌4.98 35. 66⟌2.442
36. 98⟌5.88 37. 73⟌3.869 38. 414⟌33.948 39. 824⟌32.96 40. 260⟌15.60
41. 604⟌8.456 42. 188⟌9.212 43. 428⟌14.124 44. 369⟌13.284 45. 524⟌18.864
46. 125⟌3.75 47. 321⟌24.075 48. 643⟌55.298 49. 701⟌54.131 50. 816⟌26.928

Mixed Practice

51. 6⟌17.04 52. 4⟌22.12 53. 36⟌1.7712 54. 56⟌42448 55. 461⟌299.65
56. 832⟌807.84 57. 305⟌14.945 58. 293⟌22.854 59. 65⟌35.035 60. 47⟌4.2488
61. 3⟌0.0585 62. 8⟌0.4168 63. 7⟌27.307 64. 9⟌55.896 65. 684⟌124.488
66. 63⟌154.35 67. 12⟌75.84 68. 245⟌759.5 69. 29⟌42.63 70. 52⟌29.12
71. 9⟌18.765 72. 35⟌71.75 73. 78⟌1.092 74. 316⟌25.28 75. 172⟌517.72

APPLICATIONS: Using Division

76. Five pounds of ground nutmeg cost $63.45. Find the cost of one pound?

77. Twenty kilograms of dill cost $185.80. Find the cost of one kilogram.

78. 17 ounces of paprika cost $1.87. Find the cost of 45 ounces.

79. Eight ounces of caraway seeds cost $10.32. Find the cost of 12 ounces.

80. 225 grams of sage cost $4.50. Find the cost of 375 grams.

81. Three ounces of onion salt cost $1.89. Find the cost of 16 ounces.

82. Twenty-five kilograms of vanilla beans cost $214.25. Find the cost of 450 kilograms.

DECIMALS: DIVISION 111

6-1 Dividing a Decimal by a Whole Number

To divide a decimal by a whole number, follow this procedure.

PROCEDURE To divide a decimal by a whole number (not zero):

1 Place the decimal point in the quotient directly above the decimal point in the dividend.

2 Divide as with whole numbers.

EXAMPLE 1 Divide 133.11 by 87. Check your answer.

Solution:
1 Place the decimal point in the quotient. 87⟌133.11
2 Divide as with whole numbers.

```
        1.53   Answer
87⟌133.11                         Check:     1.53
    87                                      ×  87
   461                                       1071
   435                                       1224
   261                         These should     133.11
   261                          be the same.
```

Sometimes you have to write zeros in the quotient.

EXAMPLE 2 Divide 3.298 by 194.

Solution:
1   194⟌3.298   Since 3 is not divisible by 194, write a 0 above the 3.
       0.
    194⟌3.298   Since 32 is not divisible by 194, write a 0 above the 2.
       0.0

2   194⟌3.298   Answer
      0.017
      194
      1358
      1358   The check is left for you.

REVIEW OF RELATED SKILLS

Multiply. (Pages 32–33, 36–37)

1. 42 × 13 2. 391 × 26 3. 208 × 76 4. 279 × 506 5. 404 × 168

Divide. (Pages 50–51, 54–55)

6. 7⟌91 7. 8⟌824 8. 89⟌417 9. 123⟌5658 10. 584⟌62488

110 CHAPTER 6

The **Review of Related Skills** for each skills lesson reviews prior-taught skills that are used in the lesson.

The reference is to the page where the skill was taught.

Each set of **Exercises** is referenced to the related **Example,** or steps in an **Example,** or to a **Table.**

The **Mixed Practice** exercises related to *all* the **Examples** in the lesson.

Some **Exercises** also contain **Applications.**

Problem Solving and Applications Lessons

These lessons are one-page or two-page lessons. Each immediately applies the skill(s) that was taught in the preceding lesson(s).

Each focuses on a technique for solving word problems, such as the **Hidden Question** for solving two-step word problems.

Problem Solving and Applications

Cost of Electricity

The amount of electricity used in a home is measured in kilowatt–hours. You use **one kilowatt–hour** of electricity when you use one kilowatt (1000 watts) for one hour. The tables below show the average number of kilowatt–hours used per week by each of twelve household appliances.

Appliance	Kilowatt-Hours Per Week
Air Conditioner	27
Clothes Dryer	19
Dehumidifier	7
Dishwasher	7
Microwave Oven	4
Range (self-cleaning oven)	14

Appliance	Kilo... P...
Radio	
Refrigerator–freezer (frostless)	
Television (color)	
Vacuum Cleaner	
Washing Machine	
Water Heater	

To find the cost of electricity per year for an appliance, you must first answer the question:

"How many kilowatt–hours per year are used?"

This is the hidden question in the problem. Then you can find the cost per year.

EXAMPLE Find the cost of electricity per year (52 weeks) for a radio. Suppose that electricity costs 10¢ per kilowatt–hour.

Solution: 1 Find the number of kilowatt–hours used per year. Number of kilowatt–hours used per week: 3 ◄ From table

$3 \times 52 = 156$ ◄ Kilowatt-Hours Per Week × 52 = Kilowatt-Hours Per Year

2 Find the cost per year.
$156 \times 10¢ = 1560¢$, or $15.60 ◄ Kilowatt-Hours Per Year × 10¢ =

The cost of electricity per year for the radio is **$15.60**.

34 CHAPTER 2

In general the exercises are of two types:
Those that apply the given technique in a non-verbal setting.
Those that apply the given technique to word problems.

Problem Solving and Applications

Sales Tax

Some salespersons use a table to find the amount of sales tax on a purchase. Part of a table showing amounts for a 5% sales tax is shown at the right.

EXAMPLE Find the sales tax and the total cost for a purchase of $19.50.

Solution: 1 Look at the "Amount of Sale" column in the tax table. Find the interval that includes $19.50.
Interval: **19.47 – 19.67**

2 Look in the "Tax" column directly to the right. Read the amount.
Sales Tax: **$0.98**

3 Find the total cost.
Total Cost: $19.50
+ 0.98
$20.48

Amount of Sale Interval	Tax	Amount of Sale Interval	Tax
0.01- 0.10	0.00	10.68-10.88	0.54
0.11- 0.25	0.01	10.89-11.10	0.55
0.26- 0.46	0.02	11.11-11.25	0.56
0.47- 0.67	0.03	11.26-11.46	0.57
0.68- 0.88	0.04	11.47-11.67	0.58
0.89- 1.10	0.05	11.68-11.88	0.59
1.11- 1.25	0.06	11.89-12.10	0.60
1.26- 1.46	0.07	12.11-12.25	0.61
1.47- 1.67	0.08	12.26-12.46	0.62
1.68- 1.88	0.09	12.47-12.67	0.63
1.89- 2.10	0.10	12.68-12.88	0.64
2.11- 2.25	0.11	12.89-13.10	0.65
2.26- 2.46	0.12	13.11-13.25	0.66
2.47- 2.67	0.13	13.26-13.46	0.67
2.68- 2.88	0.14	13.47-13.67	0.68
2.89- 3.10	0.15	13.68-13.88	0.69
3.11- 3.25	0.16	13.89-14.10	0.70
3.26- 3.46	0.17	14.11-14.25	0.71
3.47- 3.67	0.18	14.26-14.46	0.72
3.68- 3.88	0.19	14.47-14.67	0.73
3.89- 4.10	0.20	14.68-14.88	0.74
4.11- 4.25	0.21	14.89-15.10	0.75
4.26- 4.46	0.22	15.11-15.25	0.76
4.47- 4.67	0.23	15.26-15.46	0.77
4.68- 4.88	0.24	15.47-15.67	0.78
4.89- 5.10	0.25	15.68-15.88	0.79
5.11- 5.25	0.26	15.89-16.10	0.80
5.26- 5.46	0.27	16.11-16.25	0.81
5.47- 5.67	0.28	16.26-16.46	0.82
5.68- 5.88	0.29	16.47-16.67	0.83
5.89- 6.10	0.30	16.68-16.88	0.84
6.11- 6.25	0.31	16.89-17.10	0.85
6.26- 6.46	0.32	17.11-17.25	0.86
6.47- 6.67	0.33	17.26-17.46	0.87
6.68- 6.88	0.34	17.47-17.67	0.88
6.89- 7.10	0.35	17.68-17.88	0.89
7.11- 7.25	0.36	17.89-18.10	0.90
7.26- 7.46	0.37	18.11-18.25	0.91
7.47- 7.67	0.38	18.26-18.46	0.92
7.68- 7.88	0.39	18.47-18.67	0.93
7.89- 8.10	0.40	18.68-18.88	0.94
8.11- 8.25	0.41	18.89-19.10	0.95
8.26- 8.46	0.42	19.11-19.25	0.96
8.47- 8.67	0.43	19.26-19.46	0.97
8.68- 8.88	0.44	19.47-19.67	0.98
8.89- 9.10	0.45	19.68-19.88	0.99
9.11- 9.25	0.46	19.89-20.10	1.00
9.26- 9.46	0.47	20.11-20.25	1.01
9.47- 9.67	0.48	20.26-20.46	1.02
9.68- 9.88	0.49	20.47-20.67	1.03
9.89-10.10	0.50	20.68-20.88	1.04
10.11-10.25	0.51	20.89-21.10	1.05

Exercises

... the sales tax on each purchase.

... 19.15 2. $6.85 3. $14.50
... 21.00 5. $12.95 6. $9.00

... the sales tax and the total cost for each ... hase.

... 7.15 8. $10.58 9. $15.00
... 18.85 11. $21.25 12. $17.00
... 9.98 14. $16.75 15. $15.50

... find the sales tax and the total cost for a purchase of $19.10.

... at Hilltop Pharmacy, Mrs. Carr paid $2.25 ... r a toothbrush, $1.50 for a comb, and

Exercises

Find the number of kilowatt–hours used per year by each appliance.

1. Microwave oven 2. Dishwasher 3. Dehumidifier
4. Television (color) 5. Washing machine 6. Range
7. Refrigerator–freezer 8. Clothes dryer 9. Water heater

Suppose that electricity costs 11¢ per kilowatt–hour. Find the cost of electricity per year for each appliance.

10. Vacuum cleaner 11. Television (color) 12. Clothes dryer

Suppose that electricity costs 9¢ per kilowatt–hour. Find the cost of electricity per year for each appliance.

13. Dishwasher 14. Range 15. Water heater

16. The cost for electricity in Triple Falls is 12¢ per kilowatt–hour. Find the cost of electricity per year for a vacuum cleaner.

17. The cost for electricity in Bradford is 10¢ per kilowatt–hour. Find the cost of electricity per year for an air conditioner.

18. The cost for electricity in San Cyro is 9¢ per kilowatt–hour. Find the cost of electricity per year for a color television and a water heater.

19. Suppose that electricity for an electric clock costs 23¢ per month. Find the cost of electricity for the clock for one year.

20. The cost for electricity in North River is 11¢ per kilowatt–hour. Find the cost of electricity per year for a dehumidifier and a microwave oven.

21. Suppose that electricity for an iron costs 7¢ per hour and that a family uses the iron 4 hours per week. Find the yearly cost of electricity for the iron.

Application WHOLE NUMBERS: MULTIPLICATION 35

Review And Testing

The **Review of Related Skills** that open each chapter and the **Review of Related Skills** for each lesson provides an excellent method for continual review.

NOTE: The answers to all of the exercises in the **Review of Related Skills** are provided in the back of the book.

REVIEW OF RELATED SKILLS FOR CHAPTER 6

Multiply.   (Pages 32–33, 36–37)
1. 27 $\times31$ **2.** 46 $\times59$ **3.** 802 $\times\ 21$ **4.** 405 $\times\ 57$ **5.** 753 $\times402$ **6.** 889 $\times508$

Divide.   (Pages 50–51, 54–55)
7. $7\overline{)238}$ **8.** $6\overline{)156}$ **9.** $57\overline{)3876}$ **10.** $29\overline{)1073}$ **11.** $151\overline{)52548}$
12. $437\overline{)99636}$ **13.** $23\overline{)1518}$ **14.** $56\overline{)4984}$ **15.** $9\overline{)4716}$ **16.** $8\overline{)5928}$

Multiply each number by 10.   (Pages 102–103)
17. 0.3 **18.** 0.9 **19.** 2.19 **20.** 6.21 **21.** 0.013 **22.** 0.286
23. 3.1 **24.** 8.7 **25.** 0.017 **26.** 0.574 **27.** 4.89 **28.** 6.38

Multiply each number by 100.   (Pages 102–103)
29. 0.34 **30.** 7.72 **31.** 3.76 **32.** 0.489 **33.** 4.3 **34.** 0.8
35. 9.17 **36.** 0.29 **37.** 8.602 **38.** 6.908 **39.** 7.1 **40.** 8.9

REVIEW OF RELATED SKILLS

Round each number to the nearest ten.   (Pages 17–19)
1. 11 **2.** 18 **3.** 55 **4.** 31 **5.** 63 **6.** 94 **7.** 77 **8.** 8

Round each number to the nearest hundred.   (Pages 17–19)
9. 138 **10.** 226 **11.** 785 **12.** 197 **13.** 508 **14.** 664 **15.** 682 **16.** 651

Multiply.   (Pages 26–27)
17. 51×3 **18.** 92×8 **19.** 63×5 **20.** 34×9 **21.** 256×6 **22.** 578×8

Use an X to show where to place the first digit in the quotient.   (Pages 50–51)
23. $19\overline{)625}$ **24.** $38\overline{)105}$ **25.** $87\overline{)9936}$ **26.** $72\overline{)4324}$ **27.** 109
28. $821\overline{)9063}$ **29.** $682\overline{)31487}$ **30.** $427\overline{)10063}$ **31.** 105

Each **Chapter Review** consists of:
1. Vocabulary review
2. Skills review
3. Applications review
Note the help reference.

Chapter Review

Part 1: Vocabulary

For Exercises 1–6, choose from the box at the right the word(s) that completes each statement.

1. When dividing by a decimal, it is sometimes necessary to annex __?__ to the dividend. (Page 112)
2. Rate equals distance divided by __?__. (Page 114)
3. To divide by 100, move the decimal point 2 places to the __?__. (Page 116)
4. To divide by 0.01, move the decimal point __?__ places to the right. (Page 116)
5. Natural gas for heating is measured in __?__ units. (Page 118)
6. To find a quotient to the nearest hundredth, you first divide to the __?__ place. Then you round the quotient to the nearest hundredth. (Page 122)

zeros
cubic
two
time
three
left
thousand

Part 2: Skills

Divide.   (Pages 110–111)
7. $7\overline{)86.8}$ **8.** $5\overline{)84.65}$ **9.** $24\overline{)11.712}$ **10.** $48\overline{)163.2}$ **11.** $6\overline{)0.54}$
12. $2\overline{)0.1544}$ **13.** $36\overline{)1.7784}$ **14.** $42\overline{)49.98}$ **15.** $144\overline{)113.76}$ **16.** $305\overline{)1}$

Multiply the divisor and the dividend by 10, or by 100, or by 1000, to make the divisor a whole number.   (Pages 112–113)
17. $0.4\overline{)9.6}$ **18.** $0.3\overline{)3.92}$ **19.** $0.28\overline{)36.54}$ **20.** $6.24\overline{)238}$
21. $3.86\overline{)36.9}$ **22.** $0.046\overline{)9.2}$ **23.** $1.63\overline{)462.4}$ **24.** $1.056\overline{)28}$

Divide.   (Pages 112–113)
25. $0.7\overline{)21.77}$ **26.** $0.8\overline{)0.504}$ **27.** $4.5\overline{)14.40}$ **28.** $0.12\overline{)5.4}$
29. $4.38\overline{)22.776}$ **30.** $0.044\overline{)37.18}$ **31.** $1.22\overline{)4.392}$ **32.** $0.63\overline{)0.0}$

Divide.   (Pages 116–117)
33. $16.2 \div 10$ **34.** $1.28 \div 0.1$ **35.** $73.64 \div 0.001$ **36.** $86.3 \div 10$
37. $28.6 \div 0.001$ **38.** $0.48 \div 10$ **39.** $6.21 \div 100$ **40.** $14.85 \div 0$
41. $0.1\overline{)0.75}$ **42.** $100\overline{)5.61}$ **43.** $0.001\overline{)6.684}$ **44.** $1000\overline{)762}$

Round to the nearest whole number.   (Pages 120–121)
45. 36.84 **46.** 9.63 **47.** 0.723 **48.** 899.7 **49.** 6.578 **50.** 18

Round to the nearest tenth.   (Pages 120–121)
51. 2.856 **52.** 41.145 **53.** 5.968 **54.** 0.631 **55.** 83.453 **56.** 91

128   CHAPTER 6

Round to the nearest hundredth.   (Pages 120–121)
57. 36.609 **58.** 3.185 **59.** 0.9316 **60.** 46.249 **61.** 218.046 **62.** 1.997

Round to the nearest thousandth.   (Pages 120–121)
63. 4.3629 **64.** 91.8455 **65.** 0.0096 **66.** 25.0247 **67.** 2.81621 **68.** 42.04768

Divide. Round each quotient to the nearest tenth.   (Pages 122–123)
69. $31\overline{)41.5}$ **70.** $5.6\overline{)8.683}$ **71.** $0.56\overline{)35.2}$ **72.** $0.491\overline{)1.95418}$

Divide. Round each quotient to the nearest hundredth.   (Pages 122–123)
73. $5.9\overline{)16.59}$ **74.** $7.3\overline{)6.9}$ **75.** $0.12\overline{)3.81}$ **76.** $28.8\overline{)402.6}$

Choose the best estimate. Choose a, b, c, or d.   (Pages 126–127)
77. $32.99 + 2.15$ **a.** \$36 **b.** \$35 **c.** \$34 **d.** \$37
78. 12.3×8.9 **a.** 117 **b.** 96 **c.** 108 **d.** 100
79. $268.14 - 7.99$ **a.** \$262 **b.** \$261 **c.** \$263 **d.** \$260
80. $12.04 + 6.95$ **a.** \$19 **b.** \$18 **c.** \$20 **d.** \$17
81. $17.85 \div 3.02$ **a.** 7 **b.** 6 **c.** 8 **d.** 5
82. $49.95 - 10.05$ **a.** \$39 **b.** \$42 **c.** \$38 **d.** \$40
83. 5.95×4.2 **a.** 64 **b.** 60 **c.** 70 **d.** 74
84. $88.2 \div 10.8$ **a.** 10 **b.** 9 **c.** 8 **d.** 7

Part 3: Applications

85. Fifteen kilograms of ginger cost \$139.95. Find the cost of one kilogram. (Pages 110–111)

86. Twenty pounds of coffee cost \$51.80. Find the cost of one pound. (Pages 110–111)

87. In 1893, William Morrison built one of America's first electric automobiles. It could travel 50 miles in 2.5 hours. Find the speed of the automobile in miles per hour. (Pages 114–115)

88. The O'Reilly family used 6500 cubic feet of gas in February. They pay 39¢ per 100 cubic feet of gas. What was their total cost for heating in February? (Page 118)

89. The price of a 12–ounce can of fruit is 51¢, and the price of an 8–ounce can is 38¢. Which is the better buy? (Pages 124–126)

An Early Electric Auto

Chapter Review   DECIMALS: DIVISION   **129**

Review and Testing

Each **Chapter Test** parallels the content of the formal **Chapter Test** included in the **Teacher's Resource Book.**

An **Additional Practice** page follows each **Chapter Test.** It provides further practice for students who did not perform well on the formal **Chapter Test.**

Chapter Test

Divide.
1. 4)48.64   2. 21)0.42   3. 0.6)21.06   4. 0.15)4.5   5. 0.008)72

Divide.
6. 17.1 ÷ 100   7. 0.367 ÷ 0.001   8. 0.72 ÷ 10   9. 1000)67.9   10. 0.01)8.3

Round each number as indicated.
11. 7.83; to the nearest whole number
12. 81.839; to the nearest tenth
13. 29.645; to the nearest hundredth
14. 4.73416; to the nearest thousandth
15. 328.986; to the nearest tenth
16. 75.655; to the nearest whole number

Divide. Round each quotient to the decimal place indicated.
17. 0.3)6.483; to the nearest tenth
18. 0.14)0.3584; to the nearest tenth
19. 3.1)0.6293; to the nearest hundredth
20. 7)1.484; to the nearest hundredth

Solve.
21. Five pounds of potatoes cost $1.95. Find the cost of one pound.
22. In a track meet, Chris ran 1845 meters in 4.5 minutes. Find the speed in meters per minute.
23. The price of a 6-ounce can of frozen orange juice is 35¢, and the price of a 10-ounce can is 49¢. Which is the better buy?

In Exercises 24–25, choose the best estimate. Choose a, b, c, or d.
24. The Gonzales family used 12,000 cubic feet of natural gas in January. They pay 41¢ per 100 cubic feet of gas. Estimate the total cost.
  a. $54   b. $40
  c. $60   d. $48
25. Kerry traveled 3000 miles in 57.7 hours. Estimate her average driving speed in miles per hour.
  a. 45   b. 50
  c. 40   d. 55

130   CHAPTER 6   **Chapter Test**

Additional Practice

Skills

Divide.   (Pages 110–111)
1. 26)61.36   2. 32)52.80   3. 6)141.6   4. 8)285.6   5. 234)16.146
6. 196)6.272   7. 68)4.216   8. 89)5.963   9. 54)126.90   10. 43)185.76

(Pages 112–113)
11. 0.8)4.16   12. 0.6)2.88   13. 0.7)66.5   14. 0.4)2.492
15. 0.23)0.989   16. 1.56)4.524   17. 2.36)4.484   18. 0.59)3.717
19. 0.72)453.6   20. 0.03)14.4   21. 0.423)249.57   22. 0.561)527.34

Divide.   (Pages 116–117)
23. 13.8 ÷ 10   24. 25.6 ÷ 100   25. 38.3 ÷ 1000   26. 5.81 ÷ 0.1
27. 4.62 ÷ 0.001   28. 38.7 ÷ 0.01   29. 100)3.89   30. 0.01)14.7

Round to the nearest whole number.   (Pages 120–121)
31. 63.7   32. 48.54   33. 532.38   34. 91.45   35. 9.586   36. 12.63

Round to the nearest tenth.   (Pages 120–121)
37. 3.84   38. 16.923   39. 21.86   40. 4.953   41. 7.847   42. 2.321

Round to the nearest hundredth.   (Pages 120–121)
43. 4.637   44. 0.063   45. 43.046   46. 0.465   47. 3.421   48. 59.375

Round to the nearest thousandth.   (Pages 120–121)
49. 3.4622   50. 5.9837   51. 44.1006   52. 31.0005   53. 0.0369   54. 0.0041

Divide. Round the quotient to the nearest tenth.
(Pages 122–123)
55. 42)110.71   56. 3.9)17.277   57. 0.23)2.0608   58. 0.49)58.2

Divide. Round the quotient to the nearest hundredth.
(Pages 122–123)
59. 4.6)18.2   60. 0.18)53.94   61. 6.4)142.3   62. 42.3)186.46

Applications
63. In a 400 meter race, an athlete completed the course in 45.2 seconds. Find the rate in meters per second. Round your answer to the nearest tenth.   (Pages 114–115)
64. The Ramirez family used 12,400 cubic feet of natural gas in January. They pay 45¢ per 100 cubic feet of gas. What was their total cost of heating in January?   (Page 118)

Additional Practice   DECIMALS: DIVISION   **131**

A **Cumulative Review** appears after each of the six units. Note the multiple-choice format.

Two **Sample Competency Tests** are included: One covers Chapters 1–14. The second covers the entire text.

Cumulative Review: Chapters 5–8

Choose the correct answer. Choose a, b, c, or d.

1. Which decimal has the greatest value?
  a. 0.631   b. 0.607
  c. 0.065   d. 0.64
2. Multiply: 0.735
             × 82
  a. 60.270   b. 57.860
  c. 59.270   d. 60.027
3. Round 32.766 to the nearest

9. Add: 1.59 + 39.4 + 0.003
  a. 0.556   b. 40.993
  c. 41.02   d. 5.56
10. Subtract: 87.03
              − 5.27
  a. 71.76   b. 82.85
  c. 82.76   d. 81.76
11. Which number represents twenty-seven and sixteen

Sample Competency Test: Chapters 1–14

Choose the correct answer. Choose a, b, c, or d.

1. Add: 642
          3591
        + 46
  a. 4379   b. 4279
  c. 4281   d. 3280
2. Divide: 13)4667

5. Add: $1\frac{2}{9} + 3\frac{4}{9}$
  a. $3\frac{1}{3}$ b. $4\frac{2}{3}$ c. $4\frac{7}{9}$ d. $3\frac{5}{9}$
6. Multiply: 604
             × 83
  a. 49,132   b. 50,

Optional Features

Career lessons may be considered optional. The career areas that appear throughout focus on those that present realistic career goals for general mathematics students. Each applies the skills of the chapter.

---

career — INDUSTRY

Machinists make tools and metal parts for machines. Since all measurements are approximations, the size of each tool or part can vary by a certain amount. This amount is called the **tolerance**.

Measurement: 4.18 ± 0.05 centimeters
Tolerance: ±0.05 cm ◄ Read: "Plus or minus 0.05 centimeters."

EXAMPLE

The length of a rod is to be 4.18 ± 0.05 centimeters. Find the greatest and smallest acceptable lengths.

Solution:

The measurement 4.18 ± 0.05 means that the rod could be **as long as** 4.18 + 0.05 centimeters or **as short as** 4.18 − 0.05 centimeters.

Greatest acceptable length: 4.18 + 0.05 = **4.23 cm**
Smallest acceptable length: 4.18 − 0.05 = **4.13 cm**

The rod in the Example can be used if it is no longer than 4.23 centimeters and no shorter than 4.13 centimeters.

EXERCISES

Complete the table.

Measurement	Tolerance	Greatest Acceptable Length	Smallest Acceptable Length
1. 3.25 ± 0.05 cm	?	?	?
2. 1.19 ± 0.05 cm	?	?	?
3. 6.437 ± 0.005 mm	?	?	?
4. 2.005 ± 0.001 cm	?	?	?

5. The width of a machine part is given as 4.062 ± 0.005 centimeters. Find the greatest and smallest acceptable widths.

6. The width of an engine part is given as 85.6 ± 0.5 millimeters. Find the greatest and smallest acceptable widths.

7. A blueprint gives a measurement of 3.250 ± 0.005 centimeters. What are the greatest and smallest acceptable measurements?

8. A blueprint gives a measurement of 3.625 ± 0.002 millimeters. What are the greatest and smallest acceptable measurements?

138 CHAPTER 7   Career

OFFICE WORKER — career

Applicants for typing jobs usually take a test that shows their speed (number of words per minute) and accuracy (number of errors).

To find the net number of words per minute, you must first answer two questions:
  "What is the penalty for errors?"
  "What is the net number of words typed?"
These are the hidden questions in the problem. Then you can find the net number of words per minute.

EXAMPLE Carlos types 265 words in 5 minutes. He has 6 errors. The penalty for errors is 5 points per error. Find the net number of words per minute.

Solution:
  1 Find the amount deducted for errors.
  6 × 5 = 30 ◄ Number of Errors × 5 = Amount Deducted

  2 Find the net number of words.
  265 − 30 = 235 ◄ Number of Words Typed − Amount Deducted = Net Number of Words

  3 Find the net number of words per minute.
  235 ÷ 5 = 47 ◄ Net Number of Words ÷ Number of Minutes = Net Words Per Minute

  The net number of words per minute is **47**.

EXERCISES

For Exercises 1–6, find the net number of words per minute. The penalty for errors is 5 points per error.

1. Madeline types 415 words in 5 minutes. She has 9 errors.

2. Daniel types 200 words in 5 minutes. He has 2 errors.

3. Joyce types 315 words in 5 minutes. She has 2 errors.

4. Jerome types 250 words in 5 minutes. He has 4 errors.

5. Ramon types 398 words in 8 minutes. He has 6 errors.

6. Mijako types 389 words in 8 minutes. She has one error.

Career   WHOLE NUMBERS: DIVISION   57

The **Calculator** exercises may be considered as optional.

Each applies the use of a calculator to specific skills presented in the chapter.

Some Exercise sets contain a set of **More Challenging Exercises.**

47. One tomato contains 25 calories. How many calories do 5 tomatoes contain?

48. Four spears of asparagus contain 15 calories. How many calories are there in 16 spears?

49. Six slices of cucumber contain 5 calories. How many calories are there in 18 slices?

More Challenging Problems

Find the missing numbers.

50.	51.	52.	53.	54.
695 × ■ / 55■0	82■ × ■ / 7461	7■8 × 4 / 2■92	■0■ × 7 / 7■6	

	56.	57.	58.	59.
4■2 × 7	81■ × ■ / 1638	■■6 × 5 / 158■■	48■ × ■ / 2934	

WHOLE NUMBERS: MULTIPLICATION

ORDER OF OPERATIONS

You can use the rules for order of operations and the calculator ⊞ and ⊟ keys to solve problems with decimals.

EXAMPLE: 25.53 − 13 × 0.89 = ?

Solution: Estimated answer: 26 − 13 × 1 = 26 − 13 = **13**

Actual answer: [1] [3] [×] [.] [8] [9] [=] [M+]   11.57

  [2] [5] [.] [5] [3] [−] [MR] [=]   13.96

  Since the estimate is 13, **13.96** is a reasonable answer.

EXERCISES

First estimate each answer. Then use a calculator to find the exact answer.

Problem	Estimated Answer	Exact Answer
1. 23.91 − 14 × 0.55	?	?
2. 12.86 − 5 × 1.35	?	?
3. 57.9 − 18.1 + 14.6	?	?
4. 138.56 − 14.89 − 38.11	?	?
5. 2.8 × 450 − 49.8	?	?

Calculator   DECIMALS: DIVISION   127

Teacher's Resource Book

This paperback consists of perforated and pre-holed copying masters. You are given permission to reproduce these pages.

It consists of a
1. **Testing Program**
2. **Workbook section**
3. **Introduction to Computers**
4. **Warm-Up Exercises**
5. **Answer section**

The Testing Program

There is a supplement for each skills lesson in the workbook section.

The Workbook Section

Name _____ Date _____

CHAPTER 13   PER CENT

Write a per cent for each fraction.

1-5 ROUNDING AND ESTIMATION: WHOLE NUMBERS   (pages 17-18)

Examples: Round 7283
       a. to the nearest ten.   b. to the nearest hundred.

Solutions: a. 7283 rounded to the nearest ten is **7280**,
            because 3 (the ones place) is less than 5.

      b. 7283 rounded to the nearest hundred is **7300**,

Answers
1. _____
2. _____
3. _____
4. _____

Name_____ Date_____

CHAPTER 13   PER CENT

Write a per cent for each fraction.

1. $\frac{6}{100}$

2. $\frac{39}{100}$

Write a decimal for each per cent.

3. 51%

4. 0.7%

5. 5.6%

Write a per cent for each decimal.

6. 0.81

7. 0.726

8. 0.008

Write a fraction in lowest terms for each per cent.

9. 12%

10. $\frac{5}{6}$%

11. $7\frac{1}{2}$%

Write a per cent for each fraction or mixed number.

12. $\frac{13}{20}$

13. $8\frac{1}{4}$

14. $\frac{3}{7}$

PROBLEM SOLVING AND APPLICATIONS: MAKING CHANGE   (Page 97)

The best way of making change is to use as few bills and coins as possible.

Choose the best way of making change. Draw a circle around a, b, or c.

1.

Amount of Sale	Money Received	Change Due
$4.29	$5 - bill	$0.71

a. Two quarters, 2 dimes, 1 penny
b. Seven dimes, 1 penny
c. Five dimes, 4 nickels, 1 penny

2.

Amount of Sale	Money Received	Change Due
$8.35	$10 - bill	$1.65

a. Six quarters, 1 dime, 5 pennies
b. A $1-dollar bill, 6 dimes, 1 nickel
c. A $1-dollar bill, 2 quarters, 1 dime, 1 nickel

3.

Amount of Sale	Money Received	Change Due
$47.56	$50 -bill	$2.44

a. Eight quarters, 4 dimes, 4 pennies
b. Two $1-bills, 4 dimes, 4 pennies
c. Two $1-bills, 1 quarter, 1 dime, 1 nickel, 4 pennies

4.

Amount of Sale	Money Received	Change . Due
$82.90	$100 - bill	$17.10

a. A $10-bill, a $5-bill, two $1-bills, 1 dime
b. Three $5-bills, two $1-bills, 1 dime
c. Two $5-bills, seven $1-bills, 1 dime

For Exercises 5-14, write the number of bills and coins you would use to make change. Use as few bills and coins as possible.

	Amount of Sale	Money Received	Change Due	Answers
5.	$7.25	$10.00	$2.75	_____
6.	$31.89	$50.00	$18.11	_____
7.	$16.93	$20.00	$3.07	_____
8.	$74.98	$100.00	$25.02	_____
9.	$13.87	$15.00	$1.13	_____
10.	$108.24	$120.00	$11.76	_____
11.	$21.05	$22.00	$0.95	_____

12. Diana's bill at Hill's Pharmacy was $11.25. She gave the clerk two $10-bills.

13. Chester's bill at the record shop amounted to $53.89. He gave the clerk three $20-bills.

4

14. _____

FORM A   25

There is a supplement for most **Problem Solving and Applications** lessons.

There are two forms of each chapter test. Plus
6 cumulative tests and
3 sample competency tests.

TEACHER'S RESOURCE BOOK

In addition to receiving a copy of the Teacher's Edition, upon request, each teacher will also receive a copy of the *Teacher's Resource Book*, upon request. This paperback publication consists of copying masters that are perforated and pre-holed. This title has the following components.

Tests

It contains two forms of each chapter test. Teachers may wish to use one form as a pretest and the other form as a posttest. There are six cumulative tests, one for each of the six units. There are also three sample competency tests, — one covering Chapters 1-11, one covering Chapters 1-14, and one covering Chapters 1-20.

Workbook

There is a 112-page workbook section that contains additional practice on skills, problem solving, and applications. This material is referenced to the related pages in the text.

Warm-Ups

This section contains Warm-Up exercises for most skills lessons in Chapters 1-14, the course for Level 2. Each set of Warm-Up exercises is referenced to the related section in the text and each is designed to be used as a pre-lesson activity.

Answers

The answers for the tests and workbook exercises are included in the back of the *Teacher's Resource Book*.

NOTE: The testing program is also available as a separate 112-page, self-cover publication with perforated pages.

The 112-page workbook section is also available as a separate paperback publication with perforated pages. In addition, there is an annotated Teacher's Edition of the "Workbook".

LESSON PLAN GUIDE

Overview

Pages M-10 through M-46 consist of a *Lesson Plan Guide* for each chapter. Each consists of a listing of the objectives that are structured in three categories.

1. The objectives for the skills lessons
2. The objectives for the problem solving and applications lessons
3. The objectives for the optional topics within the chapter, such as the career lessons and the calculator exercises

The second component for each chapter is a three-level *Suggested Timetable of Assignments* chart.

Level 1: This represents a minimal course with a primary emphasis on computational skills and a secondary emphasis on word problems. (Chapters 1-13)

Level 2: This represents a course with a balance between computational skills and word problems. (Chapters 1-16)

Level 3: This represents a course in pre-algebra. (Chapters 1-20)

Codes

Three codes appear in the charts.

RRS: This represents the *Review of Related Skills* page that opens the chapter.

PSA/C: This represents the *Problem Solving and Applications* lessons and the *Career* lessons.

NOTE: Since the teacher is the best judge of which *Problem Solving and Applications* lessons or *Career* lessons are most appropriate for their students, each chart suggests only the number of days to be spent on these lessons.

S: This code appears after certain exercise groups. Because of the large number of exercises, it is suggested that the teacher Select the exercises from the indicated group.

Review and Testing

The *Suggested Timetable of Assignments* chart for each chapter includes days for review and testing. Additional days for administering cumulative tests are included in the charts for Chapters 4, 8, 11, 14, 16, and 20.

TEACHING SUGGESTIONS

Annotated Pages

Teaching suggestions are not included in the *Lesson Plan Guide*. The authors believe that teaching suggestions and other commentary for the teacher are more meaningful if they appear as annotations on the student page. You will note that each annotation is inserted in an appropriate position on the student page.

Review of Related Skills	We suggest that some or all of page viii be reviewed before proceeding with the chapter.

Skills Lesson   **Objectives**

Section 1-1 **Pages 2-3**	*To add two-digit whole numbers (Example 1)* *To add two-digit whole numbers that involves "carrying" (Example 2)*
Section 1-2 **Pages 6-7**	*To add whole numbers having three or more digits that involves "carrying" (Examples 1 and 2)*
Section 1-3 **Pages 10-11**	*To subtract whole numbers (Example 1)* *To subtract whole numbers that involves renaming once (Example 2)* *To apply the skill of subtracting whole numbers to real-life situations (Page 11)*
Section 1-4 **Pages 14-15**	*To subtract whole numbers that involves renaming more than once (Example 1)* *To subtract whole numbers that involves renaming with zeros (Example 2)*
Section 1-5 **Pages 17-18**	*To round whole numbers to the nearest ten, to the nearest hundred, to the nearest thousand, and so on (Example 1)* *To estimate the answers to problems dealing with addition and subtraction of whole numbers (Example 2)* *To apply the skill of estimating answers to problems involving addition and subtraction of whole numbers in real-life situations (Page 18)*

Problem Solving and Applications Lessons

Making Change **Page 4**	*To use a table to solve word problems*
	NOTE: This lesson applies the skill (adding two-digit whole numbers) presented in Section 1-1.
Buying a New Car **Pages 8-9**	*To use a table to solve word problems*
	NOTE: This lesson applies the skill (adding whole numbers with three or more digits) presented in Section 1-2.

Time Zones	*To use a map to solve word problems*
Pages 12-13	

NOTE: This lesson applies the skill (subtracting whole numbers) presented in Section 1-3.

Reading a	*To read a meter (Example)*
Meter	*To use meter readings to compute the number of kilowatt-hours of*
Page 16	*electricity used (Page 16)*

NOTE: This lesson applies the skills (subtraction of whole numbers that involve renaming (borrowing) more than once) presented in Section 1-4.

Optional Features

Career Lesson	*To use a table to solve word problems*
Food Services	
Page 5	

Calculator:	*To use a calculator to help solve problems that involves addition*
Addition and	*and subtraction of large whole numbers*
Subtraction of	
Whole Numbers	
Page 11	

SUGGESTED TIMETABLE OF ASSIGNMENTS

Section	Page(s)	Level One	Level Two	Level Three	
RRS	viii	1-81 S	1-81 S	Optional	
1-1	3	1-63 S	1-63 S	13-24 S	
				37-63 S	1 day
1-2	7	1-31 S	1-31 S	1-31 S	
1-3	11	1-44 S	1-44 S	1-44 S	
					1 day
1-4	15	1-58 S	1-58 S	11-20 S	
				31-58 S	
1-5	18-19	1-48 S	1-52 S	1-52 S	
PSA/C		3 days	3 days	3 days	
Review and Testing		3 days	3 days	2 days	
Total Days		12	12	8	

NOTE: The codes RRS, PSA/C, and S are explained on page M-9.

CHAPTER 2   WHOLE NUMBERS: MULTIPLICATION

Review of Related Skills

We suggest that some or all of page 24 be reviewed before proceeding with the chapter.

Skills Lessons

Objectives

Section 2-1
Pages 26-27

To multiply a whole number by a one-digit multiplier (Example 1)
To apply the skill of multiplying whole numbers by a one-digit multiplier to real-life situations (Page 27)

Section 2-2
Pages 32-33

To multiply a whole number by a two-digit multiplier (Example 1)
To multiply a whole number by a three-digit multiplier (Example 2)

Section 2-3
Pages 36-37

To multiply whole numbers when there is a zero in one of the factors (Example 1)
To multiply whole numbers when there are zeros in both factors (Example 2)

Section 2-4
Page 40

To multiply a whole number by 10, by 100, or by 1000 (Example)

Problem Solving and Applications Lessons

Ordering by Mail
Pages 28-29

To use a mail-order catalog form to solve word problems

NOTE: This lesson applies the skill (multiplication of whole numbers by a one-digit multiplier) presented in Section 2-1.

Message Units
Pages 30-31

To solve two-step problems by applying the technique of the "hidden question"

NOTE: The lesson applies the skill (multiplication of whole numbers by a one-digit multiplier) presented in Section 2-1.

Cost of Electricity
Pages 34-35

To use a table to solve two-step problems by applying the technique of the "hidden question"

NOTE: The lesson applies the skill (multiplying with larger numbers) presented in Section 2-2.

| Gross Pay and Net Pay Pages 38-39 | *To use a formula (gross pay) to solve word problems*
To use a formula (net pay) to solve word problems
To solve two-step problems by applying the technique of the "hidden question" (Example) |

NOTE: The lesson applies the skills (multiplying with larger numbers) presented in Sections 2-2 and 2-3.

Optional Features

| Career Lesson Automobile Repair Page 41 | *To read a meter and to apply the meter readings in solving problems* |

| Calculator: Multiplication of Whole Numbers Page 37 | *To use a calculator to help solve problems involving multiplication of whole numbers* |

SUGGESTED TIMETABLE OF ASSIGNMENTS

Section	Page(s)	Level One	Level Two	Level Three	
RRS	24	1-90 S	1-90 S	Optional	
2-1	27	1-49 S	1-59 S	25-59 S	⎫
					⎬ 1 day
2-2	33	1-79 S	1-79 S	63-79 S	⎭
2-3	37	1st Day: 1-22 S 2nd Day: 23-66 S	1-66 S	45-66 S	⎫
					⎬ 1 day
2-4	40	1-32 S	1-32 S	1-32 S	⎭
PSA/C		1 day	3 days	3 days	
Review and Testing		3 days	3 days	2 days	
Total Days		10	11	7	

NOTE: The codes RRS, PSA/C, and S are explained on page M-9.

Review of
Related Skills

We suggest that some or all of page 46 be reviewed before proceeding with the chapter.

Skills Lessons   **Objectives**

Section 3-1
Pages 48-49

To determine if a number is divisible by 2, by 4, by 5, or by 10 (Example 1)
To determine if a number is divisible by 3 or by 9 (Example 2)
To apply the skill of determining the divisors of whole numbers to real-life situations (Page 49)

Section 3-2
Pages 50-51

To determine where to place the first digit in a quotient (Example 1)
To divide a whole number by a nonzero, one-digit whole number (Example 2)

Section 3-3
Pages 54-55

To divide a whole number by a nonzero, two-digit whole number (Example 1)
To divide a whole number by a nonzero, three-digit whole number (Example 2)

Section 3-4
Pages 58-59

To divide a whole number by a nonzero whole number when writing a final zero in the quotient is involved (Example 1)
To divide a whole number by a nonzero whole number when writing zeros in the quotient is involved (Example 2)

Section 3-5
Pages 62-63

To apply the rules for order of operations (Table 1)
To apply the rules for order of operations in problems that involve parentheses (Table 2)

Section 3-6
Pages 64-65

To use rounding to estimate the answers to problems dealing with multiplication and division of whole numbers (Example)
To apply the skill of estimating answers to problems involving multiplication and division of whole numbers to real-life situations (Page 65)

Problem Solving and
Applications Lessons

Averages
Pages 52-53

To use a formula (average formula) to solve word problems

NOTE: This lesson applies the skills (division by one-digit divisor) presented in Section 3-2.

Finance Charges
Page 56

To solve two-step problems by applying the technique of the "hidden question"

NOTE: This lesson applies the skill (division by two- and three-digit divisors) presented in Section 3-3.

Fuel Economy of A Car
Page 60

To use a formula (fuel economy) to solve word problems

NOTE: This lesson applies the skills (division of whole numbers) presented in Sections 3-3 and 3-4.

Fuel Costs for A Car
Page 61

To solve two-step problems by applying the technique of the "hidden question"

NOTE: This lesson applies the skills (division of whole numbers) presented in Sections 3-3 and 3-4.

Optional Features

Career Lessons Office Worker
Page 57

To solve problems that involve more than one step by applying the technique of the "hidden question"

Calculator: Order of Operations
Page 63

To use a calculator to solve problems involving order of operations

Calculator: Average
Page 65

To use a calculator to solve problems involving averages
To use the skill of estimation and a calculator to solve problems involving averages

SUGGESTED TIMETABLE OF ASSIGNMENTS

Section	Page(s)	Level One	Level Two	Level Three
RRS	46	1-99 S	1-99 S	Optional
3-1	49	1-77 S	1-80 S	1-80 S
3-2	51	1-96 S	1-96 S	25-96 S ⎫
3-3	55	1st Day: 1-35 S 2nd Day: 36-85 S	1-85 S	71-85 S ⎬ 1 day
3-4	59	1st Day: 1-36 S 2nd Day: 37-84 S	1-84 S	11-84 S
3-5	63	Optional	1-46 S	1-46 S
3-6	64-65	Optional	1-14 S	1-14 S
PSA/C		1 day	2 days	3 days
Review and Testing		3 days	3 days	2 days
Total Days		11	12	10

NOTE: The codes RRS, PSA/C, and S are explained on page M-9.

CHAPTER 4   GRAPHS AND APPLICATIONS

Review of Related Skills   We suggest that some or all of page 70 be reviewed before proceeding with the chapter.

Skills Lessons   **Objectives**

Section 4-1
Pages 72-73   *To read a pictograph (Page 72)*
To use a pictograph to answer questions from real-life situations (Example)

Section 4-2
Pages 74-75   *To read a bar graph (Page 74)*
To use a bar graph to answer questions from real-life situations (Example)

Section 4-3
Pages 76-77   *To read a line graph (Page 76)*
To use a line graph to answer questions from real-life situations (Example)

Section 4-4
Pages 78-79   *To read a multiple bar graph (Page 78)*
To use a multiple bar graph to answer questions from real-life situations (Pages 78-79)

Optional Feature

Career Lesson
Government
Service   *To use a graph to solve word problems*
NOTE: This lesson applies the skill (reading a line graph) presented in Section 4-3.

SUGGESTED TIMETABLE OF ASSIGNMENTS

Section	Page(s)	Level One	Level Two	Level Three	
RRS	70	1-96 S	1-96 S	Optional	
4-1	73	1-8 S	1-10 S	1-10 S ⎫	
					1 day
4-2	75	1-10 S	1-11 S	1-11 S ⎭	
4-3	77	1st Day: 1-9	1-18	1-18	
		2nd Day: 10-18			
4-4	78-79	Optional	1-20	1-24	
PSA/C		0 days	0 days	1 day	
Review and Testing		3 days	2 days	2 days	
Cumulative Review		2 days	2 days	1 day	
Total Days		10	9	7	

NOTE: The codes RRS, PSA/C, and S are explained on page M-9.

CHAPTER 5   DECIMALS

Review of Related Skills

We suggest that some or all of page 88 be reviewed before proceeding with the chapter.

Skills Lessons   **Objectives**

Section 5-1
Pages 90-91

To give the value of any digits in a number (Example 1)
To use place value to compare decimals (Example 2)

Section 5-2
Pages 94-95

To add and subtract with decimals (Example 1)
To subtract with decimals when annexing of zeros is involved (Example 2)
To apply the skills of adding and subtracting with decimals to real-life situations (Page 95)

Section 5-3
Pages 98-99

To multiply with decimals (Example 1)
To multiply with decimals when inserting zeros in the product is involved (Example 2)

Section 5-4
Pages 102-103

To multiply a decimal by 10, by 100, or by 1000 (Example 1)
To multiply a decimal by 0.1, by 0.01, or by 0.001 (Example 2)
To apply the skill of multiplying decimals to real-life situations (Page 103)

Problem Solving and Applications Lessons

Writing Checks
Pages 92-93

To write checks
NOTE: This lesson applies the skill (decimals and place value) presented in Section 5-1.

Sales Tax
Page 96

To use a table to solve word problems
NOTE: This lesson applies the skill (adding decimals) presented in Section 5-2.

Making Change
Page 97

To make change
NOTE: This lesson applies the skills (adding and subtracting decimals) presented in Section 5-2.

Cost of Credit
Page 100

To solve problems that involve more than one step by applying the technique of the "hidden question"

NOTE: This lesson applies the skills (subtraction and multiplication with decimals) presented in Sections 5-2 and 5-3.

Optional Features

Career Lesson
Retailing
Page 101

To use a formula to find total value

Calculator:
Checking
Answers
Page 99

To use a calculator to check the answers to problems involving addition, subtraction, and multiplication of decimals

SUGGESTED TIMETABLE OF ASSIGNMENTS

Section	Page(s)	Level One	Level Two	Level Three
RRS	88	1-78 S	1-78 S	Optional
5-1	91	1-39 S	1-39 S	1-39 S
5-2	95	1-46 S	1-46 S	1-46 S
5-3	99	1st Day: 1-25 S 2nd Day: 26-50 S	1-50 S	1-50 S
5-4	103	1st Day: 1-20 2nd Day: 21-59 S	1-59 S	1-59 S
PSA/C		3 days	3 days	3 days
Review and Testing		3 days	2 days	2 days
Total Days		13	10	9

NOTE: The codes RRS, PSA/C, and S are explained on page M-9.

CHAPTER 6   DECIMALS: DIVISION

Review of Related Skills We suggest that some or all of page 108 be reviewed before proceeding with the chapter.

Skills Lessons   **Objectives**

Section 6-1
Pages 110-111
To divide a decimal by a non-zero whole number (Example 1)
To divide a decimal by a non-zero whole number when writing zeros in the quotient is involved (Example 2)
To apply the skill of dividing a decimal by a non-zero whole number to real-life situations (Page 111)

Section 6-2
Pages 112-113
To divide by a decimal (Example 1)
To divide by a decimal when annexing zeros to the dividend is involved (Example 2)

Section 6-3
Pages 116-117
To divide a decimal by 10, by 100, or by 1000 (Example 1)
To divide a decimal by 0.1, by 0.01, or by 0.001 (Example 2)

Section 6-4
Pages 120-121
To round a decimal to the nearest whole number, nearest tenth, nearest hundredth, nearest thousandth, and so on (Example)
To apply the skill of rounding decimals to real-life situations (Page 121)
NOTE: These exercises serve as a preparation for the problem-solving and applications lesson on pages 124-125.

Section 6-5
Pages 122-123
To divide by a decimal, rounding the quotient to the nearest tenth (Example 1)
To divide by a decimal, rounding the quotient to the nearest hundredth (Example 2)
To apply the skills of dividing by a decimal and rounding the quotient to a given decimal place to real-life situations (Page 123)

Section 6-6
Pages 126-127
To estimate the answers to problems dealing with addition, subtraction, multiplication, and division of decimals (Page 126)
To apply the skill of estimating answers to the problems involving decimals in real-life situations (Pages 126-127)

Problem Solving and Applications Lessons

Rate
Pages 114-115
To use a formula (distance formula) to solve word problems
NOTE: This lesson applies the skills (division of decimals) presented in Sections 6-1 and 6-2.

Heating Cost
Page 118
To solve two-step problems by applying the technique of the "hidden question"
NOTE: This lesson applies the skills presented in Section 6-3.

Comparison Shopping Pages 124-125	*To use a formula to find unit price (Example 1)*
	To use the formula for unit price to compare the cost of different sizes of the same product (Example 2)
	NOTE: This lesson applies the skills (division with remainders and rounding the quotient) presented in Sections 6-4 and 6-5.

Optional Features

Career Lesson Insurance Page 119	*To solve the problems that involve more than one step by applying the technique of the "hidden question"*
Calculator: Order of Operations Page 127	*To use a calculator to help solve problems involving order of operations*
	To use the skill of estimation and a calculator to solve problems involving order of operations

SUGGESTED TIMETABLE OF ASSIGNMENTS

Section	Page(s)	Level One	Level Two	Level Three	
RRS	108	1-94 S	1-94 S	Optional	
6-1	111	1st Day: 1-25 2nd Day: 26-82 S	1-82 S	51-82 S	⎫ ⎬ 1 day
6-2	113	1st Day: 1-8; 21-36 2nd Day: 9-20; 37-68 S	1-68 S	21-68 S	⎭
6-3	117	1st Day: 1-24 2nd Day: 25-76 S	1-76 S	1-76 S	⎫ ⎬ 1 day
6-4	120-121	1-56 S	1-62 S	1-62 S	⎭
6-5	123	1st Day: 1-20 2nd Day: 21-43	1-43 S	1-43 S	⎫ ⎬ 1 day
6-6	126	Optional	1-24	1-24 S	⎭
PSA/C		3 days	3 days	3 days	
Review and Testing		0 days	1 day	2 days	
Total Days		**13**	**11**	**8**	

NOTE: The codes RRS, PSA/C, and S are explained on page M-9.

CHAPTER 7   APPLYING METRIC MEASURES I

**Review of
Related Skills**

We suggest that some or all of page 132 be reviewed before proceeding with the chapter.

Skills Lessons   **Objectives**

Section 7-1
Page 134

To determine suitable metric units of length (Page 134)

Section 7-2
Pages 136-137

To measure the length of an object to the nearest centimeter and to the nearest millimeter (Example)

Section 7-3
Pages 140-142

To find the perimeter of a rectangle (Example 1)
To find the perimeter of a square (Example 2)
To apply the skill of finding the perimeter of a rectangle and square to real-life models (Pages 141-142)

Section 7-4
Pages 143-144

To find the area of a rectangle (Example 1)
To find the area of a square (Example 2)
To apply the skill of finding the area of a rectangle and square to real-life models (Page 144)

Section 7-5
Pages 145-146

To find the area of a parallelogram (Example 1)
To find the area of a triangle (Example 2)
To apply the skill of finding the area of a traingle to real-life models (Page 146)

Section 7-6
Pages 147-148

To find the area of a trapezoid (Example)
To apply the skill of finding the area of a trapezoid to real-life models (Page 148)

**Problem Solving and
Applications Lessons**

**Distance on
a Map
Page 135**

To use a map to solve problems
NOTE: This lesson applies the skills (metric units of length) presented in Section 7-1.

**Distance
Page 139**

To use a formula (distance formula) to solve word problems
NOTE: This lesson applies the skills (metric measurement) presented in Section 7-2.

Floor Space
Page 149

To use a floor plan to solve word problems

NOTE: This lesson applies the skills (areas of rectangles, triangles, and trapezoids) presented in Sections 7-4, 7-5, and 7-6.

Optional Features

Career Lesson
Industry
Page 138

To find the tolerance in a measurement

SUGGESTED TIMETABLE OF ASSIGNMENTS

Section	Page(s)	Level One	Level Two	Level Three
RRS	132	1-101 S	1-101 S	Optional
7-1	134	1-13	1-13 ⎫ 1 day	1-13 S ⎫ 1 day
7-2	137	1-10 S	1-10 S ⎭	1-10 S ⎭
7-3	141-142	1st Day: 1-14 S 2nd Day: 15-22	1-26 S	1-26 S
7-4	144	1st Day: 1-6 2nd Day: 7-15 S	1-15 S	1-15 S
7-5	146	Optional	1-16 S	1-16 S
7-6	148	Optional	Optional	1-19 S
PSA/C		1 day	1 day	1 day
Review and Testing		3 days	3 days	2 days
Total Days		11	9	8

NOTE: The codes RRS, PSA/C, and S are explained on page M-9.

CHAPTER 8   APPLYING METRIC MEASURES II

**Review of
Related Skills**   We suggest that some or all of page 154 be reviewed before proceeding with the chapter.

Skills Lessons   **Objectives**

Section 8-1   *To change from one unit of capacity to another (Example)*
Pages 156-157   *To apply metric units of capacity to real-life situations (Page 157)*

Section 8-2   *To change from one unit of mass to another (Example)*
Pages 158-159   *To apply metric units of mass to real-life situations (Page 159)*

Section 8-3   *To determine suitable temperatures on the Celsius scale (Page 160)*
Page 160

Section 8-4   *To find the surface area of a rectangular prism (Example)*
Pages 162-163

Section 8-5   *To find the volume of a rectangular prism (Example)*
Pages 164-165   *To apply the skill of finding the volume of a rectangular prism to real-life models (Page 165)*

Section 8-6   *To find the volume of a pyramid (Example)*
Pages 167-168   *To apply the skill of finding the volume of a pyramid to real-life models (Page 168)*

**Problem Solving and
Applications Lessons**

**Volume/
Capacity/
Mass
Page 166**   *To solve three-step problems by applying the technique of the "hidden question"*

NOTE: This lesson applies the skills (capacity, mass, and volume) presented in Sections 8-1, 8-2, and 8-5.

Optional Features

**Career Lesson
Weather
Forecasting
Page 161**   *To use tables to solve word problems*

SUGGESTED TIMETABLE OF ASSIGNMENTS

Section	Page(s)	Level One	Level Two	Level Three
RRS	154	1-100 S	1-100 S	Optional
8-1	156-157	1st Day: 1-13 2nd Day: 14-37 S	1-37 S	1-37 S
8-2	159	1st Day: 1-8 2nd Day: 9-31 S	1-31 S	1-31 S
8-3	160	1-10 S	1-10 S	1-10 S
8-4	163	Optional	1-28 S	1-28 S
8-5	164-165	1st Day: 1-9 S 2nd Day: 10-19 S	1-25 S	1-25 S
8-6	168	Optional	Optional	1-16 S
PSA/C		0 days	0 days	2 days
Review and Testing		3 days	3 days	2 days
Cumulative Review		2 days	2 days	1 day
Total Days		**13**	**11**	**10**

(Level Three 8-2, 8-3 bracketed: 1 day)

NOTE: The codes RRS, PSA/C, and S are explained on page M-9.

CHAPTER 9   FRACTIONS: ADDITION/SUBTRACTION

Review of Related Skills   We suggest that some or all of page 176 be reviewed before proceeding with the chapter.

Skills Lessons   **Objectives**

Section 9-1
Pages 178-179   *To determine whether a fraction is greater than 1, less than 1, or equal to 1 (Example 1)*
To write a mixed number for a fraction greater than 1 (Example 2)
To apply the skill of writing mixed numbers to real-life situations (Page 179)

Section 9-2
Pages 182-183   *To write a fraction in lowest terms (Example)*
To apply the skill of writing fractions in lowest terms to customary measurements (Page 183)

Section 9-3
Pages 186-187   *To add or subtract fractions with common denominators (Example 1)*
To add or subtract mixed numbers with common denominators (Example 2)
To apply the skills of adding and subtracting mixed numbers to real-life situations (Page 187)

Section 9-4
Pages 188-189   *To find the LCD of two fractions (Example 1)*
To write like fractions for unlike fractions (Example 2)

Section 9-5
Pages 190-191   *To add or subtract unlike fractions (Example 1)*
To add or subtract unlike mixed numbers (Example 2)

Section 9-6
Pages 194-195   *To subtract unlike mixed numbers when borrowing is involved (Examples 1 and 2)*

Problem Solving and Applications Lessons

Using Customary Measures
Page 180   *To measure to the nearest inch, nearest $\frac{1}{2}$-inch, nearest $\frac{1}{4}$-inch, nearest $\frac{1}{8}$-inch, and nearest $\frac{1}{16}$-inch*

NOTE: This lesson applies the skills (using fractions and mixed numbers) presented in Section 9-1.

Train Schedules
Page 184   *To use a table to solve word problems*

NOTE: This lesson applies the skills (writing a mixed number in lowest terms) presented in Sections 9-1 and 9-2.

Time Cards
Pages 192-193

To solve two-step problems by applying the technique of the "hidden question"

NOTE: This lesson applies the skill (adding unlike mixed numbers) presented in Section 9-5.

Customary Measures
Pages 196-197

To write a mixed number for a measure (Example)
To use a table to solve word problems

NOTE: This lesson applies the skills (addition and subtraction of mixed numbers in lowest terms) presented in Section 9-2 and 9-3.

Optional Features

Career Lesson Carpet Installer
Page 181

To use a table to estimate costs

Career Lesson Transportation
Page 185

To use a table to solve word problems

SUGGESTED TIMETABLE OF ASSIGNMENTS

Section	Page(s)	Level One	Level Two	Level Three	
RRS	176	1-101 S	1-101 S	Optional	
9-1	179	1-62 S	1-62 S	44-62 S	
9-2	183	1-144 S	1-153 S	1-153 S	} 1 day
9-3	187	1st Day: 1-23 2nd Day: 24-63 S	1-63 S	46-63 S	
9-4	189	1st Day: 1-41 2nd Day: 42-61	1-61 S	22-61 S	} 1 day
9-5	191	1st Day: 1-28 2nd Day: 29-64 S	1-64 S	1-64 S	
9-6	195	1st Day: 1-36 S 2nd Day: 37-72 S	1-72 S	1-72 S	
PSA/C		3 days	3 days	3 days	
Review and Testing		3 days	3 days	2 days	
Total Days		**17**	**13**	**9**	

NOTE: The codes RRS, PSA/C, and S are explained on page M-9.

CHAPTER 10   FRACTIONS: MULTIPLICATION/DIVISION

Review of Related Skills

We suggest that some or all of page 202 be reviewed before proceeding with the chapter.

Skills Lessons **Objectives**

Section 10-1
Pages 204-205

To multiply with fractions (Example 1)
To divide a numerator and denominator by the same number before multiplying fractions (Example 2)

Section 10-2
Pages 208-209

To write a fraction for a mixed number (Table Page 208)
To multiply with mixed numbers (Example)
To apply the skill of multiplying with mixed numbers to real-life situations (Page 209)

Section 10-3
Pages 212-213

To write the reciprocal of a number (Page 212)
To divide with fractions (Example)
To apply the skill of dividing with fractions to real-life situations (Page 213)

Section 10-4
Pages 214-215

To divide with mixed numbers (Example)
To apply the skill of dividing with mixed numbers to real-life situations (Page 215)

Section 10-5
Pages 218-219

To round mixed numbers (Example)
To apply the skill of estimation to problems dealing with addition, subtraction, multiplication, and division of mixed numbers (Page 218)
To apply the skill of estimating answers to problems involving mixed numbers in real-life situations (Page 219)

Problem Solving and Applications Lessons

Science
Page 206

To use multiplication to solve word problems

NOTE: This lesson applies the skill (multiplication of fractions) presented in Section 10-1.

Discount
Page 207

To solve two-step problems by applying the technique of the "hidden question"

NOTE: This lesson applies the skill (multiplication of fractions) presented in Section 10-1.

Distance Formulas
Page 210

To use a formula (distance formula) to solve word problems

NOTE: This lesson applies the skills (multiplication of fractions and mixed numbers) presented in Sections 10-1 and 10-2

Wallpapering and Estimation Page 211	*To solve two-step problems by applying the technique of the "hidden question"*

Optional Features

Career Lesson Business Page 216	*To use division of mixed numbers to solve word problems*
Career Lesson Construction Page 217	*To solve two-step problems by applying the technique of the "hidden question"*
Calculator: Multiplication of Fractions Page 219	*To use a calculator to solve problems involving multiplication of fractions*

SUGGESTED TIMETABLE OF ASSIGNMENTS

Section	Page(s)	Level One	Level Two	Level Three
RRS	202	1-121 S	1-121 S	Optional
10-1	205	1-92 S	1-92 S	49-92 S
10-2	209	1st Day: 1-28 S 2nd Day: 29-86 S	1-86 S	29-86 S
10-3	213	1st Day: 1-40 S 2nd Day: 41-79 S	1-79 S	1-79 S
10-4	215	1st Day: 1-41 S 2nd Day: 42-74 S	1-74 S	1-74 S
10-5	218-219	Optional	1-27 S	1-27 S
PSA/C		1 day	2 days	3 days
Review and Testing		3 days	3 days	2 days
Total Days		**12**	**11**	**9**

(For Level Three, rows 10-1 (49-92 S) and 10-2 (29-86 S) are bracketed together as } 1 day)

NOTE: The codes RRS, PSA/C, and S are explained on page M-9.

CHAPTER 11   CIRCLES AND APPLICATIONS

Review of Related Skills

We suggest that some or all of page 224 be reviewed before proceeding with the chapter.

Skills Lessons   **Objectives**

Section 11-1 Pages 226-227

To find the circumference of a circle using 3.14 as an approximation for π (Example)
To find the circumference of a circle using $\frac{22}{7}$ as an approximation for π (Page 227)

Section 11-2 Pages 230-231

To find the area of a circle using 3.14 as an approximation for π (Example)
To find the area of a circle using $\frac{22}{7}$ as an approximation for π (Page 231)

Section 11-3 Pages 233-234

To find the volume of a cylinder using 3.14 as an approximation for π (Example)
To find the volume of a cylinder using $\frac{22}{7}$ as an approximation for π (Page 234)

Section 11-4 Pages 236-237

To find the volume of a cone using 3.14 as an approximation for π (Example)
To find the volume of a cone using $\frac{22}{7}$ as an approximation for π (Page 237)
To apply the skill of finding the volume of a cup or cone to real-life models (Page 237)

Problem Solving and Applications Lessons

Measuring Angles Pages 228-229

To use a protractor to measure angles

Cans and Cylinders Page 235

To use a formula (surface area of a cylinder) to solve word problems

NOTE: This lesson applies the skill (area of a circle) presented in Section 11-2.

Spheres
Page 238

To use a formula (volume of a sphere) to solve word problems

Optional Features

Career Lesson
Design
Page 232

To use formulas (circumference and area of a circle) to solve word problems

NOTE: In some states and school systems, minimal competency includes only the content covered in Chapters 1-11. For this reason, a Sample Competency Test that covers the content of Chapters 1-11 is included in the Test Booklet portion of the *Teacher's Resource Book*.

If this is the case for your situation, then this will affect the number of days for testing in the following *Suggested Timetable of Assignments*.

SUGGESTED TIMETABLE OF ASSIGNMENTS

Section	Page(s)	Level One	Level Two	Level Three
RRS	224	1-82 S	1-82 S	Optional
11-1	227	1st Day: 1-12 S 2nd Day: 13-20	1-20 S	1-20 S
11-2	231	1st Day: 1-8 2nd Day: 9-16	1-16 S	1-16 S
11-3	234	1st Day: 1-8 2nd Day: 9-16	1-16 S	1-16 S
11-4	237	Optional	Optional	1-19 S
PSA/C		1 day	1 day	2 days
Review and Testing		3 days	2 days	2 days
Cumulative Review		2 days	2 days	1 day
Total Days		13	9	9

NOTE: The codes RRS, PSA/C, and S are explained on page M-9.

Review of
Related Skills

We suggest that some or all of page 246 be reviewed before proceeding with the chapter.

Skills Lessons

Objectives

Section 12-1
Pages 248-249

To review addition and subtraction of whole numbers, decimals, and fractions through the vehicle of solving equations (Examples 1 and 2)
To provide students with the equation-solving skills that will be used in Chapter 14 (Examples 1 and 2)
To solve an addition equation (Example 1)
To solve a subtraction equation (Example 2)

Section 12-2
Pages 252-253

To review multiplication and division of whole numbers, decimals, and fractions,' through the vehicle of solving equations (Examples 1 and 2)
To provide students with the equation-solving skills that will be used in Chapter 14 (Examples 1 and 2)
To solve a multiplication equation (Example 1)
To solve a division equation (Example 2)

Section 12-3
Pages 256-257

To review addition, subtraction, multiplication, and division of whole numbers, decimals, and fractions through the vehicle of solving equations (Examples 1 and 2)
To provide students with the equation-solving skills that will be used in Chapter 14 (Examples 1 and 2)
To solve an equation by using the operations of subtraction and division (Example 1)
To solve an equation by using the operations of addition and multiplication (Example 2)

Section 12-4
Pages 260-261

To write a ratio as a fraction in lowest terms (Table page 260)
To determine whether two ratios are equivalent (Example)
To apply the skill of writing a ratio as a fraction in lowest terms to real-life situations (Page 261)

Section 12-5
Pages 264-265

To solve a proportion for n (Example)
To apply the skill of solving a proportion to real-life situations (Page 265)

Problem Solving and Applications Lessons

Net Pay
Page 250

To use a formula (net pay formula) to solve word problems

NOTE: This lesson applies the skill (solving an addition equation) presented in Section 12-1.

Mortgage Loans
Page 251

To use a formula (mortgage loan formula) to solve word problems

NOTE: This lesson applies the skill (solving a subtraction equation) presented in Section 12-1.

Batting Average
Page 254

To use a formula (batting average formula) to solve word problems

NOTE: This lesson applies the skill (solving a division equation) presented in Section 12-2.

Driving Range
Page 255

To use a formula (driving range formula) to solve word problems

NOTE: This lesson applies the skill (solving a multiplication equation) presented in Section 12-2.

Overtime Pay
Page 258

To use a formula (gross earnings formula) to solve word problems

NOTE: This lesson applies the skill (using more than one operation to solve equations) presented in Section 12-3.

Renting a Car
Page 259

To use a formula (car rental formula) to solve problems

NOTE: This lesson applies the skill (using more than one operation to solve equations) presented in Section 12-3.

Energy Efficiency Ratio
Page 262

To use a formula (energy efficiency ratio formula) to solve word problems

NOTE: This lesson applies the skill (ratio) presented in Section 12-4.

Scale Drawings
Page 266

To use a proportion to find distance

NOTE: This lesson applies the skill (solving a proportion) presented in Section 12-5.

Optional Features

Career Lesson
Photography
Page 263
To use ratios to solve problems

Career Lesson
Drafting
Page 267
To use ratio and proportion to solve word problems

SUGGESTED TIMETABLE OF ASSIGNMENTS

Section	Page(s)	Level One	Level Two	Level Three
RRS	246	1-78 S	1-78 S	Optional
12-1	249	1st Day: 1-28 S 2nd Day: 29-52 S	1-52 S	1-52 S
12-2	253	1st Day: 1-30 S 2nd Day: 31-90 S	1-90 S	1-90 S
12-3	257	1st Day: 1-27 S 2nd Day: 28-64 S	1-64 S	1-64 S
12-4	261	1-64 S	1-64 S	1-64 S
12-5	265	1st Day: 1-20 2nd Day: 21-60 S	1-63 S	1-63 S
PSA/C		3 days	3 days	4 days
Review and Testing		3 days	3 days	2 days
Total Days		**16**	**12**	**11**

NOTE: The codes RRS, PSA/C, and S are explained on page M-9.

CHAPTER 13   PER CENT

Review of Related Skills We suggest that some or all of page 272 be reviewed before proceeding with the chapter.

Skills Lessons **Objectives**

Section 13-1
Pages 274-275
To write a per cent for a fraction with a denominator of 100 (Example 1)
To write a per cent for a two-place decimal (Example 2)
To apply the skill of writing a per cent for a fraction with a denominator of 100 to real-life situations (Page 275)

Section 13-2
Pages 276-277
To write a decimal for a per cent (Example 1)
To write a decimal for a per cent when inserting zeros is involved (Example 2)
To write a per cent for a decimal (Example 3)
To apply the skill of writing a decimal for a per cent to real-life situations (Page 277)

Section 13-3
Pages 278-279
To write a fraction for a per cent (Example 1)
To write a fraction for a per cent that contains a fraction (Example 2)
To apply the skill of writing a fraction for a per cent to real-life situations (Page 279)

Section 13-4
Pages 280-281
To write a per cent for a fraction or mixed number (Example 1)
To write a per cent for a fraction or mixed number when the related division problem involves a nonzero remainder. (Example 2)

Section 13-5
Pages 282-283
To find a per cent of a number by using a decimal for the per cent (Example 1)
To find a per cent of a number by using a fraction for the per cent (Example 2)
To apply the skill of finding a per cent of a number to real-life situations (Page 283)

Section 13-6
Pages 288-289
To find the amount of simple interest (Example 1)
To find the amount of compound interest (Example 2)

Section 13-7
Pages 291-293

To estimate a per cent of a number by rounding the number (Example 1)

To estimate a per cent of a number by rounding the per cent (Example 2)

Problem Solving and
Applications Lessons

Discount
Pages 284-285

To solve two-step problems by applying the technique of the "hidden question"

NOTE: This lesson applies the skill (finding a per cent of a number) presented in Section 13-5.

Commission
Pages 286-287

To use a formula (commission formula) to solve word problems (Example 1)

To solve two-step problems by applying the technique of the "hidden question" (Example 2)

NOTE: This lesson applies the skill (finding a per cent of a number) presented in Section 13-5.

Optional Features

Career Lesson
Banking
Page 290

To use a table to find compound interest

Calculator:
Writing
Per Cents
Page 281

To use a calculator to solve problems that involve writing a per cent for a mixed number

Calculator:
Finding
Discount
Page 293

To use the skill of estimation and a calculator to solve problems that involve discount

NOTE: The *Suggested Timetable of Assignments* is on the next page.

SUGGESTED TIMETABLE OF ASSIGNMENTS

Section	Page(s)	Level One	Level Two	Level Three
RRS	272	1-71 S	1-71 S	Optional
13-1	274-275	1st Day: 1-36 S 2nd Day: 37-59 S	1-59 S	37-59 S
13-2	277	1st Day: 1-40 S 2nd Day: 41-73 S	1-73 S	1-73 S
13-3	279	1st Day: 1-48 2nd Day: 49-83 S	1-83 S	49-83 S
13-4	281	1st Day: 1-30 S 2nd Day: 31-60 S	1-60 S	1-60 S
13-5	283	1st Day: 1-20 2nd Day: 21-62 S	1st Day: 1-20 2nd Day: 21-62 S	1-62 S
13-6	289	1-10	1-18 S	1-18 S
13-7	292-293	Optional	1-26 S	1-26 S
PSA/C		2 days	2 days	3 days
Review and Testing		3 days	2 days	1 day
Total Days		*19	13	10

(13-1 and 13-2 Level Three: 37-59 S and 1-73 S bracketed together as "1 day")

*An additional two days is allowed for those teachers who may wish to have Level 1 students do the Sample Competency Test: Chapters 1-14 on pages 324-327. For Level 1 students, omit items 22 and 42 on this test.

The Teacher's Resource Book contains a Sample Competency Test: Chapters 1-14 which may also be used at this time. For Level 1 students, omit items 20, 21, and 42.

NOTE: The codes RRS, PSA/C, and S are explained on page M-9.

CHAPTER 14   MORE ON PER CENT

Review of Related Skills
We suggest that some or all of page 298 be reviewed before proceeding with the chapter.

Skills Lessons   **Objectives**

Section 14-1
Pages 300-301
To find what per cent one number is of another (Example 1)
To find what per cent one number is of another when reducing fractions is involved (Example 2)

Section 14-2
Pages 303-304
To find the per cent of increase (Example 1)
To find the per cent of decrease (Example 2)
To apply the skill of finding per cent of increase and decrease to real-life situations (Page 304)

Section 14-3
Pages 306-307
To find a number when a per cent of it is known by writing the per cent as a decimal (Example 1)
To find a number when a per cent of it is known by writing the per cent as a fraction (Example 2)
To apply the skill of finding a number when a per cent of it is known to real-life situations (Page 307)
To review the three types of per cent problems (Examples 1 and 2)

Section 14-4
Pages 310-312
To find what per cent one number is of another and to find a number when a per cent of it is known (Example 2)

Section 14-5
Pages 314-316
To review solving word problems that involve per cent (Examples 1-3)
To solve word problems that involve finding a per cent of a number (Example 1)
To solve word problems that involve finding what per cent one number is of another (Example 2)
To solve word problems that involve finding a number when a per cent of it is known (Example 3)

Problem Solving and Applications Lessons

Interest Rate
Page 302
To use a formula (interest rate formula) to solve word problems

NOTE: This lesson applies the skill (finding what per cent one number is of another) presented in Section 14-1.

Sports Page 305	*To estimate per cent of increase and decrease*
	NOTE: This lesson applies the skill (finding the per cent of increase and decrease) presented in Section 14-2.
Markup and Selling Price Page 308	*To use a formula (selling price formula) to solve word problems*
	NOTE: This lesson applies the skill (finding a number given a per cent) presented in Section 14-3.
Energy Costs Page 313	*To use a table to compute costs*
	NOTE: This lesson applies the skill (finding a per cent of a number) presented in Section 14-4.
Minimum Wage Page 317	*To use per cent of increase to solve problems*
	NOTE: This lesson applies the skill (finding per cent of increase) presented in Section 14-2.

Optional Features

Career Lesson Health	*To use a table to solve word problems*

SUGGESTED TIMETABLE OF ASSIGNMENTS

Section	Page(s)	Level Two	Level Three
RRS	298	1-76 S	Optional
14-1	301	1-42 S	1-42 S
14-2	304	1-16	1-16 S
14-3	307	1-36 S	1-36 S
14-4	311-312	1-49 S	1-49 S
14-5	315-316	1-15	1-15 S
PSA/C		2 days	3 days
Review and Testing		3 days	2 days
Cumulative Review		2 days	1 day
Total Days		13	11

NOTE: The codes RRS, PSA/C, and S are explained on page M-9.

CHAPTER 15   STATISTICS

Review of Related Skills

We suggest that some or all of page 328 be reviewed before proceeding with the chapter.

Skills Lessons   **Objectives**

Section 15-1
Pages 330-331

To find the mean of a list of measures (Example 1)
To find the mode of a list of measures (Example 2)

Section 15-2
Pages 332-333

To find the median for an odd number of measures (Example 1)
To find the median for an even number of measures (Example 2)

Section 15-3
Pages 336-337

To list data by using equal intervals in a table (Example)

Section 15-4
Pages 338-339

To use a histogram to show data (Example)

Section 15-5
Pages 340-341

To use a circle graph to show data (Example)

Career Lesson
Business
Pages 334-335

To compare the mean, median, and mode

SUGGESTED TIMETABLE OF ASSIGNMENTS

Section	Page(s)	Level Two	Level Three
RRS	328	1-47 S	Optional
15-1	331	1-8	1-8 ⎫
			⎬ 1 day
15-2	333	1-6	1-6 ⎭
15-3	337	1-6	1-6
15-4	339	1-4	1-4
15-5	341	1-6 S	1-6 S
PSA/C		—	1 day
Review and Testing		2 days	2 days
Total Days		8	7

NOTE: The codes RRS, PSA/C, and S are explained on page M-9.

CHAPTER 16   PROBABILITY

Review of Related Skills   We suggest that some or all of page 346 be reviewed before proceeding with the chapter.

Skills Lessons   **Objectives**

Section 16-1
Pages 348-349   *To find the probability of an event (Exercises)*

Section 16-2
Pages 350-351   *To use a table to find the probability of an event (Example 1)*
To apply the skill of finding probability to real-life situations (Page 351)

Section 16-3
Pages 353-354   *To use a tree diagram to find the probability of an event (Example)*

Problem Solving and Applications Lessons

Chances and Choice
Pages 355-356   *To multiply probabilities*

NOTE: This lesson applies the skills (finding probabilities) presented in Section 16-1, 16-2, and 16-3.

Optional Features

Career Lesson Quality Control
Page 352   *To apply probability to sampling and quality control*

SUGGESTED TIMETABLE OF ASSIGNMENTS

Section	Page(s)	Level Two	Level Three
RRS	346	1-106 S	Optional
16-1	349	1-24	1-24
16-2	351	1-18	1-18
16-3	354	Optional	1-14
PSA/C		—	1 day
Review and Testing		2 days	2 days
Cumulative Review		1 day	1 day
Total Days		6	7

NOTE: The codes RRS, PSA/C, and S are explained on page M-9.

CHAPTER 17   SQUARES AND SQUARE ROOTS

Review of Related Skills   We suggest that some or all of page 364 be reviewed before proceeding with the chapter.

Skills Lessons   **Objectives**

Section 17-1
Pages 366-367

To square a number (Example 1)
To find the square root of a number (Example 2)
To apply the skills of squaring a number and of finding the square root of a number to real-life situations (Page 367)

Section 17-2
Pages 368-370

To use a table of squares and square roots (Example 1)
To use a table of squares and square roots to find the square roots of some numbers greater than 150 (Example 2)
To apply the skill of using a table of squares and square roots to real-life situations (Page 370)

Section 17-3
Pages 371-373

To use the Rule of Pythagoras to find the measure of the hypotenuse of a right triangle (Example 1)
To use the Rule of Pythagoras to find the measure of one leg of a right triangle (Example 2)
To apply the skill of finding the measure of a side of a right triangle to real-life situations (Page 373)

Section 17-4
Pages 374-376

To use a proportion to solve problems involving the measures of corresponding sides of similar triangles (Example)
To apply the skill of solving proportions to real-life situations (Page 376)

Section 17-5
Pages 378-380

To use the tangent ratio to find the tangent of an acute angle of a right triangle (Example 1)
To use the tangent ratio and the tangent table to find the measure of a leg of a right triangle (Example 2)
To use the skill of using the tangent ratio and the tangent table to find the measure of a leg of a right triangle to real-life situations (Page 380)

Optional Feature

Career Lesson Traffic Officer Page 377

To use a formula involving square root to solve word problems

Section	17-1	17-2	17-3	17-4	17-5	PSA/C	Rev/Test	Total
Level 3	1-96 S	1-83 S	1-10	1-10	1-17 S	1 day	2 days	7 days

1 day

NOTE: The codes PSA/C and S are explained on page M-9.

CHAPTER 18   INTEGERS: ADDITION/SUBTRACTION

Review of Related Skills

We suggest that some or all of page 386 be reviewed before proceeding with the chapter.

Skills Lessons   **Objectives**

Section 18-1
Pages 388-389

To write a positive or negative number to represent a word description (Example 1)
To write the integer represented by a point on a number line (Example 2)
To apply the skill of writing integers to real-life situations (Page 389)

Section 18-2
Pages 390-391

To write the opposite of an integer (Example 1)
To use a number line to compare integers (Example 2)
To apply the skill of comparing integers to real-life situations (Page 391)

Section 18-3
Pages 392-393

To add two positive integers on a number line (Example 1)
To add two negative integers on a number line (Example 2)
To apply the skill of adding integers on a number line to real-life situations (Page 393)

Section 18-4	*To add integers having unlike signs when the first addend is a negative integer (Example 1)*
Pages 394-395	*To add integers having unlike signs when the first addend is a positive integer (Example 2)*
	To apply the skill of adding integers to real-life situations (Page 395)

Section 18-5	*To write an addition problem for a subtraction problem (Example 1)*
Pages 396-397	*To subtract two integers on a number line (Example 2)*

Problem Solving and
Applications Lesson

Wind Chill	*To use a table to solve problems (Example 1)*
Page 398	*To use a table and subtraction of integers to solve problems (Example 2)*

NOTE: This lesson applies the skill (subtraction of integers) presented in Section 18-5.

Optional Feature

Career Lesson Automobile Maintenance Page 399	*To use a bar graph and subtraction of integers to solve word problems*

SUGGESTED TIMETABLE OF ASSIGNMENTS

Section	18-1	18-2	18-3	18-4	18-5	PSA/C	Rev/Test	Total
Level 3	1-36 S	1-43 S	1-71 S	1-65 S	1-76 S	1 day	2 days	7 days

1 day

NOTE: The codes PSA/C and S are explained on page M-9.

Review of Related Skills	We suggest that some or all of page 404 be reviewed before proceeding with the chapter.

Skills Lessons   **Objectives**

Section 19-1
Pages 406-407

To multiply two integers having unlike signs (Example)
To apply the skill of multiplying integers with unlike signs to real-life situations (Page 407)

Section 19-2
Pages 408-409

To multiply two integers having like signs (Example)

Section 19-3
Pages 410-411

To divide two integers (Example)

Section 19-4
Pages 412-413

To write a fraction for a rational number (Example 1)
To write the rational number represented by a point on a number line (Example 2)
To use the number line to arrange numbers in order (Pages 412-413)

Problem Solving and Applications Lesson

Conserving Energy
Page 414

To use a formula (heat transfer formula) and multiplication of positive and negative numbers to solve word problems

Optional Features

Career Lesson Business
Page 415

To use positive and negative numbers to solve problems related to stocks

Calculator: Multiplication
Page 409

To use a calculator to check answers to problems involving multiplication of positive and negative numbers

Calculator: Division
Page 411

To use a calculator to check answers to problems involving division of positive and negative numbers

SUGGESTED TIMETABLE OF ASSIGNMENTS

Section	19-1	19-2	19-3	19-4	PSA/C	Rev/Test	Total
Level 3	1-70 S	1-66 S	1-31	1-54 S	1 day	2 days	**7 days**

NOTE: The codes PSA/C and S are explained on page M-9.

Review of Related Skills	We suggest that some or all of page 420 be reviewed before proceeding with the chapter.

Skills Lessons   **Objectives**

Section 20-1
Pages 422-423
To name the coordinates for points on a graph (Example 1
To graph points in a coordinate plane (Example 2)

Section 20-2
Pages 426-428
To make a table of ordered pairs for an equation (Example 1)
To use ordered pairs to graph an equation (first quadrant only)
(Example 1)
To use ordered pairs to graph an equation (Example 2)

Section 20-3
Pages 429-430
To use negative integers to solve an addition equation (Example 1)
To use positive integers to solve a subtraction equation (Example 2)

Section 20-4
Pages 431-432
To use positive and negative integers to solve a multiplication equation (Example 1)
To use positive and negative integers to solve a division equation (Example 2)

Section 20-5
Pages 433-434
To use addition and division of integers to solve equations involving more than one operation (Example 1)
To use subtraction and multiplication of integers to solve equations involving more than one operation (Example 2)

Problem Solving and Applications Lesson

Latitude and Longitude
Page 424
To use latitude and longitude to locate cities on a map

NOTE: This lesson applies the skill (naming the coordinates for a point) presented in Section 20-1.

Optional Feature

Career Lesson Travel Planning
Page 425
To use a letter-number pair to locate places on a map

NOTE: The *Suggested Timetable of Assignments* is on the next page.

SUGGESTED TIMETABLE OF ASSIGNMENTS

Section	20-1	20-2	20-3	20-4	20-5	PSA/C	Rev/Test	Total
Level 3	1-18	1-36 S	1-108 S	1-72 S	1-52 S	1 day	3 days	**9 days**

NOTE: The codes PSA/C and S are explained on page M-9.

General Mathematics

SKILLS

PROBLEM SOLVING

APPLICATIONS

William J. Gerardi   **Wilmer L. Jones**   **Thomas R. Foster**

 Harcourt Brace Jovanovich, Publishers

New York   Chicago   San Francisco   Atlanta   Dallas   *and*   London

ABOUT THE AUTHORS

WILLIAM J. GERARDI
Mathematics Teacher
Boys' Latin School
Baltimore, Maryland
Formerly Principal
Baltimore Polytechnic Institute

WILMER L. JONES
Coordinator of Mathematics
Baltimore City Public Schools
Baltimore, Maryland

THOMAS R. FOSTER
Deputy Superintendent
Educational Support Services
Baltimore City Public Schools
Baltimore, Maryland

EDITORIAL ADVISORS

Dr. George Braithwaite
Assistant Principal
W. R. Thomas Junior High School
Miami, Florida

Gerlena Clark
Mathematics Coordinator
Manual Arts High School
Los Angeles, California

Donald E. Darnell
Director of Personnel Services
Formerly Supervisor of Mathematics
Kansas City Public Schools
Kansas City, Kansas

Dr. Helen S. Edens
Supervisor of Mathematics
Chesterfield School Board
Chesterfield, Virginia

Dr. Philip Halloran
Supervisor of Mathematics
Springfield, Massachusetts

George W. Saunders
Chairman, Mathematics Department
Leuzinger High School
Lawndale, California

Elgin Schilhab
Coordinator of Secondary Mathematics
Austin Independent School District
Austin, Texas

Printed in the United States of America

ISBN 0-15-353600-4

CONTENTS

UNIT I WHOLE NUMBERS

Chapter 1 Whole Numbers: Addition/Subtraction   viii

Skills   1–1 Addition: Two-Digit Numbers   2
                  1–2 Addition: Three or More Digits   6
                  1–3 Subtraction: Two-Digit Numbers   10
                  1–4 Subtraction: Three or More Digits   14
                  1–5 Rounding and Estimation   17
Problem Solving and Applications Making Change 4   •   Buying a New Car 8
   •   Time Zones 12   •   Reading a Meter 16
Features Career: Food Services 5   •   Calculator Exercises 11, 19
Review and Testing Review of Related Skills viii, 2, 7, 10, 14, 17   •   Chapter
Review 20   •   Chapter Test 22   •   Additional Practice 23

Chapter 2 Whole Numbers: Multiplication   24

Skills   2–1 One–Digit Multipliers   26
                  2–2 Two- and Three–Digit Multipliers   32
                  2–3 Zeros in Multiplication   36
                  2–4 Multiplying by 10, by 100, by 1000   40
Problem Solving and Applications Ordering by Mail 28   •   Message Units 30
   •   Cost of Electricity 34   •   Gross Pay and Net Pay 38
Features Career: Automobile Repair 41   •   Calculator Exercises 37
Review and Testing Review of Related Skills 24, 26, 32, 36, 40   •   Chapter
Review 42   •   Chapter Test 44   •   Additional Practice 45

Chapter 3 Whole Numbers: Division   46

Skills   3–1 Rules for Divisibility   48
                  3–2 One–Digit Divisors   50
                  3–3 Two- and Three–Digit Divisors   54
                  3–4 Zeros in the Quotient   58
                  3–5 Order of Operations   62
                  3–6 Rounding and Estimation   64
Problem Solving and Applications Averages 52   •   Finance Charges 56
   •   Fuel Economy 60   •   Fuel Costs for a Car 61
Features Career: Office Worker 57   •   Calculator Exercises 63, 65
Review and Testing Review of Related Skills 46, 49, 51, 55, 58, 63, 64   •   Chapter
Review 66   •   Chapter Test 68   •   Additional Practice 69

Chapter 4 Graphs and Applications   70

Skills   4–1 Pictographs and Applications   72
                  4–2 Bar Graphs and Applications   74
                  4–3 Line Graphs and Applications   76
                  4–4 Other Graphs and Applications   78
Feature Career: Government Service 80
Review and Testing Review of Related Skills 70, 72, 74, 76, 78   •   Chapter Review 81   •
Chapter Test 83   •   Additional Practice 84   •   Cumulative Review: Chapters 1–4 86

UNIT II DECIMALS/MEASUREMENT

Chapter 5 Decimals: Addition/Subtraction/Multiplication   **88**

Skills
- 5–1 Decimals and Place Value   90
- 5–2 Addition and Subtraction   94
- 5–3 Multiplication   98
- 5–4 Moving the Decimal Point   102

Problem Solving and Applications Writing Checks 92 • Sales Tax 96 • Making Change 97 • Cost of Credit 100

Features Career: Retailing 101 • Calculator Exercises 99

Review and Testing Review of Related Skills 88, 91, 94, 98, 102 • Chapter Review 104 • Chapter Test 106 • Additional Practice 107

Chapter 6 Decimals: Division   **108**

Skills
- 6–1 Dividing a Decimal by a Whole Number   110
- 6–2 Dividing by a Decimal   112
- 6–3 Dividing by 10, by 100, by 1000   116
- 6–4 Rounding Decimals   120
- 6–5 Division with Remainders   122
- 6–6 Estimation   126

Problem Solving and Applications Rate 114 • Heating Costs 118 • Comparison Shopping 124

Features Career: Insurance 119 • Calculator Exercises 127

Review and Testing Review of Related Skills 108, 110, 113, 117, 120, 122 • Chapter Review 128 • Chapter Test 130 • Additional Practice 131

Chapter 7 Applying Metric Measures I   **132**

Skills
- 7–1 Units of Length   134
- 7–2 Measurement   136
- 7–3 Perimeter and Applications   140
- 7–4 Area and Applications: Rectangles/Squares   143
- 7–5 Area and Applications: Parallelograms/Triangles   145
- 7–6 Area and Applications: Trapezoids   147

Problem Solving and Applications Distance on a Map 135 • Distance 139 • Floor Space 149

Feature Career: Industry 138

Review and Testing Review of Related Skills 132, 136, 140, 143, 146, 147 • Chapter Review 150 • Chapter Test 152 • Additional Practice 153

Chapter 8 Applying Metric Measures II   **154**

Skills
- 8–1 Units of Capacity and Applications   156
- 8–2 Units of Mass and Applications   158
- 8–3 Temperature and Applications   160
- 8–4 Surface Area and Applications   162
- 8–5 Volume and Applications   164
- 8–6 Pyramids and Applications   167

Problem Solving and Applications Volume/Capacity/Mass 166

Features Career: Weather Forecasting 161 • Calculator Exercises 161

Review and Testing Review of Related Skills 154, 156, 158, 162, 164, 167 • Chapter Review 169 • Chapter Test 171 • Additional Practice 172 • Cumulative Review: Chapters 5–8 173

UNIT III   FRACTIONS/MEASUREMENT

Chapter 9   Fractions: Addition/Subtraction   **176**
Skills   9–1   Fractions and Mixed Numbers   178
                  9–2   Lowest Terms   182
                  9–3   Addition and Subtraction: Like Fractions   186
                  9–4   Writing Like Fractions   188
                  9–5   Addition and Subtraction: Unlike Fractions   190
                  9–6   Subtraction: Mixed Numbers   194
Problem Solving and Applications   Using Customary Measures 180   ●   Train
Schedules 184   ●   Time Cards 192   ●   Customary Measures 196
Features   Careers: Carpet Installer 181   ●   Transportation 185
Review and Testing   Review of Related Skills 176, 179, 182, 186, 189, 190, 194   ●
Chapter Review 198   ●   Chapter Test 200   ●   Additional Practice 201

Chapter 10   Fractions: Multiplication/Division   **202**
Skills   10–1   Multiplication: Fractions   204
                  10–2   Multiplication: Mixed Numbers   208
                  10–3   Division: Fractions   212
                  10–4   Division: Mixed Numbers   214
                  10–5   Rounding and Estimation   219
Problem Solving and Applications   Science 206   ●   Discount 207
●   Distance Formula 210   ●   Wallpapering and Estimation 211
Features   Careers: Business 216   ●   Construction 217   ●   Calculator Exercises 219
Review and Testing   Review of Related Skills 202, 205, 208, 212, 214   ●   Chapter
Review 220   ●   Chapter Test 222   ●   Additional Practice 223

Chapter 11   Circles and Applications   **224**
Skills   11–1   Circumference and Applications   226
                  11–2   Area and Applications   230
                  11–3   Volume and Applications: Cylinders   233
                  11–4   Volume and Applications: Cones   236
Problem Solving and Applications   Measuring Angles 228   ●   Cans and
Cylinders 235   ●   Spheres 238
Features   Career: Design 232   ●   Calculator Exercises 235, 238
Review and Testing   Review of Related Skills 224, 226, 230, 233, 236   ●   Chapter
Review 239   ●   Chapter Test 241   ●   Additional Practice 242   ●
Cumulative Review: Chapters 9–11 243

UNIT IV   RATIO/PROPORTION/PER CENT

Chapter 12   Equations/Ratio and Proportion   **246**
Skills   12–1   Solving Equations: Addition/Subtraction   248
                  12–2   Solving Equations: Multiplication/Division   252
                  12–3   More on Solving Equations   256
                  12–4   Ratio   260
                  12–5   Proportion   264
Problem Solving and Applications   Net Pay 250   ●   Mortgage Loans 251   ●
Batting Average 254   ●   Driving Range 255   ●   Overtime Pay 258   ●
Renting a Car 259   ●   Energy Efficiency Ratio 262   ●   Scale Drawings 266
Features   Careers: Photography 263   ●   Drafting 267
Review and Testing   Review of Related Skills 246, 249, 252, 256, 260, 264   ●   Chapter
Review 268   ●   Chapter Test 270   ●   Additional Practice 271

Chapter 13   Per Cent   272

Skills   13–1   Meaning of Per Cent   274
           13–2   Per Cents and Decimals   276
           13–3   Writing Fractions for Per Cents   278
           13–4   Writing Per Cents for Fractions   280
           13–5   Finding a Per Cent of a Number   282
           13–6   Interest   288
           13–7   Rounding and Estimation   291

Problem Solving and Applications   Discount 284   •   Commission 286
Features   Career: Banking 290   •   Calculator Exercises 281, 293
Review and Testing   Review of Related Skills 272, 274, 277, 278, 280, 283, 288, 291 •
Chapter Review 294   •   Chapter Test 296   •   Additional Practice 297

Chapter 14   More on Per Cent   298

Skills   14–1   Finding What Per Cent a Number is of Another   300
           14–2   Per Cent of Increase or Decrease   303
           14–3   Finding a Number Given a Per Cent   306
           14–4   Review of Per Cent   310
           14–5   Review of Word Problems with Per Cent   314

Problem Solving and Applications   Interest Rate 302   •   Sports 305   •
Markup and Selling Price 308   •   Energy Costs 313   •   Minimum Wage 317
Features   Career: Health 309   •   Calculator Exercises 313
Review and Testing   Review of Related Skills 298, 301, 304, 306, 311, 315   •   Chapter Review
318   •   Chapter Test 320   •   Additional Practice 321   •   Cumulative Review:
Chapters 12–14 322   •   Sample Competency Test: Chapters 1–14 324

UNIT V   STATISTICS/PROBABILITY

Chapter 15   Statistics   328

Skills   15–1   The Mean and the Mode with Applications   330
           15–2   The Median with Applications   332
           15–3   Listing Data   336
           15–4   The Histogram with Applications   338
           15–5   Circle Graphs   340

Feature   Career: Business 334
Review and Testing   Review of Related Skills 328, 331, 333, 336, 339, 341   •   Chapter
Review 342   •   Chapter Test 344   •   Additional Practice 345

Chapter 16   Probability   346

Skills   16–1   Probability   348
           16–2   Probability and Tables   350
           16–3   Tree Diagrams   353

Problem Solving and Applications   Chances and Choices 355
Feature   Career: Quality Control 352
Review and Testing   Review of Related Skills 346, 348, 351, 353   •   Chapter Review 357   •
Chapter Test 359   •   Additional Practice 360   •   Cumulative Review: Chapters 15–16 362

UNIT VI PRE-ALGEBRA

Chapter 17   Squares and Square Roots **364**

Skills 17–1 Squares and Square Roots 366
17–2 Using a Table of Squares and Square Roots 368
17–3 Right Triangle Rule and Applications 371
17–4 Similar Triangles and Applications 374
17–5 Tangent Ratios and Applications 378

Features Career: Traffic Officer 377 ● Calculator Exercises 377
Review and Testing Review of Related Skills 364, 366, 372, 375, 379 ● Chapter
Review 381 ● Chapter Test 383 ● Additional Practice 384

Chapter 18   Integers: Addition/Subtraction **386**

Skills 18–1 Positive and Negative Numbers 388
18–2 Comparing Integers 390
18–3 Adding Integers: Like Signs 392
18–4 Adding Integers: Unlike Signs 394
18–5 Subtracting Integers 396
Problem Solving and Applications Wind Chill 398
Feature Career: Automobile Maintenance 399
Review and Testing Review of Related Skills 386, 390, 392, 395, 397 ● Chapter
Review 400 ● Chapter Test 402 ● Additional Practice 403

Chapter 19   Integers: Multiplication/Division **404**

Skills 19–1 Multiplying Integers: Unlike Signs 406
19–2 Multiplying Integers: Like Signs 408
19–3 Dividing Integers 410
19–4 Rational Numbers 412
Problem Solving and Applications Conserving Energy 414
Features Calculator Exercises 409, 411 ● Career: Business 415
Review and Testing Review of Related Skills 404, 406, 408, 411, 412 ● Chapter
Review 416 ● Chapter Test 418 ● Additional Practice 419

Chapter 20   Graphing and Equations **420**

Skills 20–1 Graphing Ordered Pairs 422
20–2 Graphing Equations 426
20–3 Equations and Integers: Addition/Subtraction 429
20–4 Equations and Integers: Multiplication/Division 431
20–5 Equations and Integers: Two Operations 433
Problem Solving and Applications Latitude and Longitude 424
Feature Career: Travel Planning 425
Review and Testing Review of Related Skills 420, 423, 427, 429, 431, 433 ● Chapter
Review 435 ● Chapter Test 437 ● Additional Practice 438 ● Cumulative Review:
Chapters 17–20 439 ● Sample Competency Test: Chapters 1–20 441

Review of Skills **445**   **Glossary** **465**
Tables of Measurement **451**   **Index** **468**
Answers to Review of Related Skills **452**   **Listing of Careers and Applications** **472**

We suggest that some or all of this page be reviewed before proceeding with the chapter.

REVIEW OF RELATED SKILLS FOR CHAPTER 1

Add.

1. 9 +6 = 15	2. 5 +9 = 14	3. 8 +6 = 14	4. 1 +4 = 5	5. 5 +8 = 13	6. 4 +2 = 6	7. 3 +5 = 8
8. 4 +8 = 12	9. 7 +0 = 7	10. 3 +1 = 4	11. 6 +4 = 10	12. 6 +6 = 12	13. 3 +2 = 5	14. 6 +3 = 9
15. 4 +3 = 7	16. 1 +5 = 6	17. 8 +2 = 10	18. 9 +1 = 10	19. 2 +7 = 9	20. 3 +3 = 6	21. 9 +2 = 11
22. 7 +1 = 8	23. 7 +7 = 14	24. 9 +9 = 18	25. 6 +1 = 7	26. 0 +8 = 8	27. 4 +4 = 8	28. 6 +2 = 8
29. 8 +9 = 17	30. 6 +7 = 13	31. 5 +2 = 7	32. 7 +3 = 10	33. 9 +5 = 14	34. 2 +8 = 10	35. 9 +7 = 16

36. 3, 5, 7, +6 = 21
37. 4, 7, 2, +9 = 22
38. 20, 50, 30, +70 = 170
39. 80, 20, 10, + 0 = 110
40. 400, 900, 300, +500 = 2100
41. 400, 500, 600, +100 = 1600

42. 80, 90, 70, +40 = 280
43. 60, 50, 80, +20 = 210
44. 400, 200, 300, +100 = 1000
45. 200, 300, 700, +600 = 1800
46. 500, 400, 900, +500 = 2300
47. 100, 400, 900, +200 = 1600

Complete.

48. 73 = __?7__ tens + __?3__ ones
49. 672 = __?6__ hundreds + __?7__ tens + __?2__ ones
50. 94 = __?9__ tens + __?4__ ones
51. 836 = __?8__ hundreds + __?3__ tens + __?6__ ones
52. 45 = 4 __?__ tens + __?__ ones (5)
53. 612 = 6 __?__ hundreds + 1 __?__ ten + __?__ ones (2)

Subtract.

54. 13 −5 = 8	55. 9 −6 = 3	56. 13 −8 = 5	57. 14 −5 = 9	58. 9 −9 = 0	59. 16 −7 = 9	60. 14 −7 = 7
61. 11 −8 = 3	62. 5 −1 = 4	63. 15 −8 = 7	64. 14 −6 = 8	65. 11 −7 = 4	66. 8 −1 = 7	67. 12 −5 = 7
68. 11 −2 = 9	69. 9 −0 = 9	70. 10 −7 = 3	71. 15 −9 = 6	72. 6 −4 = 2	73. 11 −5 = 6	74. 8 −8 = 0
75. 14 −9 = 5	76. 2 −2 = 0	77. 11 −4 = 7	78. 13 −6 = 7	79. 8 −4 = 4	80. 6 −6 = 0	81. 16 −9 = 7

Review of Related Skills

CHAPTER

1 WHOLE NUMBERS ADDITION/SUBTRACTION

SKILLS

1-1   Addition: Two-Digit Numbers
1-2   Addition: Three or More Digits
1-3   Subtraction: Two-Digit Numbers
1-4   Subtraction: Three or More Digits
1-5   Rounding and Estimation

APPLICATIONS

Making Change
Buying a New Car
Time Zones
Reading a Meter

CAREER

Food Services

1-1 Addition: Two-Digit Numbers

See the Teacher's Manual for the objectives.

To add two-digit numbers, write the numbers one under the other. Line up the "ones" on the right.

PROCEDURE To add two-digit whole numbers:

1 Add the ones.

2 Add the tens.

EXAMPLE 1 Add: **a.** $38 + 71$ **b.** $61 + 5 + 93$

Solution: Line up the ones on the right. Then add.

a.
$$\begin{array}{r} 38 \\ +71 \\ \hline \mathbf{109} \end{array}$$

b.
$$\begin{array}{r} 61 \\ 5 \\ +93 \\ \hline \mathbf{159} \end{array}$$

After completing Example 1, you may wish to have students do some or all of Exercises 1-24.

When the sum in the "ones" column is 10 or more, you add ("carry") the tens to the tens column.

EXAMPLE 2 Add: $46 + 83 + 96 + 59$

Solution: 1 Add the ones. Carry the two "tens" to the tens column.

$$6 + 3 + 6 + 9 = 24$$

$$\begin{array}{r} 2 \leftarrow \\ 46 \\ 83 \\ 96 \\ +59 \\ \hline 4 \leftarrow \end{array}$$

2 Add the tens.

$$20 + 40 + 80 + 90 + 50 = 280$$

$$\begin{array}{r} 2 \\ 46 \\ 83 \\ 96 \\ +59 \\ \hline \mathbf{284} \end{array}$$

REVIEW OF RELATED SKILLS

You may wish to use these exercises before teaching the lesson.

Add.

1.	2.	3.	4.	5.	6.	7.
2	7	7	0	9	3	5
+5	+6	+4	+9	+8	+7	+5
7	13	11	9	17	10	10

8.	9.	10.	11.	12.	13.	14.
8	2	5	8	7	5	4
+1	+3	+6	+3	+8	+7	+9
9	5	11	11	15	12	13

EXERCISES

Add. (Example 1)

1. 47 $+32$ 79	**2.** 65 $+23$ 88	**3.** 34 $+55$ 89	**4.** 53 $+36$ 89	**5.** 74 $+15$ 89	**6.** 93 $+44$ 137
7. 37 $+51$ 88	**8.** 29 $+50$ 79	**9.** 38 $+31$ 69	**10.** 62 $+25$ 87	**11.** 56 $+33$ 89	**12.** 49 $+80$ 129
13. 40 7 $+22$ 69	**14.** 2 26 $+81$ 109	**15.** 50 70 $+69$ 189	**16.** 84 71 $+33$ 188	**17.** 10 38 $+ 1$ 49	**18.** 27 39 $+ 4$ 70

19. $95 + 82 + 22$ 199

20. $57 + 60 + 22$ 139

21. $30 + 9 + 60$ 99

22. $15 + 80 + 4$ 99

23. $57 + 12 + 10$ 79

24. $81 + 45 + 32$ 158

(Example 2)

25. 63 75 28 $+47$ 213	**26.** 51 67 43 $+49$ 210	**27.** 13 29 67 $+92$ 201	**28.** 48 34 29 $+37$ 148	**29.** 58 62 17 $+35$ 172	**30.** 92 28 11 $+54$ 185
31. 78 2 69 $+35$ 184	**32.** 83 20 4 $+35$ 142	**33.** 29 40 62 $+ 7$ 138	**34.** 72 5 24 $+37$ 138	**35.** 3 29 18 $+38$ 88	**36.** 8 21 47 $+55$ 131
37. 82 46 58 $+67$ 253	**38.** 92 43 84 $+65$ 284	**39.** 73 84 7 $+21$ 185	**40.** 68 45 32 $+ 7$ 152	**41.** 59 37 83 $+32$ 211	**42.** 99 76 32 $+40$ 247

43. $57 + 84 + 2 + 37$ 180

44. $18 + 9 + 42 + 75$ 144

45. $67 + 8 + 23 + 7$ 105

46. $7 + 42 + 78 + 9$ 136

47. $91 + 82 + 67 + 49$ 289

48. $67 + 19 + 27 + 32$ 145

Mixed Practice   The Mixed Practice contains exercises that relate to both Examples 1 and 2.

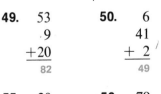

49. 53 9 $+20$ 82	**50.** 6 41 $+ 2$ 49	**51.** 23 5 1 $+80$ 109	**52.** 2 41 90 $+ 6$ 139	**53.** 93 21 7 $+ 8$ 129	**54.** 22 9 80 $+ 7$ 118
55. 20 19 28 $+ 6$ 73	**56.** 79 21 9 $+18$ 127	**57.** 8 80 78 $+92$ 258	**58.** 5 45 32 $+68$ 150	**59.** 9 8 7 $+85$ 109	**60.** 73 4 8 $+21$ 106

61. $98 + 1 + 20$ 119

62. $22 + 15 + 80$ 117

63. $29 + 31 + 9 + 18$ 87

Problem Solving and Applications

Making Change

See the Teacher's Manual for the objectives.
This lesson applies the skills presented in Section 1-1.

This list shows the amount of change needed for the cash registers of six departments in one store.

Department	Number of			Number of Rolls of				
	$10–Bills	$5–Bills	$1–Bills	$10 in Half–Dollars	$10 in Quarters	$5 in Dimes	$2 in Nickels	50¢ in Pennies
China	3	3	5	1	1	2	1	1
Furniture	8	5	10	1	1	1	1	1
Jewelry	5	4	20	1	3	3	4	2
Men's Wear	5	3	20	1	1	2	2	2
Shoes	8	5	20	4	4	2	2	2
Yard Goods	1	1	10	1	1	1	1	1

Exercises

1. How many $10–bills are needed? 30

2. How many $1–bills are needed? 85

3. How many rolls of pennies are needed? 9

4. How many rolls of half dollars are needed? 9

5. How many rolls of quarters are needed? 11

6. How many rolls of dimes are needed? 11

7. How many rolls of nickels are needed? 11

8. Find the total value of the $1–dollar bills. $85

9. Find the total value of the $5–bills. $105

10. Find the total value of the $10–bills. $300

11. Find the total value of the rolls of dimes. $55

12. Find the total value of the rolls of quarters. $110

13. With how much money does the China Department begin each day? $82.50

14. With how much money does the Shoe Department begin each day? $220

15. With how much money does the Yard Goods Department begin each day? $52.50

16. With how much money does the Jewelry Department begin each day? $154

FOOD SERVICES

Career Lessons are optional.
This lesson applies the skills presented in Section 1-1.

The following list shows the number of cases of each of eight canned vegetables that one food wholesaler has on hand in each of eight warehouses.

Item	Warehouse							
	A	B	C	D	E	F	G	H
Asparagus	32	21	18	49	12	27	10	25
Beets	46	20	45	49	44	49	41	40
Carrots	68	72	49	65	70	29	52	0
Corn	45	73	62	56	48	58	52	60
Onions	15	20	18	23	16	9	30	12
Peas	87	90	88	73	69	37	52	76
String Beans	61	86	95	83	87	51	51	72
Tomatoes	24	19	36	28	40	98	90	81

EXERCISES

Note that Exercises 1-16 are non-verbal problems. Exercises 17-22 are one-step problems.

Find the total number of cases of each item.

1. String beans 586 **2.** Beets 334 **3.** Peas 572 **4.** Carrots 405

5. Tomatoes 416 **6.** Corn 454 **7.** Asparagus 194 **8.** Onions 143

Find the total number of cases of canned vegetables in each warehouse.

9. Warehouse A 378 **10.** Warehouse B 401 **11.** Warehouse C 411 **12.** Warehouse D 426

13. Warehouse E 386 **14.** Warehouse F 358 **15.** Warehouse G 378 **16.** Warehouse H 366

17. Find the total number of cases of beets, peas, and carrots in Warehouse A. 201

18. Find the total number of cases of asparagus, corn, and onions in Warehouse H. 97

19. Find the total number of cases of tomatoes, string beans, and corn in Warehouse E. 175

20. Find the total number of cases of carrots, onions and tomatoes in Warehouse C. 103

21. Find the total number of cases of asparagus, corn, and peas in the eight warehouses. 1220

22. Find the total number of cases of beets, onions, and string beans in the eight warehouses. 1063

1-2 Addition: Three or More Digits

See the Teacher's Manual for the objectives.

Adding larger numbers is similar to adding two–digit numbers.

PROCEDURE To add larger whole numbers:

1. Add the ones.
2. Add the tens.
3. Add the hundreds, and so on.

EXAMPLE 1 Add: $456 + 361 + 902 + 893$

Solution:

1. Add the ones. Carry the "ten" to the tens column.

$$6 + 1 + 2 + 3 = 12$$

$$
\begin{array}{r}
1 \\
456 \\
361 \\
902 \\
+893 \\
\hline
2
\end{array}
$$

2. Add the tens. Carry the two "hundreds" to the hundreds column.

$$10 + 50 + 60 + 90 = 210$$

$$
\begin{array}{r}
21 \\
456 \\
361 \\
902 \\
+893 \\
\hline
12
\end{array}
$$

3. Add the hundreds.

$$200 + 400 + 300 + 900 + 800 = 2600$$

$$
\begin{array}{r}
21 \\
456 \\
361 \\
902 \\
+893 \\
\hline
2612
\end{array}
$$

After completing Example 1, you may wish to have students do some or all or Exercises 1-31.

Example 2 shows addition without "carrying." Use the method that is easier for you.

EXAMPLE 2 Add: $348 + 795 + 551 + 64$

Solution: Follow the steps in the procedure. Write each sum without carrying.

$$
\begin{array}{r}
348 \\
795 \\
551 \\
+\ 64 \\
\hline
\end{array}
$$

1. 18 ← $8 + 5 + 1 + 4$
2. 240 ← $40 + 90 + 50 + 60$
3. $\underline{1500}$ ← $300 + 700 + 500$
    1758 ← $18 + 240 + 1500$

These are the steps in the Procedure.

REVIEW OF RELATED SKILLS

You may wish to use these exercises before teaching the lesson.

Add.

1.	2.	3.	4.	5.	6.
1	2	3	2	3	5
5	6	8	8	9	8
7	9	4	9	1	2
+3	+5	+7	+0	+4	+0
16	22	22	19	17	15

7.	8.	9.	10.	11.	12.
20	10	50	800	200	300
40	40	40	600	900	400
60	30	70	800	700	700
+90	+80	+20	+700	+900	+800
210	160	180	2900	2700	2200

EXERCISES

See the suggested assignment guide in the Teacher's Manual.

Add. Use the method that is easier for you. (Examples 1 and 2)

1.	2.	3.	4.	5.
562	924	249	273	928
847	637	628	624	237
+295	+851	+385	+856	+452
1704	2412	1262	1753	1617

6.	7.	8.	9.	10.
268	109	857	254	426
537	263	290	397	538
492	581	641	583	291
+638	+674	+375	+672	+863
1935	1627	2163	1906	2118

11.	12.	13.	14.	15.
573	817	62	621	17
624	93	347	436	3268
85	314	298	29	5791
+291	+527	+115	+483	+1238
1573	1751	822	1569	10,314

16.	17.	18.	19.	20.
4283	2079	7148	71	298
6219	154	37	8615	1516
5834	62	295	9824	81
+7108	+4863	+4176	+ 562	+4083
23,444	7158	11,656	19,072	5978

21.	22.	23.	24.	25.
6840	175	3860	9308	409
27	2843	2159	72	5725
391	109	384	324	624
+ 584	+ 27	+ 67	+2185	+ 383
7842	3154	6470	11,889	7141

26. 845 + 23 + 457 + 126   1451

27. 729 + 142 + 28 + 179   1078

28. 257 + 228 + 856 + 14   1355

29. 963 + 381 + 875 + 29   2248

30. 57 + 852 + 114 + 509   1532

31. 13 + 755 + 128 + 207   1103

WHOLE NUMBERS: ADDITION/SUBTRACTION   7

Problem Solving and Applications

Buying A New Car

See the Teacher's Manual for the objectives.
This lesson applies the skills presented in Section 1-2.

To find the total cost of a new car, you add the cost of optional equipment to the base price of the car. The table at the right below shows the cost of some optional equipment.

EXAMPLE The base price of a car is $5750. Find the total cost with air conditioning, bucket seats, and power steering.

Optional Equipment	Cost
Air Conditioning	$456
Automatic Transmission	$270
Brakes (4–wheel power)	$266
Bucket Seats	$278
Defogger (rear window)	$ 77
Glass (tinted)	$ 64
Power Steering	$172
Stereo Tape, AM/FM radio	$375

Solution:

Base Price:	$5750
Air conditioning:	$ 456
Bucket Seats:	$ 278
Power Steering:	+$ 172
Total Cost:	**$6656**

Exercises

Note that Exercises 1-8 are non-verbal problems.
Exercises 9-12 are one-step problems.

Find the total cost of each car.

1.

Base Price:		$4790
Air Conditioning:	$456	?
Automatic Transmission:	$270	?
Stereo, AM/FM radio:	$375	?
Total Cost:	$5891	?

2.

Base Price:		$4680
Air Conditioning:	$456	?
Glass (tinted):	$64	?
Bucket Seats:	$278	?
Total Cost:	$5478	?

Application

3. Base Price: $5215
Air Conditioning: $456 ?
Automatic Transmission: $270 ?
Brakes (4–wheel power): $266 ?
Power Steering: $172 ?
Defogger (rear window): $77 ?
Total Cost: $6456 ?

4. Base Price: $6015
Air Conditioning: $456 ?
Automatic Transmission: $270 ?
Glass (tinted): $64 ?
Power Steering: $172 ?
Stereo, AM/FM radio: $375 ?
Total Cost: $7352 ?

5. Base Price: $5870
Automatic Transmission: $270 ?
Bucket Seats: $278 ?
Defogger (rear window): $77 ?
Glass (tinted) $64 ?
Power Steering: $172 ?
Stereo, AM/FM radio: $375 ?
Total Cost: $7106 ?

6. Base price: $6580
Air conditioning: $456 ?
Automatic Transmission: $270 ?
Bucket Seats: $278 ?
Defogger (rear window): $77 ?
Power Steering: $172 ?
Stereo, AM/FM radio: $375 ?
Total cost: $8208 ?

7. Base Price: $7512
Air Conditioning: $456 ?
Automatic Transmission: $270 ?
Brakes (4–wheel power): $266 ?
Defogger (rear window): $77 ?
Glass (tinted): $64 ?
Power Steering: $172 ?
Stereo, AM/FM radio: $375 ?
Total Cost: $9192 ?

8. Base Price: $7180
Automatic Transmission: $270 ?
Brakes (4–wheel power): $266 ?
Bucket Seats: $278 ?
Defogger (rear window): $77 ?
Glass (tinted): $64 ?
Power Steering: $172 ?
Stereo, AM/FM radio: $375 ?
Total Cost: $8682 ?

9. The base price of a car is $6590. Find the total cost with automatic transmission, tinted glass, stereo tape, AM/FM radio, and rear-window defogger. $7376

10. The base price of a car is $7150. Find the total cost with air conditioning, automatic transmission, power steering, tinted glass, and stereo tape, AM/FM radio. $8487

11. The base price of a car is $10,346. Find the total cost with automatic transmission, air conditioning, power steering, bucket seats, 4–wheel power brakes, and rear-window defogger. $11,865

12. The base price of a car is $8755. Find the total cost with 4–wheel power brakes, automatic transmission, air conditioning, power steering, and stereo tape, AM/FM radio. $10,294

1-3 Subtraction: Two-Digit Numbers See the Teacher's Manual for the objectives.

Addition and subtraction are related. That is, since $29 + 38 = 67$,
$$67 - 29 = 38 \qquad \text{and} \qquad 67 - 38 = 29.$$

Since addition and subtraction are related, you can use addition to check subtraction.

PROCEDURE To subtract two-digit whole numbers:

   1. Subtract the ones.

   2. Subtract the tens.

EXAMPLE 1 Subtract: $65 - 31$

$$\begin{array}{r} 65 \\ -31 \\ \hline 34 \end{array}$$
Same number

Check:
$$\begin{array}{r} 34 \\ +31 \\ \hline 65 \end{array}$$

After completing Example 1, you may wish to have students do some or all of Exercises 1-12.

Sometimes you have to rename in subtraction.

EXAMPLE 2 Subtract: $58 - 39$

Solution: To subtract the ones, rename the 5 tens and the 8 ones.

$$\begin{array}{r} \overset{4\ 18}{\cancel{5}\,\cancel{8}} \\ -3\ 9 \\ \hline 1\ 9 \end{array}$$

5 tens and 8 ones = 4 tens and 18 ones

Check:
$$\begin{array}{r} 19 \\ +39 \\ \hline 58 \end{array}$$

REVIEW OF RELATED SKILLS You may wish to use these exercises before teaching the lesson.

Subtract.

1.	2.	3.	4.	5.	6.	7.
$\begin{array}{r}11\\-\ 9\\\hline 2\end{array}$	$\begin{array}{r}12\\-\ 8\\\hline 4\end{array}$	$\begin{array}{r}14\\-\ 8\\\hline 6\end{array}$	$\begin{array}{r}12\\-\ 7\\\hline 5\end{array}$	$\begin{array}{r}13\\-\ 7\\\hline 6\end{array}$	$\begin{array}{r}17\\-\ 9\\\hline 8\end{array}$	$\begin{array}{r}15\\-\ 6\\\hline 9\end{array}$

8.	9.	10.	11.	12.	13.	14.
$\begin{array}{r}9\\-3\\\hline 6\end{array}$	$\begin{array}{r}12\\-\ 4\\\hline 8\end{array}$	$\begin{array}{r}15\\-\ 7\\\hline 8\end{array}$	$\begin{array}{r}8\\-2\\\hline 6\end{array}$	$\begin{array}{r}7\\-5\\\hline 2\end{array}$	$\begin{array}{r}13\\-\ 9\\\hline 4\end{array}$	$\begin{array}{r}10\\-\ 2\\\hline 8\end{array}$

Complete.

15. $18 = \underline{\ ?^{1}\ }$ ten $+ \underline{\ ?^{8}\ }$ ones

16. $59 = \underline{\ ?^{5}\ }$ tens $+ \underline{\ ?^{9}\ }$ ones

17. $43 = 4 \underline{\ ?\ } + 3 \underline{\ ?\ }$
             tens   ones

18. $754 = 7 \underline{\ ?\ } + 5 \underline{\ ?\ } + 4 \underline{\ ?\ }$
          hundreds tens   ones

EXERCISES

See the suggested assignment guide in the Teacher's Manual.

Subtract. Check your answers.   (Example 1)

1. 85	2. 63	3. 47	4. 92	5. 38	6. 53
-23	-41	-14	-30	-25	-12
62	22	33	62	13	41
7. 47	8. 68	9. 94	10. 82	11. 79	12. 88
-15	-52	-33	-51	-54	-74
32	16	61	31	25	14

(Example 2)

13. 83	14. 55	15. 46	16. 57	17. 54	18. 92
-46	-26	-27	-38	-18	-37
37	29	19	19	36	55
19. 35	20. 83	21. 36	22. 58	23. 53	24. 47
-19	$- 6$	$- 9$	-19	-24	-39
16	77	27	39	29	8

Mixed Practice The Mixed Practice contains exercises that relate to both Examples 1 and 2.

25. 23	26. 25	27. 46	28. 95	29. 64	30. 99
-12	$- 7$	$- 9$	-29	-57	-77
11	18	37	66	7	22

31. $49 - 23$ 26 **32.** $63 - 21$ 42 **33.** $75 - 27$ 48 **34.** $34 - 16$ 18 **35.** $57 - 27$ 30

36. $76 - 45$ 31 **37.** $82 - 75$ 7 **38.** $58 - 49$ 9 **39.** $93 - 67$ 26 **40.** $64 - 39$ 25

APPLICATIONS: Using Subtraction These are one-step problems that most students should be able to handle.

41. Radial tires for Maureen's car cost $73 each. Belted tires cost $37 each. How much would Maureen save by buying one belted tire? $36

42. On Monday, 93 people took the road test for a driver's license. Sixty–seven passed the test. How many failed? 26

43. There were 88 people on a bus when it left Austin. Twenty–nine got off at Houston. How many went on to the next stop? 59

44. An airplane has seats for 82 passengers. After remodeling, the plane could seat 97 passengers. How many seats were added? 15

CHECKING ADDITION/SUBTRACTION

Use a calculator to check each answer. Correct any wrong answers.

1. 5984	2. 83,455	3. 4973	4. 608,000
5979	6,908	-2198	$-419,846$
3878	96,452	2675 2775	188,254
4416	562		188,154
$+9832$	$+88,256$	5. 8901	6. 921,183
30089	275,613	-6342	$-788,285$
	275,633	2569 2559	122,898
			132,898

Problem Solving and Applications

Time Zones

See the Teacher's Manual for the objectives.
This lesson applies the skills presented in Section 1-3.

The map below shows the standard time zones in the United States.

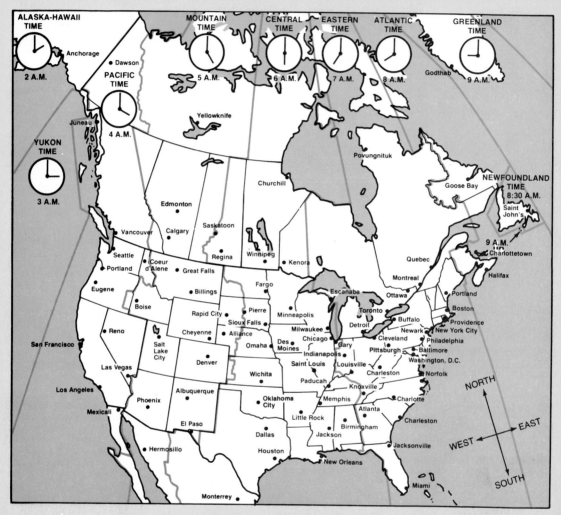

Going from east to west, subtract one hour for each zone.

EXAMPLE 1   It is 9:00 A.M. (Eastern Time) in Boston. What time (Pacific Time) is it in Seattle?

Solution: 1. Write the direction: **East to west**

2. Count the time zones from Boston to Seattle: **3**

3. Subtract 3 hours from the Boston time: $9 - 3 = 6$

It is **6 A.M.** (Pacific Time) in Seattle.

Application

Going from west to east, add one hour for each time zone.

EXAMPLE 2   It is 4:25 P.M. (Mountain Time) in Denver. What time (Central Time) is it in Chicago?

Solution: [1] Write the direction: **West to east**

[2] Count the time zones from Denver to Chicago: **1**

[3] Add 1 hour to the Denver time: **4:25 + 1 = 5:25**
It is **5:25 P.M.** (Central Time) in Chicago.

Only standard time is used in the Examples and Exercises.

Exercises   Note that Exercises 1-9 are non-verbal problems.

Use the map on page 12 to complete the table.   (Examples 1 and 2)

When it is	then it is
1. 4:00 P.M. in Denver,	__?__ P.M. in Atlanta. 6:00
2. 3:00 P.M. in New York,	__?__ P.M. in Chicago. 2:00
3. 6:30 A.M. in New York,	__?__ A.M. in Los Angeles. 3:30
4. 8:00 A.M. in St. Louis,	__?__ A.M. in Boston. 9:00
5. 8:15 A.M. in San Francisco,	__?__ A.M. in Cleveland. 11:15
6. 8:15 A.M. in San Francisco,	__?__ A.M. in Anchorage. 6:15
7. 9:25 P.M. in Omaha,	__?__ P.M. in Providence. 10:25
8. 9:25 P.M. in Omaha,	__?__ P.M. in Salt Lake City. 8:25
9. 12 noon in Dallas,	__?__ in Philadelphia. 1:00 P.M.

10. A plane leaves Denver at 9:00 A.M. (Mountain Time). The flight to Chicago takes 2 hours. At what time (Central Time) does the plane arrive in Chicago?   12 noon

11. A plane leaves New York at 2:34 P.M. (Eastern Time). The flight to Chicago takes 1 hour 25 minutes. At what time (Central Time) does the plane arrive in Chicago?   2:59 P.M.

12. A plane leaves Seattle at 12:00 noon (Pacific Time). The flight to Boston takes 6 hours 20 minutes. At what time (Eastern Time) should the plane arrive in Boston?   9:20 P.M.

1-4 Subtraction: Three or More Digits

See the Teacher's Manual for the objectives.

When subtracting larger numbers, it is sometimes necessary to rename more than once.

PROCEDURE   When necessary in subtraction:

1. Rename the tens and the ones. Subtract the ones.
2. Rename the hundreds and the tens. Subtract the tens.
3. Rename the thousands and the hundreds. Subtract the hundreds, and so on.

EXAMPLE 1   Subtract: $645 - 369$

Solution:

1. Rename the tens and the ones.

$$\begin{array}{r} 3\ 15 \\ 6\ 4\ 5 \\ -3\ 6\ 9 \\ \hline 6 \end{array}$$

◄ 4 tens + 5 ones = 3 tens + 15 ones.

2. Rename the hundreds and the tens.

$$\begin{array}{r} 5\ 13 \\ 3\ 15 \\ 6\ 4\ 5 \\ -3\ 6\ 9 \\ \hline 2\ 7\ 6 \end{array}$$

◄ 6 hundreds + 3 tens = 5 hundreds + 13 tens

The check is left for you.

After completing Example 1, you may wish to have students do some or all of Exercises 1-20.

Be careful when renaming with zeros in subtraction.

EXAMPLE 2   Subtract: **a.** $804 - 627$ **b.** $3000 - 476$

Solutions:

a.
$$\begin{array}{r} 7\ 9\ 14 \\ 8\ 0\ 4 \\ -6\ 2\ 7 \\ \hline 1\ 7\ 7 \end{array}$$

◄ 804 = 7 hundreds + 9 tens + 14 ones

b.
$$\begin{array}{r} 2\ 9\ 9\ 10 \\ 3\ 0\ 0\ 0 \\ -\ \ 4\ 7\ 6 \\ \hline 2\ 5\ 2\ 4 \end{array}$$

◄ 3000 = 2 thousands + 9 hundreds + 9 tens + 10 ones

The check is left for you.

REVIEW OF RELATED SKILLS

You may wish to use these exercises before teaching the lesson.

Add or subtract.

1. $\begin{array}{r} 7 \\ +3 \\ \hline 10 \end{array}$	**2.** $\begin{array}{r} 10 \\ -3 \\ \hline 7 \end{array}$	**3.** $\begin{array}{r} 10 \\ -7 \\ \hline 3 \end{array}$	**4.** $\begin{array}{r} 7 \\ +5 \\ \hline 12 \end{array}$	**5.** $\begin{array}{r} 12 \\ -5 \\ \hline 7 \end{array}$	**6.** $\begin{array}{r} 12 \\ -7 \\ \hline 5 \end{array}$	**7.** $\begin{array}{r} 14 \\ -9 \\ \hline 5 \end{array}$
8. $\begin{array}{r} 6 \\ +4 \\ \hline 10 \end{array}$	**9.** $\begin{array}{r} 10 \\ -6 \\ \hline 4 \end{array}$	**10.** $\begin{array}{r} 10 \\ -4 \\ \hline 6 \end{array}$	**11.** $\begin{array}{r} 8 \\ +6 \\ \hline 14 \end{array}$	**12.** $\begin{array}{r} 14 \\ -8 \\ \hline 6 \end{array}$	**13.** $\begin{array}{r} 14 \\ -6 \\ \hline 8 \end{array}$	**14.** $\begin{array}{r} 18 \\ -9 \\ \hline 9 \end{array}$

Complete.

15. 70 = __?⁷__ tens + __?⁰__ ones

16. 38 = __2?__ tens + 18 ones

17. 701 = __7?__ hundreds + __?⁰__ tens + __1?__ ones

18. 300 = __3?__ hundreds + __?⁰__ tens + __0?__ ones

19. 6 tens + 5 ones = 5 tens + __?15__ ones

20. 3 tens + 9 ones = 2 tens + __?19__ ones

21. 96 = __?⁸__ tens + 16 ones

22. 45 = __?³__ tens + 15 ones

EXERCISES

Subtract. (Example 1)

1. 645 − 257

2. 724 − 338

3. 526 − 149

4. 743 − 268

5. 553 − 277

6. 435 − 257 *(388)*

7. 226 − 149 *(386)*

8. 757 − 288 *(377)*

9. 263 − 186 *(475)*

10. 471 − 295 *(276)*

11. 436 − 279 *(178)*

12. 524 − 156 *(77)*

13. 646 − 278 *(469)*

14. 532 − 289 *(77)*

15. 663 − 386 *(176)*

16. 254 − 189 *(157)* = 65

17. 571 − 295 *(368)* = 276

18. 653 − 466 *(368)* = 187

19. 563 − 286 *(243)* = 277

20. 424 − 158 *(277)* = 266

(Example 2)

21. 905 − 328

22. 603 − 267

23. 502 − 156

24. 640 − 272

25. 506 − 159

26. 302 − 183 *(577)*

27. 509 − 267 *(336)*

28. 407 − 318 *(346)*

29. 250 − 175 *(368)*

30. 806 − 627 *(347)*

31. 903 − 267 *(119)*

32. 640 − 382 *(242)*

33. 300 − 157 *(89)*

34. 500 − 293 *(75)*

35. 750 − 369 *(179)*

36. 390 − 296 *(636)* = 94

37. 260 − 109 *(258)* = 151

38. 680 − 399 *(143)* = 281

39. 204 − 158 *(207)* = 46

40. 801 − 422 *(381)* = 379

Mixed Practice The Mixed Practice contains exercises that relate to both Examples 1 and 2.

41. 82 − 27

42. 95 − 88

43. 287 − 66

44. 469 − 54

45. 913 − 217

46. 425 − 186 *(55)* = 239

47. 4070 − 1293 *(7)* = 2777

48. 6270 − 1382 *(221)* = 4888

49. 4900 − 1913 *(415)* = 2987

50. 3800 − 2527 *(696)* = 1273

51. 2005 − 188 = 1817

52. 3004 − 297 = 2707

53. 5000 − 37 = 4963

54. 7000 − 46 = 6954

55. 8000 − 155 = 7845

56. 5600 − 1096 = 4504

57. 3800 − 1073 = 2727

58. 3844 − 1073 = 2771

Problem Solving and Applications

See the Teacher's Manual for the objectives.

Reading a Meter

To conserve energy and to save on the costs of electricity, you need to know just how much electricity you are using. One way of learning this is by reading the meter yourself.

Electricity is measured in **kilowatt-hours.** You use one kilowatt-hour of electricity when you use 1 kilowatt (1000 watts) for one hour.

EXAMPLE What is the reading on this meter?

Solution: Read the dials from left to right. When the hand is between two numbers, read the smaller number. When the hand is between 9 and 0, read 9.

The reading is **4946.** ◀ *4946 kilowatt-hours*

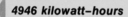

Exercises

Read each meter.

1. 2483

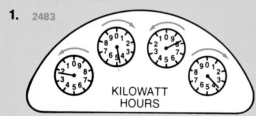

2. 6871

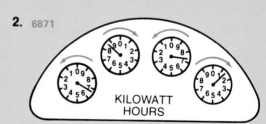

3. 4000

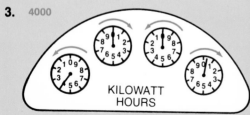

4. 1444

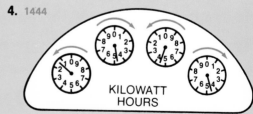

5. The reading on a meter on January 6 is 3692. The reading on February 6 is 3818. How many kilowatt-hours of electricity were used? 126

6. The reading on a meter on October 25 is 8947. The reading on November 25 is 9123. How many kilowatt-hours of electricity were used? 176

Application

1-5 Rounding and Estimation

See the Teacher's Manual for the objectives.

You can round whole numbers to the nearest ten, to the nearest hundred, and to the nearest thousand, and so on.

PROCEDURE To round whole numbers:

1. Look at the digit to the right of the place to which you are rounding.

2. a. If the digit is 5 or more, round up.
   b. If the digit is less than 5, round down.

EXAMPLE 1
a. 27 rounded to the nearest **ten** is 30.

b. 3212 rounded to the nearest **ten** is 3210.

c. 845 rounded to the nearest **hundred** is 800.

d. 12,450 rounded to the nearest **hundred** is 12,500

e. 11,850 rounded to the nearest **thousand** is 12,000.

f. 15,511 rounded to the nearest **thousand** is 16,000.

After completing Example 1, you may wish to have students do some or all of Exercises 1-36 on page 18.

You can use rounding to help you estimate answers.

EXAMPLE 2 Estimate each answer.
a. 28 + 32 + 86   b. 710 − 495

Solutions:
a. Since the numbers are greater than 10 and less than 100, round to the nearest ten.

b. Since the numbers are greater than 100 and less than 1000, round to the nearest hundred.

$$30 + 30 + 90 = 150$$ $$700 - 500 = 200$$

REVIEW OF RELATED SKILLS
You may wish to use these exercises before teaching the lesson.

Add. (Pages 6–7)

1.	2.	3.	4.	5.
450	620	170	6800	5200
+230	+580	+240	+2100	+6300
680	1200	410	8900	11,500

Subtract. (Pages 14–15)

6.	7.	8.	9.	10.
850	690	530	4800	6700
−230	−150	−290	−1300	−2800
620	540	240	3500	3900

WHOLE NUMBERS: ADDITION/SUBTRACTION **17**

EXERCISES

Round to the nearest ten.   (Example 1, a and b)

1. 13 10   **2.** 22 20   **3.** 155 160   **4.** 242 240   **5.** 1769 1770   **6.** 6258 6260

7. 8 10   **8.** 18 20   **9.** 75 80   **10.** 921 920   **11.** 836 840   **12.** 9419 9420

Round to the nearest hundred.   (Example 1, c and d)

13. 468 500   **14.** 924 900   **15.** 685 700   **16.** 505 500   **17.** 896 900   **18.** 355 400

19. 1606 1600   **20.** 2962 3000 **21.** 4805 4800 **22.** 1481 1500 **23.** 5295 5300 **24.** 2450 2500

Round to the nearest thousand.   (Example 1, e and f)

25. 6815 7000   **26.** 5820 6000   **27.** 4281 4000   **28.** 6059 6000   **29.** 8890 9000   **30.** 4051 4000

31. 14,217   **32.** 62,483   **33.** 59,860   **34.** 48,527   **35.** 19,685   **36.** 47,128
14,000   62,000   60,000   49,000   20,000   47,000

Choose the best estimate. Choose a, b, or c.   (Example 2)

37. $18 + 13 + 52$ c   **a.** $10 + 10 + 50$ **b.** $20 + 20 + 50$ **c.** $20 + 10 + 50$

38. $112 + 631$ a   **a.** $100 + 600$ **b.** $200 + 700$ **c.** $100 + 700$

39. $79 - 63$ c   **a.** $80 - 70$ **b.** $70 - 60$ **c.** $80 - 60$

40. $166 - 139$ c   **a.** $160 - 140$ **b.** $170 - 180$ **c.** $170 - 140$

41. $4280 + 3126$ b   **a.** $4200 + 3100$ **b.** $4300 + 3100$ **c.** $4200 + 3200$

42. $2655 - 1878$ b   **a.** $2600 - 1800$ **b.** $2700 - 1900$ **c.** $2600 - 1900$

Mixed Practice

Choose the best estimate. Choose a, b, c, or d.

43. $638 + 293$ a   **a.** 930   **b.** 920   **c.** 900   **d.** 950

44. $527 + 862$ a   **a.** 1390   **b.** 1400   **c.** 1300   **d.** 1350

45. $963 - 857$ b   **a.** 130   **b.** 100   **c.** 120   **d.** 90

46. $729 - 385$ d   **a.** 400   **b.** 330   **c.** 320   **d.** 340

47. $4630 + 2397$ a **a.** 7000   **b.** 7100   **c.** 6900   **d.** 7200

48. $4373 - 3790$ d **a.** 650   **b.** 550   **c.** 500   **d.** 600

APPLICATIONS: Using Estimation

49. The base price of a new car is $5750. Air conditioning costs $466, bucket seats cost $285, and power steering costs $172. Estimate the total cost to the nearest hundred dollars. b

   a. $7000   **b.** $6800

   c. $6500   **d.** $6400

50. The base price of a new car is $6850. Power steering costs $185, an automatic transmission costs $290, and tinted glass costs $74. Estimate the total cost to the nearest hundred dollars. a

   a. $7500   **b.** $8000

   c. $7000   **c.** $8500

51. A food wholesaler has 35 cases of asparagus in one warehouse, 71 cases in a second warehouse, and 29 cases in a third warehouse. Estimate the total number of cases to the nearest ten. c

a. 100   b. 130

c. 140   d. 150

52. A food wholesaler has 73 cases of canned peaches in one warehouse, 46 cases in another, and 65 cases in a third. Estimate the total number of cases to the nearest ten. d

a. 100   b. 170

c. 150   d. 190

Calculator exercises are optional.

ESTIMATION AND SUBTRACTION

Before using a calculator to find the amount of electricity used:

1 Estimate the answer to the nearest hundred kilowatt–hours.

2 Use a calculator to find the exact answer.

3 Compare the exact answer with the estimate to check whether the exact answer is reasonable.

EXAMPLE:

| Present Reading | 18,364 |
| Previous Reading | 17,887 |

Amount Used: ?

Solution: Estimated Amount: 18,400 − 17,900 = **500** ◄ *Number of kilowatt–hours*

Exact Amount: 〔 477. 〕 ◄ *18,364 − 17,887*

Since the estimate is 500 kilowatt–hours, **477** kilowatt–hours is a reasonable answer.

EXERCISES

First estimate the amount of electricity used to the nearest hundred kilowatt–hours. Then find the exact amount.

	Present Reading	Previous Reading	Estimated Amount	Exact Amount
1.	8796	8215	? 600	? 581
2.	7849	7637	? 200	? 212
3.	19,024	18,731	? 300	? 293
4.	16,128	15,739	? 400	? 389
5.	41,941	41,717	? 200	? 224

Chapter Review

These exercises review the vocabulary, skills and applications presented in the chapter as a preparation for the chapter test.

Part 1: Vocabulary

For Exercises 1–7, choose from the box at the right the word(s) or number(s) that completes the statement.

1. An example of a two–digit number is __?__. (Page 2)
   89

2. Giving an answer to the nearest ten is called __?__ the answer. (Page 17)
   rounding

3. When buying a car, items that are not part of the base price are called __?__. (Page 8) optional equipment

4. An answer obtained by using rounded numbers is an __?__ answer. (Page 17) estimated

5. Electric meters measure electricity in __?__. (Page 16)
   kilowatt-hours

6. Eastern, Central, Mountain, and Pacific are names of __?__. (Page 12) time zones

7. To check subtraction, you use the operation of __?__. (Page 10)
   addition

rounding
kilowatt–hours
521
multiplication
89
estimated
time zones
optional equipment
addition

Part 2: Skills

Add. (Pages 2–3)

8.
$$\begin{array}{r} 72 \\ +27 \\ \hline 99 \end{array}$$

9.
$$\begin{array}{r} 64 \\ +23 \\ \hline 87 \end{array}$$

10.
$$\begin{array}{r} 21 \\ 34 \\ +73 \\ \hline 128 \end{array}$$

11.
$$\begin{array}{r} 91 \\ 8 \\ +25 \\ \hline 124 \end{array}$$

12.
$$\begin{array}{r} 28 \\ 17 \\ 35 \\ +44 \\ \hline 124 \end{array}$$

13.
$$\begin{array}{r} 64 \\ 83 \\ 9 \\ +27 \\ \hline 183 \end{array}$$

14. $92 + 28 + 6$ 126
15. $43 + 32 + 9$ 84
16. $23 + 95 + 4 + 16$ 138
17. $56 + 8 + 23 + 62$ 149

(Pages 6–7)

18.
$$\begin{array}{r} 295 \\ 608 \\ +354 \\ \hline 1257 \end{array}$$

19.
$$\begin{array}{r} 3146 \\ 5495 \\ +\ 837 \\ \hline 9478 \end{array}$$

20.
$$\begin{array}{r} 458 \\ 934 \\ 276 \\ +825 \\ \hline 2493 \end{array}$$

21.
$$\begin{array}{r} 906 \\ 327 \\ 408 \\ +219 \\ \hline 1860 \end{array}$$

22.
$$\begin{array}{r} 2905 \\ 48 \\ 759 \\ +8534 \\ \hline 12,246 \end{array}$$

23.
$$\begin{array}{r} 6218 \\ 381 \\ 28 \\ +\ 542 \\ \hline 7169 \end{array}$$

24. $928 + 35 + 4701 + 7$ 5671
25. $1283 + 395 + 17 + 284$ 1979
26. $65 + 708 + 321 + 6549$ 7643

Subtract. (Pages 10–11)

27.
$$\begin{array}{r} 85 \\ -23 \\ \hline 62 \end{array}$$

28.
$$\begin{array}{r} 67 \\ -34 \\ \hline 33 \end{array}$$

29.
$$\begin{array}{r} 84 \\ -\ 5 \\ \hline 79 \end{array}$$

30.
$$\begin{array}{r} 54 \\ -\ 8 \\ \hline 46 \end{array}$$

31.
$$\begin{array}{r} 874 \\ -\ 28 \\ \hline 846 \end{array}$$

32.
$$\begin{array}{r} 962 \\ -\ 47 \\ \hline 915 \end{array}$$

(Pages 14–15)

33.
$$\begin{array}{r} 854 \\ -377 \\ \hline 477 \end{array}$$

34.
$$\begin{array}{r} 628 \\ -354 \\ \hline 274 \end{array}$$

35.
$$\begin{array}{r} 204 \\ -179 \\ \hline 25 \end{array}$$

36.
$$\begin{array}{r} 406 \\ -187 \\ \hline 219 \end{array}$$

37.
$$\begin{array}{r} 7000 \\ -\ 287 \\ \hline 6713 \end{array}$$

38.
$$\begin{array}{r} 3000 \\ -\ 465 \\ \hline 2535 \end{array}$$

39. 407 − 213 194   **40.** 506 − 88 418   **41.** 4003 − 2685 1318   **42.** 6000 − 781 5219

Round each number to the nearest ten.   (Pages 17–19)

43. 426   **44.** 825   **45.** 656   **46.** 151   **47.** 86   **48.** 98   **49.** 5   **50.** 9
    430   830   660   150   90   100   10   10

Round each number to the nearest hundred.   (Pages 17–19)

51. 685   **52.** 851   **53.** 6293   **54.** 1572   **55.** 2965   **56.** 10,096   **57.** 87   **58.** 42
    700   900   6300   1600   3000   10,100   100   0

Round each number to the nearest thousand.   (Pages 17–19)

59. 8641   **60.** 12,438   **61.** 32,115   **62.** 39,565   **63.** 43,295   **64.** 50,063
   9000   12,000   32,000   40,000   43,300   50,000

Choose the best estimate. Choose a, b, c, or d.   (Pages 17–19)

65. 318 + 491 c   **a.** 700   **b.** 850   **c.** 810   **d.** 830

66. 684 + 71 a   **a.** 750   **b.** 650   **c.** 700   **d.** 780

67. 548 − 432 d   **a.** 110   **b.** 150   **c.** 130   **d.** 120

68. 6802 − 934 c   **a.** 6000   **b.** 4900   **c.** 5900   **d.** 6900

Part 3: Applications   The use of these word problems depends on which applications were studied.

69. There are $10 in a roll of quarters and $5 in a roll of dimes. Larry has two rolls of quarters and four rolls of dimes. How much money does he have? (Page 4) $40

70. The base price of a car is $6375. The automatic transmission costs $385 and the air conditioning costs $498. What is the total price of the car? (Pages 8–9) $7258

71. Judy lives in New York. She calls her grandmother in Los Angeles at 5:00 P.M. (Eastern time). What time (Pacific time) is it in Los Angeles? (Pages 12–13) 2:00 P.M

72. There were 521 seats in the old theater in Kimball. There are 789 seats in the new theater. Estimate the difference in the number of seats to the nearest ten.
(Pages 17–19) b

   a. 260   **b.** 270

   c. 280   **d.** 290

Chapter Test

The Teacher's Resource Book contains two forms of each Chapter Test.

Add.

1. 52
    +43
    ‾95‾

2. 93
    +35
    ‾128‾

3. 82
    31
    +45
    ‾158‾

4. 51
    32
    + 4
    ‾87‾

5. 326
    42
    1731
    + 8
    ‾2107‾

6. 614 + 26 + 1093   1733

7. 25 + 391 + 2086   2502

8. 482 + 1670 + 34   2186

Subtract.

9. 99
    −26
    ‾73‾

10. 58
    −32
    ‾26‾

11. 63
    − 9
    ‾54‾

12. 42
    − 6
    ‾36‾

13. 803
    − 27
    ‾776‾

14. 5000 − 463   4537

15. 421 − 9   412

Round each number as indicated.

16. 6; to the nearest ten   10
17. 6732; to the nearest hundred   6700
18. 850; to the nearest hundred   900
19. 20,687; to the nearest thousand   21,000
20. 4681; to the nearest thousand   5000
21. 95; to the nearest ten   100

Solve each problem. The use of these word problems depends on which applications were studied.

22. Joe lives in San Francisco. He calls his sister in Boston at 6:00 P.M. (Pacific time). What time (Eastern time) is it in Boston?   9:00 P.M.

23. The base price of a car is $4991. Bucket seats cost $283 and power steering costs $179. Estimate the total price of the car to the nearest ten dollars.   a
    a. $5450   b. $5460
    c. $5470   d. $5480

24. A food wholesaler has 49 cases of canned pears in one warehouse, 62 cases in a second, and 58 cases in a third. Estimate the total number of cases to the nearest ten.   d
    a. 150   b. 180
    c. 160   d. 170

25. The cash register in the jewelry department of Slade's Department Store contains six $20–bills, two $10–bills, seven $5–bills, and eight $1–bills. How much money is in the register? $183

Additional Practice

You may wish to use all or some of these exercises depending on how well students performed on the formal chapter test.

Skills

Add.   (Pages 2–3)

| **1.** 58 $+29$ 87 | **2.** 46 $+38$ 84 | **3.** 16 19 $+48$ 83 | **4.** 24 46 $+95$ 165 | **5.** 36 5 21 $+38$ 100 | **6.** 75 82 3 $+64$ 224 |

7. $36 + 23 + 9$ 68   **8.** $43 + 78 + 7$ 128   **9.** $25 + 6 + 34 + 18$ 83   **10.** $62 + 10 + 9 + 12$ 93

(Pages 6–7)

| **11.** 462 321 $+905$ 1688 | **12.** 7287 495 $+6621$ 14,403 | **13.** 281 937 463 $+492$ 2173 | **14.** 863 988 556 $+723$ 3130 | **15.** 3416 22 864 $+ \ 6$ 4308 | **16.** 37 469 8 $+6177$ 6691 |

17. $329 + 25 + 6448 + 7$ 6809   **18.** $4436 + 8 + 560 + 25$ 5029   **19.** $43 + 688 + 4732 + 9$ 5472

Subtract.   (Pages 10–11)

| **20.** 63 -21 42 | **21.** 89 -34 55 | **22.** 63 $- \ 9$ 54 | **23.** 82 $- \ 8$ 74 | **24.** 361 $- \ 48$ 313 | **25.** 672 $- \ 36$ 636 |

26. $48 - 12$ 36   **27.** $52 - 18$ 34   **28.** $63 - 7$ 56   **29.** $483 - 18$ 465

(Pages 14–15)

| **30.** 924 -386 538 | **31.** 847 -469 378 | **32.** 303 -198 105 | **33.** 902 -657 245 | **34.** 8000 -3642 4358 | **35.** 7000 -2489 4511 |

36. $801 - 396$ 405   **37.** $408 - 199$ 209   **38.** $6002 - 1478$ 4524   **39.** $3000 - 695$ 2305

Round each number to the nearest ten.   (Pages 17–19)

40. 324 320 **41.** 689 690 **42.** 465 470 **43.** 28 30 **44.** 31 30 **45.** 375 380 **46.** 6 10 **47.** 2 0

Round each number to the nearest hundred.   (Pages 17–19)

48. 749 700 **49.** 386 400 **50.** 4228 4200 **51.** 5664 5700 **52.** 6962 7000 **53.** 3850 3900

Round each number to the nearest thousand.   (Pages 17–19)

54. 4765 5000 **55.** 8355 8000 **56.** 14,621 15,000 **57.** 21,395 21,000 **58.** 36,488 36,000 **59.** 26,862 27,000

Applications   The use of these word problems depends on which applications were studied.

60. The cash register in Gann's Delicatessen contains five $20–bills, three $10–bills, five $5–bills and seven $1–bills. How much money is in the register?   (Page 4) $162

61. A plane leaves New York at 1:45 P.M. (Eastern time). The flight to Chicago takes 1 hour 25 minutes. At what time (Central time) does the plane arrive in Chicago?   (Page 13) 2:10 P.M.

REVIEW OF RELATED SKILLS FOR CHAPTER 2

We suggest that some or all of this page be reviewed before proceeding with the chapter.

Multiply.

1. $1 \times 8 = 8$
2. $2 \times 6 = 12$
3. $3 \times 3 = 9$
4. $9 \times 9 = 81$
5. $2 \times 9 = 18$
6. $4 \times 7 = 28$
7. $9 \times 8 = 72$

8. $4 \times 6 = 24$
9. $8 \times 5 = 40$
10. $9 \times 3 = 27$
11. $1 \times 9 = 9$
12. $7 \times 0 = 0$
13. $7 \times 3 = 21$
14. $7 \times 2 = 14$

15. $9 \times 1 = 9$
16. $3 \times 2 = 6$
17. $6 \times 8 = 48$
18. $9 \times 7 = 63$
19. $3 \times 1 = 3$
20. $9 \times 4 = 36$
21. $6 \times 1 = 6$

22. $4 \times 9 = 36$
23. $5 \times 6 = 30$
24. $4 \times 0 = 0$
25. $5 \times 9 = 45$
26. $6 \times 7 = 42$
27. $6 \times 0 = 0$
28. $7 \times 4 = 28$

29. $1 \times 0 = 0$
30. $6 \times 4 = 24$
31. $3 \times 4 = 12$
32. $0 \times 4 = 0$
33. $3 \times 6 = 18$
34. $6 \times 3 = 18$
35. $3 \times 0 = 0$

36. $9 \times 6 = 54$
37. $8 \times 9 = 72$
38. $5 \times 8 = 40$
39. $4 \times 8 = 32$
40. $1 \times 7 = 7$
41. $7 \times 7 = 49$
42. $3 \times 8 = 24$

43. $8 \times 1 = 8$
44. $2 \times 1 = 2$
45. $5 \times 0 = 0$
46. $7 \times 9 = 63$
47. $1 \times 4 = 4$
48. $2 \times 0 = 0$
49. $4 \times 2 = 8$

50. $2 \times 2 = 4$
51. $8 \times 7 = 56$
52. $1 \times 1 = 1$
53. $8 \times 4 = 32$
54. $0 \times 7 = 0$
55. $7 \times 8 = 56$
56. $3 \times 9 = 27$

57. $9 \times 2 = 18$
58. $8 \times 0 = 0$
59. $7 \times 1 = 7$
60. $5 \times 5 = 25$
61. $1 \times 6 = 6$
62. $9 \times 0 = 0$
63. $8 \times 3 = 24$

64. $9 \times 5 = 45$
65. $8 \times 8 = 64$
66. $3 \times 7 = 21$
67. $7 \times 6 = 42$
68. $1 \times 2 = 2$
69. $5 \times 7 = 35$
70. $5 \times 1 = 5$

Add.   (Pages 6–7)

71. $2360 + 3975 = 6335$
72. $1184 + 8880 = 10{,}064$
73. $732 + 4900 = 5632$
74. $555 + 7300 = 7855$
75. $1325 + 4780 = 6105$

76. $1234 + 6050 = 7284$
77. $2403 + 6900 = 9303$
78. $431 + 4980 = 5411$
79. $369 + 3210 = 3579$
80. $6324 + 3910 = 10{,}234$

81. $21 + 5731 + 6500 = 12{,}252$
82. $65 + 6270 + 4500 = 10{,}835$
83. $70 + 1300 + 2400 = 3770$
84. $923 + 6420 + 3200 = 10{,}543$
85. $395 + 4100 + 8300 = 12{,}795$

86. $611 + 2109 + 3562 + 8310 = 14{,}592$
87. $765 + 1243 + 6110 + 3200 = 11{,}318$
88. $483 + 3190 + 6100 + 4000 = 13{,}773$
89. $7613 + 2111 + 220 + 4000 = 13{,}944$
90. $3370 + 2980 + 5970 + 9800 = 22{,}120$

2 WHOLE NUMBERS MULTIPLICATION

SKILLS

2-1 One-Digit Multipliers
2-2 Two- and Three-Digit Multipliers
2-3 Zeros in Multiplication
2-4 Multiplying by 10, by 100, by 1000

APPLICATIONS

Ordering by Mail
Message Units
Cost of Electricity
Gross Pay and Net Pay

CAREER

Automobile Repair

One-Digit Multipliers See the Teacher's Manual for the objectives.

This lesson shows two methods of multiplication with whole numbers. Use whichever method is easier for you.

PROCEDURE To multiply by a one–digit multiplier:

1. Multiply the ones.

2. Multiply the tens.

3. Multiply the hundreds, and so on.

EXAMPLE Multiply: 476×8

Solutions: **Method 1**   **Method 2**

476	64
$\times$ 8	476
48 $\longleftarrow$ 8×6	$\times$ 8
560 $\longleftarrow$ 8×70	3808
3200 $\longleftarrow$ 8×400	
3808 $\longleftarrow$ $48 + 560 + 3200$	

REVIEW OF RELATED SKILLS
You may wish to use these exercises before teaching the lesson.

Multiply.

1. 3 $\times9$ 27	**2.** 7 $\times7$ 49	**3.** 3 $\times7$ 21	**4.** 5 $\times9$ 45	**5.** 4 $\times0$ 0	**6.** 8 $\times5$ 40	**7.** 4 $\times6$ 24
8. 0 $\times7$ 0	**9.** 3 $\times8$ 24	**10.** 4 $\times8$ 32	**11.** 6 $\times7$ 42	**12.** 5 $\times6$ 30	**13.** 9 $\times3$ 27	**14.** 9 $\times8$ 72
15. 8 $\times4$ 32	**16.** 5 $\times7$ 35	**17.** 5 $\times8$ 40	**18.** 6 $\times0$ 0	**19.** 4 $\times9$ 36	**20.** 8 $\times8$ 64	**21.** 4 $\times7$ 28
22. 1 $\times1$ 1	**23.** 7 $\times6$ 42	**24.** 8 $\times9$ 72	**25.** 7 $\times4$ 28	**26.** 9 $\times4$ 36	**27.** 7 $\times0$ 0	**28.** 2 $\times9$ 18
29. 7 $\times8$ 56	**30.** 5 $\times0$ 0	**31.** 9 $\times6$ 54	**32.** 1 $\times0$ 0	**33.** 9 $\times5$ 45	**34.** 7 $\times3$ 21	**35.** 9 $\times9$ 81
36. 8 $\times7$ 56	**37.** 7 $\times9$ 63	**38.** 3 $\times0$ 0	**39.** 6 $\times4$ 24	**40.** 6 $\times8$ 48	**41.** 7 $\times2$ 14	**42.** 3 $\times3$ 9
43. 2 $\times2$ 4	**44.** 5 $\times5$ 25	**45.** 6 $\times3$ 18	**46.** 3 $\times4$ 12	**47.** 9 $\times7$ 63	**48.** 9 $\times1$ 9	**49.** 2 $\times6$ 12

EXERCISES

See the suggested assignment guide in the Teacher's Manual.

Multiply. Use the method that is easier for you.   (Example)

1.	267	**2.**	726	**3.**	284	**4.**	100	**5.**	857	**6.**	758
	× 3 _801_		× 2 _1452_		× 9 _2556_		× 9 _900_		× 7 _5999_		× 8 _6064_
7.	463	**8.**	643	**9.**	562	**10.**	235	**11.**	856	**12.**	489
	× 9 _4167_		× 5 _3215_		× 6 _3372_		× 8 _1880_		× 3 _2568_		× 4 _1956_
13.	815	**14.**	261	**15.**	300	**16.**	147	**17.**	513	**18.**	847
	× 5 _4075_		× 7 _1827_		× 6 _1800_		× 9 _1323_		× 8 _4104_		× 4 _3388_
19.	129	**20.**	432	**21.**	764	**22.**	483	**23.**	725	**24.**	389
	× 6 _774_		× 8 _3456_		× 9 _6876_		× 7 _3381_		× 6 _4350_		× 4 _1556_

25. 324 × 4 _1296_   **26.** 423 × 4 _1692_   **27.** 827 × 9 _7443_   **28.** 728 × 9 _6552_   **29.** 738 × 6 _4428_

30. 649 × 8 _5192_   **31.** 100 × 6 _600_   **32.** 534 × 9 _4806_   **33.** 435 × 7 _3045_   **34.** 459 × 3 _1377_

35. 593 × 4 _2372_   **36.** 359 × 5 _1795_   **37.** 491 × 2 _982_   **38.** 914 × 4 _3656_   **39.** 764 × 3 _2292_

40. 635 × 7 _4445_   **41.** 283 × 6 _1698_   **42.** 400 × 8 _3200_   **43.** 976 × 5 _4880_   **44.** 824 × 7 _5768_

APPLICATIONS: Using Multiplication

These are one-step problems that most students should be able to handle.

45. One scrambled egg contains 95 calories. How many calories are there in 3 scrambled eggs? _285_

46. One slice of whole wheat bread contains 65 calories. How many calories are there in 4 slices? _260_

47. One tomato contains 25 calories. How many calories do 5 tomatoes contain? _125_

48. Four spears of asparagus contain 15 calories. How many calories are there in 16 spears? _60_

49. Six slices of cucumber contain 5 calories. How many calories are there in 18 slices? _15_

More Challenging Problems

Find the missing numbers. More Challenging Problems are optional.

50.	695	**51.**	82■ _9_	**52.**	7■8 _4_	**53.**	¹■0■ _8_	**54.**	8■■ _2 1_
	× ■8		× ■ _9_		× 4		× 7		× 9
	55■0⁶		7461		2■92 _9_		7■6 _5_		■■89 _7 3_
55.	4■21	**56.**	81■ _9_	**57.**	■■6 _3 1_	**58.**	48■ _9_	**59.**	7■7 _7_
	× 7		× ■ _2_		× 5		× ■ _6_		× 3
	2■84 _8_		1638		158■ _0_		2934		■■31 _2 3_

WHOLE NUMBERS: MULTIPLICATION   **27**

Problem Solving and Applications

See the Teacher's Manual for the objectives.   This lesson applies the skills presented in Section 2-1.

Ordering By Mail

When you order items by mail, you find the <u>total price</u> for each kind of item. Then you find the <u>Total for Goods</u>. This is the cost of <u>all</u> the items. The **total cost of the order** includes the cost of all the items, the sales tax (if any), and any delivery costs (postage, freight, and so on.)

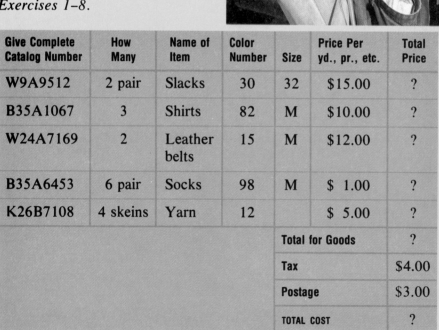

Exercises

Use this partial order form for Exercises 1–8.

Give Complete Catalog Number	How Many	Name of Item	Color Number	Size	Price Per yd., pr., etc.	Total Price
W9A9512	2 pair	Slacks	30	32	$15.00	?
B35A1067	3	Shirts	82	M	$10.00	?
W24A7169	2	Leather belts	15	M	$12.00	?
B35A6453	6 pair	Socks	98	M	$ 1.00	?
K26B7108	4 skeins	Yarn	12		$ 5.00	?
				Total for Goods		?
				Tax		$4.00
				Postage		$3.00
				TOTAL COST		?

1. Find the total price of the slacks.
   (HINT: 2 × $15.00 = _?_) $30.00

2. Find the total price of the shirts.
   (HINT: 3 × $10.00 = _?_) $30.00

3. Find the total price of the belts. $24.00

4. Find the total price of the socks. $6.00

5. Find the total price of the yarn. $20.00

6. Find the **Total for Goods.** $110.00

7. What is the charge for postage? $3.00

8. Find the TOTAL COST. $117.00

Application

Use this partial order form for Exercises 9–18.

Give Complete Catalog Number	How Many	Name of Item	Color Number	Size	Price Per yd., pr. etc.	Total Price
M8Q5624	3	Ties	9	—	$6.00	?
M8T3702	3	Sweaters	15 (1) 18 (1)	M	$18.00	?
53F0069	2 pair	Pajamas	135	M	$9.00	?
E5Z3540	2	Jacket	77 (1) 78 (1)	M	$87.00	?
B3A9612	2 pair	Jeans	18	S	$13.00	?
W9X8473	4 pair	Hose	12	A	$ 3.00	?
CID9019	2	Sweat shirts	25	S	$ 4.00	?
					Total for Goods	?
					Tax	$9.00
					Postage	$4.00
					TOTAL COST	?

9. Find the total price of the ties. $18.00

10. Find the total price of the sweaters. $54.00

11. Find the total price of the pajamas. $18.00

12. Find the total price of the jackets. $174.00

13. Find the total price of the jeans. $26.00

14. Find the total price of the hose. $12.00

15. Find the total price of the sweat shirts. $8.00

16. What is the total tax on the order? $9.00

17. Find the **Total for Goods.** $310.00

18. Find the TOTAL COST. $323.00

From a 1902 Catalog

Problem Solving and Applications

Message Units

See the Teacher's Manual for the objectives.
This lesson applies the skills presented in Section 2-1.

Message units are charges for telephone usage.
You pay one or more message units for each telephone
call, depending on how long you talk and on whether
the call is local (within a given neighboring area) or
long distance.

This map shows local and certain long–distance areas
for calls from Los Angeles.

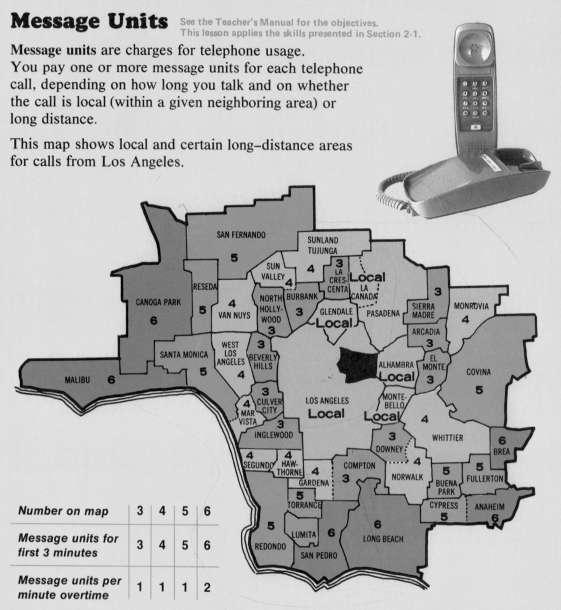

Number on map	3	4	5	6
Message units for first 3 minutes	3	4	5	6
Message units per minute overtime	1	1	1	2

The table above gives the number of message units charged for calls
from Los Angeles to each area.

To find the cost of a telephone call from Los Angeles to Anaheim,
you must first answer the question:

> How many message units were used?"

This is the <u>hidden question</u> in the problem. Then you can find the cost.

EXAMPLE Rosemary placed a call from Los Angeles to Anaheim. The call lasted 7 minutes. Find the cost of the call at 8¢ per message unit.

Solution: 1 Find the number of message units.

Number for Anaheim on map	6
Message units for first 3 minutes	6
Message units per minute overtime	2

From the table

Number of message units for first 3 minutes: 6
Number of message units for overtime: +8
Total message units: 14

7 − 3 = 4
4 × 2 = 8

2 Find the cost.

14 × 8 = 112¢, or **$1.12**

Number of message units × Cost per message unit = Cost

The cost of the call is **$1.12.**

Exercises

Note that Exercises 1-6 are one-step problems.
Exercises 7-12 are two-step problems.

Find the number of message units for each call from Los Angeles.

1. To Malibu, for 3 minutes 6
2. To Sierra Madre, for 4 minutes 4
3. To Santa Monica, for 10 minutes 12
4. To Sun Valley, for 8 minutes 9
5. To San Pedro, for 20 minutes 40
6. To San Fernando, for 35 minutes 37

Find the cost of each call from Los Angeles at 9¢ per message unit.

7. To Long Beach, for 9 minutes $1.62
8. To Whittier, for 5 minutes $0.54
9. To Covina, for 10 minutes $1.08
10. To El Monte, for 15 minutes $1.35

11. Find the cost of a 12–minute call from Los Angeles to Sun Valley at 7¢ per message unit. $0.91

12. Find the cost of a 40–minute call from Los Angeles to Canoga Park at 4¢ per message unit. $3.20

2-2 Two- and Three-Digit Multipliers

You can use the methods shown on page 26 to multiply with larger numbers.

PROCEDURE To multiply with larger numbers:

[1] Multiply by the ones.

[2] Multiply by the tens.

[3] Multiply by the hundreds, and so on.

[4] Add the products obtained in Steps 1–3.

EXAMPLE 1 Multiply: 58×76

Solutions:

Method 1

```
      58
  ×   76
     348  ←——— 6 × 58
    4060  ←——— 70 × 58
    4408  ←——— 348 + 4060
```

Method 2

```
      58
  ×   76
     348
     406
    4408
```

After completing Example 1, you may wish to have students do some or all of Exercises 1-34.

Use the method of multiplication that is easier for you.

EXAMPLE 2 Multiply: 172×349

Solutions:

Method 1

```
      172
  ×   349
     1548  ←——— 9 × 172
     6880  ←——— 40 × 172
    51600  ←——— 300 × 172
    60028
```

Method 2

```
      172
  ×   349
     1548
      688
      516
    60028
```

REVIEW OF RELATED SKILLS

Multiply.   (Pages 26–27)

1. 15 ×8 120	**2.** 31 ×9 279	**3.** 46 ×5 230	**4.** 71 ×6 426	**5.** 32 ×2 64	**6.** 85 ×4 340
7. 112 ×4 448	**8.** 923 ×5 4615	**9.** 618 ×7 4326	**10.** 425 ×9 3825	**11.** 214 ×6 1284	**12.** 393 ×3 1179

Add.   (Pages 6–7)

13.   624
+3480
‾‾‾‾
4104

14.   576
+9680
‾‾‾‾
10,256

15.   478
+2570
‾‾‾‾
3048

16.   345
+4390
‾‾‾‾
4735

17.   127
6910
+8700
‾‾‾‾ 15,737

18.   432
1990
+4500
‾‾‾‾ 6922

19.   423
8730
+3200
‾‾‾‾
12,353

20.   721
4340
+8400
‾‾‾‾
13,461

21.   812
7610
+3600
‾‾‾‾
12,022

22.   744
3560
+1400
‾‾‾‾
5704

23.   189
4500
+4200
‾‾‾‾
8889

24.   334
6500
+3400
‾‾‾‾
10,234

EXERCISES

See the suggested assignment guide in the Teacher's Manual.

Multiply.   (Example 1)

1.   27
×35 945

2.   72
×53 3816

3.   94
×26 2444

4.   49
×62 3038

5.   84
×69 5796

6.   25
×78 1950

7.   48
×96 4608

8.   37
×18 666

9.   81
×73 5913

10.   43
×34 1462

11.   45
×34 1530

12.   14
×93 1302

13.   49
×27 1323

14.   72
×49 3528

15.   64
×28 1792

16.   84
×62 5208

17.   82
×62 5084

18.   39
×57 2223

19.   67
×28 1876

20.   59
×16 944

21.   61
×59 3599

22.   43
×17 731

23.   71
×43 3053

24.   48
×75 3600

25. 83 × 68 5644   **26.** 63 × 86 5418   **27.** 59 × 16 944   **28.** 61 × 95 5795   **29.** 73 × 45 3285

30. 45 × 37 1665   **31.** 37 × 15 555   **32.** 81 × 71 5751   **33.** 45 × 76 3420   **34.** 19 × 89 1691

(Example 2)

35.   572
×293 167,596

36.   725
×392 284,200

37.   468
×342 160,056

38.   864
×243 209,952

39.   737
×265 195,305

40.   349
×115
40,135

41.   652
×733 477,916

42.   924
×576 532,224

43.   429
×765 328,185

44.   263
×185 48,655

45.   581
×632 367,192

46.   611
×429
262,119

47.   748
×327 244,596

48.   487
×723 352,101

49.   629
×328 206,312

50.   283
×296 83,768

51.   584
×186 108,624

52.   358
×763
273,154

53. 362 × 851
308,062

54. 518 × 623
322,714

55. 458 × 713
326,554

56. 854 × 137
116,998

57. 748 × 681
509,388

58. 487 × 861
419,307

59. 824 × 763
628,712

60. 673 × 284
191,132

61. 723 × 111
80,253

62. 432 × 777
335,664

Mixed Practice   The Mixed Practice contains exercises that relate to both Examples 1 and 2.

63.   58
×27 1566

64.   72
×85 6120

65.   519
× 38 19,722

66.   831
× 59 49,029

67.   625
× 74 46,250

68.   913
× 48
43,824

69.   725
× 64 46,400

70.   784
×293 229,712

71.   392
×478 187,376

72.   847
×295 249,865

73.   925
×478 442,150

74.   757
×212
160,484

75. 956 × 328
313,568

76. 928 × 356
330,368

77. 519 × 32
16,608

78. 195 × 34
6630

79. 14 × 93
1302

WHOLE NUMBERS: MULTIPLICATION   **33**

Problem Solving and Applications
Cost of Electricity

See the Teacher's Manual for the objectives.
This lesson applies the skills presented in Section 2-2.

The amount of electricity used in a home is measured in kilowatt–hours. You use **one kilowatt–hour** of electricity when you use one kilowatt (1000 watts) for one hour. The tables below show the average number of kilowatt–hours used per week by each of twelve household appliances.

Appliance	Kilowatt–Hours Per Week
Air Conditioner	27
Clothes Dryer	19
Dehumidifier	7
Dishwasher	7
Microwave Oven	4
Range (self–cleaning oven)	14

Appliance	Kilowatt–Hours Per Week
Radio	3
Refrigerator–freezer (frostless)	43
Television (color)	10
Vacuum Cleaner	1
Washing Machine	2
Water Heater	93

To find the cost of electricity per year for an appliance, you must first answer the question:

"How many kilowatt–hours per year are used?"

This is the hidden question in the problem. Then you can find the cost per year.

EXAMPLE   Find the cost of electricity per year (52 weeks) for a radio. Suppose that electricity costs 10¢ per kilowatt–hour.

Solution: **1** Find the number of kilowatt–hours used per year.

Number of kilowatt–hours used per week: 3 ◀ *From the tables*

$3 \times 52 = \mathbf{156}$ ◀ *Kilowatt–Hours Per Week* $\times 52 =$ *Kilowatt–Hours Per Year*

2 Find the cost per year.

$156 \times 10¢ = 1560¢$, or **$15.60** ◀ *Kilowatt–Hours Per Year* $\times 10¢ =$ *Cost Per Year*

The cost of electricity per year for the radio is **$15.60.**

Exercises

Note that Exercises 1-15 are non-verbal problems. Exercises 1-17 are two-step problems. Exercises 18-21 require more than two-steps.

Find the number of kilowatt–hours used per year by each appliance.

1. Microwave oven 208
2. Dishwasher 364
3. Dehumidifier 364
4. Television (color) 520
5. Washing machine 104
6. Range 728
7. Refrigerator–freezer 2236
8. Clothes dryer 988
9. Water heater 4836

Suppose that electricity costs 11¢ per kilowatt–hour. Find the cost of electricity per year for each appliance.

10. Vacuum cleaner $5.72
11. Television (color) $57.20
12. Clothes dryer $108.68

Suppose that electricity costs 9¢ per kilowatt–hour. Find the cost of electricity per year for each appliance.

13. Dishwasher $32.76
14. Range $65.52
15. Water heater $435.24

16. The cost for electricity in Triple Falls is 12¢ per kilowatt–hour. Find the cost of electricity per year for a vacuum cleaner. $6.24

17. The cost for electricity in Bradford is 10¢ per kilowatt–hour. Find the cost of electricity per year for an air conditioner. $140.40

18. The cost for electricity in San Cyro is 9¢ per kilowatt–hour. Find the cost of electricity per year for a color television and a water heater. $482.04

19. Suppose that electricity for an electric clock costs 23¢ per month. Find the cost of electricity for the clock for one year. $2.76

20. The cost for electricity in North River is 11¢ per kilowatt–hour. Find the cost of electricity per year for a dehumidifier and a microwave oven. $62.92

21. Suppose that electricity for an iron costs 7¢ per hour and that a family uses the iron 4 hours per week. Find the yearly cost of electricity for the iron. $14.56

2-3 Zeros in Multiplication See the Teacher's Manual for the objectives.

Sometimes one or both of the factors in a multiplication problem contain zeros. The **factors** are the numbers that are multiplied.

$$18 \times 5 = 90 \quad \blacktriangleleft \quad \text{Factors: 18 and 5}$$
$$\text{Product: 90}$$

Remember that the product of any number and zero is zero.

EXAMPLE 1 Multiply: 367×209

Solution:

Method 1

```
    367
  ×209
   3303  ←——— 9 × 367
   0000  ←——— 0 tens × 367
  73400  ←——— 200 × 367
  76703
```

Method 2

```
    367
  ×209
   3303
   7340
  76703
```

After completing Example 1, you may wish to have students do some or all of Exercises 1-22.

Example 2 shows multiplication with zeros in both factors.

EXAMPLE 2 Multiply: 905×307

Solution:

Method 1

```
     905
  ×  307
    6335
    0000  ←——— 0 tens × 905
  271500
  277835
```

Method 2

```
     905
  ×  307
    6335
   27150
  277835
```

Examples 1 and 2 show two methods of multiplication. Use whichever method is easier for you.

REVIEW OF RELATED SKILLS You may wish to use these exercises before teaching the lesson.

Multiply. (Pages 26–27, 32–33)

1. 37 ×0 _0_	**2.** 91 ×8 _728_	**3.** 143 ×0 _0_	**4.** 212 ×7 _1484_	**5.** 463 ×40 _18,520_	**6.** 347 ×30 _10,410_
7. 26 ×93 _2418_	**8.** 89 ×47 _4183_	**9.** 473 ×94 _44,462_	**10.** 891 ×17 _15,147_	**11.** 468 ×785 _367,380_	**12.** 529 ×398 _210,542_

EXERCISES
See the suggested assignment guide in the Teacher's Manual.

Multiply.   (Example 1)

1. 863
×108 93,204

2. 954
×309 294,786

3. 687
×403 276,861

4. 727
×807 586,689

5. 263
×408 107,304

6. 312
×704 219,648

7. 398
×105 41,790

8. 267
×505 134,835

9. 642
×503 322,926

10. 391
×406 158,746

11. 736
×508 373,888

12. 998
×103 102,794

13. 426 × 305 129,930

14. 239 × 503 120,217

15. 637 × 806 513,422

16. 429 × 308 132,132

17. 857 × 209 117,113

18. 526 × 204 107,304

19. 859 × 307 263,713

20. 624 × 704 439,296

21. 526 × 408 214,608

22. 382 × 503 192,146

(Example 2)

23. 570
×308 175,560

24. 960
×207 198,720

25. 309
×260 80,340

26. 207
×950 196,650

27. 940
×230 216,200

28. 240
×706 169,440

29. 720
×450 324,000

30. 306
×206 63,036

31. 307
×508 155,956

32. 206
×104 21,424

33. 802
×403 323,206

34. 701
×107 75,007

35. 403 × 507 204,321

36. 806 × 209 168,454

37. 490 × 306 149,940

38. 850 × 407 345,950

39. 605 × 304 183,920

40. 307 × 902 276,914

41. 509 × 306 155,754

42. 905 × 506 457,930

43. 460 × 307 141,220

44. 980 × 507 496,860

Mixed Practice

45. 415
×708 293,820

46. 975
×307 299,325

47. 320
×407 130,240

48. 597
×608 362,976

49. 108
×207 22,356

50. 122
×804 98,088

51. 305
×106 32,330

52. 307
×209 64,163

53. 206
×507 104,442

54. 275
×609 167,475

55. 420
×508 213,360

56. 903
×604 545,412

57. 310 × 510 158,100

58. 630 × 708 446,040

59. 302 × 490 147,980

60. 509 × 308 156,772

61. 407 × 728 296,296

62. 409 × 700 286,300

63. 785 × 903 708,855

64. 404 × 653 263,812

65. 305 × 777 236,985

66. 930 × 606 563,580

CHECKING MULTIPLICATION
Calculator exercises are optional.

Use a calculator to check each answer. Correct any wrong answers.

1. 692
×438
5536
2076
2768
303,096

2. 487
×566
2922
2922
2435
274,442 275,642

3. 948
×261
948
5688
1896
147,418 247,428

4. 789
×234
3156
2367
1578
184,636 184,626

5. 687
×914
2748
687
6183
626,818 627,918

6. 3068 × 789 = 2,420,652

7. 4823 × 386 = 1,861,678

8. 5723 × 267 = 1,728,041 1,528,041

9. 7206 × 808 = 6,822,488 5,822,448

10. 829 × 485 × 39 = 15,680,535

11. 368 × 473 × 25 = 4,451,600 4,351,600

12. 625 × 234 × 55 = 7,043,750 8,043,750

13. 640 × 378 × 46 = 11,128,320 11,128,320

Calculator   WHOLE NUMBERS: MULTIPLICATION   **37**

Problem Solving and Applications

Gross Pay and Net Pay

See the Teacher's Manual for the objectives.
This lesson applies the skills presented in Section 2-3.

The amount of money earned by a worker is called **gross earnings,** or **gross pay. Deductions** are the amounts subtracted from the worker's pay for taxes, health and accident insurance, and so on. **Net pay,** or **take–home pay,** is the amount the worker receives after the deductions are subtracted.

CALJON CORPORATION
STATEMENT OF EMPLOYEE EARNINGS AND DEDUCTIONS

REGULAR PAY	OVERTIME	BONUS	BENEFITS	GROSS EARNINGS
204.00	61.24			265.24

FEDERAL W.H.	F.I.C.A.	STATE W.H.		TAXES
24.70	16.26	13.26		54.22

ACT. CLUB	CHARITY	MED. INS.	LIFE INS.	D E D U C T I O N S	TOTAL DEDUCTIONS
		.92	9.80		29.47

CREDIT UNION	BONDS	RETIREMENT		
	18.75			

SOCIAL SECURITY	DEPT.	CHECK NO.	PAY PERIOD ENDING	NET PAY
243-42-7666	6740	30873	10/18	181.55

To find a worker's net pay, you must first answer the question:

> "What is the worker's gross pay?"

This is the <u>hidden question</u> in the problem. Then you can find the net pay.

EXAMPLE   Frank earns $4.00 an hour. He works 40 hours per week. His deductions per week are $29.00.
What is his net pay?

Solutions: **1** Find the gross pay.

$$40 \times \$4 = \$160 \quad \blacktriangleleft \quad \textit{Hours Worked} \times \textit{Rate Per Hour} = \textit{Gross Pay}$$

2 Find the net pay.

$$\$160 - \$29 = \$131 \quad \blacktriangleleft \quad \textit{Gross Pay} - \textit{Deductions} = \textit{Net Pay}$$

The net pay is **$131.**

To find Frank's yearly net pay, multiply the weekly net pay and 52, the number of weeks in a year.

Exercises
Note that Exercises 1-10 are non-verbal problems.

Complete the table for each worker.

	Name	Hours Worked	Rate per Hour	Gross Pay	Deductions	Net Pay
1.	T. Carter	40	$5.00	$200 ?	$31.00	? $169
2.	S. Darnello	38	$4.00	$152 ?	$27.00	? $125
3.	J. Herrara	40	$6.00	$240 ?	$42.00	? $198
4.	D. Jung	36	$7.00	$252 ?	$37.00	? $215
5.	L. McFadden	40	$15.00	$600 ?	$137.00	? $463
6.	L. Satterfield	32	$12.00	$384 ?	$61.00	? $323
7.	P. Shiller	30	$6.00	$180 ?	$24.00	? $156
8.	A. Velez	38	$10.00	$380 ?	$72.00	? $308
9.	B. Yuen	25	$9.00	$225 ?	$21.00	? $204
10.	O. Zarty	35	$12.00	$420 ?	$75.00	? $345

Solve each problem. Exercises 11-17 are two-step problems.

11. A coal miner earns $11.00 per hour and works 40 hours per week. Deductions amount to $81.00 per week. What is the net pay? $359

12. A steel worker earns $10.00 per hour and works 38 hours per week. Deductions amount to $74.00 per week. What is the net pay? $306

13. An oil–refinery worker earns $9.00 per hour and works 36 hours per week. Deductions amount to $52.00 per week. Find the net pay. $272

14. A tire factory worker earns $8.00 per hour and works 40 hours per week. Deductions amount to $48 per week. Find the net pay. $272

15. A carpenter earns $7.00 per hour and works 35 hours per week. Deductions per week amount to $21.00. Find the net pay. $224

16. A night watchman earns $4.00 per hour and works 40 hours per week. Total deductions per week amount to $23.00. Find the yearly net pay. $7124

17. A keypunch operator works 30 hours per week and earns $5.00 per hour. Total weekly deductions amount to $20.00. Find the yearly net pay. $6760

Application

WHOLE NUMBERS: MULTIPLICATION

2-4 Multiplying by 10, by 100, by 1000

See the Teacher's Manual for the objectives.

Note the pattern for multiplying by 10, by 100, by 1000.

$$
\begin{array}{c} 891 \\ \underline{\times\ 10} \\ 8910 \end{array} \quad \text{One zero} \qquad
\begin{array}{c} 891 \\ \underline{\times 100} \\ 89100 \end{array} \quad \text{Two zeros} \qquad
\begin{array}{c} 891 \\ \underline{\times 1000} \\ 891000 \end{array} \quad \text{Three zeros}
$$

PROCEDURE

1 To multiply a number by 10, write the number. Annex one zero on the right.

2 To multiply a number by 100, write the number. Annex two zeros on the right.

3 To multiply a number by 1000, write the number. Annex three zeros on the right.

EXAMPLE Multiply. Annex one, two, or three zeros on the right.

a. 263×10 **b.** 900×100 **c.** 119×10000

Solutions:

a. $263 \times 10 = 2630$ **b.** $900 \times 100 = 90{,}000$ **c.** $119 \times 1000 = 119{,}000$

You can follow the same method to multiply by 10,000, by 100,000, and so on.

REVIEW OF RELATED SKILLS

You may wish to use these exercises before teaching the lesson.

Multiply. (Pages 26-27)

1. 100×5 500 **2.** 100×9 900 **3.** 300×4 1200 **4.** 400×6 2400 **5.** 200×9 1800 **6.** 700×1 700

7. 200×8 1600 **8.** 600×5 3000 **9.** 100×7 700 **10.** 500×2 1000 **11.** 900×4 3600 **12.** 300×4 1200

EXERCISES

See the suggested assignment guide in the Teacher's Manual.

Multiply.

1. 497×10 4970 **2.** 864×10 8640 **3.** 7251×10 72,510 **4.** 8433×10 84,330 **5.** 873×10 8730

6. 468×10 4680 **7.** 407×10 4070 **8.** 290×10 2900 **9.** 2003×10 20,030 **10.** 4200×10 42,000

11. 463×100 46,300 **12.** 825×100 82,500 **13.** 4686×100 468,600 **14.** 3937×100 393,700 **15.** 271×100 27,100

16. 864×100 86,400 **17.** 100×36 3600 **18.** 100×75 7500 **19.** 100×811 81,100 **20.** 100×283 28,300

21. 57×1000 57,000 **22.** 73×1000 73,000 **23.** 264×1000 264,000 **24.** 819×1000 819,000

25. 473×1000 473,000 **26.** 1000×4324 4,324,000 **27.** 5862×1000 5,862,000 **28.** 1000×297 297,000

29. 843×1000 843,000 **30.** 1000×180 180,000 **31.** 1000×456 456,000 **32.** 1000×1135 1,135,000

AUTOMOBILE REPAIR

Career lessons are optional.
This lesson applies the skills presented in Section 2-4.

When an automobile engine is "tuned", it uses less fuel. To tune an engine, a tune–up technician must know the <u>number of revolutions per minute</u> (abbreviated: rpm) that the engine turns. To learn this, the technician uses a <u>tachometer</u>.

EXAMPLE Give the number of revolutions per minute shown on the dial of this tachometer.

Solution:
1. Read the number on the dial: **56**
2. Multiply by 100.

    $56 \times 100 =$ **5600**

The reading is **5600 rpm.**

EXERCISES

Give the number of revolutions per minute shown on each dial.

1. 7000

2. 3500

3. 5300

4. 1200

5. 2400

6. 7700

Chapter Review

Part 1: Vocabulary

For Exercises 1–7, choose from the box at the right the word(s) that completes the statement.

1. When you order by mail, the cost for all the items is called the __?__. (Page 28) total for goods

2. When you use one kilowatt of electricity for one hour, you have used one __?__. (Page 34) kilowatt-hour

3. In a multiplication problem, the numbers you multiply are called __?__. (Page 36) factors

4. The total amount of money earned by a worker is called __?__. (Page 38) gross pay

5. Money taken from your salary to pay taxes is called a __?__. (Page 38) deduction

6. Another word for take–home pay is __?__. (Page 38) net pay

7. To multiply a number by 100, you annex __?__ zeros to the number. (Page 40) two

net pay
factors
one
gross pay
total for goods
addends
deduction
two
kilowatt–hour
message unit

Part 2: Skills

Multiply. (Pages 26–27)

8. 321 × 4 1284
9. 435 × 6 2610
10. 428 × 7 2996
11. 643 × 4 2572
12. 932 × 8 7456
13. 572 × 6 3432

14. 223 × 7 1561
15. 276 × 5 1380
16. 178 × 4 712
17. 712 × 8 5696
18. 128 × 6 768
19. 233 × 7 1631

20. 491 × 9 4419
21. 746 × 3 2238
22. 825 × 7 5775
23. 686 × 6 4116
24. 569 × 9 5121

25. 129 × 8 1032
26. 263 × 5 1315
27. 483 × 2 966
28. 516 × 3 1548
29. 759 × 4 3036

30. 883 × 7 6181
31. 496 × 8 3968
32. 927 × 4 3708
33. 645 × 5 3225
34. 334 × 9 3006

35. 276 × 3 828
36. 535 × 7 3745
37. 656 × 6 3936
38. 163 × 4 652
39. 384 × 5 1920

(Page 32–33)

40. 62 ×47 2914
41. 38 ×17 646
42. 865 ×228 197,220
43. 932 ×429 399,828
44. 486 × 28 13,608
45. 732 × 46 33,672

46. 24 ×37 888
47. 75 ×49 3675
48. 36 ×18 648
49. 23 ×49 1127
50. 315 × 18 5670
51. 285 × 43 12,255

52. 72 × 45 3240
53. 66 × 98 6468
54. 356 × 732 260,592
55. 215 × 111 23,865
56. 715 × 34 24,310

57. 84 × 65 5460
58. 47 × 96 4512
59. 548 × 173 94,804
60. 237 × 141 33,417
61. 159 × 48 7632

62. 77 × 54 4158
63. 98 × 41 4018
64. 47 × 28 1316
65. 19 × 27 513
66. 612 × 18 11,016

67. 846 × 213 180,198
68. 148 × 562 83,176
69. 281 × 492 138,252
70. 775 × 431 334,025
71. 422 × 584 246,448

Chapter Review

(Pages 36–37)

72. 451   **73.** 398   **74.** 280   **75.** 490   **76.** 703   **77.** 408
  ×807 363,957   ×206 81,988   ×309 86,520   ×605 296,450   ×106 74,518   ×307
                                                                            125,256

78. 180   **79.** 610   **80.** 260   **81.** 714   **82.** 321   **83.** 806
  ×305 54,900   ×105 64,050   ×204 53,040   ×203 144,942   ×506 162,426   ×304
                                                                            245,024

84. 640 × 709 453,760   **85.** 590 × 904 533,360   **86.** 408 × 647 263,976   **87.** 506 × 748 378,488

88. 704 × 216 152,064   **89.** 480 × 609 292,320   **90.** 615 × 803 493,845   **91.** 208 × 941 195,728

92. 707 × 504 356,328   **93.** 906 × 501 453,906   **94.** 983 × 306 300,798   **95.** 344 × 502 172,688

(Page 40)

96. 62 × 10 620   **97.** 49 × 10 490   **98.** 78 × 100 7800   **99.** 931 × 1000 931,000

100. 10 × 403 4030   **101.** 306 × 100 30,600   **102.** 703 × 1000 703,000   **103.** 1000 × 502 502,000

104. 644 × 100 64,400   **105.** 10 × 509 5090   **106.** 583 × 1000 583,000   **107.** 100 × 296 29,600

Part 3: Applications The use of these word problems depends on which applications were studied.

108. Three strips of bacon contain 237 calories. How many calories are there in 9 strips of bacon? (Page 27) 711

109. Jeans cost $14.95 a pair and ties cost $5.99 each. What is the total cost of 3 pairs of jeans and 4 ties? (Page 28) $68.81

110. Suppose that electricity for the Lopez family's toaster costs 8¢ per hour. How much money will the Lopez family pay per year if they use the toaster 3 hours per week? (Pages 34–35) $12.48

111. A gas station attendant works 40 hours per week and earns $3.50 per hour. Deductions amount to $36.00 per week. Find the net pay. (Page 38–39) $104

112. A house painter earns $8.00 per hour and works 35 hours per week. Weekly deductions amount to $72.00. Find the yearly net pay. (Page 38–39) $10,816

Chapter Test

Multiply.

1. 521
    × 9
    ––––
    4689

2. 468
    × 3
    ––––
    1404

3. 78
    ×17
    ––––
    1326

4. 96
    ×24
    ––––
    2304

5. 324
    × 46
    ––––
    14,904

6. 498
    ×364
    ––––
    181,272

7. 687
    ×472
    ––––
    324,264

8. 988
    × 39
    ––––
    38,532

9. 438
    ×302
    ––––
    132,276

10. 587
    ×601
    ––––
    352,787

11. 309
    ×405
    ––––
    125,145

12. 720
    ×609
    ––––
    438,480

13. 486 × 10 4860

14. 507 × 1000 507,000

15. 821 × 100 82,100

16. 647 × 309 199,923

17. 604 × 1000 604,000

18. 324 × 10 3240

19. 574 × 386 221,564

20. 962 × 100 96,200

The use of these word problems depends on which applications were studied.

21. One slice of cheese contains 112 calories. How many calories are there in 6 slices? 672

22. Sweatshirts cost $5.95 each. How much will 3 sweatshirts cost? $17.85

23. Suppose that electricity for a night light costs 13¢ per month. Find the cost of electricity for the light for for one year. $1.56

24. A stock clerk earns $3.15 per hour and works 35 hour per week. Deductions total $29.00. Find the weekly net pay. $81.25

25. An electrician earns $9.00 per hour and works 40 hours per week. Total weekly deductions amount to $96.00. Find the yearly net pay.

$13,728

Additional Practice

You may wish to use all or some of these exercises depending on how well students performed on the formal chapter test.

Skills

Multiply.   (Pages 26–27)

1.   231
$\times$ 5 1155

2.   162
$\times$ 4 648

3.   328
$\times$ 4 1312

4.   412
$\times$ 9 3708

5.   612
$\times$ 2 1224

6.   145
$\times$ 8 1160

7.   512
$\times$ 3 1536

8.   416
$\times$ 2 832

9.   854
$\times$ 3 2562

10.   463
$\times$ 6 2778

11.   239
$\times$ 4 956

12.   266
$\times$ 8 2128

13.   932
$\times$ 5 4660

14.   519
$\times$ 9 4671

15.   572
$\times$ 7 4004

16.   743
$\times$ 8 5944

17.   189
$\times$ 6 1134

18.   224
$\times$ 7 1568

19. 382×6 2292   **20.** 915×3 2745   **21.** 725×4 2900   **22.** 437×6 2622   **23.** 198×5 990

(Pages 32–33)

24.   45
$\times 18$ 810

25.   62
$\times 31$ 1922

26.   28
$\times 24$ 672

27.   91
$\times 26$ 2366

28.   43
$\times 78$ 3354

29.   18
$\times 96$ 1728

30.   281
$\times$ 45 12,645

31.   714
$\times$ 26 18,564

32.   625
$\times$ 73 45,625

33.   268
$\times$ 29 7772

34.   743
$\times$ 38 28,234

35.   218
$\times$ 46 10,028

36.   612
$\times$ 13 7956

37.   429
$\times$ 37 15,873

38.   356
$\times 213$ 75,828

39.   475
$\times 224$ 106,400

40.   381
$\times 356$ 135,636

41.   672
$\times 158$ 106,176

42. 472×21 9912   **43.** 398×36 14,328   **44.** 226×319 72,094   **45.** 463×313 144,919   **46.** 645×91 58,695

(Pages 36–37)

47.   381
$\times 401$ 152,781

48.   642
$\times 309$ 198,378

49.   480
$\times 406$ 194,880

50.   920
$\times 603$ 554,760

51.   605
$\times 702$ 424,710

52.   803
$\times 509$ 408,727

53.   633
$\times 401$ 253,833

54.   435
$\times 307$ 133,545

55.   560
$\times 109$ 61,040

56.   480
$\times 206$ 98,880

57.   308
$\times 409$ 125,972

58.   509
$\times 607$ 308,963

59. 688×307 211,216   **60.** 436×508 221,488   **61.** 620×307 190,340   **62.** 360×903 325,080   **63.** 407×309 125,763

64. 903×406 366,618   **65.** 806×402 324,012   **66.** 303×506 153,318   **67.** 621×308 191,268   **68.** 743×904 671,672

(Page 40)

69. 38×10 380   **70.** 47×1000 47,000   **71.** 52×100 5200   **72.** 1000×68 68,000

73. 321×100 32,100   **74.** 486×10 4860   **75.** 596×1000 596,000   **76.** 224×100 22,400

77. 100×308 30,800   **78.** 506×10 5060   **79.** 409×100 40,900   **80.** 1000×607 607,000

81. 286×1000 286,000   **82.** 100×361 36,100   **83.** 592×10 5920   **84.** 464×1000 464,000

Applications   The use of these word problems depends on which applications were studied.

85. Jeans cost $22.50 a pair and shirts cost $14.95 each. What is the total cost of 4 pairs of jeans and 3 shirts?   (Page 28) $134.85

86. A stock clerk works 40 hours per week and earns $3.25 per hour. Deductions amount to $32.50 per week. Find the net pay.   (Page 39) $97.50

REVIEW OF RELATED SKILLS FOR CHAPTER 3

We suggest that some or all of this page be reviewed before proceeding with the chapter.

Add.

1. $3 + 5$ 8   **2.** $2 + 4$ 6   **3.** $5 + 6$ 11   **4.** $3 + 1 + 2$ 6   **5.** $4 + 7 + 5$ 16

6. $8 + 7 + 5 + 2$ 22   **7.** $1 + 2 + 9 + 3$ 15   **8.** $1 + 1 + 7 + 3$ 12   **9.** $2 + 4 + 5 + 4$ 15

Add or subtract.   (Pages 2–3, 10–11)

10. 63	**11.** 43	**12.** 71	**13.** 46	**14.** 81	**15.** 53
$+58$	-19	-28	$+38$	-26	$+47$
121	24	43	84	55	100

Subtract.   (Pages 14–15)

16. 523	**17.** 185	**18.** 472	**19.** 1625	**20.** 8143	**21.** 4000
$-\ 95$	$-\ 36$	-291	$-\ 388$	-2457	-2488
428	149	181	1237	5686	1512

Round each number to the nearest ten.   (Pages 17–19)

22. 13 10   **23.** 36 40   **24.** 786 790   **25.** 723 720   **26.** 45 50   **27.** 8 10

Round each number to the nearest hundred.   (Pages 17–19)

28. 861 900   **29.** 69 100   **30.** 643 600   **31.** 6824 6800   **32.** 3582 3600   **33.** 152 200

Round each number to the nearest thousand.   (Pages 17–19)

34. 4849 5000   **35.** 2499 2000   **36.** 17,523 18,000   **37.** 29,483 29,000   **38.** 887 1000   **39.** 1264 1000

Multiply.   (Pages 26–27)

40. 139	**41.** 248	**42.** 123	**43.** 275	**44.** 343	**45.** 196
$\times\ 3$	$\times\ 5$	$\times\ 8$	$\times\ 6$	$\times\ 7$	$\times\ 2$
417	1240	984	1650	2401	392

46. 275	**47.** 114	**48.** 436	**49.** 368	**50.** 674	**51.** 482
$\times\ 4$	$\times\ 5$	$\times\ 2$	$\times\ 4$	$\times\ 5$	$\times\ 9$
1100	570	872	1472	3370	4338

52. 546	**53.** 629	**54.** 438	**55.** 248	**56.** 217	**57.** 568
$\times\ 3$	$\times\ 3$	$\times\ 7$	$\times\ 3$	$\times\ 5$	$\times\ 7$
1638	1887	3066	744	1085	3976

Divide.

58. $10 \div 2$ 5   **59.** $20 \div 5$ 4   **60.** $36 \div 6$ 6   **61.** $36 \div 9$ 4   **62.** $12 \div 3$ 4   **63.** $21 \div 7$ 3

64. $16 \div 4$ 4   **65.** $15 \div 3$ 5   **66.** $24 \div 8$ 3   **67.** $45 \div 9$ 5   **68.** $56 \div 8$ 7   **69.** $63 \div 7$ 9

70. $72 \div 8$ 9   **71.** $49 \div 7$ 7   **72.** $12 \div 4$ 3   **73.** $81 \div 9$ 9   **74.** $32 \div 8$ 4   **75.** $40 \div 5$ 8

76. $54 \div 6$ 9   **77.** $40 \div 4$ 10   **78.** $27 \div 3$ 9   **79.** $30 \div 5$ 6   **80.** $48 \div 6$ 8   **81.** $42 \div 7$ 6

82. $35 \div 5$ 7   **83.** $18 \div 2$ 9   **84.** $24 \div 3$ 8   **85.** $16 \div 2$ 8   **86.** $12 \div 6$ 2   **87.** $24 \div 4$ 6

88. $14 \div 2$ 7   **89.** $21 \div 3$ 7   **90.** $36 \div 4$ 9   **91.** $35 \div 7$ 5   **92.** $18 \div 9$ 2   **93.** $56 \div 7$ 8

94. $25 \div 5$ 5   **95.** $42 \div 6$ 7   **96.** $64 \div 8$ 8   **97.** $27 \div 9$ 3   **98.** $80 \div 8$ 10   **99.** $18 \div 6$ 3

3 WHOLE NUMBERS DIVISION

SKILLS

3-1　Rules for Divisibility
3-2　One-Digit Divisors
3-3　Two- and Three-Digit Divisors
3-4　Zeros in the Quotient
3-5　Order of Operations
3-6　Rounding and Estimation

APPLICATIONS

Averages
Finance Charges
Fuel Economy
Fuel Costs for a Car

CAREER

Office Worker

3-1 Rules for Divisibility

See the Teacher's Manual for the objectives.

A number is **divisible** by another number if the remainder is 0. Thus, in the division problem at the right, 28 is divisible by 7.

$$\begin{array}{r} 4 \leftarrow \text{Quotient} \\ 7\overline{)28} \leftarrow \text{Dividend} \\ 28 \\ \hline 0 \leftarrow \text{Remainder} \end{array}$$

Divisor ⟶ 7)28 ← Dividend

PROCEDURE A number is divisible by

2 if its last digit is 0, 2, 4, 6, or 8.
4 if the number represented by its last two digits is divisible by 4.
5 if its last digit is 0 or 5.
10 if its last digit is 0.

EXAMPLE 1 Determine whether each number is divisible by 2, by 4, by 5, or by 10. Give a reason for each answer.

Number	Divisible by 2?	Divisible by 4?	Divisible by 5?	Divisible by 10?
a. 768	Yes; last digit is 8.	Yes; 68 is divisible by 4.	No; last digit is not 0 or 5.	No; last digit is not 0.
b. 80	Yes; last digit is 0.	Yes; 80 is divisible by 4.	Yes; last digit is 0.	Yes; last digit is 0.
c. 925	No; last digit is not 0, 2, 4, 6, or 8.	No; 25 is not divisible by 4.	Yes; last digit is 5.	No; last digit is not 0.

After completing Example 1, you may wish to have students do some or all of Exercises 1-35.

You can also determine whether a number is divisible by 3 or by 9.

PROCEDURE A number is divisible by

3 if the sum of its digits is divisible by 3.
9 if the sum of its digits is divisible by 9.

EXAMPLE 2 Determine whether each number is divisible by 3 or by 9. Give a reason for each answer.

Number	Sum of Digits	Divisible by 3?	Divisible by 9?
a. 81	$8 + 1 = 9$	Yes; $9 \div 3 = 3$	Yes; $9 \div 9 = 1$
b. 498	$4 + 9 + 8 = 21$	Yes; $21 \div 3 = 7$	No; 21 is not divisible by 9.

48 CHAPTER 3

REVIEW OF RELATED SKILLS

You may wish to use these exercises before teaching the lesson.

Find the sum of digits of each number.

1. 29   **2.** 74   **3.** 217   **4.** 345

$2 + 9 = $ __?__ 11 $7 + 4 = $ __?__ 11 $2 + 1 + 7 = $ __?__ 10 $3 + 4 + 5 = $ __?__ 12

5. 2215 10   **6.** 7136 17   **7.** 6043 13   **8.** 9005 14   **9.** 8000 8   **10.** 812,946 30

EXERCISES

See the suggested assignment guide in the Teacher's Manual.

Determine whether each number is divisible by 2, by 4, by 5, or by 10.

(Example 1) The numbers in Exercises 3, 11, 12, 13, 14, 17, 24, 30, and 32 are not divisible by 2, 4, 5, or 10.

1. 42 2   **2.** 28 2, 4   **3.** 511   **4.** 685 5   **5.** 125 5   **6.** 390 2, 5, 10   **7.** 630 2, 5, 10

8. 850 2, 5, 10   **9.** 540 2, 4, 5, 10   **10.** 252 2, 4   **11.** 647   **12.** 473   **13.** 317   **14.** 931

15. 248 2, 4   **16.** 672 2, 4   **17.** 139   **18.** 85 5   **19.** 55 5   **20.** 550 2, 5, 10   **21.** 440 2, 4, 5, 10

22. 304 2, 4   **23.** 536 2, 4   **24.** 743   **25.** 626 2   **26.** 506 2   **27.** 808 2, 4   **28.** 412 2, 4

29. 515 5   **30.** 633   **31.** 316 2, 4   **32.** 109   **33.** 842 2   **34.** 696 2, 4   **35.** 748 2, 4

The numbers in Exercises 37, 41, 42, 45, 51, and 52 are not divisible by 3 or 9.

Determine whether each number is divisible by 3 or by 9.   **(Example 2)**

36. 423 3, 9   **37.** 131   **38.** 816 3   **39.** 117 3, 9   **40.** 243 3, 9   **41.** 235   **42.** 415

43. 624 3   **44.** 318 3   **45.** 221   **46.** 450 3, 9   **47.** 750 3   **48.** 621 3, 9   **49.** 315 3, 9

50. 834 3   **51.** 409   **52.** 347   **53.** 657 3, 9   **54.** 216 3, 9   **55.** 1197 3, 9   **56.** 2196 3, 9

Mixed Practice

The numbers in Exercises 60, 61, 66, 73, 74, and 75 are not divisible by 2, 3, 4, 5, 9, or 10.

Determine whether each number is divisible by 2, 3, 4, 5, 9, or 10.

57. 424 2, 4   **58.** 608 2, 4   **59.** 111 3   **60.** 421   **61.** 313   **62.** 627 3   **63.** 333 3, 9

64. 580 2, 4, 5, 10   **65.** 920 2, 4, 5, 10   **66.** 257   **67.** 36 2, 3, 4, 9   **68.** 48 2, 3, 4   **69.** 245 5   **70.** 625 5

71. 75 3, 5   **72.** 15 3, 5   **73.** 389   **74.** 811   **75.** 721   **76.** 225 3, 5, 9   **77.** 135 3, 5, 9

APPLICATIONS: Using the Rules for Divisibility

These are one-step problems that most students should be able to handle.

78. Audrey has 350 books. She wishes to build shelves holding 10 books each. Will the books fit exactly on the 35 shelves? Yes

79. The Sterner family has 4 members. Can a box of 144 pencils be divided equally among them? Yes

80. Nine people caught 176 fish. Will they be able to divide the catch so that each has the same number of fish? No

3-2 One-Digit Divisors

See the Teacher's Manual for the objectives.

Placing the first digit in the quotient is an important step in division. First count the number of digits in the divisor. Then draw a line after the same number of digits in the dividend.

EXAMPLE 1 Use an **X** to show where to place the first digit in the quotient of $385 \div 5$.

Solution: The divisor has one digit. Draw a line after the "3" in the dividend.

$5\overline{)3|85}$ ◀ **3 is less than 5. Draw a new line.** ⟶ $5\overline{)38|5}$ ◀ **38 is greater than 5. Place the X over the "8."** ⟶ $\overset{\text{X}}{5\overline{)38|5}}$

After completing Example 1, you may wish to have students do some or all of Exercises 1-24.

Follow this procedure to divide with one-digit divisors.

PROCEDURE To divide with one-digit divisors:

1 Determine where to place the first digit in the quotient.

2 Divide.

Example 2 shows how to use multiplication to check division.

EXAMPLE 2 Divide. Check your answer.

a. $944 \div 8$ **b.** $257 \div 6$

Solutions:

a. 1 $8\overline{)9|44}$ with X over the 4

2 $8\overline{)944}$
$\underline{8}$
14
$\underline{8}$
64
$\underline{64}$
0

quotient: 118

These should be the same.

Check:
118
$\times\ \ 8$
$\overline{944}$

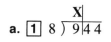

b. 1 $6\overline{)2|57}$ ◀ **2 is less than 6. Draw a new line.**

$6\overline{)25|7}$

2 $6\overline{)257}$
$\underline{24}$
17
$\underline{12}$
5 ◀ **Remainder**

quotient: 42 ◀ **Answer: 42 r 5**

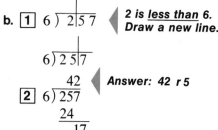

Check:
42
$\times\ \ 6$
$\overline{252}$
$+\ \ \ 5$ ◀ **Add the remainder.**
$\overline{257}$

REVIEW OF RELATED SKILLS

You may wish to use these exercises before teaching the lesson.

Subtract. (Pages 10–11, 14–15)

1. 9	2. 21	3. 32	4. 43	5. 1064	6. 5000
−5	− 6	−14	−28	− 875	−1999
4	15	18	15	189	3001

Divide.

7. 27 ÷ 3 9   8. 28 ÷ 7 4   9. 36 ÷ 6 6   10. 18 ÷ 2 9   11. 16 ÷ 4 4   12. 18 ÷ 9 2

13. 81 ÷ 9 9   14. 42 ÷ 6 7   15. 16 ÷ 2 8   16. 25 ÷ 5 5   17. 24 ÷ 4 6   18. 45 ÷ 5 9

19. 21 ÷ 7 3   20. 72 ÷ 8 9   21. 63 ÷ 7 9   22. 54 ÷ 9 6   23. 64 ÷ 8 8   24. 0 ÷ 8 0

25. 72 ÷ 9 8   26. 56 ÷ 8 7   27. 20 ÷ 5 4   28. 28 ÷ 4 7   29. 48 ÷ 8 6   30. 24 ÷ 8 3

31. 35 ÷ 7 5   32. 49 ÷ 7 7   33. 27 ÷ 9 3   34. 18 ÷ 6 3   35. 36 ÷ 4 9   36. 32 ÷ 4 8

37. 42 ÷ 7 6   38. 56 ÷ 7 8   39. 48 ÷ 6 8   40. 21 ÷ 3 7   41. 20 ÷ 4 5   42. 16 ÷ 8 2

43. 12 ÷ 3 4   44. 63 ÷ 9 7   45. 36 ÷ 9 4   46. 35 ÷ 5 7   47. 0 ÷ 7 0   48. 12 ÷ 6 2

EXERCISES

See the suggested assignment guide in the Teacher's Manual.

Use an X to show where to place the first digit in each quotient. (Example 1)

1. 6)492   2. 7)378   3. 5)165   4. 4)256   5. 7)364   6. 3)414

7. 9)378   8. 3)502   9. 9)477   10. 2)516   11. 3)465   12. 6)324

13. 7)546   14. 6)444   15. 8)272   16. 6)114   17. 9)648   18. 5)345

19. 4)512   20. 5)360   21. 7)238   22. 9)567   23. 8)752   24. 4)732

Divide. Check each answer. (Example 2a)   55. 1313   56. 2244

25. 5)35 7   26. 6)54 9   27. 3)54 18   28. 7)84 12   29. 6)72 12   30. 2)64 32

31. 8)96 12   32. 7)35 5   33. 8)64 8   34. 4)64 16   35. 3)84 28   36. 3)27 9

37. 5)215 43   38. 3)225 75   39. 4)324 81   40. 6)312 52   41. 9)468 52   42. 5)425 85

43. 6)444 74   44. 8)224 28   45. 7)525 75   46. 3)522 174   47. 7)518 74   48. 4)524 131

49. 6)348 58   50. 9)756 84   51. 7)245 35   52. 3)165 55   53. 8)592 74   54. 2)728 364

55. 4)5252   56. 3)6732   57. 8)4336 542   58. 7)4564 652   59. 6)3906 651   60. 9)3924 436

61. 3)2673 891   62. 5)4325 865   63. 4)1824 456   64. 6)5316 886   65. 5)4315 863   66. 7)2513 359

(Example 2b)

67. 84r3 5)423   68. 266r1 2)533   69. 64r2 8)514   70. 58r1 3)175   71. 214r1 2)429   72. 73r2 6)440

73. 3)685   74. 4)421   75. 7)374 53r3   76. 6)325 54r1   77. 5)643   78. 8)356 44r4

79. 9)291 32r3   80. 7)827   81. 5)632 126r2   82. 7)246 35r1   83. 6)329 54r5   84. 7)278 39r5

85. 4)627   86. 5)623   87. 4)715   88. 5)728   89. 7)941   90. 6)511 85r1

91. 7)5217   92. 5)3217   93. 7)5295   94. 2)6375   95. 8)4674   96. 4)2137 534r1

745r2   643r2   756r3   3187r1   584r2

73. 228r1   74. 105r1   77. 128r3   80. 118r1   85. 156r3
86. 124r3   87. 178r3   88. 145r3   89. 134r3

WHOLE NUMBERS: DIVISION   **51**

Problem Solving and Applications

Averages

See the Teacher's Manual for the objectives.
This lesson applies the skills presented in Section 3-2.

This table shows the number of rainy days in New York City for the first six months of a recent year. You can use this information or **data** to find the **average or mean** number of rainy days for the six months.

Month	Rainy Days
January	3
February	2
March	5
April	18
May	5
June	3

$$\text{Average} = \frac{\textbf{Sum of Measures}}{\textbf{Number of Measures}}$$

EXAMPLE Find the average number of rainy days for the 6 months.

Solution: $\text{Average} = \dfrac{3 + 2 + 5 + 18 + 5 + 3}{6}$ ◀ **Sum of rainy days / Number of months**

$$= \frac{36}{6}$$

$$= 6 \quad \text{The average number of rainy days was } \textbf{6.}$$

Note that no month had the average number of rainy days.

Exercises

Note that Exercises 1-8 are non-verbal problems.

1.

Month	Rainy Days
January	2
February	3
March	7
April	20
May	8
June	3

Average number of rainy days (Jan.–June): __?__ 7

2.

Month	Sunless Days
July	2
August	4
September	4
October	2
November	8
December	5

Average number of sunless days (July–Dec.): __?__ 4

3.

Cost of Textbooks	
English	$ 9.00
Social Studies	$10.50
Mathematics	$ 9.50
Science	$11.00

Average cost: __?__ $10.00

4.

Total Summer Earnings	
J. Azumo	$660.00
D. Suarez	$818.00
B. Tanaka	$503.00
J. Vines	$591.00

Average summer earnings: __?__
$643.00

Application

5.

Weekly Pay Before Taxes	
Shoe–factory worker	$165
Clothing worker	$165
Laundry worker	$153
Retail–trade worker	$148
Leather–goods worker	$168

Average weekly pay: __?__ $159.80

6.

Age at First Inaugural	
G. Washington	57
J. Adams	61
T. Jefferson	57
J. Madison	57
J. Monroe	58

Average age: __?__ 58

7.

Barrels of Oil Produced Per Day	
Canada	1,470,000
China	2,120,000
Iraq	3,300,000
Mexico	1,910,000
Saudi Arabia	9,776,000
United States	8,690,000
Venezuela	2,050,000

Average number of barrels produced per day: __?__ 4,188,000

8.

Price of A New Car in Several Cities	
Los Angeles	$5,287
New York	$5,268
Denver	$5,206
San Francisco	$5,683
Minneapolis	$5,028
Seattle	$5,157
Houston	$5,093

Average Price: __?__ $5,246

Nancy Lopez, Professional Golfer

9. Annual salaries for starting players on a professional football team were $90,000, $123,000, $225,000, $178,000 and $137,000. What is the average salary for a starter on the team? $150,600

10. A player scored 78, 75, 71, and 72 to win a golf tournament. What was the average score? 74

11. A player in a Football League set a rushing record of 2002 yards gained in a 14–game season. What was the average number of yards gained per game? 143

12. A basketball player scored 1875 points in 75 games. Find the average number of points scored per game. 25

Application

3-3 Two-and Three-Digit Divisors

See the Teacher's Manual for the objectives.

When dividing by two- or three–digit divisors, it is sometimes helpful to use rounding to find a trial divisor.

PROCEDURE To divide by two- or three–digit divisors:

1. Determine where to place the first digit in the quotient.

2. Find a trial divisor.

3. Divide.

EXAMPLE 1 Divide 3554 by 58.

Solution:

1. $58\overline{)35|54}$ *35 is less than 58. Draw a new line.* → $58\overline{)355|4}$

2. 58 rounded to the nearest ten is 60. *Trial divisor*

   Think: $60\overline{)355}$ → 5 Try 5 for the first digit.

3.
$$
\begin{array}{r} 5 \\ 58\overline{)355} \\ 290 \\ \hline 65 \end{array}
$$
Since 65 is greater than 58, 5 is not enough. Try 6.

$$
\begin{array}{r} 61 \\ 58\overline{)3554} \\ 348 \\ \hline 74 \\ 58 \\ \hline 16 \end{array}
$$
$60\overline{)74}$ → 1

Answer: **61 r 16**

After completing Example 1, you may wish to have students do some or all of Exercises 1-35.

Follow the same procedure when dividing by a three–digit divisor.

EXAMPLE 2 Divide 19612 by 241.

Solution:

1. $241\overline{)196|12}$ *196 is less than 241. Draw a new line.* → $241\overline{)1961|2}$

2. 241 rounded to the nearest hundred is 200. *Trial Divisor*

   Think: $200\overline{)1961}$ → 9 Try 9 for the first digit.

3.
$$
\begin{array}{r} 9 \\ 241\overline{)19612} \\ 2169 \end{array}
$$
9 is too much. Try 8.

$$
\begin{array}{r} 81 \\ 241\overline{)19612} \\ 1928 \\ \hline 332 \\ 241 \\ \hline 91 \end{array}
$$
$200\overline{)332}$ → 1

Answer: **81 r 91**

Round each number to the nearest ten. (Pages 17–19)

1. 11 10 **2.** 18 20 **3.** 55 60 **4.** 31 30 **5.** 63 60 **6.** 94 90 **7.** 77 80 **8.** 8 10

Round each number to the nearest hundred. (Pages 17-19)

9. 138 100 **10.** 226 200 **11.** 785 800 **12.** 197 200 **13.** 508 500 **14.** 664 700 **15.** 682 700 **16.** 651 700

Multiply. (Pages 26-27)

1536

17. 51×3 153 **18.** 92×8 736 **19.** 63×5 315 **20.** 34×9 306 **21.** 256×6 **22.** 578×8 4624

Use an X to show where to place the first digit in the quotient. (Pages 50-51)

23. $19\overline{)625}$ **24.** $38\overline{)105}$ **25.** $87\overline{)9936}$ **26.** $72\overline{)4324}$ **27.** $109\overline{)2235}$
28. $821\overline{)9063}$ **29.** $682\overline{)31487}$ **30.** $427\overline{)10063}$ **31.** $105\overline{)11095}$ **32.** $208\overline{)17783}$

EXERCISES
See the suggested assignment guide in the Teacher's Manual.

24. 134r10   26. 120r15   29. 61r36   32. 41r86

Divide. Check each answer. (Example 1)

1. $17\overline{)51}$ 3   **2.** $23\overline{)46}$ 2   **3.** $36\overline{)92}$ 2r20   **4.** $41\overline{)93}$ 2r11   **5.** $29\overline{)91}$ 3r4

6. $59\overline{)84}$ 1r25   **7.** $28\overline{)83}$ 2r27   **8.** $19\overline{)85}$ 4r9   **9.** $21\overline{)63}$ 3   **10.** $12\overline{)84}$ 7

11. $39\overline{)455}$ 11r26 **12.** $23\overline{)897}$ 39 **13.** $29\overline{)464}$ 16 **14.** $34\overline{)728}$ 21r14 **15.** $27\overline{)642}$ 23r21

16. $25\overline{)375}$ 15 **17.** $75\overline{)450}$ 6 **18.** $63\overline{)495}$ 7r54 **19.** $44\overline{)283}$ 6r19 **20.** $52\overline{)884}$ 17

21. $21\overline{)1197}$ 57 **22.** $37\overline{)2368}$ 64 **23.** $95\overline{)6555}$ 69 **24.** $62\overline{)8318}$ **25.** $78\overline{)2560}$ 32r64

26. $65\overline{)7815}$ **27.** $84\overline{)3024}$ 36 **28.** $54\overline{)3672}$ 68 **29.** $43\overline{)2659}$ **30.** $82\overline{)3582}$ 43r56

31. $72\overline{)4561}$ 63r25 **32.** $92\overline{)3858}$ **33.** $81\overline{)4212}$ 52 **34.** $55\overline{)3905}$ 71 **35.** $98\overline{)4658}$ 47r52

(Example 2)   46. 5r178   48. 22r187   49. 26r138   52. 20r315   54. 11r480   56. 12r575   57. 7r428

36. $231\overline{)693}$ 3   **37.** $113\overline{)339}$ 3 **38.** $158\overline{)790}$ 5   **39.** $485\overline{)970}$ 2   **40.** $516\overline{)842}$ 1r326

41. $284\overline{)862}$ 3r10 **42.** $593\overline{)618}$ 1r25 **43.** $395\overline{)790}$ 2 **44.** $291\overline{)873}$ 3   **45.** $337\overline{)8531}$ 25r106

46. $957\overline{)4963}$ **47.** $591\overline{)9456}$ 16 **48.** $375\overline{)8437}$ **49.** $267\overline{)7080}$ **50.** $219\overline{)9417}$ 43

51. $229\overline{)8015}$ 35 **52.** $438\overline{)9075}$ **53.** $854\overline{)9394}$ 11 **54.** $585\overline{)6915}$ **55.** $415\overline{)3842}$ 9r107

56. $624\overline{)8063}$ **57.** $917\overline{)6847}$ **58.** $247\overline{)9386}$ 38 **59.** $362\overline{)2968}$ **60.** $265\overline{)6367}$ 24r7

61. $267\overline{)72438}$ **62.** $584\overline{)27448}$ **63.** $327\overline{)84328}$ **64.** $829\overline{)47253}$ 57 **65.** $423\overline{)69417}$ 164r45

66. $857\overline{)48621}$ **67.** $295\overline{)22420}$ **68.** $854\overline{)75687}$ **69.** $149\overline{)38293}$ **70.** $393\overline{)50137}$

Mixed Practice

76   88r535   257   127r226

96r4   154r46   58r78   14r358

71. $67\overline{)7438}$ 111r1 **72.** $29\overline{)2788}$ **73.** $48\overline{)7438}$ **74.** $84\overline{)4950}$ **75.** $621\overline{)9052}$

76. $483\overline{)5917}$ **77.** $958\overline{)7664}$ 8 **78.** $723\overline{)92374}$ **79.** $722\overline{)39521}$ **80.** $49\overline{)3626}$ 74

81. $378\overline{)14742}$ **82.** $28\overline{)9508}$ **83.** $34\overline{)6370}$ **84.** $289\overline{)13583}$ 47 **85.** $879\overline{)12306}$ 14

59. 8r72   61. 271r81   62. 47   63. 257r289   66. 56r629
76. 12r121   78. 127r553   79. 54r533   81. 39   82. 339r16
83. 187r12

Problem Solving and Applications

Finance Charges

When you borrow money from a bank or other lending agency, you pay interest or a **finance charge** for the use of the money. Usually the amount borrowed plus the finance charge is paid back in equal monthly payments over a specified number of months.

To find the amount of each monthly payment, you must first answer the question:

"What is the total amount owed?"

This is the <u>hidden question</u> in the problem. Then you can find the monthly payment.

EXAMPLE   A bank lends a customer $2500 for 12 months. Finance charges are $176. Find the amount of each monthly payment.

Solution: 1   Find the total amount owed.

Amount owed: $2500 + $176 = **$2676** ◀ $\dfrac{Amount}{Borrowed} + \dfrac{Finance}{Charge} = \dfrac{Amount}{Owed}$

2   Divide the total amount owed by the number of months.

$$\begin{array}{r} 223 \\ 12\overline{)2676} \end{array}$$ The monthly payment is **$223**.

Exercises   NOTE: These are two-step problems.

Complete the table.

	Amount Borrowed	Finance Charge	Total Amount Owed	Number of Months To Repay	Monthly Payment
1.	$1000	$ 68	? $1068	12	? $89
2.	$1000	$ 548	? $1548	36	? $43
3.	$1000	$ 860	? $1860	60	? $31
4.	$3500	$1252	? $4752	36	? $132

5. Alma Clay borrowed $1000 and agreed to pay back the money in 18 months in equal monthly installments. Finance charges will amount to $122.84. Find the amount of each monthly payment. $62.38

6. Roy Beebe borrowed $3000 and agreed to repay the loan in equal monthly installments over 2 years. Finance charges amount to $735.12. Find the amount of each monthly payment. $155.63

Application

OFFICE WORKER

Career lessons are optional.
This lesson applies the skills presented in Section 8-3 plus multiplication and subtraction.

Applicants for typing jobs usually take a test that shows their speed (number of words per minute) and accuracy (number of errors).

To find the net number of words per minute, you must first answer two questions:

"What is the penalty for errors?"
"What is the net number of words typed?"

These are the <u>hidden questions</u> in the problem. Then you can find the net number of words per minute.

EXAMPLE   Carlos types 265 words in 5 minutes. He has 6 errors. The penalty for errors is 5 points per error. Find the net number of words per minute.

Solution:

1 Find the amount deducted for errors.

$6 \times 5 = 30$ ◀ **Number of Errors** $\times$ **5** $=$ **Amount Deducted**

2 Find the net number of words.

$265 - 30 = 235$ ◀ **Number of Words Typed** $-$ **Amount Deducted** $=$ **Net Number of Words**

3 Find the net number of words per minute.

$235 \div 5 = 47$ ◀ **Net Number of Words** $\div$ **Number of Minutes** $=$ **Net Words Per Minute**

The net number of words per minute is **47**.

EXERCISES   NOTE: These are three-step problems.

For Exercises 1–6, find the net number of words per minute. The penalty for errors is 5 points per error.

1. Madeline types 415 words in 5 minutes. She has 9 errors. 74

2. Daniel types 200 words in 5 minutes. He has 2 errors. 38

3. Joyce types 315 words in 5 minutes. She has 2 errors. 61

4. Jerome types 250 words in 5 minutes. He has 4 errors. 46

5. Ramon types 398 words in 8 minutes. He has 6 errors. 46

6. Mijako types 389 words in 8 minutes. She has one error. 48

3-4 Zeros in the Quotient See the Teacher's Manual for the objectives.

Sometimes you have to write zeros in the quotient. Example 1 shows a quotient that ends in zero.

Note that the numbered steps in the Examples refer to the numbered steps in the Procedure on page 54.

EXAMPLE 1   Divide 29148 by 62.

Solution:

$\boxed{1}$ $62\overline{)291\,48}$

$\boxed{2}$ Trial divisor: 60 $60\overline{)291}$ (4)   ◄ **Try 4 for the first digit.**

$\boxed{3}$
$$
\begin{array}{r}
470 \\
62\overline{)29148} \\
\underline{248} \\
434 \\
\underline{434} \\
8
\end{array}
$$
◄ **8 is less than 62. Write a "0" in the quotient.**   **Answer: 470 r 8**

The check is left for you.

After completing Example 1, you may wish to have students do some or all of Exercises 1-36.

Sometimes the zero is not the last digit in the quotient.

EXAMPLE 2   Divide 9778 by 94.

Solution:

$\boxed{1}$ $94\overline{)97\,78}$

$\boxed{2}$ Trial divisor: 90 $90\overline{)97}$ (1)   ◄ **Try 1 for the first digit.**

$\boxed{3}$
$$
\begin{array}{r}
104 \\
94\overline{)9778} \\
\underline{94} \\
37 \\
\underline{00} \\
378 \\
\underline{376} \\
2
\end{array}
$$
◄ **37 is less than 94. Write a "0" in the quotient.**

Answer: 104 r 2

The check is left for you.

REVIEW OF RELATED SKILLS   You may wish to use these exercises before teaching the lesson.

Round each number to the nearest ten.   (Pages 17–19)

1. 9 10   **2.** 15 20   **3.** 8 10   **4.** 82 80   **5.** 46 50   **6.** 31 30   **7.** 78 80

8. 12 10   **9.** 6 10   **10.** 5 10   **11.** 63 60   **12.** 89 90   **13.** 58 60   **14.** 27 30

Round each number to the nearest hundred. (Pages 17–19)

15. 96 _100_ **16.** 121 _100_ **17.** 356 _400_ **18.** 858 _900_ **19.** 647 _600_ **20.** 432 _400_ **21.** 59 _100_

22. 506 _500_ **23.** 84 _100_ **24.** 729 _700_ **25.** 186 _200_ **26.** 225 _200_ **27.** 937 _900_ **28.** 74 _100_

Multiply. (Pages 26–27)

29. 226 × 3 **30.** 431 × 5 **31.** 945 × 9 **32.** 321 × 9 **33.** 439 × 8 **34.** 623 × 6
_678_ _2155_ _8505_ _2889_ _3512_ _3738_

Use an X to show where to place the first digit in the quotient. (Pages 50–51)

35. 18$\overset{x}{)}$109 **36.** 56$\overset{x}{)}$3907 **37.** 210$\overset{x}{)}$5067 **38.** 903$\overset{x}{)}$8006 **39.** 103$\overset{x}{)}$1076

EXERCISES

See the suggested assignment guide in the Teacher's Manual.

Divide. Check each answer. (Example 1)

1. 21$)$639 _30r9_ **2.** 31$)$938 _30r8_ **3.** 18$)$725 _40r5_ **4.** 17$)$692 _40r12_

5. 14$)$985 _70r5_ **6.** 23$)$927 _40r7_ **7.** 21$)$849 _40r9_ **8.** 43$)$872 _20r12_

9. 63$)$3163 _50r13_ **10.** 73$)$3668 _50r18_ **11.** 58$)$2355 _40r35_ **12.** 56$)$3375 _60r15_

13. 75$)$3055 _40r55_ **14.** 42$)$6325 _150r25_ **15.** 43$)$5615 _130r25_ **16.** 37$)$8912 _240r32_

17. 67$)$17432 _260r12_ **18.** 57$)$20538 _360r18_ **19.** 41$)$11085 _270r15_ **20.** 51$)$14291 _280r11_

21. 88$)$24656 _280r16_ **22.** 23$)$13582 _590r12_ **23.** 33$)$16198 _490r28_ **24.** 69$)$29696 _430r26_

25. 261$)$8044 _30r214_ **26.** 371$)$7480 _20r60_ **27.** 459$)$9381 _20r201_ **28.** 349$)$7182 _20r202_

29. 774$)$8164 _10r424_ **30.** 842$)$9235 _10r815_ **31.** 943$)$9782 _10r352_ **32.** 521$)$5634 _10r424_

33. 642$)$25795 _40r115_ **34.** 732$)$22285 _30r325_ **35.** 284$)$36985 _130r65_ **36.** 385$)$92658
_240r258_

(Example 2)

37. 47$)$9647 _205r12_ **38.** 56$)$5779 _103r11_ **39.** 89$)$9296 _104r40_ **40.** 97$)$9809 _101r12_

41. 74$)$7795 _105r25_ **42.** 38$)$7850 _206r22_ **43.** 48$)$9718 _202r22_ **44.** 21$)$6420 _305r15_

45. 39$)$80124 _2054r18_ **46.** 49$)$99083 _2022r5_ **47.** 72$)$15108 _209r60_ **48.** 82$)$17042 _207r68_

49. 37$)$11414 _308r18_ **50.** 65$)$26615 _409r30_ **51.** 75$)$38142 _508r42_ **52.** 41$)$16718 _407r31_

53. 638$)$69573 _109r31_ **54.** 729$)$78642 _107r639_ **55.** 317$)$66045 _208r109_ **56.** 219$)$67332 _307r99_

57. 943$)$99901 _105r886_ **58.** 184$)$74915 _407r27_ **59.** 175$)$70610 _403r85_ **60.** 568$)$60430
_106r222_

Mixed Practice

61. 57$)$609 _10r39_ **62.** 68$)$715 _10r35_ **63.** 43$)$4491 _104r19_ **64.** 54$)$5715 _105r45_

65. 185$)$7515 _40r115_ **66.** 293$)$31742 _108r98_ **67.** 891$)$91775 _103r2_ **68.** 104$)$62875 _604r59_

69. 84$)$25916 _308r44_ **70.** 73$)$22191 _303r72_ **71.** 42$)$33745 _803r19_ **72.** 33$)$19942 _604r10_

73. 79$)$71474 _904r58_ **74.** 57$)$11594 _203r23_ **75.** 48$)$10044 _209r12_ **76.** 52$)$26243 _504r35_

77. 841$)$91752 _109r83_ **78.** 527$)$55970 _106r108_ **79.** 438$)$47893 _109r151_ **80.** 591$)$60952 _103r79_

81. 334$)$67142 _201r8_ **82.** 626$)$87642 _140r2_ **83.** 413$)$94990 _230_ **84.** 39$)$7995 _205_

Problem Solving and Applications

This lesson applies the skills presented in Sections 3-3 and 3-4.   See the Teacher's Manual for the objectives.

Fuel Economy of a Car

The **fuel economy** of a car refers to how many miles it can travel on one gallon of gasoline. You can use this rule to find fuel economy.

$$\frac{\text{Fuel}}{\text{Economy}} = \frac{\text{Number of}}{\text{Miles}} \div \frac{\text{Number of}}{\text{Gallons}}$$

EXAMPLE   A car traveled 512 miles on 24 gallons of gasoline. Find the fuel economy for the car.

Solution: Divide the number of miles by the number of gallons.

Fuel Economy $= 512 \div 24$

$= \textbf{21 r 8}$

Since there is a remainder, round <u>down</u> to be on the safe side.

The fuel economy of the car is **21 miles per gallon** (abbreviated: mpg).

Exercises

These are one-step problems.
Note that Exercises 1-6 are non-verbal problems.

Find the fuel economy for each car.

	Car	Miles Driven	Gallons Used	Fuel Economy	
1.	A	395	15	__?__ miles per gallon	26
2.	B	300	13	__?__ miles per gallon	23
3.	C	605	25	__?__ miles per gallon	24
4.	D	349	11	__?__ miles per gallon	31
5.	E	750	24	__?__ miles per gallon	31
6.	F	400	12	__?__ miles per gallon	33

7. A car travels 725 miles on 24 gallons of gasoline. Find its fuel economy. 30

8. A car travels 2186 miles on 95 gallons of gasoline. Find its fuel economy. 23

9. Mrs. Carr drove her station wagon 4890 miles and used 153 gallons of gasoline. What is the fuel economy of the station wagon? 31

10. The Lopez family drove their station wagon 3728 miles and used 120 gallons of gasoline. What is the fuel economy of the station wagon? 31

Problem Solving and Applications

This lesson applies the skills presented in Sections 3-3 and 3-4 plus multiplication. See the Teacher's Manual for the objectives.

Fuel Costs for a Car

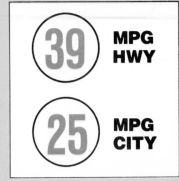

Advertisements for new cars give both the **City** mpg and the **Highway** mpg. You can use these estimates to calculate the cost of gasoline for driving a car a given number of miles in city traffic or on the highway.

To find the cost of gasoline, you must first answer the question:

"How many gallons of gasoline were used?"

This is the <u>hidden question</u> in the problem. Then you can find the cost.

EXAMPLE The City mpg estimate for a certain car is 20. Suppose that the cost for gasoline is $1.40 per gallon. About how much will it cost to drive the car 1800 miles in city driving?

Solution: **1** Find the number of gallons used.

$$1800 \div 20 = 90 \quad \blacktriangleleft \quad \textbf{Number of } \div \textbf{ City } = \textbf{Number of} \atop \textbf{Miles} \qquad \textbf{MPG} \qquad \textbf{Gallons}$$

2 Find the cost of gasoline.

$$90 \times 1.40 = 126.00 \quad \blacktriangleleft \quad \textbf{Number of } \times \textbf{ Cost Per } = \textbf{Total} \atop \textbf{Gallons} \qquad \textbf{Gallon} \qquad \textbf{Cost}$$

The cost of the gasoline is **$126.00.**

Exercises   These are two-step problems.

1. The City mpg for a certain car is 29. Suppose that gasoline costs $1.40 per gallon. About how much will it cost to drive the car 1160 miles in city traffic? $56.00

2. The Highway mpg for a certain car is 25. Suppose that gasoline costs $1.30 per gallon. About how much will it cost to drive the car 2250 miles in highway driving conditions? $117.00

3. The Highway mpg for a certain car is 42. Suppose that gasoline costs $1.50 per gallon. About how much will it cost to drive the car 8400 miles in highway driving conditions? $300

4. The City mpg for a certain car is 26. Suppose that gasoline costs $1.60 per gallon. About how much will it cost to drive the car 10,400 miles in city traffiic? $640

3-5 Order of Operations

When working with more than one operation ($+$, $-$, $\times$, $\div$), you need to know which operation to do first.

PROCEDURE

1. When the only operations are addition and subtraction, add and subtract in order from left to right.

2. When the only operations are multiplication and division, multiply and divide in order from left to right.

3. When three or four operations are involved, multiply and divide <u>before</u> you add and subtract.

TABLE 1

Problem	Order of Operations	Solution
$18 + 9 - 4$	**a.** Add. **b.** Subtract.	$18 + 9 - 4 = 27 - 4$ $= 23$
$36 \div 9 \times 2$	**a.** Divide. **b.** Multiply.	$36 \div 9 \times 2 = 4 \times 2$ $= 8$
$9 \times 2 - 12 \div 3$	**a.** Multiply. **b.** Divide. **c.** Subtract.	$9 \times 2 - 12 \div 3 = 18 - 12 \div 3$ $= 18 - 4$ $= 14$
$36 - 18 \div 3 \times 4$	**a.** Divide. **b.** Multiply. **c.** Subtract.	$36 - 18 \div 3 \times 4 = 36 - 6 \times 4$ $= 36 - 24$ $= 12$

Whenever parentheses are used with $+$, $-$, $\times$, $\div$, do the computations inside the parentheses **first**.

TABLE 2

Problem	Order of Operations	Solution
$(18 + 6) \div (4 \times 3)$	**a.** Do the work inside the parentheses. **b.** Divide.	$(18 + 6) \div (4 \times 3) = 24 \div 12$ $= 2$
$56 + (24 \div 8)$	**a.** Do the work inside the parentheses. **b.** Add.	$56 + (24 \div 8) = 56 + 3$ $= 59$

Find each answer.   (Pages 2–3, 10–11, 32–33, 54–55)

1. $18 + 84$ 102   **2.** $25 + 35$ 60   **3.** $41 - 26$ 15   **4.** $60 - 14$ 46   **5.** 23×12 276

6. 40×81 3240   **7.** $80 \div 16$ 5   **8.** $72 \div 24$ 3   **9.** $896 \div 32$ 28   **10.** $324 \div 12$ 27

EXERCISES

See the suggested assignment guide in the Teacher's Manual.

Find each answer.   (Table 1)

1. $42 - 7 - 18$ 17   **2.** $10 + 53 - 60$ 3   **3.** $43 + 26 - 11$ 58   **4.** $37 - 5 + 10$ 42

5. $24 \div 4 \times 3$ 18   **6.** $18 + 9 \div 3$ 21   **7.** $16 + 24 \div 6$ 20   **8.** $72 \div 9 - 5$ 3

9. $17 - 2 \times 5$ 7   **10.** $6 \times 5 \div 10$ 3   **11.** $19 - 5 \times 2$ 9   **12.** $12 + 48 \div 16$ 15

13. $8 + 9 \times 2$ 26   **14.** $2 + 7 \times 3$ 23   **15.** $21 - 6 \times 3$ 3   **16.** $11 - 2 \times 5$ 1

17. $48 \div 16 \times 2$ 6   **18.** $100 \div 10 \times 2$ 20   **19.** $9 \times 8 \div 3$ 24   **20.** $5 \times 4 \div 2$ 10

21. $132 \div 4 + 3$ 36   **22.** $39 \div 13 - 1$ 2   **23.** $14 + 2 \times 30$ 74   **24.** $80 - 4 \times 6$ 56

25. $15 \times 3 \div 9$ 5   **26.** $6 \div 3 \times 21$ 42   **27.** $81 \div 9 + 4$ 13   **28.** $48 - 7 \times 3$ 27

(Table 2)

29. $(3 + 8) \times 3$ 33   **30.** $(8 - 4) \div 4$ 1   **31.** $9 - (2 + 3)$ 4   **32.** $12 - (8 + 2)$ 2

33. $(13 - 7) \div 2$ 3   **34.** $(7 + 5) \times 5$ 60   **35.** $(12 - 2) \div 5$ 2   **36.** $145 \div (8 - 3)$ 29

37. $(32 \div 4) \times 7$ 56   **38.** $14 + (3 \times 12)$ 50   **39.** $42 - (3 \times 4)$ 30   **40.** $(5 + 3) \times 2$ 16

41. $(24 \div 6) + (8 \times 9)$ 76   **42.** $(50 - 4) + (2 \times 9)$ 64   **43.** $25 - (7 \times 3) + 10$ 14

44. $(18 + 12) \div (45 \div 3)$ 2   **45.** $(4 \times 12) - (5 \times 2)$ 38   **46.** $(144 \div 2) + (6 \times 5)$ 102

Calculator exercises are optional.
ORDER OF OPERATIONS

You can use the [M+] (memory) and [MR] (memory recall) keys to solve problems involving order of operations.

EXAMPLE: Solve: **a.** $80 - 4 \times 6$ **b.** $25 \div (8 - 3)$

Solutions:

a. [4] [×] [6] [=] [M+] [8] [0] [−] [MR] [=]   [M] *55.*

b. [8] [−] [3] [=] [M+] [2] [5] [÷] [MR] [=]   [M] *5.*

EXERCISES   Use a calculator to solve Exercises 4, 9, 11, 15, 16, 24, 28, 31, 32, and 38. Clear the memory before you start a new problem.

3-6 Rounding and Estimation See the Teacher's Manual for the objectives.

You can use rounding to help you estimate answers to multiplication and division problems. The symbol $\approx$ means **"is approximately equal to."**

—— EXAMPLE   Estimate each answer: **a.** 42×38 **b.** $1889 \div 98$

Solutions: **a.** Round each number to the nearest ten.

Think: $42 \times 38 \approx 40 \times 40$

≈ 1600

b. Round each number to the nearest hundred.

Think: $1889 \div 98 \approx 1900 \div 100$

≈ 19

REVIEW OF RELATED SKILLS   You may wish to use these exercises before teaching the lesson.

Round each number to the nearest ten.   (Pages 17–19)

1. 11 10   **2.** 23 20   **3.** 65 70   **4.** 639 640   **5.** 172 170   **6.** 429 430   **7.** 569 570

Round each number to the nearest hundred.   (Pages 17–19)

8. 103 100   **9.** 416 400   **10.** 387 400   **11.** 296 300   **12.** 449 400   **13.** 238 200   **14.** 255 300

Round each number to the nearest thousand.   (Pages 17–19)

15. 5299 5000   **16.** 1886 2000   **17.** 995 1000   **18.** 4090 4000   **19.** 3505 4000   **20.** 16,811 17,000

EXERCISES ————

See the suggested assignment guide in the Teacher's Manual.

Choose the best estimate. Choose a, b, or c.

1. 52×48 c   **a.** 30×40 **b.** 30×50 **c.** 50×50

2. 185×307 a   **a.** 200×300 **b.** 100×300 **c.** 200×400

3. 476×18 c   **a.** 480×10 **b.** 500×20 **c.** 480×20

4. $813 \div 89$ a   **a.** $810 \div 90$ **b.** $800 \div 90$ **c.** $820 \div 80$

5. $773 \div 68$ c   **a.** $770 \div 60$ **b.** $780 \div 65$ **c.** $770 \div 70$

Choose the best estimate. Choose a, b, c, or d.

6. 29×38 d   **a.** 600   **b.** 700   **c.** 900   **d.** 1200

7. 701×18 d   **a.** 20,000   **b.** 18,000   **c.** 16,000   **d.** 14,000

8. $332 \div 27$ b   **a.** 40   **b.** 10   **c.** 20   **d.** 30

9. $2847 \div 72$ a   **a.** 40   **b.** 30   **c.** 300   **d.** 41

10. $5559 \div 595$ b   **a.** 6   **b.** 10   **c.** 100   **d.** 5

APPLICATIONS: Using Estimation

The use of these word problems depends on which applications were taught.

Choose the best estimate. Choose a, b, c, or d.

11. A basketball player scored 1401 points in 69 games. Estimate the average number of points scored per game. d

    a. 32   **b.** 28

    c. 25   **d.** 20

12. A bank lends a customer $2200 for 12 months. Finance charges are $199. Estimate the monthly payment to the nearest hundred dollars. b

    a. $240   **b.** $200

    c. $180   **d.** $300

13. The Juarez family drove their car 3604 miles and used 102 gallons of gasoline. Estimate the fuel economy of their car. a

    a. 36   **b.** 32

    c. 34   **d.** 28

14. The Highway mpg for a certain car is 30. Gasoline costs $1.49 per gallon. Estimate the cost to drive the car 1200 miles on a highway. a

    a. $60   **b.** $58

    c. $56   **d.** $54

FINDING AVERAGES

Calculator exercises are optional.

You can use a calculator to find an average.

EXAMPLE:

Newspapers Sold	
Monday	52
Tuesday	54
Wednesday	62
Thursday	48
Friday	69

Solution: Estimate the average.

$$50 + 50 + 60 + 50 + 70 = 280$$
$$280 \div 5 = 56 \blacktriangleleft \textit{Estimated average}$$

Exact Average: 57.

EXERCISES

1.

Population: Six Districts	
District 1	494,000
District 2	540,000
District 3	507,000
District 4	484,000
District 5	538,000
District 6	536,000

Estimated average: __?__ 500,000

Actual average: __?__ 516,500

2.

Pieces of Mail Handled	
January	193,000
February	210,000
March	230,000
April	217,000
May	194,000
June	174,000

Estimated average: __?__ 200,000

Actual average: __?__ 203,000

Chapter Review

These exercises review the vocabulary, skills, and applications presented in the chapter as preparation for the chapter test.

Part I: Vocabulary

1. A number is __?__ by another number if the remainder is zero. (Page 48) <small>divisible</small>

2. The result obtained when one number is divided by another is the __?__. (Page 48) <small>quotient</small>

3. Information used to compute an average is called __?__. (Page 52) <small>data</small>

4. Another word for average is __?__. (Page 52) <small>mean</small>

5. When you borrow money, the amount you pay for the use of the money is the __?__. (Page 56) <small>finance charge</small>

6. The abbreviation for miles per gallon is __?__. (Page 60) <small>mpg</small>

| mean |
| divisible |
| quotient |
| finance charge |
| data |
| product |
| mpg |

Part 2: Skills

Determine whether each number is divisible by 2, 3, 4, 5, 9, or 10.
(Pages 48–49) <small>The numbers in Exercises 13, 17, 18, 25, and 28 are not divisible by 2, 3, 4, 5, 9, or 10.</small>

7. 35 <small>5</small> **8.** 117 <small>3, 9</small> **9.** 214 <small>2</small> **10.** 938 <small>2</small> **11.** 722 <small>2</small> **12.** 51 <small>3</small> **13.** 803 **14.** 792 <small>2, 3, 4, 9</small>

15. 46 <small>2</small> **16.** 52 <small>2, 4</small> **17.** 647 **18.** 811 **19.** 415 <small>5</small> **20.** 336 <small>2, 3, 4</small> **21.** 621 <small>3, 9</small> **22.** 834 <small>2, 3</small>

23. 750 <small>2, 3, 5, 10</small> **24.** 507 <small>3</small> **25.** 313 **26.** 920 <small>2, 4, 5, 10</small> **27.** 1197 <small>3, 9</small> **28.** 67 **29.** 865 <small>5</small> **30.** 333 <small>3, 9</small>

Divide. (Pages 50–51)

31. $7\overline{)63}$ <small>9</small> **32.** $3\overline{)341}$ <small>113r2</small> **33.** $4\overline{)232}$ <small>58</small> **34.** $8\overline{)72}$ <small>9</small> **35.** $3\overline{)176}$ <small>58r2</small>

36. $5\overline{)3215}$ <small>643</small> **37.** $9\overline{)4671}$ <small>519</small> **38.** $6\overline{)5319}$ <small>886r3</small> **39.** $7\overline{)4317}$ <small>616r5</small> **40.** $9\overline{)648}$ <small>72</small>

(Pages 54–55)

41. $18\overline{)54}$ <small>3</small> **42.** $24\overline{)72}$ <small>3</small> **43.** $29\overline{)463}$ <small>15r28</small> **44.** $52\overline{)597}$ <small>11r25</small> **45.** $31\overline{)4561}$ <small>147r4</small>

46. $36\overline{)4858}$ <small>134r34</small> **47.** $486\overline{)843}$ <small>1r357</small> **48.** $114\overline{)465}$ <small>4r9</small> **49.** $278\overline{)1473}$ <small>5r83</small> **50.** $622\overline{)91436}$ <small>147r2</small>

(Pages 58–59)

51. $21\overline{)429}$ <small>20r9</small> **52.** $185\overline{)7566}$ <small>40r166</small> **53.** $73\overline{)3694}$ <small>50r44</small> **54.** $42\overline{)857}$ <small>20r17</small> **55.** $891\overline{)80766}$ <small>90r576</small>

56. $54\overline{)5738}$ <small>106r14</small> **57.** $103\overline{)52430}$ <small>509r3</small> **58.** $62\overline{)1873}$ <small>30r13</small> **59.** $43\overline{)4592}$ <small>106r34</small> **60.** $307\overline{)61753}$ <small>201r46</small>

Find each answer. (Pages 62–63)

61. $4 + 3 \times 2$ <small>10</small> **62.** $14 - 6 + 2$ <small>10</small> **63.** $12 + 3 \times 2$ <small>18</small> **64.** $8 + 6 \div 3$ <small>10</small> **65.** $19 - 8 \times 1$ <small>11</small>

66. $54 - 8 - 6$ <small>40</small> **67.** $(8 - 5) \times 9$ <small>27</small> **68.** $9 + 8 \div 2$ <small>13</small> **69.** $3 \times 8 \div 2$ <small>12</small> **70.** $5 \times 12 \div 4$ <small>15</small>

71. $4 + 6 \times 3$ <small>22</small> **72.** $(4 + 5) \div 3$ <small>3</small> **73.** $49 + 7 + 5$ <small>61</small> **74.** $12 - 2 \times 5$ <small>2</small> **75.** $17 - 5 \div 5$ <small>16</small>

76. $3 + 25 \div 5 \times 2$ <small>13</small> **77.** $24 - (7 \times 3) + 12$ <small>15</small> **78.** $(24 \div 8) + (10 \times 2)$ <small>23</small> **79.** $6 \times 7 - 30 \div 10$ <small>39</small>

Choose the best estimate. Choose a, b, c, or d.   (Pages 64–65)

80. 377×18 b   **a.** 370×20 **b.** 380×20 **c.** 380×10 **d.** 370×10

81. $642 \div 79$ a   **a.** $640 \div 80$ **b.** $640 \div 70$ **c.** $650 \div 70$ **d.** $650 \div 80$

82. $295 - 178$ b   **a.** $300 - 170$ **b.** $300 - 180$ **c.** $290 - 180$ **d.** $290 - 170$

83. $671 \div 62$ d   **a.** $670 \div 70$ **b.** $680 \div 70$ **c.** $680 \div 60$ **d.** $670 \div 60$

84. $929 + 43$ d   **a.** $930 + 50$ **b.** $920 + 40$ **c.** $920 + 50$ **d.** $930 + 40$

85. 603×19 b   **a.** $10,000$ **b.** $12,000$ **c.** 7000 **d.** 9000

86. $52 + 49$ a   **a.** 100 **b.** 110 **c.** 90 **d.** 80

87. $418 \div 21$ d   **a.** 18 **b.** 19 **c.** 23 **d.** 21

88. $381 - 29$ b   **a.** 340 **b.** 350 **c.** 330 **d.** 320

89. $597 \div 18$ b   **a.** 34 **b.** 30 **c.** 32 **d.** 18

Part 3: Applications   The use of these word problems depends on which applications were studied.

90. Alfredo has 117 books. His bookcase has 3 shelves. Can he put an equal number of books on each shelf?   (Page 49)   Yes

91. The price of running shoes in five stores follows: $19.95, $23.95, $30.00, $24.95, and $21.00. Find the average price.   (Pages 52–53)
$23.97

92. Louise borrowed $3000 from a bank. She must pay back the money over 2 years in equal monthly installments. Finance charges amount to $878.88. How much is each monthly payment? (Page 56) $161.62

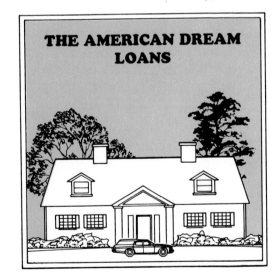

THE AMERICAN DREAM LOANS

93. Carlos borrowed $504. He will pay it back in 10 equal monthly installments. The finance charge is $33. Estimate the amount of a monthly payment.   (Page 56)   b

a. $57   **b.** $53

c. $65   **d.** $48

94. The Highway mpg of a car is 29. Estimate the number of gallons of gasoline it will take to travel 6604 miles under highway conditions.   c
(Page 61)

a. 230   **b.** 225

c. 220   **d.** 215

95. The City mpg for a certain car is 26. Suppose that gasoline costs $1.60 per gallon. About how much will it cost to drive the car 41,600 miles in city traffic?   (Page 61) $2560

Chapter Test

The Teacher's Resource Book contains two forms of each Chapter Test.

Determine whether each number is divisible by 2, 3, 4, 5, 9, or 10.

1. 64 2, 4   **2.** 123 3   **3.** 1450 2, 5, 10   **4.** 321,468 2, 3, 4   **5.** 75,625 5

Divide.

6. $8\overline{)432}$ 54   **7.** $7\overline{)413}$ 59   **8.** $17\overline{)959}$ 56r7   **9.** $34\overline{)952}$ 28

10. $47\overline{)506}$ 10r36   **11.** $53\overline{)16043}$ 302r37   **12.** $64\overline{)19771}$ 308r59   **13.** $257\overline{)53566}$ 208r110

Find each answer.

14. $4 + 16 \div 2 - 3$ 9   **15.** $(6 \times 5) - (2 + 17)$ 11   **16.** $4 \times 9 \div (6 - 3)$ 12   **17.** $17 - 4 \times 3 + 8$ 13

Choose the best estimate. Choose a, b, c, or d.

18. $27 + 42$ c   **a.** $20 + 40$ **b.** $30 + 50$ **c.** $30 + 40$ **d.** $20 + 50$

19. $422 \div 21$ a   **a.** $420 \div 20$ **b.** $430 \div 20$ **c.** $430 \div 0$ **d.** $420 \div 30$

20. $563 \div 38$ b   **a.** 20   **b.** 14   **c.** 10   **d.** 18

21. 712×19 c   **a.** 13,800   **b.** 14,400   **c.** 14,200   **d.** 14,000

The use of these word problems depends on which applications were studied.

22. Joe bought eight books. He paid the following prices: $3.75, $9.87, $4.53, $2.50, $4.25, $12.00, $3.69, and $1.97. Find the average price. $5.32

23. Maria borrowed $3288 from a bank. She must pay it back over two years in equal monthly installments. The finance charge is $1320. Find the amount of each monthly payment. $192

24. The City mpg for a new car is 27. How many gallons of gasoline will be needed to drive 540 miles in city traffic? 20

25. A player in a golf tournament had scores of 80, 78, 71, and 71. What was the player's average score? 75

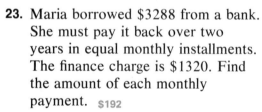

Chapter Test

Additional Practice

You may wish to use some or all of these exercises depending on how well students performed on the formal chapter test.

Skills

Determine whether each number is divisible by 2, 3, 4, 5, 9 or 10.
(Pages 48–49)

1. 46 2   **2.** 28 2, 4   **3.** 45 3,5,9   **4.** 81 3, 9   **5.** 99 3, 9   **6.** 560 2, 4, 5, 10   **7.** 39 3   **8.** 56 2, 4

9. 42 2, 3   **10.** 54 2,3,9 **11.** 36 2, 3, 4, 9   **12.** 58 2   **13.** 75 3, 5   **14.** 63 3, 9   **15.** 30 2, 3, 5, 10   **16.** 48 2, 3, 4

Divide.   (Pages 50–51)

17. $8\overline{)256}$ 32   **18.** $4\overline{)384}$ 96   **19.** $5\overline{)1810}$ 362   **20.** $3\overline{)894}$ 298   **21.** $7\overline{)2989}$ 427

22. $7\overline{)1113}$ 159   **23.** $3\overline{)384}$ 128   **24.** $8\overline{)1912}$ 239   **25.** $7\overline{)2275}$ 325   **26.** $9\overline{)2286}$ 254

27. $9\overline{)2085}$ 231r6 **28.** $6\overline{)2127}$ 354r3 **29.** $6\overline{)1543}$ 257r1 **30.** $2\overline{)1301}$ 650r1 **31.** $8\overline{)1871}$ 233r7

32. $5\overline{)1572}$ 314r2 **33.** $2\overline{)863}$ 431r1 **34.** $4\overline{)479}$ 119r3 **35.** $9\overline{)5230}$ 581r1 **36.** $3\overline{)980}$ 326r2

(Pages 54–55)

37. $21\overline{)63}$ 3   **38.** $13\overline{)65}$ 5   **39.** $25\overline{)625}$ 25   **40.** $42\overline{)882}$ 21   **41.** $56\overline{)1624}$ 29

42. $34\overline{)1924}$ 56r20 **43.** $24\overline{)2146}$ 89r10 **44.** $18\overline{)1715}$ 95r5 **45.** $29\overline{)1639}$ 56r15 **46.** $31\overline{)2950}$ 95r5

47. $332\overline{)6972}$ 21 **48.** $425\overline{)7225}$ 17 **49.** $175\overline{)7875}$ 45 **50.** $218\overline{)7848}$ 36 **51.** $516\overline{)11352}$ 22

52. $621\overline{)14483}$ 23r200 **53.** $486\overline{)12358}$ 25r208 **54.** $378\overline{)10516}$ 27r310 **55.** $236\overline{)13416}$ 56r200 **56.** $462\overline{)16382}$ 35r212

(Pages 58–59)   **62.** 60r200   **63.** 340r28   **65.** 203r200   **69.** 60r214

57. $26\overline{)1314}$ 50r14 **58.** $336\overline{)34272}$ 102 **59.** $53\overline{)10812}$ 204 **60.** $71\overline{)6416}$ 90r26 **61.** $502\overline{)51706}$ 103

62. $221\overline{)13460}$ **63.** $56\overline{)19068}$ **64.** $42\overline{)1281}$ 30r21 **65.** $306\overline{)62318}$ **66.** $18\overline{)12966}$

67. $34\overline{)3621}$ 106r17 **68.** $29\overline{)5980}$ 206r6 **69.** $461\overline{)27874}$ **70.** $32\overline{)9768}$ 305r8 **71.** $423\overline{)88941}$

72. $118\overline{)35675}$ **73.** $38\overline{)19399}$ **74.** $218\overline{)8841}$ **75.** $83\overline{)17204}$ **76.** $24\overline{)12080}$ 503r8

302r39   510r19   40r121   207r23

Find each answer.   (Pages 62–63)   **66.** 720r6   **71.** 210r111

77. $5 + 6 \div 3$ 7   **78.** $4 + 10 \div 5$ 6   **79.** $3 \times 9 - 2$ 25   **80.** $6 \times 8 + 4$ 52

81. $14 - 9 \div 3$ 11   **82.** $24 - 6 \times 2$ 12   **83.** $13 + 10 \times 4$ 53   **84.** $26 + 3 \times 2$ 32

85. $21 \div 3 \times 2$ 14   **86.** $14 \div 7 \times 4$ 8   **87.** $6 \times 12 \div 2$ 36   **88.** $3 \times 8 \div 2$ 12

89. $4 + 14 \div 7 + 5$ 11   **90.** $24 - 8 \times 2 + 6$ 14   **91.** $3 \times 15 - 6 \div 2$ 42

92. $(4 + 6) \div (7 - 5)$ 2   **93.** $(3 \times 9) - (4 \times 2)$ 19   **94.** $28 \div (3 + 4)$ 4

95. $(3 + 9) \div (2 \times 3)$ 2   **96.** $(17 - 5) \div (18 \div 3)$ 2   **97.** $22 \times 2 + (4 \times 2)$ 52

Applications

The use of these word problems depends on which applications were studied.

98. The price of a record album in six stores is as follows: $7.98, $6.99, $5.97, $7.98, $8.29, and $6.95. Find the average price of the album. (Pages 52–53) $7.36

99. The Highway mpg for a car is 33. Suppose gasoline costs $1.60 per gallon. How much will it cost to drive the car 8250 miles in highway conditions? (Page 61) $400

REVIEW OF RELATED SKILLS FOR CHAPTER 4

We suggest that you use some or all of this page before proceeding with the chapter.

Multiply. (Page 40)

1. 80×10 800 2. 190×100 19,000 3. $321 \times 10,000$ 3,210,000 4. 42×1000 42,000
5. $8 \times 10,000$ 80,000 6. 3467×10 34,670 7. 283×1000 283,000 8. 4624×10 46,240
9. 689×100 68,900 10. 731×1000 731,000 11. 33×100 3300 12. $486 \times 10,000$ 4,860,000
13. 2813×10 28,130 14. 46×100 4600 15. 74×1000 74,000 16. $7 \times 10,000$ 70,000

Round each number to the nearest ten. (Pages 17–19)

17. 59 60 18. 13 10 19. 55 60 20. 87 90 21. 98 100 22. 62 60 23. 71 70
24. 901 900 25. 157 160 26. 118 120 27. 255 260 28. 803 800 29. 349 350 30. 736 740

Round each number to the nearest hundred. (Pages 17–19)

31. 381 400 32. 298 300 33. 450 500 34. 358 400 35. 620 600 36. 249 200
37. 4463 4500 38. 5981 6000 39. 4972 5000 40. 3380 3400 41. 2162 2200 42. 5850 5900

Round each number to the nearest thousand. (Pages 17–19)

43. 8604 9000 44. 3229 3000 45. 6546 7000 46. 9500 10,000 47. 4498 4000
48. 63,481 63,000 49. 72,563 73,000 50. 81,500 82,000 51. 43,562 44,000 52. 39,500 40,000

Round each number to the nearest ten thousand. (Pages 17–19)

53. 26,907 30,000 54. 42,318 40,000 55. 55,293 60,000 56. 39,700 40,000 57. 62,349 60,000
58. 164,981 160,000 59. 285,780 290,000 60. 395,406 400,000 61. 478,324 480,000 62. 681,965 680,000

Round each number to the nearest million. (Pages 17–19)

63. 4,685,431 5,000,000 64. 9,746,329 10,000,000 65. 21,382,496 21,000,000 66. 43,499,564 43,000,000

Subtract. (Pages 10–11, 14–15)

67. $\begin{array}{r}58\\-9\\\hline\end{array}$ 49	68. $\begin{array}{r}63\\-8\\\hline\end{array}$ 55	69. $\begin{array}{r}71\\-5\\\hline\end{array}$ 66	70. $\begin{array}{r}82\\-7\\\hline\end{array}$ 75	71. $\begin{array}{r}54\\-8\\\hline\end{array}$ 46	72. $\begin{array}{r}28\\-9\\\hline\end{array}$ 19
73. $\begin{array}{r}63\\-24\\\hline\end{array}$ 39	74. $\begin{array}{r}48\\-39\\\hline\end{array}$ 9	75. $\begin{array}{r}54\\-18\\\hline\end{array}$ 36	76. $\begin{array}{r}60\\-42\\\hline\end{array}$ 18	77. $\begin{array}{r}21\\-13\\\hline\end{array}$ 8	78. $\begin{array}{r}42\\-17\\\hline\end{array}$ 25
79. $\begin{array}{r}98\\-38\\\hline\end{array}$ 60	80. $\begin{array}{r}56\\-26\\\hline\end{array}$ 30	81. $\begin{array}{r}50\\-25\\\hline\end{array}$ 25	82. $\begin{array}{r}42\\-38\\\hline\end{array}$ 4	83. $\begin{array}{r}56\\-27\\\hline\end{array}$ 29	84. $\begin{array}{r}45\\-16\\\hline\end{array}$ 29
85. $\begin{array}{r}6300\\-255\\\hline\end{array}$ 6045	86. $\begin{array}{r}8200\\-290\\\hline\end{array}$ 7910	87. $\begin{array}{r}6400\\-483\\\hline\end{array}$ 5917	88. $\begin{array}{r}2400\\-176\\\hline\end{array}$ 2224	89. $\begin{array}{r}7300\\-289\\\hline\end{array}$ 7011	90. $\begin{array}{r}6100\\-376\\\hline\end{array}$ 5724
91. $\begin{array}{r}7000\\-2814\\\hline\end{array}$ 4186	92. $\begin{array}{r}3000\\-1498\\\hline\end{array}$ 1502	93. $\begin{array}{r}5000\\-1834\\\hline\end{array}$ 3166	94. $\begin{array}{r}9000\\-7961\\\hline\end{array}$ 1039	95. $\begin{array}{r}6000\\-2638\\\hline\end{array}$ 3362	96. $\begin{array}{r}8000\\-3547\\\hline\end{array}$ 4453

4 GRAPHS AND APPLICATIONS

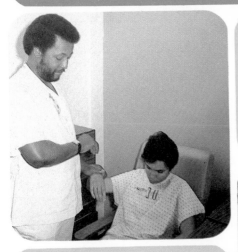

SKILLS/APPLICATIONS

4-1 Pictographs and Applications
4-2 Bar Graphs and Applications
4-3 Line Graphs and Applications
4-4 Other Graphs and Applications

CAREER

Government Service

4-1 Pictographs and Applications See the Teacher's Manual for the objectives.

In a **pictograph,** a picture or symbol is used to represent a number. The **key** tells how many are represented by each symbol.

The pictograph at the right shows how many boxes of oranges were produced in the United States in four different years.

U.S. Production of Oranges

1980	🍊 🍊 🍊 🍊 🍊
1975	🍊 🍊 🍊 🍊 🍊
1970	🍊 🍊 🍊 🍊
1965	🍊 🍊 🍊

Key: Each 🍊 represents 50,000,000 boxes of oranges.

PROCEDURE To read a pictograph:

1 Look for the key.

2 Use the key to interpret the graph.

EXAMPLE Use the pictograph above to answer each question.

Questions	Solutions
a. How many boxes of oranges does one orange represent?	**a.** **50,000,000 boxes** ◀ *From the key*
b. How many boxes were produced in 1975?	**b.** There are 5 oranges for 1975. So $5 \times 50,000,000 = $ **250,000,000 boxes.**
c. How many more boxes were produced in 1970 than in 1965?	**c.** The graph shows one more orange for 1970 than for 1965. So **50,000,000** more boxes were produced in 1970.
d. In which two years were the same number of boxes produced?	**d.** **1980 and 1975**

REVIEW OF RELATED SKILLS You may wish to use these exercises before teaching the lesson.

5. 9,182,000   10. 8,620,000

Multiply.   (Page 40)

1. 70×10 700

2. 980×10 9800

3. 416×100 41,600

4. 1319×100 131,900

5. 9182×1000

6. 62×1000 62,000

7. 589×100 58,900

8. 257×100 25,700

9. $6 \times 10,000$ 60,000

10. $862 \times 10,000$

11. $7 \times 10,000$ 70,000

12. $12 \times 10,000$ 120,000

13. 9×1000 9000

14. 6×1000 6000

15. 21×1000 21,000

16. 10×1000 10,000

17. 21×100 2100

18. 3150×100 315,000

19. 7×100 700

20. 910×100 91,000

21. 10×100 1000

22. 100×100 10,000

23. 100×1000 100,000

24. 1000×1000 1,000,000

See the suggested assignment guide in the Teacher's Manual.

The pictograph below shows the average number of miles that the buses of ten cities were driven in a recent year.

1. How many miles are represented by one symbol? 10,000

2. In which city were the buses driven more than 40,000 miles? Los Angeles

3. In which cities were the buses driven more than 30,000 miles?
Los Angeles, Denver, Chicago, Atlanta, Detroit, Dallas

4. In which cities were the buses driven fewer than 30,000 miles?
New York, Washington, Philadelphia, Boston

5. In which city were the buses driven a little less than 25,000 miles? Boston

6. In which cities (2) were the buses driven about 30,000 miles? New York Washington

7. In which city were the buses driven about 10,000 miles more than in Detroit? Los Angeles

8. In which city were the buses driven about 10,000 miles more than in Washington? Denver

Average Yearly Mileage for a City Bus

Los Angeles	◎ ◎ ◎ ◎ ◖
Denver	◎ ◎ ◎ ◖
Chicago	◎ ◎ ◎ ◖
Atlanta	◎ ◎ ◎ ◖
Detroit	◎ ◎ ◎ ◖
Dallas	◎ ◎ ◎ ◖
New York	◎ ◎ ◖
Washington	◎ ◎ ◖
Philadelphia	◎ ◎ ◖
Boston	◎ ◎ ◖

Key: Each ◎ represents 10,000 miles.

APPLICATION: Constructing Pictographs These exercises may be considered optional.

Use the given information to construct a pictograph. Be sure to include the key.

9. **Leading Potato Growing States in a Recent Year**

State	Idaho	Washington	Maine	California	North Dakota
Number of Bags	80,000,000	35,000,000	30,000,000	25,000,000	20,000,000
	16 potatoes	7 potatoes	6 potatoes	5 potatoes	4 potatoes

Key: 🥔 represents 5,000,000 bags

10. **Leading Horse Raising States in a Recent Year**

State	Texas	California	Tennessee	Oklahoma	Ohio
Number of Horses	700,000	650,000	300,000	250,000	200,000
	7 horses	6½ horses	3 horses	2½ horses	2 horses

Key: Each 🐎 represents 100,000 horses.

4-2 Bar Graphs and Applications

A **bar graph** has two axes, a horizontal axis and a vertical axis. On a bar graph, the length of each bar represents a number. The **scale** on one of the axes tells you how to find the number.

This bar graph shows average July temperatures for five cities.

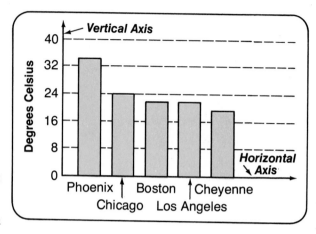

PROCEDURE   To read a bar graph:

1. Look for the number scale on one of the axes.

2. Use the scale to interpret the graph.

EXAMPLE   Use the bar graph above to answer each question.

Questions

a. Which city has the lowest average July temperature?

b. For which cities are average July temperatures the same?

c. Which of the cities have average July temperatures between 16°C and 28°C?

Solutions

a. Cheyenne ◀ *Cheyenne has the shortest bar.*

b. Boston and Los Angeles ◀ *The bars are equal in height.*

c. Boston, Chicago, Los Angeles, and Cheyenne

REVIEW OF RELATED SKILLS

You may wish to use these exercises before teaching the lesson.

Round each number to the nearest ten.   (Pages 17–19)

1. 58   60   **2.** 61   60   **3.** 88   90   **4.** 96   100   **5.** 345   350   **6.** 801   800   **7.** 177   180

Round each number to the nearest thousand.   (Pages 17–19)

8. 7805   8000   **9.** 3450   3000   **10.** 4199   4000   **11.** 6700   7000   **12.** 9050   9000   **13.** 6832   7000

14. 51,100   51,000   **15.** 78,015   78,000   **16.** 42,716   43,000   **17.** 15,806   16,000   **18.** 12,517   13,000   **19.** 25,328   25,000

Round each number to the nearest ten thousand.   (Pages 17–19)

20. 99,586   100,000   **21.** 83,419   80,000   **22.** 60,008   60,000   **23.** 123,905   120,000   **24.** 145,187   150,000

EXERCISES

See the suggested assignment guide in the Teacher's Manual.

The horizontal bar graph at the right shows the number of metric tons of wheat produced by 6 countries in a recent year. Use this graph for Exercises 1–6.

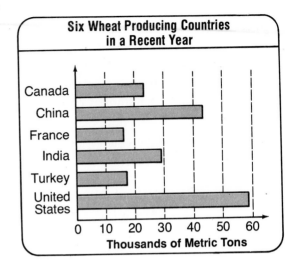

1. Which country produced the most wheat? United States

2. Which country produced almost as much wheat as Turkey? France

3. Which country produced about half as much wheat as the United States? India

4. About how many metric tons of wheat did the United States produce? 60,000

5. Which country produced about 23,000 metric tons of wheat? Canada

6. Which countries produced less than 20,000 metric tons of wheat? France, Turkey

The vertical bar graph at the right shows different ways of transporting freight in the United States. Use this graph for Exercises 7–10.

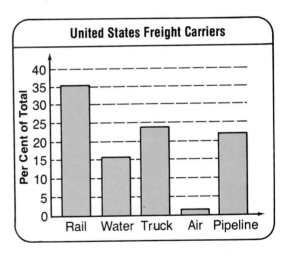

7. Which carrier transported about 15% of the freight? Water

8. Which carriers (2) transported from 20–25% of the freight? Truck Pipeline

9. Which carrier transported the most freight? Rail

10. Which carrier transported less than 5% of the freight? Air

APPLICATION: **Constructing a Bar Graph**   This exercise may be considered optional.

Use the given information to construct a bar graph. Refer to the scale given in the problem.

11. **Record Attendance at a Baseball Game in a Recent Year**

1 inch   6 inches   8 inches   7 inches   5 inches

City	Cleveland	Detroit	New York	Philadelphia	Seattle
Attendance	10,000	60,000	80,000	70,000	50,000

Scale: Let 1 centimeter represent 10,000 people.

4-3 Line Graphs and Applications See the Teacher's Manual for the objectives.

Line graphs show the amount of <u>change</u> over a certain period of time. A line graph has a <u>horizontal</u> axis and a <u>vertical</u> axis. One axis shows the period of time. The other shows the amount of change.

This line graph shows the average amount of rainfall in New Orleans for each month of the year.

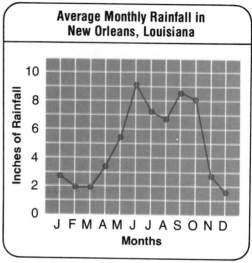

Average Monthly Rainfall in New Orleans, Louisiana

PROCEDURE To read a line graph:

1. Find the given number or time on one axis.

2. Use the second axis to find the unknown number or time.

EXAMPLE Use the line graph above to answer each question.

Questions

a. Which month has the most rainfall?

b. Which month has the least amount of rainfall?

c. Which two months have about the same amount of rainfall?

d. Between which two months does the amount of rainfall decrease the most?

Solutions

a. June *Highest point on the graph.*

b. December *Lowest point on the graph.*

c. February and March

d. October and November *The line between the dots is the longest and steepest.*

REVIEW OF RELATED SKILLS
You may wish to use these exercises before teaching the lesson.

Subtract.   (Pages 10–11)

1. 20 $-\ 9$ 11	**2.** 23 $-\ 8$ 15	**3.** 32 $-\ 7$ 25
4. 30 $-\ 6$ 24	**5.** 27 $-\ 8$ 19	**6.** 31 $-\ 5$ 26
7. 80 -12 68	**8.** 70 -11 59	**9.** 92 -18 74
10. 65 -19 46	**11.** 96 -17 79	**12.** 83 -16 67
13. 45 -29 16	**14.** 62 -35 27	**15.** 98 -26 72
16. 87 -38 49	**17.** 95 -25 70	**18.** 83 -27 56

The line graph at the right shows average temperatures in Portland, Oregon for each month of the year. Use this graph for Exercises 1–9.

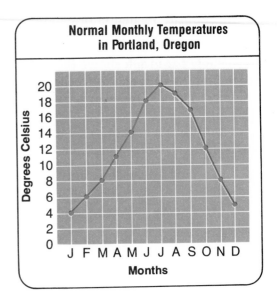

Normal Monthly Temperatures in Portland, Oregon

1. What information is given on the horizontal axis? months
2. What scale is given on the vertical axis? degrees Celsius
3. Which is the warmest month? July
4. Which are the two coldest months? Jan., Dec.
5. For which months are the temperatures higher than 16 degrees? June, July, Aug., Sept.
6. For how many months are the temperatures between 7 degrees and 15 degrees? 5
7. Which months have temperatures of less than 8 degrees? Jan., Feb., Dec.
8. Between which two months do temperatures increase the most? May and June
9. Between which two months do temperatures decrease the most? September & October

This graph shows a patient's pulse rate over a 24-hour period. Use this graph for Exercises 10–18.

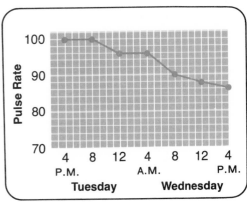

10. What information is given on the vertical axis? pulse rate
11. What information is given on the horizontal axis? time of day
12. When was the patient's pulse rate the fastest? from 4-8 P.M. Tuesday
13. When was the patient's pulse rate the slowest? 4 P.M. Wednesday
14. For which 4–hour period did the patient's pulse rate decrease the most? 4-8 A.M. Wednesday
15. For which two 4–hour periods was there no change in the patient's pulse rate? 4-8 P.M. Tues., 12-4 A.M. Wed.
16. For which two 4–hour periods did the patient's pulse rate decrease by the same amount? 8-12 and 12-4, Wed.
17. What was the patient's pulse rate at 8 P.M. on Tuesday? 100
18. What was the patient's pulse rate at 8 A.M. on Wednesday? 90

GRAPHS AND APPLICATIONS   **77**

4-4 Other Graphs and Applications

This lesson may be considered optional for Level 1 students.

You can compare related information by placing two graphs on the same axis.

This **multiple bar graph** shows the mileage from San Francisco to each of six different cities in two ways, by road and by air.

PROCEDURE   To read a multiple bar graph:

1 Read the information given on each axis.

2 Look for the key.

3 Use both of these to interpret the graph.

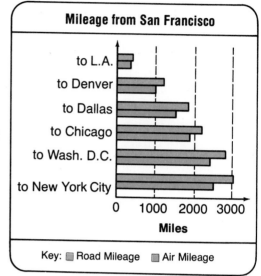

Mileage from San Francisco

to L.A.
to Denver
to Dallas
to Chicago
to Wash. D.C.
to New York City

0   1000 2000 3000
Miles

Key: ■ Road Mileage   ■ Air Mileage

REVIEW OF RELATED SKILLS

You may wish to use these exercises before teaching the lesson.

Subtract.   (Pages 14–15)

1. 3000	2. 2000	3. 5100	4. 6000	5. 3500
− 500	− 150	− 175	−2575	− 475
2500	1850	4925	3425	3025

Round each number to the nearest million.   (Pages 17–19)

6. 19,100,000   19,000,000 **7.** 21,800,000   22,000,000 **8.** 3,500,000   4,000,000 **9.** 3,900,000   4,000,000

10. 13,225,000   13,000,000**11.** 11,987,000   12,000,000**12.** 17,153,000   17,000,000**13.** 6,555,000   7,000,000

EXERCISES

See the suggested assignment guide in the Teacher's Manual.

Use the multiple bar graph above for Exercises 1–8.

1. What scale is given on the horizontal axis?   miles

2. What information is given on the vertical axis?   cities

3. What information is given in the key?   kind of mileage shown by the bars

4. Which is greater in every case, the road mileage or the air mileage?   road

5. Which cities are less than 1500 miles from San Francisco by road?   L.A. Denver

6. Which cities are more than 2000 miles from San Francisco by air?   Wash. D.C.   New York City

7. For which city is the difference between the road mileage and the air mileage the least?   L.A.

8. For which city is the difference between the road mileage and the air mileage about 500 miles?   New York City

78   CHAPTER 4

This graph shows the U. S. population for certain age groups in 1975 and the estimated population for these same groups in 1985. Use this graph for Exercises 9–20.

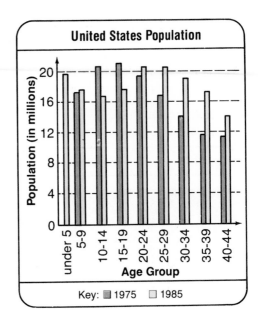

United States Population

Key: ■1975 □1985

9. What information is given on the horizontal axis? Age Groups

10. What information is given on the vertical axis? Population

11. What information is given in the key? the years represented by the bars

12. Which was the largest age group in 1975? 15-19

13. By 1985, which two groups will be the largest? 20-24, 25-29

14. For which age groups will there be an increase in population between 1975 and 1985? 5-9, 20-24, 25-29, 30-34, 35-39, 40-44

15. For which age groups will there be a decrease in population between 1975 and 1985? 10-14, 15-19

16. For which age group will there be almost no change in population between 1975 and 1985? 5-9

17. For which age groups was the population over 20 million in 1975? 10-14 15-19

18. For which age groups will the population be over 20 million in 1985? 20-24 25-29

19. For which age groups will the population in 1985 be between 16 and 20 million? under 5, 5-9, 10-14, 15-19, 30-34, 35-39

20. For which age group will the population in 1985 be between 12 and 16 million? 40-44

More Challenging Problems   These exercises are optional.

This graph shows the average rainfall per month in Cincinnati, Ohio (solid line) and Phoenix, Arizona (dashed line). Use this graph for Exercises 21–24.

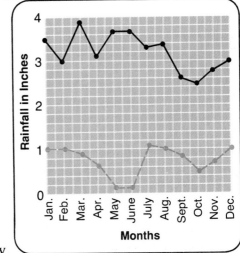

21. During which month does Phoenix have the most rain? July

22. During which month does Cincinnati have the least rain? Oct.

23. During which month does Cincinnati have three times as much rain as Phoenix? February

24. Find the difference in the amount of rainfall in the two cities for February.

2 inches

Career lessons are optional.

Every five years, the Federal government requires a **census** (count) of the population of the United States. The graph below shows the growth of the population of the United States since 1790.

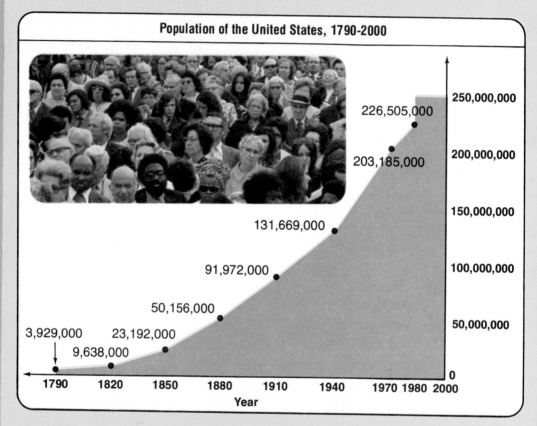

Population of the United States, 1790-2000

250,000,000

226,505,000

203,185,000

200,000,000

150,000,000

131,669,000

91,972,000

100,000,000

50,156,000

50,000,000

3,929,000   23,192,000

9,638,000

0

| 1790 | 1820 | 1850 | 1880 | 1910 | 1940 | 1970 1980 2000 |

Year

EXERCISES

1. What was the population of the United States in 1790? 3,929,000

2. What was the population of the United States in 1820? 9,638,000

3. What was the increase in population in the United States from 1790 to 1820? 5,709,000

4. In what year shown on the graph was the population of the United States close to 50,000,000? 1880

5. What was the increase in population in the United States from 1970 to 1980? 23,320,000

6. Over what 30-year period did the population of the United States reach 200 million? 1940-1970

7. Over what 30-year period was there the greatest increase in the population of the United States? 1940-1970

8. Over what 30-year period was there the least increase in the population of the United States? 1790-1820

Chapter Review

These exercises review the vocabulary, skills, and applications presented in the chapter as a preparation for the chapter test.

Part I: Vocabulary

For Exercises 1–6, choose from the box at the right the word(s) that completes each statement.

1. In a pictograph, a picture or symbol is used to represent __?__.
   (Page 72) numbers

2. In a pictograph, the __?__ tells how many are represented by each symbol. (Page 72) key

3. On a bar graph, the __?__ of the bar represents a number.
   (Page 74) length

4. On a bar graph, the __?__ tells you how to find the number represented by each bar. (Page 74) scale

5. On a bar graph, the bars can be either vertical or __?__.
   (Page 75) horizontal

6. Line graphs show the amount of __?__ over a certain period of time. (Page 76) change

| bar |
| key |
| width |
| horizontal |
| scale |
| multiple |
| numbers |
| length |
| change |

Part 2: Skills and Applications

This pictograph shows the number of automobile registrations in the United States every five years from 1960 to 1980. Use this pictograph for Exercises 7–12. (Pages 72–73)

United States Automobile Registration

1960	
1965	
1970	
1975	
1980	

Key: Each 🚗 represents 10 million cars.

7. How many cars does one symbol represent? 10 million

8. In which year were 90 million cars registered? 1970

9. In which year were more than 130 million cars registered? 1980

10. In which year were 110 million cars registered? 1975

11. Over which 5–year period did the number of registered cars increase by about 15 million? 1965-1970

12. Over which 10–year period did the number of registered cars increase by about 45 million? 1970-1980

Chapter Review   GRAPHS AND APPLICATIONS   **81**

The horizontal bar graph below shows the length of the growing season for the area around eight cities. Use this graph for Exercises 13–20. (Pages 74–75)

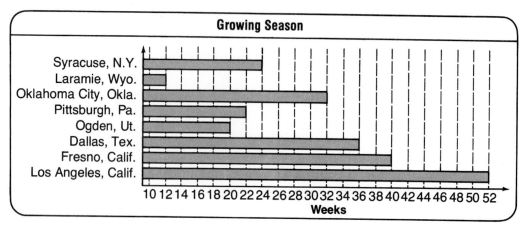

Growing Season

13. What scale is given on the horizontal axis? weeks 10 to 52

14. What information is given on the vertical axis? names of cities

15. Which city has the shortest growing season? Laramie, Wyo.

16. Which city has the longest growing season? Los Angeles, Calif.

17. How many weeks long is the growing season in Fresno? 40

18. How many weeks long is the growing season in Pittsburgh? 22

19. Which city has a growing season that is twice as long as the growing season in Laramie? Syracuse, N.Y.

20. How much longer than the growing season in Oklahoma City is the growing season in Los Angeles? 20 weeks

The line graph at the right shows Tina's bowling scores for 12 games. Use this graph for Exercises 21–26. (Pages 76–77)

21. What scale is given on the vertical axis? scores 100 to 190

22. What information is given on the horizontal axis? games 1 to 12

23. What is the highest score shown on the graph? 185

24. For which game did Tina bowl the lowest score shown on the graph? 5

25. For which three games did Tina have the same score? 7, 10, 11

26. By how much did Tina increase her score from Game 2 to Game 3? 10 points

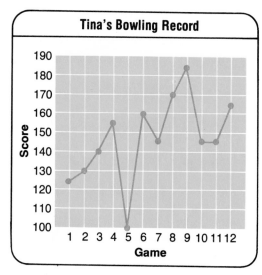

Tina's Bowling Record

Chapter Test

This pictograph shows a baseball player's hits over one month.

1. How many hits does one baseball represent? 2

2. How many of the player's hits were home runs? 6

3. How many hits were doubles? 10

4. How many more singles than home runs did the player hit? 16

5. How many more doubles than triples did the player hit? 8

6. What was the total number of hits for this player over one month? 40

A Baseball Player's Record of Hits in One Month

Home runs

Triples

Doubles

Singles

Key: Each ⚾ represents two hits.

This bar graph shows predicted energy sources for the United States in 1985.

7. What information is given on the vertical axis? energy sources

8. How many quadrillion units of energy are represented by one unit on the horizontal axis? 5

9. What will be our greatest source of energy in 1985? oil

10. From which source will we receive the least amount of energy in 1985? hydropower

11. About how many units of energy will come from nuclear power? 7.5 quadrillion

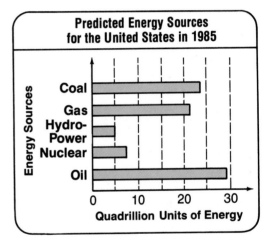

Predicted Energy Sources for the United States in 1985

Energy Sources: Coal, Gas, Hydro-Power, Nuclear, Oil

Quadrillion Units of Energy

This line graph shows the length of the first day of every month for a year.

12. What scale is given on the vertical axis? minutes of daylight

13. For which months do the first days have the same length? Jan. and Dec. June and July

14. For which two consecutive months does the length of the first day decrease the most? Sept. and Oct.

15. How many minutes long is the first day in January? 550

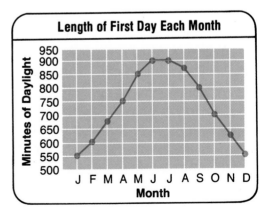

Length of First Day Each Month

Minutes of Daylight

Month

J F M A M J J A S O N D

Additional Practice

You may wish to use some or all of these exercises depending on how well students performed on the formal chapter test.

Number of Hits in a Season	
Player	**Hits**
Carew	⚾⚾⚾⚾⚾ ⚾⚾⚾⚾⚾ ⚾
McRae	⚾⚾⚾⚾⚾ ⚾⚾⚾⚾(
Allen	⚾⚾⚾⚾⚾ ⚾⚾
Garr	⚾⚾⚾⚾⚾ ⚾⚾⚾⚾⚾ (
Fisk	⚾⚾⚾⚾⚾ ⚾⚾⚾(
Gross	⚾⚾⚾⚾⚾ ⚾⚾⚾⚾

Key: Each ⚾ represents 20 hits.

The pictograph above shows the number of hits in a season by six baseball players. Use this graph for Exercises 1–10. (Pages 72–73)

1. How many hits are represented by one symbol? **20**

2. Which two players had the same number of hits? **McRae and Fisk**

3. Which player had the fewest hits? **Allen**

4. Which player had 180 hits? **Gross**

5. Which player had the most hits for the season? **Carew**

6. Which players had more than 200 hits? **Carew and Garr**

7. How many more hits did Carew have than Allen? **80**

8. How many more hits did Garr have than Fisk? **20**

9. Which player had 40 more hits than McRae? **Garr**

10. Which player had 30 fewer hits than Garr? **Gross**

The bar graph at the right shows the heights of five buildings. Use the graph for Exercises 11–15. (Pages 74–75).

11. Which building is the tallest? **Empire State**

12. Which building is the shortest? **Tenneco**

13. About how tall is the Prudential Building? **750 feet**

14. About how tall is the Empire State Building? **1500 feet**

15. The Empire State Building is about how much taller than the Chrysler Building? **500 feet**

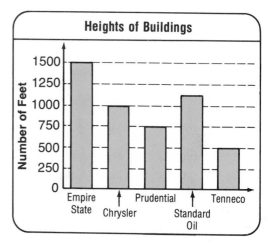

Heights of Buildings

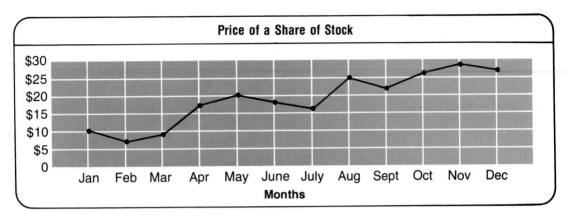

Price of a Share of Stock

The line graph above shows the changes in the price of a share of stock. Use this graph for Exercises 16–21. (Pages 76–77)

16. What information is given on the horizontal axis? Months

17. What scale is given on the vertical axis? 0 to $30

18. In which month was the price the highest? Nov.

19. In which month was the price the lowest? Feb.

20. For which months was the price higher than $25? Oct., Nov., Dec.

21. For which months was the price lower than $15? Jan., Feb., Mar.

The multiple bar graph at the right shows the high and low normal temperatures for January in several cities.

Use the graph for Exercises 22–27. (Pages 78–79)

22. Which city has the highest temperature? New Orleans

23. Which city has the lowest temperature? Chicago

24. Which city has the greatest difference between its high and low temperatures? New Orleans

25. Which city has a low temperature that is 4 degrees higher than the high temperature in Boston? San Francisco

26. What is the difference between the high temperatures of New Orleans and Chicago? 31°

27. What is the difference between the low temperatures of San Francisco and Boston? 19°

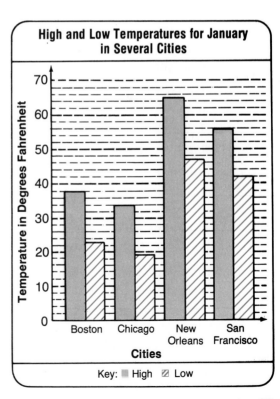

High and Low Temperatures for January in Several Cities

Key: ■ High ▨ Low

Cumulative Review: Chapters 1–4

You may also wish to use at this time the cumulative review titled *Review of Skills* on page 445 that reviews only the skills presented in Chapters 1-4.

Choose the correct answer. Choose a, b, c, or d.

1. Add: 4729
117
+3813   c

   a. 8749   **b.** 8649

   c. 8659   **d.** 8750

2. Round 138,499 to the nearest thousand.   b

   a. 139,000   **b.** 138,000

   c. 140,000   **d.** 130,000

3. Multiply: 783
× 29   c

   a. 12,707   **b.** 22,607

   c. 22,707   **d.** 8613

4. Divide: 32)8005   a

   a. 250 R 5   **b.** 218 R 25

   c. 281 R 13   **d.** 255

5. Add: 6 + 19 + 33 + 2   b

   a. 40   **b.** 60   **c.** 54   **d.** 58

6. Multiply: 63
×1000   b

   a. 6,300   **b.** 63,000

   c. 630   **d.** 631,000

7. Round 174 to the nearest ten.   c

   a. 200   **b.** 160   **c.** 170   **d.** 180

8. Divide: 534)24030   c

   a. 46   **b.** 47   **c.** 45   **d.** 44

9. Multiply: 709
×210   d

   a. 14,970   **b.** 14,889

   c. 142,590   **d.** 148,890

10. Divide: 176)35728   c

   a. 23   **b.** 230   **c.** 203   **d.** 2003

11. Subtract: 8742 − 3695   a

   a. 5047   **b.** 4047

   c. 5147   **d.** 4147

12. Which numbers divide 42 evenly?   a

   a. 2 and 3   **b.** 2 and 5

   c. 4 and 5   **d.** 2 and 10

13. Subtract: 6004 − 158   d

   a. 5954   **b.** 5946

   c. 6956   **d.** 5846

14. Multiply: 31 × 27   a

   a. 837   **b.** 627   **c.** 737   **d.** 279

15. Subtract: 67
−18   b

   a. 51   **b.** 49   **c.** 59   **d.** 41

16. Multiply: 802 × 100   b

   a. 8020   **b.** 80,200

   c. 8200   **d.** 802,000

17. Divide: 9)1944   c

   a. 238   **b.** 214   **c.** 216   **d.** 218

18. How many graduates are represented by

Key: 🎓 represents 10 graduates.   d

a. 5   b. 500   c. 5000   d. 50

19. Read the meter.   a

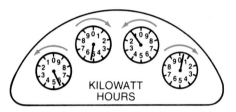

KILOWATT HOURS

a. 5510   b. 6611

c. 6100   d. 6510

20. Use the graph below to tell how many more books were sold in March than in January.   b

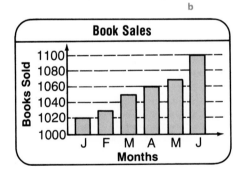

Book Sales

Books Sold: 1100, 1080, 1060, 1040, 1020, 1000

Months: J F M A M J

a. 10   b. 30   c. 25   d. 300

21. On a summer job, Myra earned $213 in June, $492 in July, and $576 in August. Find the average monthly salary.   a

a. $427   b. $394

c. $1171   d. $1281

22. What is the total value of twenty $5-bills, three $10-bills, and fifteen $20 bills?   b

a. $1330   b. $430

c. $330   d. $38

23. Frank earns $8.00 per hour and works 35 hours per week. Deductions amount to $63.00. Find the net pay.   b

a. $106   b. $217

c. $212   d. $343

24. Use the graph below to find how many people rode buses in 1930.   a

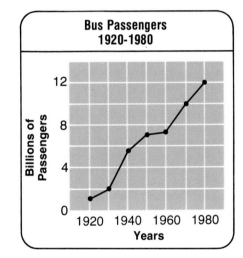

Bus Passengers 1920-1980

Billions of Passengers: 12, 8, 4, 0

Years: 1920 1940 1960 1980

a. 2 billion   b. 1 billion

c. 3 billion   d. 4 billion

25. The base price of a new car is $7290. Power steering costs $215 and an automatic transmission costs $303. Estimate the total cost to the nearest hundred dollars.   d

a. $7700   b. $7900

c. $8000   d. $7800

REVIEW OF RELATED SKILLS FOR CHAPTER 5

We suggest that some or all of this page be reviewed before proceeding with the chapter.

Divide each number by 10.

1. 40 ⁴ **2.** 90 ⁹ **3.** 70 ⁷ **4.** 60 ⁶ **5.** 900 ⁹⁰ **6.** 500 ⁵⁰ **7.** 300 ³⁰ **8.** 400 ⁴⁰

Divide each number by 100.

9. 600 ⁶ **10.** 700 ⁷ **11.** 200 ² **12.** 300 ³ **13.** 4000 ⁴⁰ **14.** 9000 ⁹⁰ **15.** 5000 ⁵⁰

Divide each number by 1000.

16. 7000 ⁷ **17.** 10,000 ¹⁰ **18.** 30,000 ³⁰ **19.** 9000 ⁹ **20.** 6000 ⁶ **21.** 5000 ⁵

Add. (Pages 6–7)

22.	**23.**	**24.**	**25.**	**26.**	**27.**
68	49	186	36	430	325
+295	+716	47	349	17	27
363	765	+ 19	+ 12	+ 4	+ 3
		252	397	451	355

28.	**29.**	**30.**	**31.**	**32.**	**33.**
425	507	116	2119	48,691	54,701
16	62	2193	315	7,850	4,213
+398	+309	247	8048	10,009	15,892
839	878	+3086	+ 217	+ 963	+ 316
		5642	10,699	67,513	75,122

34. 98 + 62,501 + 309 + 51,006 113,914   **35.** 72,828 + 174 + 43,668 + 25 116,695

36. 53,010 + 7 + 819 + 892 54,728   **37.** 21 + 62,593 + 1705 + 754 65,073

Subtract. (Pages 14–15)

38.	**39.**	**40.**	**41.**	**42.**	**43.**
139	486	1703	4030	3000	5000
−127	−267	− 898	− 277	−1682	−4283
12	219	805	3753	1318	717

44. 503 − 247 256   **45.** 760 − 191 569   **46.** 9000 − 8658 342   **47.** 3801 − 774 3027

Multiply. (Pages 26–27, 32–33, 36–37)

48.	**49.**	**50.**	**51.**	**52.**	**53.**
63	29	58	79	276	416
× 7 441	× 5 145	×13 754	×22 1738	×321 88,596	×504 209,664

54.	**55.**	**56.**	**57.**	**58.**	**59.**
2456	108	507	6008	1050	4849
× 238 584,528	× 27 2916	× 83 42,081	× 203 1,219,624	× 480 504,000	× 197 955,253

60. 103 × 26 2678   **61.** 3000 × 201 603,000 **62.** 724 × 92 66,608   **63.** 6500 × 41 266,500

Multiply. (Page 40)

64. 7 × 10 70   **65.** 70 × 10 700   **66.** 700 × 10 7000 **67.** 7000 × 10 70,000   **68.** 715 × 10 7,150

69. 9 × 100 900 **70.** 90 × 100 9,000 **71.** 900 × 100 90,000 **72.** 93 × 100 9,300 **73.** 93 × 1000 93,000

74. 6 × 1000 6,000   **75.** 61 × 1000 61,000   **76.** 52 × 1000 52,000   **77.** 10 × 1000 10,000   **78.** 100 × 1000 100,000

SKILLS

5-1 Decimals and Place Value
5-2 Addition and Subtraction
5-3 Multiplication
5-4 Moving the Decimal Point

APPLICATIONS

Writing Checks
Sales Tax
Making Change
Cost of Credit

CAREER

Retailing

5-1 Decimals and Place Value See the Teacher's Manual for the objectives.

In our decimal system, the value of each decimal place is <u>ten</u> times the value of the place to its right.

PROCEDURE To give the value of any digit in a number:

    1 Identify the place name.

    2 Use the digit and the place name to give the value.

TABLE

Place Names							
Thousands							Thousand**ths**
	Hundreds					Hundred**ths**	
		Tens			Tenths		
			Ones	.			
a. 4	3	6	5	.	7	9	2
b.		5	8	.	4		
c.			9	.	0	0	4

┌ **EXAMPLE 1** Give the value of the "4" for each number in the table.

    1 **Place Name**   **2** **Value**

Solutions: **a.** Thousands   **a.** 4000 ◀ *Read: "four thousand."*

          b. Tenths   **b.** 0.4 ◀ *Read: "four tenths."*

          c. Thousandths   **c.** 0.004 ◀ *Read: "four thousandths."*

After completing Example 1, you may wish to have students do some or all of Exercises 1-18.

PROCEDURE To compare decimals:

    1 Write the decimals one under the other. Line up the decimal points.

    2 Starting from the left, compare the first digits that are <u>not</u> alike. Annex final zeros when necessary.

    3 Compare the decimals in the same order as the unlike digits in Step 2.

    NOTE: Annexing final zeros does <u>not</u> change the value of a decimal. The symbols $>$ and $<$ are used to compare numbers.

    ">" means "**is greater than.**"   "<" means "**is less than.**"

Replace the ● with <, =, or >.

a. 5.42 ● 5.39   b. 0.003 ● 0.0031

Solutions:

		a.	b.
1	Write the decimals one under the other.	5.42 5.39	0.003 0.0031
2	Compare the first digits that are <u>not</u> alike. Start from the left.	5.42 5.39 4 > 3	0.0030 ◀ Annex one zero. 0.0031 0 < 1
3	Compare the decimals in the same order.	5.42 > 5.39	0.003 < 0.0031

REVIEW OF RELATED SKILLS
You may wish to use these exercises before teaching the lesson.

Divide each number by 10.

1. 30 3   2. 90 9   3. 50 5   4. 70 7   5. 60 6   6. 80 8   7. 100 10   8. 500 50

Divide each number by 100.

9. 100 1   10. 400 4   11. 300 3   12. 700 7   13. 900 9   14. 200 2   15. 1000 10   16. 7000 70

Divide each number by 1000.

17. 1000 1   18. 3000 3   19. 6000 6   20. 8000 8   21. 10,000 10   22. 20,000 20

EXERCISES
See the suggested assignment guide in the Teacher's Manual.

For Exercises 1–18, give the place value of the underlined digit in each number. (Example 1)

1. 13.<u>5</u> 5 tenths   2. 13.0<u>5</u> 5 hundredths   3. 1<u>5</u>.03 5 ones   4. 13.176<u>5</u> 5 ten-thousandths   5. 13.2<u>5</u> 5 hundredths   6. <u>2</u>3.14 2 tens

7. <u>2</u>56.8 2 hundreds   8. 100.<u>2</u>5 2 tenths   9. <u>2</u>001.5 2 thousandths   10. 3<u>2</u>976.4 2 thousandths   11. 1<u>7</u>5.4 7 tens   12. 2.51<u>7</u> 7 thousandths

13. <u>7</u>.586 7 ones   14. 4.<u>0</u>7 0 tenths   15. 9.<u>7</u>58 7 tenths   16. <u>1</u>0045.79 1 ten-thousand   17. 9.00<u>1</u>5 1 thousandth   18. 628.<u>1</u>9 1 tenth

For Exercises 19–39, replace the ● with <, =, or >. (Example 2)

19. 6.51 ● 6.48 >   20. 0.02 ● 0.027 <   21. 14.075 ● 14.07 >

22. 7.01 ● 7.89 <   23. 0.1005 ● 0.10036 >   24. 1.63 ● 1.632 <

25. 0.50 ● 0.500 =   26. 0.319 ● 0.32 <   27. 0.72 ● 0.7 >

28. 0.200 ● 0.2 =   29. 0.45 ● 0.450 =   30. 0.241 ● 0.24 >

31. 1.007 ● 0.07 >   32. 3.05 ● 3.005 >   33. 0.628 ● 0.625 >

34. 0.421 ● 0.422 <   35. 0.09 ● 0.9 <   36. 0.302 ● 0.305 <

37. 0.610 ● 0.61 =   38. 0.914 ● 0.92 <   39. 0.01 ● 0.15 <

Problem Solving and Applications

Writing Checks

See the Teacher's Manual for the objectives.
This lesson applies the skills presented in Section 5-1.

Many people make payments by check because it saves time and it makes record keeping easier. On a check, the amount being paid is written both in <u>decimals</u> and in <u>words</u>.

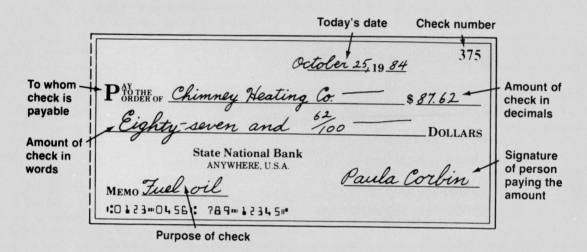

Today's date

Check number

To whom check is payable

Amount of check in decimals

Amount of check in words

Signature of person paying the amount

Purpose of check

Exercises

For Exercises 1-10, write each amount in words as it would appear on a check.

1. Twenty-five and $\frac{12}{100}$ 3. Fourteen and $\frac{00}{100}$ 5. Three hundred twenty-five and $\frac{75}{100}$

2. Thirty-six and $\frac{72}{100}$ 4. One hundred eighteen and $\frac{00}{100}$

1. $25.12   **2.** $36.72   **3.** $14.00   **4.** $118.00   **5.** $325.75

6. $481.29   **7.** $19.08   **8.** $206.05   **9.** $1725.00   **10.** $3005.00

6. Four hundred eighty-one and $\frac{29}{100}$ 7. Nineteen and $\frac{08}{100}$ 8. Two hundred six and $\frac{05}{100}$

For Exercises 11–14, find what is missing on each check. Correct any errors.

11.

276

The date is missing.

P AY TO THE ORDER OF *Tyson Department Store* $ 115.00

One hundred fifteen and $\frac{00}{100}$ — DOLLARS

State National Bank
ANYWHERE, U.S.A.

MEMO *Clothing*   *Joann Murphy*

⑆0123⑈0456⑆ 789⑈12345⑈

9. One thousand seven hundred twenty-five and $\frac{00}{100}$ 10. Three thousand five and $\frac{00}{100}$

12. 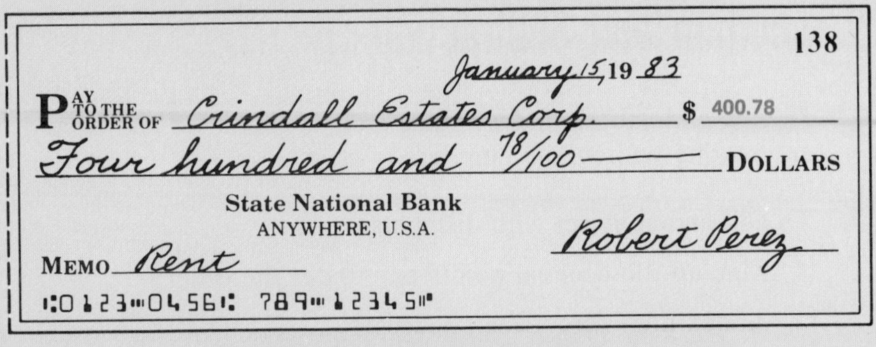

138
January 15, 19 83
PAY TO THE ORDER OF Crindall Estates Corp. $ 400.78
Four hundred and 78/100 DOLLARS
State National Bank
ANYWHERE, U.S.A.
MEMO Rent
Robert Perez
⑆0123⑈0456⑆ 789⑈12345⑈

13. 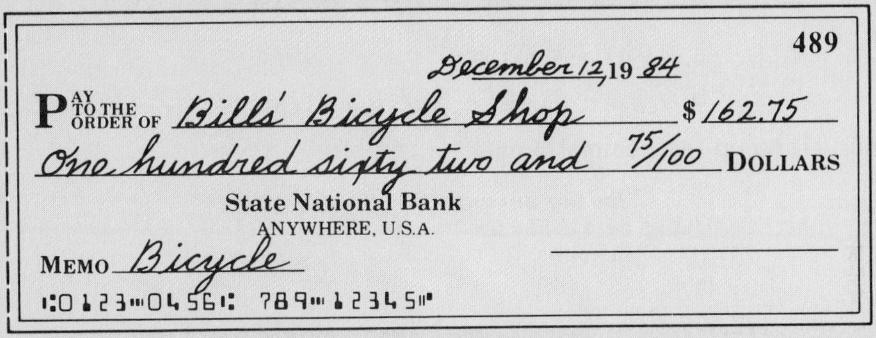

489
December 12, 19 84
PAY TO THE ORDER OF Bills' Bicycle Shop $ 162.75
One hundred sixty two and 75/100 DOLLARS
State National Bank
ANYWHERE, U.S.A.
MEMO Bicycle
⑆0123⑈0456⑆ 789⑈12345⑈

Signature is missing.

14. 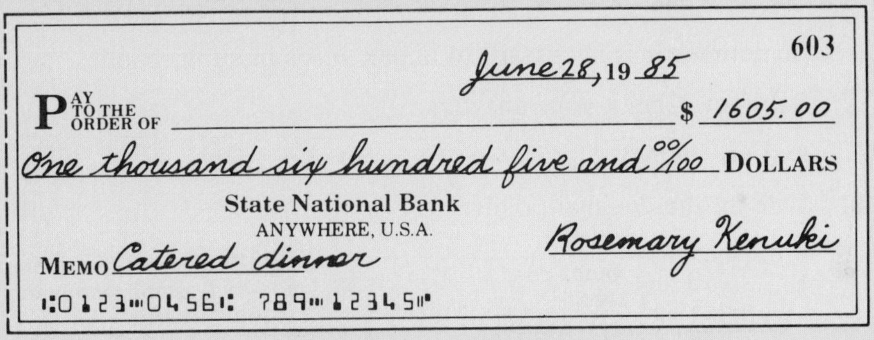

603
June 28, 19 85
PAY TO THE ORDER OF $ 1605.00
One thousand six hundred five and 00/100 DOLLARS
State National Bank
ANYWHERE, U.S.A.
MEMO Catered dinner
Rosemary Kenuki
⑆0123⑈0456⑆ 789⑈12345⑈

Name of payee is missing.

For each of Exercises 15–16, first copy a check form shown above. Then write out a check as indicated.

15. On August 30, Janet Keefe wrote check number 305 to Midway Dental Clinic for $68.75.

16. On October 8, Anthony Bi Blasi wrote check number 117 to Uptown Electric Company for $31.00.

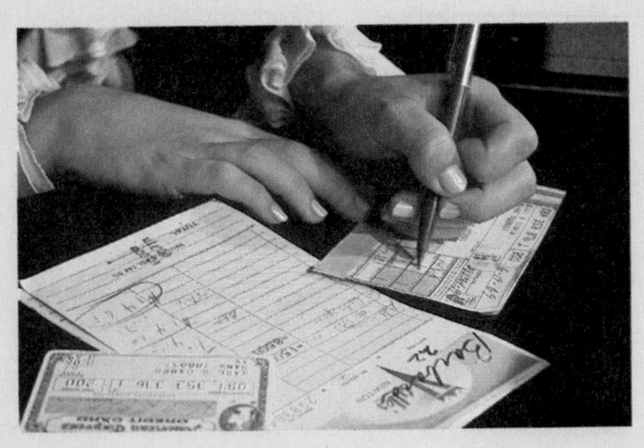

5-2 Addition and Subtraction See the Teacher's Manual for the objectives.

Adding and subtracting with decimals is similar to adding and subtracting with whole numbers.

PROCEDURE To add and subtract with decimals:

1. Line up the decimal points one under the other.

2. Annex final zeros when necessary.

3. Add or subtract as with whole numbers.

EXAMPLE 1 Add: **a.** $16.07 + 5.203 + 91.532$
b. $9.369 + 51.001 + 83.878 + 212.6$

After completing Example 1, you may wish to have students do some or all of Exercises 1-18.

Solutions: Line up the decimal points.

a.
$$
\begin{array}{r}
\overset{1}{1}\overset{1}{6}.070 \\
5.203 \\
+91.532 \\
\hline
112.805
\end{array}
$$
You can annex a zero to line up the ones.

b.
$$
\begin{array}{r}
\overset{11}{9}.\overset{11}{3}69 \\
51.001 \\
83.878 \\
+212.600 \\
\hline
356.848
\end{array}
$$

Sometimes it is necessary to annex zeros in subtraction.

EXAMPLE 2 Subtract. Check your answers.

a. $2.45 - 0.983$

b. $3 - 1.999$

Solutions: Line up the decimal points.

a.
$$
\begin{array}{r}
\overset{1}{2}.\overset{34}{4}\overset{10}{5}0 \\
-0.983 \\
\hline
1.467
\end{array}
$$
Annex one zero.

b.
$$
\begin{array}{r}
\overset{2}{3}.\overset{99}{0}\overset{10}{0}0 \\
-1.999 \\
\hline
1.001
\end{array}
$$
Insert the decimal point. Annex three zeros.

Check: a.
$$
\begin{array}{r}
1.467 \\
+0.983 \\
\hline
2.450
\end{array}
$$
$2.450 = 2.45$

b.
$$
\begin{array}{r}
1.001 \\
+1.999 \\
\hline
3.000
\end{array}
$$
$3.000 = 3$

REVIEW OF RELATED SKILLS You may wish to use these exercises before teaching the lesson.

Add or subtract as indicated. (Pages 6–7, 14–15)

1. $52,986 + 20,050 + 9644 + 828$ 83,508

2. $33,456 + 65,897 + 4765 + 675$ 104,793

3. $93 - 81$ 12   4. $75 - 39$ 36   5. $1802 - 945$ 857   6. $452 - 65$ 387   7. $2100 - 1348$ 752

EXERCISES

See the suggested assignment guide in the Teacher's Manual.

Add. (Example 1)

1. 4.75 11.04 + 9.13 24.92	**2.** 6.26 12.58 + 3.91 22.75	**3.** 28.257 6.096 +19.318 53.671	**4.** 7.946 36.552 +19.318 63.816	**5.** 156.04 2.95 + 32.21 191.20
6. 26.1 3.951 + 8.492 38.543	**7.** 19.406 4.8 + 9.07 33.276	**8.** 67.008 1.1 + 0.95 69.058	**9.** 0.33 21.56 +38.2 60.09	**10.** 126.2 73.08 + 1.38 200.66

11. 48.65 + 3.27 + 15.98 + 1.52 69.42

12. 5.93 + 12.41 + 16.88 + 3.48 38.70

13. 16.709 + 8.951 + 3.463 + 6.005 35.128

14. 59.681 + 24.053 + 17.009 + 6.208 106.951

15. 8.43 + 26.05 + 31.62 + 4.77 70.87

16. 8.085 + 26.459 + 7.202 + 8.4999 50.2459

17. 74.656 + 8.9 + 5.013 + 713.85 802.419

18. 57.09 + 878.015 + 6.02 + 5.535 946.660

Subtract. Check each answer. (Example 2)

19. 16.78 − 9.43 7.35	**20.** 83.79 −17.66 66.13	**21.** 4.968 −2.375 2.593	**22.** 5.284 −3.197 2.087	**23.** 9.06 −4.18 4.88
24. 7.475 −0.3551 7.1199	**25.** 3.62 −2.485 1.135	**26.** 8.19 −6.959 1.231	**27.** 1.7 −0.87 0.83	**28.** 21.195 − 7.2325 13.9625

29. 4 − 0.45 3.55

30. 7 − 0.904 6.096

31. 6 − 2.62 3.38

32. 15 − 6.073 8.927

33. 29 − 3.251 25.749

34. 38 − 8.326 29.674

35. 10 − 1.13 8.87

36. 1000 − 99.98 900.02

37. 26 − 0.605 25.395

38. 28.95 − 19.36 9.59

39. 9 − 0.048 8.952

40. 17.484 − 12.813 4.671

41. 61.33 − 9.746 51.584

42. 5.608 − 2.35 3.258

43. 59.375 − 6.76 52.615

44. 11.06 − 8.633 2.427

These are one-step problems that most students should be able to handle.

APPLICATIONS: Using Decimals

45. In the 800-meter relay, Nathan ran the first leg in 29.2 seconds, Ted ran the second leg in 28.6 seconds, Bill ran the third leg in 28.0 seconds, and Jamie ran the fourth leg in 30.2 seconds. Find their total time. 116 seconds

46. One year, the record for the women's 100-meter freestyle swimming meet was 58.9 seconds. Ten years later, the record was 55.41 seconds. How much faster was the second record? 3.49 seconds

DECIMALS **95**

Problem Solving and Applications

Sales Tax
See the Teacher's Manual for the objectives.
This lesson applies the skills presented in Section 5-2.

Some salespersons use a table to find the amount of sales tax on a purchase. Part of a table showing amounts for a 5% sales tax is shown at the right.

EXAMPLE Find the sales tax and the total cost for a purchase of $19.50.

Solution:

1 Look at the "Amount of Sale" column in the tax table. Find the interval that includes $19.50.

Interval: **19.47 – 19.67**

2 Look in the "Tax" column directly to the right. Read the amount.

Sales Tax: **$0.98**

3 Find the total cost.

$19.50
+ 0.98
Total Cost: **$20.48**

Exercises
These are two-step problems that involve reading a table and addition.

Find the sales tax on each purchase.

1. $19.15 $0.96
2. $6.85 $0.34
3. $14.50 $0.73
4. $21.00 $1.05
5. $12.95 $0.65
6. $9.00 $0.45
11. $1.06, $22.31
12. $0.85, $17.85

Find the sales tax and the total cost for each purchase.

7. $7.15 $0.36, $7.51
8. $10.58 $0.53, $11.11
9. $15.00 $0.75, $15.75
10. $18.85 $0.94, $19.79
11. $21.25
12. $17.00
13. $9.98 $0.50, $10.48
14. $16.75 $0.84, $17.59
15. $15.50 $0.78, $16.28

16. Find the sales tax and the total cost for a purchase of $19.10. $0.95, $20.05

17. At Hilltop Pharmacy, Mrs. Carr paid $2.25 for a toothbrush, $1.50 for a comb, and $3.89 for shampoo. Find the sales tax and the total cost. $0.38, $8.02

Amount of Sale Interval	Tax	Amount of Sale Interval	Tax
0.01- 0.10	0.00	10.68-10.88	0.54
0.11- 0.25	0.01	10.89-11.10	0.55
0.26- 0.46	0.02	11.11-11.25	0.56
0.47- 0.67	0.03	11.26-11.46	0.57
0.68- 0.88	0.04	11.47-11.67	0.58
0.89- 1.10	0.05	11.68-11.88	0.59
1.11- 1.25	0.06	11.89-12.10	0.60
1.26- 1.46	0.07	12.11-12.25	0.61
1.47- 1.67	0.08	12.26-12.46	0.62
1.68- 1.88	0.09	12.47-12.67	0.63
1.89- 2.10	0.10	12.68-12.88	0.64
2.11- 2.25	0.11	12.89-13.10	0.65
2.26- 2.46	0.12	13.11-13.25	0.66
2.47- 2.67	0.13	13.26-13.46	0.67
2.68- 2.88	0.14	13.47-13.67	0.68
2.89- 3.10	0.15	13.68-13.88	0.69
3.11- 3.25	0.16	13.89-14.10	0.70
3.26- 3.46	0.17	14.11-14.25	0.71
3.47- 3.67	0.18	14.26-14.46	0.72
3.68- 3.88	0.19	14.47-14.67	0.73
3.89- 4.10	0.20	14.68-14.88	0.74
4.11- 4.25	0.21	14.89-15.10	0.75
4.26- 4.46	0.22	15.11-15.25	0.76
4.47- 4.67	0.23	15.26-15.46	0.77
4.68- 4.88	0.24	15.47-15.67	0.78
4.89- 5.10	0.25	15.68-15.88	0.79
5.11- 5.25	0.26	15.89-16.10	0.80
5.26- 5.46	0.27	16.11-16.25	0.81
5.47- 5.67	0.28	16.26-16.46	0.82
5.68- 5.88	0.29	16.47-16.67	0.83
5.89- 6.10	0.30	16.68-16.88	0.84
6.11- 6.25	0.31	16.89-17.10	0.85
6.26- 6.46	0.32	17.11-17.25	0.86
6.47- 6.67	0.33	17.26-17.46	0.87
6.68- 6.88	0.34	17.47-17.67	0.88
6.89- 7.10	0.35	17.68-17.88	0.89
7.11- 7.25	0.36	17.89-18.10	0.90
7.26- 7.46	0.37	18.11-18.25	0.91
7.47- 7.67	0.38	18.26-18.46	0.92
7.68- 7.88	0.39	18.47-18.67	0.93
7.89- 8.10	0.40	18.68-18.88	0.94
8.11- 8.25	0.41	18.89-19.10	0.95
8.26- 8.46	0.42	19.11-19.25	0.96
8.47- 8.67	0.43	19.26-19.46	0.97
8.68- 8.88	0.44	19.47-19.67	0.98
8.89- 9.10	0.45	19.68-19.88	0.99
9.11- 9.25	0.46	19.89-20.10	1.00
9.26- 9.46	0.47	20.11-20.25	1.01
9.47- 9.67	0.48	20.26-20.46	1.02
9.68- 9.88	0.49	20.47-20.67	1.03
9.89-10.10	0.50	20.68-20.88	1.04
10.11-10.25	0.51	20.89-21.10	1.05
10.26-10.46	0.52	21.11-21.25	1.06
10.47-10.67	0.53	21.26-21.46	1.07

Application

Problem Solving and Applications

Making Change

The best way to make change is to use as few bills and coins as possible.

Exercises

Choose the best way of making change. Choose a, b, or c.

1.

Amount of Sale	Money Received	Change Due
$3.20	$5–bill	$1.80

a

a. A $1–bill, 3 quarters, one nickel
b. A $1–bill and 8 dimes
c. A $1–bill, 2 quarters, 3 dimes

2.

Amount of Sale	Money Received	Change Due
$4.12	$5–bill	$0.88

c

a. Two quarters, 7 nickels, 3 pennies
b. Two quarters, 3 dimes, 8 pennies
c. Three quarters, 1 dime, 3 pennies

3.

Amount of Sale	Money Received	Change Due
$7.65	$10–bill	$2.35

a

a. Two $1–bills, 1 quarter, 1 dime
b. Two $1–bills, 1 quarter, 2 nickels
c. Two $1–bills, 3 dimes, one nickel

4.

Amount of Sale	Money Received	Change Due
$36.85	Two $20–bills	$3.15

c

a. Three $1–bills and 15 pennies
b. Twelve quarters and 15 pennies
c. Three $1–dollar bills, a dime, one nickel.

Make a chart like the one shown below. Write the number of bills and coins in the boxes to show the best way to make change. The first one is done for you.

	Amount of Sale	Money Received	Change Due	Change: Number of						
				$10–bills	$5–bills	$1–bills	Quarters	Dimes	Nickels	Pennies
5.	$ 6.19	$10	$ 3.81	None	None	3	3	None	1	1
6.	$ 8.55	$10	$ 1.45	? None	? None	? 1	? 1	? 2	? None	? None
7.	$ 3.89	$20	$16.11	? 1	? 1	? 1	? None	? 1	? None	? 1
8.	$12.60	$20	$ 7.40	? None	? 1	? 2	? 1	? 1	? 1	? None

5-3 Multiplication

See the Teacher's Manual for the objectives.

Multiplying with decimals involves counting the number of decimal places in the factors in order to place the decimal point in the product. The **number of decimal places** means the number of digits to the <u>right</u> of the decimal point.

PROCEDURE To multiply with decimals:

1. Multiply as with whole numbers.

2. Count the number of decimal places in the factors. Starting at the right and moving left, count the same number of decimal places in the product. Insert the decimal point.

EXAMPLE 1 Multiply: **a.** 96×0.07 **b.** 11.08×1.05

Decimal Places

Solutions: **a.**
$$\begin{array}{r} 96 \longleftarrow \quad 0 \\ \times 0.07 \longleftarrow \quad 2 \\ \hline 6.72 \longleftarrow \quad 0+2, \text{ or } 2 \end{array}$$

Decimal Places

b.
$$\begin{array}{r} 11.08 \longleftarrow \quad 2 \\ \times \ 1.05 \longleftarrow \quad 2 \\ \hline 5540 \\ 00000 \\ 11080 \\ \hline 11.6340 \longleftarrow \quad 2+2, \text{ or } 4 \end{array}$$

After completing Example 1, you may wish to have students do some or all of Exercises 1-25.

Sometimes you have to insert zeros in a product.

EXAMPLE 2 Multiply: **a.** 1.2×0.004 **b.** 0.12×0.0014

Decimal Places

Solutions: **a.**
Insert two zeros to make 4 decimal places.
$$\begin{array}{r} 1.2 \longleftarrow \quad 1 \\ \times 0.004 \longleftarrow \quad 3 \\ \hline 0.0048 \end{array}$$

Decimal Places

b.
$$\begin{array}{r} 0.12 \longleftarrow \quad 2 \\ \times 0.0014 \longleftarrow \quad 4 \\ \hline 48 \\ 120 \\ \hline 0.000168 \end{array}$$
Insert three zeros to make 6 decimal places.

REVIEW OF RELATED SKILLS

You may wish to use these exercises before teaching the lesson.

Multiply. (Pages 26–27, 32–33, 36–37)

1. $\begin{array}{r} 87 \\ \times \ 9 \\ \hline 783 \end{array}$	**2.** $\begin{array}{r} 65 \\ \times \ 5 \\ \hline 325 \end{array}$	**3.** $\begin{array}{r} 702 \\ \times \ 44 \\ \hline 30888 \end{array}$	**4.** $\begin{array}{r} 513 \\ \times 109 \\ \hline 55917 \end{array}$	**5.** $\begin{array}{r} 6254 \\ \times \ 287 \\ \hline 1,794,898 \end{array}$	**6.** $\begin{array}{r} 2498 \\ \times \ 543 \\ \hline 1,356,414 \end{array}$

EXERCISES

Copy each product. Then insert the decimal point.   (Example 1)

1.   15
×0.7
105   *10.5*

2.   1.5
×0.7
105   *1.05*

3.   1.5
× 7
105   *10.5*

4.   0.15
× 7
105   *1.05*

5.   1.50
× 0.7
1050   *1.050*

Multiply.   (Example 1)

6.   45
×0.6
27.0 or 27.

7.   26
×0.8
20.8

8.   39
×2.3
89.7

9.   92
×1.5
138.0 or 138.

10.   7
×0.04
0.28

11.   8
×0.05
0.40 or 0.4

12.   121
×0.01
1.21

13.   473
×0.02
9.46

14.   5631
×0.09
506.79

15.   9742
×0.08
779.36

16.   2.09
×3.89
8.1301

17.   21.06
× 1.02
21.4812

18.   3.51
×0.74
2.5974

19.   3.14
×0.13
0.4082

20.   9.08
× 1.5
13.620 or 13.62

21.   8.71
× 1.5
13.065

22.   59.3
×0.61
36.173

23.   47.6
×0.59
28.084

24.   13.72
× 21.5
294.980 or 294.98

25.   45.16
× 35.2
1589.632

Copy each product. Then insert the decimal point.   (Example 2)

26.   0.18
×0.06
108   *0.0108*

27.   0.018
× 0.06
108   *0.00108*

28.   0.18
×0.006
108   *0.00108*

29.   0.018
×0.006
108   *0.000108*

30.   0.018
×0.060
108   *0.00108*

Multiply.   (Example 2)

31.   3.4
×.002
0.0068

32.   2.5
×.005
0.0125

33.   1.6
×0.03
0.048

34.   1.9
×.007
0.0133

35.   8.1
×0.0009
0.00729

36.   2.81
×0.007
0.01967

37.   0.6
×0.001
0.0006

38.   0.5
×0.002
0.0010

39.   0.08
×0.06
0.0048

40.   0.12
×0.07
0.0084

41.   0.61
×0.0032
0.001952

42.   6.05
×0.0027
0.016335

43.   0.23
×0.0038
0.000874

44.   0.13
×0.0052
0.000676

45.   0.144
×0.0028
0.0004032

46.   1.13
×0.0052
0.005876

47.   2.63
×0.0001
0.000263

48.   91.31
×0.0005
0.045655

49.   0.003
×0.0015
0.0000045

50.   7.642
×0.0101
0.0771842

CHECKING ANSWERS

Calculator exercises are optional.

Use a calculator to check each answer. Correct any wrong answers.

1. $2.9 + 49.6 + 58.47 + 0.60 = 110.66$ *111.57*   **2.** $0.86 + 37.09 + 6.6 + 9.75 = 54.3$ *372.9*

3. $20.5 - 16.609 = 3.891$ **4.** $880 - 264.54 = 615.46$ **5.** $809.8 - 436.9 = 371.9$ *0.1792*

6. $95.2 \times 1.25 = 119.3$ *119.0*   **7.** $4.5 \times 0.37 = 2.665$ *1.665*   **8.** $2.8 \times 0.064 = 1.792$

Calculator   DECIMALS   **99**

Problem Solving and Applications

Cost of Credit

Sometimes buyers do not wish to pay cash for a purchase. Instead, they may prefer to buy "on credit." They agree to pay an extra amount called the **cost of credit.**

To find the cost of credit, you must first answer the question:

"What is the total amount paid?"

This is the hidden question in the problem. Then you find the cost of credit.

EXAMPLE   Automobile tires are selling for a cash price of $150. They can also be bought by paying $14.75 per month for 12 months. Find the cost of credit.

Solution: ☐1 Find the amount paid in 12 months.

$14.75 \times 12 = $177

☐2 Find the cost of credit.

$177 - $150 = $27   ◀ **Total Monthly** − **Cash** = **Cost of**
                        Payments   **Price**   **Credit**

The cost of credit is **$27.**

Exercises   Exercises 1-4 are one-step problems.

1. Rosa's monthly payment on a portable television set is $8.25. How much will she pay in 20 months? $165.00

2. Stanislaus makes monthly payments of $72.85 on his car. How much will he pay in 12 months? $874.20

3. Mr. Harvey is paying $37.50 per month for a new carpet. How much will he pay in 15 months? $562.50

4. The Garcias pay $109.90 a month for a new dining room set. How much will they pay in 23 months? $2527.70

In Exercises 5–8, find the cost of credit. Exercises 5-8 are two-step problems.

5. A washing machine sells for a cash price of $284.95. It can also be purchased by paying $15.50 per month for 24 months. $87.05

6. A home freezer sells for a cash price of $329.95. It can also be bought by paying $13.50 per month for 27 months. $34.55

7. A sofa sells for a cash price of $600. It can also be bought by paying $53.22 a month for 12 months. $38.64

8. A color television sells for a cash price of $595. It can also be bought by paying $22.85 a month for 30 months. $90.50

RETAILING

Career lessons are optional.
This lesson applies the skills presented in Section 5-3 and addition.

Salesworkers in some stores help to take inventory once or twice a year. An **inventory** is a count of all the merchandise. The inventory may also give the value of the merchandise. To find this value, you multiply the <u>unit cost</u> (cost per item) by the number of items.

EXERCISES

For Exercises 1–5, find the value of the inventory for each item. Then find the value of the combined inventory for lamps.

	Item	Inventory	Unit Cost (Cost Per Item)	Value	
1.	Desk lamps	45	$ 25.30	$25.30 × 45 = __?__	$1,138.50
2.	Table lamps	15	$110.85	$110.85 × 15 = __?__	$1,662.75
3.	Standing lamps	10	$ 95.75	$95.75 × 10 = __?__	$957.50
4.	Chandeliers	3	$527.90	$527.90 × 3 = __?__	$1,583.70
5.				Value of lamp inventory: __?__	$5,342.45

For Exercises 6–10, find the value of the inventory for each item. Then find the value of the combined inventory for blouses.

	Item	Inventory	Unit Cost (Cost Per Item)	Value	
6.	Silk blouses	18	$43.70	__?__	$786.60
7.	Cotton blouses	45	$30.85	__?__	$1388.25
8.	Tee-shirts	21	$ 7.80	__?__	$163.80
9.	Polyester blouses	31	$22.75	__?__	$705.25
10.			Value of blouse inventory:	__?__	$3043.90

5-4 Moving the Decimal Point See the Teacher's Manual for the objectives.

You can multiply by 10, by 100, by 1000, and so on, by moving the decimal point to the <u>right</u>.

PROCEDURE To multiply a decimal by   10 by 100, or by 1000:

1 Move the decimal point one,   two, or   three places to the <u>right</u>.

2 When necessary, annex zeros in order to have the correct number of decimal places.

EXAMPLE 1 Multiply: **a.** 5.84×10 **b.** 0.9×100 **c.** 21.3×1000

Solutions: **a.** $5.84 \times 10 = 5\,8.4$ **b.** $0.9 \times 100 = 90$ ◀ *Annex one zero*

c. $21.3 \times 1000 = 21\,300$ ◀ *Annex two zeros.*

After completing Example 1, you may wish to have students do some or all of Exercises 1-20.

You can multiply by 0.1, by 0.01, by 0.001, and so on by moving the decimal point to the <u>left</u>.

PROCEDURE To multiply a decimal   by 0.1,   by 0.01, or by 0.001:

1 Move the decimal point   one,   two,   or   three places to the <u>left</u>.

2 When necessary, insert zeros in order to have the correct number of decimal places.

EXAMPLE 2 Multiply: **a.** 3.8×0.1 **b.** 176.3×0.01 **c.** 2.156×0.001

Solutions: **a.** $3.8 \times 0.1 = 0.3\,8$ **b.** $176.3 \times 0.01 = 1.76\,3$

c. $2.156 \times 0.001 = 0.002\,156$ ◀ *Insert two zeros.*

REVIEW OF RELATED SKILLS You may wish to use these exercises before teaching the lesson.

Multiply.   (Page 40)

1. 5×10 50   **2.** 52×10 520   **3.** 514×10 5140   **4.** 5696×10 56960   **5.** 783×10 7830

6. 9×100 900   **7.** 47×100 4700   **8.** 983×100 98300 **9.** 7821×100 782100   **10.** 25×100 2500

11. 3×1000 3,000   **12.** 83×1000 83,000   **13.** 426×1000 426,000   **14.** 3826×1000 3,826,000   **15.** 228×1000 228,000

EXERCISES

See the suggested assignment guide in the Teacher's Manual.

Multiply. (Example 1)

1. 4.59×10 45.9   **2.** 3.15×10 31.5   **3.** 4.59×100 459.   **4.** 3.15×100 315

5. 4.59×1000 4590   **6.** 3.15×1000 3150   **7.** 0.035×10 0.35   **8.** 17.5×10 175

9. 0.035×100 3.5   **10.** 17.5×100 1750   **11.** 17.5×1000 17500.   **12.** 0.035×1000 35

13. 4.608×10 46.08   **14.** 0.5×10 5   **15.** 4.608×100 460.8   **16.** 0.5×100 50

17. 4.608×1000 4608   **18.** 0.5×1000 500   **19.** 1.1×100 110   **20.** 1.1×1000 1100

Multiply. (Example 2)

21. 0.71×0.1 0.071   **22.** 51.5×0.1 5.15   **23.** 9.71×0.01 0.0971   **24.** 51.5×0.01 0.515

25. 9.71×0.001 0.00971   **26.** 51.5×0.001 0.0515   **27.** 1.7×0.1 0.17   **28.** 0.83×0.1 0.083

29. 1.7×0.01 0.017   **30.** 0.83×0.01 0.0083   **31.** 1.7×0.01 0.017   **32.** 0.83×0.001 0.00083

33. 1.7×0.001 0.0017   **34.** 0.143×0.01 0.00143   **35.** 143×0.001 0.143   **36.** 9.71×0.01 0.0971

Mixed Practice

37. 4.9×0.1 0.49   **38.** 43.96×0.1 4.396   **39.** 3.8×10 38   **40.** 3.35×10 33.5

41. 313.43×0.001 **42.** 60.25×0.001 **43.** 85.9×100 8590   **44.** 1.063×100 106.3

45. 0.621×1000 621   **46.** 0.07×1000 70   **47.** 0.1592×0.1 **48.** 0.0225×0.1 0.00225

49. 10.8×0.01 0.108   **50.** 154×0.01 1.54   **51.** 5.52×10 55.2   **52.** 50.38×10 503.8

53. 67.7×0.001 0.0677   **54.** 8.29×0.001 0.00829   **55.** 3.7×100 370   **56.** 0.4×100 40

41. 0.31343   42. 0.06025   47. 0.01592

APPLICATIONS: **Moving the Decimal Point**

These are one-step problems that most students should be able to handle.

57. Mr. and Mrs. Rubin earn $35,300 year. They give one-tenth of this to charity. How much do they give to charity? $3,530

58. The foreman in a light factory estimates that 0.01 of the bulbs produced each day are defective. About how many defective bulbs are there on a day on which 25,000 bulbs are produced?   250

59. After the installation of new equipment, the factory foreman estimates that 0.001 of the bulbs produced are defective. About how many defective bulbs will there be in a batch of 100,000 bulbs?   100

Chapter Review

These exercises review the vocabulary, skills, and applications presented in the chapter as a preparation for the chapter test.

Part 1: Vocabulary

For Exercises 1–4, choose from the box at the right the word(s) that completes the statement.

1. The 2 in 253 has a __?__ of 200. (Page 90) value
2. The place name of the 5 in 22.35 is __?__. (Page 90) hundredths
3. To place the decimal point in a product, you find the sum of the number of __?__ places in the factors. (Page 98) decimal
4. Another name for finance charge is __?__. (Page 100)
   cost of credit

hundredths
cost of credit
value
thousandths
decimal

Part 2: Skills

For Exercises 5–14, give the value of the underlined digit in each number. (Pages 90–91)

5. 481.7<u>2</u> 7 tenths
6. 36<u>7</u>.58 7 ones
7. 29.0<u>7</u> 7 hundredths
8. 238.36<u>7</u> 7 thousandths
9. <u>7</u>4.36 7 tens
10. 52.1<u>3</u> 3 hundredths
11. <u>3</u>85.7 3 hundred
12. 200.3<u>6</u> 3 tenths
13. <u>3</u>047.61 3 thousand
14. 9372.80<u>3</u> 3 thousandths

For Exercises 15–20, replace the ● with <, =, or >. (Pages 90–91)

15. 3.28 ● 3.31 <
16. 0.008 ● 0.0082 <
17. 21.0462 ● 21.0463 <
18. 5.003 ● 6.003 <
19. 4.506 ● 4.5055 >
20. 2.06 ● 2.068 <

Add. (Pages 94–95)

21. 36.86
    9.25
    +15.38
    _____
    61.49

22. 1.38
    16.24
    + 8.39
    _____
    26.01

23. 23.728
    2.597
    + 6.362
    _____
    32.687

24. 2.516
    6.24
    +4.518
    _____
    13.274

25. 6.27
    7.4
    +21.836
    _____
    35.506

26. 3.17 + 14.38 + 6.53 + 2.45 26.53
27. 2.75 + 4.35 + 21.96 + 1.84 30.90

Subtract. (Pages 94–95)

28. 7.64
    −3.59
    _____
    4.05

29. 18.5
    − 9.8
    _____
    8.7

30. 28.03
    − 6.95
    _____
    21.08

31. 2.36
    −1.034
    _____
    1.326

32. 28.6
    −19.732
    _____
    8.868

33. 5 − 0.63 4.37
34. 32 − 3.71 28.29
35. 700 − 35.64 664.36
36. 3000 − 981.42 2018.58

Multiply. (Pages 98–99)

37. 47
    ×0.8
    _____
    37.6

38. 92
    ×0.6
    _____
    55.2

39. 321
    × 0.9
    _____
    288.9

40. 462
    × 2.1
    _____
    970.2

41. 3.24
    ×9.06
    _____
    29.3544

42. 6.8
    ×0.002
    _____
    0.0136

43. 3.4
    ×0.008
    _____
    0.0272

44. 0.09
    ×0.05
    _____
    0.0045

45. 0.123
    ×0.002
    _____
    0.000246

46. 7.6
    ×0.002
    _____
    0.0152

Multiply.   (Pages 102–103)

47. 6.21×10 62.1
48. 4.8×10 48.
49. 6.21×100 621.
50. 4.8×100 480.

51. 6.21×1000 6210.
52. 4.8×1000 4800.
53. 23.8×0.1 2.38
54. 1.62×0.1 .162

55. 23.8×0.01 0.238
56. 1.62×0.01 0.0162
57. 23.8×0.001 0.0238
58. 1.62×0.001 0.00162

59. 4.8×0.1 0.48
60. 51.25×10 512.5
61. 3.96×0.001 0.00396
62. 1.073×100 107.3

63. 5.62×0.01 0.0562
64. 169×1000 169000.
65. 0.621×100 62.1
66. 0.0345×0.1 0.00345

Part 3: Applications The use of these word problems depends on which applications were studied.

Use this check for Exercises 67–70.   (Pages 92–93)

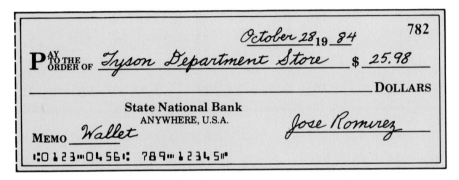

67. What is the number of this check? 782
68. What is the date of this check? October 28, 1984

69. What is missing on this check? The amount in words.
70. Write the amount in words. Twenty-five and $\frac{98}{100}$

71. In the 800–meter relay, Sue ran the first leg in 33.8 seconds, Terry ran the second leg in 32.94 seconds, Maria ran the third leg in 33.0 seconds, and Kim ran the fourth leg in 34.6 seconds. Find the total time. (Pages 94–95) 134.34 seconds

72. Use the table below to find the sales tax and the total cost for a purchase of $14.95.   (Page 96)

Sales tax: $0.75
Total cost: $15.70

Amount of Sale Interval	Tax
14.68-14.88	0.74
14.89-15.10	0.75
15.11-15.25	0.76

73. Marita made a $3.98 purchase with a $10–bill. Find the best way to make change.   (Page 97) One $5-bill, one $1-bill, and 2 pennies
74. Gordon made a $2.19 purchase with a $5–bill. Find the best way to make change.   (Page 97) Two $1-bills, 3 quarters, 1 nickel, and 1 penny

75. A color television set sells for a cash price of $285. It can also be purchased by paying $30 a month for 12 months. Find the cost of credit. (Page 100) $75.00
76. A foreman in a camera factory estimates that 0.001 of the 3500 shutters produced each day are defective. About how many of the shutters are defective?   (Page 103) 3.5

Chapter Test

The Teacher's Resource Book contains two forms of each Chapter Test.

For Exercises 1–3, replace the ● with <, =, or >.

1. 7.41 ● 7.38 >

2. 0.04 ● 0.047 <

3. 4.34 ● 4.341 <

Add.

4.
```
  2.19
  5.46
+4.83
```
12.48

5.
```
  32.6
143.72
+  8.61
```
184.93

6.
```
  3.15
  .186
+57.9
```
61.236

7. 632.1 + 93.62 + 8.461 + 0.7   734.881

8. 6.053 + .97 + 28.61 + 6.2   41.833

Subtract.

9.
```
 26.4
−19.8
```
6.6

10.
```
 32.5
− 1.62
```
30.88

11.
```
  2.8
−0.37
```
2.43

12. 17 − 5.87   11.13

13. 300 − 19.96   280.04

Multiply.

14.
```
  52
×0.9
```
46.8

15.
```
 3.8
×1.2
```
4.56

16.
```
 6.21
× 0.3
```
1.863

17.
```
  8.9
×0.004
```
0.0356

18.
```
    21
×0.0006
```
0.0126

19. 72 × 10   720

20. 8.6 × 0.1   0.86

21. 32.8 × 1000   32800.

22. 1.4 × 0.01   0.014

23. 3.9 × 0.001   0.0039

24. 0.08 × 100   8

25. 0.1 × 0.01   0.001

26. 0.5 × 1000   500

The use of these word problems depends on which applications were studied.

Solve each problem.

27. Paula ran the 100–meter dash in 11.39 seconds. Rose ran it in 11.52 seconds. How much faster did Paula run?   0.13 seconds

28. Richard made a purchase of $6.73. He gave the sales clerk a $10–bill. Find the best way for the sales clerk to make change.   Three $1-bills, 1 quarter, and 2 pennies

29. A carpet sells for a cash price of $99.95. It can also be purchased by paying $37.50 a month for 3 months. Find the cost of credit. $12.55

30. Iva scored 38.39 points in high diving. Renita scored 40.03 points. Find the difference between the two scores.   1.64 points

Additional Practice

You may wish to use some or all of these exercises depending on how well students performed on the formal chapter test.

Skills

For Exercises 1–10, give the value of the underlined digit in each number. (Pages 90–91)

1. 262.0<u>4</u> hundredths

2. <u>4</u>28.3 hundreds

3. 6<u>4</u>.95 ones

4. 28.<u>4</u>6 tenths

5. <u>4</u>85.03 hundreds

6. 246.7<u>5</u> tenths

7. 3<u>7</u>2.9 tens

8. 0.00<u>7</u> thousandths

9. 4.0<u>7</u>6 hundredths

10. 2<u>7</u>.58 ones

For Exercises 11–16, replace the ● with <, =, or >. (Pages 90–91)

11. 0.005 ● 0.050 <

12. 4.36 ● 4.036 >

13. 0.177 ● 1.770 <

14. 0.351 ● 0.352 <

15. 1.63 ● 1.603 >

16. 0.08 ● 1.08 <

Add. (Pages 94–95)

17.
2.7
3.5
+0.8
7.0

18.
20.4
7.5
+ 5.61
33.51

19.
23.2
4.68
+ 7.932
35.812

20.
25.004
2.3
+ 0.96
28.264

21.
178.3
4.75
+ 21.2
204.25

22. 7.23 + 18.65 + 10.624 + 4.2 40.704

23. 19.5 + 10.367 + 4.2 + 12.13 46.197

Subtract. (Pages 94–95)

24.
27.3
− 9.5
17.8

25.
4.283
−2.15
2.133

26.
6.9
−3.46
3.44

27.
17
− 4.99
12.01

28.
25.75
− 3.2
22.55

29. 8.27 − 3.1 5.17

30. 9 − 6.78 2.22

31. 42 − 3.59 38.41

32. 15.62 − 5.9 9.72

Multiply. (Pages 98–99)

33.
49
×0.7
34.3

34.
56
×0.9
50.4

35.
582
×0.04
23.28

36.
4.6
×0.008
0.0368

37.
0.13
×0.0062
0.000806

38.
36.4
×0.06
2.184

39.
48.2
×1.03
49.646

40.
5.63
×2.17
12.2171

41.
9.47
×3.26
30.8722

42.
.387
×2.09
0.80883

Multiply. (Pages 102–103)

43. 4.7 × 10 47

44. 5.86 × 10 58.6

45. 347.8 × 10 3478

46. 9.732 × 10 97.32

47. 0.23 × 100 23

48. 48.3 × 100 4830

49. 5.76 × 100 576

50. 578.2 × 100 57820

51. 0.8 × 1000 800

52. 1.9 × 1000 1900

53. 42.8 × 1000 42800

54. 3.266 × 1000 3266

Applications The use of these word problems depends on which applications were studied.

55. A stereo receiver sells for $299. It can also be purchased by paying $30 a month for 12 months. Find the cost of credit. (Page 100)
$61

56. A foreman in a radio factory estimates that 0.01 of the 4600 transistors produced each day are defective. About how many are defective? (Page 103) 46

REVIEW OF RELATED SKILLS FOR CHAPTER 6

We suggest that some or all of this page be reviewed before proceeding with the chapter.

Multiply.   (Pages 32–33, 36–37)

1. 27	**2.** 46	**3.** 802	**4.** 405	**5.** 753	**6.** 889
×31	×59	× 21	× 57	×402	×508
837	2714	16842	23085	302706	451612

Divide.   (Pages 50–51, 54–55)

7. 7)238 34 228   **8.** 6)156 26 66   **9.** 57)3876 68   **10.** 29)1073 37 89   **11.** 151)52548 348

12. 437)99636   **13.** 23)1518   **14.** 56)4984   **15.** 9)4716 524   **16.** 8)5928 741

Multiply each number by 10.   (Pages 102–103)

17. 0.3 3   **18.** 0.9 9   **19.** 2.19 21.9   **20.** 6.21 62.1   **21.** 0.013 0.13   **22.** 0.286 2.86

23. 3.1 31   **24.** 8.7 87   **25.** 0.017 0.17   **26.** 0.574 5.74   **27.** 4.89 48.9   **28.** 6.38 63.8

Multiply each number by 100.   (Pages 102–103)

29. 0.34 34   **30.** 7.72 772   **31.** 3.76 376   **32.** 0.489 48.9   **33.** 4.3 430   **34.** 0.8 80

35. 0.17 17   **36.** 0.29 29   **37.** 8.602 860.2   **38.** 6.908 690.8   **39.** 7.1 710   **40.** 8.9 890

Multiply each number by 1000.   (Pages 102–103)

41. 6.809 6809   **42.** 4.393 4393   **43.** 84.7 84700   **44.** 68.3 68300   **45.** 5.08 5080   **46.** 2.95 2950

47. 39.96 39960   **48.** 51.905 51905   **49.** 2.8 2800   **50.** 16.49 16490   **51.** 25.031 25031   **52.** 7.3 7300

Multiply.   (Pages 102–103)

53. 0.3 × 0.1 0.03   **54.** 1.7 × 0.1 0.17   **55.** 36.1 × 0.1 3.61   **56.** 234.3 × 0.1 23.43

57. 0.3 × 0.01 0.003   **58.** 4.5 × 0.01 0.045   **59.** 613.4 × 0.01 6.134   **60.** 11.9 × 0.01 0.119

61. 7.2 × 0.001 0.0072   **62.** 0.3 × 0.001 0.0003   **63.** 334.5 × 0.001 0.3345   **64.** 48.2 × 0.001 0.0482

Round to the nearest ten.   (Pages 17–19)

65. 57 60   **66.** 8 10   **67.** 66 70   **68.** 23 20   **69.** 225 230   **70.** 4115 4120

Round to the nearest hundred.   (Pages 17–19)

71. 87 100   **72.** 125 100   **73.** 253 300   **74.** 327 300   **75.** 8255 8300   **76.** 7488 7500

Round to the nearest thousand.   (Pages 17–19)

77. 8513 9000   **78.** 978 1000   **79.** 6266 6000   **80.** 5499 5000   **81.** 2323 2000   **82.** 8580 9000

Give the place value of the "6" in each number.   (Pages 90–91)

83. 46.81 6 ones   **84.** 63.28 6 tens   **85.** 83.67 6 tenths   **86.** 71.062 6 hundredths   **87.** 1.076 6 thousandths   **88.** 8.1546 6 ten-thousandths

Give the place value of the "8" in each number.

89. 0.8 8 tenths   **90.** 800.3 8 hundreds   **91.** 57.98 8 hundredths   **92.** 18.8 8 ones   **93.** 0.008 8 thousandths   **94.** 1.0508 8 ten-thousandths

CHAPTER

6 DECIMALS DIVISION

SKILLS

6-1   Dividing a Decimal by a
       Whole Number
6-2   Dividing by a Decimal
6-3   Dividing by 10, by 100, by 1000
6-4   Rounding Decimals
6-5   Division with Remainders
6-6   Estimation

APPLICATIONS

Rate
Heating Costs
Comparison Shopping

CAREER

Insurance

6-1 Dividing a Decimal by a Whole Number

See the Teacher's Manual for the objectives.

To divide a decimal by a whole number, follow this procedure.

PROCEDURE   To divide a decimal by a whole number (not zero):

1. Place the decimal point in the quotient directly above the decimal point in the dividend.

2. Divide as with whole numbers.

EXAMPLE 1   Divide 133.11 by 87. Check your answer.

Solution:
1. Place the decimal point in the quotient. $87 \overline{)133.11}$

2. Divide as with whole numbers.

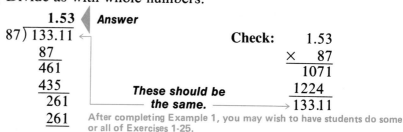

Sometimes you have to write zeros in the quotient.

EXAMPLE 2   Divide 3.298 by 194.

Solution:

1. $194 \overline{)3.298}$ quotient 0.   Since 3 is not divisible by 194, write a 0 above the 3.

$194 \overline{)3.298}$ quotient 0.0   Since 32 is not divisible by 194, write a 0 above the 2.

2.
```
      0.017  ◄ Answer
194 ) 3.298
      194
      1358
      1358
```
The check is left for you.

REVIEW OF RELATED SKILLS   You may wish to use these exercises before teaching the lesson.

Multiply.   (Pages 32–33, 36–37)

1. 42 × 13 546   2. 391 × 26 10,166   3. 208 × 76 15,808   4. 279 × 506 141,174   5. 404 × 168 67,872

Divide.   (Pages 50–51, 54–55)

6. $7 \overline{)91}$ 13   7. $8 \overline{)824}$ 103   8. $89 \overline{)4717}$ 53   9. $123 \overline{)5658}$ 46   10. $584 \overline{)62488}$ 107

EXERCISES

See the suggested assignment guide in the Teacher's Manual.

Divide. Check your answers. (Example 1)

1. 6)$\overline{20.88}$ (3.48) **2.** 3)$\overline{7.23}$ (2.41) **3.** 5)$\overline{3.580}$ (0.716) **4.** 7)$\overline{43.96}$ (6.28) **5.** 26)$\overline{35.88}$ (1.38)

6. 17)$\overline{59.67}$ (3.51) **7.** 31)$\overline{25.637}$ (0.827) **8.** 93)$\overline{191.58}$ (2.06) **9.** 42)$\overline{49.56}$ (1.18) **10.** 86)$\overline{474.72}$ (5.52)

11. 49)$\overline{165.13}$ (3.37) **12.** 23)$\overline{8.28}$ (0.36) **13.** 44)$\overline{40.656}$ (0.924) **14.** 82)$\overline{33.62}$ (0.41) **15.** 986)$\overline{5324.4}$ (5.4)

16. 705)$\overline{380.70}$ (0.54) **17.** 677)$\overline{798.86}$ (1.18) **18.** 215)$\overline{451.5}$ (2.1) **19.** 624)$\overline{4804.8}$ (7.7) **20.** 885)$\overline{5221.5}$ (5.9)

21. 411)$\overline{2301.6}$ (5.6) **22.** 191)$\overline{349.53}$ (1.83) **23.** 182)$\overline{43.68}$ (0.24) **24.** 348)$\overline{87.348}$ (0.251) **25.** 306)$\overline{96.696}$ (0.316)

(Example 2)

26. 8)$\overline{0.4544}$ (0.0568) **27.** 6)$\overline{0.5886}$ (0.0981) **28.** 4)$\overline{0.232}$ (0.058) **29.** 9)$\overline{0.585}$ (0.065) **30.** 65)$\overline{3.185}$ (0.049)

31. 43)$\overline{2.236}$ (0.052) **32.** 37)$\overline{3.182}$ (0.086) **33.** 21)$\overline{0.462}$ (0.022) **34.** 83)$\overline{4.98}$ (0.06) **35.** 66)$\overline{2.442}$ (0.037)

36. 98)$\overline{5.88}$ (0.06) **37.** 73)$\overline{3.869}$ (0.053) **38.** 414)$\overline{33.948}$ (0.082) **39.** 824)$\overline{32.96}$ (0.04) **40.** 260)$\overline{15.60}$ (0.06)

41. 604)$\overline{8.456}$ (0.014) **42.** 188)$\overline{9.212}$ (0.049) **43.** 428)$\overline{14.124}$ (0.033) **44.** 369)$\overline{13.284}$ (0.036) **45.** 524)$\overline{18.864}$ (0.036)

46. 125)$\overline{3.75}$ (0.03) **47.** 321)$\overline{24.075}$ (0.075) **48.** 643)$\overline{55.298}$ (0.086) **49.** 703)$\overline{54.131}$ (0.077) **50.** 816)$\overline{26.928}$ (0.033)

Mixed Practice The Mixed Practice contains exercises that relate to both Examples 1 and 2.

51. 6)$\overline{17.04}$ (2.84) **52.** 4)$\overline{22.12}$ (5.53) **53.** 36)$\overline{1.7712}$ (0.0492) **54.** 56)$\overline{4.2448}$ (0.0758) **55.** 461)$\overline{299.65}$ (0.65)

56. 832)$\overline{307.84}$ (0.37) **57.** 305)$\overline{14.945}$ (0.049) **58.** 293)$\overline{22.854}$ (0.078) **59.** 65)$\overline{35.035}$ (0.539) **60.** 47)$\overline{4.2488}$ (0.0904)

61. 3)$\overline{0.0585}$ (0.0195) **62.** 8)$\overline{0.4168}$ (0.0521) **63.** 7)$\overline{27.307}$ (3.901) **64.** 9)$\overline{55.836}$ (6.204) **65.** 684)$\overline{124.488}$ (0.182)

66. 63)$\overline{154.35}$ (2.45) **67.** 12)$\overline{75.84}$ (6.32) **68.** 245)$\overline{759.5}$ (3.1) **69.** 29)$\overline{42.63}$ (1.47) **70.** 52)$\overline{29.12}$ (0.56)

71. 9)$\overline{18.765}$ (2.085) **72.** 35)$\overline{71.75}$ (2.05) **73.** 78)$\overline{1.092}$ (.014) **74.** 316)$\overline{25.28}$ (0.08) **75.** 172)$\overline{517.72}$ (3.01)

APPLICATIONS: Using Division These are one-step problems that most students should be able to handle.

76. Five pounds of ground nutmeg cost $63.45. Find the cost of one pound? $12.69

77. Twenty kilograms of dill cost $185.80. Find the cost of one kilogram. $9.29

78. 17 ounces of paprika cost $1.87. Find the cost of 45 ounces. $4.95

79. Eight ounces of caraway seeds cost $10.32. Find the cost of 12 ounces. $15.48

80. 225 grams of sage cost $4.50. Find the cost of 375 grams. $7.50

81. Three ounces of onion salt cost $1.89. Find the cost of 16 ounces. $10.08

82. Twenty-five kilograms of vanilla beans costs $214.25. Find the cost of 450 kilograms. $3856.50

6-2 Dividing by a Decimal

See the Teacher's Manual for the objectives.

The first step in dividing by a decimal is to multiply both the divisor and the dividend by the <u>same</u> number in order to obtain a whole–number divisor.

PROCEDURE   To divide by a decimal:

1. Multiply both the divisor and the dividend by 10, or by 100, or by 1000, and so on, to obtain a whole number divisor.
2. Divide.

EXAMPLE 1   Divide 326.986 by 0.89. Check your answer.

Solution: 1. Since the divisor is 89 <u>hundredths</u>, multiply the divisor and the dividend by <u>100</u>.

$$0.89 \overline{\smash{)}326.98\,6}$$

Move the decimal point two places to the right.

$$
\begin{array}{r}
367.4 \\
2.\ 89\overline{\smash{)}32698.6} \\
\underline{267} \\
599 \\
\underline{534} \\
658 \\
\underline{623} \\
356 \\
\underline{356}
\end{array}
$$

Check:

$$
\begin{array}{r}
367.4 \\
\times\ 0.89 \\
\hline
33066 \\
29392 \\
\hline
326.986
\end{array}
$$

After completing Example 1, you may wish to have students do some or all of Exercises 1-8 and 21-36.

Sometimes you have to annex zeros to the dividend. You can annex as many <u>final zeros after the decimal point</u> as you need.

EXAMPLE 2   Divide: **a.** $62.5 \div 0.25$ **b.** $1.2 \div 4.8$

Solutions:

a. 1. $0.25 \overline{\smash{)}62.50}$ **Annex one zero.**

$$
\begin{array}{r}
250 \\
2.\ 25\overline{\smash{)}6250} \\
\underline{50} \\
125 \\
\underline{125} \\
00 \\
\underline{00}
\end{array}
$$

    Answer: **250**

b. 1. $4.8 \overline{\smash{)}1.2}$

$$
\begin{array}{r}
0.25 \\
2.\ 48\overline{\smash{)}12.00} \\
\underline{9\ 6} \\
2\ 40 \\
\underline{2\ 40}
\end{array}
$$

  Annex two zeros.

    Answer: **0.25**

The checks are left for you.

Multiply each number by 10.   (Pages 102–103)

1. 0.5 ⁵   **2.** 1.67 ¹⁶·⁷   **3.** 20.458 ²⁰⁴·⁵⁸ **4.** 15 ¹⁵⁰   **5.** 0.09 ⁰·⁹   **6.** 1.405 ¹⁴·⁰⁵

Multiply each number by 100.   (Pages 102–103)

7. 0.17 ¹⁷   **8.** 0.05 ⁵   **9.** 7.309 ⁷³⁰·⁹ **10.** 21.6 ²¹⁶⁰ **11.** 0.8 ⁸⁰   **12.** 4.665 ⁴⁶⁶·⁵

Multiply each number by 1000.   (Pages 102–103)

13. 5.612 ⁵⁶¹² **14.** 21.009 ²¹⁰⁰⁹ **15.** 9.73 ⁹⁷³⁰   **16.** 0.08 ⁸⁰   **17.** 5.1 ⁵¹⁰⁰ **18.** 5.652 ⁵⁶⁵²

EXERCISES

See the suggested assignment guide in the Teacher's Manual.

Multiply the divisor and the dividend by 10, or by 100, or by 1000, to make the divisor a whole number.   (Example 1, Step 1) 2. 48)006.2   3. 5)261.5

1. 0.32)8.96 ³²⁾⁸⁹⁶   **2.** 0.48)0.062   **3.** 0.5)26.15   **4.** 7.5)2.25 ⁷⁵⁾²²·⁵

5. 3.224)0.1863   **6.** 0.961)3.8840   **7.** 0.432)7.2295   **8.** 4.2)2.8813 ⁴²⁾²⁸·⁸¹³
    ³²²⁴⁾⁰¹⁸⁶·³   ⁹⁶¹⁾³⁸⁸⁴·⁰   ⁴³²⁾⁷²²⁹·⁵
(Example 2, Step 1)

9. 0.12)2.4 ¹²⁾²⁴⁰   **10.** 0.45)3.5 ⁴⁵⁾³⁵⁰ **11.** 0.7)28 ⁷⁾²⁸⁰   **12.** 0.5)25 ⁵⁾²⁵⁰

13. 0.485)13.58   **14.** 0.36)7.2 ³⁶⁾⁷²⁰ **15.** 7.28)254.8   **16.** 11.4)6874.2 ¹¹⁴⁾⁶⁸⁷⁴²

17. 0.095)58.9   **18.** 0.224)5.6   **19.** 0.09)8.1 ⁹⁾⁸¹⁰   **20.** 0.64)2.5 ⁶⁴⁾²⁵⁰

Mixed Practice   13. 485)13580   15. 728)25480   17. 95)58900   18. 224)5600

21. 0.4)3.76 ⁹·⁴   **22.** 0.8)0.496 ⁰·⁶²   **23.** 5.6)43.68 ⁷·⁸   **24.** 5.5)153.45 ²⁷·⁹

25. 0.75)0.225 ⁰·³   **26.** 2.20)1.342 ⁰·⁶¹   **27.** 4.38)1.1388 ⁰·²⁶   **28.** 0.714)27.132 ³⁸·

29. 0.09)14.31 ¹⁵⁹·   **30.** 0.11)94.82 ⁸⁶²·   **31.** 0.704)3.5904 ⁵·¹   **32.** 0.013)0.1482 ¹¹·⁴

33. 0.23)10.488 ⁴⁵·⁶   **34.** 2.6)1.066 ⁰·⁴¹   **35.** 4.3)2.365 ⁰·⁵⁵   **36.** 3.48)1.0092 ⁰·²⁹

37. 0.154)69.3 ⁴⁵⁰·   **38.** 0.004)14.68 ³⁶⁷⁰   **39.** 0.73)664.3 ⁹¹⁰·   **40.** 0.43)881.5 ²⁰⁵⁰·

41. 0.433)2294.9 ⁵³⁰⁰·   **42.** 0.08)20.4 ²⁵⁵·   **43.** 0.12)4.2 ³⁵·   **44.** 0.055)42.9 ⁷⁸⁰·

45. 78.5)2355 ³⁰·   **46.** 8.2)328 ⁴⁰·   **47.** 0.68)30.6 ⁴⁵·   **48.** 0.98)264.6 ²⁷⁰·

49. 0.68)61.2 ⁹⁰·   **50.** 0.7)238 ³⁴⁰·   **51.** 0.9)657 ⁷³⁰·   **52.** 18.2)5096 ²⁸⁰·

53. 0.7)20.02 ²⁸·⁶   **54.** 0.56)511.84 ⁹¹⁴·   **55.** 0.25)16.5 ⁶⁶·   **56.** 0.004)21.88 ⁵⁴⁷⁰·

57. 0.16)57.12 ³⁵⁷·   **58.** 0.38)2682.8 ⁷⁰⁶⁰·   **59.** 0.93)1441.5 ¹⁵⁵⁰·   **60.** 0.006)5340.6 ⁸⁹⁰¹⁰⁰·

61. 8.1)5070.6 ⁶²⁶·   **62.** 0.708)38.232 ⁵⁴·   **63.** 0.05)9.15 ¹⁸³·   **64.** 0.211)700.52 ³³²⁰·

65. 4.92)14.5632 ²·⁹⁶   **66.** 0.03)121.71 ⁴⁰⁵⁷·   **67.** 0.044)36.74 ⁸³⁵·   **68.** 0.36)205.632 ⁵⁷¹·²

Problem Solving and Applications

Rate

You can use the following rule to find rate, or speed.

Rate = Distance ÷ Time

This table shows some units that are used in measuring distance, time, and rate.

Distance	Time	Rate
miles	hours	miles per hour
feet	seconds	feet per second
kilometers	hours	kilometers per hour
meters	seconds	meters per second

EXAMPLE 1 A cheetah was timed running 91.64 meters in 2.9 seconds. Find the cheetah's average speed in meters per second.

Solution: Distance: 91.64 meters   Time: 2.9 seconds   Rate: __?__

Rate = 91.64 ÷ 2.9 ◀ *Rate = Distance ÷ Time*
= **31.6**

The cheetah's average speed was **31.6 meters per second.**

You use the same rule to find the rate in miles per hour.

EXAMPLE 2 In 1932, Amelia Earhart Putnam flew her plane from Newfoundland to Ireland in 14.9 hours. The distance covered was 2024.91 miles. Find her average speed in miles per hour.

Solution: Distance: 2024.91 miles   Time: 14.9 hours   Rate: __?__

Rate = 2024.91 ÷ 14.9 ◀ *Rate = Distance ÷ Time*
= **135.9**

The average speed was **135.9 miles per hour.**

Exercises
Note that Exercises 1-8 are non-verbal.

For Exercises 1–8, find the rate.

1. Distance: 280 kilometers
   Time: 3.5 hours 80 kilometers per hour

2. Distance: 120 kilometers
   Time: 1.6 hours 75 kilometers per hour

3. Distance: 187.5 miles
   Time: 3.75 hours 50 kilometers per hour

4. Distance: 278.25 miles
   Time: 5.25 hours 53 kilometers per hour

On December 3, 1980, Janice Brown made the first solar–powered flight in the Solar Challenger.

5. Distance: 45,000 meters
   Time: 4.5 seconds   10,000 meters per second

6. Distance: 800 meters
   Time: 1.25 minutes   640 meters per minute

7. Distance: 6105 feet
   Time: 5.5 seconds   1,110 feet per second

8. Distance: 63,504 feet
   Time: 6.3 seconds   10,080 feet per second

Solve each problem.   Exercises 9-14 are one-step word problems that involve using a formula.

9. On December 3, 1980, Janice Brown made the first solar–powered flight. The flight lasted 20 minutes and covered 6 miles. Find the rate in miles per minute.   0.3 miles per minute

10. In a cross–country skiing race, a record was set by the competitor who travelled 15 kilometers in 1.25 hours. Find the rate in kilometers per hour.   12 kilometers per hour

11. At a point in Lake Superior, it takes sound waves 0.27 seconds to reach the bottom of the lake. The depth of the lake at this point is 394.2 meters. Find the speed of the sound waves in meters per second.   1460 meters per second

12. On a certain day, it takes light from the moon 1.2 seconds to reach the earth. The distance from the moon to the earth is 360,000,000 meters. Find the speed of light in meters per second.
    300,000,000 meters per second

13. A radio wave travels 30,000 meters in 0.0001 seconds. What is the average speed of the wave in meters per second?   300,000,000 meters per second

14. In 1927, Charles Lindberg flew the *Spirit of St. Louis* from New York to Paris, a distance of about 3611.3 miles in 33.5 hours. Find his average rate in miles per hour.
    107.8 miles per hour

Application

6-3 Dividing by 10, by 100, by 1000 See the Teacher's Manual for the objectives.

You can divide by 10, by 100, by 1000, and so on, simply by moving the decimal point to the left.

PROCEDURE   To divide a decimal   by 10, by 100, or by 1000:

> ↓   ↓   ↓

1. Move the decimal point in the dividend one,   two,   or   three places to the left.

2. When necessary, insert zeros in order to have the correct number of decimal places.

EXAMPLE 1   Divide: **a.** $13.6 \div 10$ **b.** $10\overline{)4.96}$

c. $100\overline{)4.32}$ **d.** $6.9 \div 1000$

Solutions:

a. $13.6 \div 10 = 13.6$
$= 1.36$

b. $10\overline{)4.96} = 4.96$
$= 0.496$

c. $100\overline{)4.32} = 04.32$ ◀ *Insert one zero.*
$= 0.0432$

d. $6.9 \div 1000 = 006.9$ ◀ *Insert two zeros.*
$= 0.0069$

After completing Example 1, you may wish to have students do some or all of Exercises 1-24.

You can divide by 0.1, by 0.01, by 0.001 and so on, simply by moving the decimal point to the right.

PROCEDURE   To divide a decimal   by 0.1, by 0.01, or by 0.001:

> ↓   ↓   ↓

1. Move the decimal point in the dividend one,   two,   or   three places to the right.

2. When necessary, annex zeros in order to have the correct number of decimal places.

EXAMPLE 2   Divide: **a.** $0.1\overline{)1.36}$ **b.** $8.94 \div 0.01$

c. $43.2 \div 0.01$ **d.** $0.001\overline{)6.8}$

Solutions:

a. $0.1\overline{)1.36} = 1.36$

$= 13.6$

b. $8.94 \div 0.01 = 8.94$

$= 894$

c. $43.2 \div 0.01 = 43.20$ ◀ *Annex one zero.*

$= 4320$

d. $0.001\overline{)6.8} = 6.800$ ◀ *Annex two zeros.*

$= 6800$

You may wish to use these exercises before
teaching the lesson.

Multiply. (Pages 102–103)

1. 0.5×0.1 0.05 **2.** 1.3×0.1 0.13 **3.** 23.2×0.1 2.32 **4.** 156.1×0.1 15.61

5. 0.5×0.01 0.005 **6.** 3.7×0.01 0.037 **7.** 362×0.01 3.62 **8.** 75.5×0.01 0.755

9. 9.4×0.001 0.0094 **10.** 0.5×0.001 0.0005 **11.** 124.8×0.001 0.1248 **12.** 39.2×0.001 0.0392

EXERCISES

See the suggested assignment guide in the Teacher's Manual.

Divide by moving the decimal point one, two, or three places to the left. (Example 1)

1. $15.8 \div 10$ 1.58 **2.** $174.5 \div 10$ 17.45 **3.** $383.15 \div 100$ 3.8315 **4.** $49.72 \div 100$ 0.4972

5. $1000 \overline{)46.8}$ 0.0468 **6.** $1000 \overline{)6.1}$ 0.0061 **7.** $10 \overline{)0.06}$ 0.006 **8.** $10 \overline{)60.05}$ 6.005

9. $1000 \overline{)0.9}$ 0.0009 **10.** $3.2 \div 1000$ 0.0032 **11.** $100 \overline{)11.5}$ 0.115 **12.** $0.36 \div 100$ 0.0036

13. $3.67 \div 100$ 0.0367 **14.** $0.48 \div 1000$ 0.00048 **15.** $1000 \overline{)11.62}$ 0.01162 **16.** $100 \overline{)58.25}$ 0.5825

17. $38.9 \div 10$ 3.89 **18.** $100 \overline{)0.35}$ 0.0035 **19.** $7.24 \div 100$ 0.0724 **20.** $10 \overline{)0.29}$ 0.029

21. $10 \overline{)0.73}$ 0.073 **22.** $10 \overline{)7.34}$ 0.734 **23.** $8.69 \div 1000$ 0.00869 **24.** $8.69 \div 100$ 0.0869

Divide by moving the decimal point one, two, or three places to the right. (Example 2)

25. $13.80 \div 0.1$ 138 **26.** $2.431 \div 0.1$ 24.31 **27.** $0.65 \div 0.01$ 65 **28.** $3.97 \div 0.01$ 397

29. $0.001 \overline{)9.65}$ 9650 **30.** $0.001 \overline{)14.93}$ 14,930 **31.** $0.01 \overline{)0.884}$ 88.4 **32.** $0.01 \overline{)3.418}$ 341.8

33. $58.2 \div 0.1$ 582 **34.** $0.1 \overline{)83.7}$ 837 **35.** $46.8 \div 0.001$ 46800 **36.** $0.001 \overline{)21.36}$ 21,360

37. $73.1 \div 0.1$ 731 **38.** $0.28 \div 0.1$ 2.8 **39.** $0.01 \overline{)0.275}$ 27.5 **40.** $0.01 \overline{)76.21}$ 7621

41. $11.32 \div 0.001$ **42.** $19.9 \div 0.001$ 19,900 **43.** $39 \div 0.01$ 3900 **44.** $761 \div 0.01$ 76,100

45. $0.1 \overline{)43.6}$ 436 **46.** $0.1 \overline{)0.98}$ 9.8 **47.** $0.001 \overline{)425}$ 425,000 **48.** $0.001 \overline{)83.7}$ 83,700

41. 11,320

Mixed Practice The Mixed Practice contains exercises that relate to both Examples 1 and 2.

Divide.

49. $17.21 \div 10$ 1.721 **50.** $18.36 \div 10$ 1.836 **51.** $17.46 \div 0.1$ 174.6 **52.** $19.38 \div 0.1$ 193.8

53. $0.001 \overline{)255.7}$ **54.** $0.001 \overline{)1433.7}$ **55.** $100 \overline{)9416}$ 94.16 **56.** $100 \overline{)8892}$ 88.92

57. $847.3 \div 1000$ **58.** $475.29 \div 1000$ **59.** $0.398 \div 0.001$ 398 **60.** $0.7453 \div 0.001$ 745.3

61. $0.1 \overline{)3}$ 30 **62.** $0.1 \overline{)7}$ 70 **63.** $1000 \overline{)18}$ 0.018 **64.** $1000 \overline{)75}$ 0.075

65. $19 \div 0.01$ 1900 **66.** $29 \div 0.01$ 2900 **67.** $756 \div 100$ 7.56 **68.** $389 \div 100$ 3.89

69. $10 \overline{)1936}$ 193.6 **70.** $10 \overline{)2149}$ 214.9 **71.** $0.1 \overline{)8.6}$ 86 **72.** $0.1 \overline{)7.5}$ 75

73. $432 \div 0.001$ 432,000 **74.** $100 \overline{)756.2}$ 7.562 **75.** $10 \overline{)95.2}$ 9.52 **76.** $49.3 \div 0.01$ 4930

53. 255,700 54. 1,433,700 57. 0.8473 58. 0.47529

Problem Solving and Applications

Heating Costs

See the Teacher's Manual for the objectives.
This lesson applies the skills presented in Section 6-3 and multiplication.

Natural gas for heating is measured in **cubic feet.**
The cost is given in cents per 100 cubic feet.

To find total heating costs, you must <u>first</u> answer
the question:

> "How many 100's are there in the
> number of cubic feet of gas used?"

This is the <u>hidden question</u> in the problem. Then
you can find the total cost.

EXAMPLE   Find the cost of 85,000 cubic feet of
natural gas at 35¢ per 100 cubic feet.

Solution: [1] Find the number of 100's in 85,000: $85,000 \div 100 = 850$

[2] Find the total cost.
$850 \times \$0.35 = \$297.50$ $\blacktriangleleft$ $\dfrac{Cubic\ Feet}{in\ 100's} \times \dfrac{Cost\ Per\ 100}{Cubic\ Feet} = \dfrac{Total}{Cost}$

The total cost is **$297.50.**

Exercises

Note that Exercises 1-12 are non-verbal.
These are two-step problems that involve division by 100 and multiplication.

For Exercises 1–6, suppose that natural gas costs 36¢ per 100 cubic feet.
Find the cost for each number of cubic feet.

1. 900	**2.** 2100	**3.** 3000	**4.** 10,000	**5.** 100,000	**6.** 87,000
$3.24	$7.56	$10.80	$36.00	$360.00	$313.20

For Exercises 7–12, suppose that natural gas costs 40¢ per 100 cubic feet.
Find the cost for each number of cubic feet.

7. 800	**8.** 1700	**9.** 48,000	**10.** 92,000	**11.** 276,000	**12.** 3,000,000
$3.20	$6.80	$192.00	$368.00	$1104.00	$12,000.00

13. One month, the Johnson's used
14,200 cubic feet of gas. They pay
42¢ for each 100 cubic feet of gas.
What was the total cost? $59.64

14. The Rodriguez family used 11,300
cubic feet of natural gas in March.
They pay 45¢ per 100 cubic feet
of gas. What was the total cost? $50.85

15. The Davis family used 36,600 cubic
feet of gas for heating last year.
They paid 43¢ per 100 cubic feet
of gas. What was the total cost? $157.38

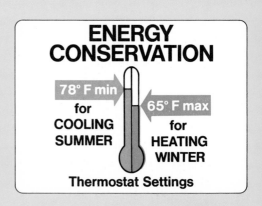

ENERGY CONSERVATION

78° F min for COOLING SUMMER

65° F max for HEATING WINTER

Thermostat Settings

INSURANCE

Career lessons are optional.
This lesson applies the skills presented in Section 6-3 and multiplication.

Underwriters or **insurance salespersons** help employers in setting up group life insurance plans for their employees. Usually the amount of insurance purchased for each employee is based on earnings (see the table at the right).

To find the cost per month, you <u>first</u> ask the question:

"How many thousands are there in the amount of insurance?"

This is the <u>hidden question</u> in the problem. Then you can find the cost.

Annual Earnings		
Over	But Not More Than	Insurance
$10,000	$12,000	$22,000
12,000	15,000	27,000
15,000	20,000	35,000
20,000	25,000	45,000
25,000	——	50,000

EXAMPLE

Tim Zok earns $24,000 per year. He pays $0.65 per month for each $1000 of group life insurance. How much does he pay per month?

Solution:

1 Use the table to find the amount of insurance.

Locate the interval that contains 24,000. Read the amount from the column directly to the right.

Over	But Not More Than	Insurance
20,000	25,000	45,000

2 Find the number of 1000's in 45,000: $45,000 \div 1000 = \textbf{45}$

3 Find the cost: $45 \times \$0.65 = \$29.25$ ◄ $\underset{\text{1000's}}{\text{Number of}} \times \underset{\$1000}{\text{Cost Per}} = \text{Cost}$

Tim pays **$29.25 per month.**

EXERCISES

These are three-step problems that involve reading a table, division by 1000, and multiplication.

Suppose that the employees of Topp Limited pay $0.65 per month for each $1000 of group life insurance. Use the table above to find the cost of insurance per month for each annual salary.

$14.30 $22.75 $29.25 $32.50

1. $11,000   **2.** $17,000   **3.** $22,000   **4.** $30,000   **5.** $15,000 $17.55

6. Dawn pays $0.65 per month per $1000 of life insurance. She is insured for $40,000. How much does she pay per month? $26.00

7. Jason is paying $0.60 per month per $1000 of life insurance. He is insured for $30,000. How much does he pay per month? $18.00

6-4 Rounding Decimals

See the Teacher's Manual for the objectives.

The procedure for rounding decimals is similar to that for rounding whole numbers.

PROCEDURE To round a decimal, look at the digit to the <u>right</u> of the place to which you are rounding.

1. If the digit is 5 or more, round <u>up</u>.

2. If the digit is less than 5, round <u>down</u>.

EXAMPLE
a. 7.8532 rounded to the nearest whole number is **8.**

b. 7.8352 rounded to the nearest tenth is **7.8.**

c. 7.8352 rounded to the nearest hundredth is **7.84.**

d. 7.8352 rounded to the nearest thousandth is **7.835.**

REVIEW OF RELATED SKILLS
You may wish to use these exercises before teaching the lesson.

Round to the nearest ten.   (Pages 17–19)

1. 23 20   **2.** 9 10   **3.** 55 60   **4.** 148 150   **5.** 1613 1610   **6.** 21,978 21,980

Round to the nearest hundred.   (Pages 17–19)

7. 95 100   **8.** 226 200   **9.** 582 600   **10.** 2651 2700   **11.** 5902 5900   **12.** 50,105 50,100

Round to the nearest thousand.   (Pages 17–19)

13. 5156 5000   **14.** 7231 7000   **15.** 4862 5000   **16.** 10,602 11,000   **17.** 52,526 53,000   **18.** 195,583 196,000

For Exercises 19–24, give the place value of the "9" in each number. (Pages 90–91)

19. 29.81   **20.** 28.19   **21.** 281.009   **22.** 2.98   **23.** 8.1539   **24.** 91.5

9 ones   9 hundredths   9 thousandths   9 tenths   9 ten-thousandths   9 tens

EXERCISES
See the suggested assignment guide in the Teacher's Manual.

Round to the nearest whole number.   (Example, a)

1. 9.2351 9   **2.** 73.058 73   **3.** 32.887 33   **4.** 192.81 193   **5.** 8.5469 9   **6.** 9.45 9

7. 4.9962 5   **8.** 52.618 53   **9.** 138.62 139   **10.** 9299.4 9299   **11.** 105.9 106   **12.** 1892.31 1892

Round to the nearest tenth.   (Example, b)

13. 3.1415 3.1   **14.** 86.449 86.4   **15.** 1.7729 1.8   **16.** 532.95 533.0   **17.** 1.4397 1.4   **18.** 8.439 8.4

19. 5.579 5.6   **20.** 0.0816 .1   **21.** 72.388 72.4   **22.** 31.3922 31.4   **23.** 5.55 5.6   **24.** 3.05 3.1

Round to the nearest hundredth.   (Example, c)

25. 34.509 _{34.51} **26.** 4.175 _{4.18} **27.** 4.8429 _{4.84} **28.** 0.84199 _{0.84} **29.** 0.0653 _{0.07} **30.** 32.549 _{32.55}

31. 421.165 _{421.17} **32.** 84.9569 _{84.96} **33.** 2.604 _{2.60} **34.** 319.905 _{319.91} **35.** 0.001 _{0.00} **36.** 12.005 _{12.01}

Round to the nearest thousandth.   (Example, d)

37. 5.3451 _{5.345} **38.** 4.6679 _{4.668} **39.** 77.2465 _{77.247} **40.** 20.4394 _{20.439} **41.** 38.0958 _{38.096} **42.** 5.9986 _{5.999}

43. 0.36054 _{0.361} **44.** 12.3109 _{12.311} **45.** 67.1302 _{67.130} **46.** 1.9645 _{1.965} **47.** 85.0081 _{85.008} **48.** 12.3012 _{12.301}

APPLICATIONS: Using Rounding   Most students should be able to do these applications.

For Exercises 49–52, round each decimal to the nearest whole number.

49. In 1975, Americans consumed 14.5 pounds of cheese per person. ₁₅

50. In 1975, Americans consumed 120.1 pounds of beef per person. ₁₂₀

51. In 1975, Americans consumed 17.8 pounds of apples per person. ₁₈

52. In 1975, Americans consumed 90.2 pounds of refined sugar per person. ₉₀

For Exercises 53–56, round each decimal to the nearest tenth.

53. An object dropped from the top of the Sears Building in Chicago would take 9.53 seconds to reach the ground. _{9.5}

54. An object dropped from the top of the Renaissance Center in Detroit would take 5.47 seconds to reach the ground. _{5.5}

55. An object dropped from the top of the torch of the Statue of Liberty would take 3.07 seconds to reach the ground. _{3.1}

56. An object dropped from the top of the Space Needle in Seattle would take 6.14 seconds to reach the ground. _{6.1}

Use the table below for Exercises 57–62. Round each decimal to the nearest hundredth.

POPULATION (IN MILLIONS)

City	1970	1976	1980
New York City	7.895	7.422	8.476
Chicago	3.369	3.074	3.447
Los Angeles	2.812	2.744	3.782
Philadelphia	1.950	1.797	1.751

57. What was the population of New York City in 1976? _{7.42 million}

58. What was the population of Los Angeles in 1980? _{3.78 million}

59. What was the population of Philadelphia in 1980? _{1.75 million}

60. What was the population of Philadelphia in 1970? _{1.95 million}

61. What was the population of Chicago in 1976? _{3.07 million}

62. What was the population of New York City in 1980? _{8.48 million}

6-5 Division with Remainders

See the Teacher's Manual for the objectives.

It is sometimes useful to round a quotient to a given decimal place.

PROCEDURE   To find a quotient to a given decimal place:

1. Carry the division to one additional decimal place.

2. Round the quotient to the given decimal place.

EXAMPLE 1   Divide 74.1 by 23. Round the quotient to the nearest tenth.

Solution: 1. Carry the division to hundredths.

$$
\begin{array}{r}
3.22 \\
23\overline{)74.10} \\
\underline{69} \\
51 \\
\underline{46} \\
50 \\
\underline{46} \\
4
\end{array}
$$

◀ **Annex one zero.**

2. Round the quotient.

3.22 rounded to the nearest <u>tenth</u> is **3.2.**

After completing Example 1, you may wish to have students do some or all of Exercises 1-20.

When rounding a quotient to the nearest hundredth, you carry out the division to thousandths.

EXAMPLE 2   Divide 4.8 by 5.4. Round the quotient to the nearest hundredth.

Solution: 1. Carry the division to thousandths.

$$
\begin{array}{r}
0.888 \\
5.4\overline{)4.8\,000} \\
\underline{43\,2} \\
4\,80 \\
\underline{4\,32} \\
480 \\
\underline{432} \\
48
\end{array}
$$

◀ **Annex three zeros.**

2. Round the quotient.

0.888 rounded to the nearest <u>hundredth</u> is **0.89.**

REVIEW OF RELATED SKILLS

You may wish to use these exercises before teaching the lesson.

Round each number to the nearest tenth.   (Pages 120–121)

1. 6.71 _6.7_   **2.** 0.905 _0.9_   **3.** 3.65 _3.7_   **4.** 0.7064 _0.7_   **5.** 73.113 _73.1_   **6.** 109.05 _109.1_

Round each number to the nearest hundredth.   (Pages 120–121)

7. 7.327 _7.33_   **8.** 4.932 _4.93_   **9.** 11.9852 _11.99_   **10.** 7.5016 _7.50_   **11.** 0.40895 _0.41_   **12.** 5.051 _5.05_

Round each number to the nearest thousandth.   (Pages 120–121)

13. 0.0069   **14.** 5.9801   **15.** 71.1135   **16.** 182.0073   **17.** 0.6355   **18.** 4.0005
    0.007   5.980   71.114   182.007   0.636   4.001

Divide.   (Pages 112–113)

19. 0.7)3.22 4.6   **20.** 0.7)49 70   **21.** 0.13)0.741 5.7   **22.** 4.08)0.816 0.2

23. 0.006)0.0588 9.8   **24.** 0.408)0.0816 0.2   **25.** 0.05)446 8920   **26.** 0.005)3 600

27. 0.09)81 900   **28.** 0.012)87.6 7300   **29.** 2.7)1.62 0.6   **30.** 0.03)0.063 2.1

EXERCISES

See the suggested assignment guide in the Teacher's Manual.

Divide. Round each quotient to the nearest tenth.   (Example 1)

1. 29)41.8 1.4   **2.** 18)93.9 5.2   **3.** 3.9)6.8 1.7   **4.** 24)71.4 3.0   **5.** 5.6)42.2 7.5

6. 6.7)46.7 7.0   **7.** 3)1.3 0.4   **8.** 51)74.5 1.5   **9.** 45)42.1 0.9   **10.** 0.83)527 634.9

11. 94)334.2 3.6   **12.** 6.6)59.1 9.0   **13.** 29)88.4 3.0   **14.** 35)28.5 0.8   **15.** 7.1)43.8 6.2

16. 0.58)34.1 58.8   **17.** 0.17)1.09 6.4   **18.** 1.6)38.56 24.1   **19.** 57)845.2 14.8   **20.** 1.08)200 185.2

Divide. Round each quotient to the nearest hundredth.   (Example 2)

21. 6.3)35.3 5.60   **22.** 41)22.65 0.55   **23.** 3.6)5.7 1.58   **24.** 5.8)16.56 2.86   **25.** 7.6)6.2 0.82

26. 7.3)4.35 0.60   **27.** 92)5.49 0.06   **28.** 34)221.44   **29.** 8.8)4.9 0.56   **30.** 0.11)2.45 22.27

31. 87)521.6 6.00   **32.** 2.6)64.37   **33.** 82)165.3 2.02   **34.** 0.66).46 0.70   **35.** 0.49)5.6 11.43

36. 2.8)8.24 2.94   **37.** 97)347 3.58   **38.** 24)8.16 0.34   **39.** 14.4)105.6 7.33   **40.** 5.4)0.48 0.09

28. 6.51   32. 24.76

APPLICATIONS: Using Division   These are one-step problems that most students should be able to handle.

For Exercises 41–43, round each answer to the nearest whole number.

41. A certain car travels 344 miles on a full tank of gasoline. The tank holds 13.2 gallons when full. How far can the car travel on one gallon? 26 miles

42. The fuel tank of a sports car holds 24.9 gallons when full. The car travels 254 miles on a full tank. How far can it travel on one gallon of fuel? 10 miles

43. A compact car travels 310 miles on a full tank of fuel. The fuel tank holds 17.2 gallons when full. How far can the car travel on one gallon of fuel? 18 miles

Problem Solving and Applications

See the Teacher's Manual for the objectives.
This lesson applies the skills presented in Section 6-5.

Comparison Shopping

Shoppers use <u>unit price</u> to compare the cost of different sizes of the same product. **Unit price** is the price per gram, per ounce, and so on. You can use this formula to find unit price.

Unit Price = Price of an Item ÷ Number of Units

EXAMPLE 1   The cost of this 12–ounce can of peaches is 91¢. Find the unit price. Round your answer to the nearest tenth of a cent.

Solution: Price: 91¢   Number of Units: 12 ounces
Unit Price: 91 ÷ 12

$$\begin{array}{r} 7.58 \\ 12\overline{)91.00} \end{array}$$ ◀ *Round to the nearest tenth.*

The unit price is **7.6¢.**

After completing Example 1, you may wish to have students do some or all of Exercises 1-15.

To find the <u>better buy</u>, shoppers compare the unit price of two or more sizes of the same product. The size with the lower unit price is the **better buy.** (This assumes that the items being compared are of the same quality.)

When the price of an item is one dollar or more, change the price to cents before dividing.

EXAMPLE 2   The cost of a 16–ounce can of peaches is $1.17.

a. Find the unit price. Round your answer to the nearest tenth of a cent.

b. Compare the unit price with the unit price in Example 1 to determine the better buy.

Solution: Price: $1.17   Number of Units: 16 ounces
Unit Price: 117 ÷ 16

$$\begin{array}{r} 7.31 \\ 16\overline{)117.00} \end{array}$$ ◀ *Round to the nearest tenth.*

a. The unit price is **7.3¢.**

b. The **16–ounce can** has the <u>lower</u> unit price. Therefore, it is the better buy.

Exercises

For Exercises 1–15, find the unit price. Round each answer to the nearest tenth of a cent.

	Price	Size		Price	Size		Price	Size
1.	29¢	4 ounces 7.3¢	**6.**	$1.19	4 bars 29.8¢	**11.**	$3.30	8 liters 41.3¢
2.	94¢	60 grams 1.6¢	**7.**	25¢	16 ounces 1.6¢	**12.**	53¢	3 liters 17.7¢
3.	81¢	20 ounces 4.1¢	**8.**	$4.00	30 pounds 13.3¢	**13.**	$1.96	5 kilograms 39.2¢
4.	42¢	400 grams 0.1¢	**9.**	$1.65	4 quarts 41.3¢	**14.**	$1.01	2 kilograms 50.5¢
5.	$1.01	3 bars 33.7¢	**10.**	93¢	2 liters 46.5¢	**15.**	81¢	250 milliliters 0.3¢

16. The price of a two–quart container of orange juice is $1.11. The price of a one–quart container is 60¢. Which is the better buy? Two-quart container

17. The price of an 18–ounce box of bread crumbs is 69¢. The price of a 40–ounce box is $1.44. Which is the better buy? 40-ounce box

18. The price of a 12–ounce tube of toothpaste is 85¢ and the price of a 20–ounce tube is $1.35. Which is the better buy? 20-ounce tube

19. Trash bags can be bought in boxes of 20 bags for $2.19 or in boxes of 8 bags for $1.02. Which is the better buy? Box of 20 bags

20. Muffins can be bought in boxes of 12 for 79¢ or in boxes of 6 for 43¢. Which is the better buy? Box of 12

21. The price of a 24–ounce container of coconut is $2.28, and the price of a 15–ounce container is $1.69. Which is the better buy? 24-ounce container

22. A brand of soap is selling at 3 bars for $1.00 and at 5 bars for $1.58. Which is the better buy? 5 bars for $1.50

6-6 Estimation

See the Teacher's Manual for the objectives.
This lesson may be considered optional for some students.

The rules for rounding decimals (see pages 120–121) can help you to estimate answers.

EXERCISES

See the suggested assignment guide in the Teacher's Manual.

Choose the best estimate. Choose a, b, or c.

1. $21.95 + $1.03 c   **a.** $21 + $1   **b.** $22 + $2   **c.** $22 + $1
2. $6.90 + $0.15 a   **a.** $7 + $0   **b.** $7 + $1   **c.** $6 + $0
3. $141.27 − $78.95 b   **a.** $142 − $75   **b.** $141 − $79   **c.** $141 − $70
4. $99.65 − $10.09 b   **a.** $95 − $10   **b.** $100 − $10   **c.** $99 − $11
5. 49.9 × 0.93 a   **a.** 50 × 1   **b.** 49 × 2   **c.** 40 × 1
6. 11.08 × 1.02 b   **a.** 12 × 2   **b.** 11 × 1   **c.** 11 × 2
7. 12.1 ÷ 5.9 a   **a.** 12 ÷ 6   **b.** 15 ÷ 5   **c.** 15 ÷ 6
8. 14.88 ÷ 3.01 c   **a.** 14 ÷ 2   **b.** 14 ÷ 4   **c.** 15 ÷ 3

Choose the best estimate. Choose a, b, c, or d.

9. 16.7 + 3.9 + 21.2 c   **a.** 40   **b.** 41   **c.** 42   **d.** 43
10. 9.1 + 8.6 + 11.9 a   **a.** 30   **b.** 29   **c.** 31   **d.** 28
11. 11.22 − 4.5 b   **a.** 7   **b.** 6   **c.** 5   **d.** 10
12. 22.7 − 19.8 b   **a.** 2   **b.** 3   **c.** 4   **d.** 1
13. 2.7 × 3.9 c   **a.** 9   **b.** 8   **c.** 12   **d.** 6
14. 1.3 × 10.5 d   **a.** 10   **b.** 22   **c.** 20   **d.** 11
15. 17.5 ÷ 6.3 c   **a.** 1   **b.** 4   **c.** 3   **d.** 2
16. 99.7 ÷ 24.6 d   **a.** 5   **b.** 3   **c.** 2   **d.** 4

APPLICATIONS: Using Estimation

The use of these word problems depends on which applications were studied.

17. In a speed–skating contest, an athlete skated 1800 meters in 3.3 minutes. Estimate the number of meters per minute. c
 a. 550   **b.** 450
 c. 600   **d.** 500

18. A train traveled a distance of 123.8 miles in 2 hours. Estimate the average speed in miles per hour. a
 a. 62   **b.** 40
 c. 53   **d.** 80

19. A certain brand of trash bags can be bought in boxes of 20 bags for $2.19. Estimate the cost of one trash bag. b
 a. 15¢   **b.** 10¢
 c. 9¢   **d.** 20¢

20. In a certain store the price of a four–quart container of milk is $2.39. Estimate the cost of one quart. b
 a. 75¢   **b.** 60¢
 c. 55¢   **d.** 70¢

21. At Timber Hardware, Jed paid
$3.10 for nails, $12.65 for paints,
and $4.17 for a hammer. The tax
was 61¢. Estimate the total bill. b
a. $10.00   b. $21.00
c. $23.00   d. $15.00

22. Gloria bought earrings for $10.75
and a bracelet for $25.30. She
gave the clerk a $50-bill. Estimate
the amount of change she should
receive. a
a. $14.00   b. $15.00
c. $12.00   d. $10.00

23. Estimate the total value of this
inventory. d

Item	Inventory	Unit Cost
Sandals	10	$18.20
Sport shoes	30	$39.95

a. $60.00   b. $1000.00
c. $1200.00   d. $1380.00

24. John Whiteagle bought a jacket for
$24.98 and 3 pairs of jeans at
$38.40 per pair. He gave the clerk
two $100-bills. Estimate the amount
of change he should receive. d
a. $145.00   b. $90.00
c. $100.00   d. $55.00

ORDER OF OPERATIONS

You can use the rules for order of operations and the calculator [M+]
and [MR] keys to solve problems with decimals.

EXAMPLE: $25.53 - 13 \times 0.89 = $ __?__

Solution: Estimated answer: $26 - 13 \times 1 = 26 - 13 = $ **13**

Actual answer:
    [=] [M+] | *11.57* |

 [−] [MR] [=]   [M] | *13.96* |

Since the estimate is 13, **13.96** is a reasonable answer.

EXERCISES

*First estimate each answer. Then use a calculator to find the exact
answer.*

Problem	Estimated Answer	Exact Answer
1. $23.91 - 14 \times 0.55$	? 10	? 16.21
2. $12.86 - 5 \times 1.35$	? 8	? 6.11
3. $57.9 - 18.1 + 14.6$	? 55	? 54.4
4. $138.56 - 14.89 - 38.11$	? 85	? 85.56
5. $2.8 \times 450 - 49.8$	? 130	? 1210.2

Chapter Review

Part 1: Vocabulary

For Exercises 1–6, choose from the box at the right the word(s) that completes each statement.

zeros
cubic
two
time
three
left
thousandths

1. When dividing by a decimal, it is sometimes necessary to annex __?__ to the dividend. (Page 112) *zeros*

2. Rate equals distance divided by __?__. (Page 114) *time*

3. To divide by 100, move the decimal point 2 places to the __?__. (Page 116) *left*

4. To divide by 0.01, move the decimal point __?__ places to the right. (Page 116) *two*

5. Natural gas for heating is measured in __?__ units. *cubic* (Page 118)

6. To find a quotient to the nearest hundredth, you first divide to the __?__ place. Then you round the quotient to the nearest hundredth. (Page 122) *thousandths*

Part 2: Skills

Divide. (Pages 110–111)

7. $7\overline{)86.8}$ *12.4*   8. $5\overline{)84.65}$ *16.93*   9. $24\overline{)11.712}$ *0.488*   10. $48\overline{)163.2}$ *3.4*   11. $6\overline{)0.5472}$ *0.0912*

12. $2\overline{)0.1544}$ *0.0772*   13. $36\overline{)1.7784}$ *0.0494*   14. $42\overline{)49.98}$ *1.19*   15. $144\overline{)113.76}$ *0.79*   16. $305\overline{)15.25}$ *0.05*

Multiply the divisor and the dividend by 10, or by 100, or by 1000, to make the divisor a whole number. (Pages 112–113)

17. $0.4\overline{)9.6}$ 18. $0.3\overline{)3.92}$ 19. $0.28\overline{)36.54}$ 20. $6.24\overline{)238.1}$

21. $3.86\overline{)36.9}$ 22. $0.046\overline{)9.2}$ 23. $1.63\overline{)462.4}$ 24. $1.056\overline{)285.9}$

Divide. (Pages 112–113)

25. $0.7\overline{)21.77}$ *31.1*   26. $0.8\overline{)0.504}$ *0.63*   27. $4.5\overline{)14.40}$ *3.2*   28. $0.12\overline{)5.4}$ *45.*

29. $4.38\overline{)22.776}$ *5.2*   30. $0.044\overline{)37.18}$ *845.*   31. $1.22\overline{)4.392}$ *3.6*   32. $0.63\overline{)0.0252}$ *0.04*

Divide. (Pages 116–117)

33. $16.2 \div 10$ *1.62*   34. $1.28 \div 0.1$ *12.8*   35. $73.64 \div 0.001$ *73,640*   36. $86.3 \div 1000$ *0.0863*

37. $28.6 \div 0.001$ *28,600*   38. $0.48 \div 10$ *0.048*   39. $6.21 \div 100$ *0.0621*   40. $14.85 \div 0.01$ *1485*

41. $0.1\overline{)0.75}$ *7.5*   42. $100\overline{)5.61}$ *0.0561*   43. $0.001\overline{)6.684}$ *6684*   44. $1000\overline{)762.81}$ *0.76281*

Round to the nearest whole number. (Pages 120–121)

45. 36.84 *37*   46. 9.63 *10*   47. 0.723 *1*   48. 899.7 *900* 49. 6.578 *7*   50. 186.94 *187*

Round to the nearest tenth. (Pages 120–121)

51. 2.856 *2.9*   52. 41.145 *41.1*   53. 5.968 *6.0*   54. 0.631 *0.6*   55. 83.453 *83.5* 56. 91.72 *91.8*

Round to the nearest hundredth. (Pages 120–121)

57. 36.609   **58.** 3.185   **59.** 0.9316   **60.** 46.249   **61.** 218.046   **62.** 1.997
      36.61   3.19   0.93   46.25   218.05   2.00

Round to the nearest thousandth. (Pages 120–121)

63. 4.3629   **64.** 91.8455   **65.** 0.0096   **66.** 25.0247   **67.** 2.81621   **68.** 42.04768
      4.363   91.846   0.010   25.025   2.816   42.048

Divide. Round each quotient to the nearest tenth. (Pages 122–123)

69. 31$\overline{)41.5}$ 1.3   **70.** 5.6$\overline{)8.683}$ 1.6   **71.** 0.56$\overline{)35.2}$ 62.9   **72.** 0.491$\overline{)1.95418}$ 4.0

Divide. Round each quotient to the nearest hundredth. (Pages 122–123)

73. 5.9$\overline{)16.59}$ 2.81   **74.** 7.3$\overline{)6.9}$ 0.95   **75.** 0.12$\overline{)3.81}$ 31.75   **76.** 28.8$\overline{)402.6}$ 13.98

Choose the best estimate. Choose a, b, c, or d. (Pages 126–127)

77. $32.99 + $2.15 b   **a.** $36   **b.** $35   **c.** $34   **d.** $37

78. 12.3 × 8.9 c   **a.** 117   **b.** 96   **c.** 108   **d.** 100

79. $268.14 − $7.99 d   **a.** $262   **b.** $261   **c.** $263   **d.** $260

80. $12.04 + $6.95 a   **a.** $19   **b.** $18   **c.** $20   **d.** $17

81. 17.85 ÷ 3.02 b   **a.** 7   **b.** 6   **c.** 8   **d.** 5

82. $49.95 − $10.05 d   **a.** $39   **b.** $42   **c.** $38   **d.** $40

83. 15.95 × 4.2 a   **a.** 64   **b.** 60   **c.** 70   **d.** 74

84. 88.2 ÷ 10.8 c   **a.** 10   **b.** 9   **c.** 8   **d.** 7

Part 3: Applications   The use of these word problems depends on which applications were studied.

85. Fifteen kilograms of ginger cost $139.95. Find the cost of one kilogram. (Pages 110–111) $9.33

86. Twenty pounds of coffee cost $51.80. Find the cost of one pound. (Pages 110–111) $2.59

87. In 1893, William Morrison built one of America's first electric automobiles. It could travel 50 miles in 2.5 hours. Find the speed of the automobile in miles per hour. (Pages 114–115) 20 mph

88. The O'Reilly family used 6500 cubic feet of gas in February. They pay 39¢ per 100 cubic feet of gas. What was their total cost for heating in February? (Page 118) $25.35

89. The price of a 12–ounce can of fruit is 51¢, and the price of an 8–ounce can is 38¢. Which is the better buy? (Pages 124–126) The 12-ounce can

An Early Electric Auto

Chapter Test

The Teacher's Resource Book contains two forms of each Chapter Test.

Divide.

1. $4\overline{)48.64}$ 12.16   **2.** $21\overline{)0.42}$ 0.02   **3.** $0.6\overline{)21.06}$ 35.1   **4.** $0.15\overline{)4.5}$ 30   **5.** $0.008\overline{)72}$ 9000

Divide.

6. $17.1 \div 100$
0.171

7. $0.367 \div 0.001$
367

8. $0.72 \div 10$
0.072

9. $1000\overline{)67.9}$
0.0679

10. $0.01\overline{)8.3}$
830

Round each number as indicated.

11. 7.83; to the nearest whole number 8   **12.** 81.839; to the nearest tenth 81.8

13. 29.645; to the nearest hundredth   29.65   **14.** 4.73416; to the nearest thousandth 4.734

15. 328.986; to the nearest tenth 329.0   **16.** 75.655; to the nearest whole number 76

Divide. Round each quotient to the decimal place indicated.

17. $0.3\overline{)6.483}$; to the nearest tenth   21.6   **18.** $0.14\overline{)0.3584}$; to the nearest tenth 2.6

19. $3.1\overline{)0.6293}$; to the nearest hundredth   0.20   **20.** $7\overline{)1.484}$; to the nearest hundredth   0.21

Solve. The use of these word problems depends on which applications were studied.

21. Five pounds of potatoes cost $1.95. Find the cost of one pound. $0.39

22. In a track meet, Chris ran 1845 meters in 4.5 minutes. Find the speed in meters per minute. 410 meters per minute

23. The price of a 6–ounce can of frozen orange juice is 35¢, and the price of a 10–ounce can is 49¢. Which is the better buy? The 10-ounce can

In Exercises 24–25, choose the best estimate. Choose a, b, c, or d.

24. The Gonzales family used 12,000 cubic feet of natural gas in January. They pay 41¢ per 100 cubic feet of gas. Estimate the total cost. d

a. $54   **b.** $40

c. $60   **d.** $48

25. Kerry traveled 3000 miles in 57.7 hours. Estimate her average driving speed in miles per hour. b

a. 45   **b.** 50

c. 40   **d.** 55

Additional Practice

You may wish to use some or all of these exercises depending on how well students performed on the formal chapter test.

Skills

Divide.   (Pages 110–111)

1. $26\overline{)61.36}$ 2.36 **2.** $32\overline{)52.80}$ 1.65 **3.** $6\overline{)141.6}$ 23.6 **4.** $8\overline{)285.6}$ 35.7 **5.** $234\overline{)16.146}$ 0.069

6. $196\overline{)6.272}$ 0.032 **7.** $68\overline{)4.216}$ 0.062 **8.** $89\overline{)5.963}$ 0.067 **9.** $54\overline{)126.90}$ 2.35 **10.** $43\overline{)185.76}$ 4.32

(Pages 112–113)

11. $0.8\overline{)4.16}$ 5.2 **12.** $0.6\overline{)2.88}$ 4.8 **13.** $0.7\overline{)66.5}$ 95 **14.** $0.4\overline{)2.492}$ 6.23

15. $0.23\overline{)0.989}$ 4.3 **16.** $1.56\overline{)4.524}$ 2.9 **17.** $2.36\overline{)4.484}$ 1.9 **18.** $0.59\overline{)3.717}$ 6.3

19. $0.72\overline{)453.6}$ 630 **20.** $0.03\overline{)14.4}$ 480 **21.** $0.423\overline{)249.57}$ 590 **22.** $0.561\overline{)527.34}$ 940

Divide.   (Pages 116–117)

23. $13.8 \div 10$ 1.38 **24.** $25.6 \div 100$ 0.256 **25.** $38.3 \div 1000$ 0.0383 **26.** $5.81 \div 0.1$ 58.1

27. $4.62 \div 0.001$ 4620 **28.** $38.7 \div 0.01$ 3870 **29.** $100\overline{)3.89}$ 0.0389 **30.** $0.01\overline{)14.7}$ 1470

Round to the nearest whole number.   (Pages 120–121)

31. 63.7 64 **32.** 48.54 49 **33.** 532.38 532 **34.** 91.45 91 **35.** 9.586 10 **36.** 12.63 13

Round to the nearest tenth.   (Pages 120–121)

37. 3.84 3.8 **38.** 16.923 16.9 **39.** 21.86 21.9 **40.** 4.953 5.0 **41.** 7.847 7.8 **42.** 2.321 2.3

Round to the nearest hundredth.   (Pages 120–121)

43. 4.637 4.64 **44.** 0.063 0.06 **45.** 43.046 43.05 **46.** 0.465 0.47 **47.** 3.421 3.42 **48.** 59.375 59.38

Round to the nearest thousandth.   (Pages 120–121)

49. 3.4622 3.462 **50.** 5.9837 5.984 **51.** 44.1006 44.101 **52.** 31.0005 31.001 **53.** 0.0369 0.037 **54.** 0.0041 0.004

Divide. Round the quotient to the nearest tenth.
(Pages 122–123)

55. $42\overline{)110.71}$ 2.6 **56.** $3.9\overline{)17.277}$ 4.4 **57.** $0.23\overline{)2.0608}$ 9.0 **58.** $0.49\overline{)58.2}$ 118.8

Divide. Round the quotient to the nearest hundredth.
(Pages 122–123)

59. $4.6\overline{)18.2}$ 3.96 **60.** $0.18\overline{)53.94}$ 299.67 **61.** $6.4\overline{)142.3}$ 22.23 **62.** $42.3\overline{)186.46}$ 4.41

Applications   The use of these word problems depends on which applications were studied.

63. In a 400 meter race, an athlete completed the course in 45.2 seconds. Find the rate in meters per second. Round your answer to the nearest tenth.   (Pages 114–115)
8.8 meters per second

64. The Ramirez family used 12,400 cubic feet of natural gas in January. They pay 45¢ per 100 cubic feet of gas. What was their total cost of heating in January?   (Page 118) $55.80

REVIEW OF RELATED SKILLS FOR CHAPTER 7

We suggest that some or all of this page be reviewed before proceeding with the chapter.

Round each number to the nearest ten.   (Pages 17–19)

1. 7 10   **2.** 3 0   **3.** 23 20   **4.** 19 20   **5.** 41 40   **6.** 58 60   **7.** 45 50

8. 65 70   **9.** 36 40   **10.** 79 80   **11.** 68 70   **12.** 97 100   **13.** 102 100   **14.** 213 210

15. 466 470   **16.** 558 560   **17.** 335 340   **18.** 675 680   **19.** 896 900   **20.** 399 400   **21.** 231 230

Round each decimal to the nearest whole number.   (Pages 120–121)

22. 8.3 8   **23.** 4.2 4   **24.** 9.6 10   **25.** 7.9 8   **26.** 5.5 6   **27.** 8.5 9

28. 21.3 21   **29.** 34.1 34   **30.** 16.9 17   **31.** 19.8 20   **32.** 42.9 43   **33.** 58.7 59

34. 23.5 24   **35.** 81.5 82   **36.** 64.8 65   **37.** 72.6 73   **38.** 31.4 31   **39.** 29.3 29

40. 100.6 101   **41.** 200.8 201   **42.** 322.4 322   **43.** 684.1 684   **44.** 309.5 310   **45.** 410.5 411

Add.   (Pages 2–3, 94–95)

46. $2 + 3 + 2 + 3$ 10   **47.** $4 + 8 + 4 + 8$ 24   **48.** $16 + 20 + 16 + 20$ 72

49. $49 + 31 + 49 + 31$ 160   **50.** $78 + 16 + 78 + 16$ 188   **51.** $53 + 17 + 53 + 17$ 140

52. $6.8 + 9.2 + 3.9$ 19.9   **53.** $4.5 + 7.8 + 6.1$ 18.4   **54.** $8.6 + 9.7 + 3.2$ 21.5

55. $5.3 + 7.2 + 9.9$ 22.4   **56.** $42.8 + 6.4 + 8$ 57.2   **57.** $15.9 + 7.8 + 6$ 29.7

58. $62.3 + 71.5 + 80.4$ 214.2   **59.** $48.9 + 19.3 + 20.1$ 88.3   **60.** $82.4 + 93.9 + 41.7$ 218

61. $74.8 + 92.3 + 14.6$ 181.7   **62.** $25.6 + 31.9 + 14.4$ 71.9   **63.** $63.9 + 80.5 + 16.2$ 160.6

Multiply.   (Pages 26–27, 32–33, 36–37)

64. 14×3 42   **65.** 21×9 189   **66.** 15×8 120   **67.** 17×9 153

68. 22×12 264   **69.** 11×13 143   **70.** 16×21 336   **71.** 14×18 252

72. 43×40 1720   **73.** 62×60 3720   **74.** 71×73 5183   **75.** 84×87 7308

(Pages 98–99)

76. 8.2×7.4 60.68   **77.** 9.3×6.9 64.17   **78.** 4.9×3.4 16.66   **79.** 6.5×8.3 53.95

80. 10.6×12.2 129.32   **81.** 13.1×14.5 189.95   **82.** 21.2×19.1 404.92   **83.** 17.6×11.3 198.88

Find each answer.   (Pages 62–63)

84. $27 \times 30 \div 2$ 405   **85.** $12 \times 14 \div 2$ 84   **86.** $40 \times 35 \div 2$ 700

87. $24 \times 20 \div 2$ 240   **88.** $16 \times 18 \div 2$ 144   **89.** $15 \times 16 \div 2$ 120

90. $4.2 \times 3.8 \div 2$ 7.98   **91.** $6.4 \times 5.9 \div 2$ 18.88   **92.** $2.8 \times 1.7 \div 2$ 2.38

93. $3.6 \times 3.9 \div 2$ 7.02   **94.** $20 \times 14.6 \div 2$ 146   **95.** $30 \times 15.1 \div 2$ 226.5

96. $21.2 \times 3.6 \div 2$ 38.16   **97.** $13.4 \times 8.9 \div 2$ 59.63   **98.** $17.8 \times 9.2 \div 2$ 81.88

99. $14.7 \times 9.3 \div 2$ 68.355   **100.** $21.4 \times 22.8 \div 2$ 243.96   **101.** $36.4 \times 28.9 \div 2$ 525.98

7 APPLYING METRIC MEASURES I

SKILLS/APPLICATIONS

7-1   Units of Length
7-2   Measurement
7-3   Perimeter and Applications
7-4   Area and Applications: Rectangles/Squares
7-5   Area and Applications: Parallelograms/Triangles
7-6   Area and Applications: Trapezoids

OTHER APPLICATIONS

Distance on a Map
Distance Formula
Floor Space

CAREER

Industry

7-1 Units of Length

This table shows the most commonly used units of length in the metric system.

One **millimeter** (abbreviated: **mm**) is about the thickness of a dime.

One **centimeter** (abbreviated: **cm**) is about the width of this paper clip.

One **meter** (abbreviated: **m**) is about the width of a door.

One **kilometer** (abbreviated: **km**) is about the length of ten football fields.

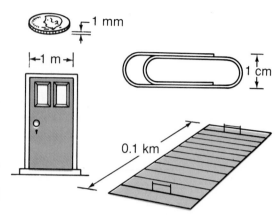

TABLE

PROCEDURE   To determine a suitable metric unit of length:

1 Compare with the measurements show in the table.

2 Choose a similar unit of length.

EXERCISES

Choose the most suitable measure. Choose a, b, or c.

1. The width of a quarter   a | **a.** 23 mm | **b.** 23 cm | **c.** 23 m
2. The length of a toothbrush   b | **a.** 8 mm | **b.** 16 cm | **c.** 1 m
3. The height of a doorknob from the floor.   b | **a.** 1 cm | **b.** 1 m | **c.** 1 km
4. The distance from Chicago to Los Angeles   c | **a.** 3400 cm | **b.** 3400 m | **c.** 3400 km
5. The width of a room   b | **a.** 8 cm | **b.** 8 m | **c.** 8 km
6. The length of a safety pin   a | **a.** 26 mm | **b.** 20 cm | **c.** 20 m
7. The width of a button   a | **a.** 20 mm | **b.** 20 cm | **c.** 20 m
8. The length of a dollar bill   b | **a.** 15.6 mm | **b.** 15.6 cm | **c.** 15.6 m
9. The width of a dollar bill   b | **a.** 6.6 mm | **b.** 6.6 cm | **c.** 6.6 m
10. The length of a ballpoint pen   b | **a.** 14 mm | **b.** 14 cm | **c.** 14 m
11. The length of a car   b | **a.** 3 cm | **b.** 3 m | **c.** 3 km
12. The height of a building   b | **a.** 10 cm | **b.** 10 m | **c.** 10 km
13. The thickness of this book   c | **a.** 2.4 m | **b.** 2.4 mm | **c.** 2.4 cm

Problem Solving and Applications

Distance on a Map

This map shows air distances in kilometers between some cities of the United States.

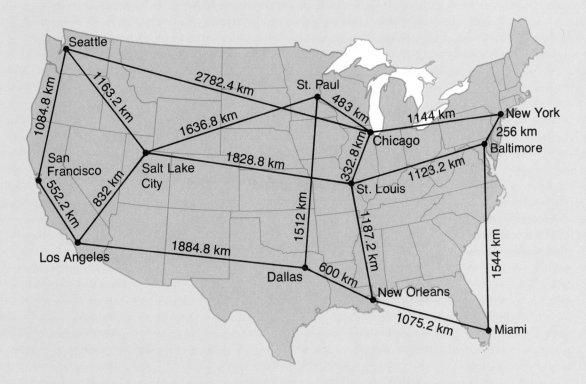

Exercises

For Exercises 1–8, use the air distances shown on the map.

1. How far is it from New York to Chicago? 1144 km

2. How far is it from St. Paul to Dallas? 1512 km

3. How far is it from Baltimore to New Orleans by way of Miami? 2619.2 km

4. How far is it from Baltimore to New Orleans by way of St. Louis? 2310.4 km

5. How far is it from New York to Los Angeles by way of Chicago, St. Louis, and Salt Lake City? 4137.6 km

6. How far is it from New York to Los Angeles by way of Baltimore, Miami, New Orleans, and Dallas? 5360 km

7. Which is the shorter route: Dallas to St. Paul to Chicago or Dallas to New Orleans to St. Louis to Chicago? Dallas to Saint Paul to Chicago How much shorter is it? 125 km shorter

8. Which is the shorter route: San Francisco to Los Angeles to Dallas to St. Paul or San Francisco to Los Angeles to Salt Lake City to St. Paul? How much shorter is it? 928 km shorter

8. San Francisco to Los Angeles to Salt Lake City to St. Paul

7-2 Measurement

See the Teacher's Manual for the objectives.

You measure the length of an object to the nearest meter, to the nearest centimeter, to the nearest millimeter, and so on. Measurements are <u>never</u> exact.

PROCEDURE To measure the length of an object to the nearest centimeter:

1. Determine the two centimeter measurements, one larger and one smaller, between which the length of the object lies.

2. Choose the closer measurement.

EXAMPLE Give the length of the arrowhead:
a. to the nearest centimeter

b. to the nearest millimeter.

Solutions: **a.**

The tip is closer to 6 cm than to 7 cm.

Length: **6 cm** (nearest centimeter)

b.

The tip is closer to 63 mm than to 64 mm.

Length: **63 mm** (nearest millimeter)

When you give a measurement to the nearest unit, you are actually **rounding** the measure.

REVIEW OF RELATED SKILLS

You may wish to use these exercises before teaching the lesson.

Round each number to the nearest ten.   (Pages 17–19)

1. 8 10   **2.** 15 20   **3.** 11 10   **4.** 19 20   **5.** 21 20   **6.** 57 60   **7.** 81 80   **8.** 97 100

9. 14 10   **10.** 46 50   **11.** 22 20   **12.** 88 90   **13.** 162 160   **14.** 171 170   **15.** 145 150   **16.** 228 230

Round each decimal to the nearest whole number.   (Pages 120–121)

17. 8.9 9   **18.** 5.3 5   **19.** 46.9 47   **20.** 33.7 34   **21.** 90.8 91   **22.** 68.7 69

23. 14.5 15   **24.** 75.5 76   **25.** 100.3 100   **26.** 126.2 126   **27.** 289.9 290   **28.** 305.1 305

EXERCISES

See the suggested assignment guide in the Teacher's Manual.

Measure the length of each object to the given measurement.

1. Nearest centimeter 2 cm **2.** Nearest centimeter 3 cm **3.** Nearest centimeter 3 cm

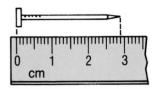

4. Nearest millimeter 30 mm **5.** Nearest millimeter 25 mm **6.** Nearest millimeter 18 mm

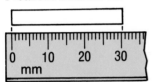
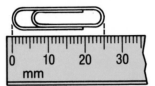
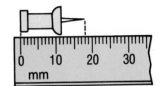

Measure each side of each figure. Give each measurment to the nearest millimeter. Use this information to answer the questions in the third column.

Figure	Measurements	Questions
7. Rectangle	side *a*: __?__ mm (36) side *b*: __?__ mm (15) side *c*: __?__ mm (36) side *d*: __?__ mm (15)	Does the length of side *a* equal the length of side *c*? Yes Does the length of side *b* equal the length of side *d*? Yes
8. Square	side *a*: __?__ mm (15) side *b*: __?__ mm (15) side *c*: __?__ mm (15) side *d*: __?__ mm (15)	Do the sides have equal lengths? Yes
9. Isosceles Triangle	side *a*: __?__ (25 mm) side *b*: __?__ mm (25) side *c*: __?__ (39 mm)	Are **two sides** of the isosceles triangle equal in length? Yes
10. Equilateral Triangle	side *a*: __?__ (21 mm) side *b*: __?__ mm (21) side *c*: __?__ mm (21)	Are all three sides of the equilateral triangle equal in length? Yes

career

Career lessons are optional.

Machinists make tools and metal parts for machines. Since all measurements are approximations, the size of each tool or part can vary by a certain amount. This amount is called the **tolerance.**

Measurement: 4.18 ± 0.05 centimeters

Tolerance: ±0.05 cm ◀ *Read: "Plus or minus 0.05 centimeters."*

EXAMPLE

The length of a rod is to be 4.18 ± 0.05 centimeters. Find the greatest and smallest acceptable lengths.

Solution:

The measurement 4.18 ± 0.05 means that the rod could be **as long as 4.18 + 0.05** centimeters or **as short as 4.18 − 0.05** centimeters.

Greatest acceptable length: 4.18 + 0.05 = **4.23 cm**

Smallest acceptable length: 4.18 − 0.05 = **4.13 cm**

The rod in the Example can be used if it is no longer than 4.23 centimeters and no shorter than 4.13 centimeters.

EXERCISES Note that Exercises 1-4 are non-verbal.

Complete the table.

Measurement	Tolerance	Greatest Acceptable Length	Smallest Acceptable Length
1. 3.25 ± 0.05 cm	±0.05 cm ?	? 3.30 cm	? 3.20 cm
2. 1.19 ± 0.05 cm	±0.05 ? cm	? 1.24 cm	? 1.14 cm
3. 6.437 ± 0.005 mm	±0.005 ? mm	? 6.442 mm	? 6.432 mm
4. 2.005 ± 0.001 cm	±0.001 ? cm	? 2.006 cm	? 2.004 cm

5. The width of a machine part is given as 4.062 ± 0.005 centimeters. Find the greatest and smallest acceptable widths. 4.067 cm, 4.057 cm

6. The width of an engine part is is given as 85.6 ± 0.5 millimeters. Find the greatest and smallest acceptable widths. 86.1 mm, 85.1 mm

7. A blueprint gives a measurement of 3.250 ± 0.005 centimeters. What are the greatest and smallest acceptable measurements? 3.255 cm, 3.245 cm

8. A blueprint gives a measurement of 3.625 ± 0.002 millimeters. What are the greatest and smallest acceptable measurements? 3.627 mm; 3.623 mm

Problem Solving and Applications

Distance See the Teacher's Manual for the objectives.

Sound travels in water at a rate of **1460 meters per second.** You can use the speed of sound in water and the following rule to find water depth.

Distance = Rate × Time

EXAMPLE At a point in Lake Tahoe in Nevada, it takes sound waves 0.33 seconds to reach the bottom of the lake. What is the depth at this point?

Lake Tahoe

Solution: Time: 0.33 seconds
Rate: 1460 meters per second   Distance: ___?___

Distance = 1460 × 0.33   **◀ Distance = Rate × Time**

= **481.8**   The depth is **481.8 meters.**

Exercises These exercises apply the technique of using a formula to solve word problems.

1. At a point in Crater Lake in Oregon, it takes sound waves 0.40 seconds to reach the bottom of the lake. What is the depth? 584 meters

2. At a point in Lake Champlain in Vermont, sound waves take 0.08 seconds to reach the bottom of the lake. What is the depth? 116.8 meters

3. At a point in Lake Erie, it takes sound waves 0.15 seconds to reach the bottom of the lake. Find the depth at this point. 219 meters

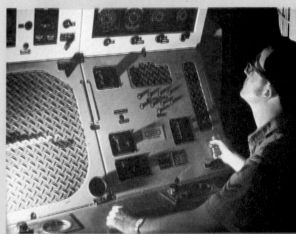

4. The deepest point in the Atlantic Ocean is called the Milwaukee Deep. It takes 5.92 seconds for sound waves to reach the bottom at this point. Find the depth. 8643.2 meters

5. The deepest point in the Pacific Ocean is called the Challenger Deep. It takes 7.55 seconds for sound waves to reach the bottom at this point. Find the depth. 11,023 meters

Sonar Technician at Work

7-3 Perimeter and Applications

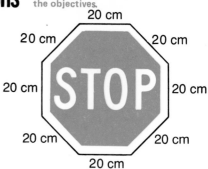

To find the perimeter, *P*, of the "STOP" sign at the right, add the lengths of the sides.

$P = 20 + 20 + 20 + 20 + 20 + 20 + 20 + 20$
$P = 160$ centimeters

You can use a **formula** to find the perimeter of a rectangle and of a square. The opposite sides of a rectangle have the same length.

PROCEDURE To find the perimeter, *P*, of a rectangle, add twice the length, *l*, to twice the width, *w*.

$$P = 2l + 2w$$

EXAMPLE 1 A draftsman's board is 66 centimeters long and 54 centimeters wide. Find the perimeter.

Solution: $P = 2l + 2w$ ◀ $l = 66$ *cm*
$w = 54$ *cm*

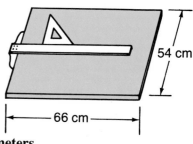

$P = 2 \times 66 + 2 \times 54$
$P = 132 + 108$
$P = 240$ The perimeter is **240 centimeters.**

The sides of a square have equal lengths.

PROCEDURE To find the perimeter, *P*, of a square, multiply the length of a side, *s*, by 4.

$$P = 4 \times s$$

EXAMPLE 2 Each side of a square picture frame is 31 centimeters long. Find the perimeter.

Solution: $P = 4 \times s$ ◀ $s = 31$ *cm*

$P = 4 \times 31$
$P = 124$ The perimeter is **124 centimeters.**

REVIEW OF RELATED SKILLS

You may wish to use these exercises before teaching the lesson.

Add.   (Pages 2–3, 94–95)

1. $15 + 18 + 15 + 18$ 66

2. $93 + 87 + 93 + 87$ 360

3. $4.0 + 6.2 + 7.8$ 18

4. $9.6 + 8.9 + 7.3$ 25.8

5. $21.6 + 50.8 + 9$ 81.4

6. $23.4 + 90.1 + 56.2$

169.7

EXERCISES

See the suggested assignment guide in the Teacher's Manual.

Find the perimeter of each rectangle or square. (Examples 1 and 2)

1. Parking Lot 350 m

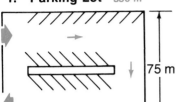

75 m

100 m

2. Garden 20 m

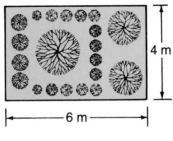

4 m

6 m

3. City Square 380 m

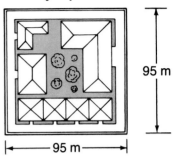

95 m

95 m

4. Fountain 34 m

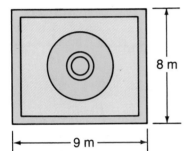

8 m

9 m

5. Swimming Pool 14 m

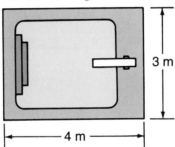

3 m

4 m

6. Baseball Diamond 109.6 m

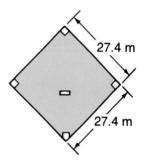

27.4 m

27.4 m

	Length	Width	Perimeter	
7.	5 cm	3 cm	?	16 cm
8.	14 m	4 m	?	36 m
9.	6.2 cm	5.1 cm	?	22.6 cm
10.	9.8 m	3.4 m	?	26.4 m

	Length	Width	Perimeter	
11.	30 cm	30 cm	?	120 cm
12.	10 m	9 m	?	38 m
13.	6.7 cm	3.9 cm	?	21.2 cm
14.	4.0 m	2.8 m	?	13.6 m

APPLICATIONS: Using Perimeter   Most students should be able to do Exercises 15-18.

15. Two tennis courts are laid out side by-side as shown below. Find the perimeter. 116.6 m

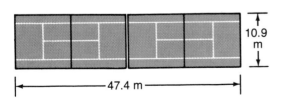

10.9 m

47.4 m

16. A park has the shape of a square. Each side of the park is 175 meters long. Find the perimeter. 700 m

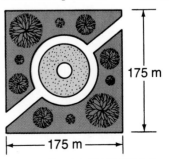

175 m

175 m

APPLYING METRIC MEASURES I   **141**

17. Find the perimeter of the roof shown below. 30.4 m

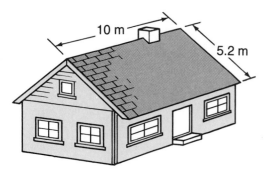

10 m

5.2 m

18. Find the perimeter of the roof shown below. 172 m

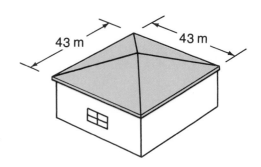

43 m   43 m

The plan below shows the dimensions of some of the rooms of the first floor of a house. For example, the dimensions 4.2 m × 4 m for the dining room mean that it is 4.2 meters long and 4 meters wide. Use this plan for Exercises 19–22. Exercises 19-26 may be considered optional for some students.

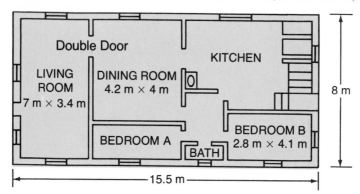

Double Door

LIVING ROOM
7 m × 3.4 m

DINING ROOM
4.2 m × 4 m

KITCHEN

8 m

BEDROOM A

BATH

BEDROOM B
2.8 m × 4.1 m

15.5 m

19. What is the perimeter of the dining room? 16.4 m

20. What is the perimeter of the living room? 20.8 m

21. What is the perimeter of bedroom B? 13.8 m

22. What is the perimeter of the outside walls? 47 m

For Exercises 23–26, first draw a rectangle or a square. Use the information in the problem to mark the lengths of the sides. Then solve the problem.

23. The rectangular building in which spacecraft are assembled at Cape Kennedy in Florida is 199.33 meters long and 144.47 meters wide. Find the perimeter. 687.6 m

24. The base of the Great Pyramid of Egypt is a square. Each side of the square is 236.4 meters long. Find the perimeter of the base. 945.6 m

25. One side of a square rug is 9.5 meters long. Find the perimeter of the rug. 38 m

26. A rectangular swimming pool is 55 meters long and 27 meters wide. Find its perimeter. 164 m

7-4 Area and Applications: Rectangles / Squares

See the Teacher's Manual for the objectives.

Each side of the square at the right is 1 centimeter long. The square has an area of 1×1, or 1 square centimeter (abbreviated: 1 cm²).

1 cm²

Area is measured in **square units.** You can use a formula to find the area of some figures.

PROCEDURE   To find the area, A, of a rectangle, multiply the length, l, and the width, w.

$$A = l \times w$$

EXAMPLE 1   A soccer field is 119 meters long and 91 meters wide. Find the area of the field.

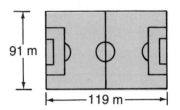

Solution: $A = l \times w$ ◀ $l = 119\ m$ $w = 91\ m$

$A = 119 \times 91$

$A = \mathbf{10{,}829}$ The area is **10,829 m².**

You can also use a formula to find the area of a square.

PROCEDURE   To find the area, A, of a square, multiply the length of any two sides.

$$A = s \times s \text{ or } A = s^2 \quad ◀ \quad s^2 \text{ means } s \times s.$$

EXAMPLE 2   Storm warning flags have the shape of a square. Each side of the square is 1.2 meters. Find the area of the flag.

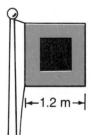

Solution: $A = s \times s$ ◀ $s = 1.2\ m$

$A = 1.2 \times 1.2$

$A = \mathbf{1.44}$ The area is **1.44 m².**

REVIEW OF RELATED SKILLS

You may wish to use these exercises before teaching the lesson.

Multiply.   (Pages 26–27, 32–33, 36–37, 98–99)

1. 17×8 136
2. 19×21 399
3. 42×50 2100
4. 3.2×5 16

5. 17.5×28 490
6. 7.6×1.2 9.12
7. 10.3×9.5 97.85
8. 16.9×32.8 554.32

EXERCISES

See the suggested assignment guide in the Teacher's Manual.

Find the area of each rectangle or square.

1. Gym Floor 1134 m²

42 m

←27 m→

2. Solar Panel 961 m²

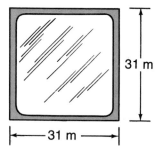

31 m

├─── 31 m ───┤

3. Rug 1.21 m²

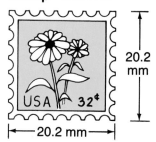

1.1 m

├──1.1 m──┤

4. Dollar Bill 100.75 cm²

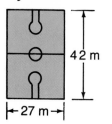

6.5 cm

├──── 15.5 cm ────┤

5. Business Card 4518 mm²

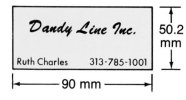

Dandy Line Inc.

Ruth Charles   313-785-1001

50.2 mm

├──── 90 mm ────┤

6. Stamp 408.04 mm²

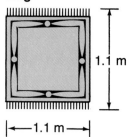

USA 32¢

20.2 mm

├── 20.2 mm ──┤

	Length	Width	Area
7.	4 cm	3 cm	12 cm² ?
8.	5 m	4.6 m	23 m² ?
9.	8 km	8 km	64 km² ?

	Length	Width	Area
10.	2 m	2 m	4m² ?
11.	13 mm	2.8 mm	36.4 mm² ?
12.	7.5 m	2.8 m	21 m² ?

APPLICATIONS: Using Area

Most students should be able to do Exercises 13-15.

13. The flag that hangs from the George Washington Bridge on holidays is 18 meters wide and 27 meters long. Find its area. 486 m²

14. The top of a rectangular table is 1 meter long and 0.8 meters wide. Find the area of the table top. 0.8 m²

15. Floor tiles are sold in boxes containing 10 tiles. Each tile is a square with sides that are 30 centimeters long. Find the number of square centimeters that can be covered by one box of floor tiles. 9000 cm²

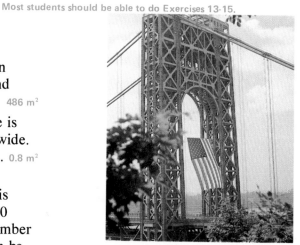

**George Washington Bridge
New York City**

7-5 Area and Applications: Parallelograms / Triangles

A parallelogram can be changed into a rectangle of equal area.

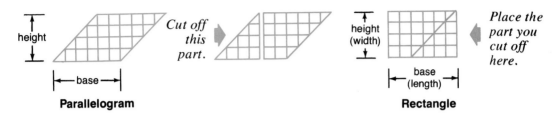

| height | Cut off this part. | height (width) | Place the part you cut off here. |

base — Parallelogram

base (length) — Rectangle

Thus, the formula for finding the area of a parallelogram is similar to the formula for finding the area of a rectangle.

PROCEDURE To find the area, A, of a parallelogram, multiply the base, b, and the height, h.

$$A = b \times h$$

EXAMPLE 1 An address plate on an apartment building has the shape of a parallelogram. The plate is 24 centimeters long and 15.5 centimeters high. Find the area.

193

15.5 cm

|← 24 cm →|

Solution: $A = b \times h$ $\begin{cases} b = 24 \text{ cm} \\ h = 15.5 \text{ cm} \end{cases}$

$A = 24 \times 15.5 = 372$ The area is **372 cm².**

A parallelogram can be changed into two triangles with equal area. The area of each triangle is one half the area of the parallelogram.

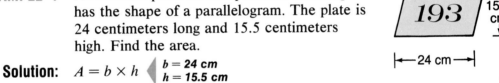

PROCEDURE To find the area, A, of a triangle, multiply the base, b, and the height, h. Then divide by 2.

$$A = \frac{b \times h}{2}$$

EXAMPLE 2 The base of a triangular sail is 6 meters and the height is 8.6 meters. Find the area of the sail.

8.6 m

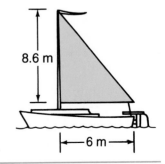

Solution: $A = \frac{b \times h}{2}$ $\begin{cases} b = 6 \text{ m} \\ h = 8.6 \text{ m} \end{cases}$

$A = \frac{6 \times 8.6}{2}$

6 m

$A = 25.8$ The area is **25.8 m².**

Find each answer. (Pages 62–63)

1. $21 \times 30 \div 2$ ³¹⁵   **2.** $18 \times 43 \div 2$ ³⁸⁷   **3.** $6.1 \times 5.4 \div 2$ ¹⁶·⁴⁷

1. $21 \times 30 \div 2$ 315   **2.** $18 \times 43 \div 2$ 387   **3.** $6.1 \times 5.4 \div 2$ 16.47

4. $19.8 \times 10.3 \div 2$ 101.97   **5.** $20 \times 15.6 \div 2$ 156   **6.** $27.2 \times 10 \div 2$ 136

EXERCISES

See the suggested assignment guide in the Teacher's Manual.

Find the area of each parallelogram or triangle.

1. Parking Lot 63 m²

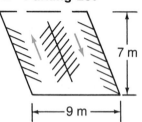

7 m

9 m

2. Table Top .35 m²

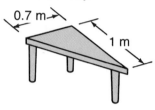

0.7 m

1 m

3. Tie Back 175 cm²

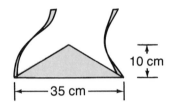

10 cm

35 cm

4. Side of a Chest .48 m²

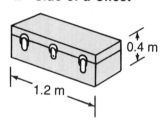

0.4 m

1.2 m

5. Flag 5.75 m²

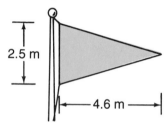

2.5 m

4.6 m

6. Gable of a Roof 5.7 m²

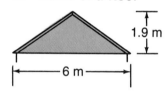

1.9 m

6 m

Figure	Base	Height	Area
7. Parallelogram	4 cm	6 cm	? 24 cm²
8. Triangle	3 cm	4 cm	? 6 cm²
9. Parallelogram	5 cm	2 cm	? 10 cm²
10. Parallelogram	6.6 m	5 m	? 33 m²

Figure	Base	Height	Area
11. Triangle	6 m	4.2 m	? 12.6 m²
12. Triangle	3.5 cm	2.6 cm	? 4.55 cm²
13. Parallelogram	7.9 m	4.6 m	? 36.34 m²
14. Parallelogram	4.1 cm	3.9 cm	? 15.99 cm²

APPLICATIONS: Using Area
Most students should be able to solve these word problems.

15. Each side of a steeple has the shape of a triangle. The base of the triangle is 3.6 meters long and the height is 55 meters. Find the total area of the four sides of the steeple. 396 m²

16. The sides of the Transamerica Building in San Francisco are triangular in shape. The base of the triangle is 34.7 meters and the height is 257 meters. Find the area of one side of the building. 4458.95 m²

**Transamerica Building
San Francisco**

7-6 Area and Applications: Trapezoids

See the Teacher's Manual for the objectives.
This lesson may be considered optional for some students.

A trapezoid can be separated into two triangles. The area of the trapezoid is the sum of the areas of the triangles.

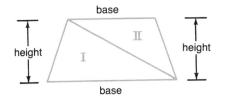
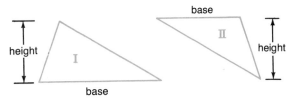

| Area of Trapezoid | = | Area of Triangle I | + | Area of Triangle II |

PROCEDURE To find the area of a trapezoid:

1. Separate the trapezoid into two triangles. Find the area of each triangle.

2. Find the sum of the areas of the triangles.

EXAMPLE Two sides of this wheelbarrow have the shape of a trapezoid. The bases of the trapezoid are 100 centimeters and 75 centimeters long. The height is 50 centimeters. Find the area.

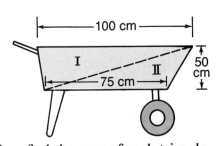

Solution: 1. Draw a line separating the trapezoid into two triangles. Then find the area of each triangle.

Triangle 1: $A = \dfrac{b \times h}{2}$ $b = 100$ cm $h = 50$ cm

$$A = \frac{100 \times 50}{2}$$

$$A = 2500$$ The area is 2500 cm².

Triangle II: $A = \dfrac{b \times h}{2}$ $b = 75$ cm $h = 50$ cm

$$A = \frac{75 \times 50}{2}$$

$$A = 1875$$ The area is 1875 cm².

2. Find the sum of the areas: $2500 + 1875 = 4375$

The area of the side of the wheelbarrow is **4375 cm².**

REVIEW OF RELATED SKILLS

You may wish to use these exercises before teaching the lesson.

Find each answer. (Pages 62–63)

1. $7 \times 10 \div 2$ 35

2. $15 \times 18 \div 2$ 135

3. $9.1 \times 6.5 \div 2$ 29.575

4. $2.1 \times 9.6 \div 2$ 10.08

5. $18.1 \times 11.7 \div 2$ 105.885

6. $21.5 \times 100 \div 2$ 1075

EXERCISES

See the suggested assignment guide in the Teacher's Manual.

Find the area of each trapezoid.

1. Side of a Tent 6.5 m²

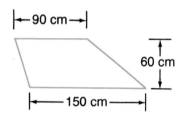

2.5 m

2 m

4 m

2. Side of a Tool Shed 5700 cm²

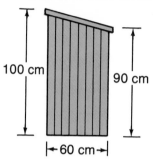

100 cm

90 cm

60 cm

3. Window Box 0.27 m²

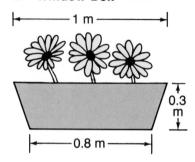

1 m

0.3 m

0.8 m

4. Slab of Cement 7200 cm²

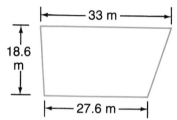

90 cm

60 cm

150 cm

5. Plot of Land 563.58 m²

33 m

18.6 m

27.6 m

6. Airplane Wing 27.2 m²

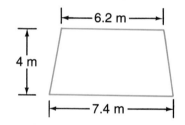

6.2 m

4 m

7.4 m

	Upper Base	Lower Base	Height	Area		Upper Base	Lower Base	Height	Area
7.	4 cm	6 cm	4 cm	? 20 cm²	**12.**	7.6 cm	10.4 cm	5 cm	?45 cm²
8.	3 cm	17 cm	3.5 cm	? 35 cm²	**13.**	6 m	4 m	3.5 m	?17.5 m²
9.	20 cm	35 cm	25 cm	?	**14.**	2.8 m	3.6 m	2 m	?6.4 m²
10.	5 cm	9 m	2.5 cm	?	**15.**	6.3 cm	8.5 cm	4 cm	?29.6 cm²
11.	9.1 m	12.3 m	2 m	? 21.4 m²	**16.**	16.5 m	21.5 m	10 m	?190 m²

APPLICATIONS: Using Area

9. 687.5 cm²   10. 17.5 cm²

17. A garden has the shape of a trapezoid. The bases of the trapezoid are 4.5 meters and 10 meters long. The height is 6.6 meters. Find the area of the garden. 47.85 m²

18. A patio having the shape of a trapezoid has a height of 2 meters. The bases of the trapezoid are 3 meters and 2.5 meters. Find the area of the patio. 5.5 m²

19. Find the amount of waste in the piece of sheet metal shown at the right. Round your answer to the nearest whole number. 7.8 m²

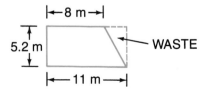

8 m

5.2 m

WASTE

11 m

Problem Solving and Applications

Floor Space

See the Teacher's Manual for the objectives.
This lesson applies the skills presented in Sections 7-4, 7-5, and 7-6.

This plan shows the floor space (floor area) allowed for five shops in a new shopping center.

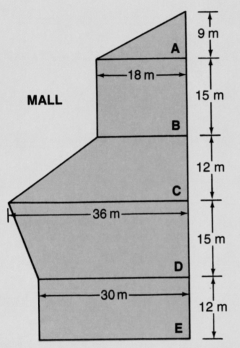

Exercises

1. Find the floor area for Shop B. 270 m²
2. Find the floor area for Shop E. 360 m²
3. Find the floor area for Shop A. 81 m²
4. Find the floor area for Shop D. 495 m²

Monthly rent for the shops in the center will be about $25.00 per square meter of floor space. Use this information for Exercises 5–12. Exercises 5-8 are two-step problems.

5. How much more will it cost per month to rent shop B rather than shop A? $4725

6. How much more will it cost per month to rent shop D rather than shop C? $4275

7. How much more will it cost per month to rent shop D rather than shop E? $3375

8. How much more will it cost per month to rent shop C rather than shop A? $6075

9. What is the total cost of rent per month for the five shops? $38,250

10. What is the cost of rent per year for shop B? $81,000

11. What is the cost of rent per year for shop A? $24,300

12. What is the cost of rent per year for shop C? $97,200

Application

Chapter Review

These exercises review the vocabulary, skills, and applications presented in the chapter as a preparation for the chapter test.

Part 1: Vocabulary

For Exercises 1–7, choose from the box at the right the word(s) that completes each statement.

always
cm
$A = l \times w$
$P = 2l + 2w$
km
length
same
$A = \dfrac{b \times h}{2}$
square

1. A centimeter is a unit of __?__ in the metric system. (Page 134) *length*
2. The abbreviation for kilometer is __?__. (Page 134) *km*
3. All sides of a square have the __?__ length. (Page 140) *same*
4. The formula for the perimeter of a rectangle is __?__.
   (Page 140) *$P = 2l + 2w$*
5. Area is measured in __?__ units. (Page 143) *square*
6. The formula for the area of a rectangle is __?__. (Page 143) *$A = l \times w$*
7. The formula for the area of a triangle is __?__. (Page 145) *$A = \dfrac{b \times h}{2}$*

Part 2: Skills

Choose the most suitable measure. Choose a, b, or c.   (Page 134)

8. The diameter of a baseball   *b*   **a.** 8 mm   **b.** 8 cm   **c.** 8 m
9. The length of a new pencil   *a*   **a.** 18 cm   **b.** 18 m   **c.** 18 km
10. The height of a tall building   *c*   **a.** 381 mm   **b.** 381 cm   **c.** 381 m
11. The thickness of a magazine   *c*   **a.** 5 cm   **b.** 5 m   **c.** 5 mm

Measure the length of each object to the given measurement.
(Pages 136–137)

12. Nearest centimeter   *3.5 cm*

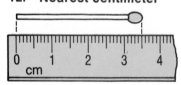

13. Nearest centimeter   *1.3 cm*

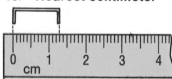

14. Nearest millimeter   *35 mm*

Find the perimeter.   (Pages 140–142)

15. Book Cover   *86 cm*

24 cm

←19 cm→

16. Table Top   *4.2 m*

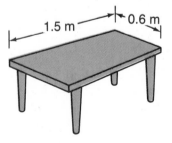

1.5 m — 0.6 m

17. Checker Board   *1.56 m*

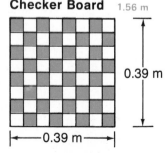

0.39 m

←0.39 m→

Find the area of each rectangle or square.   (Pages 143–144)

18. Football Field 5390 m²

49 m

110 m

19. Kitchen 27.04 m²

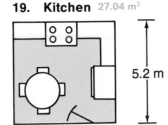

5.2 m

5.2 m

20. Calendar 933.9 cm²

| JANUARY |
| S M T W T F S |
| 1 2 3 |
| 4 5 6 7 8 9 10 |
| 11 12 13 14 15 16 17 |
| 18 19 20 21 22 23 24 |
| 25 26 27 28 29 30 31 |

28.3 cm

33 cm

Figure	Length	Width	
21. Rectangle	9 cm	4 cm	36 cm²
22. Rectangle	2.8 m	1.9 m	5.32 m²
23. Square	21 mm	21 mm	441 mm²

Figure	Length	Width	
24. Rectangle	42.1 m	47 m	1978.7 m²
25. Square	5.6 cm	5.6 cm	31.36 cm²
26. Rectangle	24 mm	18 mm	432 mm²

Find the area of each parallelogram or triangle.   (Pages 145–146)

Figure	Base	Height	
27. Parallelogram	6 cm	3 cm	18 cm²
28. Triangle	5 cm	4 cm	10 cm²
29. Triangle	21 cm	18 cm	189 cm²

Figure	Base	Height	
30. Triangle	3.2 m	4.6 m	7.36 m²
31. Parallelogram	9.8 cm	12.3 cm	120.54 cm²
32. Parallelogram	4.9 m	3.8 m	18.62 m²

Find the area of each trapezoid.   (Pages 147–148)

33. Piece of Slate 6425.5 cm²   **34. Trough** 504 cm²   **35. Side of a Stairway** 10.15 m²

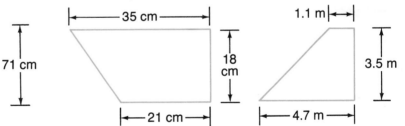

85 cm

71 cm

96 cm

35 cm

18 cm

21 cm

1.1 m

3.5 m

4.7 m

Part 3: Applications   The use of these word problems depends on which applications were studied.

36. A blanket is 190 centimeters long and 140 centimeters wide. Find the perimeter of the blanket. (Pages 140–142)   660 cm

37. One side of a square garden is 6.2 meters long. Find the area of the garden. (Pages 143–144)   38.44 m²

38. Each side of a steeple has the shape of a triangle. The base of the triangle is 4.3 meters long and the height is 50 meters. Find the area of one side of the steeple. (Pages 145–146)   107.5 m²

39. The Wong family's lawn is shaped like a parallelogram. The base of the lawn is 7 meters long and its height is 6.5 meters. What is the area of the lawn? (Pages 145–146)   45.5 m²

Chapter Test

The Teacher's Resource Book contains two forms of each chapter test.

Find the perimeter.

1. Window 4.4 m

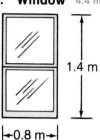

1.4 m

|←0.8 m→|

2. Bookmark 34 cm

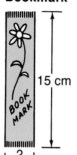

15 cm

|←2 cm→|

3. Record Jacket

120 cm

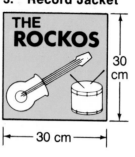

THE ROCKOS

30 cm

|← 30 cm →|

4. Door 7.2 m

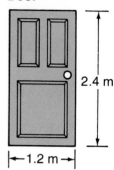

2.4 m

|←1.2 m→|

Find the area of each rectangle or square.

Figure	Length	Width
5. Rectangle	2.3 mm	1.9 mm 4.37 mm²
6. Square	7 cm	7 cm 49 cm²
7. Square	8.3 m	8.3 m 68.89 m²

Figure	Length	Width
8. Rectangle	9.1 cm	3.8 cm 34.58 cm²
9. Rectangle	10 mm	6.2 mm 62 mm²
10. Square	3.1 m	3.1 m 9.61 m²

Find each area.

Figure	Base	Height
11. Parallelogram	3 m	2 m 6 m²
12. Parallelogram	4.1 cm	5.6 cm 22.96 cm²
13. Triangle	6 cm	5 cm 15 cm²

Figure	Base	Height
14. Parallelogram	1.9 m	2 m 3.8 m²
15. Triangle	4.2 m	2.9 m 6.09 m²
16. Triangle	10 cm	8.6 cm 43 cm²

Solve. The use of these word problems depends on which applications were studied.

17. A rectangular plot of land is 27.1 meters long and 5 meters wide. Find the perimeter of the lot. 64.2 m

18. A square shipping label is 60 millimeters long on each side. Find the area of the label. 3600 m²

19. A window has the shape of a triangle. The base is 0.8 meters long and the height is 0.6 meters. Find the area of the window. 0.24 m²

20. Mrs. Chou wants to carpet her bedroom which is 5.2 meters long and 4 meters wide. How much carpet does Mrs. Chou need to buy? 20.8 m²

Additional Practice

You may wish to use some or all of these exercises depending on how well students performed on the Chapter Test.

Skills

Find the perimeter. (Pages 140–142)

1. Newspaper 130 cm

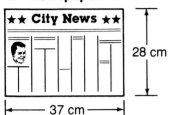

28 cm

37 cm

2. Backgammon Board 160 cm

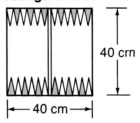

40 cm

40 cm

3. Telephone Book 100 cm

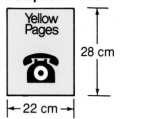

28 cm

22 cm

Find the area of each rectangle or square. (Pages 143–144)

Figure	Length	Width	
4. Rectangle	8 cm	5 cm	40 cm²
5. Rectangle	3.4 cm	2.1 cm	7.14 cm²
6. Square	4.2 cm	4.2 cm	17.64 cm²

Figure	Length	Width	
7. Rectangle	25.1 m	9.8 m	245.98 m²
8. Rectangle	3.2 cm	1.9 cm	6.08 cm²
9. Square	16 mm	16 mm	256 mm²

Find the area of each parallelogram or triangle. (Pages 145–146)

Figure	Base	Height	
10. Parallelogram	3.5 cm	6 cm	21 cm²
11. Triangle	3 m	2.5 m	3.75 m²
12. Triangle	16 cm	14 cm	112 cm²

Figure	Base	Height	
13. Parallelogram	16.7 cm	10.2 cm	170.34 cm²
14. Parallelogram	3.4 cm	5.6 cm	19.04 cm²
15. Parallelogram	45 mm	30 mm	1350 mm²

Find the area of each trapezoid. (Pages 147–148)

16. Car Window 1575 cm²

45 cm
30 cm
60 cm

17. Quilt Patch 564.775 cm²

25.1 cm
20.5 cm
30 cm

18. Cushion 1360 cm²

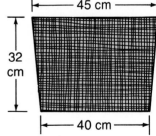

45 cm
32 cm
40 cm

Applications

The use of these word problems depends on which applications were studied.

19. A tablecloth is 2 meters long and 1.5 meters wide. Find the perimeter. (Pages 140–142) 7 m

20. A triangular pennant has a base of 20 centimeters and a height of 40 centimeters. Find the area. (Pages 145–146) 400 cm²

REVIEW OF RELATED SKILLS FOR CHAPTER 8

Complete. (Pages 102–103)

1. To multiply by 1000, move the decimal point __?__ 3 places to the __?__. right

2. To multiply by 0.001, move the decimal point __?__ 3 places to the __?__. left

Multiply. (Pages 102–103)

3. 6×1000 6000   **4.** 48×1000 48,000   **5.** 716×1000 716,000   **6.** 11.8×1000 11,800

7. 7×1000 7000   **8.** 37×1000 37,000   **9.** 293×1000 293,000   **10.** 9.2×1000 9200

11. 2.1×0.001 0.0021   **12.** 0.986×0.001 0.000986   **13.** 712.3×0.001 0.7123   **14.** 91×0.001 0.091

15. 3.5×0.001 0.0035   **16.** 0.48×0.001 0.00048   **17.** 844.1×0.001 0.8441   **18.** 20×0.001 0.02

19. 27.36×1000 27360   **20.** 8.72×0.001 0.00872   **21.** 398.27×0.001 0.398270   **22.** 4.2×1000 4200

23. 85.23×0.001 0.08523   **24.** 720.3×1000 720,300   **25.** 9.872×1000 9872   **26.** 3.6×0.001 0.0036

27. 79.38×1000 79,380   **28.** 0.2184×1000 218.4   **29.** 0.21×0.001 0.00021   **30.** 9.3×0.001 0.0093

Multiply. (Pages 26–27, 32–33, 98–99)

31. $2 \times 6 \times 11$ 132   **32.** $14 \times 4 \times 8$ 448   **33.** $16 \times 2 \times 9$ 288   **34.** $21 \times 5 \times 4$ 420

35. $8 \times 7 \times 6$ 336   **36.** $10 \times 3 \times 7$ 210   **37.** $40 \times 8 \times 12$ 3840   **38.** $9 \times 25 \times 8$ 1800

39. $1 \times 14 \times 8$ 112   **40.** $21 \times 16 \times 2$ 672   **41.** $8 \times 9 \times 41$ 2952   **42.** $3 \times 13 \times 6$ 234

43. $73 \times 21 \times 3$ 4599   **44.** $30 \times 4 \times 11$ 1320   **45.** $54 \times 10 \times 8$ 4320   **46.** $67 \times 6 \times 9$ 3618

47. $23.6 \times 8 \times 4$ 755.2   **48.** $6 \times 13.9 \times 7$ 583.8   **49.** $9.5 \times 4 \times 3.1$ 117.8   **50.** $6.1 \times 8 \times 2$ 97.6

51. $36.2 \times 4 \times 3.4$ 492.32   **52.** $1.8 \times 8.1 \times 1$ 14.58   **53.** $6.7 \times 10 \times 9.5$ 636.5   **54.** $1.3 \times 7 \times 2$ 18.2

55. $24.9 \times 6 \times 5$ 747   **56.** $8 \times 13 \times 4.6$ 478.4   **57.** $3 \times 44.7 \times 7$ 938.7   **58.** $4.5 \times 3 \times 0$ 0

59. $16.7 \times 3 \times 1.5$ 75.15   **60.** $43.1 \times 4.3 \times 4$ 741.32   **61.** $6 \times 8.5 \times 18.1$ 923.1   **62.** $2 \times 6.8 \times 7$ 95.2

Find each answer. (Pages 62–63)

63. $3 + 8 \times 12$ 99   **64.** $2 + 2 \times 9$ 20   **65.** $34 + 8 \times 6$ 82   **66.** $7 + 23 \times 6$ 145

67. $4 + 6 \times 3$ 22   **68.** $1 + 7 \times 8$ 57   **69.** $16 + 9 \times 14$ 142   **70.** $3 + 10 \times 9$ 93

71. $9 + 13 \times 2$ 35   **72.** $26 + 8 \times 16$ 154   **73.** $15 + 24 \times 40$ 975   **74.** $82 + 7 \times 9$ 145

75. $3 \times 6 + 8 \times 9$ 90   **76.** $4 \times 5 + 3 \times 15$ 65   **77.** $19 \times 4 + 7 \times 6$ 118   **78.** $4 + 24 \times 3$ 76

79. $4 + 2 \times 17$ 38   **80.** $31 \times 4 + 6 \times 9$ 178   **81.** $5 \times 13 + 4 \times 8$ 97   **82.** $9 + 5 \times 7$ 44

83. $7 + 76 \times 5$ 387   **84.** $82 \times 6 + 4 \times 3$ 504   **85.** $29 \times 1 + 9 \times 3$ 56   **86.** $4 + 7 \times 44$ 312

87. $5 \times 9 \div 3$ 15   **88.** $5 \times 12 \div 3$ 20   **89.** $8 \times 6 \div 3$ 16   **90.** $6 \times 4 \div 3$ 8

91. $3.6 \times 5 \div 3$ 6   **92.** $5.1 \times 4.2 \div 3$ 7.14   **93.** $6.3 \times 9.7 \div 3$ 20.37   **94.** $5 \times 8.7 \div 3$ 14.5

95. $13.5 \times 1.6 \div 3$ 7.2   **96.** $9.3 \times 0.25 \div 3$ 0.775   **97.** $4.6 \times 3.1 \times 0.6 \div 3$ 2.852

98. $6 \times 0.27 \times 2.3 \div 3$ 1.242   **99.** $0.51 \times 7.3 \times 4 \div 3$ 4.964   **100.** $7.2 \times 6.8 \times 1.1 \div 3$ 17.952

8 APPLYING METRIC MEASURES II

SKILLS/APPLICATIONS

8-1   Units of Capacity and Applications

8-2   Units of Mass and Applications

8-3   Temperature and Applications

8-4   Surface Area and Applications

8-5   Volume and Applications

8-6   Pyramids and Applications

OTHER APPLICATIONS

Volume / Capacity / Mass

CAREER

Weather Forecasting

8-1 Units of Capacity and Applications See the Teacher's Manual for the objectives.

This table shows the most commonly used units of capacity in the metric system.

TABLE An eyedropper holds about 1 milliliter (abbreviated: **mL**) of liquid.

A milk carton (one–quart size) contains a little less than 1 liter (abbreviated: **L**).

You use this relationship to change liters to milliliters and to change milliliters to liters.

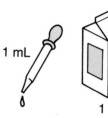

1 mL

1 L

1000 milliliters = 1 liter

PROCEDURE To change <u>from liters to milliliters</u>, multiply by 1000.

To change <u>from milliliters to liters</u>, multiply by 0.001.

EXAMPLE **a.** 3 L = __?__ mL **b.** 46 mL = __?__ L

Solutions: **a.** 3 L = (3 × 1000) mL **b.** 46 mL = (46 × 0.001) L

= **3000 mL** = **0.046 L**

REVIEW OF RELATED SKILLS You may wish to use these exercises before teaching the lesson.

Complete.   (Pages 102–103)

1. To multiply by 1000, move the decimal point __?__ **3** places to the __?__ **right**.

2. To multiply by 0.001, move the decimal point __?__ **3** places to the __?__ **left**.

Multiply.   (Pages 102–103)

3. 6 × 1000 6000 4. 65 × 1000 65,000 5. 659 × 1000 659,000 6. 2.8 × 1000 2800

7. 9857 × 0.001 9.857 8. 98.57 × 0.001 0.09857 9. 985.7 × 0.001 0.9857 10. 9.857 × 0.001 0.009857

11. 0.9857 × 1000 985.7 12. 0.09 × 1000 90 13. 0.09 × 0.001 0.00009 14. 0.9857 × 0.001 0.0009857

EXERCISES See the suggested assignment guide in the Teacher's Manual.

Choose the most suitable measure. Choose a or b.   (Table)

1. A spoonful of medicine a **a.** milliliter **b.** liter

2. A tank of gasoline for a car b **a.** milliliter **b.** liter

3. A can of oil for a car b **a.** milliliter **b.** liter

4. A glass of milk a **a.** milliliter **b.** liter

5. A drop from an eyedropper a **a.** milliliter **b.** liter

Choose the most suitable measure. Choose a, b, or c.   (Table)

6. Coffee cup b

a. 2 L
b. 200 mL
c. 50 mL

7. Water pitcher a

a. 1 L
b. 2 mL
c. 200 L

8. Punch bowl b

a. 325 mL
b. 2 L
c. 3 mL

9. Can of soup b

a. 3 L
b. 300 mL
c. 30 mL

10. Pail b

a. 20 mL
b. 10 L
c. 200 L

11. Kettle b

a. 20 L
b. 2 L
c. 0.2 L

12. Aquarium a

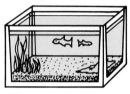

a. 25 L
b. 25 mL
c. 250 mL

13. Thermos c

a. 1900 mL
b. 19 L
c. 1 L

Complete. (Example)

14. $162 \text{ L} = \underline{?} \text{ mL}$ 162,000
15. $200 \text{ L} = \underline{?} \text{ mL}$ 200,000
16. $77 \text{ L} = \underline{?} \text{ mL}$ 77,000
17. $19 \text{ L} = \underline{?} \text{ mL}$ 19,000

18. $9.2 \text{ L} = \underline{?} \text{ mL}$ 9200
19. $8.8 \text{ L} = \underline{?} \text{ mL}$ 8800
20. $0.5 \text{ L} = \underline{?} \text{ mL}$ 500
21. $0.1 \text{ L} = \underline{?} \text{ mL}$ 100

22. $6212 \text{ mL} = \underline{?} \text{ L}$ 6.212
23. $8906 \text{ mL} = \underline{?} \text{ L}$ 8.906
24. $160 \text{ mL} = \underline{?} \text{ L}$ 0.16
25. $500 \text{ mL} = \underline{?} \text{ L}$ 0.5

26. $5 \text{ mL} = \underline{?} \text{ L}$ 0.005
27. $8 \text{ mL} = \underline{?} \text{ L}$ 0.008
28. $9.2 \text{ mL} = \underline{?} \text{ L}$ 0.0092
29. $4.3 \text{ mL} = \underline{?} \text{ L}$ 0.0043

30. $490 \text{ L} = \underline{?} \text{ mL}$ 490,000
31. $49 \text{ mL} = \underline{?} \text{ L}$ 0.049
32. $3.01 \text{ mL} = \underline{?} \text{ L}$ 0.00301
33. $30.1 \text{ L} = \underline{?} \text{ mL}$ 30,100

APPLICATIONS: Using Units of Capacity   These are one-step problems that most students should be able to handle.

34. One teaspoon contains 5 milliliters. How many teaspoons can be poured from a bottle containing 225 milliliters?   45

35. One tablespoon contains 15 milliliters. How many tablespoons can be poured from a bottle containing 225 milliliters?   15

36. A drinking glass contains 250 milliliters. How many glasses can be poured from a 1-liter pitcher?   4

37. How many liters of milk will be needed to pour 12 glasses of milk?   3

8-2 Units of Mass and Applications See the Teacher's Manual for the objectives.

This table shows the most commonly used units of **mass** in the metric system.

TABLE
The mass of the wing of a bee is about 1 milligram (abbreviated: **mg**).

The mass of a paper clip is about 1 gram (abbreviated: **g**).

The mass of a pair of shoes (adult size) is about 1 kilogram (abbreviated: **kg**).

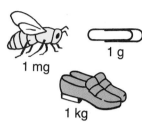

1 mg

1 g

1 kg

The following relationships are useful in changing from one of the units in the table to another.

1 kilogram = 1000 grams   **1 gram = 1000 milligrams**

PROCEDURE
To change <u>from kilograms to grams</u>, multiply by 1000.

To change <u>from grams to kilograms</u>, multiply by 0.001.

To change <u>from grams to milligrams</u>, multiply by 1000.

To change <u>from milligrams to grams</u>, multiply by 0.001.

EXAMPLE
a. 5 kg = ___?___ gm
c. 237 mg = ___?___ gm

b. 58.5 g = ___?___ mg
d. 78,000 g = ___?___ kg

Solutions:
a. 5 kg = (5 × 1000)gm
      = 5000 gm

c. 237 mg = (237 × 0.001)gm
      = 0.237 gm

b. 58.5 g = (58.5 × 1000)mg
      = 58,500 mg

d. 78,000 g = (78,000 × 0.001)kg
      = 78 kg

REVIEW OF RELATED SKILLS
You may wish to use these exercises before teaching the lesson.

Complete.   (Pages 102–103)

1. To multiply by 1000, move the decimal point __?__ 3 places to the __?__ right

2. To multiply by 0.001, move the decimal point __?__ 3 places to the __?__ left

Multiply.   (Pages 102–103)

3. 3.5 × 1000   3500   **4.** 0.35 × 1000   350   **5.** 0.358 × 1000   358   **6.** 0.7 × 1000   700

7. 958 × 0.001   0.958   **8.** 95 × 0.001   0.095   **9.** 9 × 0.001   0.009   **10.** 0.09 × 0.001   0.00009

11. 0.95 × 0.001   0.00095   **12.** 0.958 × 0.001   0.000958   **13.** 50 × 1000   50,000   **14.** 1.006 × 1000   1006

EXERCISES
See the suggested assignment guide in the Teacher's Manual.

Choose the most suitable measure. Choose a, b, or c. (Table)

1. Nickel b

a. 5 mg
b. 5 g
c. 5 kg

2. Automobile c

a. 2181 mg
b. 2181 g
c. 2181 kg

3. Can of Tomatoes b

a. 453 mg
b. 453 g
c. 453 kg

4. Egg b

a. 40 kg
b. 40 g
c. 40 mg

5. Toothbrush b

a. 30 kg
b. 30 g
c. 30 mg

6. Sofa c

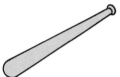

a. 38 kg
b. 380 kg
c. 3800 kg

7. Baseball Bat b

a. 800 kg
b. 800 g
c. 8000 kg

8. Piano c

a. 4 kg
b. 400 kg
c. 4000 kg

Complete. (Example)

9. 500 kg = __?__ g *500,000*

10. 100 kg = __?__ g *100,000*

11. 8 kg = __?__ g *8000*

12. 25 kg = __?__ g *25,000*

13. 50 g = __?__ mg *50,000*

14. 4 g = __?__ mg *4000*

15. 6 g = __?__ mg *6000*

16. 73 g = __?__ mg *73,000*

17. 108 mg = __?__ g *0.108*

18. 220 mg = __?__ g *0.220*

19. 25 mg = __?__ g *0.025*

20. 67 mg = __?__ g *0.067*

21. 5100 g = __?__ kg *5.1*

22. 789 g = __?__ kg *0.789*

23. 50 g = __?__ kg *0.05*

24. 36 g = __?__ kg *0.36*

25. 9 kg = __?__ g *9000*

26. 30 kg = __?__ g *30,000*

27. 2000 g = __?__ kg *2*

28. 94 g = __?__ kg *0.094*

These are one-step problems that most students should be able to handle.

APPLICATIONS: Using Units of Mass

29. An airplane is carrying 125 passengers. The average mass of each passenger is 83 kilograms. Find the total mass of the passengers. *10,375*

30. The average mass of the luggage for each passenger in Exercise 29 is 45 kilograms. Find the total mass of the luggage. *5625*

31. Find the total mass of the passengers and the luggage on the plane. *16,000*

APPLYING METRIC MEASURES II **159**

8-3 Temperature and Applications

See the Teacher's Manual for the objectives.

In the metric system, the Celsius thermometer is used to measure temperature.

Freezing Point of Water

0° C ◀ *Read: "Zero degrees Celsius."*

Here are some ways to think about Celsius temperatures.

100° C: Water boils

37° C: Normal body temperature

35° C: Hot summer day

22° C to 26° C: Comfortable room temperature

0° C: Water freezes

PROCEDURE To determine a suitable temperature, compare with the temperatures above.

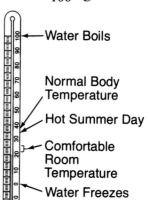

Boiling Point of Water

100° C

Water Boils

Normal Body Temperature

Hot Summer Day

Comfortable Room Temperature

Water Freezes

Celsius Scale Thermometer

EXERCISES

See the suggested assignment guide in the Teacher's Manual.

Choose the most suitable temperature. Choose a, b, or c.

1. The temperature of a pleasant summer day b   **a.** 2° C   **b.** 25° C   **c.** 50° C

2. The temperature of a cold winter day   a   **a.** −5° C   **b.** 15° C   **c.** 30° C

3. Comfortable room temperature   b   **a.** 0° C   **b.** 20° C   **c.** 30° C

4. The temperature of a person with a fever   c   **a.** 35° C   **b.** 37° C   **c.** 37.8° C

5. The temperature of a cup of hot tea   c   **a.** 15° C   **b.** 40° C   **c.** 80° C

6. The temperature of an ice cube   a   **a.** 0° C   **b.** 10° C   **c.** 15° C

7. The temperature of a moderately cool day   b   **a.** 0° C   **b.** 12° C   **c.** 35° C

8. The outdoor temperature is 25° C. Would you go ice skating or water skiing?   water skiing

9. The room temperature is 40° C. Would you turn on the air conditioning or raise the setting on the thermostat?   turn on the air conditioning

10. The outdoor temperature is 33° C. Would you wear a warm jacket or light summer clothing to go for a 2-mile walk?   light summer clothing

Career lessons are optional.

Here are some averages used in weather forecasting.

Average daily temperature: Add the high and low temperatures. Then divide by 2.

Average monthly temperature: Add the daily average temperatures. Then divide by the number of days in the month.

Average yearly temperature: Add the average monthly temperatures. Then divide by 12.

EXERCISES

In Exercises 1–6, find the average daily temperature for each city.

City	High	Low	
1. Atlanta	23°C	11°C	17°C
2. Boston	21°C	15°C	18°C
3. Kansas City	19°C	5°C	12°C

City	High	Low	
4. Los Angeles	29°C	19°C	24°C
5. Seattle	21°C	10°C	15.5°C
6. Tampa	26°C	22°C	24°C

The table below shows average monthly temperatures for four cities.

City	AVERAGE MONTHLY TEMPERATURE IN °C											
	J	F	M	A	M	J	J	A	S	O	N	D
Key West	22	22	23	24	26	28	28	29	29	26	23	22
Yuma	13	15	18	21	24	29	33	35	30	23	16	13
Portland	4	6	8	11	14	17	18	18	16	13	8	5
New Orleans	13	14	20	21	24	27	28	28	26	22	16	13

Find the average yearly temperature for each city. Use paper and pencil or use a calculator.

7. Key West   25.2   8. Yuma   22.5

9. Portland   11.5   10. New Orleans   21

11. In tropical climates, the average temperature each month is above 18°C. Which cities in the table have a tropical climate?   Key West

Penny Griego, Weather Forecaster

12. In warm temperature climates, average temperatures in January and February are between 3° below zero and 18°. Which cities have a warm temperature climate?   Yuma, Portland, New Orleans

8-4 Surface Area and Applications

See the Teacher's Manual for the objectives.

This lesson may be considered optional for some students.

A **rectangular prism** is a solid such as the shoe box at the right. Each of its six sides or **faces** is a rectangle. **Opposite faces** such as the top and bottom have equal areas. The **surface area** of a rectangular prism is the sum of the areas of the six faces.

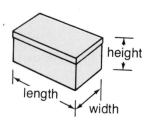

PROCEDURE To find the surface area of a rectangular prism add the areas of the six faces.

Surface Area	=	Area of Top and Bottom	+	Area of Front and Back	+	Area of Sides
A	=	$2 \times l \times w$	+	$2 \times l \times h$	+	$2 \times w \times h$

EXAMPLE Find the surface area of the box of paper clips shown at the right.

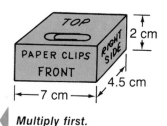

Solution: $l = 7$ cm; $w = 4.5$ cm; $h = 2$ cm

$A = 2 \times l \times w + 2 \times l \times h + 2 \times w \times h$

$A = 2 \times 7 \times 4.5 + 2 \times 7 \times 2 + 2 \times 4.5 \times 2$ ◀ *Multiply first.*

$A = \quad\ 63 \quad + \quad 28 \quad + \quad 18$

$A = 109$ The surface area is **109 cm²**.

A cube is a special kind of rectangular prism. The length, width, and height are the same. You can use this formula to find its surface area, A.

$$A = 6 \times s \times s$$ ◀ *s = length of any side*

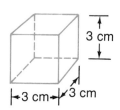

REVIEW OF RELATED SKILLS

You may wish to use these exercises before teaching the lesson.

Find each answer.   (Pages 62–63)

1. $13 + 4 \times 24$ 109 **2.** $62 + 5 \times 12$ 122 **3.** $25 + 40 \times 15$ 625 **4.** $30 + 4 \times 17$ 98

5. $21 + 2 \times 41$ 103 **6.** $36 + 7 \times 3$ 57 **7.** $18 + 9 \times 7$ 81 **8.** $4 + 48 \times 16$ 772

9. $21 \times 7 + 1 \times 3$ 150 **10.** $16 \times 2 + 8 \times 3$ 56 **11.** $7 \times 9 + 21 \times 3$ 126 **12.** $4 \times 7 + 16 \times 5$ 108

EXERCISES

See the suggested assignment guide in the Teacher's Manual.

Find the surface area of each rectangular solid.

1. Package   3120 cm²

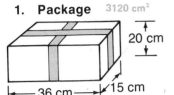

20 cm
36 cm
15 cm

2. Match Box   68 cm²

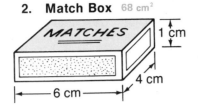

MATCHES
1 cm
6 cm
4 cm

3. Refrigerator   10 m²

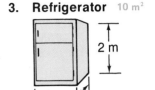

2 m
1 m
1 m

4. Packing Crate   4600 cm²

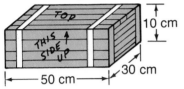

TOP
THIS SIDE UP
10 cm
50 cm
30 cm

5. Cabinet   22 m²

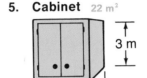

3 m
2 m
1 m

6. Cereal Box   1720 cm²

PUFFO CEREAL
25 cm
20 cm
8 cm

7. Shoe Box   1900 cm²

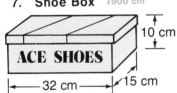

ACE SHOES
10 cm
32 cm
15 cm

8. Book   1084 cm²

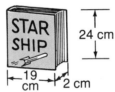

STAR SHIP
24 cm
19 cm
2 cm

9. Planter   1000 cm²

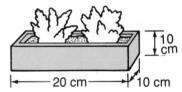

10 cm
20 cm
10 cm

10. Door   10.6 m²

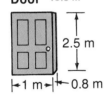

2.5 m
1 m
0.8 m

11. Paper Weight   8272 mm²

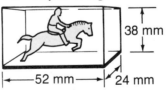

38 mm
52 mm
24 mm

12. Stereo Speaker   4456 cm²

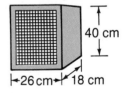

40 cm
26 cm
18 cm

	Length	Width	Height	
13.	5 cm	10 cm	16 cm	580 cm²
14.	45 cm	60 cm	30 cm	11,700 cm²
15.	8 m	5 m	2.5 m	145 m²
16.	28 cm	24 cm	7 cm	2072 cm²
17.	5 m	5 m	5 m	150 m²
18.	0.7 m	1.5 m	3 m	15.3 m²
19.	0.3 m	0.3 m	0.3 m	0.54 m²
20.	1.1 m	2.4 m	6 m	47.28 m²

	Length	Width	Height	
21.	3.4 cm	4 cm	6.5 cm	123.4 cm²
22.	40 cm	29 cm	10.2 cm	3727.6 cm²
23.	6 m	4 m	2.3 m	94 m²
24.	8 cm	5 cm	4.1 cm	186.6 cm²
25.	3.4 m	4.8 m	3 m	81.84 m²
26.	9 cm	9 cm	9 cm	486 cm²
27.	39 cm	15 cm	30 cm	4410 cm²
28.	11 m	15 m	3 m	486 m²

8-5 Volume and Applications See the Teacher's Manual for the objectives.

The **volume** of a rectangular prism is the amount of space it contains. The prism at the right has a volume of **one cubic centimeter** (abbreviated: **1 cm³**). Each side has a length of one centimeter.

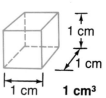

1 cm

1 cm

1 cm

1 cm³

PROCEDURE To find the volume of a rectangular prism, find the product of the length, width, and height.

$$\text{Volume} = \text{Length} \times \text{Width} \times \text{Height}$$
$$V \quad = \quad l \quad \times \quad w \quad \times \quad h$$

EXAMPLE Find the volume of this box of soap powder.

Solution: $V = l \times w \times h$ ◀ $l = 18$ cm; $w = 5$ cm; $h = 24$ cm

$V = 18 \times 5 \times 24$

$V = \mathbf{2160}$ The volume of the box is **2160 cm³**.

Super Suds SOAP

24 cm

18 cm   5 cm

REVIEW OF RELATED SKILLS You may wish to use these exercises before teaching the lesson.

Multiply.   (Pages 26–27, 32–33, 98–99)

1. $9 \times 7 \times 12$ 756
2. $15 \times 12 \times 18$ 3240
3. $32 \times 10 \times 19$ 6080
4. $10 \times 10 \times 10$ 1000
5. $9.5 \times 10 \times 18$ 1710
6. $12.9 \times 11 \times 5$ 709.5
7. $40.2 \times 35.8 \times 7$ 10074.12
8. $0.5 \times 9.1 \times 8$ 36.4
9. $2.4 \times 3.5 \times 4$ 33.6
10. $21.2 \times 20 \times 3$ 1272
11. $16.4 \times 9.2 \times 6$ 905.28
12. $2.7 \times 3.1 \times 5$ 41.85

EXERCISES

See the suggested assignment guide in the Teacher's Manual.

Find the volume.

1. Truck 8.448 m³

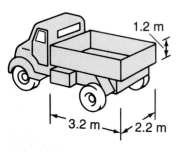

1.2 m

3.2 m   2.2 m

2. Refrigerator 3 m³

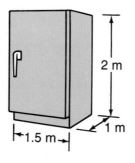

2 m

1 m

1.5 m

3. Railroad Box Car 218.120 m³

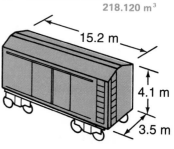

15.2 m

4.1 m

3.5 m

4. Loaf Pan 1760 cm³

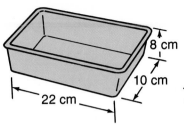

8 cm
10 cm
22 cm

5. Ice Cube Tray 1440 cm³

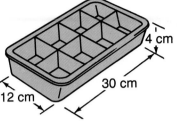

4 cm
30 cm
12 cm

6. Shoe Box 10,500 cm³

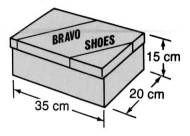

BRAVO SHOES
15 cm
20 cm
35 cm

7. Fish Tank 33,750 cm³

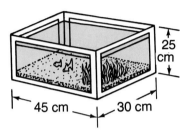

25 cm
45 cm
30 cm

8. Shed 3 m³

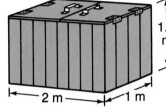

1.5 m
2 m
1 m

9. Suitcase 24,000 m³

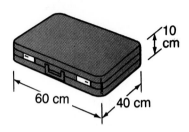

10 cm
60 cm
40 cm

	Length	Width	Height	
10.	8 cm	4 cm	8 cm	256 cm³
11.	6 cm	18 cm	2 cm	216 cm³
12.	25 cm	13 cm	5 cm	1625 cm³
13.	10 m	10 m	10 m	1000 m³
14.	4.5 m	6.8 m	3 m	91.8 m³

	Length	Width	Height	
15.	3.1 cm	2.4 cm	5 cm	37.2 cm³
16.	0.5 m	0.5 m	0.5 m	0.125 m³
17.	7 cm	3.2 cm	4 cm	89.6 cm³
18.	2.9 m	5 m	3 m	43.5 m³
19.	100 cm	100 cm	5.4 cm	54,000 cm³

APPLICATIONS: Using Volume These are one-step problems that most students should be able to handle.

20. A bookcase is 68 centimeters long, 20.2 centimeters wide, and 90 centimeters high. Find the volume. 123,624 cm³

21. A sand box is 30 centimeters long, 34 centimeters wide, and 10 centimeters deep. Find the volume. 10,200 cm³

22. A storage closet for linen is 2 meters long, 1 meter wide, and 0.8 meters high. Find the volume. 1.6 m³

23. A desk drawer is 30.5 centimeters wide, 45 centimeters long, and 15 centimeters deep. Find its volume. 20,587.5 cm³

24. Suppose that each measurement in Exercise 23 is doubled. Find the new volume. 164,700 cm³

25. A wall oven is 150 centimeters wide, 125 centimeters deep, and 100 centimeters high. Find the volume of the oven. 1,875,000 cm³

APPLYING METRIC MEASURES II **165**

Problem Solving and Applications

Volume/Capacity/Mass
See the Teacher's Manual for the objectives.
This lesson may be considered optional for some students.

Metric units of volume, capacity, and mass are related.

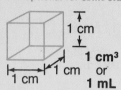

1 cubic centimeter = 1 milliliter

1 milliliter of water has a mass of 1 gram.

1 liter of water has a mass of 1 kilogram.

To find the mass of the water in the fish tank below, you must first answer the questions:

> "What is the volume of the tank?" and
> "What is the capacity of the tank in liters?"

These are the <u>hidden questions</u> in the problem. Then you can find the mass.

Exercises
These exercises apply the skills presented in Sections 8-1, 8-2, and 8-5.

1. Find the volume of this fish tank. 18,000 cm³

2. Find the capacity of the tank in liters.

$$1 \text{ cm}^3 = 1 \text{ mL}$$
$$18,000 \text{ cm}^3 = \underline{\ ?\ }^{18,000} \text{ mL}$$
$$18,000 \text{ mL} = \underline{\ ?\ }^{18} \text{ L} \blacktriangleleft \ \textbf{1000 mL = 1L}$$

3. Find the mass of 18 liters of water.

   1 L has a mass of 1 kg.

   18 L have a mass of $\underline{\ ?\ }^{18}$ kg.

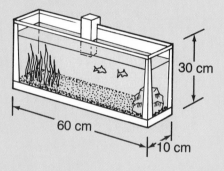

4158 cm³

4. Find the volume of the container of gasoline.

5. Find the capacity of the container in liters.

$$1 \text{ cm}^3 = 1 \text{ mL}$$
$$4158 \text{ cm}^3 = \underline{\ ?\ } \text{ mL } 4158$$
$$4158 \text{ mL} = \underline{\ ?\ } \text{ L } 4.158$$

6. One liter of gasoline has a mass of 0.7 kilograms. Find the mass of 4.158 liters. 2.9106 kg

One liter of milk has a mass of about 0.99 kilograms. Use this information for Exercises 7–8.

7. The average yearly milk production per cow in the United States in a recent year was 4,557 liters. What is the mass of this amount of milk? 4511.43 kg

8. Dairy plants in the United States process about 24 billion liters of the milk produced per year. Find the mass of this amount of milk. 23.76 billion liters

Application

8-6 Pyramids and Applications

It takes <u>three</u> pyramid-shaped containers to fill the box.

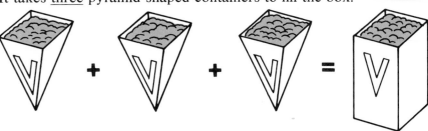

When a pyramid and a rectangular prism have equal heights and bases that are equal in area, the volume of the pyramid is $\frac{1}{3}$ of the volume of the rectangular prism.

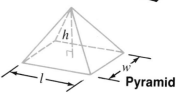

Pyramid

PROCEDURE To find the volume of a pyramid multiply the area of the base and the height. Then divide by 3.

$$\text{Volume} = \frac{\text{Area of Base} \times \text{Height}}{3} \quad \text{or} \quad V = \frac{l \times w \times h}{3}$$

EXAMPLE The Great Pyramid of Egypt has a square base. Each side of the base is 230 meters long. The height of the pyramid is 147 meters. Find the volume.

Solution: $V = \frac{l \times w \times h}{3}$ ◁ $l = 230\ m;\ w = 230\ m;\ h = 147\ m$

$V = \frac{230 \times 230 \times 147}{3} = \frac{7,776,300}{3}$

$V = 2,592,100$ The volume is **2,592,100 m³**.

REVIEW OF RELATED SKILLS
You may wish to use these exercises before teaching the lesson.

Find each answer. (Pages 62–63)

1. $9 \times 6 \div 3$ 18
2. $18 \times 21 \div 3$ 126
3. $7 \times 9 \div 3$ 21
4. $17 \times 15 \div 3$ 85
5. $6.3 \times 9 \div 3$ 18.9
6. $3.3 \times 8 \div 3$ 8.8
7. $4.2 \times 7 \div 3$ 9.8
8. $9.1 \times 6 \div 3$ 18.2
9. $0.27 \times 1.5 \div 3$ 0.135
10. $2.1 \times 2.4 \div 3$ 1.68
11. $3.9 \times 4.6 \div 3$ 5.98
12. $3.6 \times 2.9 \times 4 \div 3$ 13.92
13. $7.8 \times 2.5 \times 8 \div 3$ 52
14. $8.6 \times 7.9 \times 6 \div 3$ 135.88

EXERCISES
See the suggested assignment guide in the Teacher's Manual.

Find the volume of each pyramid.

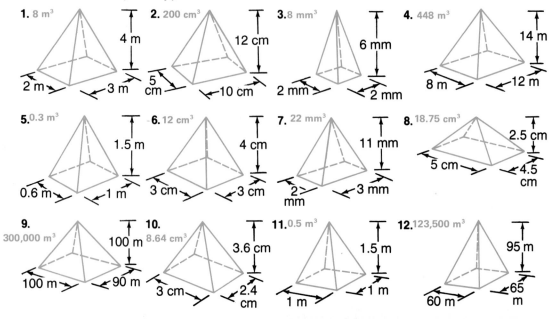

1. 8 m³   4 m   2 m   3 m

2. 200 cm³   12 cm   5 cm   10 cm

3. 8 mm³   6 mm   2 mm   2 mm

4. 448 m³   14 m   8 m   12 m

5. 0.3 m³   1.5 m   0.6 m   1 m

6. 12 cm³   4 cm   3 cm   3 cm

7. 22 mm³   11 mm   2 mm   3 mm

8. 18.75 cm³   2.5 cm   5 cm   4.5 cm

9. 300,000 m³   100 m   100 m   90 m

10. 8.64 cm³   3.6 cm   3 cm   2.4 cm

11. 0.5 m³   1.5 m   1 m   1 m

12. 123,500 m³   95 m   60 m   65 m

APPLICATIONS: Using Volume

13. Two girls pitched a tent that has the shape of a pyramid. The base of the tent is a rectangle that is 2.1 meters long and 2.4 meters wide. The tent is 2 meters high. Find the volume.   3.36 m³

14. A pyramid–shaped popcorn container has a rectangular base. The base is 13 centimeters long and 9 centimeters wide. The container is 22.5 centimeters high. Find the volume.   877.5 cm³

In Exercises 15–16, look for <u>hidden questions</u>.   Exercises 15-16 are two-step problems.

15. A parking lot has pyramid–shaped markers with rectangular bases. The markers are 0.3 meters wide, 0.4 meters long, and 0.8 meters high. How many cubic meters of concrete will be needed to make 40 of these markers?   1.28 m³

16. The entrance to the parking lot has two pyramid–shaped pillars with square bases. Each side of a base is 1.2 meters long and each pillar is 2.1 meters high. Find the total volume of the pillars.   2.016 m³

Chapter Review

Part 1: Vocabulary

For Exercises 1–7, choose from the box at the right the word(s) or number(s) that completes each statement.

square meter
0
1000
gram
0.001
rectangular
100
meter
cubic centimeter

1. To change from liters to milliliters, multiply by __?__. 1000 (Page 156)

2. To change from grams to kilograms, multiply by __?__. 0.001 (Page 158)

3. A unit of mass in the metric system is the __?__. gram (Page 158)

4. Water freezes at __?__ degrees Celsius. 0 (Page 160)

5. Water boils at __?__ degrees Celsius. 100 (Page 160)

6. A shoe box is an example of a __?__ prism. rectangular (Page 162)

7. A unit of volume in the metric system is the __?__. (Page 164) cubic centimeter

Part 2: Skills

Choose the most suitable measure. Choose a, b, or c.   (Pages 156–157)

8. Soup bowl b	**a.** 3 L	**b.** 300 mL	**c.** 30 mL
9. Gas can a	**a.** 4 L	**b.** 40 L	**c.** 40 mL
10. Water glass c	**a.** 2.5 L	**b.** 25 L	**c.** 250 mL
11. Can of oil c	**a.** 950 L	**b.** 950 mL	**c.** 1 L
12. Bathtub a	**a.** 150 L	**b.** 15 mL	**c.** 150 mL

Complete.   (Pages 156–157)

13. 23 L = __?__ mL 23,000
14. 400 mL = __?__ L 0.4
15. 3.9 L = __?__ mL 3900
16. 0.62 mL = __?__ L 0.00062
17. 46 L = __?__ mL 46,000
18. 348 mL = __?__ L 0.348

Choose the most suitable measure. Choose a, b, or c.   (Pages 158–159)

19. Dime b	**a.** 3 mg	**b.** 3 g	**c.** 3 kg
20. Magazine c	**a.** 0.5 mg	**b.** 0.5 g	**c.** 0.5 kg
21. Bowling ball c	**a.** 8 mg	**b.** 8 g	**c.** 8 kg
22. Tennis racquet c	**a.** 1 kg	**b.** 1 g	**c.** 500 g
23. Tea bag b	**a.** 1 mg	**b.** 1 g	**c.** 1 kg

Complete.   (Pages 158–159)

24. 2.1 kg = __?__ g 2100
25. 47 g = __?__ mg 47,000
26. 46.1 g = __?__ kg 0.0461
27. 0.73 g = __?__ mg 730
28. 5.9 kg = __?__ g 5900
29. 28 mg = __?__ g 0.028

For Exercises 30–36, find the surface area of each rectangular prism.
(Pages 162–163)

30. Trunk 3.66 m²

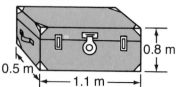

0.5 m
0.8 m
1.1 m

31. Radio 1242 m²

18 cm
24 cm
4.5 cm

32. Suitcase 11,550 cm²

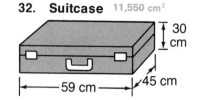

30 cm
59 cm
45 cm

	Length	Width	Height	
33.	8 cm	4 cm	3 cm	136 cm²
34.	4.6 m	1.2 m	0.6 m	18 m²

	Length	Width	Height	
35.	9 m	5 m	2.3 m	154.4 m²
36.	21 cm	10 cm	5 cm	730 cm²

For Exercises 37–43, find the volume. (Pages 164–165)

37. Refrigerator 0.56 m³

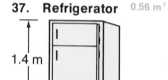

1.4 m
0.8 m 0.5 m

38. Cabinet 0.864 m³

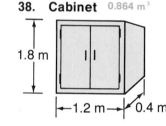

1.8 m
1.2 m 0.4 m

39. Drawer 0.21 m³

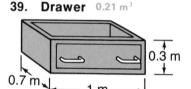

0.3 m
0.7 m
1 m

	Length	Width	Height	
40.	5 cm	3 cm	4 cm	60 cm³
41.	6.1 m	4.2 m	5 m	128.1 m³

	Length	Width	Height	
42.	4 cm	4 cm	4 cm	64 cm³
43.	3.2 m	1.8 m	2 m	11.52 m³

Find the volume of each pyramid. (Pages 167–168)

44. 192 m³

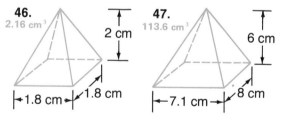

12 m
12 m 4 m

45. 15 m³

5 m
3 m 3 m

46. 2.16 cm³

2 cm
1.8 cm 1.8 cm

47. 113.6 cm³

6 cm
7.1 cm 8 cm

Part 3: Applications

48. One teaspoon contains 5 milliliters. How many teaspoons can be poured from a bottle containing 250 milliliters? (Pages 156–157) 50

49. An elevator is carrying 10 people. The average mass of each person is 83 kilograms. Find the total mass of the people. (Pages 158–159) 830

50. The room temperature is 15°C. Would you turn on the air conditioning or turn on a heater? (Page 160) heater

51. The outdoor temperature is 30°C. Is this temperature more typical of winter or of summer? (Page 160) summer

Chapter Test

The Teacher's Resource Book contains two forms of each chapter test.

Choose the most suitable measure. Choose a, b, or c.

1. Can of juice b   **a.** 50 L   **b.** 500 mL   **c.** 50 mL
2. Automobile c   **a.** 2200 mg   **b.** 2200 g   **c.** 2200 kg
3. Tablespoon c   **a.** 15 L   **b.** 150 mL   **c.** 15 mL
4. Postcard a   **a.** 2 g   **b.** 2 kg   **c.** 2 mg
5. Thermos bottle c   **a.** 1900 mL   **b.** 19 L   **c.** 1 L

Complete.

        4200   30,100   0.78   0.0296

6. 4.2 L = __?__ mL   **7.** 30.1 kg = __?__ g   **8.** 780 mL = __?__ L   **9.** 29.6 mg = __?__ g

Find the surface area of each rectangular prism.

10. Book 2278.5 cm²   **11. Jewelry Box** 1181 cm²   **12. Packing Crate** 16 m²

20 cm   45.5 cm   3.5 cm

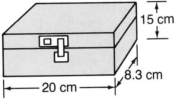
15 cm   20 cm   8.3 cm

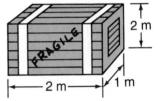
2 m   2 m   1 m

Find the volume of each rectangular prism.

	Length	Width	Height	
13.	4 cm	3 cm	2 cm	24 cm³
14.	6.2 m	4.1 m	5 m	127.1 m³

	Length	Width	Height	
15.	8 cm	8 cm	8 cm	512 cm³
16.	1.9 m	1.7 m	1.5 m	4.845 m³

Solve.

17. One tablespoon contains 15 milliliters. How many tablespoons can be poured from a bottle containing 240 milliliters? 16

18. An airplane is carrying 120 passengers. The average mass of each passenger is 80 kilograms. Find the total mass. 9600 kg

19. The outdoor temperature on a day in February is 25°C. Is this temperature more typical of Arizona or Maine? Arizona

20. The room temperature is 30°C. Would you turn on the air conditioner or raise the setting on the thermostat? air conditioner

Additional Practice

Skills

Complete. (Pages 156–157)

1. 48 L = ? mL 48,000
2. 220 mL = ? L 0.22
3. 4.2 L = ? mL 4200
4. 300 L = ? mL 300,000
5. 0.2 mL ? L 0.0002
6. 2.3 L = ? mL 2300
7. 3.81 mL = ? L 0.00381
8. 3.9 mL = ? L 0.0039

(Pages 158–159)

9. 4.3 kg = ? g 4300
10. 23 g = ? mg 23,000
11. 5.6 mg = ? g 0.0056
12. 320 g = ? kg 0.32
13. 0.02 g = ? kg 0.00002
14. 320 mg = ? g 0.32
15. 0.08 g = ? mg 80
16. 0.9 kg = ? g 900

For Exercises 17–23, find the surface area. (Pages 162–163)

17. Cereal Box 800 cm²

22 cm

Wheat Flakes KRAGER

12 cm   4 cm

18. Shoe Box 2880 cm²
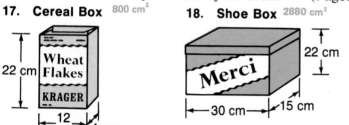
22 cm
Merci
30 cm   15 cm

19. File Cabinet 3.52 m²
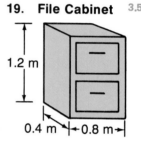
1.2 m
0.4 m   0.8 m

	Length	Width	Height	
20.	5 cm	2 cm	4 cm	76 cm²
21.	12.8 cm	9.4 cm	3.1 cm	378.28 cm²

	Length	Width	Height	
22.	8 cm	6 m	3.9 m	205.2 m²
23.	16 cm	14 cm	8 cm	928 cm²

For Exercises 24–27, find the volume. (Pages 164–165)

	Length	Width	Height	
24.	9 cm	6 m	5.1 m	275.4 m³
25.	14 cm	12 cm	8 cm	1344 cm³

	Length	Width	Height	
26.	9 cm	9 cm	9 cm	729 cm³
27.	2.1 m	1.9 m	1 m	3.99 m³

Find the volume of each pyramid. (Pages 167–168)

28. 15 m³
5 m
3 m   3 m

29. 3400 cm³
17 cm   20 cm

30 20 mm³
30 cm
3 mm   2 mm

31. 84 m³
10 mm
4.5 m
8 m   7 m

Applications

32. A drinking glass contains 250 milliliters. How many glasses can be poured from a 1 liter bottle? (Pages 156–157)   4

33. A bus is carrying 45 people. The average mass of each person is 75 kilograms. Find the total mass. (Pages 158–159)   3375 kg

Cumulative Review: Chapters 5–8

You may also wish to use at this time the cumulative review on page 446 titled Review of Skills that reviews only the skills presented in Chapters 1-8.

Choose the correct answer. Choose a, b, c, or d.

1. Which decimal has the greatest value? d

  a. 0.631   **b.** 0.607

  c. 0.065   **d.** 0.64

2. Multiply: a $\begin{array}{r} 0.735 \\ \times \quad 82 \end{array}$

  a. 60.270   **b.** 57.860

  c. 59.270   **d.** 60.027

3. Round 32.766 to the nearest hundredth. d

  a. 32.700   **b.** 32.800

  c. 32.760   **d.** 32.770

4. Multiply: 53.2×0.001 b

  a. 0.532   **b.** 0.0532

  c. 5.32   **d.** 5320

5. Divide: $3.05\overline{)0.00122}$ b

  a. 0.0400   **b.** 0.0004

  c. 0.4   **d.** 4000

6. Which is the most appropriate temperature for a hot summer day? c

  a. 2°C   **b.** 78°C   **c.** 33°C   **d.** 95°C

7. Multiply: 2.09×0.007 c

  a. 14.63   **b.** 14.063

  c. 0.01463   **d.** 1.4063

8. Divide: $18\overline{)8.28}$ a

  a. 0.46   **b.** 4.6   **c.** 1.46   **d.** 46

9. Add: $1.59 + 39.4 + 0.003$ b

  a. 0.556   **b.** 40.993

  c. 41.02   **d.** 5.56

10. Subtract: d $\begin{array}{r} 87.03 \\ - \quad 5.27 \end{array}$

  a. 71.76   **b.** 82.85

  c. 82.76   **d.** 81.76

11. Which number represents twenty–seven and sixteen thousandths? b

  a. 2716   **b.** 27.016

  c. 27.160   **d.** 16.27

12. Which unit would you use to measure the distance from Miami to Dallas? a

  a. kilometers   **b.** meters

  c. liters   **d.** millimeters

13. Complete: $8 \text{ kg} = \underline{} \text{ g}$ d

  a. 80   **b.** 0.008   **c.** 800   **d.** 8000

14. In 5371.0964, which digit is in the thousandths place? b

  a. 5   **b.** 6   **c.** 4   **d.** 9

15. Find the perimeter. c

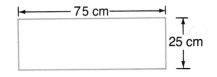

  a. 625   **b.** 100   **c.** 200   **d.** 450

16. Which shows the numbers 0.4, 0.04, and 4.4 listed from smallest to largest? c

a. 0.4, 0.04, 4.4
b. 0.4, 4.4, 0.04
c. 0.04, 0.4, 4.4
d. 0.04, 4.4, 0.4

17. How many square centimeters are there in the area of this stamp? b

2.1 cm

|←2.1 cm→|

a. 44.1
b. 4.41
c. 0.441
d. 4.2

18. Divide: $3.27\overline{)4.873}$ d
Round the quotient to the nearest tenth.

a. 1.490
b. 1.4
c. 1.49
d. 1.5

19. Divide: $3.86 \div 0.01$ a

a. 386
b. 38.6
c. 0.386
d. 0.0386

20. Which unit would you use to measure a glass of water? d

a. grams
b. liters
c. meters
d. milliliters

21. Find the cost of 7300 cubic feet of natural gas at 41¢ per 100 cubic feet. a

a. $29.93
b. $3.00
c. $2.99
d. $2993.00

22. Subtract: $8 - 2.9$ c

a. 6.9
b. 6.1
c. 5.1
d. 5.9

23. Find the volume in cubic meters of this packing crate. b

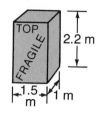

a. 33
b. 3.3
c. 0.33
d. 330

24. Give the length of the nail to the nearest millimeter. c

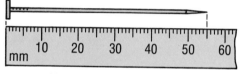

a. 60
b. 50
c. 55
d. 5.5

25. Add: $34 + 0.47 + 1.983$ a

a. 36.453
b. 37.553
c. 2064
d. 20.64

26. Multiply: 0.042×1000 b

a. 4.2
b. 42
c. 420
d. 0.42

27. In 34.07<u>8</u>, give the value of the underlined digit. d

a. tens
b. hundredths
c. tenths
d. thousandths

28. Choose the best estimate. c
$$15.2 \div 2.9$$
a. 3
b. 4
c. 5
d. 6

29. Choose the best estimate. b
$$19.8 \times 4.1$$
a. 5
b. 80
c. 60
d. 4

30. A refrigerator costs $888.00. It can also be bought on credit by paying $41.50 a month for 24 months. Find the cost of credit. a

  a. $108.00   **b.** $112.00

  c. $996.00   **d.** $929.50

31. A teaspoon contains 5 milliliters. How many teaspoons are there in 125 milliliters? c

  a. 40   **b.** 0.04   **c.** 25   **d.** 15

32. A rectangular rug is 4.1 meters long and 1.9 meters wide. Find the perimeter in meters. b

  a. 7.79   **b.** 12   **c.** 6   **d.** 15.58

33. Sound travels in water at a rate of 1460 meters per second. At one point in the Atlantic Ocean, it takes 5.39 seconds for sound waves to reach the bottom. Find the depth in meters. b

  a. 786.94   **b.** 7869.4

  c. 7859.5   **d.** 7738.1

34. Choose the best way to make change. b

Amount of Sale	Money Received	Change Due
$8.75	$10-bill	$1.25

  a. Four quarters, 2 dimes, 1 nickel

  b. One $1-bill, 1 quarter

  c. One $1-bill, 2 dimes, 1 nickel

  d. Four quarters, 5 nickels

35. Fifteen pounds of coffee cost $45.35. Estimate the cost of one pound. b

  a. $2   **b.** $3   **c.** $4   **d.** $5

36. In a speed-skating contest, one athlete skated 1800 meters in 3.2 minutes. Find the rate in meters per minute. d

  a. 56.25   **b.** 5625

  c. 0.5625   **d.** 562.5

37. A rectangular box is 4.5 centimeters long, 3 centimeters wide, and 3.5 centimeters deep. Find the volume in cubic centimeters. a

  a. 47.25   **b.** 11

  c. 42   **d.** 45.25

38. A triangular sail has a height of 7 meters. The base of the sail is 8.5 meters wide. Find the area in square meters. a

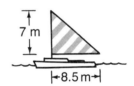

  a. 29.75

  b. 59.5

  c. 56.5

  d. 29.5

39. The cost of a 1.6-liter bottle of fruit is $1.09. Find the unit price. Round your answer to the nearest tenth of a cent. c

  a. 68.2¢   **b.** 68.0¢

  c. 68.1¢   **d.** 51.0¢

40. Find the surface area in square centimeters of this box. c

  a. 900   **b.** 800   **c.** 950   **d.** 1500

REVIEW OF RELATED SKILLS FOR CHAPTER 9

Add. (Pages 2–3)

1. $13 + 26$ 39   2. $15 + 14$ 29   3. $21 + 17$ 38   4. $32 + 43$ 75   5. $19 + 17$ 36

6. $15 + 27$ 42   7. $25 + 17$ 42   8. $62 + 39$ 101   9. $47 + 53$ 100   10. $18 + 24$ 42

11. $28 + 29$ 57   12. $17 + 16$ 33   13. $23 + 36$ 59   14. $28 + 38$ 66   15. $64 + 18$ 82

Subtract. (Pages 10–11)

16. $23 - 9$ 14   17. $32 - 17$ 15   18. $43 - 28$ 15   19. $34 - 6$ 28   20. $23 - 18$ 5

21. $36 - 19$ 17   22. $41 - 26$ 15   23. $52 - 35$ 17   24. $26 - 17$ 9   25. $63 - 51$ 12

26. $72 - 60$ 12   27. $83 - 46$ 37   28. $42 - 19$ 23   29. $54 - 37$ 17   30. $81 - 78$ 3

Multiply. (Pages 26–27)

31. 31×7 217   32. 14×8 112   33. 22×6 132   34. 45×5 225   35. 12×7 84

36. 16×4 64   37. 50×3 150   38. 26×8 208   39. 31×9 279   40. 38×5 190

41. 13×6 78   42. 12×9 108   43. 11×4 44   44. 16×8 128   45. 24×9 216

46. 25×8 200   47. 27×4 108   48. 21×3 63   49. 18×7 126   50. 17×9 153

State whether the first two numbers are divisible by the third number.
Answer <u>Yes</u> <u>or</u> <u>No</u>. (Pages 48–49)

51. 75 and 40 by 5   Yes   52. 14 and 24 by 2   Yes   53. 26 and 28 by 4   No

54. 51 and 37 by 3   No   55. 39 and 48 by 3   Yes   56. 70 and 60 by 10   Yes

57. 18 and 27 by 2   No   58. 51 and 33 by 9   No   59. 36 and 54 by 9   Yes

60. 72 and 48 by 4   Yes   61. 40 and 55 by 10   No   62. 60 and 52 by 5   No

63. 63 and 72 by 9   Yes   64. 44 and 28 by 4   Yes   65. 46 and 52 by 4   No

Divide. (Pages 50–51, 54–55)

66. $35 \div 7$ 5   67. $42 \div 3$ 14   68. $56 \div 4$ 14   69. $90 \div 9$ 10   70. $48 \div 3$ 16

71. $22 \div 2$ 11   72. $49 \div 7$ 7   73. $72 \div 6$ 12   74. $60 \div 5$ 12   75. $64 \div 4$ 16

76. $200 \div 25$ 8   77. $336 \div 16$ 21   78. $108 \div 12$ 9   79. $240 \div 16$ 15   80. $144 \div 12$ 12

81. $378 \div 18$ 21   82. $192 \div 16$ 12   83. $154 \div 14$ 11   84. $120 \div 15$ 8   85. $153 \div 17$ 9

Replace the ● with $<$, $=$, or $>$.
(Pages 50–51, 54–55, 90–91, 110–111, 112–113)

86. $1.7 ● 1$ $>$ 87. $0.8 ● 1$ $<$ 88. $0.99 ● 1$ $<$ 89. $2.34 ● 1$ $>$

90. $4.3 ● 1$ $>$ 91. $0.95 ● 1$ $<$ 92. $1.00 ● 1$ $=$ 93. $0.63 ● 1$ $<$

94. $(14 \div 7) ● 1$ $>$ 95. $(32 \div 48) ● 1$ $<$ 96. $(21 \div 21) ● 1$ $=$ 97. $(7 \div 9) ● 1$ $<$

98. $(6 \div 0.25) ● 1$ $>$ 99. $(1.2 \div 3) ● 1$ $<$ 100. $(2 \div 2.6) ● 1$ $<$ 101. $(3.7 \div 2) ● 1$ $>$

SKILLS

9-1   Fractions and Mixed Numbers
9-2   Lowest Terms
9-3   Addition and Subtraction: Like Fractions
9-4   Writing Like Fractions
9-5   Addition and Subtraction: Unlike Fractions
9-6   Subtraction: Mixed Numbers

APPLICATIONS

Customary Measures
Train Schedules
Time Cards
Customary Measures

CAREERS

Carpet Installer
Transportation

9-1 Fractions and Mixed Numbers

See the Teacher's Manual for the objectives.

A **fraction** is the quotient of two whole numbers. That is,

$$2 \div 3 \text{ can be written as } \tfrac{2}{3}. \quad \blacktriangleleft \textbf{\textit{Fraction}}$$

In the fraction $\tfrac{2}{3}$, the numerator is 2 and the denominator is 3. The denominator of a fraction can <u>never</u> be zero. Fractions can represent a number greater than 1, less than 1, or equal to 1.

PROCEDURE To determine whether a fraction is greater than 1, less than 1, or equal to 1, compare the numerator with the denominator.

a. When the numerator is less than the denominator, the fraction is less than 1.

b. When the numerator equals the denominator, the fraction equals 1.

c. When the numerator is greater than the denominator, the fraction is greater than 1.

EXAMPLE 1 Replace each ● with $<$, $=$, or $>$. Give a reason for each answer.

a. $\tfrac{6}{5}$ ● 1   **b.** $\tfrac{0}{1}$ ● 1   **c.** $\tfrac{15}{15}$ ● 1   **d.** $\tfrac{3}{5}$ ● 1

Solutions: **a.** $\tfrac{6}{5} > 1$ because $6 > 5$.   **b.** $\tfrac{0}{1} < 1$ because $0 < 1$.

c. $\tfrac{15}{15} = 1$ because $15 = 15$.   **d.** $\tfrac{3}{5} < 1$ because $3 < 5$.

After completing Example 1, you may wish to have students do some or all of Exercises 1-15.

A fraction greater than 1 can be written as a **mixed number.**

PROCEDURE To write a mixed number for a fraction greater than 1:

[1] Divide the numerator by the denominator.

[2] Write a fraction for the remainder.

EXAMPLE 2 Write a mixed number for $\tfrac{21}{5}$.

Solution: [1] $\tfrac{21}{5}$ means $21 \div 5$. ◀——— $5\overline{)21}$ with quotient 4, $\tfrac{20}{1}$

[2] Quotient: **4** $r\,1$, or $4\tfrac{1}{5}$ ◀——— Remainder
                                              ◀——— Divisor

Thus, $\tfrac{21}{5} = 4\tfrac{1}{5}$ ◀ **\textit{Mixed number}**

Divide.   (Pages 50–51, 54–55)

1. $12 \div 4$ 3
2. $15 \div 3$ 5
3. $8 \div 8$ 1
4. $20 \div 20$ 1
5. $132 \div 11$ 12

6. $100 \div 5$ 20
7. $20 \div 4$ 5
8. $81 \div 3$ 27
9. $133 \div 7$ 19
10. $169 \div 13$ 13

Replace each ● *with* <, =, *or* >.   (Pages 50–51, 54–55, 90–91, 110–111, 112–113)

11. 0 ● 1 <
12. 3 ● 1 >
13. 1.9 ● 1 >
14. 0.5 ● 1 <

15. $(3 \div 3)$ ● 1 =
16. $(32 \div 16)$ ● 1 >
17. $(8 \div 0.25)$ ● 1 >
18. $(50 \div 50)$ ● 1 =

EXERCISES
See the suggested assignment guide in the Teacher's Manual.

Replace each ● *with* <, =, *or* >.   (Example 1)

1. $\frac{1}{3}$ ● 1 <
2. $\frac{3}{3}$ ● 1 =
3. $\frac{7}{3}$ ● 1 >
4. $\frac{5}{3}$ ● 1 >
5. $\frac{1}{9}$ ● 1 <

6. $\frac{8}{9}$ ● 1 <
7. $\frac{9}{8}$ ● 1 >
8. $\frac{8}{8}$ ● 1 =
9. $\frac{5}{4}$ ● 1 >
10. $\frac{4}{5}$ ● 1 <

11. $\frac{5}{5}$ ● 1 =
12. $\frac{10}{5}$ ● 1 >
13. $\frac{19}{20}$ ● 1 <
14. $\frac{8}{5}$ ● 1 >
15. $\frac{1}{1}$ ● 1 =

Write a mixed number for each fraction.   (Example 2)

16. $\frac{5}{4}$ $1\frac{1}{4}$
17. $\frac{5}{2}$ $2\frac{1}{2}$
18. $\frac{9}{8}$ $1\frac{1}{8}$
19. $\frac{9}{4}$ $2\frac{1}{4}$
20. $\frac{5}{3}$ $1\frac{2}{3}$
21. $\frac{7}{3}$ $2\frac{1}{3}$
22. $\frac{7}{5}$ $1\frac{2}{5}$

23. $\frac{8}{5}$ $1\frac{3}{5}$
24. $\frac{9}{7}$ $1\frac{2}{7}$
25. $\frac{9}{6}$ $1\frac{3}{6}$
26. $\frac{6}{4}$ $1\frac{2}{4}$
27. $\frac{7}{4}$ $1\frac{3}{4}$
28. $\frac{8}{3}$ $2\frac{2}{3}$
29. $\frac{10}{3}$ $3\frac{1}{3}$

30. $\frac{10}{4}$ $2\frac{2}{4}$
31. $\frac{11}{2}$ $5\frac{1}{2}$
32. $\frac{17}{6}$ $2\frac{5}{6}$
33. $\frac{15}{2}$ $7\frac{1}{2}$
34. $\frac{13}{4}$ $3\frac{1}{4}$
35. $\frac{15}{4}$ $3\frac{3}{4}$
36. $\frac{18}{5}$ $3\frac{3}{5}$

37. $\frac{21}{5}$ $4\frac{1}{5}$
38. $\frac{21}{8}$ $2\frac{5}{8}$
39. $\frac{25}{8}$ $3\frac{1}{8}$
40. $\frac{21}{10}$ $2\frac{1}{10}$
41. $\frac{21}{11}$ $1\frac{10}{11}$
42. $\frac{35}{13}$ $2\frac{9}{13}$
43. $\frac{45}{12}$ $3\frac{9}{12}$

Mixed Practice The Mixed Practice contains exercises that relate to both Examples 1 and 2.

Replace each ● *with* <, =, *or* >. *Then write a mixed number for each fraction greater than 1.*

44. $\frac{18}{25}$ ● 1 <
45. $\frac{27}{25}$ ● 1 >; $1\frac{2}{25}$
46. $\frac{25}{25}$ ● 1 =
47. $\frac{51}{25}$ ● 1 >; $2\frac{1}{25}$
48. $\frac{20}{23}$ ● 1 <

49. $\frac{13}{20}$ ● 1 <
50. $\frac{30}{20}$ ● 1 >; $1\frac{10}{20}$
51. $\frac{33}{33}$ ● 1 =
52. $\frac{64}{12}$ ● 1 >; $5\frac{4}{12}$
53. $\frac{24}{64}$ ● 1 <

54. $\frac{10}{7}$ ● 1 >; $1\frac{3}{7}$
55. $\frac{15}{4}$ ● 1 >; $3\frac{3}{4}$
56. $\frac{9}{11}$ ● 1 <
57. $\frac{17}{20}$ ● 1 <
58. $\frac{13}{3}$ ● 1 >; $4\frac{1}{3}$

APPLICATIONS: Using Fractions

Write a mixed number for each fraction.

59. In 1980, the cost of first-class postage was $\frac{5}{2}$ times the cost in 1970. $2\frac{1}{2}$

60. In 1980, the cost of laundry services was $\frac{8}{4}$ times the cost in 1970. 2

61. In 1980, the cost of developing film was $\frac{4}{3}$ times the cost in 1970. $1\frac{1}{3}$

62. In 1980, the cost of auto insurance was $\frac{19}{10}$ times the cost in 1970. $1\frac{9}{10}$

Problem Solving and Applications

Using Customary Measures

See the Teacher's Manual for the objectives.

This lesson combines the concepts presented in Section 9-1 with using customary measures of length.

You can measure the length of an object to the nearest inch, to the nearest $\frac{1}{2}$-inch, to the nearest $\frac{1}{4}$-inch, and so on.

EXAMPLE Give the length of the pencil to the nearest unit.

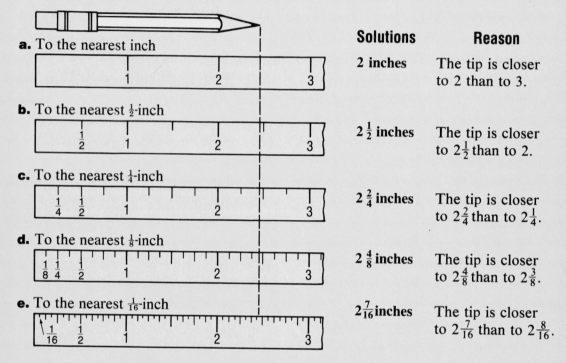

Solutions | **Reason**

a. To the nearest inch

2 inches — The tip is closer to 2 than to 3.

b. To the nearest $\frac{1}{2}$-inch

$2\frac{1}{2}$ inches — The tip is closer to $2\frac{1}{2}$ than to 2.

c. To the nearest $\frac{1}{4}$-inch

$2\frac{2}{4}$ inches — The tip is closer to $2\frac{2}{4}$ than to $2\frac{1}{4}$.

d. To the nearest $\frac{1}{8}$-inch

$2\frac{4}{8}$ inches — The tip is closer to $2\frac{4}{8}$ than to $2\frac{3}{8}$.

e. To the nearest $\frac{1}{16}$-inch

$2\frac{7}{16}$ inches — The tip is closer to $2\frac{7}{16}$ than to $2\frac{8}{16}$.

Exercises

Give the length of each object to the nearest indicated unit.

1. To the nearest $\frac{1}{4}$-inch $\quad 1\frac{1}{4}$ inches

2. To the nearest $\frac{1}{2}$-inch. $\quad 1\frac{1}{2}$ inches

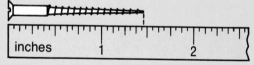

3. To the nearest $\frac{1}{8}$-inch $\quad \frac{6}{8}$ inch

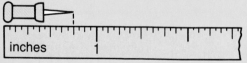

4. To the nearest $\frac{1}{16}$-inch $\quad 1\frac{9}{16}$ inches

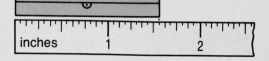

Application

CARPET INSTALLER

Career Lessons are optional.
This lesson combines the skill of reading a table with rounding and multiplication of decimals.

Carpet installers use a table such as the one below to **estimate** the number of packages of carpet squares needed to cover a floor. Each carpet square covers <u>one</u> <u>square foot</u>. Thus, a package of 10 covers 10 square feet.

Room Length	Room Width									
	4	**6**	**8**	**9**	**10**	**12**	**14**	**16**	**18**	**20**
4	2	3	4	4	4	5	6	7	8	8
6	3	4	5	6	6	8	9	10	11	12
8	4	5	7	8	8	10	12	13	15	16
9	4	6	8	9	9	11	13	15	17	18
10	4	6	8	9	10	12	14	16	18	20
12	5	8	10	11	12	15	17	20	22	24

EXAMPLE

A package of 10 carpet squares costs $9.95. Estimate the cost of carpeting a room that is $11\frac{1}{4}$ feet long and $9\frac{1}{2}$ feet wide.

Solution:

1 Round the length and the width to the <u>next largest</u> foot.

$11\frac{1}{4}$ $\longrightarrow$ 12 feet $9\frac{1}{2}$ $\longrightarrow$ 10 feet

2 Read the table to find the number of packages needed.

About **12 packages** will be needed.

3 Estimate the cost. Round $9.95 to $10.

$12 \times \$10 = \$120$ The carpet squares will cost about **$120.**

EXERCISES   Note that Exercises 1-3 are non-verbal.

For Exercises 1–3, estimate the cost of carpet tiles for each room.

	Room		Number of Packages	Cost per Package of 10	Total Cost	
	Length	Width				
1.	8 feet	14 feet	_?_ 12	$ 9.80	_?_	$120
2.	$11\frac{3}{4}$ feet	$11\frac{1}{4}$ feet	_?_ 15	$10.95	_?_	$165
3.	$11\frac{1}{2}$ feet	$17\frac{2}{3}$ feet	_?_ 22	$11.80	_?_	$264

4. Estimate the cost of carpeting a room $9\frac{3}{4}$ feet long and $13\frac{2}{3}$ feet wide. The cost per package of 10 carpet squares is $14.85.

5. Estimate the cost of carpeting a room $11\frac{7}{8}$ feet long and 16 feet wide. The cost per package of 10 carpet squares is $13.98.

14 × 15 = $210   20 × 14 = $280

9-2 Lowest Terms

See the Teacher's Manual for the objectives.

A fraction is in **lowest terms** when the numerator <u>and</u> denominator <u>cannot</u> be divided evenly by the same number except one. To write a fraction in lowest terms, follow this procedure.

PROCEDURE To write a fraction in lowest terms:

$\boxed{1}$ Divide the numerator <u>and</u> the denominator by a number that will divide evenly into both.

$\boxed{2}$ Repeat Step 1 until the numerator and denominator cannot be divided evenly by the same number except 1.

EXAMPLE Write in lowest terms. Then write a mixed number for any fraction greater than 1.

a. $\frac{18}{24}$　　　　　　**b.** $\frac{45}{12}$

Solutions:

a. $\frac{18}{24} = \frac{18 \div 2}{24 \div 2}$

$= \frac{9}{12}$ ◀ *Not in lowest terms*

$= \frac{9 \div 3}{12 \div 3}$

$= \frac{3}{4}$ ◀ *Lowest terms*

b. $\frac{45}{12} = \frac{45 \div 3}{12 \div 3}$

$= \frac{15}{4}$ ◀ *Write as a mixed number.*

$= 3\frac{3}{4}$

REVIEW OF RELATED SKILLS

You may wish to use these exercises before teaching the lesson.

Divide. (Pages 50–51, 54–55)

1. $21 \div 7$ ₃ **2.** $90 \div 10$ ₉ **3.** $48 \div 16$ ₃ **4.** $625 \div 25$ ₂₅ **5.** $225 \div 9$ ₂₅

6. $84 \div 6$ ₁₄ **7.** $48 \div 3$ ₁₆ **8.** $164 \div 4$ ₄₁ **9.** $168 \div 12$ ₁₄ **10.** $432 \div 6$ ₇₂

11. $228 \div 4$ ₅₇ **12.** $121 \div 11$ ₁₁ **13.** $325 \div 25$ ₁₃ **14.** $618 \div 6$ ₁₀₃ **15.** $135 \div 5$ ₂₇

State whether the first two numbers are both divisible by the third number. Answer <u>Yes</u> *or* <u>No</u>. (Pages 48–49)

16. 85 and 102 by 5 No
17. 35 and 50 by 5 Yes
18. 20 and 36 by 4 Yes

19. 18 and 32 by 4 No
20. 6 and 20 by 2 Yes
21. 33 and 93 by 3 Yes

22. 10 and 80 by 10 Yes
23. 36 and 45 by 4 No
24. 6 and 42 by 3 Yes

25. 18 and 81 by 9 Yes
26. 24 and 80 by 3 No
27. 63 and 72 by 9 Yes

28. 56 and 64 by 4 Yes
29. 20 and 35 by 5 Yes
30. 21 and 28 by 3 No

31. 18 and 21 by 2 No
32. 14 and 24 by 4 No
33. 39 and 48 by 3 Yes

EXERCISES

Write in lowest terms. Then write a mixed number for any fraction greater than one.

1. $\frac{4}{10}$ $\frac{2}{5}$
2. $\frac{6}{9}$ $\frac{2}{3}$
3. $\frac{5}{7}$ $\frac{5}{7}$
4. $\frac{12}{64}$ $\frac{3}{16}$
5. $\frac{45}{80}$ $\frac{9}{16}$
6. $\frac{8}{24}$ $\frac{1}{3}$
7. $\frac{21}{36}$ $\frac{7}{12}$
8. $\frac{14}{30}$ $\frac{7}{15}$

9. $\frac{25}{90}$ $\frac{5}{18}$
10. $\frac{13}{39}$ $\frac{1}{3}$
11. $\frac{6}{12}$ $\frac{1}{2}$
12. $\frac{12}{60}$ $\frac{1}{5}$
13. $\frac{14}{35}$ $\frac{2}{5}$
14. $\frac{13}{15}$ $\frac{13}{15}$
15. $\frac{15}{45}$ $\frac{1}{3}$
16. $\frac{8}{12}$ $\frac{2}{3}$

17. $\frac{10}{80}$ $\frac{1}{8}$
18. $\frac{7}{12}$ $\frac{7}{12}$
19. $\frac{16}{28}$ $\frac{4}{7}$
20. $\frac{5}{25}$ $\frac{1}{5}$
21. $\frac{9}{36}$ $\frac{1}{4}$
22. $\frac{16}{21}$ $\frac{16}{21}$
23. $\frac{11}{22}$ $\frac{1}{2}$
24. $\frac{1}{8}$ $\frac{1}{8}$

25. $\frac{3}{12}$ $\frac{1}{4}$
26. $\frac{3}{15}$ $\frac{1}{5}$
27. $\frac{2}{16}$ $\frac{1}{8}$
28. $\frac{4}{16}$ $\frac{1}{4}$
29. $\frac{6}{15}$ $\frac{2}{5}$
30. $\frac{6}{14}$ $\frac{3}{7}$
31. $\frac{5}{15}$ $\frac{1}{3}$
32. $\frac{15}{25}$ $\frac{3}{5}$

33. $\frac{4}{14}$ $\frac{2}{7}$
34. $\frac{4}{18}$ $\frac{2}{9}$
35. $\frac{6}{18}$ $\frac{1}{3}$
36. $\frac{6}{24}$ $\frac{1}{4}$
37. $\frac{12}{40}$ $\frac{3}{10}$
38. $\frac{14}{28}$ $\frac{1}{2}$
39. $\frac{14}{32}$ $\frac{7}{16}$
40. $\frac{8}{36}$ $\frac{2}{9}$

41. $\frac{12}{16}$ $\frac{3}{4}$
42. $\frac{12}{18}$ $\frac{2}{3}$
43. $\frac{10}{16}$ $\frac{5}{8}$
44. $\frac{14}{16}$ $\frac{7}{8}$
45. $\frac{12}{20}$ $\frac{3}{5}$
46. $\frac{24}{30}$ $\frac{4}{5}$
47. $\frac{35}{42}$ $\frac{5}{6}$
48. $\frac{20}{32}$ $\frac{5}{8}$

49. $\frac{21}{24}$ $\frac{7}{8}$
50. $\frac{6}{32}$ $\frac{3}{16}$
51. $\frac{15}{48}$ $\frac{5}{16}$
52. $\frac{45}{80}$ $\frac{9}{16}$
53. $\frac{28}{30}$ $\frac{14}{15}$
54. $\frac{36}{45}$ $\frac{4}{5}$
55. $\frac{24}{64}$ $\frac{3}{8}$
56. $\frac{39}{48}$ $\frac{13}{16}$

57. $\frac{29}{58}$ $\frac{1}{2}$
58. $\frac{100}{300}$ $\frac{1}{3}$
59. $\frac{50}{75}$ $\frac{2}{3}$
60. $\frac{23}{46}$ $\frac{1}{2}$
61. $\frac{9}{54}$ $\frac{1}{6}$
62. $\frac{21}{66}$ $\frac{7}{22}$
63. $\frac{9}{12}$ $\frac{3}{4}$
64. $\frac{18}{81}$ $\frac{2}{9}$

65. $\frac{75}{500}$ $\frac{3}{20}$
66. $\frac{42}{60}$ $\frac{7}{10}$
67. $\frac{57}{90}$ $\frac{19}{30}$
68. $\frac{58}{60}$ $\frac{29}{30}$
69. $\frac{40}{200}$ $\frac{1}{5}$
70. $\frac{10}{40}$ $\frac{1}{4}$
71. $\frac{18}{21}$ $\frac{6}{7}$
72. $\frac{14}{18}$ $\frac{7}{9}$

73. $\frac{10}{4}$ $\frac{5}{2}$; $2\frac{1}{2}$
74. $\frac{33}{9}$ $\frac{11}{3}$; $3\frac{2}{3}$
75. $\frac{50}{12}$ $\frac{25}{6}$; $4\frac{1}{6}$
76. $\frac{80}{21}$ $3\frac{17}{21}$
77. $\frac{120}{64}$ $\frac{15}{8}$; $1\frac{7}{8}$
78. $\frac{18}{10}$ $\frac{9}{5}$; $1\frac{4}{5}$
79. $\frac{6}{4}$ $\frac{3}{2}$; $1\frac{1}{2}$
80. $\frac{12}{9}$ $\frac{4}{3}$; $1\frac{1}{3}$

81. $\frac{34}{6}$ $\frac{17}{3}$; $5\frac{2}{3}$
82. $\frac{14}{8}$ $\frac{7}{4}$; $1\frac{3}{4}$
83. $\frac{60}{16}$ $\frac{15}{4}$; $3\frac{3}{4}$
84. $\frac{28}{16}$ $\frac{7}{4}$; $1\frac{3}{4}$
85. $\frac{45}{6}$ $\frac{15}{2}$; $7\frac{1}{2}$
86. $\frac{45}{20}$ $\frac{9}{4}$; $2\frac{1}{4}$
87. $\frac{38}{24}$ $\frac{19}{12}$; $1\frac{7}{12}$
88. $\frac{36}{24}$ $\frac{3}{2}$; $1\frac{1}{2}$

89. $\frac{55}{25}$ $\frac{11}{5}$; $2\frac{1}{5}$
90. $\frac{75}{50}$ $\frac{3}{2}$; $1\frac{1}{2}$
91. $\frac{60}{58}$ $\frac{30}{29}$; $1\frac{1}{29}$
92. $\frac{21}{18}$ $\frac{7}{6}$; $1\frac{1}{6}$
93. $\frac{16}{10}$ $\frac{8}{5}$; $1\frac{3}{5}$
94. $\frac{45}{10}$ $\frac{9}{2}$; $4\frac{1}{2}$
95. $\frac{24}{21}$ $\frac{8}{7}$; $1\frac{1}{7}$
96. $\frac{36}{8}$ $\frac{9}{2}$; $4\frac{1}{2}$

97. $\frac{15}{6}$ $\frac{5}{2}$; $2\frac{1}{2}$
98. $\frac{55}{15}$ $\frac{11}{3}$; $3\frac{2}{3}$
99. $\frac{32}{14}$
100. $\frac{60}{42}$
101. $\frac{100}{9}$ $\frac{100}{9}$; $11\frac{1}{9}$
102. $\frac{54}{16}$ $\frac{27}{8}$; $3\frac{3}{8}$
103. $\frac{85}{60}$ $\frac{17}{12}$; $1\frac{5}{12}$
104. $\frac{84}{90}$ $\frac{14}{15}$

105. $\frac{9}{54}$ $\frac{1}{6}$
106. $\frac{5}{80}$ $\frac{1}{16}$
107. $\frac{16}{54}$ $\frac{8}{27}$
108. $\frac{27}{45}$ $\frac{3}{5}$
109. $\frac{32}{64}$ $\frac{1}{2}$
110. $\frac{25}{125}$ $\frac{1}{5}$
111. $\frac{27}{36}$ $\frac{3}{4}$
112. $\frac{19}{76}$ $\frac{1}{4}$

113. $\frac{36}{20}$ $\frac{9}{5}$; $1\frac{4}{5}$
114. $\frac{75}{45}$ $\frac{5}{3}$; $1\frac{2}{3}$
115. $\frac{22}{20}$ $\frac{11}{10}$; $1\frac{1}{10}$
116. $\frac{24}{15}$ $\frac{8}{5}$; $1\frac{3}{5}$
117. $\frac{72}{18}$ 4
118. $\frac{21}{14}$ $\frac{3}{2}$; $1\frac{1}{2}$
119. $\frac{72}{69}$
120. $\frac{17}{12}$

121. $\frac{16}{24}$ $\frac{2}{3}$
122. $\frac{22}{88}$ $\frac{1}{4}$
123. $\frac{120}{45}$ $\frac{8}{3}$; $2\frac{2}{3}$
124. $\frac{360}{125}$
125. $\frac{72}{28}$ $\frac{18}{7}$; $2\frac{4}{7}$
126. $\frac{30}{32}$ $\frac{15}{16}$
127. $\frac{45}{72}$ $\frac{5}{8}$
128. $\frac{54}{4}$

129. $\frac{24}{40}$ $\frac{3}{5}$
130. $\frac{63}{54}$ $\frac{7}{6}$; $1\frac{1}{6}$
131. $\frac{200}{50}$ 4
132. $\frac{21}{84}$ $\frac{1}{4}$
133. $\frac{80}{32}$ $\frac{5}{2}$; $2\frac{1}{2}$
134. $\frac{60}{144}$ $\frac{5}{12}$
135. $\frac{12}{30}$ $\frac{2}{5}$
136. $\frac{96}{99}$ $\frac{32}{33}$

137. $\frac{36}{16}$ $\frac{9}{4}$; $2\frac{1}{4}$
138. $\frac{7}{42}$ $\frac{1}{6}$
139. $\frac{40}{24}$ $\frac{5}{3}$; $1\frac{2}{3}$
140. $\frac{105}{70}$ $\frac{3}{2}$; $1\frac{1}{2}$
141. $\frac{36}{16}$ $\frac{9}{4}$; $2\frac{1}{4}$
142. $\frac{52}{56}$ $\frac{13}{14}$
143. $\frac{49}{63}$ $\frac{7}{9}$
144. $\frac{81}{83}$ $\frac{81}{83}$

99. $\frac{16}{7}$; $2\frac{2}{7}$ 100. $\frac{10}{7}$; $1\frac{3}{7}$ 119. $\frac{24}{23} = 1\frac{1}{23}$ 120. $\frac{17}{12}$; $1\frac{5}{12}$ 124. $\frac{72}{25}$; $2\frac{22}{25}$ 128. $\frac{27}{2}$; $13\frac{1}{2}$

APPLICATIONS: Using Fractions and Customary Measures

Write each measurement as a fraction as indicated.

145. $\frac{8}{16}$ inch $= \frac{?}{8}$ inch $\frac{4}{8}$
146. $\frac{48}{64}$ inch $= \frac{?}{8}$ inch $\frac{6}{8}$
147. $\frac{24}{32}$ inch $= \frac{?}{4}$ inch $\frac{3}{4}$

148. $\frac{40}{64}$ inch $= \frac{?}{32}$ inch $\frac{20}{32}$
149. $\frac{4}{64}$ inch $= \frac{?}{16}$ inch $\frac{1}{16}$
150. $\frac{8}{64}$ inch $= \frac{?}{8}$ inch $\frac{1}{8}$

151. $\frac{4}{16}$ pound $= \frac{?}{4}$ pound $\frac{1}{4}$
152. $\frac{20}{32}$ pound $= \frac{?}{8}$ pound $\frac{5}{8}$
153. $\frac{21}{24}$ pound $= \frac{?}{8}$ pound $\frac{7}{8}$

Problem Solving and Applications

Train Schedules

See the Teacher's Manual for the objectives.
This lesson applies the skills presented in Section 9-2.

The table below shows how long it takes to travel by Superliner from New York to three cities along the same route.

SUPERLINER TRAIN SERVICE

Express	Local
To Philadelphia 1 hour 25 minutes	To Philadelphia 1 hour 25 minutes
To Baltimore 2 hours 45 minutes	To Baltimore 3 hours 40 minutes
To Washington 3 hours 30 minutes	To Washington 4 hours 20 minutes

You can write a mixed number for the time it takes for each trip.

EXAMPLE Write a mixed number for the time it takes to travel from New York to Philadelphia by express service.

Solution: **1** Find the time for the trip: **1 hour 25 minutes** ◄ **From the table**

2 Change 25 minutes to hours.

60 minutes = 1 hour

25 minutes = $\frac{25}{60}$ hour ◄ **Write in lowest terms.**

25 minutes = $\frac{5}{12}$ hour   So 1 hour 25 minutes = $1\frac{5}{12}$ hours.

Exercises

Write a mixed number for the time it takes for each trip.

1. New York to Baltimore, by express service $2\frac{3}{4}$ hours

2. New York to Washington, by express service $3\frac{1}{2}$ hours

3. New York to Baltimore, by local service $3\frac{2}{3}$ hours

4. New York to Washington, by local service $4\frac{1}{3}$ hours

5. New York to Philadelphia and return, by local service $2\frac{5}{6}$ hours

6. New York to Washington and return, by local service $8\frac{2}{3}$ hours

7. New York to Baltimore and return, by express service $5\frac{1}{2}$ hours

8. New York to Baltimore and return, by local service $7\frac{1}{3}$ hours

9. From Philadelphia to Baltimore, by local service $2\frac{1}{4}$ hours

10. From Philadelphia to Baltimore, by express service $1\frac{1}{3}$ hour

Career Lessons are optional.
This lesson combines the concept of fraction with the skills of addition and multiplication of decimals.

Taxi fares are usually based on parts or **fractions** of a mile. As the sign at the right shows, one taxi service charges $1.00 for the first $\frac{1}{7}$ mile, and 10¢ for each additional $\frac{1}{7}$ mile.

DILSON TAXI
RATES

$1.00   1st $\frac{1}{7}$ MILE

10¢   Each Additional $\frac{1}{7}$ MILE

EXERCISES

Use the rates for the Dilson Taxi Service for Exercises 1–6.

1. What is the charge for the first $\frac{1}{7}$ mile? $1.00

2. What is the charge for the second $\frac{1}{7}$ mile? 10¢

3. What is the charge for a ride of $\frac{2}{7}$ mile? $1.10
(HINT: $1.00 + 1 × $0.10 = __?__)

4. What is the charge for a ride of $\frac{5}{7}$ mile? $1.40
(HINT: $1.00 + 4 × $0.10 = __?__)

5. What is the charge for a ride of one mile? $1.60
(HINT: $1.00 + 6 × $0.10 = __?__)

6. What is the charge for a ride of 2 miles? $2.30
(HINT: $1.00 + 13 × $0.10 = __?__)

Use the rates for the Rush Taxi Service for Exercises 7–10.

RUSH TAXI SERVICE
RATES

$1.15   1st $\frac{1}{5}$ MILE

15¢ EACH ADDITIONAL $\frac{1}{5}$ MILE

7. What is the charge for the first $\frac{1}{5}$ mile? $1.15

8. What is the charge for the second $\frac{1}{5}$ mile? 15¢

9. What is the charge for a ride of 1 mile? $1.75

10. What is the charge for a ride of $2\frac{1}{5}$ miles? $2.65

9-3 Addition and Subtraction: Like Fractions

Fractions such as $\frac{1}{3}$ and $\frac{2}{3}$ are **like fractions** because they have a **common denominator**, 3.

PROCEDURE To add or subtract like fractions:

1 Add or subtract the numerators.

2 Write the sum or difference over the common denominator.

3 Write the answer in lowest terms.

EXAMPLE 1 **a.** $\frac{7}{10} + \frac{1}{10} = \underline{\ ?\ }$ **b.** $\frac{5}{6} - \frac{1}{6} = \underline{\ ?\ }$

Solutions: **a.** $\begin{array}{r}\frac{7}{10}\\ +\frac{1}{10}\\ \hline \frac{8}{10}=\frac{4}{5}\end{array}$ ◀ **Lowest terms**   **b.** $\begin{array}{r}\frac{5}{6}\\ -\frac{1}{6}\\ \hline \frac{4}{6}=\frac{2}{3}\end{array}$ ◀ **Lowest terms**

After completing Example 1, you may wish to have students do some or all of Exercises 1-23.

PROCEDURE To add or subtract mixed numbers:

1 Add or subtract the fractional parts.

2 Add or subtract the whole numbers.

3 Write the answer in lowest terms.

EXAMPLE 2 **a.** $2\frac{1}{4} + 3\frac{1}{4} = \underline{\ ?\ }$ **b.** $9\frac{7}{8} - 2\frac{1}{8} = \underline{\ ?\ }$

Solutions: **a.** $\begin{array}{r}2\frac{1}{4}\\ +3\frac{1}{4}\\ \hline 5\frac{2}{4}=5\frac{1}{2}\end{array}$ ◀ **Lowest terms**   **b.** $\begin{array}{r}9\frac{7}{8}\\ -2\frac{1}{8}\\ \hline 7\frac{6}{8}=7\frac{3}{4}\end{array}$ ◀ **Lowest terms**

REVIEW OF RELATED SKILLS   You may wish to use these exercises before teaching the lesson.

Add.   (Pages 2–3)

1. $12 + 30$ 42 **2.** $19 + 6$ 25 **3.** $28 + 7$ 35 **4.** $26 + 18$ 44 **5.** $39 + 15$ 54

Subtract.   (Pages 10–11)

6. $25 - 6$ 19 **7.** $51 - 8$ 43 **8.** $42 - 9$ 33 **9.** $65 - 12$ 53 **10.** $38 - 29$ 9

Write each fraction in lowest terms.   (Pages 182–183)

11. $\frac{6}{12}$ $\frac{1}{2}$ **12.** $\frac{3}{18}$ $\frac{1}{6}$ **13.** $\frac{9}{4}$ $2\frac{1}{4}$ **14.** $\frac{15}{21}$ $\frac{5}{7}$ **15.** $\frac{8}{36}$ $\frac{2}{9}$ **16.** $\frac{48}{96}$ $\frac{1}{2}$ **17.** $\frac{48}{84}$ $\frac{4}{7}$ **18.** $\frac{81}{99}$ $\frac{9}{11}$

EXERCISES
See the suggested assignment guide in the Teacher's Manual.

Add or subtract. Write each answer in lowest terms. (Example 1)

1. $\dfrac{1}{3}$
$+\dfrac{1}{3}$ $\dfrac{2}{3}$

2. $\dfrac{1}{5}$
$+\dfrac{1}{5}$ $\dfrac{2}{5}$

3. $\dfrac{3}{4}$
$-\dfrac{2}{4}$ $\dfrac{1}{4}$

4. $\dfrac{4}{5}$
$-\dfrac{3}{5}$ $\dfrac{1}{5}$

5. $\dfrac{1}{5}$
$+\dfrac{2}{5}$ $\dfrac{3}{5}$

6. $\dfrac{1}{8}$
$+\dfrac{1}{8}$ $\dfrac{1}{4}$

7. $\dfrac{7}{8}$
$-\dfrac{6}{8}$ $\dfrac{1}{8}$

8. $\dfrac{9}{10}$
$-\dfrac{8}{10}$ $\dfrac{1}{10}$

9. $\dfrac{2}{5}$
$+\dfrac{2}{5}$ $\dfrac{4}{5}$

10. $\dfrac{1}{8}$
$+\dfrac{2}{8}$ $\dfrac{3}{8}$

11. $\dfrac{4}{5}$
$-\dfrac{2}{5}$ $\dfrac{2}{5}$

12. $\dfrac{3}{8}$
$+\dfrac{3}{8}$ $\dfrac{3}{4}$

13. $\dfrac{1}{4}$
$+\dfrac{1}{4}$ $\dfrac{1}{2}$

14. $\dfrac{3}{8}$
$+\dfrac{1}{8}$ $\dfrac{1}{2}$

15. $\dfrac{4}{6}$
$-\dfrac{1}{6}$ $\dfrac{1}{2}$

16. $\dfrac{5}{8}$
$-\dfrac{1}{8}$ $\dfrac{1}{2}$

17. $\dfrac{2}{12}$
$+\dfrac{4}{12}$ $\dfrac{1}{2}$

18. $\dfrac{5}{8}$
$-\dfrac{3}{8}$ $\dfrac{1}{4}$

19. $\dfrac{9}{10} - \dfrac{4}{10}$ $\dfrac{1}{2}$

20. $\dfrac{7}{10} - \dfrac{3}{10}$ $\dfrac{2}{5}$

21. $\dfrac{3}{20} + \dfrac{7}{20}$ $\dfrac{1}{2}$

22. $\dfrac{3}{10} + \dfrac{3}{10}$ $\dfrac{3}{5}$

23. $\dfrac{1}{12} + \dfrac{3}{12}$ $\dfrac{1}{3}$

Add or subtract. Write each answer in lowest terms. (Example 2)

24. $3\dfrac{1}{5}$
$+2\dfrac{2}{5}$ $5\dfrac{3}{5}$

25. $1\dfrac{1}{4}$
$+5\dfrac{2}{4}$ $6\dfrac{3}{4}$

26. $7\dfrac{2}{5}$
$-3\dfrac{1}{5}$ $4\dfrac{1}{5}$

27. $9\dfrac{2}{3}$
$-6\dfrac{1}{3}$ $3\dfrac{1}{3}$

28. $4\dfrac{3}{8}$
$+1\dfrac{4}{8}$ $5\dfrac{7}{8}$

29. $10\dfrac{7}{10}$
$-\ 2\dfrac{2}{10}$ $8\dfrac{1}{2}$

30. $7\dfrac{3}{4}$
$-4\dfrac{2}{4}$ $3\dfrac{1}{4}$

31. $9\dfrac{3}{5}$
$-5\dfrac{2}{5}$ $4\dfrac{1}{5}$

32. $8\dfrac{1}{3}$
$+1\dfrac{1}{3}$ $9\dfrac{2}{3}$

33. $5\dfrac{1}{4}$
$+3\dfrac{2}{4}$ $8\dfrac{3}{4}$

34. $9\dfrac{5}{7}$
$-3\dfrac{3}{7}$ $6\dfrac{2}{7}$

35. $12\dfrac{9}{10}$
$-\ 3\dfrac{7}{10}$ $9\dfrac{1}{5}$

36. $2\dfrac{1}{8}$
$+1\dfrac{3}{8}$ $3\dfrac{1}{2}$

37. $3\dfrac{1}{4}$
$+4\dfrac{1}{4}$ $7\dfrac{1}{2}$

38. $4\dfrac{3}{6}$
$-1\dfrac{1}{6}$ $3\dfrac{1}{3}$

39. $5\dfrac{8}{9}$
$-2\dfrac{5}{9}$ $3\dfrac{3}{9}$

40. $7\dfrac{1}{8}$
$+1\dfrac{1}{8}$ $8\dfrac{1}{4}$

41. $5\dfrac{1}{8}$
$+7\dfrac{3}{8}$ $12\dfrac{1}{2}$

42. $9\dfrac{7}{12} - 5\dfrac{5}{12}$ $4\dfrac{1}{6}$

43. $8\dfrac{1}{4} + 9\dfrac{1}{4}$ $17\dfrac{1}{2}$

44. $6\dfrac{3}{6} + 5\dfrac{1}{6}$ $11\dfrac{2}{3}$

45. $3\dfrac{11}{12} - 1\dfrac{7}{12}$ $2\dfrac{1}{3}$

Mixed Practice   The Mixed Practice contains exercises that relate to both Examples 1 and 2.

46. $\dfrac{11}{12}$
$+\dfrac{9}{12}$ $1\dfrac{2}{3}$

47. $\dfrac{5}{17}$
$+\dfrac{29}{17}$ 2

48. $3\dfrac{3}{8}$
$-1\dfrac{1}{8}$ $2\dfrac{1}{4}$

49. $\dfrac{32}{35}$
$-\dfrac{27}{35}$ $\dfrac{1}{7}$

50. $8\dfrac{1}{6}$
$+7$ $15\dfrac{1}{6}$

51. 13
$+\ 5\dfrac{6}{7}$ $18\dfrac{6}{7}$

52. $20\dfrac{2}{5}$
$-11\dfrac{1}{5}$ $9\dfrac{1}{5}$

53. $18\dfrac{5}{6}$
$-18\dfrac{5}{6}$ 0

54. $\dfrac{41}{80}$
$+\dfrac{39}{80}$ 1

55. $2\dfrac{3}{20}$
$+5\dfrac{9}{20}$ $7\dfrac{3}{5}$

56. $9\dfrac{3}{4}$
$-4\dfrac{3}{4}$ 5

57. $27\dfrac{7}{8}$
$-14\dfrac{5}{8}$ $13\dfrac{1}{4}$

58. $12\dfrac{1}{3} + 5$ $17\dfrac{1}{3}$

59. $34 + 33\dfrac{1}{8}$ $67\dfrac{1}{8}$

60. $28\dfrac{2}{3} - 17$ $11\dfrac{2}{3}$

61. $12\dfrac{8}{9} - 10$ $2\dfrac{8}{9}$

These are one-step problems that most students should be able to handle.

APPLICATIONS: Using Fractions and Customary Measures

62. Michelle jogged $2\dfrac{3}{4}$ miles on Monday, $3\dfrac{1}{4}$ miles on Tuesday, and $1\dfrac{3}{4}$ miles on Wednesday. How many miles did she jog in all? $7\dfrac{3}{4}$ miles

63. In October, Pedro's height was $5\dfrac{3}{8}$ feet. By the following March, his height was $5\dfrac{5}{8}$ feet. How much did he grow?   3 inches

9-4 Writing Like Fractions See the Teacher's Manual for the objectives.

The **least common denominator** (abbreviated: LCD) of two or more fractions is the <u>smallest</u> number that is a multiple of the denominators of the fractions. You can find the <u>multiple</u> of a number by multiplying the number by 1, by 2, by 3, and so on.

PROCEDURE   To find the LCD of two fractions, write the multiple of one of the denominators. Stop when you find a <u>common multiple</u> of <u>both</u> denominators.

EXAMPLE 1   Find the LCD of $\frac{1}{6}$ and $\frac{3}{10}$.

Solution: Write multiples of 6 until you reach a number that is <u>also</u> a multiple of 10.

$6 \times 1 = 6$ $6 \times 2 = 12$ $6 \times 3 = 18$ $6 \times 4 = 24$ $6 \times 5 = 30$ ◀ **Stop! 30 is also a multiple of 10.**

LCD of $\frac{1}{6}$ and $\frac{3}{10}$: **30**

After completing Example 1, you may wish to have students do some or all of Exercises 1-41.

You can use the LCD to write like fractions for unlike fractions.

Unlike fractions are fractions such as $\frac{2}{3}$ and $\frac{3}{4}$. Their denominators, 3 and 4, are <u>not</u> the same.

PROCEDURE   To write like fractions for unlike fractions:

1 Find the LCD.

2 Multiply both the numerator and denominator of each fraction by a number that will make the denominator equal to the LCD.

EXAMPLE 2   Write like fractions for $\frac{1}{6}$ and $\frac{3}{10}$.

Solutions: 1 LCD: 30 ◀ *From Example 1*

2 $\frac{1}{6} = \frac{1 \times 5}{6 \times 5}$ $\frac{3}{10} = \frac{3 \times 3}{10 \times 3}$

$\frac{1}{6} = \frac{5}{30}$ $\frac{3}{10} = \frac{3}{30}$

└── **Like fractions** ──┘

You can use like fractions to compare two or more fractions.

188   CHAPTER 9

EXAMPLE 3 Which is greater, $\frac{3}{5}$, or $\frac{1}{2}$?

Solution: ☐1 Write like fractions: $\frac{3}{5} = \frac{6}{10}$ $\frac{1}{2} = \frac{5}{10}$

$\overset{6 > 5}{}$

☐2 Compare the numerators. The fraction with the greater numerator is greater.

Since $6 > 5$, $\frac{3}{5} > \frac{1}{2}$.

Fractions such as $\frac{1}{6}$ and $\frac{5}{30}$ are <u>equivalent fractions</u>. Equivalent fractions are equal.

REVIEW OF RELATED SKILLS
You may wish to use these exercises before teaching the lesson.

Multiply.   (Pages 26–27)

1. 7×6 42 **2.** 30×3 90 **3.** 15×5 75 **4.** 14×7 98 **5.** 16×5 80 **6.** 20×8 160

7. 10×4 40 **8.** 9×6 54 **9.** 9×4 36 **10.** 11×3 33 **11.** 8×12 96 **12.** 16×7 112

EXERCISES
See the suggested assignment guide in the Teacher's Manual.

10. 13,26,39,52,65   11. 11,22,33,44,55   12. 20,40,60,80,100   13. 15,30,45,60,75   14. 100,200,300,400,500

Write the first 5 multiples of each number.   (Example 1)
6. 7,14,21,28,35
7. 9,18,27,36,45
10,20,30,40,50

1. 2 2,4,6,8,10 **2.** 4 4,8,12,16, **3.** 5 5,10,15,20, **4.** 8 8,16,24,32,40 **5.** 10 **6.** 7 **7.** 9
20
25

8. 3 3,6,9,12,15 **9.** 6 6,12,18, **10.** 13 **11.** 11 **12.** 20 **13.** 15 **14.** 100
24,30

15. 12 12,24, **16.** 50 **17.** 14 14,28, **18.** 200 200,400, **19.** 16 16,32, **20.** 25 25,50, **21.** 17
36, 48, 60 50,100,150,200,250 42,56,70 600,800,1000 48,64,80 75,100,125 17,34,51,
68,85

Find the LCD of each pair of fractions.   (Example 1)

22. $\frac{1}{2}$ and $\frac{5}{6}$ 6 **23.** $\frac{2}{3}$ and $\frac{4}{9}$ 9 **24.** $\frac{3}{7}$ and $\frac{5}{14}$ 14 **25.** $\frac{1}{8}$ and $\frac{5}{24}$ 24 **26.** $\frac{1}{3}$ and $\frac{1}{12}$ 12

27. $\frac{4}{5}$ and $\frac{3}{10}$ 10 **28.** $\frac{5}{12}$ and $\frac{14}{24}$ 24 **29.** $\frac{2}{3}$ and $\frac{1}{6}$ 6 **30.** $\frac{1}{7}$ and $\frac{2}{21}$ 21 **31.** $\frac{3}{8}$ and $\frac{1}{2}$ 8

32. $\frac{1}{2}$ and $\frac{1}{14}$ 14 **33.** $\frac{1}{4}$ and $\frac{9}{16}$ 16 **34.** $\frac{1}{2}$ and $\frac{1}{3}$ 6 **35.** $\frac{1}{3}$ and $\frac{1}{4}$ 12 **36.** $\frac{1}{2}$ and $\frac{1}{5}$ 10

37. $\frac{1}{3}$ and $\frac{1}{5}$ 15 **38.** $\frac{1}{5}$ and $\frac{1}{6}$ 30 **39.** $\frac{2}{3}$ and $\frac{5}{8}$ 24 **40.** $\frac{4}{5}$ and $\frac{7}{8}$ 40 **41.** $\frac{3}{4}$ and $\frac{2}{5}$ 20

Write like fractions for each pair. Then compare the fractions.   (Examples 2–3)

42. $\frac{1}{4}$ and $\frac{2}{3}$ $\frac{3}{12} < \frac{8}{12}$ **43.** $\frac{2}{5}$ and $\frac{1}{6}$ $\frac{12}{30} > \frac{5}{30}$ **44.** $\frac{1}{2}$ and $\frac{3}{5}$ $\frac{5}{10} < \frac{6}{10}$ **45.** $\frac{1}{2}$ and $\frac{1}{3}$ $\frac{3}{6} > \frac{2}{6}$ **46.** $\frac{3}{4}$ and $\frac{1}{5}$

47. $\frac{1}{6}$ and $\frac{3}{4}$ $\frac{2}{12} < \frac{9}{12}$ **48.** $\frac{5}{6}$ and $\frac{4}{5}$ $\frac{25}{30} > \frac{24}{30}$ **49.** $\frac{1}{3}$ and $\frac{4}{5}$ $\frac{5}{15} < \frac{12}{15}$ **50.** $\frac{1}{8}$ and $\frac{1}{4}$ $\frac{1}{8} < \frac{2}{8}$ **51.** $\frac{1}{8}$ and $\frac{1}{2}$

52. $\frac{3}{8}$ and $\frac{2}{3}$ $\frac{9}{24} < \frac{16}{24}$ **53.** $\frac{7}{8}$ and $\frac{1}{5}$ $\frac{35}{40} > \frac{8}{40}$ **54.** $\frac{3}{10}$ and $\frac{2}{5}$ $\frac{3}{10} < \frac{4}{10}$ **55.** $\frac{1}{10}$ and $\frac{3}{4}$ **56.** $\frac{7}{10}$ and $\frac{1}{6}$

57. $\frac{1}{18}$ and $\frac{5}{6}$ $\frac{1}{18} < \frac{15}{18}$ **58.** $\frac{5}{9}$ and $\frac{5}{6}$ $\frac{10}{18} < \frac{15}{18}$ **59.** $\frac{1}{3}$ and $\frac{6}{7}$ $\frac{7}{21} < \frac{18}{21}$ **60.** $\frac{7}{8}$ and $\frac{1}{6}$ $\frac{21}{24} > \frac{4}{24}$ **61.** $\frac{1}{2}$ and $\frac{9}{18}$ $\frac{9}{18} > \frac{2}{18}$

46. $\frac{15}{20} > \frac{4}{20}$ 51. $\frac{1}{8} < \frac{4}{8}$ 55. $\frac{2}{10} < \frac{15}{20}$ 56. $\frac{21}{30} > \frac{5}{30}$ FRACTIONS: ADDITION/SUBTRACTION   **189**

9-5 Addition and Subtraction/Unlike Fractions

See the Teacher's Manual for the objectives.

Writing like fractions for unlike fractions is an important step in adding and subtracting with fractions.

PROCEDURE To add or subtract unlike fractions:

1. Find the LCD (least common denominator).
2. Use the LCD to write like fractions.
3. Add or subtract.
4. Write your answer in lowest terms.

EXAMPLE 1   **a.** $\frac{1}{6} + \frac{7}{10} = $ _?_   **b.** $\frac{1}{4} - \frac{1}{12} = $ _?_

Solutions: **a.** LCD: 30   **b.** LCD: 12

$$\frac{1}{6} = \frac{5}{30} \quad \boxed{\frac{1 \times 5}{6 \times 5}}$$

$$+\frac{7}{10} = +\frac{21}{30} \quad \boxed{\frac{7 \times 3}{10 \times 3}}$$

$$\frac{26}{30} = \frac{13}{15} \quad \boxed{\text{Lowest terms}}$$

$$\frac{1}{4} = \frac{3}{12}$$

$$-\frac{1}{12} = -\frac{1}{12}$$

$$\frac{2}{12} = \frac{1}{6}$$

After completing Example 1, you may wish to have students do some or all of Exercises 1-28.

Adding or subtracting with mixed numbers is similar to adding or subtracting with unlike fractions.

EXAMPLE 2   **a.** $4\frac{1}{2} + 2\frac{2}{3} = $ _?_   **b.** $7\frac{9}{10} - 4\frac{5}{6} = $ _?_

Solutions: **a.** LCD: 6   **b.** LCD: 30

$$4\frac{1}{2} = \quad 4\frac{3}{6}$$

$$+2\frac{2}{3} = +2\frac{4}{6}$$

$$6\frac{7}{6} = 6 + 1\frac{1}{6} \quad \boxed{\frac{7}{6} = 1\frac{1}{6}}$$

$$= 7\frac{1}{6}$$

$$7\frac{9}{10} = \quad 7\frac{27}{30}$$

$$-4\frac{5}{6} = -4\frac{25}{30}$$

$$3\frac{2}{30} = 3\frac{1}{15}$$

REVIEW OF RELATED SKILLS

You may wish to use these exercises before teaching the lesson.

Multiply.   (Pages 26–27)

1. 7×6 42   **2.** 30×3 90   **3.** 15×5 75   **4.** 14×7 98   **5.** 19×5 95   **6.** 18×6 108

7. 13×9 117   **8.** 16×5 80   **9.** 13×8 104   **10.** 21×5 105   **11.** 17×6 102   **12.** 4×14 56

13. 22×8 176   **14.** 25×9 225   **15.** 34×7 238   **16.** 12×8 96   **17.** 18×4 72   **18.** 19×3 57

19. $\frac{8}{12}$ $\frac{2}{3}$ **20.** $\frac{16}{12}$ $1\frac{1}{3}$ **21.** $\frac{21}{24}$ $\frac{7}{8}$ **22.** $\frac{36}{48}$ $\frac{3}{4}$ **23.** $\frac{25}{10}$ $2\frac{1}{2}$ **24.** $\frac{42}{27}$ $1\frac{5}{9}$

EXERCISES
See the suggested assignment guide in the Teacher's Manual.

Add. Write each answer in lowest terms. (Example 1a)

1. $\frac{2}{3}$
$+\frac{5}{8}$ $1\frac{7}{24}$

2. $\frac{5}{6}$
$+\frac{2}{5}$ $1\frac{7}{30}$

3. $\frac{3}{7}$
$+\frac{11}{14}$ $1\frac{3}{14}$

4. $\frac{1}{5}$
$+\frac{2}{3}$ $\frac{13}{15}$

5. $\frac{7}{9}$
$+\frac{3}{4}$ $1\frac{19}{36}$

6. $\frac{1}{4}$
$+\frac{5}{6}$ $1\frac{1}{12}$

7. $\frac{7}{8}$
$+\frac{1}{3}$ $1\frac{5}{24}$

8. $\frac{9}{10}$
$+\frac{7}{20}$ $1\frac{1}{4}$

9. $\frac{1}{7}$
$+\frac{3}{4}$ $\frac{25}{28}$

10. $\frac{4}{5}$
$+\frac{3}{8}$ $1\frac{7}{40}$

11. $\frac{1}{2}$
$+\frac{5}{6}$ $1\frac{1}{3}$

12. $\frac{2}{9}$
$+\frac{2}{3}$ $\frac{8}{9}$

13. $\frac{5}{8}+\frac{3}{16}$ $\frac{13}{16}$ **14.** $\frac{3}{11}+\frac{8}{22}$ $\frac{7}{11}$ **15.** $\frac{1}{5}+\frac{3}{4}$ $\frac{19}{20}$ **16.** $\frac{5}{8}+\frac{10}{16}$ $1\frac{1}{4}$ **17.** $\frac{7}{9}+\frac{1}{6}$ $\frac{17}{18}$

Subtract. Write each answer in lowest terms. (Example 1b)

18. $\frac{2}{3}$
$-\frac{1}{6}$ $\frac{1}{2}$

19. $\frac{3}{4}$
$-\frac{1}{5}$ $\frac{11}{20}$

20. $\frac{2}{3}$
$-\frac{1}{9}$ $\frac{5}{9}$

21. $\frac{5}{6}$
$-\frac{1}{2}$ $\frac{1}{3}$

22. $\frac{8}{9}$
$-\frac{1}{3}$ $\frac{5}{9}$

23. $\frac{6}{10}$
$-\frac{3}{20}$ $\frac{9}{20}$

24. $\frac{5}{12}-\frac{1}{4}$ $\frac{1}{6}$ **25.** $\frac{4}{5}-\frac{6}{10}$ $\frac{1}{5}$ **26.** $\frac{7}{8}-\frac{1}{4}$ $\frac{5}{8}$ **27.** $\frac{1}{2}-\frac{3}{8}$ $\frac{1}{8}$ **28.** $\frac{4}{5}-\frac{3}{10}$ $\frac{1}{2}$

Add. Write each answer in lowest terms. (Example 2a)

29. $5\frac{1}{2}$
$+2\frac{1}{4}$ $7\frac{3}{4}$

30. $8\frac{4}{5}$
$+5\frac{1}{3}$ $14\frac{2}{15}$

31. $9\frac{3}{8}$
$+8\frac{1}{6}$ $17\frac{13}{24}$

32. $2\frac{5}{8}$
$+1\frac{1}{2}$ $4\frac{1}{8}$

33. $5\frac{2}{3}$
$+5\frac{2}{3}$ $11\frac{1}{3}$

34. $20\frac{1}{8}$
$+15\frac{3}{5}$ $35\frac{29}{40}$

35. $1\frac{5}{6}$
$+\ \frac{3}{4}$ $2\frac{7}{12}$

36. $1\frac{3}{10}$
$+\ \frac{2}{5}$ $1\frac{7}{10}$

37. $6\frac{3}{4}$
$+1\frac{2}{8}$ 8

38. $12\frac{1}{7}$
$+\ 9\frac{2}{3}$ $21\frac{17}{21}$

39. $6\frac{2}{5}$
$+\ \frac{3}{4}$ $7\frac{3}{20}$

40. $12\frac{1}{2}$
$+11\frac{1}{8}$ $23\frac{5}{8}$

41. $24\frac{3}{8}+22\frac{1}{3}$ $46\frac{17}{24}$ **42.** $12\frac{1}{12}+13\frac{1}{4}$ $25\frac{1}{3}$ **43.** $54\frac{7}{8}+13\frac{1}{3}$ $68\frac{5}{24}$ **44.** $19\frac{2}{5}+17\frac{1}{2}$ $36\frac{9}{10}$

Subtract. Write each answer in lowest terms. (Example 2b)

45. $5\frac{3}{4}$
$-2\frac{1}{2}$ $3\frac{1}{4}$

46. $11\frac{1}{2}$
$-11\frac{6}{12}$ 0

47. $5\frac{11}{12}$
$-4\frac{3}{8}$ $1\frac{13}{24}$

48. $2\frac{5}{6}$
$-\ \frac{3}{4}$ $2\frac{1}{12}$

49. $7\frac{7}{10}$
$-\ \frac{2}{5}$ $7\frac{3}{10}$

50. $8\frac{7}{8}$
$-6\frac{3}{4}$ $2\frac{1}{8}$

51. $28\frac{2}{3}-26\frac{4}{9}$ $2\frac{2}{9}$ **52.** $33\frac{1}{2}-32\frac{1}{4}$ $1\frac{1}{4}$ **53.** $46\frac{8}{15}-\frac{2}{5}$ $46\frac{2}{15}$ **54.** $71\frac{4}{10}-\frac{7}{20}$ $71\frac{1}{20}$

Mixed Practice

55. $7\frac{3}{5}$
$+2\frac{1}{3}$ $9\frac{14}{15}$

56. $8\frac{1}{3}$
$+7\frac{3}{4}$ $16\frac{1}{12}$

57. $2\frac{1}{2}$
$-1\frac{3}{8}$ $1\frac{1}{8}$

58. $7\frac{3}{4}$
$-3\frac{1}{3}$ $4\frac{5}{12}$

59. $4\frac{11}{15}$
$+6\frac{3}{5}$ $11\frac{1}{3}$

60. $11\frac{3}{12}$
$+\ 2\frac{1}{3}$ $13\frac{7}{12}$

61. $11\frac{1}{3}-6\frac{1}{6}$ $5\frac{1}{6}$ **62.** $18\frac{5}{16}+13\frac{1}{4}$ $31\frac{9}{16}$ **63.** $26\frac{1}{2}+23\frac{1}{8}$ $49\frac{5}{8}$ **64.** $38\frac{3}{4}-35\frac{1}{2}$ $3\frac{1}{4}$

Problem Solving and Applications

Time Cards

See the Teacher's Manual for the objectives.
This lesson applies the skills presented in Sections 9-3, 9-4, and 9-5.

In many businesses, workers must "punch" in and out of work by inserting cards in a time clock. The time card provides a record of the hours at work.

To determine the total number of hours worked per week, you must first answer the question:

"How many hours are worked each day?"

This is the <u>hidden question</u> in the problem. Then you can find the total number of hours worked per week.

EXAMPLE
a. Find the number of hours worked on Day 1.
b. Find the total number of hours worked for the week.

DAYS	IN	OUT	IN	OUT	DAILY TOTALS
1	9:00	12:30	1:30	5:15	?
2	9:00	12:30	1:30	5:00	7
3	9:30	12:30	1:30	5:00	$7\frac{1}{2}$
4	8:30	12:30	1:30	5:15	$7\frac{3}{4}$
5	9:00	12:30	1:30	5:30	$7\frac{1}{2}$

Solutions:

a. 9:00 to 12:30: $\quad 3\frac{1}{2}$ hours $= \quad 3\frac{2}{4}$

$\quad$ 1:30 to $\:$ 5:15: $\quad 3\frac{3}{4}$ hours $= \quad +3\frac{3}{4}$

$\qquad\qquad$ TOTAL $\qquad 6\frac{5}{4} = 7\frac{1}{4}$ **hours** ◀ *Hours worked on Day 1*

b. Add the Daily Totals.

$7\frac{1}{4} = \quad 7\frac{1}{4}$

$7 \: = \quad 7$

$7\frac{1}{2} = \quad 7\frac{2}{4}$

$7\frac{3}{4} = \quad 7\frac{3}{4}$

$+7\frac{1}{2} = +7\frac{2}{4}$

$\qquad\qquad 35\frac{8}{4} = 35 + 2 = 37$ **hours** ◀ *Total hours for the week*

Exercises

Exercises 1 and 2 are one-step problems.

1. Reynaldo worked $6\frac{1}{2}$ hours on Monday, $5\frac{3}{4}$ hours on Wednesday, and $4\frac{1}{2}$ hours on Friday. Find the total number of hours worked. $16\frac{3}{4}$ hours

2. Mary Chu worked $3\frac{1}{2}$ hours on Tuesday, $3\frac{3}{4}$ hours on Friday, and $8\frac{1}{4}$ hours on Saturday. Find the total number of hours worked. $15\frac{1}{2}$ hours

Application

For Exercises 3–8, find the number of hours worked each day. Note that Exercises 3-8 are non-verbal.
Then find the total number of hours worked for the week. Exercises 9-10 involve more than two steps.

3.

WEEK ENDING ___11/14___ 19 82
NAME *O'saka, D.*

DAYS	IN	OUT	IN	OUT	DAILY TOTALS	
1	9:00	12:00	1:00	5:00	?	7
2	9:00	12:15	1:15	5:30	?	$7\frac{1}{2}$
3	8:30	12:00	1:00	4:00	?	$6\frac{1}{2}$
4	8:45	12:00	1:00	4:15	?	$6\frac{1}{2}$
5	9:00	12:00	1:00	4:45	?	$6\frac{3}{4}$

Week's total: $34\frac{1}{4}$ hours

4.

WEEK ENDING ___5/26___ 19 82
NAME *Sheehan, J.*

DAYS	IN	OUT	IN	OUT	DAILY TOTALS	
1	9:00	12:30	1:30	5:00	?	7
2	9:00	12:30	1:30	4:30	?	$6\frac{1}{2}$
3	8:00	12:30	1:30	4:30	?	$7\frac{1}{2}$
4	9:00	12:30	1:30	4:15	?	$6\frac{1}{4}$
5	9:00	12:30	1:30	4:45	?	$6\frac{3}{4}$

Week's total: 34 hours

5.

WEEK ENDING ___8/12___ 19 82
NAME *Beebe, R.*

DAYS	IN	OUT	IN	OUT	DAILY TOTALS	
1	8:00	12:00	1:00	4:15	?	$7\frac{1}{4}$
2	8:00	12:00	1:00	3:30	?	$6\frac{1}{2}$
3	8:00	12:00	1:00	4:45	?	$7\frac{3}{4}$
4	8:00	12:00	1:00	4:30	?	$7\frac{1}{2}$
5	8:00	12:00	1:00	3:15	?	$6\frac{1}{4}$

Week's total: $35\frac{1}{4}$ hours

6.

WEEK ENDING ___2/28___ 19 82
NAME *Suarez, R.*

DAYS	IN	OUT	IN	OUT	DAILY TOTALS	
1	9:00	11:30	12:30	5:30	?	$7\frac{1}{2}$
2	8:45	11:30	12:30	5:15	?	$7\frac{1}{2}$
3	8:45	12:00	1:00	5:00	?	$7\frac{1}{4}$
4	8:30	12:15	1:15	4:45	?	$7\frac{1}{4}$
5	8:30	12:00	1:00	4:00	?	$6\frac{1}{2}$

Week's total: 36 hours

7.

WEEK ENDING ___8/5___ 19 82
NAME *Liebowitz, T.*

DAYS	IN	OUT	IN	OUT	DAILY TOTALS	
1	9:00	1:00	2:00	5:30	?	$7\frac{1}{2}$
2	9:00	1:00	2:00	5:45	?	$7\frac{3}{4}$
3	8:15	12:00	1:00	5:15	?	8
4	8:30	12:00	1:00	5:15	?	$7\frac{3}{4}$
5	9:00	12:00	1:00	5:15	?	$7\frac{1}{4}$

Week's total: $38\frac{1}{4}$ hours

8.

WEEK ENDING ___9/15___ 19 82
NAME *Dolan, C.*

DAYS	IN	OUT	IN	OUT	DAILY TOTALS	
1	9:00	12:15	1:15	5:15	?	$7\frac{1}{4}$
2	8:30	12:15	1:15	5:00	?	$7\frac{1}{2}$
3	8:30	12:15	1:15	5:15	?	$7\frac{3}{4}$
4	8:30	12:15	1:15	4:45	?	$7\frac{1}{4}$
5	8:30	12:15	1:15	4:30	?	7

Week's total: $36\frac{3}{4}$ hours

9. Flora worked from 9 A.M. to 4:15 P.M. on Monday, from 8:30 A.M. to 4:45 P.M. on Tuesday, and from 8:30 A.M. to 5:15 P.M. on Friday. She took an hour off for lunch each day.
Find the total number of hours worked. $21\frac{1}{4}$ hours

10. Yoshiro worked from 8:30 A.M. to 4:15 P.M. on Thursday, from 8:15 A.M. to 4:45 P.M. on Friday, and from 8:00 A.M. to 4:15 P.M. on Saturday. He took an hour off for lunch each day.
Find the total number of hours worked. $21\frac{1}{2}$ hours

9-6 Subtraction: Mixed Numbers

See the Teacher's Manual for the objectives.

When subtracting with mixed numbers, it is sometimes necessary to "borrow" from the whole number.

PROCEDURE   To subtract with mixed numbers:

1. Find the LCD.

2. Use the LCD to write like fractions. "Borrow" from the whole number when necessary.

3. Subtract.

4. Write the answer in lowest terms.

EXAMPLE 1 $7\frac{1}{6} - 4\frac{2}{3} = \underline{\ \ ?\ \ }$

Solution: LCD: 6

$$
\begin{array}{rcl}
7\frac{1}{6} & = & 7\frac{1}{6} \\
-4\frac{2}{3} & = & -4\frac{4}{6}
\end{array}
$$

Since $\frac{1}{6}$ is less than $\frac{4}{6}$, borrow 1, or $\frac{6}{6}$, from 7.

$$
\begin{array}{rcl}
7\frac{1}{6} & = & 6\frac{7}{6} \\
-4\frac{2}{3} & = & -4\frac{4}{6} \\
\hline
 & & 2\frac{3}{6} = 2\frac{1}{2}
\end{array}
$$

◀ $\frac{1}{6} + \frac{6}{6} = \frac{7}{6}$

Here is another Example that shows how to "borrow."

EXAMPLE 2 $5\frac{2}{3} - 2\frac{6}{7} = \underline{\ \ ?\ \ }$

Solution: LCD: 21

$$
\begin{array}{rcl}
5\frac{2}{3} & = & 5\frac{14}{21} \\
-2\frac{6}{7} & = & -2\frac{18}{21}
\end{array}
$$

Since $\frac{14}{21}$ is less than $\frac{18}{21}$, borrow 1, or $\frac{21}{21}$, from 5.

$$
\begin{array}{rcl}
5\frac{2}{3} & = & 4\frac{35}{21} \\
-2\frac{6}{7} & = & -2\frac{18}{21} \\
\hline
 & & 2\frac{17}{21}
\end{array}
$$

◀ $\frac{14}{21} + \frac{21}{21} = \frac{35}{21}$

REVIEW OF RELATED SKILLS

You may wish to use these exercises before teaching the lesson.

Complete.   (Pages 178–179)

1. $\frac{?}{4} = 1$ 4

2. $\frac{?}{3} = 1$ 3

3. $\frac{?}{5} = 1$ 5

4. $\frac{?}{10} = 1$ 10

5. $\frac{?}{400} = 1$ 400

Write in lowest terms.   (Pages 182–183)

6. $\frac{4}{10}$ $\frac{2}{5}$

7. $\frac{3}{27}$ $\frac{1}{9}$

8. $\frac{21}{36}$ $\frac{7}{12}$

9. $\frac{18}{45}$ $\frac{2}{5}$

10. $\frac{9}{12}$ $\frac{3}{4}$

11. $\frac{8}{30}$ $\frac{4}{15}$

Find the LCD for each pair of fractions.   (Pages 188–189)

12. $\frac{1}{6}$ and $\frac{3}{4}$ 12

13. $\frac{2}{5}$ and $\frac{1}{4}$ 20

14. $\frac{1}{3}$ and $\frac{4}{5}$ 15

15. $\frac{5}{6}$ and $\frac{4}{9}$ 18

16. $\frac{3}{5}$ and $\frac{7}{8}$ 40

EXERCISES

See the suggested assignment guide in the Teacher's Manual.

Subtract. Write each answer in lowest terms.

1. $5\frac{1}{4}$
$\underline{-1\frac{3}{4}}$ $3\frac{1}{2}$

2. $3\frac{1}{8}$
$\underline{-1\frac{3}{8}}$ $1\frac{3}{4}$

3. $7\frac{1}{6}$
$\underline{-4\frac{1}{2}}$ $2\frac{2}{3}$

4. $10\frac{3}{10}$
$\underline{-5\frac{3}{5}}$ $4\frac{7}{10}$

5. $8\frac{7}{30}$
$\underline{-2\frac{7}{10}}$ $5\frac{8}{15}$

6. $9\frac{1}{12}$
$\underline{-3\frac{2}{3}}$
$5\frac{5}{12}$

7. 14
$\underline{-12\frac{1}{2}}$ $1\frac{1}{2}$

8. 5
$\underline{-\frac{1}{3}}$ $4\frac{2}{3}$

9. $18\frac{5}{6}$
$\underline{-11\frac{1}{12}}$ $7\frac{3}{4}$

10. $1\frac{3}{8}$
$\underline{-\frac{11}{24}}$ $\frac{11}{12}$

11. $4\frac{1}{4}$
$\underline{-1\frac{3}{8}}$ $2\frac{7}{8}$

12. $17\frac{5}{12}$
$\underline{-8\frac{2}{3}}$
$8\frac{3}{4}$

13. $3\frac{1}{8}$
$\underline{-1\frac{3}{4}}$ $1\frac{3}{8}$

14. $5\frac{1}{14}$
$\underline{-3\frac{1}{2}}$ $1\frac{4}{7}$

15. $2\frac{1}{6}$
$\underline{-\frac{1}{3}}$ $1\frac{5}{6}$

16. $11\frac{1}{2}$
$\underline{-\frac{5}{6}}$ $10\frac{2}{3}$

17. 6
$\underline{-5\frac{2}{3}}$ $\frac{1}{3}$

18. $5\frac{3}{8}$
$\underline{-3\frac{3}{4}}$ $1\frac{5}{8}$

19. $3\frac{1}{4}$
$\underline{-\frac{1}{2}}$ $2\frac{3}{4}$

20. $9\frac{2}{3}$
$\underline{-4\frac{11}{12}}$ $4\frac{3}{4}$

21. $30\frac{3}{5}$
$\underline{-14\frac{4}{5}}$ $15\frac{4}{5}$

22. $4\frac{1}{3}$
$\underline{-2\frac{2}{3}}$ $1\frac{2}{3}$

23. 11
$\underline{-8\frac{1}{4}}$ $2\frac{3}{4}$

24. 8
$\underline{-2\frac{9}{10}}$ $5\frac{1}{10}$

25. $10\frac{3}{16}$
$\underline{-5\frac{7}{8}}$ $4\frac{5}{16}$

26. $23\frac{5}{8}$
$\underline{-1\frac{3}{4}}$ $21\frac{7}{8}$

27. $5\frac{2}{11}$
$\underline{-1\frac{5}{22}}$ $3\frac{21}{22}$

28. $3\frac{5}{12}$
$\underline{-1\frac{1}{2}}$ $1\frac{11}{12}$

29. $1\frac{1}{3}$
$\underline{-\frac{2}{3}}$ $\frac{2}{3}$

30. $16\frac{5}{6}$
$\underline{-6\frac{7}{8}}$
$9\frac{23}{24}$

31. $5\frac{1}{8}$
$\underline{-3\frac{1}{5}}$ $1\frac{37}{40}$

32. $10\frac{1}{6}$
$\underline{-7\frac{3}{4}}$ $2\frac{5}{12}$

33. $14\frac{1}{2}$
$\underline{-11\frac{3}{5}}$ $2\frac{9}{10}$

34. $9\frac{1}{3}$
$\underline{-8\frac{1}{2}}$ $\frac{5}{6}$

35. $3\frac{1}{4}$
$\underline{-1\frac{2}{3}}$ $1\frac{7}{12}$

36. $2\frac{1}{3}$
$\underline{-\frac{1}{2}}$ $1\frac{5}{6}$

37. $8\frac{1}{5}$
$\underline{-2\frac{1}{2}}$ $5\frac{7}{10}$

38. $4\frac{1}{3}$
$\underline{-1\frac{3}{5}}$ $2\frac{11}{15}$

39. $7\frac{1}{5}$
$\underline{-2\frac{5}{12}}$ $4\frac{47}{60}$

40. $12\frac{1}{4}$
$\underline{-2\frac{2}{5}}$ $9\frac{17}{20}$

41. $9\frac{1}{10}$
$\underline{-6\frac{1}{2}}$ $2\frac{3}{5}$

42. 5
$\underline{-\frac{1}{2}}$ $4\frac{1}{2}$

43. 6
$\underline{-1\frac{2}{3}}$ $4\frac{1}{3}$

44. $8\frac{1}{3}$
$\underline{-5\frac{3}{8}}$ $2\frac{23}{24}$

45. 1
$\underline{-\frac{1}{3}}$ $\frac{2}{3}$

46. $2\frac{7}{8}$
$\underline{-1\frac{1}{3}}$ $1\frac{13}{24}$

47. $5\frac{1}{6}$
$\underline{-1\frac{1}{2}}$ $3\frac{2}{3}$

48. $2\frac{3}{5}$
$\underline{-\frac{7}{8}}$ $1\frac{29}{40}$

49. $7\frac{1}{4}$
$\underline{-3\frac{5}{6}}$ $3\frac{5}{12}$

50. $4\frac{3}{4}$
$\underline{-1\frac{11}{12}}$ $2\frac{5}{6}$

51. $1\frac{2}{3}$
$\underline{-\frac{3}{4}}$ $\frac{11}{12}$

52. $8\frac{1}{3}$
$\underline{-3\frac{4}{5}}$ $4\frac{8}{15}$

53. $15\frac{1}{4}$
$\underline{-8\frac{2}{3}}$ $6\frac{7}{12}$

54. $11\frac{1}{5}$
$\underline{-3\frac{1}{2}}$
$7\frac{7}{10}$

55. $7\frac{1}{4}$
$\underline{-2\frac{3}{8}}$ $4\frac{7}{8}$

56. $6\frac{1}{6}$
$\underline{-4\frac{4}{5}}$ $1\frac{11}{30}$

57. $9\frac{1}{4}$
$\underline{-2\frac{3}{10}}$ $6\frac{19}{20}$

58. $4\frac{1}{12}$
$\underline{-1\frac{1}{4}}$ $2\frac{5}{6}$

59. $2\frac{1}{6}$
$\underline{-\frac{3}{8}}$ $1\frac{19}{24}$

60. $8\frac{1}{7}$
$\underline{-4\frac{1}{5}}$ $3\frac{33}{35}$

61. $21\frac{3}{8}-3\frac{11}{12}$ $17\frac{11}{24}$

62. $6\frac{1}{2}-4\frac{5}{7}$ $1\frac{11}{14}$

63. $11\frac{1}{8}-3\frac{2}{3}$ $7\frac{11}{24}$

64. $1\frac{5}{6}-\frac{8}{9}$ $\frac{17}{18}$

65. $17\frac{1}{2}-\frac{2}{3}$ $16\frac{5}{6}$

66. $7\frac{1}{12}-3\frac{2}{9}$ $3\frac{31}{36}$

67. $8\frac{1}{8}-2\frac{1}{4}$ $5\frac{7}{8}$

68. $3\frac{1}{6}-1\frac{2}{3}$
$1\frac{1}{2}$

69. $11\frac{1}{5}-6\frac{1}{3}$ $4\frac{13}{15}$

70. $12\frac{2}{7}-2\frac{1}{3}$ $9\frac{20}{21}$

71. $9\frac{3}{8}-2\frac{1}{3}$ $7\frac{1}{24}$

72. $4\frac{3}{16}-1\frac{1}{4}$
$3\frac{15}{16}$

FRACTIONS: ADDITION/SUBTRACTION **195**

Problem Solving and Applications

Customary Measures

See the Teacher's Manual for the objectives.

This table shows some commonly used units in the customary system of measurement. Note that the abbreviations for customary measures which formerly ended with a period now have no period.

Length	Capacity	
12 inches (in) = 1 foot (ft)	2 cups (c) = 1 pint (pt)	
3 feet = 1 yard (yd)	2 pints = 1 quart (qt)	
36 inches = 1 yard	4 quarts = 1 gallon (gal)	
5280 feet = 1 mile (mi)	**Weight**	
	16 ounces (oz) = 1 pound (lb)	
	2000 pounds = 1 ton (T)	

You can write a mixed number for a measure such as 3 feet 9 inches.

EXAMPLE Complete. Write each answer as a mixed number.

    a. 3 ft 9 in = __?__ ft   **b.** 5 lb 2 oz = __?__ lb

Solutions: **a.** Since 12 in = 1 ft,

$$9 \text{ in} = \frac{9}{12}, \text{ or } \frac{3}{4} \text{ ft.} \quad \blacktriangleleft \text{ Lowest terms}$$

Thus, 3 ft 9 in = $3\frac{3}{4}$ **ft.**

    b. Since 16 oz = 1 lb,

$$2 \text{ oz} = \frac{2}{16}, \text{ or } \frac{1}{8} \text{ lb.}$$

Thus, 5 lb 2 oz = $5\frac{1}{8}$ **lb.**

Exercises

Exercises 1-12 apply the skills presented in Section 9-2.

Complete. Write each answer as a mixed number.

1. 4 gal 2 qt = __?__ gal $4\frac{1}{2}$ **2.** 2 yd 12 in = __?__ yd $2\frac{1}{3}$ **3.** 5 qt 1 pt = __?__ qt $5\frac{1}{2}$

4. 6 ft 9 in = __?__ ft $6\frac{3}{4}$ **5.** 98 lb 8 oz = __?__ lb $98\frac{1}{2}$ **6.** 1 yd 5 ft = __?__ yd $2\frac{2}{3}$

7. 5 yd 2 ft = __?__ yd $5\frac{2}{3}$ **8.** 1 qt 5 pt = __?__ qt $3\frac{1}{2}$ **9.** 1 mi 528 ft = $1\frac{1}{10}$__?__ mi

10. 8 yd 24 in = __?__ yd $8\frac{2}{3}$ **11.** 5 pt 1 c = __?__ pt $5\frac{1}{2}$ **12.** 3 lb 10 oz = __?__ lb $3\frac{5}{8}$

The skills used in solving Exercises 13-35 are related to the skills presented in Sections 9-3, 9-4, 9-5, and 9-6.

Use the table to add or subtract as indicated. The first one in each row is done for you.

13.   2 ft 6 in

       +1 ft 9 in

          3 ft 15 in = 3 ft + 1 ft 3 in

              = 4 ft 3 in

              = $4\frac{1}{4}$ ft

14.   1 ft 7 in

       +2 ft 7 in $4\frac{1}{6}$ ft

15.   5 ft 9 in

       +2 ft 3 in   8 ft

16.   5 ft 6 in

       +9 ft 2 in $14\frac{2}{3}$ ft

17.   12 ft 4 in

       + 6 ft 6 in

              $18\frac{5}{6}$ ft

18.
$$9 \text{ yd } 2 \text{ ft}$$
$$\underline{+4 \text{ yd } 2 \text{ ft}}$$
$$13 \text{ yd } \underline{4 \text{ ft}} = 13 \text{ yd} + \underline{1 \text{ yd } 1 \text{ ft}}$$
$$= 14 \text{ yd } 1 \text{ ft}$$
$$= 14\tfrac{1}{3} \text{ yd}$$

19.
$$1 \text{ yd } 2 \text{ ft}$$
$$\underline{+8 \text{ yd } 1 \text{ ft}}$$
10 yd

20.
$$6 \text{ yd } 2 \text{ ft}$$
$$\underline{+5 \text{ yd } 2 \text{ ft}}$$
$$12\tfrac{1}{3} \text{ yd}$$

21.
$$8 \text{ yd } 2 \text{ ft}$$
$$\underline{+ \qquad 3 \text{ ft}}$$
$$9\tfrac{2}{3} \text{ yd}$$

22.
$$4 \text{ yd } 1 \text{ ft}$$
$$\underline{+3 \text{ yd } 1 \text{ ft}}$$
$$7\tfrac{2}{3} \text{ yd}$$

23.
$$4 \text{ gal } 2 \text{ qt}$$
$$\underline{+3 \text{ gal } 3 \text{ qt}}$$
$$7 \text{ gal } \underline{5 \text{ qt}} = 7 \text{ gal} + \underline{1 \text{ gal } 1 \text{ qt}}$$
$$= 8 \text{ gal } 1 \text{ qt}$$
$$= 8\tfrac{1}{4} \text{ gal}$$

24.
$$5 \text{ gal } 2 \text{ qt}$$
$$\underline{+7 \text{ gal } 3 \text{ qt}}$$
$$13\tfrac{1}{4} \text{ gal}$$

25.
$$4 \text{ gal } 3 \text{ qt}$$
$$\underline{+3 \text{ gal } 3 \text{ qt}}$$
$$8\tfrac{1}{2} \text{ gal}$$

26.
$$1 \text{ gal } 1 \text{ qt}$$
$$\underline{+9 \text{ gal } 2 \text{ qt}}$$
$$10\tfrac{3}{4} \text{ gal}$$

27.
$$6 \text{ gal } 3 \text{ qt}$$
$$\underline{+7 \text{ gal } 1 \text{ qt}}$$
14 gal

28.
$$3 \text{ lb } \;\; 9 \text{ oz}$$
$$\underline{+2 \text{ lb } 15 \text{ oz}}$$
$$5 \text{ lb } \underline{24 \text{ oz}} = 5 \text{ lb} + \underline{1 \text{ lb } 8 \text{ oz}}$$
$$= 6 \text{ lb } 8 \text{ oz}$$
$$= 6\tfrac{1}{2} \text{ lb}$$

29.
$$7 \text{ lb } 15 \text{ oz}$$
$$\underline{+3 \text{ lb } \;\; 5 \text{ oz}}$$
$$11\tfrac{1}{4} \text{ lb}$$

30.
$$98 \text{ lb } 10 \text{ oz}$$
$$\underline{+17 \text{ lb } 11 \text{ oz}}$$
$$116\tfrac{5}{6} \text{ lb}$$

31.
$$2 \text{ lb } 4 \text{ oz}$$
$$\underline{+7 \text{ lb } 12 \text{ oz}}$$
10 lb

32.
$$53 \text{ lb } 1 \text{ oz}$$
$$\underline{+27 \text{ lb } 3 \text{ oz}}$$
$$80\tfrac{1}{4} \text{ lb}$$

33. Mary measured the amount of water collected from a dripping faucet.

Monday: 1 gallon 2 quarts
Tuesday: 1 gallon 3 quarts

Find the total amount collected in the two days. Write your answer as a mixed number. $3\tfrac{1}{4}$ gallons

34. Larry wishes to replace the weather-stripping at the top and on one side of a door. The height of the door is 6 feet 11 inches and the width is 2 feet 9 inches. How many feet of weather-stripping will be needed? $9\tfrac{2}{3}$ feet

35. A Lunar Rover carrying an astronaut wearing a space suit and backpack weighs 880 pounds 5 ounces. The astronaut wearing a space suit and backpack weighs 379 pounds 13 ounces. Find the weight of the Lunar Rover. Write your answer as a mixed number. $500\tfrac{1}{2}$ pounds

Application

FRACTIONS: ADDITION/SUBTRACTION   **197**

Chapter Review

These exercises review the vocabulary, skills and applications presented in the chapter as a preparation for the chapter test.

Part 1: Vocabulary

For Exercises 1–6, choose from the box at the right the word(s) that completes each statement.

1. A fraction is greater than 1 when the numerator is __?__ than the denominator. (Page 178) greater

2. The denominator of a fraction can never equal __?__. (Page 178) zero

3. A fraction greater than 1 can be written as a __?__. (Page 178) mixed number

4. The abbreviation for least common denominator is __?__. (Page 188) LCD

5. $\frac{2}{3}$ and $\frac{3}{4}$ are __?__ fractions. (Page 188) unlike

6. $\frac{1}{2}$ and $\frac{2}{4}$ are __?__ fractions. (Page 189) equivalent

| unlike |
| zero |
| like |
| mixed number |
| equivalent |
| LCD |
| greater |
| whole number |

Part 2: Skills

Replace each ● with <, =, or >. (Pages 178–179)

7. $\frac{5}{8}$ ● 1 <
8. $\frac{3}{3}$ ● 1 =
9. $\frac{14}{11}$ ● 1 >
10. $\frac{9}{7}$ ● 1 >
11. $\frac{1}{6}$ ● 1 <

12. $\frac{4}{13}$ ● 1 <
13. $\frac{10}{4}$ ● 1 >
14. $\frac{3}{4}$ ● 1 <
15. $\frac{4}{4}$ ● 1 =
16. $\frac{9}{3}$ ● 1 >

Write a mixed number for each fraction. (Pages 178–179)

17. $\frac{9}{4}$ $2\frac{1}{4}$
18. $\frac{20}{17}$ $1\frac{3}{17}$
19. $\frac{11}{2}$ $5\frac{1}{2}$
20. $\frac{8}{3}$ $2\frac{2}{3}$
21. $\frac{10}{7}$ $1\frac{3}{7}$
22. $\frac{24}{7}$ $3\frac{3}{7}$
23. $\frac{17}{4}$ $4\frac{1}{4}$

24. $\frac{15}{2}$ $7\frac{1}{2}$
25. $\frac{10}{3}$ $3\frac{1}{3}$
26. $\frac{7}{4}$ $1\frac{3}{4}$
27. $\frac{15}{11}$ $1\frac{4}{11}$
28. $\frac{25}{6}$ $4\frac{1}{6}$
29. $\frac{13}{3}$ $4\frac{1}{3}$
30. $\frac{22}{7}$ $3\frac{1}{7}$

Write in lowest terms. Then write a mixed number for any fraction greater than 1. (Pages 182–183)

31. $\frac{12}{9}$ $\frac{4}{3}$; $1\frac{1}{3}$
32. $\frac{6}{9}$ $\frac{2}{3}$
33. $\frac{21}{49}$ $\frac{3}{7}$
34. $\frac{16}{14}$ $\frac{8}{7}$; $1\frac{1}{7}$
35. $\frac{24}{36}$ $\frac{2}{3}$
36. $\frac{5}{25}$ $\frac{1}{5}$
37. $\frac{18}{15}$ $\frac{6}{5}$; $1\frac{1}{5}$

38. $\frac{22}{4}$ $\frac{11}{2}$; $5\frac{1}{2}$
39. $\frac{14}{28}$ $\frac{1}{2}$
40. $\frac{15}{12}$ $\frac{5}{4}$; $1\frac{1}{4}$
41. $\frac{7}{21}$ $\frac{1}{3}$
42. $\frac{36}{45}$ $\frac{4}{5}$
43. $\frac{32}{24}$ $\frac{4}{3}$; $1\frac{1}{3}$
44. $\frac{64}{80}$ $\frac{4}{5}$

Add or subtract. Write each answer in lowest terms. (Pages 186–187)

45. $\frac{3}{7}$ $+\frac{4}{7}$ 1
46. $\frac{5}{8}$ $+\frac{7}{8}$ $1\frac{1}{2}$
47. $\frac{10}{11}$ $-\frac{8}{11}$ $\frac{2}{11}$
48. $\frac{12}{13}$ $-\frac{6}{13}$ $\frac{6}{13}$
49. $2\frac{3}{8}$ $+1\frac{3}{8}$ $3\frac{3}{4}$
50. $6\frac{7}{10}$ $-4\frac{2}{10}$ $2\frac{1}{2}$

51. $5\frac{9}{14}$ $+6$ $11\frac{9}{14}$
52. $14\frac{5}{6}$ -7 $7\frac{5}{6}$
53. $5\frac{18}{24}$ -1 $4\frac{3}{4}$
54. $7\frac{14}{18}$ $-3\frac{12}{18}$ $4\frac{1}{9}$
55. $7\frac{2}{3}$ $+1\frac{1}{3}$ 9
56. $9\frac{1}{2}$ $+3\frac{1}{2}$ 13

57. $32\frac{10}{18} - 22\frac{7}{18}$ $10\frac{1}{6}$
58. $6\frac{5}{8} + 4\frac{3}{8}$ 11
59. $13\frac{3}{5} + 9\frac{1}{5}$ $22\frac{4}{5}$
60. $22\frac{2}{3} - 17\frac{1}{3}$ $5\frac{1}{3}$

198   CHAPTER 9

Chapter Review

Find the LCD for each pair of fractions. (Pages 188–189)

61. $\frac{1}{3}$ and $\frac{3}{6}$ 6   **62.** $\frac{2}{5}$ and $\frac{7}{10}$ 10   **63.** $\frac{2}{3}$ and $\frac{3}{4}$ 12   **64.** $\frac{1}{2}$ and $\frac{3}{5}$ 10   **65.** $\frac{1}{7}$ and $\frac{3}{8}$ 56

Write like fractions for each pair. Then compare the fractions. (Pages 188–189)

66. $\frac{1}{4}$ and $\frac{1}{2}$ $\frac{1}{4} < \frac{2}{4}$ **67.** $\frac{3}{10}$ and $\frac{1}{5}$ $\frac{3}{10} > \frac{2}{10}$ **68.** $\frac{6}{8}$ and $\frac{4}{5}$ $\frac{30}{40} < \frac{32}{40}$ **69.** $\frac{2}{5}$ and $\frac{3}{4}$ $\frac{8}{20} < \frac{15}{20}$ **70.** $\frac{1}{2}$ and $\frac{4}{9}$ $\frac{9}{18} > \frac{8}{18}$

Add or subtract. Write each answer in lowest terms. (Pages 190–191)

71. $\frac{1}{2}$ $+\frac{1}{4}$ $\frac{3}{4}$

72. $\frac{2}{3}$ $+\frac{1}{6}$ $\frac{5}{6}$

73. $23\frac{3}{4}$ $-11\frac{1}{2}$ $12\frac{1}{4}$

74. $4\frac{5}{8}$ $-2\frac{1}{4}$ $2\frac{3}{8}$

75. $6\frac{2}{3}$ $+3\frac{1}{8}$ $9\frac{19}{24}$

76. $17\frac{14}{15}$ $-4\frac{2}{3}$ $13\frac{4}{15}$

77. $6\frac{2}{5}$ $+4\frac{1}{4}$ $10\frac{13}{20}$

78. $2\frac{5}{8}$ $-1\frac{1}{6}$ $1\frac{11}{24}$

79. $16\frac{4}{5}$ $-12\frac{2}{7}$ $4\frac{18}{35}$

80. $21\frac{2}{5}$ $+5\frac{3}{4}$ $27\frac{3}{20}$

81. $19\frac{1}{2}$ $-3\frac{1}{9}$ $6\frac{7}{18}$

82. $17\frac{2}{5}$ $+6\frac{7}{8}$ $24\frac{9}{356}$

83. $22\frac{3}{4} + 5\frac{2}{3}$ $28\frac{5}{12}$ **84.** $16\frac{1}{8} + 15\frac{5}{6}$ $31\frac{23}{24}$ **85.** $27\frac{3}{4} - 14\frac{1}{5}$ $13\frac{11}{20}$ **86.** $15\frac{7}{8} - 12\frac{5}{8}$ $3\frac{11}{40}$

Subtract. Write each answer in lowest terms. (Pages 194–195)

87. $4\frac{1}{3}$ $-2\frac{2}{3}$ $1\frac{2}{3}$

88. $6\frac{1}{5}$ $-4\frac{3}{5}$ $1\frac{3}{5}$

89. $7\frac{2}{3}$ $-4\frac{5}{6}$ $2\frac{5}{6}$

90. $10\frac{1}{2}$ $-5\frac{3}{4}$ $4\frac{3}{4}$

91. 6 $-3\frac{1}{8}$ $2\frac{7}{8}$

92. 19 $-2\frac{7}{10}$ $16\frac{3}{10}$

93. $16\frac{1}{4}$ $-3\frac{2}{5}$ $12\frac{17}{20}$

94. $7\frac{3}{8}$ $-4\frac{4}{5}$ $2\frac{23}{40}$

95. $3\frac{1}{2}$ $-\frac{7}{9}$ $2\frac{13}{18}$

96. $24\frac{2}{3}$ $-\frac{7}{8}$ $23\frac{19}{24}$

97. $4\frac{1}{9}$ $-3\frac{3}{4}$ $\frac{13}{36}$

98. $6\frac{1}{2}$ $-5\frac{5}{7}$ $\frac{11}{14}$

99. $5\frac{1}{3} - 4\frac{3}{8}$ $\frac{23}{24}$ **100.** $1\frac{5}{18} - \frac{3}{4}$ $\frac{19}{36}$ **101.** $3\frac{1}{9} - 1\frac{1}{5}$ $1\frac{41}{45}$ **102.** $12\frac{3}{10} - 2\frac{1}{2}$ $9\frac{4}{5}$

Part 3: Applications The use of these word problems depends on which applications were studied.

103. The school record for the high jump was 6 feet $4\frac{7}{8}$ inches. Juan jumped 6 feet $2\frac{3}{8}$ inches.
Find the difference between the two jumps. (Pages 186–187) $2\frac{1}{2}$ inches

104. Kyoki worked from 8:00 A.M. to 4:30 P.M. on Monday, from 8:15 A.M. to 4:30 P.M. on Tuesday, and from 8:30 A.M. to 5:15 P.M. on Wednesday. He took an hour for lunch each day. Find the total number of hours worked. (Pages 192–193) $22\frac{1}{2}$ hours

Chapter Test

The Teacher's Resource Book contains two forms of each chapter test.

Write in lowest terms. Then write a mixed number for any fraction greater than 1.

1. $\frac{2}{4}$ $\frac{1}{2}$ **2.** $\frac{6}{4}$ $\frac{3}{2}; 1\frac{1}{2}$ **3.** $\frac{3}{9}$ $\frac{1}{3}$ **4.** $\frac{14}{21}$ $\frac{2}{3}$ **5.** $\frac{16}{12}$ $\frac{4}{3}; 1\frac{1}{3}$ **6.** $\frac{18}{14}$ $\frac{9}{7}; 1\frac{2}{7}$ **7.** $\frac{15}{20}$ $\frac{3}{4}$

Add or subtract. Write each answer in lowest terms.

8. $\begin{array}{r} \frac{5}{8} \\ +\frac{7}{8} \\ \hline 1\frac{1}{2} \end{array}$
  9. $\begin{array}{r} \frac{10}{12} \\ -\frac{7}{12} \\ \hline \frac{1}{4} \end{array}$
  10. $\begin{array}{r} 3\frac{3}{4} \\ +1\frac{2}{4} \\ \hline 5\frac{1}{4} \end{array}$
  11. $\begin{array}{r} 5\frac{7}{9} \\ +6\frac{4}{9} \\ \hline 12\frac{2}{9} \end{array}$
  12. $\begin{array}{r} 13\frac{12}{13} \\ -9\frac{4}{13} \\ \hline 4\frac{8}{13} \end{array}$
  13. $\begin{array}{r} 25\frac{16}{18} \\ -9\frac{7}{18} \\ \hline 16\frac{1}{2} \end{array}$

Write like fractions for each pair. Then compare the fractions.

14. $\frac{3}{4}$ and $\frac{1}{2}$ $\frac{3}{4} > \frac{2}{4}$ **15.** $\frac{2}{3}$ and $\frac{5}{6}$ $\frac{4}{6} < \frac{5}{6}$ **16.** $\frac{1}{6}$ and $\frac{3}{8}$ $\frac{4}{24} < \frac{9}{24}$ **17.** $\frac{3}{5}$ and $\frac{1}{4}$ $\frac{12}{20} > \frac{5}{20}$ **18.** $\frac{7}{8}$ and $\frac{1}{7}$ $\frac{49}{56} > \frac{8}{56}$

Add or subtract. Write each answer in lowest terms.

19. $\begin{array}{r} 1\frac{1}{2} \\ +2\frac{3}{4} \\ \hline 4\frac{1}{4} \end{array}$
  20. $\begin{array}{r} 4\frac{1}{3} \\ +2\frac{4}{6} \\ \hline 7 \end{array}$
  21. $\begin{array}{r} 3\frac{5}{6} \\ -1\frac{1}{2} \\ \hline 2\frac{1}{3} \end{array}$
  22. $\begin{array}{r} 15\frac{7}{8} \\ -2\frac{3}{4} \\ \hline 13\frac{1}{8} \end{array}$
  23. $\begin{array}{r} 12\frac{2}{3} \\ +3\frac{3}{4} \\ \hline 16\frac{5}{12} \end{array}$
  24. $\begin{array}{r} 14\frac{2}{5} \\ +7\frac{1}{4} \\ \hline 21\frac{13}{20} \end{array}$

25. $\begin{array}{r} 16\frac{2}{3} \\ -6\frac{1}{5} \\ \hline 10\frac{7}{15} \end{array}$
  26. $\begin{array}{r} 22\frac{4}{5} \\ -11\frac{2}{7} \\ \hline 11\frac{18}{35} \end{array}$
  27. $\begin{array}{r} 14 \\ -1\frac{1}{3} \\ \hline 12\frac{2}{3} \end{array}$
  28. $\begin{array}{r} 23\frac{1}{8} \\ -12\frac{3}{8} \\ \hline 10\frac{5}{8} \end{array}$
  29. $\begin{array}{r} 14\frac{1}{2} \\ -12\frac{3}{4} \\ \hline 1\frac{3}{4} \end{array}$
  30. $\begin{array}{r} 7\frac{1}{3} \\ -4\frac{4}{5} \\ \hline 2\frac{8}{15} \end{array}$

Solve. The use of these word problems depends on which applications were studied.

31. Neil jogged $2\frac{3}{7}$ miles on Monday and $3\frac{2}{5}$ miles on Wednesday. How many miles did he jog on the two days? $5\frac{29}{35}$ miles

32. The school record for running the mile was $4\frac{3}{4}$ minutes. Jerry's record is $5\frac{1}{4}$ minutes. Find the difference between the two records. $\frac{1}{2}$ minute

33. One year a fox was 1 foot 11 inches tall. The next year it was 2 feet 6 inches tall. How much did it grow in that year? 7 inches

Additional Practice

You may wish to use some or all of these exercises depending on how well students performed on the formal chapter test.

Skills

Replace each ● *with* <, =, *or* >. (Pages 178–179)

1. $\frac{3}{4}$ ● 1 < **2.** $\frac{9}{5}$ ● 1 > **3.** $\frac{3}{3}$ ● 1 = **4.** $\frac{7}{8}$ ● 1 < **5.** $\frac{10}{7}$ ● 1 >

Write a mixed number for each fraction. (Pages 178–179)

6. $\frac{3}{2}$ $1\frac{1}{2}$ **7.** $\frac{10}{3}$ $3\frac{1}{3}$ **8.** $\frac{27}{5}$ $5\frac{2}{5}$ **9.** $\frac{32}{7}$ $4\frac{4}{7}$ **10.** $\frac{41}{3}$ $13\frac{2}{3}$ **11.** $\frac{29}{2}$ $14\frac{1}{2}$ **12.** $\frac{23}{4}$ $5\frac{3}{4}$ **13.** $\frac{15}{8}$ $1\frac{7}{8}$

Write in lowest terms. Then write a mixed number for any fraction greater than 1.
(Pages 182–183)

14. $\frac{2}{10}$ $\frac{1}{5}$ **15.** $\frac{12}{8}$ $\frac{3}{2}$; $1\frac{1}{2}$ **16.** $\frac{50}{35}$ $\frac{10}{7}$; $1\frac{3}{7}$ **17.** $\frac{18}{21}$ $\frac{6}{7}$ **18.** $\frac{27}{24}$ $\frac{9}{8}$; $1\frac{1}{8}$ **19.** $\frac{3}{12}$ $\frac{1}{4}$ **20.** $\frac{12}{15}$ $\frac{4}{5}$ **21.** $\frac{48}{36}$ $\frac{4}{3}$; $1\frac{1}{3}$

Add or subtract. Write each answer in lowest terms.
(Pages 186–187)

22. $\frac{2}{9}$ $+\frac{5}{9}$ $\frac{7}{9}$ **23.** $\frac{12}{13}$ $-\frac{8}{13}$ $\frac{4}{13}$ **24.** $\frac{10}{14}$ $-\frac{6}{14}$ $\frac{2}{7}$ **25.** $\frac{3}{8}$ $+\frac{7}{8}$ $1\frac{1}{4}$ **26.** $1\frac{5}{9}$ $+2\frac{2}{9}$ $3\frac{7}{9}$ **27.** $6\frac{4}{7}$ $+3$ $9\frac{4}{7}$

28. $5\frac{3}{4}-2$ $3\frac{3}{4}$ **29.** $3\frac{11}{12}-2\frac{5}{12}$ $1\frac{1}{2}$ **30.** $4\frac{1}{3}+9\frac{2}{3}$ 14 **31.** $3\frac{7}{8}+2\frac{5}{8}$ $6\frac{1}{2}$

Write like fractions for each pair. Then compare the fractions.
(Pages 188–189)

32. $\frac{3}{4}$ and $\frac{1}{3}$ $\frac{9}{12} > \frac{4}{12}$ **33.** $\frac{2}{3}$ and $\frac{4}{7}$ $\frac{14}{21} > \frac{12}{21}$ **34.** $\frac{3}{8}$ and $\frac{2}{5}$ $\frac{15}{40} < \frac{16}{40}$ **35.** $\frac{4}{7}$ and $\frac{3}{4}$ $\frac{16}{28} < \frac{21}{28}$ **36.** $\frac{1}{2}$ and $\frac{5}{9}$ $\frac{9}{18} < \frac{10}{18}$

Add or subtract. Write each answer in lowest terms.
(Pages 190–191)

37. $\frac{4}{9}$ $+\frac{2}{3}$ $1\frac{1}{9}$ **38.** $\frac{3}{4}$ $+\frac{4}{7}$ $1\frac{9}{28}$ **39.** $\frac{1}{2}$ $-\frac{1}{3}$ $\frac{1}{6}$ **40.** $\frac{5}{6}$ $-\frac{2}{5}$ $\frac{13}{30}$ **41.** $5\frac{2}{3}$ $+2\frac{1}{6}$ $7\frac{5}{6}$ **42.** $6\frac{3}{4}$ $-1\frac{1}{3}$ $5\frac{5}{12}$

43. $6\frac{1}{3}+2\frac{1}{5}$ $8\frac{8}{15}$ **44.** $2\frac{1}{6}+3\frac{5}{12}$ $5\frac{7}{12}$ **45.** $4\frac{7}{12}-3\frac{3}{8}$ $1\frac{5}{24}$ **46.** $5\frac{2}{5}+1\frac{1}{2}$ $6\frac{9}{10}$

(Pages 194–195)

47. $4\frac{3}{5}$ $-2\frac{2}{3}$ $1\frac{14}{15}$ **48.** 9 $-2\frac{7}{8}$ $6\frac{1}{8}$ **49.** $8\frac{1}{3}$ $-4\frac{7}{8}$ $3\frac{11}{24}$ **50.** $7\frac{1}{4}$ $-1\frac{7}{8}$ $5\frac{3}{8}$ **51.** 10 $-3\frac{4}{5}$ $6\frac{1}{5}$ **52.** $4\frac{1}{5}$ $-2\frac{2}{3}$ $1\frac{8}{15}$

53. $8\frac{1}{4}-3\frac{1}{6}$ $5\frac{1}{12}$ **54.** $8\frac{1}{2}-4\frac{3}{8}$ $4\frac{1}{8}$ **55.** $6-2\frac{2}{3}$ $3\frac{1}{3}$ **56.** $12-6\frac{3}{4}$ $5\frac{1}{4}$

Applications The use of these word problems depends on which applications were studied.

57. Sue worked $7\frac{1}{5}$ hours on Wednesday and $6\frac{1}{2}$ hours on Thursday. How many hours did she work on the two days? (Page 193) $13\frac{7}{10}$ hours

58. In January, Jim's height was 4 feet 10 inches. In September, his height was 5 feet 2 inches. How much did Jim grow? (Page 197) 4 inches

We suggest that some or all of this page be reviewed before proceeding with the chapter.

Multiply. (Pages 26–27)

1. 21×8 168
2. 31×5 155
3. 23×3 69
4. 11×3 33
5. 27×7 189
6. 19×4 76
7. 22×6 132
8. 25×5 125
9. 26×7 182
10. 75×6 450
11. 43×9 387
12. 30×9 270
13. 19×4 76
14. 29×3 87
15. 40×7 280
16. 12×8 96
17. 51×2 102
18. 16×9 144
19. 15×8 120
20. 44×7 308
21. 14×2 28
22. 24×6 144
23. 30×8 240
24. 43×8 344
25. 23×8 184
26. 15×6 90
27. 21×4 84
28. 13×7 91
29. 27×6 162
30. 60×3 180

Divide the first two numbers by the third. (Pages 48–49, 50–51)

31. 81 and 27 by 9 9, 3
32. 28 and 30 by 2 14, 15
33. 18 and 21 by 3 6, 7
34. 35 and 90 by 5 7, 18
35. 32 and 28 by 4 8, 7
36. 25 and 40 by 5 5, 8
37. 9 and 12 by 3 3, 4
38. 16 and 48 by 4 4, 12
39. 14 and 26 by 2 7, 13
40. 36 and 45 by 9 4, 5
41. 40 and 90 by 10 4, 9
42. 8 and 12 by 4 2, 3
43. 24 and 40 by 4 6, 10
44. 6 and 8 by 2 3, 4
45. 18 and 27 by 9 2, 3
46. 15 and 48 by 3 5, 16
47. 10 and 25 by 5 2, 5
48. 39 and 48 by 3 13, 16
49. 25 and 70 by 5 5, 14
50. 60 and 100 by 10 6, 10
51. 10 and 22 by 2 5, 11

Write a mixed number for each fraction. (Pages 178–179)

52. $\frac{10}{3}$ $3\frac{1}{3}$
53. $\frac{11}{6}$ $1\frac{5}{6}$
54. $\frac{9}{2}$ $4\frac{1}{2}$
55. $\frac{16}{9}$ $1\frac{7}{9}$
56. $\frac{14}{5}$ $2\frac{4}{5}$
57. $\frac{7}{4}$ $1\frac{3}{4}$
58. $\frac{12}{7}$ $1\frac{5}{7}$
59. $\frac{8}{5}$ $1\frac{3}{5}$
60. $\frac{7}{2}$ $3\frac{1}{2}$
61. $\frac{13}{3}$ $4\frac{1}{3}$
62. $\frac{13}{6}$ $2\frac{1}{6}$
63. $\frac{15}{7}$ $2\frac{1}{7}$
64. $\frac{5}{2}$ $2\frac{1}{2}$
65. $\frac{17}{4}$ $4\frac{1}{4}$
66. $\frac{23}{6}$ $3\frac{5}{6}$
67. $\frac{11}{4}$ $2\frac{3}{4}$
68. $\frac{11}{2}$ $5\frac{1}{2}$
69. $\frac{17}{5}$ $3\frac{2}{5}$
70. $\frac{17}{3}$ $5\frac{2}{3}$
71. $\frac{25}{7}$ $3\frac{4}{7}$
72. $\frac{25}{8}$ $3\frac{1}{8}$
73. $\frac{26}{9}$ $2\frac{8}{9}$
74. $\frac{22}{5}$ $4\frac{2}{5}$
75. $\frac{47}{8}$ $5\frac{7}{8}$
76. $\frac{22}{3}$ $7\frac{1}{3}$
77. $\frac{13}{6}$ $2\frac{1}{6}$
78. $\frac{15}{2}$ $7\frac{1}{2}$
79. $\frac{45}{7}$ $6\frac{3}{7}$
80. $\frac{73}{8}$ $9\frac{1}{8}$
81. $\frac{29}{3}$ $9\frac{2}{3}$
82. $\frac{36}{5}$ $7\frac{1}{5}$
83. $\frac{21}{2}$ $10\frac{1}{2}$
84. $\frac{49}{9}$ $5\frac{4}{9}$
85. $\frac{19}{9}$ $2\frac{1}{9}$
86. $\frac{19}{4}$ $4\frac{3}{4}$

Write each fraction in lowest terms. (Pages 182–183)

87. $\frac{8}{20}$ $\frac{2}{5}$
88. $\frac{6}{16}$ $\frac{3}{8}$
89. $\frac{4}{20}$ $\frac{1}{5}$
90. $\frac{15}{18}$ $\frac{5}{6}$
91. $\frac{9}{18}$ $\frac{1}{2}$
92. $\frac{6}{8}$ $\frac{3}{4}$
93. $\frac{4}{16}$ $\frac{1}{4}$
94. $\frac{4}{12}$ $\frac{1}{3}$
95. $\frac{9}{36}$ $\frac{1}{4}$
96. $\frac{12}{36}$ $\frac{1}{3}$
97. $\frac{16}{48}$ $\frac{1}{3}$
98. $\frac{9}{27}$ $\frac{1}{3}$
99. $\frac{8}{12}$ $\frac{2}{3}$
100. $\frac{4}{6}$ $\frac{2}{3}$
101. $\frac{6}{9}$ $\frac{2}{3}$
102. $\frac{6}{45}$ $\frac{2}{15}$
103. $\frac{5}{15}$ $\frac{1}{3}$
104. $\frac{4}{8}$ $\frac{1}{2}$
105. $\frac{8}{24}$ $\frac{1}{3}$
106. $\frac{12}{24}$ $\frac{1}{2}$
107. $\frac{14}{16}$ $\frac{7}{8}$
108. $\frac{8}{32}$ $\frac{1}{4}$
109. $\frac{9}{15}$ $\frac{3}{5}$
110. $\frac{20}{28}$ $\frac{5}{7}$
111. $\frac{20}{24}$ $\frac{5}{6}$
112. $\frac{18}{20}$ $\frac{9}{10}$
113. $\frac{16}{18}$ $\frac{8}{9}$
114. $\frac{12}{16}$ $\frac{3}{4}$
115. $\frac{3}{6}$ $\frac{1}{2}$
116. $\frac{2}{16}$ $\frac{1}{8}$
117. $\frac{4}{32}$ $\frac{1}{8}$
118. $\frac{15}{33}$ $\frac{5}{11}$
119. $\frac{7}{21}$ $\frac{1}{3}$
120. $\frac{6}{14}$ $\frac{3}{7}$
121. $\frac{16}{28}$ $\frac{4}{7}$

CHAPTER 10

FRACTIONS MULTIPLICATION/ DIVISION

SKILLS

10-1   Multiplication: Fractions
10-2   Multiplication: Mixed Numbers
10-3   Division: Fractions
10-4   Division: Mixed Numbers
10-5   Rounding and Estimation

APPLICATIONS

Science
Discount
Distance Formula
Wallpapering and Estimation

CAREERS

Business
Construction

10-1 Multiplication: Fractions

See the Teacher's Manual for the objectives.

You can use rectangles to show multiplication with fractions.

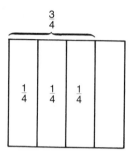

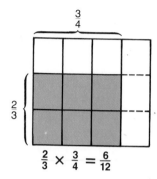

$$\frac{2}{3} \times \frac{3}{4} = \frac{6}{12}$$

Thus, $\frac{2}{3} \times \frac{3}{4} = \frac{2 \times 3}{3 \times 4} = \frac{6}{12} = \frac{1}{2}$. ◀ *Lowest terms*

PROCEDURE To multiply with fractions:

1 Multiply the numerators and multiply the denominators.

2 Write the answer in lowest terms.

EXAMPLE 1 Multiply: **a.** $\frac{5}{6} \times \frac{7}{10}$ **b.** $14 \times \frac{2}{3}$

Solutions: **a.** 1 $\frac{5}{6} \times \frac{7}{10} = \frac{5 \times 7}{6 \times 10}$

$= \frac{35}{60}$ ◀ *Write in lowest terms.*

2 $= \frac{7}{12}$

b. $14 \times \frac{2}{3} = \frac{14}{1} \times \frac{2}{3}$ ◀ $14 = \frac{14}{1}$

1 $= \frac{14 \times 2}{1 \times 3}$

$= \frac{28}{3}$ ◀ *Write a mixed number for $\frac{28}{3}$.*

2 $= 9\frac{1}{3}$

After completing Example 1, you may wish to have students do some or all of Exercises 1-48.

Sometimes you can divide a numerator and a denominator by the same number before you multiply.

EXAMPLE 2 Multiply: **a.** $\frac{2}{3} \times \frac{5}{12}$ **b.** $\frac{7}{9} \times \frac{18}{21}$

Solutions: **a.** $\frac{2}{3} \times \frac{5}{12} = \frac{2}{3} \times \frac{5}{\underset{6}{\cancel{12}}}^{1}$ ◀ $\begin{array}{l} 2 \div 2 = 1 \\ 12 \div 2 = 6 \end{array}$

$= \frac{1 \times 5}{3 \times 6}$

$= \frac{5}{18}$

b. $\frac{7}{9} \times \frac{18}{21} = \frac{7}{\underset{1}{\cancel{9}}} \times \frac{\overset{2}{\cancel{18}}}{\underset{3}{\cancel{21}}}$

$= \frac{1 \times 2}{1 \times 3}$

$= \frac{2}{3}$

Write a mixed number for each fraction.　　(Pages 178–179)　　$7\frac{3}{11}$

1. $\frac{10}{7}$　$1\frac{3}{7}$　2. $\frac{26}{9}$　$2\frac{8}{9}$　3. $\frac{52}{9}$　$5\frac{7}{9}$　4. $\frac{100}{3}$　$33\frac{1}{3}$　5. $\frac{48}{5}$　$9\frac{3}{5}$　6. $\frac{51}{4}$　$12\frac{3}{4}$　7. $\frac{91}{12}$　$7\frac{7}{12}$　8. $\frac{80}{11}$

Write each fraction in lowest terms.　　(Pages 182–183)　　$\frac{2}{3}$

9. $\frac{21}{42}$　$\frac{1}{2}$　10. $\frac{18}{48}$　$\frac{3}{8}$　11. $\frac{20}{50}$　$\frac{2}{5}$　12. $\frac{36}{64}$　$\frac{9}{16}$　13. $\frac{36}{48}$　$\frac{3}{4}$　14. $\frac{49}{98}$　$\frac{1}{2}$　15. $\frac{16}{64}$　$\frac{1}{4}$　16. $\frac{96}{144}$

EXERCISES

Multiply. Write the answer in lowest terms.　　(Example 1a)　　$\frac{3}{35}$

1. $\frac{1}{4} \times \frac{1}{2}$　$\frac{1}{8}$　2. $\frac{1}{3} \times \frac{1}{5}$　$\frac{1}{15}$　3. $\frac{3}{4} \times \frac{1}{4}$　$\frac{3}{16}$　4. $\frac{3}{5} \times \frac{1}{2}$　$\frac{3}{10}$　5. $\frac{4}{5} \times \frac{1}{7}$　$\frac{4}{35}$　6. $\frac{3}{5} \times \frac{1}{7}$

7. $\frac{3}{5} \times \frac{2}{7}$　$\frac{6}{35}$　8. $\frac{4}{5} \times \frac{3}{7}$　$\frac{12}{35}$　9. $\frac{2}{9} \times \frac{4}{5}$　$\frac{8}{45}$　10. $\frac{3}{11} \times \frac{5}{7}$　$\frac{15}{77}$　11. $\frac{1}{2} \times \frac{1}{3}$　$\frac{1}{6}$　12. $\frac{1}{2} \times \frac{3}{5}$　$\frac{3}{10}$

13. $\frac{3}{5} \times \frac{1}{8}$　$\frac{3}{40}$　14. $\frac{4}{7} \times \frac{1}{5}$　$\frac{4}{35}$　15. $\frac{1}{5} \times \frac{8}{9}$　$\frac{8}{45}$　16. $\frac{3}{4} \times \frac{3}{5}$　$\frac{9}{20}$　17. $\frac{3}{8} \times \frac{7}{11}$　$\frac{21}{88}$　18. $\frac{4}{5} \times \frac{2}{3}$　$\frac{8}{15}$

19. $\frac{5}{9} \times \frac{4}{7}$　$\frac{20}{63}$　20. $\frac{5}{6} \times \frac{2}{7}$　$\frac{5}{21}$　21. $\frac{5}{8} \times \frac{1}{12}$　$\frac{5}{96}$　22. $\frac{5}{7} \times \frac{11}{12}$　$\frac{55}{84}$　23. $\frac{2}{5} \times \frac{1}{6}$　$\frac{1}{15}$　24. $\frac{2}{7} \times \frac{1}{6}$　$\frac{1}{21}$

(Example 1b)　　$10\frac{1}{2}$

25. $2 \times \frac{1}{5}$　$\frac{2}{5}$　26. $4 \times \frac{1}{5}$　$\frac{4}{5}$　27. $3 \times \frac{1}{10}$　$\frac{3}{10}$　28. $5 \times \frac{1}{8}$　$\frac{5}{8}$　29. $\frac{1}{10} \times 7$　$\frac{7}{10}$　30. $21 \times \frac{1}{2}$

31. $16 \times \frac{1}{5}$　$3\frac{1}{5}$　32. $\frac{2}{5} \times 18$　$7\frac{1}{5}$　33. $\frac{3}{5} \times 27$　$16\frac{1}{5}$　34. $12 \times \frac{4}{5}$　$9\frac{3}{5}$　35. $11 \times \frac{1}{2}$　$5\frac{1}{2}$　36. $7 \times \frac{1}{6}$　$1\frac{1}{6}$

37. $\frac{5}{6} \times 19$　$15\frac{5}{6}$　38. $\frac{3}{4} \times 21$　$15\frac{3}{4}$　39. $12 \times \frac{1}{5}$　$2\frac{2}{5}$　40. $9 \times \frac{2}{7}$　$2\frac{4}{7}$　41. $32 \times \frac{2}{3}$　$21\frac{1}{3}$　42. $\frac{3}{4} \times 81$　$60\frac{3}{4}$

43. $\frac{3}{4} \times 15$　$11\frac{1}{4}$　44. $42 \times \frac{3}{5}$　$25\frac{1}{5}$　45. $\frac{1}{8} \times 11$　$1\frac{3}{8}$　46. $\frac{1}{6} \times 5$　$\frac{5}{6}$　47. $3 \times \frac{1}{8}$　$\frac{3}{8}$　48. $5 \times \frac{1}{6}$　$\frac{5}{6}$

(Example 2)

49. $\frac{4}{5} \times \frac{5}{7}$　$\frac{4}{7}$　50. $\frac{3}{4} \times \frac{4}{5}$　$\frac{3}{5}$　51. $\frac{3}{5} \times \frac{2}{3}$　$\frac{2}{5}$　52. $\frac{4}{7} \times \frac{3}{4}$　$\frac{3}{7}$　53. $\frac{1}{3} \times \frac{3}{5}$　$\frac{1}{5}$　54. $\frac{7}{8} \times \frac{8}{9}$　$\frac{7}{9}$

55. $\frac{1}{2} \times \frac{4}{5}$　$\frac{2}{5}$　56. $\frac{1}{4} \times \frac{8}{9}$　$\frac{2}{9}$　57. $\frac{5}{9} \times \frac{7}{10}$　$\frac{7}{18}$　58. $\frac{4}{5} \times \frac{7}{12}$　$\frac{7}{15}$　59. $\frac{9}{10} \times \frac{1}{3}$　$\frac{3}{10}$　60. $\frac{10}{11} \times \frac{3}{5}$　$\frac{6}{11}$

61. $\frac{5}{9} \times \frac{3}{7}$　$\frac{5}{21}$　62. $\frac{3}{4} \times \frac{2}{5}$　$\frac{3}{10}$　63. $\frac{4}{5} \times \frac{5}{8}$　$\frac{1}{2}$　64. $\frac{2}{3} \times \frac{3}{8}$　$\frac{1}{4}$　65. $\frac{2}{9} \times \frac{3}{4}$　$\frac{1}{6}$　66. $\frac{9}{10} \times \frac{5}{6}$　$\frac{3}{4}$

67. $\frac{2}{3} \times \frac{9}{10}$　$\frac{3}{5}$　68. $\frac{5}{8} \times \frac{4}{15}$　$\frac{1}{6}$　69. $\frac{3}{4} \times \frac{8}{15}$　$\frac{2}{5}$　70. $\frac{7}{16} \times \frac{4}{21}$　$\frac{1}{12}$　71. $\frac{4}{9} \times \frac{3}{8}$　$\frac{1}{6}$　72. $\frac{12}{15} \times \frac{3}{4}$　$\frac{3}{5}$

Mixed Practice　The Mixed Practice contains exercises that relate to both Examples 1 and 2.

73. $\frac{5}{8} \times \frac{11}{25}$　$\frac{11}{40}$　74. $\frac{5}{6} \times \frac{4}{5}$　$\frac{2}{3}$　75. $\frac{10}{21} \times \frac{14}{15}$　$\frac{4}{9}$　76. $\frac{9}{10} \times \frac{8}{15}$　$\frac{12}{25}$　77. $\frac{4}{3} \times \frac{3}{4}$　1

78. $\frac{1}{9} \times 6$　$\frac{2}{3}$　79. $\frac{1}{9} \times \frac{3}{8}$　$\frac{1}{24}$　80. $\frac{1}{9} \times \frac{6}{7}$　$\frac{2}{21}$　81. $\frac{3}{8} \times \frac{6}{7}$　$\frac{9}{28}$　82. $\frac{8}{9} \times \frac{9}{8}$　1

83. $\frac{3}{4} \times \frac{4}{9}$　$\frac{1}{3}$　84. $\frac{2}{3} \times \frac{3}{4}$　$\frac{1}{2}$　85. $\frac{3}{8} \times \frac{8}{9}$　$\frac{1}{3}$　86. $\frac{9}{10} \times \frac{5}{6}$　$\frac{3}{4}$　87. $\frac{21}{75} \times \frac{75}{84}$　$\frac{1}{4}$

88. $\frac{8}{9} \times \frac{5}{6}$　$\frac{20}{27}$　89. $\frac{3}{4} \times 8$　6　90. $\frac{5}{6} \times 12$　10　91. $\frac{3}{4} \times \frac{8}{11}$　$\frac{6}{11}$　92. $\frac{5}{6} \times \frac{12}{13}$　$\frac{10}{13}$

Problem Solving and Applications

Science

See the Teacher's Manual for the objectives.
This lesson applies the skills presented in Section 10-1.

A **bathyscaph** is a small submarine. Scientists use bathyscaphs to descend as far as 10,000 meters into the ocean to explore and to perform experiments.

EXAMPLE In 1934, an American naturalist named William Beebe used a bathyscaph to descend into the ocean. He descended $\frac{2}{25}$ of 10,000 meters. How many meters was this?

Solution: Find $\frac{2}{25}$ of 10,000. ◀ $\frac{2}{25} \times 10{,}000$

$$\frac{2}{25} \times 10{,}000 = \frac{2}{\underset{1}{25}} \times \frac{\overset{400}{\cancel{10\ 000}}}{1} \quad ◀ \quad \begin{array}{l} 10{,}000 \div 25 = 400 \\ 25 \div 25 = 1 \end{array}$$

$$= \frac{2 \times 400}{1 \times 1}$$

$$= \frac{800}{1}, \text{ or } \mathbf{800} \qquad \text{The bathyscaph descended } \mathbf{800 \ meters.}$$

Exercises

Note that these are one-step problems.

1. In the 1880's, divers used suits with hoses to descend about $\frac{3}{500}$ as far as a bathyscaph. How many meters was this? 60 meters

2. The Aluminaut is a small submarine that carries a crew of six. It can descend $\frac{9}{20}$ as far as a bathyscaph. How many meters can it descend? 4500 meters

3. The U.S. Navy uses a plastic sphere to descend $\frac{9}{500}$ as far as a bathyscaph. How many meters is this? 180 meters

4. In 1965, Scott Carpenter, one of the original astronauts, spent 30 days in the U.S. Navy's Sealab II. Sealab II was at a depth that was $\frac{3}{1000}$ of the depth of a bathyscaph. At what depth was Sealab II? 30 meters

The Aluminaut

Sealab II

Problem Solving and Applications

Discount

See the Teacher's Manual for the objectives.
This lesson applies the skills presented in Section 10-1.

Items on sale are sold at a discount from the regular price. The **discount** is the amount the customer saves. Sometimes the rate of discount is given as a fraction, such as "$\frac{1}{3}$ off." The **net price** is the amount the customer actually pays for the item.

To find the net price, first answer the question:

"What is the amount of discount?"

This is the <u>hidden question</u> in the problem.

**Sale!
1/3 OFF**

**BaseBall
Gloves**

REGULARLY $24.90

EXAMPLE   Find the net price of the baseball gloves in the advertisement.

Solution   [1] Find the discount.

$$\frac{1}{3} \times \overset{8.30}{\underset{1}{24.90}} = 8.30 \qquad \blacktriangleleft \quad \textit{Rate of Discount} \times \textit{Regular Price} = \textit{Discount}$$

[2] Find the net price.

$$24.90 - 8.30 = 16.60 \qquad \blacktriangleleft \quad \textit{Regular Price} - \textit{Discount} = \textit{Net Price}$$

The net price is **$16.60**.

Exercises

Note that these are two-step problems.

Find the net price.

1. Alexander Hoff bought a camera for $\frac{1}{5}$ off the regular price of $113.00. What was the discount? $22.60

2. Laura Montez bought a clock radio for $\frac{1}{4}$ off the regular price of $62.96. What was the discount? $15.74

3. The regular price of an 8–track tape is $6.80. At a sale, the tapes are marked "$\frac{1}{5}$ OFF." Find the net price. $5.44

4. The regular price of a television set is $510.00. The set is marked "$\frac{1}{4}$ OFF." Find the net price. $382.50

5. The regular price of a rug is $150.00. The rug is marked "$\frac{1}{5}$ OFF." Find the net price. $120.00

Application   FRACTIONS: MULTIPLICATION/DIVISION   **207**

10-2 Multiplication: Mixed Numbers

See the Teacher's Manual for the objectives.

This table shows how to write a fraction for a mixed number.

Mixed Numbers	PROCEDURE		
	1 Multiply the denominator and the whole number.	**2** Add this product to the numerator.	**3** Write this sum over the denominator.
$3\frac{2}{5}$	$5 \times 3 = 15$	$15 + 2 = 17$	$\frac{17}{5}$ $3\frac{2}{5} = \frac{17}{5}$
$1\frac{7}{8}$	$8 \times 1 = 8$	$8 + 7 = 15$	$\frac{15}{8}$ $1\frac{7}{8} = \frac{15}{8}$

Writing a fraction for each mixed number is the first step in multiplying with mixed numbers.

PROCEDURE To multiply with mixed numbers:

1 Write a fraction for each mixed number.

2 Multiply the fractions.

3 Write the answer in lowest terms.

EXAMPLE Multiply: **a.** $8 \times 3\frac{1}{16}$ **b.** $4\frac{2}{3} \times 3\frac{1}{7}$

Solutions:

a. **1** $8 \times 3\frac{1}{16} = \frac{8}{1} \times \frac{49}{16}$

2 $\qquad = \frac{\overset{1}{\cancel{8}}}{1} \times \frac{49}{\underset{2}{\cancel{16}}}$

$\qquad = \frac{49}{2}$ $\boxed{\frac{1 \times 49}{1 \times 2}}$

3 $\qquad = 24\frac{1}{2}$

b. **1** $4\frac{2}{3} \times 3\frac{1}{7} = \frac{14}{3} \times \frac{22}{7}$

2 $\qquad = \frac{\overset{2}{\cancel{14}}}{3} \times \frac{22}{\underset{1}{\cancel{7}}}$

$\qquad = \frac{44}{3}$ $\boxed{\frac{2 \times 22}{3 \times 1}}$

3 $\qquad = 14\frac{2}{3}$

REVIEW OF RELATED SKILLS

You may wish to use these exercises before teaching the lesson.

Write a mixed number for each fraction. (Pages 178–179)

1. $\frac{9}{2}$ $\quad 4\frac{1}{2}$ **2.** $\frac{11}{5}$ $\quad 2\frac{1}{5}$ **3.** $\frac{27}{5}$ $\quad 5\frac{2}{5}$ **4.** $\frac{59}{6}$ $\quad 9\frac{5}{6}$ **5.** $\frac{46}{7}$ $\quad 6\frac{4}{7}$ **6.** $\frac{37}{4}$ $\quad 9\frac{1}{4}$ **7.** $\frac{14}{3}$ $\quad 4\frac{2}{3}$ **8.** $\frac{73}{8}$ $\quad 9\frac{1}{8}$

Write each fraction in lowest terms. (Pages 182–183)

9. $\frac{30}{45}$ $\quad \frac{2}{3}$ **10.** $\frac{21}{63}$ $\quad \frac{1}{3}$ **11.** $\frac{24}{72}$ $\quad \frac{1}{3}$ **12.** $\frac{125}{225}$ $\quad \frac{5}{9}$ **13.** $\frac{13}{78}$ $\quad \frac{1}{6}$ **14.** $\frac{18}{96}$ $\quad \frac{3}{16}$ **15.** $\frac{32}{40}$ $\quad \frac{4}{5}$ **16.** $\frac{54}{63}$ $\quad \frac{6}{7}$

Write a fraction for each mixed number.   (Example, Step 1) $\frac{93}{8}$

1. $2\frac{1}{2}$ $\frac{5}{2}$ 2. $4\frac{1}{3}$ $\frac{13}{3}$ 3. $6\frac{1}{5}$ $\frac{31}{5}$ 4. $5\frac{3}{4}$ $\frac{23}{4}$ 5. $3\frac{3}{4}$ $\frac{15}{4}$ 6. $9\frac{3}{8}$ $\frac{75}{8}$ 7. $11\frac{5}{8}$

8. $5\frac{1}{6}$ $\frac{31}{6}$ 9. $2\frac{2}{3}$ $\frac{8}{3}$ 10. $3\frac{4}{7}$ $\frac{25}{7}$ 11. $7\frac{1}{8}$ $\frac{57}{8}$ 12. $8\frac{7}{9}$ $\frac{79}{9}$ 13. $16\frac{1}{12}$ $\frac{193}{12}$ 14. $12\frac{11}{10}$

15. $1\frac{1}{16}$ $\frac{17}{16}$ 16. $7\frac{1}{6}$ $\frac{43}{6}$ 17. $8\frac{4}{5}$ $\frac{44}{5}$ 18. $12\frac{1}{5}$ $\frac{61}{5}$ 19. $2\frac{13}{16}$ $\frac{45}{16}$ 20. $3\frac{3}{16}$ $\frac{51}{16}$ 21. $7\frac{1}{12}$

22. $4\frac{5}{7}$ $\frac{33}{7}$ 23. $3\frac{7}{16}$ $\frac{55}{16}$ 24. $6\frac{5}{7}$ $\frac{47}{7}$ 25. $1\frac{7}{15}$ $\frac{22}{15}$ 26. $4\frac{3}{20}$ $\frac{83}{20}$ 27. $8\frac{9}{10}$ $\frac{89}{10}$ 28. $6\frac{1}{25}$

14. $\frac{131}{10}$ 21. $\frac{85}{12}$ 28. $\frac{151}{25}$

Multiply.   (Example)

29. $3\frac{1}{2} \times 2$ ^{7} 30. $5\frac{1}{3} \times 4$ $21\frac{1}{3}$ 31. $4 \times 1\frac{1}{2}$ ^{6} 32. $6 \times 2\frac{1}{3}$ ^{14} 33. $2\frac{1}{4} \times 4$ ^{9}

34. $3\frac{3}{5} \times 5$ ^{18} 35. $4\frac{1}{3} \times 9$ ^{39} 36. $6\frac{1}{2} \times 3$ $19\frac{1}{2}$ 37. $7 \times 4\frac{1}{7}$ ^{29} 38. $8 \times 4\frac{5}{6}$ $38\frac{2}{3}$

39. $3\frac{1}{3} \times \frac{3}{5}$ ^{2} 40. $2\frac{1}{5} \times \frac{5}{6}$ $1\frac{5}{6}$ 41. $5\frac{3}{4} \times \frac{2}{3}$ $3\frac{5}{6}$ 42. $4\frac{1}{2} \times \frac{2}{9}$ ^{1} 43. $\frac{1}{2} \times 3\frac{1}{5}$ $1\frac{3}{5}$

44. $\frac{5}{6} \times 3\frac{3}{10}$ $2\frac{3}{4}$ 45. $\frac{5}{8} \times 2\frac{1}{5}$ $1\frac{3}{8}$ 46. $\frac{5}{8} \times 6\frac{1}{4}$ $3\frac{29}{32}$ 47. $\frac{7}{8} \times 4\frac{1}{2}$ $3\frac{15}{16}$ 48. $\frac{3}{5} \times 2\frac{1}{2}$ $1\frac{1}{2}$

49. $2\frac{1}{2} \times 3\frac{1}{2}$ $8\frac{3}{4}$ 50. $1\frac{3}{4} \times 4\frac{1}{2}$ $7\frac{7}{8}$ 51. $2\frac{1}{4} \times 3\frac{1}{3}$ $7\frac{1}{2}$ 52. $4\frac{1}{2} \times 2\frac{3}{5}$ $11\frac{7}{10}$ 53. $5\frac{2}{3} \times 2\frac{1}{5}$ $12\frac{7}{15}$

54. $5\frac{1}{2} \times 6\frac{1}{3}$ $34\frac{5}{6}$ 55. $4\frac{2}{3} \times 5\frac{1}{6}$ $24\frac{4}{9}$ 56. $9\frac{1}{8} \times 4\frac{3}{5}$ $41\frac{39}{40}$ 57. $8\frac{2}{3} \times 4\frac{3}{8}$ $37\frac{11}{12}$ 58. $7\frac{1}{3} \times 8\frac{1}{2}$ $62\frac{1}{3}$

59. $1\frac{1}{6} \times 1\frac{4}{5}$ $2\frac{1}{10}$ 60. $\frac{1}{8} \times 3\frac{3}{4}$ $\frac{15}{32}$ 61. $3\frac{3}{5} \times \frac{2}{3}$ $2\frac{2}{5}$ 62. $2\frac{1}{2} \times \frac{4}{5}$ ^{2} 63. $5\frac{1}{2} \times 20$ ^{110}

64. $3\frac{1}{5} \times 25$ ^{80} 65. $1\frac{7}{8} \times 6\frac{2}{5}$ ^{12} 66. $3\frac{1}{2} \times 4\frac{2}{3}$ $16\frac{1}{3}$ 67. $1\frac{1}{2} \times 1\frac{5}{9}$ $2\frac{1}{3}$ 68. $1\frac{7}{8} \times 3\frac{2}{3}$ $6\frac{7}{8}$

69. $3\frac{1}{2} \times 1\frac{1}{8}$ $3\frac{15}{16}$ 70. $1\frac{1}{2} \times 2\frac{3}{4}$ $4\frac{1}{8}$ 71. $1\frac{1}{4} \times 1\frac{1}{4}$ $1\frac{9}{16}$ 72. $3\frac{2}{3} \times 3\frac{2}{3}$ $13\frac{4}{9}$ 73. $28 \times 1\frac{3}{8}$ $38\frac{1}{2}$

74. $8 \times 1\frac{5}{6}$ $14\frac{2}{3}$ 75. $4\frac{1}{2} \times 2\frac{1}{3}$ $10\frac{1}{2}$ 76. $3\frac{1}{8} \times 3\frac{1}{3}$ $10\frac{5}{12}$ 77. $3\frac{3}{4} \times 120$ ^{450} 78. $7\frac{2}{3} \times 81$ ^{621}

79. $52 \times 9\frac{1}{4}$ ^{481} 80. $18\frac{1}{3} \times 39$ ^{715} 81. $85 \times 42\frac{3}{5}$ ^{3621} 82. $72 \times 9\frac{3}{8}$ ^{675} 83. $66 \times 8\frac{1}{11}$ ^{534}

APPLICATIONS: Using Mixed Numbers and Customary Measures
These are one-step problems that most students should be able to handle.

84. A carpenter is repairing the four legs of a stool. A piece of lumber $13\frac{3}{8}$ inches long is needed for each leg. How many inches of lumber are needed for the four legs? $53\frac{1}{2}$

85. A plank is $11\frac{3}{4}$ inches wide. A carpenter wishes to cut four strips each $2\frac{3}{4}$ inches wide. Can the carpenter cut the four strips from the plank? Yes

86. Each board in a stack of roofing boards is $\frac{13}{16}$ inch thick. There are 32 boards in the stack. How high is the stack? 26 inches

FRACTIONS: MULTIPLICATION/DIVISION   **209**

Problem Solving and Applications

Distance Formula See the Teacher's Manual for the objectives.

You can use a formula to find the distance traveled when you know the **rate** (speed) and the **time.**

$$\text{Distance} = \text{rate} \times \text{time} \quad \text{or} \quad d = r \times t$$

EXAMPLE Because of the rotation of the earth, all points on the equator are moving eastward at a speed of 1660 kilometers per hour. How far does a point on the equator travel in $5\frac{1}{2}$ hours?

Solution: Use the distance formula.

$$d = r \times t \quad \begin{cases} r = 1660 \\ t = 5\frac{1}{2} \end{cases}$$

$$d = 1660 \times 5\frac{1}{2}$$

$$d = \overset{830}{\cancel{1660}} \times \frac{11}{\underset{1}{\cancel{2}}}$$

$$d = 9130 \quad \text{A point on the equator travels } \textbf{9130 meters} \text{ in } 5\frac{1}{2} \text{ hours.}$$

The Earth as Seen From 400,000 Kilometers in Space

Exercises

These exercises combine the skills of using a formula to solve problems and multiplication with fractions and mixed numbers.

1. A baseball pitcher threw a ball that traveled at the rate of 46 meters per second for $\frac{2}{5}$ second. How far did the ball travel? $18\frac{2}{5}$ meters

2. A driver travels the length of the Pennsylvania turnpike in $6\frac{9}{10}$ hours at an average rate of 50 miles per hour. How long is the turnpike? 345 miles

3. The attention of a driver traveling at the rate of 75 feet per second (50 miles per hour) wanders for $\frac{1}{2}$ second. How many feet does the car travel during this time? $37\frac{1}{2}$ feet

4. A snail travels at a "snail's pace" of 0.5 meters per hour. How many meters does it travel in $8\frac{1}{2}$ hours? 4.25 meters

5. A home run ball traveling at a rate of 135 feet per second was caught by a fan $2\frac{3}{5}$ seconds after the batter hit the ball. How many feet did the ball travel? 351 feet

Application

Problem Solving and Applications

Wallpapering and Estimation

See the Teacher's Manual for the objectives.
This lesson combines the skills of reading a table, addition and subtraction of fractions and mixed numbers, and rounding.

To find the amount of wallpaper needed for a room, you can use a table such as the one at the right.

To find the number of rolls needed, first answer the question:

"How much must be subtracted for doors and windows?"

This is the <u>hidden question</u> in the problem. Then you can find the number of rolls.

CEILING HEIGHT	8 Feet	9 Feet	10 Feet
Size of Room in Feet	NUMBER OF SINGLE ROLLS		
8 × 10	9	10	11
10 × 10	10	11	13
10 × 12	11	12	14
10 × 14	12	14	15
12 × 12	12	14	15
12 × 14	13	15	16

NOTE: Subtract 1 roll for every door. Subtract 1 roll for every two windows.

EXAMPLE

A room is $9\frac{1}{2}$ feet wide and $11\frac{3}{4}$ feet long. The ceiling is 8 feet high. The room has 2 doors and 3 windows. How many single rolls of wallpaper are needed?

Solution:

1. Round $9\frac{1}{2}$ and $11\frac{3}{4}$ up to the next foot. ⟶ **10 × 12**

2. Use the table to find the number of rolls. ⟶ **11**

3. Calculate the allowance for windows and doors.

2 doors:	2 rolls	*From the note in the table*
3 windows:	$1\frac{1}{2}$ rolls	
Total allowance:	$3\frac{1}{2}$	

4. Subtract. $11 - 3\frac{1}{2} = 7\frac{1}{2}$

Number of rolls needed: **8 single rolls** ◀ *Round up to the next whole number.*

Exercises

Note that these problems involve more than two steps.

Find the number of single rolls of wallpaper needed for each room.

Room	Length	Width	Ceiling Height	Number of Doors	Number of Windows
1. Den	$9\frac{1}{2}$ ft	$9\frac{1}{2}$ ft	8 ft	2	4 6
2. Kitchen	$7\frac{3}{4}$ ft	$9\frac{1}{2}$ ft	9 ft	1	5 7
3. Living Room	$11\frac{1}{2}$ ft	12 ft	10 ft	3	4 10
4. Bedroom	$9\frac{1}{2}$ ft	$13\frac{1}{2}$ ft	8 ft	2	3 9

Application   FRACTIONS: MULTIPLICATION/DIVISION

10-3 Division: Fractions See the Teacher's Manual for the objectives.

Two numbers whose product is one are **reciprocals** of each other.

$$\frac{3}{5} \times \frac{5}{3} = 1 \quad \textbf{Reciprocals: } \frac{3}{5} \text{ and } \frac{5}{3} \qquad 8 \times \frac{1}{8} = 1 \quad \textbf{Reciprocals: 8 and } \frac{1}{8}$$

Dividing by a number is the <u>the same</u> as multiplying by the reciprocal of the number.

PROCEDURE To divide with fractions:

  1 Use the reciprocal of the divisor to write the corresponding multiplication problem.

  2 Multiply.

  3 Write the answer in lowest terms.

EXAMPLE Divide.

  a. $\frac{5}{8} \div \frac{3}{4}$

  b. $\frac{2}{3} \div 9$

Solutions:

a. 1 $\frac{5}{8} \div \frac{3}{4} = \frac{5}{8} \times \frac{4}{3}$ ◀ *The reciprocal of $\frac{3}{4}$ is $\frac{4}{3}$.*

  2 $= \frac{5}{\overset{}{\underset{2}{8}}} \times \frac{\overset{1}{4}}{3}$

  3 $= \frac{5}{6}$

b. 1 $\frac{2}{3} \div 9 = \frac{2}{3} \times \frac{1}{9}$ ◀ *The reciprocal of 9 is $\frac{1}{9}$.*

  2 $= \frac{2 \times 1}{3 \times 9}$

  3 $= \frac{2}{27}$

REVIEW OF RELATED SKILLS You may wish to use these exercises before teaching the lesson.

Write each fraction in lowest terms.   (Pages 182–183)

1. $\frac{22}{24}$ $\frac{11}{12}$ 2. $\frac{10}{18}$ $\frac{5}{9}$ 3. $\frac{18}{30}$ $\frac{3}{5}$ 4. $\frac{12}{60}$ $\frac{1}{5}$ 5. $\frac{13}{39}$ $\frac{1}{3}$ 6. $\frac{24}{80}$ $\frac{3}{10}$ 7. $\frac{46}{69}$ $\frac{2}{3}$ 8. $\frac{32}{100}$ $\frac{8}{25}$

9. $\frac{35}{50}$ $\frac{7}{10}$ 10. $\frac{30}{42}$ $\frac{5}{7}$ 11. $\frac{81}{90}$ $\frac{9}{10}$ 12. $\frac{28}{42}$ $\frac{2}{3}$ 13. $\frac{33}{77}$ $\frac{3}{7}$ 14. $\frac{32}{48}$ $\frac{2}{3}$ 15. $\frac{56}{77}$ $\frac{8}{11}$ 16. $\frac{45}{54}$ $\frac{5}{6}$

Multiply. Write each answer in lowest terms.   (Pages 204–205)

17. $\frac{5}{4} \times \frac{4}{5}$ 1 18. $\frac{7}{9} \times \frac{9}{7}$ 1 19. $6 \times \frac{1}{6}$ 1 20. $\frac{1}{9} \times 9$ 1 21. $\frac{4}{9} \times \frac{27}{16}$ $\frac{3}{4}$ 22. $\frac{5}{6} \times \frac{18}{35}$ $\frac{3}{7}$

23. $10 \times \frac{21}{100}$ $2\frac{1}{10}$ 24. $\frac{7}{9} \times 63$ 49 25. $\frac{1}{3} \times \frac{3}{4}$ $\frac{1}{4}$ 26. $\frac{5}{2} \times \frac{4}{5}$ 2 27. $\frac{35}{16} \times \frac{4}{5}$ $1\frac{3}{4}$ 28. $\frac{9}{16} \times \frac{8}{3}$ $1\frac{1}{2}$

29. $\frac{3}{8} \times 32$ 12 30. $20 \times \frac{63}{100}$ $12\frac{3}{5}$ 31. $\frac{8}{9} \times \frac{9}{16}$ $\frac{1}{2}$ 32. $\frac{4}{7} \times \frac{3}{4}$ $\frac{3}{7}$ 33. $\frac{54}{15} \times \frac{5}{6}$ 3 34. $\frac{2}{9} \times \frac{3}{8}$ $\frac{1}{12}$

EXERCISES

See the suggested assignment guide in the Teacher's Manual.

Write the reciprocal of each number. (Example, Step 1)

1. $\frac{1}{3}$ 3 **2.** $\frac{1}{4}$ 4 **3.** $\frac{3}{5}$ $\frac{5}{3}$ **4.** $\frac{4}{7}$ $\frac{7}{4}$ **5.** 8 $\frac{1}{8}$ **6.** 4 $\frac{1}{4}$ **7.** $\frac{9}{10}$ $\frac{10}{9}$ **8.** $\frac{7}{9}$ $\frac{9}{7}$

9. $\frac{5}{6}$ $\frac{6}{5}$ **10.** $\frac{7}{20}$ $\frac{20}{7}$ **11.** $\frac{11}{5}$ $\frac{5}{11}$ **12.** $\frac{18}{11}$ $\frac{11}{18}$ **13.** $\frac{21}{4}$ $\frac{4}{21}$ **14.** $\frac{13}{4}$ $\frac{4}{13}$ **15.** 21 $\frac{1}{21}$ **16.** $9\frac{1}{9}$

Divide. (Example)

17. $\frac{1}{2} \div \frac{3}{4}$ $\frac{2}{3}$ **18.** $\frac{1}{4} \div \frac{1}{3}$ $\frac{3}{4}$ **19.** $\frac{3}{5} \div \frac{4}{5}$ $\frac{3}{4}$ **20.** $\frac{1}{2} \div \frac{2}{3}$ $\frac{3}{4}$ **21.** $\frac{2}{5} \div \frac{7}{12}$ $\frac{24}{35}$ **22.** $\frac{1}{4} \div \frac{3}{4}$ $\frac{1}{3}$

23. $\frac{5}{8} \div \frac{5}{6}$ $\frac{3}{4}$ **24.** $\frac{2}{3} \div \frac{4}{5}$ $\frac{5}{6}$ **25.** $\frac{7}{8} \div \frac{3}{4}$ $1\frac{1}{6}$ **26.** $\frac{4}{7} \div \frac{7}{12}$ $\frac{48}{49}$ **27.** $\frac{1}{3} \div \frac{5}{9}$ $\frac{3}{5}$ **28.** $\frac{1}{8} \div \frac{1}{4}$ $\frac{1}{2}$

29. $\frac{5}{9} \div \frac{11}{12}$ $\frac{20}{33}$ **30.** $\frac{1}{9} \div \frac{8}{21}$ $\frac{7}{24}$ **31.** $\frac{3}{5} \div \frac{5}{12}$ $1\frac{11}{25}$ **32.** $\frac{6}{7} \div \frac{9}{14}$ $1\frac{1}{3}$ **33.** $\frac{3}{8} \div \frac{1}{6}$ $2\frac{1}{4}$ **34.** $\frac{7}{9} \div \frac{14}{15}$ $\frac{5}{6}$

35. $\frac{4}{5} \div \frac{4}{5}$ 1 **36.** $\frac{3}{7} \div \frac{3}{7}$ 1 **37.** $\frac{1}{2} \div 6$ $\frac{1}{12}$ **38.** $\frac{1}{2} \div 2$ $\frac{1}{4}$ **39.** $\frac{1}{5} \div 2$ $\frac{1}{10}$ **40.** $\frac{1}{5} \div 6$ $\frac{1}{30}$

41. $\frac{1}{6} \div 5$ $\frac{1}{30}$ **42.** $7 \div \frac{1}{3}$ 21 **43.** $9 \div \frac{1}{3}$ 27 **44.** $3 \div \frac{1}{4}$ 12 **45.** $8 \div \frac{1}{4}$ 32 **46.** $4 \div \frac{1}{7}$ 28

47. $\frac{1}{8} \div \frac{3}{4}$ $\frac{1}{6}$ **48.** $\frac{2}{3} \div 9$ $\frac{2}{27}$ **49.** $4 \div \frac{2}{3}$ 6 **50.** $\frac{5}{6} \div \frac{2}{3}$ $1\frac{1}{4}$ **51.** $1 \div \frac{4}{5}$ $1\frac{1}{4}$ **52.** $1 \div \frac{2}{3}$ $1\frac{1}{2}$

53. $5 \div \frac{2}{3}$ $7\frac{1}{2}$ **54.** $\frac{5}{6} \div 10$ $\frac{1}{12}$ **55.** $\frac{8}{27} \div 16$ $\frac{1}{54}$ **56.** $\frac{3}{5} \div \frac{5}{6}$ $\frac{18}{25}$ **57.** $\frac{3}{8} \div \frac{2}{3}$ $\frac{9}{16}$ **58.** $\frac{5}{6} \div \frac{3}{5}$ $1\frac{7}{18}$

59. $\frac{2}{3} \div \frac{3}{8}$ $1\frac{7}{9}$ **60.** $\frac{5}{9} \div \frac{5}{12}$ $1\frac{1}{3}$ **61.** $\frac{3}{8} \div \frac{3}{10}$ $1\frac{1}{4}$ **62.** $1 \div \frac{3}{8}$ $2\frac{2}{3}$ **63.** $2 \div \frac{3}{8}$ $5\frac{1}{3}$ **64.** $\frac{1}{2} \div \frac{3}{8}$ $1\frac{1}{3}$

65. $\frac{1}{3} \div \frac{3}{8}$ $\frac{8}{9}$ **66.** $\frac{3}{10} \div \frac{3}{8}$ $\frac{4}{5}$ **67.** $\frac{3}{8} \div 64$ $\frac{3}{512}$ **68.** $6 \div \frac{3}{8}$ 16 **69.** $\frac{8}{9} \div \frac{3}{4}$ $1\frac{5}{27}$ **70.** $\frac{1}{5} \div \frac{10}{11}$ $\frac{11}{50}$

71. $\frac{7}{8} \div \frac{1}{6}$ $5\frac{1}{4}$ **72.** $\frac{3}{8} \div \frac{3}{4}$ $\frac{1}{2}$ **73.** $\frac{24}{36} \div 12$ $\frac{1}{18}$ **74.** $10 \div \frac{1}{2}$ 20 **75.** $\frac{2}{3} \div \frac{1}{6}$ 4 **76.** $\frac{3}{7} \div \frac{3}{7}$ 1

APPLICATIONS: Using Fractions and Customary Measures

These are one-step problems that most students should be able to handle.

77. When buying ground meat, Tom Lee estimates that he will need $\frac{1}{4}$ pound per serving. How many servings are there in 2 pounds of ground meat? 8

78. A cookbook advises buying $\frac{3}{4}$ pound of spinach per serving. How many servings are there in 6 pounds of spinach? 8

79. A cookbook advises buying $\frac{1}{3}$ pound of cauliflower per serving. How many servings are there in 2 pounds of cauliflower? 6

Division: Mixed Numbers See the Teacher's Manual for the objectives.

Writing a fraction for each mixed number is the first step in dividing with mixed numbers.

PROCEDURE To divide with mixed numbers:

1. Write a fraction for each mixed number.

2. Divide the fractions.

3. Write the answer in lowest terms.

EXAMPLE Divide.

a. $6\frac{1}{4} \div 1\frac{1}{2}$ 　　　　　　　　　　　　**b.** $6 \div 3\frac{1}{5}$

Solutions:

a. 1 $6\frac{1}{4} \div 1\frac{1}{2} = \frac{25}{4} \div \frac{3}{2}$ 　　　**b.** 1 $6 \div 3\frac{1}{5} = \frac{6}{1} \div \frac{16}{5}$

2 　　　$= \frac{25}{4} \times \frac{2}{3}$ ◀ The reciprocal of $\frac{3}{2}$ is $\frac{2}{3}$. 　　　2 　　$= \frac{6}{1} \times \frac{5}{16}$

$= \frac{25}{\overset{2}{4}} \times \frac{\overset{1}{2}}{3}$ 　　　　　　　　$= \frac{\overset{3}{6}}{1} \times \frac{5}{\underset{8}{16}}$

$= \frac{25}{6}$ ◀ Write a mixed number for $\frac{25}{6}$. 　　　　$= \frac{15}{8}$

3 　　　$= 4\frac{1}{6}$ 　　　　　　　　　　　　3 　　$= 1\frac{7}{8}$

REVIEW OF RELATED SKILLS You may wish to use these exercises before teaching the lesson.

Write a fraction for each mixed number.　　(Pages 208–209)

1. $2\frac{1}{3}$ $\frac{7}{3}$ **2.** $7\frac{1}{8}$ $\frac{57}{8}$ **3.** $9\frac{3}{5}$ $\frac{48}{5}$ **4.** $12\frac{2}{3}$ $\frac{38}{3}$ **5.** $16\frac{7}{8}$ $\frac{135}{8}$ **6.** $11\frac{1}{9}$ $\frac{100}{9}$ **7.** $1\frac{1}{10}$ $\frac{11}{10}$ **8.** $4\frac{5}{6}$ $\frac{29}{6}$

Write the reciprocal for each number.　　(Pages 212–213)

9. $\frac{5}{8}$ $\frac{8}{5}$ **10.** $\frac{6}{7}$ $\frac{7}{6}$ **11.** $\frac{1}{15}$ 15 **12.** 21 $\frac{1}{21}$ **13.** $\frac{41}{50}$ $\frac{50}{41}$ **14.** 18 $\frac{1}{18}$ **15.** $\frac{1}{50}$ 50 **16.** $\frac{9}{25}$ $\frac{25}{9}$

Multiply.　　(Pages 204–205, 208–209)

17. $\frac{3}{4} \times \frac{5}{2}$ $1\frac{7}{8}$ **18.** $\frac{6}{25} \times \frac{5}{4}$ $\frac{3}{10}$ **19.** $\frac{7}{9} \times 3$ $2\frac{1}{3}$ **20.** $\frac{1}{45} \times 10$ $\frac{2}{9}$ **21.** $2\frac{1}{3} \times 1\frac{1}{9}$ $2\frac{16}{27}$ **22.** $1\frac{1}{4} \times 3\frac{5}{9}$ $4\frac{4}{9}$

23. $\frac{1}{6} \times \frac{9}{2}$ $\frac{3}{4}$ **24.** $\frac{14}{18} \times \frac{3}{7}$ $\frac{1}{3}$ **25.** $\frac{1}{6} \times 4$ $\frac{2}{3}$ **26.** $\frac{1}{50} \times 25$ $\frac{1}{2}$ **27.** $2\frac{1}{2} \times 3\frac{1}{5}$ 8 **28.** $2\frac{5}{8} \times 1\frac{1}{7}$ 3

EXERCISES
See the suggested assignment guide in the Teacher's Manual.

Write the reciprocal of each mixed number. (Example, Steps 1 and 2) $\frac{16}{165}$

1. $1\frac{2}{3}$ $\frac{3}{5}$ **2.** $6\frac{1}{12}$ $\frac{12}{73}$ **3.** $4\frac{5}{8}$ $\frac{8}{37}$ **4.** $2\frac{1}{2}$ $\frac{2}{5}$ **5.** $5\frac{1}{10}$ $\frac{10}{51}$ **6.** $1\frac{5}{7}$ $\frac{7}{12}$ **7.** $9\frac{3}{25}$ $\frac{25}{228}$ **8.** $10\frac{5}{16}$

9. $21\frac{4}{5}$ $\frac{5}{109}$ **10.** $15\frac{1}{6}$ $\frac{6}{91}$ **11.** $1\frac{1}{10}$ $\frac{10}{11}$ **12.** $17\frac{1}{3}$ $\frac{3}{52}$ **13.** $2\frac{7}{9}$ $\frac{9}{25}$ **14.** $11\frac{5}{9}$ $\frac{9}{104}$ **15.** $18\frac{3}{4}$ $\frac{4}{75}$ **16.** $9\frac{4}{25}$

$\frac{25}{229}$

Divide. (Example)

17. $\frac{1}{3} \div 3\frac{3}{5}$ $\frac{5}{54}$ **18.** $\frac{5}{8} \div 6\frac{1}{4}$ $\frac{1}{10}$ **19.** $\frac{2}{5} \div 7\frac{1}{8}$ $\frac{16}{285}$ **20.** $\frac{3}{4} \div 4\frac{1}{12}$ $\frac{9}{49}$ **21.** $2\frac{1}{2} \div \frac{5}{8}$ 4

22. $9\frac{1}{2} \div \frac{3}{4}$ $12\frac{2}{3}$ **23.** $6\frac{2}{3} \div \frac{5}{8}$ $10\frac{2}{3}$ **24.** $3\frac{5}{6} \div \frac{7}{12}$ $6\frac{4}{7}$ **25.** $7\frac{1}{2} \div 1\frac{1}{4}$ 6   **26.** $6\frac{3}{4} \div 2\frac{1}{4}$ 3

27. $9\frac{3}{4} \div 3\frac{1}{4}$ 3   **28.** $6\frac{6}{7} \div 2\frac{2}{7}$ 3   **29.** $6\frac{1}{3} \div 1\frac{1}{3}$ $4\frac{3}{4}$ **30.** $8\frac{1}{5} \div 2\frac{1}{2}$ $3\frac{7}{25}$ **31.** $4\frac{2}{3} \div 1\frac{5}{6}$ $2\frac{6}{11}$

32. $3\frac{1}{3} \div 1\frac{1}{5}$ $2\frac{7}{9}$ **33.** $2\frac{1}{4} \div 3\frac{3}{8}$ $\frac{2}{3}$ **34.** $1\frac{3}{5} \div 3\frac{1}{5}$ $\frac{1}{2}$ **35.** $2\frac{1}{12} \div 5\frac{3}{4}$ $\frac{25}{69}$ **36.** $3\frac{1}{4} \div 6\frac{1}{2}$ $\frac{1}{2}$

37. $4 \div 1\frac{1}{3}$ 3   **38.** $2 \div 1\frac{1}{4}$ $1\frac{3}{5}$ **39.** $6 \div 4\frac{1}{2}$ $1\frac{1}{3}$ **40.** $7 \div 2\frac{1}{2}$ $2\frac{4}{5}$ **41.** $5 \div 3\frac{1}{2}$ $1\frac{3}{7}$

42. $2 \div 3\frac{1}{3}$ $\frac{3}{5}$ **43.** $8 \div 2\frac{1}{2}$ $3\frac{1}{5}$ **44.** $10 \div 4\frac{1}{5}$ $2\frac{8}{21}$ **45.** $8 \div 4\frac{1}{3}$ $1\frac{11}{13}$ **46.** $24 \div 5\frac{1}{3}$ $4\frac{1}{2}$

47. $3\frac{5}{8} \div 3$ $1\frac{5}{24}$ **48.** $5\frac{2}{3} \div 2$ $2\frac{5}{6}$ **49.** $4\frac{4}{5} \div 6$ $\frac{4}{5}$ **50.** $12\frac{7}{8} \div 6$ $2\frac{7}{48}$ **51.** $4\frac{1}{3} \div 8$ $\frac{13}{24}$

52. $1\frac{3}{8} \div 4$ $\frac{11}{32}$ **53.** $2\frac{1}{7} \div 7$ $\frac{15}{49}$ **54.** $1\frac{1}{3} \div 2$ $\frac{2}{3}$ **55.** $4\frac{1}{3} \div 4$ $1\frac{1}{12}$ **56.** $3\frac{1}{2} \div 4$ $\frac{7}{8}$

57. $9\frac{5}{8} \div 11$ $\frac{7}{8}$ **58.** $6\frac{1}{4} \div 25$ $\frac{1}{4}$ **59.** $4\frac{1}{3} \div 13$ $\frac{1}{3}$ **60.** $3\frac{1}{2} \div \frac{3}{4}$ $4\frac{2}{3}$ **61.** $\frac{7}{8} \div 6$ $\frac{7}{48}$

62. $\frac{7}{8} \div 3\frac{1}{7}$ $\frac{49}{176}$ **63.** $6\frac{2}{3} \div 1\frac{3}{4}$ $3\frac{17}{21}$ **64.** $5\frac{7}{8} \div 6\frac{2}{5}$ $\frac{235}{256}$ **65.** $4 \div 6\frac{1}{4}$ $\frac{16}{25}$ **66.** $16 \div \frac{5}{8}$ $25\frac{3}{5}$

67. $3\frac{7}{8} \div 4$ $\frac{31}{32}$ **68.** $8\frac{1}{2} \div 6$ $1\frac{5}{12}$ **69.** $9\frac{1}{7} \div 8\frac{1}{2}$ $1\frac{9}{119}$ **70.** $5\frac{1}{4} \div 6\frac{7}{8}$ $\frac{42}{55}$ **71.** $8 \div 2\frac{1}{2}$ $3\frac{1}{5}$

APPLICATIONS: Using Mixed Numbers and Customary Measures
These are one-step problems that most students should be able to handle.

72. A tailor has $45\frac{1}{2}$ yards of material with which to make suits. Each suit requires $3\frac{1}{4}$ yards. How many suits can the tailor make?   14

73. Pam Dee has 22 yards of taffeta. She wishes to use the material to make dresses, each of which requires $2\frac{3}{4}$ yards. How many dresses can she make?   8

74. Costumes for a school play each require $3\frac{1}{3}$ yards of material. How many costumes can be made from a bolt of material that contains 40 yards?   12

FRACTIONS: MULTIPLICATION/DIVISION   **215**

career

Career Lessons are optional.
This lesson applies the skills presented in Section 10-4.

BUSINESS

AIRLINES		ALUMINUM		AUTO		BEVERAGES		BUILDING MATERIALS		CONTAINERS	
AMR	2 7	AL	2 2	AMO	6	GTY	6 3 5	BCC	2 9 5	ACK	3 5 6
NWA	2 9 5	AMX	3 3 4	CHM	3 7	FAL	6 6	GP	4 8 1	CCK	1 9 4
EAL	1 9 5	HAR	1 9 6	F	6 2 4	KO	0 2 3	JWC	3 7 3	CCC	3 7 2
PN	1 3	KLU	3 0 2	FTR	3 6 7	PEP	5 5 4	MOH	3 5 3	NAC	2 6 6
TWA	2 7 7	RLM	2 6 7	WH	2 3 6	SH	2 5 4	MRP	2 7 4	PPG	3 2 4

ELECTRONICS

When you own a <u>share of stock</u>, you own part of a company. The prices of shares of stock are given in fractions of a dollar. Thus, a price of **$42\frac{3}{8}$** means **$42\frac{3}{8}$.**

EXAMPLE   Jane Tate wishes to invest $10,850 in a stock that has a market price of $27\frac{1}{8}$ per share. How many shares can she purchase?

Solution: Divide the total amount by the price of one share.

$$10{,}850 \div 27\frac{1}{8} = 10{,}850 \div \frac{217}{8}$$

$$= \overset{50}{\cancel{10{,}850}} \times \frac{8}{\underset{1}{\cancel{217}}}$$

$$= 50 \times 8 = \textbf{400}\qquad \text{Jane can buy } \textbf{400 shares.}$$

EXERCISES   Note that Exercises 1-6 are one-step problems.

1. Julio Ortega wishes to invest $14,250 in a stock that has a market value of $47\frac{1}{2}$ per share. How many shares can he purchase? 300

2. The Keene family decides to invest $4450 in a stock that has a market value of $22\frac{1}{4}$ per share. How many shares can they purchase? 200

3. The Okimi family agree to invest $6,780 in stock that has a market value of $42\frac{3}{8}$ per share. How many shares can they purchase? 160

4. Tony Wong wishes to invest $400 in a stock that has a market value of $12\frac{1}{2}$ per share. How many shares can he purchase? 32

5. Mary Silverheels received $850 for stock which she sold at $1\frac{1}{16}$ per share. How many shares was this? 800

6. An investor received $18,750 for stock which he sold at $18\frac{3}{4}$ per share. How many shares was this? 1000

CONSTRUCTION career

Carpenters use <u>fractions</u> and <u>customary units</u> <u>of length</u> in their calculations, such as in building a staircase. The figure at the right shows the **total rise** (height from floor to floor) of a staircase.

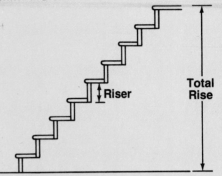

To find the number of risers in a staircase, first answer the question:

"What is the total rise?"

This is the <u>hidden question</u> in the problem.

EXAMPLE   A staircase has a total rise of 7 feet 6 inches. Each riser is $7\frac{1}{2}$ inches high. How many risers are there?

Solution: [1] Find the number of inches in 7 feet 6 inches.

1 foot = 12 inches.
So 7 feet 6 inches = $12 \times 7 + 6 = 84 + 6 =$ **90 inches.**

[2] Find the number of risers.

$$90 \div 7\frac{1}{2} = 90 \div \frac{15}{2} \quad \blacktriangleleft \quad \frac{\text{Number of}}{\text{Risers}} = \frac{\text{Total}}{\text{Rise}} \div \frac{\text{Height of One}}{\text{Riser}}$$

$$= \overset{6}{90} \times \frac{2}{\underset{1}{15}}$$

$$= 12 \quad \text{The staircase will have \textbf{12 risers}.}$$

EXERCISES   Note that Exercises 1-5 are two-step problems.

In Exercises 1–5, find the number of risers in each staircase.

1. Total rise: 10 feet
   Height of one riser: $7\frac{1}{2}$ inches ₁₆

2. Total rise: 8 feet 9 inches
   Height of one riser: $7\frac{1}{2}$ inches ₁₄

3. Total rise: 8 feet 8 inches
   Height of one riser: $6\frac{1}{2}$ inches ₁₆

4. A staircase will have a total rise of 9 feet. The height of each riser will be $6\frac{3}{4}$ inches. How many risers will the staircase have? ₁₆

5. The total rise of a staircase is 12 feet 1 inch. Each riser is $7\frac{1}{4}$ inches high. Find the number of risers. ₂₀

10-5 Rounding and Estimation

This lesson may be considered optional for some students.

Rounding a mixed number is similar to rounding a fraction.

PROCEDURE To round a mixed number, look at the fractional part.

a. If the fraction is less than $\frac{1}{2}$, round <u>down</u> to the nearest whole number.

b. If the fraction is greater than or equal to $\frac{1}{2}$, round <u>up</u> to the next whole number.

EXAMPLE **a.** $3\frac{1}{5}$ rounded to the nearest whole number is **3**.

b. $16\frac{1}{2}$ rounded to the nearest whole number is **17**.

c. $9\frac{7}{8}$ rounded to the nearest whole number is **10**.

The rules for rounding can help you to estimate answers.

EXERCISES

Round to the nearest whole number.

1. $1\frac{1}{12}$ 1   **2.** $3\frac{5}{6}$ 4   **3.** $8\frac{1}{2}$ 9   **4.** $5\frac{7}{9}$ 6   **5.** $7\frac{2}{3}$ 8   **6.** $10\frac{1}{16}$ 10   **7.** $1\frac{3}{4}$

8. $15\frac{1}{8}$ 15   **9.** $21\frac{4}{9}$ 21   **10.** $72\frac{3}{4}$ 73   **11.** $73\frac{1}{20}$ 73   **12.** $31\frac{1}{2}$ 32   **13.** $19\frac{7}{8}$ 20   **14.** $1\frac{15}{16}$

Choose the best estimate. Choose a, b, c, or d.

15. $1\frac{3}{4}+5\frac{7}{8}$ c   **a.** $1+5$ **b.** $0+6$ **c.** $2+6$ **d.** $2+5$

16. $109\frac{2}{3}+11\frac{1}{6}$ a   **a.** $110+11$ **b.** $110+10$ **c.** $110+12$ **d.** $109+10$

17. $3\frac{1}{4}-1\frac{3}{8}$ a   **a.** $3-1$ **b.** $3-2$ **c.** $2-2$ **d.** $4-1$

18. $87\frac{2}{3}-21\frac{1}{6}$ c   **a.** $85-20$ **b.** $90-15$ **c.** $88-21$ **d.** $87-22$

19. $14\frac{1}{9}\div\frac{8}{9}$ a   **a.** $14\div1$ **b.** $10\div\frac{1}{2}$ **c.** $15\div\frac{1}{2}$ **d.** $20\div\frac{1}{2}$

20. $1\frac{15}{16}\div1\frac{19}{20}$ b   **a.** $0\div1$ **b.** $2\div2$ **c.** $2\div\frac{1}{2}$ **d.** $1\div\frac{1}{2}$

21. $2\frac{3}{4}+4\frac{1}{6}$ c   **a.** 8   **b.** 10   **c.** 7   **d.** 6

22. $59\frac{5}{8}-12\frac{1}{3}$ b   **a.** 40   **b.** 48   **c.** 55   **d.** 72

23. $3\frac{1}{9}-1\frac{2}{3}$ a   **a.** 1   **b.** 2   **c.** 3   **d.** 0

24. $\frac{1}{3}\times6\frac{1}{8}$ a   **a.** 2   **b.** 1   **c.** 3   **d.** 4

25. $12\frac{1}{10}\div\frac{1}{4}$ c   **a.** 12   **b.** 3   **c.** 48   **d.** 42

218   CHAPTER 10

Choose the best estimate. Choose a, b, c, or d.

26. The regular price of a stereo receiver is $199.95. At a sale, the receiver is marked "$\frac{1}{5}$ OFF."

Estimate the discount. b

- **a.** $30
- **b.** $40
- **c.** $50
- **d.** $60

27. A carpenter is building a bookcase. She wants each of the four shelves to be $2\frac{7}{8}$ feet long.

About how much wood does she need? b

- **a.** 10 feet
- **b.** 12 feet
- **c.** 14 feet
- **d.** 16 feet

MULTIPLYING FRACTIONS

Most calculators do not have fraction keys. However, you can use a calculator to multiply and divide with fractions. The calculator gives the answer as an equivalent decimal.

EXAMPLE: $\frac{7}{25} \times \frac{9}{80} \times \frac{2}{5} = \underline{\quad ? \quad}$

Solution: Multiply the denominators. Enter the product in the memory. Multiply the numerators. Then divide.

EXERCISES

Use a calculator to find each answer.

1. $\frac{15}{16} \times \frac{39}{5} \times \frac{27}{8}$ 24.679687

2. $\frac{8}{15} \times \frac{3}{2} \times \frac{3}{50}$ 0.048

3. $\frac{11}{15} \times \frac{32}{39} \times \frac{9}{20}$ 0.2707692

4. $\frac{9}{48} \times \frac{13}{21} \times \frac{17}{52}$ 0.0379464

5. $\frac{33}{100} \times \frac{27}{40} \times \frac{1}{9}$ 0.02475

6. $\frac{7}{16} \times \frac{5}{12} \times \frac{9}{400}$ 0.0041015

Chapter Review

Part 1: Vocabulary

For Exercises 1–6, choose from the box at the right the word(s) that completes each statement.

multiplying
fraction
discount
net price
time
reciprocals

1. The amount a customer saves by buying items on sale is the __?__. (Page 207) discount
2. Sometimes the rate of discount is given as a __?__. (Page 207) fraction
3. The difference between the regular price and the discount is the __?__. (Page 207) net price
4. Distance = rate × __?__. (Page 210) time
5. Two numbers whose product is one are __?__ of each other. (Page 212) reciprocals
6. Dividing by a number is the same as __?__ by the reciprocal of the number. (Page 212) multiplying

Part 2: Skills

Multiply. Write each answer in lowest terms. (Pages 204–205)

7. $\frac{2}{3} \times \frac{4}{9}$ $\frac{8}{27}$
8. $\frac{3}{4} \times \frac{5}{7}$ $\frac{15}{28}$
9. $4 \times \frac{1}{3}$ $1\frac{1}{3}$
10. $\frac{2}{7} \times 8$ $2\frac{2}{7}$
11. $\frac{4}{7} \times \frac{5}{12}$ $\frac{5}{21}$
12. $\frac{5}{8} \times \frac{8}{9}$ $\frac{5}{9}$

13. $\frac{1}{9} \times 12$ $1\frac{1}{3}$
14. $15 \times \frac{2}{3}$ 10
15. $\frac{8}{15} \times \frac{3}{4}$ $\frac{2}{5}$
16. $\frac{2}{3} \times \frac{6}{8}$ $\frac{1}{2}$
17. $\frac{21}{30} \times \frac{5}{7}$ $\frac{1}{2}$
18. $\frac{2}{15} \times \frac{3}{4}$ $\frac{1}{10}$

Write a fraction for each mixed number. (Pages 208–209)

19. $6\frac{2}{3}$ $\frac{20}{3}$
20. $5\frac{4}{7}$ $\frac{39}{7}$
21. $3\frac{4}{5}$ $\frac{19}{5}$
22. $7\frac{9}{10}$ $\frac{79}{10}$
23. $4\frac{1}{15}$ $\frac{61}{15}$
24. $2\frac{7}{15}$ $\frac{37}{15}$
25. $7\frac{1}{6}$ $\frac{43}{6}$

Multiply. Write each answer in lowest terms. (Pages 208–209)

26. $4\frac{1}{6} \times 9$ $37\frac{1}{2}$
27. $5\frac{3}{4} \times 2$ $11\frac{1}{2}$
28. $3\frac{3}{5} \times \frac{2}{3}$ $2\frac{2}{5}$
29. $\frac{4}{5} \times 7\frac{1}{2}$ 6
30. $2\frac{3}{5} \times 1\frac{1}{6}$ $3\frac{1}{30}$

31. $1\frac{1}{5} \times 4\frac{3}{8}$ $5\frac{1}{4}$
32. $8\frac{1}{4} \times \frac{5}{6}$ $6\frac{7}{8}$
33. $2\frac{2}{3} \times 6\frac{3}{4}$ 18
34. $2\frac{1}{2} \times 3\frac{3}{4}$ $9\frac{3}{8}$
35. $4\frac{1}{2} \times 2\frac{2}{3}$ 12

Write the reciprocal of each number. (Pages 212–213)

36. $\frac{2}{3}$ $\frac{3}{2}$
37. $\frac{1}{6}$ 6
38. 7 $\frac{1}{7}$
39. 5 $\frac{1}{5}$
40. $\frac{21}{4}$ $\frac{4}{21}$
41. $\frac{5}{8}$ $\frac{8}{5}$
42. $\frac{16}{15}$ $\frac{15}{16}$
43. 3 $\frac{1}{3}$

Divide. Write each answer in lowest terms. (Pages 212–213)

44. $\frac{3}{4} \div \frac{3}{5}$ $1\frac{1}{4}$
45. $\frac{2}{3} \div \frac{2}{5}$ $1\frac{2}{3}$
46. $\frac{2}{5} \div 4$ $\frac{1}{10}$
47. $\frac{9}{10} \div 3$ $\frac{3}{10}$
48. $3 \div \frac{6}{10}$ 5
49. $8 \div \frac{4}{5}$ 10

50. $\frac{5}{12} \div \frac{1}{3}$ $1\frac{1}{4}$
51. $\frac{3}{16} \div \frac{3}{4}$ $\frac{1}{4}$
52. $\frac{3}{5} \div \frac{9}{10}$ $\frac{2}{3}$
53. $\frac{3}{7} \div \frac{9}{14}$ $\frac{2}{3}$
54. $\frac{4}{5} \div \frac{8}{15}$ $1\frac{1}{2}$
55. $\frac{3}{4} \div \frac{1}{8}$ 6

Write the reciprocal of each mixed number. (Pages 214–215)

56. $3\frac{1}{2}$ $\frac{2}{7}$
57. $4\frac{7}{8}$ $\frac{8}{39}$
58. $5\frac{1}{4}$ $\frac{4}{21}$
59. $6\frac{2}{3}$ $\frac{3}{20}$
60. $4\frac{3}{10}$ $\frac{10}{43}$
61. $7\frac{1}{8}$ $\frac{8}{57}$
62. $9\frac{4}{5}$ $\frac{5}{49}$

Divide. Write each answer in lowest terms. (Pages 214–215)

63. $\frac{1}{3} \div 4\frac{2}{3}$ $\frac{1}{14}$ 　　64. $\frac{3}{7} \div 6\frac{3}{7}$ $\frac{1}{15}$ 　　65. $2\frac{2}{3} \div \frac{10}{21}$ $5\frac{3}{5}$ 　　66. $3\frac{3}{4} \div \frac{5}{8}$ 6 　　67. $6\frac{1}{8} \div 7\frac{7}{8}$

68. $5\frac{5}{6} \div 14$ $\frac{5}{12}$ 　　69. $3\frac{1}{2} \div 1\frac{3}{4}$ 2 　　70. $9\frac{3}{7} \div 5\frac{1}{2}$ $1\frac{5}{7}$ 　　71. $4\frac{2}{3} \div 1\frac{3}{4}$ $2\frac{2}{3}$ 　　72. $2\frac{1}{2} \div 3\frac{1}{8}$ $\frac{4}{5}$

73. $1\frac{1}{3} \div 3\frac{2}{3}$ $\frac{4}{11}$ 　　74. $2\frac{3}{4} \div 1\frac{7}{8}$ $1\frac{7}{15}$ 　75. $3\frac{5}{6} \div 1\frac{2}{3}$ $2\frac{3}{10}$ 　76. $2\frac{3}{8} \div 1\frac{5}{16}$ $1\frac{17}{21}$ 　77. $1\frac{5}{9} \div 3\frac{1}{3}$ $\frac{7}{15}$

78. $3\frac{3}{8} \div 2\frac{1}{2}$ $1\frac{7}{20}$ 　79. $1\frac{1}{2} \div 3\frac{3}{8}$ $\frac{4}{9}$ 　　80. $7\frac{1}{3} \div 4\frac{2}{3}$ $1\frac{4}{7}$ 　　81. $1\frac{7}{10} \div 3\frac{2}{5}$ $\frac{1}{2}$ 　　82. $4\frac{2}{3} \div 1\frac{7}{9}$

$2\frac{5}{8}$

Round to the nearest whole number. (Pages 218–219)

83. $1\frac{1}{4}$ 1 　　84. $3\frac{3}{4}$ 4 　　85. $5\frac{7}{8}$ 6 　　86. $6\frac{1}{2}$ 7 　　87. $4\frac{3}{7}$ 4 　　88. $13\frac{1}{3}$ 13 　　89. $20\frac{5}{9}$ 21

90. $1\frac{7}{9}$ 2 　　91. $1\frac{1}{5}$ 1 　　92. $5\frac{1}{4}$ 5 　　93. $2\frac{5}{6}$ 3 　　94. $4\frac{4}{5}$ 5 　　95. $3\frac{3}{10}$ 3 　　96. $8\frac{2}{9}$ 8

Choose the best estimate. Choose a, b, c, or d. (Pages 218–219)

97. $6\frac{7}{8} + 3\frac{1}{2}$ b 　　a. 12 　　b. 11 　　c. 9 　　d. 8

98. $14\frac{2}{3} - 4\frac{1}{8}$ a 　　a. 11 　　b. 10 　　c. 9 　　d. 8

99. $7\frac{5}{6} \times 8\frac{7}{8}$ c 　　a. 64 　　b. 63 　　c. 72 　　d. 56

100. $9\frac{1}{3} \times 6\frac{3}{4}$ a 　　a. 63 　　b. 54 　　c. 70 　　d. 60

101. $12\frac{1}{9} \div 2\frac{9}{10}$ d 　　a. 6 　　b. 5 　　c. 3 　　d. 4

Part 3: Applications
The use of these word problems depends on which applications were studied.

102. Anna Young bought a camera for $\frac{1}{3}$ off the regular price of $135.00. What was the discount? (Page 207) $45.00

103. The regular price of a desk is listed as $118.00. At a sale, the desk is marked "$\frac{1}{4}$ OFF." Find the net price. (Page 207) $88.50

104. A carpenter wishes to cut 4 strips, each $2\frac{1}{4}$ inches wide, from a plank. The plank is $10\frac{1}{2}$ inches wide. Can the carpenter cut the four strips from the plank? (Pages 208–209) Yes

105. A fly ball traveling at a rate of 120 feet per second was caught by the center fielder $2\frac{4}{5}$ seconds after the batter hit the ball. How many feet did it travel? 336 feet (Page 210)

Chapter Review　　　　　　FRACTIONS: MULTIPLICATION/DIVISION　　**221**

Chapter Test

The Teacher's Resource Book contains two forms of each chapter test.

Multiply. Write each answer in lowest terms.

1. $\frac{1}{2} \times \frac{3}{5}$ $\frac{3}{10}$ **2.** $\frac{2}{3} \times 4$ $2\frac{2}{3}$ **3.** $5 \times \frac{3}{4}$ $3\frac{3}{4}$ **4.** $\frac{2}{3} \times \frac{9}{10}$ $\frac{3}{5}$ **5.** $\frac{5}{7} \times \frac{14}{15}$ $\frac{2}{3}$

6. $1\frac{1}{2} \times 2\frac{5}{6}$ $4\frac{1}{4}$ **7.** $3 \times 4\frac{7}{12}$ $13\frac{3}{4}$ **8.** $9\frac{1}{8} \times 3\frac{1}{5}$ $29\frac{1}{5}$ **9.** $4\frac{2}{3} \times 6\frac{3}{7}$ 30 **10.** $8\frac{1}{2} \times 3\frac{3}{7}$

$29\frac{1}{7}$

Divide. Write each answer in lowest terms.

11. $\frac{2}{3} \div \frac{4}{9}$ $1\frac{1}{2}$ **12.** $3 \div \frac{3}{8}$ 8 **13.** $\frac{9}{10} \div \frac{3}{5}$ $1\frac{1}{2}$ **14.** $\frac{6}{7} \div 12$ $\frac{1}{14}$ **15.** $1\frac{1}{2} \div 2\frac{1}{4}$

$\frac{2}{3}$

16. $6\frac{1}{8} \div 3\frac{1}{16}$ 2 **17.** $2\frac{2}{3} \div 4\frac{1}{8}$ $\frac{64}{99}$ **18.** $5\frac{3}{5} \div 2\frac{1}{3}$ $2\frac{2}{5}$ **19.** $12\frac{1}{2} \div 2\frac{1}{2}$ 5 **20.** $4\frac{5}{7} \div 5\frac{1}{2}$

$\frac{6}{7}$

Round to the nearest whole number.

21. $7\frac{2}{3}$ 8 **22.** $9\frac{1}{2}$ 10 **23.** $4\frac{1}{16}$ 4 **24.** $10\frac{3}{4}$ 11 **25.** $10\frac{3}{14}$ 10 **26.** $17\frac{6}{11}$ 18 **27.** $24\frac{8}{9}$

25

Solve each problem.   The use of these word problems depends on which applications were studied.

28. The regular price of a dress is listed as $54.97. At a sale, the dress is marked "$\frac{1}{3}$ OFF." Find the net price. $36.65

29. A carpenter wishes to cut 5 strips, each $3\frac{1}{8}$ inches wide, from a plank. The plank is $16\frac{3}{4}$ inches wide. Can the carpenter cut the 5 strips? Yes

30. Sue Chi drove to her brother's home in $7\frac{2}{3}$ hours. Her average speed was 50 miles per hour. Find the distance she traveled. $383\frac{1}{3}$ miles

Additional Practice

You may wish to use some or all of these exercises depending on how well students performed on the formal chapter test.

Skills

Multiply. Write each answer in lowest terms. (Pages 204–205) $\frac{3}{20}$

1. $\frac{1}{4} \times \frac{3}{5}$ $\frac{3}{20}$ **2.** $\frac{1}{2} \times \frac{5}{6}$ $\frac{5}{12}$ **3.** $\frac{1}{2} \times 5$ $2\frac{1}{2}$ **4.** $\frac{3}{4} \times 15$ $11\frac{1}{4}$ **5.** $\frac{2}{3} \times \frac{9}{16}$ $\frac{3}{8}$ **6.** $\frac{4}{5} \times \frac{3}{16}$

7. $\frac{1}{5} \times \frac{3}{8}$ $\frac{3}{40}$ **8.** $\frac{2}{5} \times \frac{5}{8}$ $\frac{1}{4}$ **9.** $6 \times \frac{3}{5}$ $3\frac{3}{5}$ **10.** $\frac{4}{5} \times \frac{1}{2}$ $\frac{2}{5}$ **11.** $\frac{4}{21} \times \frac{7}{8}$ $\frac{1}{6}$ **12.** $\frac{4}{5} \times \frac{7}{8}$ $\frac{7}{10}$

13. $\frac{3}{10} \times \frac{5}{12}$ $\frac{1}{8}$ **14.** $4 \times \frac{3}{8}$ $1\frac{1}{2}$ **15.** $\frac{9}{10} \times \frac{2}{3}$ $\frac{3}{5}$ **16.** $60 \times \frac{4}{5}$ 48 **17.** $16 \times \frac{5}{8}$ 10 **18.** $\frac{8}{9} \times \frac{3}{4}$ $\frac{2}{3}$

Write a fraction for each mixed number. (Pages 208–209)

19. $3\frac{1}{8}$ $\frac{25}{8}$ **20.** $5\frac{3}{4}$ $\frac{23}{4}$ **21.** $9\frac{1}{3}$ $\frac{28}{3}$ **22.** $8\frac{4}{9}$ $\frac{76}{9}$ **23.** $6\frac{9}{10}$ $\frac{69}{10}$ **24.** $5\frac{5}{8}$ $\frac{45}{8}$

Multiply. Write each answer in lowest terms. (Pages 208–209) $16\frac{1}{3}$

25. $2\frac{1}{4} \times 8$ 18 **26.** $1\frac{1}{3} \times 6$ 8 **27.** $1\frac{1}{2} \times \frac{2}{3}$ 1 **28.** $4\frac{1}{5} \times 2\frac{1}{2}$ $10\frac{1}{2}$ **29.** $3\frac{1}{2} \times 4\frac{2}{3}$

30. $1\frac{2}{3} \times 3\frac{1}{5}$ $5\frac{1}{3}$ **31.** $1\frac{1}{4} \times 3\frac{1}{2}$ $4\frac{3}{8}$ **32.** $2\frac{3}{4} \times \frac{2}{9}$ $\frac{11}{18}$ **33.** $8 \times 2\frac{1}{2}$ 20 **34.** $4 \times 3\frac{7}{8}$ $15\frac{1}{2}$

Write the reciprocal of each number. (Pages 212–213)

35. $\frac{3}{5}$ $\frac{5}{3}$ **36.** $\frac{18}{7}$ $\frac{7}{18}$ **37.** 6 $\frac{1}{6}$ **38.** $\frac{4}{9}$ $\frac{9}{4}$ **39.** $\frac{13}{2}$ $\frac{2}{13}$ **40.** 10 $\frac{1}{10}$ **41.** $\frac{7}{10}$ $\frac{10}{7}$ **42.** $\frac{5}{9}$ $\frac{9}{5}$

Divide. Write each answer in lowest terms. (Pages 212–213)

43. $6 \div \frac{1}{2}$ 12 **44.** $\frac{1}{2} \div 4$ $\frac{1}{8}$ **45.** $\frac{8}{9} \div \frac{3}{2}$ $\frac{16}{27}$ **46.** $3 \div \frac{2}{5}$ $7\frac{1}{2}$ **47.** $\frac{2}{5} \div \frac{4}{15}$ $1\frac{1}{2}$ **48.** $\frac{3}{4} \div \frac{1}{8}$ 6

49. $\frac{5}{6} \div \frac{1}{3}$ $2\frac{1}{2}$ **50.** $\frac{4}{9} \div \frac{3}{4}$ $\frac{16}{27}$ **51.** $\frac{4}{9} \div 4$ $\frac{1}{9}$ **52.** $\frac{5}{8} \div \frac{4}{3}$ $\frac{15}{32}$ **53.** $\frac{6}{7} \div \frac{12}{21}$ $1\frac{1}{2}$ **54.** $\frac{11}{12} \div \frac{5}{6}$ $1\frac{1}{10}$

Write the reciprocal of each mixed number. (Pages 214–215)

55. $2\frac{3}{8}$ $\frac{8}{19}$ **56.** $1\frac{2}{3}$ $\frac{3}{5}$ **57.** $2\frac{1}{4}$ $\frac{4}{9}$ **58.** $5\frac{2}{5}$ $\frac{5}{27}$ **59.** $3\frac{3}{4}$ $\frac{4}{15}$ **60.** $8\frac{1}{6}$ $\frac{6}{49}$

Divide. Write each answer in lowest terms. (Pages 214–215) $2\frac{5}{8}$

61. $7\frac{1}{5} \div \frac{1}{5}$ 36 **62.** $3\frac{4}{5} \div 2$ $1\frac{9}{10}$ **63.** $3\frac{1}{2} \div 7$ $\frac{1}{2}$ **64.** $\frac{1}{5} \div 2\frac{2}{5}$ $\frac{1}{12}$ **65.** $4\frac{2}{3} \div 1\frac{7}{9}$

66. $1\frac{1}{2} \div 3\frac{3}{8}$ $\frac{4}{9}$ **67.** $\frac{3}{8} \div 4\frac{1}{2}$ $\frac{1}{12}$ **68.** $1\frac{1}{2} \div \frac{1}{2}$ 3 **69.** $1\frac{7}{10} \div 3\frac{2}{5}$ $\frac{1}{2}$ **70.** $5\frac{1}{4} \div 4\frac{3}{8}$ $1\frac{1}{5}$

Applications The use of these word problems depends on which applications were studied.

71. Maria Lopez bought a dress for $\frac{1}{4}$ off the regular price of $36.00.
  a. What was the amount of discount? $9
  b. What did she pay for the dress? $27
  (Page 207)

72. A football traveling at a rate of 20 yards per second was caught by a receiver $2\frac{1}{4}$ seconds after it was thrown.
How many yards did it travel?
(Page 210) 45 yards

REVIEW OF RELATED SKILLS FOR CHAPTER 11

Tell whether each number is divisible by 3. Answer Yes or No.
(Pages 48–49)

1. 42 Yes   **2.** 513 Yes   **3.** 64 No   **4.** 78 Yes   **5.** 21 Yes   **6.** 329 No   **7.** 48 Yes

8. 56 No   **9.** 325 No   **10.** 126 Yes   **11.** 460 No   **12.** 14 No   **13.** 39 Yes   **14.** 414 Yes

Multiply.   (Pages 98–99)

15. 3×3.14 9.42   **16.** 9×3.14 28.26   **17.** 12×3.14 37.68   **18.** 16×3.14 50.24

19. 2.3×3.14 7.222   **20.** 6.8×3.14 21.352   **21.** 2.7×3.14 8.478   **22.** 17.1×3.14 53.694

23. $2 \times 3.14 \times 6$ 37.68   **24.** $2 \times 3.14 \times 9$ 56.52   **25.** $2 \times 3.14 \times 7$ 43.96   **26.** $2 \times 3.14 \times 4$ 25.12

Round each decimal to the nearest whole number.   (Pages 120–121)

27. 0.62 1   **28.** 1.98 2   **29.** 14.2 14   **30.** 25.3 25   **31.** 46.54 47   **32.** 99.5 100

33. 62.28 62   **34.** 25.31 25   **35.** 17.93 18   **36.** 36.81 37   **37.** 85.9 86   **38.** 103.2 103

Find the volume of each rectangular prism.   (Pages 164–165)

39. $l = 5$ cm   **40.** $l = 3$ cm   **41.** $l = 7$ cm   **42.** $l = 10$ cm
$w = 4$ cm $w = 3$ cm $w = 4$ cm $w = 8$ cm
$h = 5$ cm 100 cm³ $h = 3$ cm 27 cm³ $h = 6$ cm 168 cm³ $h = 12$ cm 960 cm³

43. $l = 9$ cm   **44.** $l = 2.1$ cm   **45.** $l = 4.8$ cm   **46.** $l = 2.9$ cm
$w = 9$ cm $w = 2$ cm $w = 3.2$ cm $w = 2.3$ cm
$h = 9$ cm 729 cm³ $h = 3$ cm 12.6 cm³ $h = 4.1$ cm 62.976 cm³ $h = 2$ cm 13.34 cm³

Write a fraction for each mixed number.   (Pages 208–209)

47. $2\frac{2}{3}$ $\frac{8}{3}$ **48.** $1\frac{1}{8}$ $\frac{9}{8}$ **49.** $9\frac{3}{4}$ $\frac{39}{4}$ **50.** $6\frac{1}{2}$ $\frac{13}{2}$ **51.** $12\frac{3}{8}$ $\frac{99}{8}$ **52.** $14\frac{5}{6}$ $\frac{89}{6}$

53. $21\frac{1}{3}$ $\frac{64}{3}$ **54.** $3\frac{5}{16}$ $\frac{53}{16}$ **55.** $16\frac{1}{2}$ $\frac{33}{2}$ **56.** $21\frac{3}{10}$ $\frac{213}{10}$ **57.** $13\frac{9}{10}$ $\frac{139}{10}$ **58.** $25\frac{1}{2}$ $\frac{51}{2}$

Multiply.   (Pages 204–205, 208–209)

59. $14 \times \frac{22}{7}$ 44   **60.** $21 \times \frac{22}{7}$ 66   **61.** $56 \times \frac{22}{7}$ 176   **62.** $7 \times \frac{22}{7}$ 22

63. $2 \times 28 \times \frac{22}{7}$ 176   **64.** $2 \times 35 \times \frac{22}{7}$ 220   **65.** $2 \times 63 \times \frac{22}{7}$ 396   **66.** $2 \times 77 \times \frac{22}{7}$ 484

67. $2 \times 2\frac{4}{5} \times 3\frac{1}{7}$ $17\frac{3}{5}$ **68.** $2 \times 4\frac{2}{3} \times 3\frac{1}{7}$ $29\frac{1}{3}$ **69.** $2 \times 5\frac{1}{4} \times 3\frac{1}{7}$ 33   **70.** $2 \times 2\frac{1}{10} \times 3\frac{1}{7}$ $13\frac{1}{5}$

Round each fraction or mixed number to the nearest whole number.
(Pages 218–219)

71. $\frac{1}{3}$ 0   **72.** $\frac{7}{8}$ 1   **73.** $\frac{5}{6}$ 1   **74.** $\frac{1}{4}$ 0   **75.** $2\frac{2}{3}$ 3   **76.** $3\frac{1}{5}$ 3

77. $9\frac{7}{8}$ 10   **78.** $8\frac{3}{4}$ 9   **79.** $6\frac{1}{2}$ 7   **80.** $19\frac{1}{2}$ 20   **81.** $21\frac{3}{8}$ 21   **82.** $13\frac{1}{3}$ 13

CIRCLES AND APPLICATIONS

SKILLS/APPLICATIONS

11-1 Circumference and Applications
11-2 Area and Applications
11-3 Volume and Applications: Cylinders
11-4 Volume and Applications: Cones

OTHER APPLICATIONS

Measuring Angles
Cans and Cylinders
Spheres

CAREER

Design

11-1 Circumference and Applications

See the Teacher's Manual for the objectives.

The **diameter** and **radius** of a circle such as this bicycle wheel are shown at the right. In any circle, the diameter is twice the radius. That is,

$$d = 2 \times r.$$ ◀ **d = diameter**
r = radius

The **circumference**, C, of a circle, is the distance around the circle. For all circles, the quotient $\dfrac{\text{circumference}}{\text{diameter}}$ is the same.

It is the number π (Greek letter "pi").
As a decimal, π is about 3.14. As a fraction, π is about $\frac{22}{7}$.

PROCEDURE To find the circumference, C, of a circle, find the product of the radius and 2π <u>or</u> the product of the diameter and π.

$$C = 2 \times \pi \times r \quad \text{or} \quad C = \pi \times d$$

EXAMPLE The radius of this bicycle wheel is 32 centimeters.
Find the circumference. Round your answer to the nearest whole number.

Solutions:

Method 1

$C = 2 \times \ \pi \ \times \ r$ ◀ **r = 32 cm**
$C = 2 \times 3.14 \times 32$
$C = 200.96$

Method 2

$C = \ \pi \ \times \ d$
$C = 3.14 \times 64$ ◀ **d = 2 × r**
d = 2 × 32
$C = 200.96$

The circumference is about **201 cm.** ◀ **Rounded to the nearest whole number**

REVIEW OF RELATED SKILLS You may wish to use these exercises before teaching the lesson.

Multiply. (Pages 98–99)

1. 2×3.14 6.28 **2.** 10×3.14 31.4 **3.** 59×3.14 185.26 **4.** 1.6×3.14 5.024

5. 72.5×3.14 227.65 **6.** 19.6×3.14 61.544 **7.** $2 \times 3.14 \times 9.5$ 59.66 **8.** $2 \times 3.14 \times 27.8$
174.584

Write a fraction for each mixed number. (Pages 208–209)

9. $3\frac{1}{7}$ $\frac{22}{7}$ **10.** $1\frac{3}{4}$ $\frac{7}{4}$ **11.** $5\frac{1}{4}$ $\frac{21}{4}$ **12.** $10\frac{7}{8}$ $\frac{87}{8}$ **13.** $25\frac{2}{3}$ $\frac{77}{3}$ **14.** $12\frac{5}{16}$ $\frac{197}{16}$ **15.** $18\frac{5}{6}$ $\frac{113}{6}$ **16.** $100\frac{4}{5}$
$\frac{504}{5}$

Multiply.   (Pages 204–205, 208–209)

17. $2 \times 49 \times \frac{22}{7}$ 308   **18.** $2 \times 280 \times \frac{22}{7}$ 1760   **19.** $2 \times 350 \times \frac{22}{7}$ 2200   **20.** $2 \times 25 \times \frac{22}{7}$ $157\frac{1}{7}$

Round to the nearest whole number.   (Pages 120–121, 218–219)

21. 21.3 21   **22.** 73.5 74   **23.** 54.8 55   **24.** 34.72 35   **25.** 61.55 62   **26.** 41.32 41

27. $\frac{3}{4}$ 1   **28.** $5\frac{1}{8}$ 5   **29.** $23\frac{5}{8}$ 24   **30.** $152\frac{11}{12}$ 153   **31.** $301\frac{1}{2}$ 302   **32.** $27\frac{9}{10}$ 28

EXERCISES

See the suggested assignment guide in the Teacher's Manual.

Metric Measures

Find the circumference. Use 3.14 for π. Round answers to the nearest whole number.

1. Auto Tire   **2. Bicycle Wheel**   **3. Tennis Ball**   **4. Record**

$r = 30$ cm $r = 33$ cm $r = 3.2$ cm $r = 12.7$ cm
188 cm   207 cm   20 cm   80 cm

5. Tractor Tire   **6. Earth**   **7. Basketball**   **8. Skating Rink**

$d = 1.3$ m $d = 12{,}766$ km $r = 12.1$ cm $d = 20$ m
4 m   40,085 km   76 cm   63 m

9. Doorknob   **10. Bowling Ball**   **11. Grapefruit**   **12. Sun**

$d = 5$ cm $r = 34.5$ cm $d = 11$ cm $r = 696{,}000$ km
16 cm   217 cm   35 cm   4,370,880 km

Customary Measures

Find the circumference. Use $\frac{22}{7}$ for π. Round answers to the nearest whole number.

13. Fountain Base   **14. Bicycle Gear**   **15. Clock**   **16. Moon**

$r = 7\frac{1}{2}$ ft 47 ft $r = 4\frac{2}{5}$ in 28 in $d = 13\frac{1}{2}$ in 42 in $d = 2250$ mi
                                                                                                 7071 mi

17. Douglas Fir   **18. Mars**   **19. Softball**   **20. Reel of Tape**

$r = 2$ yd $d = 11{,}152$ mi $d = 12$ in $r = 3\frac{1}{2}$ in
13 yd   35049 mi   38 in   22 in

Problem Solving and Applications

Measuring Angles

See the Teacher's Manual for the objectives.

The **degree** (symbol: "°") is the standard unit for measuring an angle. You can use a **protractor** to measure an angle. A protractor is one half a circle, or a **semicircle**.

Ray

Vertex

Ray

To use a protractor to measure an angle:

1 Place the center of the base of the protractor at the vertex of the angle.

2 Place the protractor so that one ray of the angle passes through "0" on the protractor.

3 Read the measure of the angle from the second ray.

Angle	Measure	Name
Read the measure from this ray. This ray passes through 0. Place the center of the base at the vertex. Base	60°	**Acute.** An **acute angle** has a measure of less than 90°.
The ray passes through 90° exactly.	90°	**Right.** A **right angle** has a measure of 90°. The sides of a right angle are **perpendicular** to each other.
The ray passes through 120° exactly.	120°	**Obtuse.** An **obtuse angle** has a measure of more than 90° but less than 180°.

The sum of the angles of any triangle is 180°.

Application

Exercises

Use a protractor to find the measure of each angle to the nearest degree.

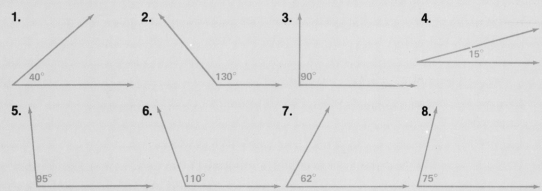

1. 40° 2. 130° 3. 90° 4. 15°

5. 95° 6. 110° 7. 62° 8. 75°

For each of Exercises 9–15, the measure of an angle is given. Tell whether the angle is acute, right, or obtuse.

9. 25°
acute

10. 90°
right

11. 130°
obtuse

12. 45°
acute

13. 175°
obtuse

14. 99°
obtuse

15. 12°
acute

Measure each angle in each figure to the nearest degree. Then find the sum of the angles of each figure. Answer the questions in the fourth column.

	Figure	Angle Measures	Sum of the Angle Measures	Questions
16.	2 1 3 **Acute Triangle**	angle 1: __?__ 50° angle 2: __?__ 70° angle 3: __?__ 60°	__?__ 180°	Are all of the angles of an acute triangle less than 90°? Yes
17.	2 1 3 **Right Triangle**	angle 1: __?__ 90° angle 2: __?__ 55° angle 3: __?__ 35°	__?__ 180°	What is the sum of the acute angles of the right triangle? 90°
18.	2 1 3 **Obtuse Triangle**	angle 1: __?__ 125° angle 2: __?__ 25° angle 3: __?__ 30°	__?__ 180°	Are any of the angles of an obtuse triangle greater than 90°? Yes

11-2 Area and Applications

See the Teacher's Manual for the objectives.

The formulas for the area of a parallelogram and of a circle are similar.

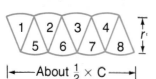

|←——About $\frac{1}{2}$ × C——→|

Cut a circle into 8 equal pieces.

Arrange pieces like this.

Area of parallelogram: $A = b \times h$

Area of circle: $A = \frac{1}{2} \times C \times r$

$A = \frac{1}{2} \times 2 \times \pi \times r \times r$

$A = \pi \times r \times r$

PROCEDURE To find the area of a circle, multiply π times the radius times the radius.

$$A = \pi \times r \times r \quad \text{or} \quad A = \pi \times r^2 \quad \blacktriangleleft \; r^2 \text{ means } r \times r.$$

EXAMPLE The top of a round table has a radius of 0.5 meter. Find the area. Use 3.14 for π. Round your answer to the nearest whole number.

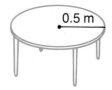

0.5 m

Solution: $A = \pi \times r^2 \quad \blacktriangleleft \; r^2 \text{ means } r \times r.$

$A = 3.14 \times 0.5 \times 0.5$

$A = 0.785$ The area is about 1 m^2. $\blacktriangleleft$ **Nearest whole number**

REVIEW OF RELATED SKILLS

You may wish to use these exercises before teaching the lesson.

Multiply. (Pages 98–99)

1. $3.14 \times 4 \times 4$ 50.24
2. $3.14 \times 10 \times 10$ 314
3. $3.14 \times 0.1 \times 0.1$ 0.0314
4. $3.14 \times 2.5 \times 2.5$ 19.625

Write a fraction for each mixed number. (Pages 208–209)

5. $3\frac{1}{7}$ $\frac{22}{7}$
6. $3\frac{1}{10}$ $\frac{31}{10}$
7. $2\frac{1}{8}$ $\frac{17}{8}$
8. $11\frac{1}{2}$ $\frac{23}{2}$
9. $9\frac{3}{5}$ $\frac{48}{5}$
10. $12\frac{9}{16}$ $\frac{201}{16}$
11. $6\frac{2}{3}$ $\frac{20}{3}$
12. $51\frac{9}{20}$ $\frac{1029}{20}$

Multiply. (Pages 204–205, 208–209)

13. $\frac{22}{7} \times 21 \times 21$ 1386
14. $\frac{22}{7} \times 9 \times 9$ $254\frac{4}{7}$
15. $\frac{22}{7} \times \frac{21}{5} \times \frac{21}{5}$ $55\frac{11}{12}$
16. $\frac{22}{7} \times \frac{35}{11} \times \frac{35}{11}$ $31\frac{9}{11}$

17. $3\frac{1}{7} \times 14 \times 14$ 616
18. $3\frac{1}{7} \times \frac{9}{2} \times \frac{9}{2}$ $63\frac{9}{14}$
19. $3\frac{1}{7} \times 8\frac{2}{3} \times 8\frac{2}{3}$ $236\frac{4}{63}$
20. $3\frac{1}{7} \times 5\frac{1}{4} \times 5\frac{1}{4}$ $86\frac{5}{8}$

Round each decimal to the nearest whole number. (Pages 120–121)

21. 0.87   1
22. 1.83   2
23. 9.27   9
24. 30.21   30
25. 15.14   15
26. 4.89   5

Round each fraction to the nearest whole number. (Pages 218–219)

27. $21\frac{1}{2}$ 22
28. $17\frac{3}{5}$ 18
29. $63\frac{2}{5}$ 63
30. $84\frac{7}{8}$ 85
31. $50\frac{21}{24}$ 51
32. $94\frac{10}{11}$ 95

EXERCISES

See the suggested assignment guide in the Teacher's Manual.

Metric Measures

Find the area. Use 3.14 for π. Round answers to the nearest whole number. 1963 mm²

1. Tray 1256 cm²

$r = 20$ cm

2. Mirror 1661 cm²

$r = 23$ cm

3. Rug 2 m²

$r = 0.8$ m

4. Camera Lens

$r = 25$ mm

5. Plate 408 cm²

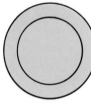

$r = 11.4$ cm

6. Pool Cover Top
28 m²

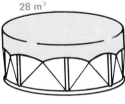

$r = 3$ m

7. Garden 23 m²

$r = 2.7$ m

8. Top of a Jar 38 cm²

$r = 3.5$ cm

Customary Measures

Find the area. Use $\frac{22}{7}$ for π. Round answers to the nearest whole number.

9. Paper Doily 50 in²

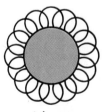

$r = 4$ in

10. Target 7 ft²

$r = 1\frac{1}{2}$ ft

11. Flower Center
13 in²

$r = 2$ in

12. Clock Face 24 in²

$r = 2\frac{3}{4}$ in

13. Top of a Drum
227 in²

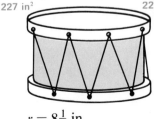

$r = 8\frac{1}{2}$ in

14. Hassock Top
225 in²

$r = 9$ in

15. Emblem
16 in²

$r = 2\frac{1}{4}$ in

16. Window
201 ft²

$r = 8$ ft

CIRCLES AND APPLICATIONS **231**

career
Career Lessons are optional.
This lesson applies the skills presented in Sections 11-1 and 11-2.

Landscape architects help plan and design the arrangement of trees, walks, and gardens for projects such as parks and playgrounds. The plan below shows a tulip garden surrounded by a gravel walk.

EXERCISES

For Exercises 1–10, use $\pi = 3.14$. Round your answers to the nearest tenth.

The radius of the red–tulip section of the garden is 1.5 meters.

1. Find the circumference of the red–tulip section of the garden. 9.4 m

2. Find the area of the red–tulip section of the garden. 7.1 m²

The radius of the red– and orange–tulip sections of the garden is 2.5 meters.

3. Find the circumference of the red– and orange–tulip sections of the garden. 15.7 m

4. Find the area of the red– and orange–tulip sections of the garden. 19.6 m²

The total radius of the tulip garden is 4 meters.

5. Find the circumference of the garden. 25.1 m

6. Find the area of the tulip garden. 50.2 m²

7. How much of the total area of the garden is planted with orange tulips? 12.5 m²

8. How much of the total area of the garden is planted with yellow tulips? 30.6 m²

9. A gravel walk, one meter wide, surrounds the garden. Find the total area of the garden and the walk. 78.5 m²

10. Find the area of the gravel walk only. (Hint: Area of garden and walk − Area of garden = __?__) 28.3 m²

11-3 Volume and Applications: Cylinders See the Teacher's Manual for the objectives.

Finding the volume of a cylinder is similar to finding the volume of a rectangular prism. Volume is measured in **cubic units.**

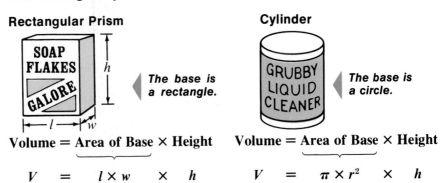

Rectangular Prism

The base is a rectangle.

Volume = **Area of Base** × **Height**

$$V = l \times w \times h$$

Cylinder

The base is a circle.

Volume = **Area of Base** × **Height**

$$V = \pi \times r^2 \times h$$

PROCEDURE To find the volume, V, of a cylinder, multiply the area of the base and the height.

$$V = \pi \times r \times r \times h \quad \text{or} \quad V = \pi \times r^2 \times h$$

EXAMPLE Find the volume of this can of soup. The radius is 3.3 centimeters. Use 3.14 for π. Round your answer to the nearest whole number.

Champs CHICKEN SOUP

Solution: $V = \pi \times r^2 \times h$ ◀ r^2 *means* $r \times r$.

$$V = 3.14 \times 3.3 \times 3.3 \times 10$$

$V = \textbf{341.946}$ The volume is about **342 cm³.**

REVIEW OF RELATED SKILLS You may wish to use these exercises before teaching the lesson.

Find the volume of each rectangular prism.   (Pages 164–165)

1. $l = 8$ cm
$w = 5$ cm
$h = 6$ cm
240 cm³

2. $l = 4$ cm
$w = 4$ cm
$h = 4$ cm
64 cm³

3. $l = 8.5$ cm
$w = 3$ cm
$h = 9$ cm
229.5 cm³

4. $l = 8.2$ cm
$w = 4.9$ cm
$h = 10$ cm
401.8 cm³

Round each decimal to the nearest whole number.   (Pages 120–121)

5. 12.5 13   **6.** 35.7 36   **7.** 9.62 10   **8.** 81.08 81   **9.** 116.331 116   **10.** 402.4496 402

Round each fraction to the nearest whole number.   (Pages 218–219)

11. $3\frac{2}{3}$ 4   **12.** $8\frac{5}{7}$ 9   **13.** $12\frac{5}{12}$ 12   **14.** $403\frac{11}{14}$ 404   **15.** $1022\frac{4}{7}$ 1023   **16.** $5339\frac{29}{56}$ 5340

EXERCISES

See the suggested assignment guide in the Teacher's Manual.

Metric Measures

Find the volume. Use 3.14 for π. Round answers to the nearest whole number.

1. Hasty Oats

$r = 5$ cm; $h = 18$ cm
1413 cm³

2. Baking Powder

$r = 3$ cm; $h = 6$ cm
170 cm³

3. Corn

$r = 4$ cm; $h = 10.5$ cm
528 cm³

4. Orange Juice

$r = 2$ cm; $h = 9$ cm
177 cm³

5. Mug

$r = 4$ cm; $h = 8$ cm
402 cm³

6. Sauce Pan

$r = 6.5$ cm; $h = 6$ cm
796 cm³

7. Planter

$r = 0.8$ m; $h = 1$ m
2 m³

8. Can of Varnish

$r = 7$ cm; $h = 15$ cm
2308 cm³

Customary Measures

Find the volume. Use $\frac{22}{7}$ for π. Round answers to the nearest whole number.

9. Glass

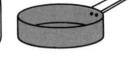

$r = 2$ in; $h = 6$ in
75 in³

10. Vase

$r = 1\frac{1}{2}$ in; $h = 11$ in
78 in³

11. Water Tower

$r = 15$ ft; $h = 50$ ft
35,357 ft³

12. Fruit Juice Can

$r = 3$ in; $h = 8$ in
226 in³

13. Cookie Tin

$r = 4\frac{1}{2}$ in; $h = 5$ in
318 in³

14. Waste Basket

$r = 7\frac{1}{4}$ in; $h = 13$ in
2148 in³

15. Trash Can

$r = 9$ in; $h = 22\frac{1}{2}$ in
5728 in³

16. Flour Canister

$r = 3$ in; $h = 7\frac{1}{2}$ in
212 in³

Problem Solving and Applications

Cans and Cylinders See the Teacher's Manual for the objectives.

To find the amount of metal needed to make a paint can, the manufacturer uses a formula which is based on the formulas for the area of a circle and of a rectangle.

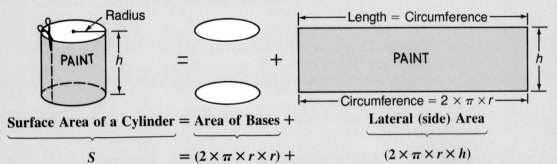

Surface Area of a Cylinder = **Area of Bases** + **Lateral (side) Area**

$$S = (2 \times \pi \times r \times r) + (2 \times \pi \times r \times h)$$

EXAMPLE The radius of a paint can is 3 centimeters and its height is 14 centimeters. Find its surface area. Use 3.14 for π. Round your answer to the nearest whole number.

Solution: Use paper and pencil or use a calculator.

$S = (2 \times \pi \times r \times r) + (2 \times \pi \times r \times h)$
$S = (2 \times 3.14 \times 3 \times 3) + (2 \times 3.14 \times 3 \times 14)$
$S = \qquad 56.62 \qquad + \qquad 263.76$
$S = 320.28 \qquad$ The surface area is about **320 cm²**.

Exercises

For Exercises 1–4, round each answer to the nearest whole number.

1. The radius of a snare drum is 19 centimeters and its height is 25 centimeters. Find the surface area. Use 3.14 for π. 5250 cm²

2. The radius of a box of bread crumbs is $1\frac{1}{2}$ inches and its height is 6 inches. Find the surface area. Use $\frac{22}{7}$ for π. 71 in²

3. A hot water tank is to be insulated. The radius of the tank is 0.4 meters and its height is 1.5 meters. How much insulation will be needed? Use 3.14 for π. 5 m²

4. The radius of a box of salt is $1\frac{1}{2}$ inches and its height is 5 inches. How much heavy cardboard will be needed to make 2,000,000 such boxes? Use $\frac{22}{7}$ for π. 122,571,429 in²

Application   CIRCLES AND APPLICATIONS   **235**

11-4 Volume and Applications: Cones

See the Teacher's Manual for the objectives.

This lesson may be considered optional for some students.

It takes three of the cone–shaped cups to fill <u>one</u> glass (cylinder).

The base of a cone is a circle. When a cone and a cylinder have equal radii (plural of radius) and equal heights, the volume of the cone is one third the volume of the cylinder.

PROCEDURE To find the volume of a cone, find the product of $\frac{1}{3}$ the area of the base and the height.

$$\text{Volume} = \frac{1}{3} \times \underbrace{\text{Area of Base}} \times \text{Height}$$

$$V = \frac{1}{3} \times \quad \pi \times r \times r \quad \times \quad h$$

EXAMPLE Find the volume of this paper cup. Use 3.14 for π. Round your answer to the nearest whole number.

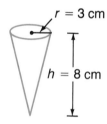

Solution: $V = \frac{1}{3} \times \pi \times r \times r \times h$ ◀ $r = 3$
$h = 8$

$V = \frac{1}{3} \times 3.14 \times 3 \times 3 \times 8$

$V = 75.36$ The volume is about **75 cm³**.

REVIEW OF RELATED SKILLS You may wish to use these exercises before teaching the lesson

Tell whether each number is divisible by 3. Answer <u>Yes</u> *or* <u>No</u>.
(Pages 48–49)

1. 81 Yes   **2.** 111 Yes **3.** 612 Yes   **4.** 580 No   **5.** 901 No   **6.** 720 Yes   **7.** 222
Yes

Round to the nearest whole number.   (Pages 120–121)

8. 10.3 10   **9.** 17.1 17   **10.** 100.5 101 **11.** 89.8 90   **12.** 67.4 67   **13.** 9.05 9   **14.** 4.81
5
(Pages 218–219)

15. $18\frac{1}{5}$ 18   **16.** $9\frac{2}{3}$ 10   **17.** $12\frac{1}{2}$ 13   **18.** $16\frac{3}{4}$ 17   **19.** $\frac{9}{10}$ 1   **20.** $15\frac{9}{8}$ 16   **21.** $\frac{1}{6}$ 0

Multiply.   (Pages 98–99, 204–205)

22. $\frac{1}{3} \times 3.14 \times 27$ **23.** $\frac{1}{3} \times 3.14 \times 81$ **24.** $\frac{1}{3} \times \frac{22}{7} \times 399$ 418   **25.** $\frac{1}{3} \times \frac{22}{7} \times 105$
28.26   84.78   110

EXERCISES

Metric Measures

Find the volume. Use 3.14 for π. Round answers to the nearest whole number.

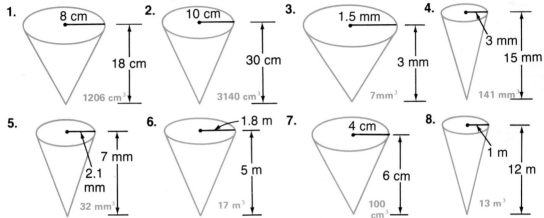

1. 8 cm — 18 cm — 1206 cm³
2. 10 cm — 30 cm — 3140 cm³
3. 1.5 mm — 3 mm — 7mm³
4. 3 mm — 15 mm — 141 mm³
5. 7 mm — 2.1 mm — 32 mm³
6. 1.8 m — 5 m — 17 m³
7. 4 cm — 6 cm — 100 cm³
8. 1 m — 12 m — 13 m³

Customary Measures

Find the volume. Use $\frac{22}{7}$ for π. Round answers to the nearest whole number.

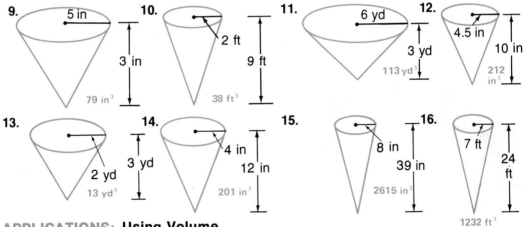

9. 5 in — 3 in — 79 in³
10. 2 ft — 9 ft — 38 ft³
11. 6 yd — 3 yd — 113 yd³
12. 4.5 in — 10 in — 212 in³
13. 2 yd — 3 yd — 13 yd³
14. 4 in — 12 in — 201 in³
15. 8 in — 39 in — 2615 in³
16. 7 ft — 24 ft — 1232 ft³

APPLICATIONS: Using Volume

17. Find the volume of the cylinder-shaped cup. Round your answer to the nearest cubic centimeter. 452 cm³

18. Find the volume of the cup shaped like a cone. Round your answer to the nearest cubic centimeter. 151 cm³

19. Which cup has the greater volume? How much greater is it? 3 times as great

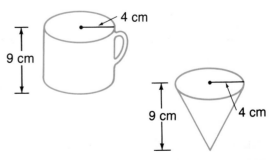

4 cm — 9 cm

9 cm — 4 cm

Problem Solving and Applications

Spheres

Some storage tanks have the shape of a **sphere**.
You can use this formula to find the volume of
a sphere.

$$V = \tfrac{4}{3} \times \pi \times r \times r \times r$$

EXAMPLE The radius of this storage tank is
7.2 meters. Find the volume of the
tank. Use 3.14 for π. Round your
answer to the nearest whole
number.

Solution: Use paper and pencil or use a calculator.

$V = \tfrac{4}{3} \times \pi \times r \times r \times r$ ◀ **r = 7.2**

$V = \tfrac{4}{3} \times 3.14 \times 7.2 \times 7.2 \times 7.2$

$$\boxed{4}\ \boxed{\times}\ \boxed{3}\ \boxed{.}\ \boxed{1}\ \boxed{4}\ \boxed{\times}\ \boxed{7}\ \boxed{.}\ \boxed{2}\ \boxed{\times} \qquad \boxed{90.432}$$

$$\boxed{7}\ \boxed{.}\ \boxed{2}\ \boxed{\times}\ \boxed{7}\ \boxed{.}\ \boxed{2}\ \boxed{\div}\ \boxed{3}\ \boxed{=} \qquad \boxed{1562.6649}$$

The volume is about **1563 m³**. ◀ *Nearest whole number*

Exercises

For Exercises 1–4, round each answer to the nearest whole number.

1. Find the volume of a basketball
   that has a radius of 12 centimeters.
   Use 3.14 for π. 7235 cm³

2. Find the volume of a volleyball that
   has a radius of $4\tfrac{1}{5}$ inches. Use $\tfrac{22}{7}$
   for π. 310 in³

3. A spherical storage tank for natural
   gas has a radius of 36 feet. Find the
   volume of the tank. Use $\tfrac{22}{7}$ for π. 195511 ft³

4. The kettle at the right has a radius
   of 29 centimeters. Find the volume
   of the bottom half of the kettle
   (half a sphere or a **hemisphere**).
   Use 3.14 for π. 51054 cm³

Chapter Review

These exercises review the vocabulary, skills, and applications presented in the chapter as a preparation for the chapter test.

Part 1: Vocabulary

For Exercises 1–5, choose from the box at the right the word(s) that completes each statement.

1. The distance around a circle is its __?__. (Page 226) circumference

2. The formula for the circumference of a circle is __?__. (Page 226)
$C = 2 \times \pi \times r$

3. The standard unit of measurement for an angle is the __?__. (Page 228)
degree

4. An angle with a measurement less than 90° is an __?__ angle. (Page 228)
acute

5. The formula for the area of a circle is __?__. (Page 230)
$A = \pi \times r \times r$

| degree |
| circumference |
| $A = \pi \times r \times r$ |
| acute |
| $C = 2 \times \pi \times r$ |
| obtuse |

Part 2: Skills

Find the circumference. Round each answer to the nearest whole number.
(Pages 226–227)

6. Garden

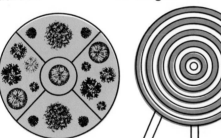

$r = 3.5$ m

$\pi = 3.14$

22 m

7. Target

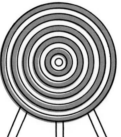

$d = 35$ in

$\pi = \frac{22}{7}$

110 in

8. Sunflower Center

$r = 3\frac{1}{2}$ in

$\pi = 3\frac{1}{7}$

22 in

9. Checker

$d = 3$ cm

$\pi = 3.14$

9 cm

Use a protractor to find the measure of each angle to the nearest degree. (Pages 228–229)

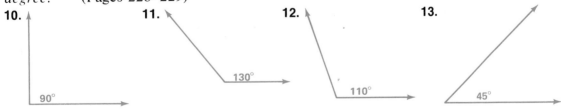

10.

90°

11.

130°

12.

110°

13.

45°

For Exercises 16–22, tell whether the given measure indicates an acute, right, or obtuse angle. (Pages 228–229)

14. 30°　　**15.** 96°　　**16.** 80°　　**17.** 90°　　**18.** 160°　　**19.** 23°　　**20.** 134°

acute　　　obtuse　　　acute　　　right　　　obtuse　　　acute　　　obtuse

Chapter Review　　　　　　　　CIRCLES AND APPLICATIONS　　**239**

Find the area. Round each answer to the nearest whole number.
(Pages 230–231)

21. Quarter

$r = 1.2$ cm

$\pi = 3.14$
5 cm²

22. Sauce Pan Lid

$r = 2\frac{1}{2}$ inches

$\pi = 3\frac{1}{7}$
20 in²

23. Flashlight Face

$r = 1$ inch

$\pi = \frac{22}{7}$
3 in²

24. Roller Skate Wheel

$r = 2.2$ cm

$\pi = 3.14$
15 cm²

Find the volume of each cylinder. Round each answer to the nearest whole number. (Pages 233–234)

25. Salt Container

$r = 4$ cm

$\pi = 3.14$

$h = 16$ cm
804 cm³

26. Can of Tuna

$r = 2$ inches

$\pi = \frac{22}{7}$

$h = 2\frac{1}{4}$ inches
28 in³

27. Candle

$r = 1\frac{1}{2}$ inches

$\pi = 3\frac{1}{7}$

$h = 7$ inches
50 in³

28. Pencil Holder

$r = 3.3$ cm

$\pi = 3.14$

$h = 10$ cm
342 cm³

Find the volume of each cone. Round each answer to the nearest whole number. (Pages 236–237)

29.

8 in
3 in

$\pi = \frac{22}{7}$ 75 in³

30.

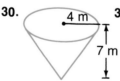

4 m
7 m

$\pi = 3.14$ 117 m³

31.

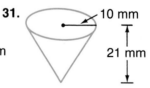

10 mm
21 mm

$\pi = 3.14$ 2198 mm³

32.

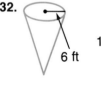

11 ft
6 ft

$\pi = 3\frac{1}{7}$ 415 ft³

Part 3: Applications   The use of these word problems depends on which applications were studied.

For Exercises 33–34, round each answer to the nearest whole number.

33. The radius of a can of soup is 3.2 centimeters and its height is 10 centimeters. Find the surface area. Use 3.14 for π. (Page 235) 265 cm²

34. A cone–shaped hanging planter has a radius of 7 centimeters and a height of 15 centimeters. Find the volume. Use 3.14 for π. (Pages 236–237) 769 cm³

Chapter Test

Find the circumference. Round each answer to the nearest whole number.

1. Watch Face

$d = 2$ cm

$\pi = 3.14$

6 cm

2. Key Ring

$r = 1.5$ cm

$\pi = 3.14$

9 cm

3. Lamp Base

$d = 7$ in

$\pi = \frac{22}{7}$

22 in

4. Top of Thimble

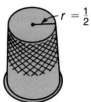

$r = \frac{1}{2}$ in

$r = \frac{1}{2}$ in

$\pi = 3\frac{1}{7}$

3 in

Use a protractor to find the measure of each angle to the nearest degree.

5.
105°

6.
90°

7.
80°

8.
75°

Tell whether each of the given angles is acute, right, or obtuse.

9. 25° acute   **10.** 48° acute   **11.** 103° obtuse   **12.** 96° obtuse   **13.** 90° right   **14.** 82° acute

For Exercises 15–20, round each answer to the nearest whole number.
For Exercises 15–16, find the area.   *For Exercises 17–18, find the volume.*

15. Top of Scale

$r = 10$ cm

$\pi = 3.14$ 314 cm²

16. Bottom of Pan

$r = 7$ in

$\pi = \frac{22}{7}$ 154 in²

17. Jar of Pickles

$\pi = 3.14$

804 cm³

18. Cone

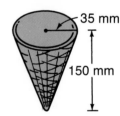

$\pi = \frac{22}{7}$

192,500 mm²

The use of these word problems depends on which applications were studied.

19. A cylinder–shaped salt shaker has a radius of 3 centimeters and its height is 6 centimeters. Find the surface area. Use 3.14 for π.   170 cm²

20. A candle has the shape of a cone. Its radius is 2 inches and its height is 7 inches. Find the volume. Use $\frac{22}{7}$ for π.   29 in³

Additional Practice

You may wish to use some or all of these exercises depending on how well students performed on the formal chapter test.

Skills

Find the circumference. Round each answer to the nearest whole number. (Pages 226–227)

1. Basketball

$r = 12.4$ cm

$\pi = 3.14$

78 cm

2. Table Fan

$r = 4\frac{1}{2}$ in

$\pi = \frac{22}{7}$

28 in

3. Rim of a Dish

$r = 5$ cm

$\pi = 3.14$

31 cm

4. Rim of a Pool

$r = 7$ feet

$\pi = \frac{22}{7}$

44 ft

Use a protractor to find the measure of each angle to the nearest degree. (Pages 228–229)

5.

30°

6.

90°

7.

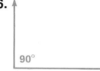

165°

8.

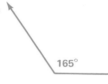

50°

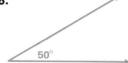

Find the area. Round each answer to the nearest whole number. (Pages 230–231)

9. Tractor Tire

$r = 0.6$ m

$\pi = 3.14$

1 m²

10. Circular Mirror

$r = 6$ in

$\pi = \frac{22}{7}$

113 in²

11. Wagon Wheel

$r = 5$ cm

$\pi = 3.14$

79 cm²

12. Quarter

$r = \frac{1}{2}$ in

$\pi = \frac{22}{7}$

1 in²

Find the volume of each cylinder. Round each answer to the nearest whole number. (Pages 233–234)

13. Drum

$r = 9.5$ cm

$\pi = 3.14$

$h = 10.5$ cm

2976 cm³

14. Vase

$r = 2\frac{3}{4}$ in

$\pi = \frac{22}{7}$

$h = 12$ in

285 in³

15. Wastebasket

$r = 7$ in

$\pi = \frac{22}{7}$

$h = 15$ in

2310 in³

16. Water Tower

$r = 5.2$ m

$\pi = 3.14$

$h = 16.6$ m

1409 in³

Applications

The use of these word problems depends on which applications were studied.

17. The radius of a can of tuna fish is 5 centimeters and its height is 6 centimeters. Find the surface area. Use 3.14 for π. (Page 235) 345 cm²

18. A cone-shaped paper cup has a radius of $1\frac{1}{2}$ inches and a height of $3\frac{3}{4}$ inches. Find the volume. Use $\frac{22}{7}$ for π. (Pages 236–237) 9 in³

Cumulative Review: Chapters 9–11

You may also wish to use at this time the cumulative review on page 447 titled *Review of Skills* that reviews *only* the skills presented in Chapters 1-11.

Choose the correct answer. Choose a, b, c, or d.

1. Write $\frac{12}{18}$ in lowest terms. ᵃ

  a. $\frac{2}{3}$ **b.** $\frac{6}{9}$ **c.** $\frac{4}{6}$ **d.** $\frac{1}{2}$

2. Add. Write the answer in lowest terms. ᶜ

$$\frac{3}{8} + \frac{1}{8}$$

  a. $\frac{4}{8}$ **b.** $\frac{4}{16}$ **c.** $\frac{1}{2}$ **d.** $\frac{1}{4}$

3. Find the number of centimeters ᵇ in the circumference of this plate. Use $C = 2 \times \pi \times r$ with $\pi = 3.14$.

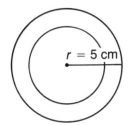

r = 5 cm

  a. 7   **b.** 31.4   **c.** 25   **d.** 15.7

4. Divide. Write the answer in lowest terms. ᵃ

$$\frac{3}{5} \div \frac{15}{26}$$

  a. $1\frac{1}{25}$ **b.** $\frac{9}{26}$ **c.** $\frac{45}{130}$ **d.** $\frac{78}{75}$

5. Add. Write the answer in lowest terms. ᵈ

$$\frac{1}{6} + \frac{5}{8}$$

  a. $\frac{38}{48}$ **b.** $\frac{3}{7}$ **c.** $\frac{6}{14}$ **d.** $\frac{19}{24}$

6. Divide. Write the answer in lowest terms. ᵃ

$$18 \div 2\frac{2}{5}$$

  a. $7\frac{1}{2}$ **b.** $43\frac{1}{5}$ **c.** $\frac{90}{12}$ **d.** $\frac{45}{6}$

7. Write a fraction for $3\frac{4}{5}$. ᵈ

  a. $\frac{43}{5}$ **b.** $\frac{12}{5}$ **c.** $\frac{7}{5}$ **d.** $\frac{19}{5}$

8. Write the reciprocal of $3\frac{1}{5}$. ᵃ

  a. $\frac{5}{16}$ **b.** $\frac{16}{5}$ **c.** $5\frac{1}{3}$ **d.** $\frac{16}{3}$

9. Find the number of meters in the ᵈ volume of this tank. Use $V = \pi \times r \times r \times h$ with $\pi = 3.14$.

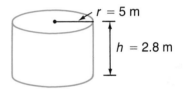

r = 5 m   *h = 2.8 m*

  a. 70   **b.** 230   **c.** 44   **d.** 219.8

10. Multiply. Write the answer in lowest terms. ᵇ

$$\frac{5}{12} \times \frac{16}{25}$$

  a. $\frac{80}{300}$ **b.** $\frac{4}{15}$ **c.** $\frac{125}{192}$ **d.** $\frac{8}{30}$

11. Subtract. Write the answer in lowest terms. ᶜ

$$7\frac{2}{3} - 3\frac{3}{4}$$

  a. $4\frac{1}{12}$ **b.** $4\frac{1}{7}$ **c.** $3\frac{11}{12}$ **d.** $\frac{11}{12}$

12. Choose the word that best describes the angle shown below. ᵃ

  a. acute   **b.** obtuse

  c. right   **d.** none of these

13. Which fractions are arranged in order from least to greatest? ᵇ

a. $\frac{1}{8}, \frac{1}{6}, \frac{1}{7}, \frac{1}{5}$

b. $\frac{1}{8}, \frac{1}{7}, \frac{1}{6}, \frac{1}{5}$

c. $\frac{1}{5}, \frac{1}{6}, \frac{1}{7}, \frac{1}{8}$

d. $\frac{1}{5}, \frac{1}{7}, \frac{1}{6}, \frac{1}{8}$

14. Subtract. Write the answer in lowest terms. ᵈ

$$\frac{5}{8}$$
$$-\frac{1}{3}$$

a. $\frac{4}{5}$ b. $\frac{5}{24}$ c. $\frac{1}{6}$ d. $\frac{7}{24}$

15. Which fraction is greater than 1? ᵇ

a. $\frac{99}{100}$ b. $\frac{6}{5}$ c. $\frac{9}{9}$ d. $\frac{0}{1}$

16. Subtract. Write the answer in lowest terms. ᵇ

$$7 - 3\frac{1}{5}$$

a. $4\frac{4}{5}$ b. $3\frac{4}{5}$ c. $10\frac{1}{5}$ d. $4\frac{1}{5}$

17. Find the number of square meters in the area of this circular garden. Use $A = \pi \times r \times r$ with $\pi = 3.14$. ᵈ

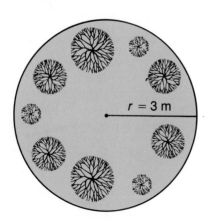

$r = 3$ m

a. 11   b. 21   c. 30   d. 28.26

18. Change $\frac{43}{7}$ to a mixed number. ᵇ

a. $4\frac{3}{7}$ b. $6\frac{1}{7}$ c. $5\frac{6}{7}$ d. $3\frac{4}{7}$

19. Complete. Write your answer as a mixed number. ᵈ

5 gal 2 qt = _?_ gal

a. 5   b. $5\frac{1}{4}$ c. $5\frac{2}{3}$ d. $5\frac{1}{2}$

20. Multiply. Write the answer in lowest terms. ᵈ

$$1\frac{3}{5} \times 5\frac{7}{10}$$

a. $5\frac{21}{50}$ b. $\frac{16}{57}$ c. $\frac{2}{3}$ d. $9\frac{3}{25}$

21. Add. Write the answer in lowest terms. ᵃ

$$3\frac{2}{5}$$
$$+5\frac{1}{4}$$

a. $8\frac{13}{20}$ b. $8\frac{1}{3}$ c. $8\frac{3}{20}$ d. $\frac{3}{20}$

22. Which fractions are equivalent? ᵈ

a. $\frac{1}{3}$ and $\frac{3}{10}$ b. $\frac{3}{5}$ and $\frac{0}{15}$

c. $\frac{3}{4}$ and $\frac{9}{16}$ d. $\frac{2}{3}$ and $\frac{4}{6}$

23. How many cubic centimeters are there in the volume of this paper cup? Use $V = \frac{1}{3} \times \pi \times r \times r \times h$ with $\pi = 3.14$. ᵃ

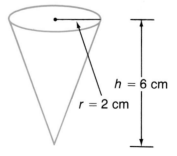

$h = 6$ cm

$r = 2$ cm

a. 25.12   b. 75.36

c. 12.56   d. 8

24. It takes 1 hour 15 minutes for the
  b Speedliner Express Train to go
  from New York to Philadelphia.
  Write the time as a mixed number.

  a. $1\frac{1}{15}$ **b.** $1\frac{1}{4}$ **c.** $1\frac{15}{24}$ **d.** $1\frac{3}{8}$

25. Give the length of the key to the
  a nearest $\frac{1}{4}$-inch.

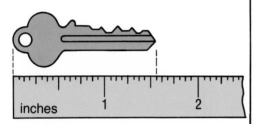

  a. $1\frac{2}{4}$ inches **b.** $1\frac{1}{4}$ inches

  c. $1\frac{3}{4}$ inches **d.** $1\frac{1}{8}$ inches

26. Bill drove to his sister's house at
  a an average rate of 38 miles per

  hour. The trip took $4\frac{1}{2}$ hours. How

  many miles did he travel? Use the
  formula $d = r \times t$.

  a. 171 **b.** $152\frac{1}{2}$ **c.** 342 **d.** $8\frac{4}{9}$

27. Jill bought a coat that was on sale
  a for $\frac{1}{3}$ off the regular price of $79.98.

  What was the discount on the coat?

  a. $26.66 **b.** $106.64

  c. $53.32 **d.** $54.00

28. An interior decorator wishes to
  c cover 10 chairs. Each chair requires

  $2\frac{4}{5}$ yards of material. Estimate the

  number of yards needed.

  a. 25 **b.** 17 **c.** 30 **d.** 18

29. Lyndon bought 2 pounds 10 ounces
  c of salami and 1 pound 12 ounces
  of bologna. How many pounds of
  meat did he buy? Write the answer
  as a mixed number.

  a. $3\frac{3}{8}$ **b.** 5 **c.** $4\frac{3}{8}$ **d.** $4\frac{5}{6}$

30. How many cubic centimeters are
  a there in the volume of a beach ball
  that has a radius of 10.5 centimeters?

  Use $V = \frac{4}{3} \times \pi \times r \times r \times r$ and

  $\pi = 3.14$.

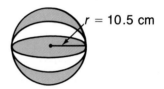

  a. 2726 **b.** 4847 **c.** 462 **d.** 882

31. Use the time card below to find the
  d number of hours worked on
  Monday.

In	Out	In	Out	Total
9:00	12:15	1:00	5:15	?

  a. $8\frac{1}{2}$ **b.** 7 **c.** $7\frac{3}{4}$ **d.** $7\frac{1}{2}$

32. Merle rode her bike $5\frac{3}{4}$ kilometers
  d on Saturday and $3\frac{3}{4}$ kilometers on
  Sunday. Find the total number of
  kilometers she rode.

  a. $8\frac{1}{2}$ **b.** $8\frac{3}{4}$ **c.** $9\frac{1}{4}$ **d.** $9\frac{1}{2}$

33. A cook uses $\frac{1}{6}$ dozen eggs to make
  b an omelet for one person. How
  many people can be served with
  $3\frac{1}{2}$ dozen eggs?

  a. 12 **b.** 21 **c.** 15 **d.** 10

REVIEW OF RELATED SKILLS FOR CHAPTER 12

Add. (Pages 2–3)

1. $15 + 6$ ²¹ **2.** $23 + 14$ ³⁷ **3.** $36 + 25$ ⁶¹ **4.** $17 + 94$ ¹¹¹ **5.** $28 + 16$ ₄₄

Subtract. (Pages 10–11)

6. $15 - 8$ ⁷ **7.** $39 - 16$ ²³ **8.** $42 - 17$ ²⁵ **9.** $51 - 19$ ³² **10.** $27 - 13$ ₁₄

Multiply. (Pages 26–27, 32–33)

11. 30×6 ¹⁸⁰ **12.** 16×8 ¹²⁸ **13.** 217×6 ¹³⁰² **14.** 68×25 ¹⁷⁰⁰ **15.** 241×13 ₃₁₃₃

Divide. (Pages 50–51, 54–55)

16. $84 \div 6$ ¹⁴ **17.** $115 \div 5$ ²³ **18.** $133 \div 7$ ¹⁹ **19.** $54 \div 3$ ¹⁸ **20.** $286 \div 13$ ₂₂

Add. (Pages 94–95)

21. $3.2 + 1.6$ ⁴·⁸ **22.** $8.1 + 5.9$ ¹⁴ **23.** $2.7 + 4.7$ ⁷·⁴ **24.** $6.2 + 9.9$ ¹⁶·¹ **25.** $4.7 + 2.8$ ₇.₅

Subtract. (Pages 94–95)

26. $3.7 - 1.6$ ²·¹ **27.** $4.5 - 2.6$ ¹·⁹ **28.** $2.4 - 0.8$ ¹·⁶ **29.** $3.2 - 1.4$ ¹·⁸ **30.** $40.5 - 2.7$ ₃₇.₈

Multiply. (Pages 98–99)

31. 3×4.1 ¹²·³ **32.** 16.2×9 ¹⁴⁵·⁸ **33.** 0.7×21 ¹⁴·⁷ **34.** 18×0.4 ⁷·² **35.** 3.2×5.5 ₁₇.₆

36. 7.2×4.8 ₃₄.₅₆ **37.** 0.3×6.1 ₁.₈₃ **38.** 2.9×4.5 ₁₃.₀₅ **39.** 6.7×9.3 ₆₂.₃₁ **40.** 8.9×0.9 ₈.₀₁

Divide. (Pages 110–113)

41. $13 \div 2.6$ ⁵ **42.** $29 \div 2.5$ ¹¹·⁶ **43.** $7.2 \div 1.6$ ⁴·⁵ **44.** $4.2 \div 3.5$ ¹·² **45.** $1.08 \div 4.5$ ₀.₂₄

46. $5.27 \div 8.5$ ₀.₆₂ **47.** $10.4 \div 26$ ₀.₄ **48.** $36 \div 3.6$ ¹⁰ **49.** $10.8 \div 1.08$ ¹⁰ **50.** $69.3 \div 33$ ₂.₁

Write each fraction in lowest terms. (Pages 182–183)

51. $\frac{6}{12}$ $\frac{1}{2}$ **52.** $\frac{18}{21}$ $\frac{6}{7}$ **53.** $\frac{24}{30}$ $\frac{4}{5}$ **54.** $\frac{13}{39}$ $\frac{1}{3}$ **55.** $\frac{10}{45}$ $\frac{2}{9}$ **56.** $\frac{70}{90}$ $\frac{7}{9}$ **57.** $\frac{96}{108}$ $\frac{8}{9}$ **58.** $\frac{66}{121}$ $\frac{6}{11}$

Add. (Pages 190–191)

59. $\frac{2}{3} + \frac{1}{6}$ $\frac{5}{6}$ **60.** $\frac{4}{5} + \frac{1}{8}$ $\frac{37}{40}$ **61.** $\frac{1}{2} + \frac{8}{9}$ $1\frac{7}{18}$ **62.** $\frac{7}{8} + \frac{3}{4}$ $1\frac{5}{8}$ **63.** $\frac{6}{7} + \frac{1}{3}$ $1\frac{4}{21}$

64. $\frac{3}{7} + \frac{1}{4}$ $\frac{19}{28}$ **65.** $\frac{5}{12} + \frac{1}{4}$ $\frac{2}{3}$ **66.** $\frac{5}{8} + \frac{1}{7}$ $\frac{43}{56}$ **67.** $\frac{1}{2} + \frac{3}{7}$ $\frac{13}{14}$ **68.** $\frac{5}{6} + \frac{3}{8}$ $1\frac{5}{24}$

Subtract. (Pages 190–191)

69. $\frac{6}{7} - \frac{1}{2}$ $\frac{5}{14}$ **70.** $\frac{4}{5} - \frac{1}{8}$ $\frac{27}{40}$ **71.** $\frac{11}{12} - \frac{5}{6}$ $\frac{1}{12}$ **72.** $\frac{5}{8} - \frac{1}{4}$ $\frac{3}{8}$ **73.** $\frac{2}{3} - \frac{1}{6}$ $\frac{1}{2}$

74. $\frac{8}{9} - \frac{2}{3}$ $\frac{2}{9}$ **75.** $\frac{3}{5} - \frac{1}{2}$ $\frac{1}{10}$ **76.** $\frac{4}{5} - \frac{3}{4}$ $\frac{1}{20}$ **77.** $\frac{6}{7} - \frac{2}{3}$ $\frac{4}{21}$ **78.** $\frac{1}{3} - \frac{1}{4}$ $\frac{1}{12}$

12 EQUATIONS RATIO AND PROPORTION

SKILLS

12-1   Solving Equations:
        Addition/Subtraction
12-2   Solving Equations:
        Multiplication/Division
12-3   More on Solving Equations
12-4   Ratio
12-5   Proportion

APPLICATIONS

Net Pay
Mortgage Loans
Batting Average
Driving Range
Overtime Pay
Renting a Car
Energy Efficiency Ratio
Scale Drawings

CAREERS

Photography
Drafting

12-1 Solving Equations: Addition/Subtraction

See the Teacher's Manual for the objectives.

An **equation** is a sentence that uses "=". Here are some examples of equations.

$$n + 5 = 19 \qquad n - 1.2 = 7.5 \qquad n - \frac{1}{2} = \frac{3}{4}$$

To solve an equation for n, you have to get n **alone on one side of the equation.**

PROCEDURE To solve an addition equation such as $n + 5 = 19$, subtract 5 from each side of the equation.

EXAMPLE 1 Solve and check: **a.** $n + 1.2 = 7.5$ **b.** $n + \frac{1}{2} = \frac{3}{4}$

Solutions: **a.** $n + 1.2 = 7.5$ ◀ Subtract 1.2 from each side. **b.** $n + \frac{1}{2} = \frac{3}{4}$ ◀ Subtract $\frac{1}{2}$ from each side.

$n + 1.2 - 1.2 = 7.5 - 1.2$ $\qquad n + \frac{1}{2} - \frac{1}{2} = \frac{3}{4} - \frac{1}{2}$

$n = \textbf{6.3}$ $\qquad\qquad\qquad n = \frac{1}{4}$

Check: $n + 1.2 = 7.5$ ◀ Replace n with 6.3. **Check:** $n + \frac{1}{2} = \frac{3}{4}$ ◀ Replace n with $\frac{1}{4}$.

$6.3 + 1.2 \overset{?}{=} 7.5$ $\qquad\qquad \frac{1}{4} + \frac{1}{2} \overset{?}{=} \frac{3}{4}$

$7.5 \overset{?}{=} 7.5$ Yes ✔ $\qquad\qquad \frac{3}{4} \overset{?}{=} \frac{3}{4}$ Yes ✔

After completing Example 1, you may wish to have students do some or all of Exercises 1-2, and 5-28.

An equation such as $n - 2.5 = 6.1$ is a subtraction equation.

PROCEDURE To solve a subtraction equation such as $n - 64 = 75$, add 64 to each side of the equation.

EXAMPLE 2 Solve and check: **a.** $n - 64 = 75$ **b.** $n - 9.8 = 12.3$

Solutions: **a.** $n - 64 = 75$ ◀ Add 64 to each side. **b.** $n - 9.8 = 12.3$ ◀ Add 9.8 to each side.

$n - 64 + 64 = 75 + 64$ $\qquad n - 9.8 + 9.8 = 12.3 + 9.8$

$n = \textbf{139}$ $\qquad\qquad\qquad n = \textbf{22.1}$

Check: $n - 64 = 75$ $\qquad\qquad$ **Check:** $n - 9.8 = 12.3$

$139 - 64 \overset{?}{=} 75$ $\qquad\qquad\qquad 22.1 - 9.8 \overset{?}{=} 12.3$

$75 \overset{?}{=} 75$ Yes ✔ $\qquad\qquad\qquad 12.3 \overset{?}{=} 12.3$ Yes ✔

After solving an equation, you should always check the answer in the original equation.

REVIEW OF RELATED SKILLS

Subtract.   (Pages 10–11)

1. $17 - 6$ 11   **2.** $38 - 10$ 28   **3.** $7 - 7$ 0   **4.** $92 - 4$ 88   **5.** $26 - 19$ 7

(Pages 94–95)

6. $9.8 - 4.3$ 5.5 **7.** $1.7 - 0.8$ 0.9 **8.** $61.5 - 18.7$ 42.8 **9.** $40.5 - 23.8$ 16.7 **10.** $15.72 - 1.89$
13.83

(Pages 190–191)

11. $\frac{3}{4} - \frac{1}{2}$ $\frac{1}{4}$ **12.** $\frac{5}{8} - \frac{1}{4}$ $\frac{3}{8}$ **13.** $\frac{5}{6} - \frac{2}{3}$ $\frac{1}{6}$ **14.** $\frac{11}{12} - \frac{5}{8}$ $\frac{7}{24}$ **15.** $\frac{4}{5} - \frac{1}{4}$ $\frac{11}{20}$

Add.   (Pages 2–3)

16. $19 + 5$ 24   **17.** $26 + 10$ 36   **18.** $43 + 9$ 52   **19.** $67 + 8$ 75   **20.** $94 + 7$ 101

(Pages 94–95)

21. $1.3 + 7.6$ 8.9 **22.** $1.5 + 6.2$ 7.7 **23.** $0.9 + 1.3$ 2.2   **24.** $4.7 + 9.8$ 14.5 **25.** $6.8 + 0.9$ 7.7

(Pages 190–191)

26. $\frac{1}{8} + \frac{5}{6}$ $\frac{23}{24}$ **27.** $\frac{1}{3} + \frac{1}{2}$ $\frac{5}{6}$ **28.** $\frac{1}{4} + \frac{2}{3}$ $\frac{11}{12}$ **29.** $\frac{7}{8} + \frac{5}{12}$ $1\frac{7}{24}$ **30.** $\frac{5}{6} + \frac{1}{9}$ $\frac{17}{18}$

EXERCISES —

*For Exercises 1–4, write the number you would add or subtract to each side
of the equation in order to solve for n.*   (Examples 1 and 2, step 1)

1. $n + 2 = 15$ –2   **2.** $n + 17 = 20$ –17   **3.** $n - 16 = 9$ +16   **4.** $n - 17 = 50$
+17

Solve for n. Check each answer.   (Example 1)

5. $n + 8 = 14$ 6   **6.** $n + 5 = 7$ 2   **7.** $n + 4 = 8$ 4   **8.** $n + 2 = 19$ 17
9. $n + 5 = 10$ 5   **10.** $n + 25 = 51$ 26   **11.** $n + 13 = 72$ 59   **12.** $n + 20 = 93$ 73
13. $n + 1.8 = 2.5$ 0.7   **14.** $n + 1.2 = 7.5$ 6.3 **15.** $n + 5.7 = 10.3$ 4.6 **16.** $n + 9.1 = 16.5$ 7.4
17. $n + 3.6 = 4.8$ 1.2   **18.** $n + 1.9 = 3.4$ 1.5 **19.** $n + 4.1 = 13.6$ 9.5 **20.** $n + 7.4 = 10.2$ 2.8
21. $n + \frac{1}{4} = \frac{1}{2}$ $\frac{1}{4}$ **22.** $n + \frac{3}{8} = \frac{7}{8}$ $\frac{1}{2}$ **23.** $n + \frac{1}{5} = \frac{4}{5}$ $\frac{3}{5}$ **24.** $n + \frac{1}{3} = \frac{5}{6}$ $\frac{1}{2}$
25. $n + \frac{1}{8} = \frac{1}{2}$ $\frac{3}{8}$ **26.** $n + \frac{3}{8} = \frac{3}{4}$ $\frac{3}{8}$ **27.** $n + \frac{1}{3} = \frac{3}{4}$ $\frac{5}{12}$ **28.** $n + \frac{1}{6} = \frac{1}{3}$ $\frac{1}{6}$

(Example 2)

29. $n - 9 = 10$ 19   **30.** $n - 14 = 25$ 39   **31.** $n - 6 = 65$ 71   **32.** $n - 13 = 7$ 20
33. $n - 11 = 46$ 57   **34.** $n - 7 = 18$ 25   **35.** $n - 9 = 36$ 45   **36.** $n - 50 = 40$ 90
37. $n - 3.4 = 4.5$ 7.9 **38.** $n - 1.4 = 5.6$ 7   **39.** $n - 2.1 = 1.7$ 3.8   **40.** $n - 3.8 = 4.2$ 8
41. $n - 4.9 = 6.3$ 11.2 **42.** $n - 7.5 = 7.5$ 15 **43.** $n - 0.5 = 1$ 1.5   **44.** $n - 3.6 = 8.5$ 12.1
45. $n - \frac{1}{2} = \frac{1}{2}$ 1   **46.** $n - \frac{1}{3} = \frac{2}{3}$ 1   **47.** $n - \frac{3}{4} = \frac{1}{2}$ $1\frac{1}{4}$ **48.** $n - \frac{1}{6} = \frac{5}{6}$ 1
49. $n - \frac{1}{6} = \frac{1}{2}$ $\frac{2}{3}$ **50.** $n - \frac{3}{4} = \frac{1}{3}$ $1\frac{1}{12}$ **51.** $n - \frac{2}{3} = \frac{1}{2}$ $1\frac{1}{6}$ **52.** $n - \frac{1}{8} = \frac{1}{4}$ $\frac{3}{8}$

Problem Solving and Applications

Net Pay

See the Teacher's Manual for the objectives.
The lesson applies the skills presented in Section 12-1.

Equations can be used to solve many problems that occur in everyday life. Equations used in this way are called **formulas.**

You can use this formula to find net pay or take-home pay. **Net pay** is the amount left when all **deductions** such as taxes have been subtracted. **Gross earnings** is the amount actually earned.

Net Pay + **Total Deductions** = **Gross Earnings,** or

$$n \quad + \quad d \quad = \quad g$$

EXAMPLE Martha earns $500.00 per week (gross earnings). Her total deductions amount to $101.95. Find her net pay.

Solution: $n + d = g$ ◀ **Replace d with 101.95 and g with 500.**

$$n + 101.95 = 500$$

$$n + 101.95 - 101.95 = 500 - 101.95$$

$$n = 398.05 \quad \text{Martha's net pay is } \$398.05. \quad ◀ \text{ The check is left for you.}$$

Exercises

Note that Exercises 1-8 are non-verbal.
In Exercises 11-12, students are asked to solve for d.

For Exercises 1–12, use the formula $n + d = g$.

	Total Deductions	Gross Earnings	Net Pay			Total Deductions	Gross Earnings	Net Pay
1.	$121.69	$560.00	? $438.31		**5.**	$ 9.18	$ 80.00	? $70.82
2.	$108.33	$600.00	? $491.67		**6.**	$49.78	$370.00	? $320.22
3.	$ 55.37	$392.00	? $336.63		**7.**	$58.48	$295.80	? $237.32
4.	$ 59.21	$411.00	? $351.79		**8.**	$88.95	$452.00	? $363.05

9. Last week, Scott's gross earnings were $458.16. Total deductions were $106.05. Find his net pay. $352.11

10. Lisa's gross earnings each week amount to $460.85. Deductions total $125.09. Find her net pay. $335.76

11. The gross pay for one worker for Wilde Elm Lumber Company amounted to $375.00. Net pay for the worker was $306.25. Find the total deductions. $68.75

12. The net pay for an employee of Gibson's Pharmacy amounted to $317.90. The employee's gross earnings were $368.50. Find the total deductions. $50.60

Problem Solving and Applications

Mortgage Loans

When you borrow money from a bank to buy a house, you agree to pay **interest** on the **mortgage loan.** The loan plus the interest is paid over a certain period of time, such as 20 or 30 years. The <u>longer</u> the mortgage runs, the <u>greater</u> is the amount of interest you pay.

You can use this formula to find the total amount repaid on a mortgage loan.

Amount Repaid $-$ Amount Borrowed $=$ Amount of Interest, or

$$r \quad - \quad b \quad = \quad i$$

EXAMPLE   The Dolan family borrowed $45,500 to buy a house. Over a period of 30 years, they paid $110,603.20 in interest on the loan. Find the total amount repaid.

Solution: $r - b = i$ ◀ **Replace b with 45,500 and i with 110,603.20.**

$$r - 45,500 = 110,603.20$$

$$r - 45,500 + 45,500 = 110,603.20 + 45,500$$

$$r = \mathbf{156{,}103.20} \quad \text{The total amount repaid was } \mathbf{\$156{,}103.20.}$$

Exercises   Note that Exercises 1-4 are non-verbal.

For Exercises 1–10, use the formula $r - b = i$.

Amount Borrowed	Amount of Interest	Amount Repaid		Amount Borrowed	Amount of Interest	Amount Repaid
1. $50,000	$107,964.40	? $157,964.40	**5.**	$40,000	$75,560.00	? $115,560.00
2. $50,000	$116,890.00	? $166,890.00	**6.**	$55,500	$101,842.50	? $157,342.50
3. $45,000	$106,308.00	? $151,308.00	**7.**	$60,000	$117,551.50	? $177,551.50
4. $65,000	$96,148.00	? $161,148.00	**8.**	$58,000	$140,986.00	? $198,986.00

9. The Hernandez family borrowed $25,000 to buy a house. Over a period of 25 years, they paid $53,975 in interest on the loan. Find the total amount repaid. $78,975.00

10. The Norton family borrowed $60,000 to buy some property. Over a period of 30 years, they paid $230,469.60 in interest on the mortgage. Find the total amount repaid.
$290,469.60

Application   EQUATIONS/RATIO AND PROPORTION   **251**

12-2 Solving Equations: Multiplication/Division

See the Teacher's Manual for the objectives.

The equation $4n = 68$ is a multiplication equation. ◀ **4n means 4 × n.**

PROCEDURE To solve an multiplication equation such as $4 \times n = 68$, divide each side by 4.

EXAMPLE 1 Solve and check: **a.** $4n = 68$ **b.** $1.6n = 48$

Solutions: **a.** $4n = 68$ ◀ **Divide each side by 4.**

$$\frac{4n}{4} = \frac{68}{4}$$

$$n = 17$$

b. $1.6n = 48$ ◀ **Divide each side by 1.6.**

$$\frac{1.6n}{1.6} = \frac{48}{1.6}$$

$$n = 30$$

Check: $4n = 68$ ◀ **Replace n with 17.**

$4 \times 17 \stackrel{?}{=} 68$

$68 \stackrel{?}{=} 68$ Yes ✔

Check: $1.6n = 48$ ◀ **Replace n with 30.**

$1.6 \times 30 \stackrel{?}{=} 48$

$48 \stackrel{?}{=} 48$ Yes ✔

After completing Example 1, you may wish to have students do some or all of Exercises 1-30.

An expression such as $n \div 20$ can be written as $\frac{n}{20}$.

PROCEDURE To solve a division equation such as $\frac{n}{20} = 15$, multiply each side by 20.

EXAMPLE 2 Solve and check: **a.** $\frac{n}{20} = 15$ **b.** $\frac{n}{15} = 7.2$

Solutions: **a.** $\frac{n}{20} = 15$ ◀ **Multiply each side by 20.**

$$\frac{n}{20} \times 20 = 15 \times 20$$

$$n = 300$$

b. $\frac{n}{15} = 7.2$ ◀ **Multiply each side by 15.**

$$\frac{n}{15} \times 15 = 7.2 \times 15$$

$$n = 108$$

Check: $\frac{n}{20} = 15$ ◀ **Replace n with 300.**

$\frac{300}{20} \stackrel{?}{=} 15$

$15 \stackrel{?}{=} 15$ Yes ✔

Check: $\frac{n}{15} = 7.2$ ◀ **Replace n with 108.**

$\frac{108}{15} \stackrel{?}{=} 7.2$

$7.2 \stackrel{?}{=} 7.2$ Yes ✔

REVIEW OF RELATED SKILLS
You may wish to use these exercises before teaching the lesson.

Divide.   (Pages 50–51, 112–113)

1. $9 \div 9$ 1   **2.** $56 \div 4$ 14   **3.** $91 \div 7$ 13   **4.** $116 \div 4$ 29   **5.** $132 \div 6$ 22

6. $16 \div 3.2$ 5   **7.** $24 \div 1.5$ 16   **8.** $27 \div 2.7$ 10   **9.** $4.2 \div 2.8$ 1.5   **10.** $1.5 \div 0.75$ 2

Multiply.   (Pages 26–27, 32–33)

11. 20×9 180   **12.** 15×8 120   **13.** 11×12 132   **14.** 125×13 1625   **15.** 90×100 9000

(Pages 98–99)

16. 6×7.5 45   **17.** 10.9×10 109   **18.** 0.4×36 14.4   **19.** 5.8×1.4 8.12   **20.** 5.4×3.6 19.44

EXERCISES

See the suggested assignment guide in the Teacher's Manual.

In Exercises 1–5, write the number by which you would divide each side of the equation in order to solve for n.   (Example 1, step 1)

1. $6n = 30$ 6   **2.** $9n = 45$ 9   **3.** $1.2n = 72$ 1.2   **4.** $0.3n = 2.7$ 0.3   **5.** $4.9n = 4.9$
4.9

Solve and check.   (Example 1)

6. $5n = 45$ 9   **7.** $4n = 16$ 4   **8.** $7n = 105$ 15   **9.** $20n = 1800$ 90   **10.** $3n = 48$ 16

11. $4n = 116$ 29   **12.** $7n = 91$ 13   **13.** $9n = 729$ 81   **14.** $6n = 132$ 22   **15.** $8n = 96$ 12

16. $3.2n = 16$ 5   **17.** $1.8n = 9$ 5   **18.** $2.4n = 36$ 15   **19.** $1.5n = 24$ 16   **20.** $4.5n = 27$ 6

21. $4.2n = 63$ 15   **22.** $2.5n = 50$ 20   **23.** $6.4n = 80$ 12.5   **24.** $7.2n = 27$ 3.75   **25.** $0.3n = 42$
140

26. $2.8n = 4.2$ 1.5   **27.** $0.4n = 3.2$ 8   **28.** $5.6n = 8.4$ 1.5   **29.** $2.5n = 6.25$ 2.5   **30.** $0.75n = 15$
20

In Exercises 31–35, write the number by which you would multiply each side of the equation in order to solve for n.   (Example 2, step 1)

31. $\frac{n}{6} = 14$ 6   **32.** $\frac{n}{9} = 13$ 9   **33.** $\frac{n}{15} = 18$ 15   **34.** $\frac{n}{13} = 4.1$ 13   **35.** $\frac{n}{3} = 9.1$ 3

Solve and check.   (Example 2)

36. $\frac{n}{5} = 6$ 30   **37.** $\frac{n}{8} = 2$ 16   **38.** $\frac{n}{20} = 9$ 180   **39.** $\frac{n}{4} = 36$ 144   **40.** $\frac{n}{10} = 3$ 30

41. $\frac{n}{9} = 8$ 72   **42.** $\frac{n}{6} = 12$ 72   **43.** $\frac{n}{5} = 11$ 55   **44.** $\frac{n}{7} = 5$ 35   **45.** $\frac{n}{15} = 4$ 60

46. $\frac{n}{3} = 7$ 21   **47.** $\frac{n}{9} = 10$ 90   **48.** $\frac{n}{7} = 8$ 56   **49.** $\frac{n}{2} = 3$ 6   **50.** $\frac{n}{11} = 6$ 66

51. $\frac{n}{5} = 1.1$ 5.5   **52.** $\frac{n}{7} = 4.1$ 28.7   **53.** $\frac{n}{6} = 7.5$ 45   **54.** $\frac{n}{4} = 0.4$ 1.6   **55.** $\frac{n}{10} = 10.9$
109

56. $\frac{n}{3} = 13.5$ 40.5   **57.** $\frac{n}{11} = 18.3$ 201.3   **58.** $\frac{n}{2} = 1.06$ 2.12   **59.** $\frac{n}{8} = 1.1$ 8.8   **60.** $\frac{n}{12} = 0.6$ 7.2

61. $\frac{n}{9} = 5.7$ 51.3   **62.** $\frac{n}{36} = 2.2$ 79.2   **63.** $\frac{n}{81} = 0.9$ 72.9   **64.** $\frac{n}{58} = 1.4$ 81.2   **65.** $\frac{n}{72} = 3.1$
223.2

Mixed Practice   The Mixed Practice contains exercises that relate to both Examples 1 and 2.

66. $\frac{n}{8} = 3$ 24   **67.** $\frac{n}{11} = 15$ 165   **68.** $\frac{n}{9} = 4$ 36   **69.** $\frac{n}{6} = 8.3$ 49.8   **70.** $\frac{n}{2} = 1.6$ 3.2

71. $5n = 60$ 12   **72.** $9n = 45$ 5   **73.** $4n = 32$ 8   **74.** $20n = 180$ 9   **75.** $7n = 140$ 20

76. $2.6n = 13$ 5   **77.** $7.2n = 36$ 5   **78.** $3.5n = 21$ 6   **79.** $3.6n = 5.4$ 1.5   **80.** $3.8n = 26.6$ 7

81. $\frac{n}{15} = 2.5$ 37.5   **82.** $\frac{n}{10} = 12$ 120   **83.** $\frac{n}{16} = 4$ 64   **84.** $\frac{n}{12} = 1.2$ 14.4   **85.** $\frac{n}{18} = 7.4$ 133.2

86. $\frac{n}{12} = 0.1$ 1.2   **87.** $\frac{n}{5} = 0.6$ 3   **88.** $\frac{n}{13} = 0.5$ 6.5   **89.** $\frac{n}{100} = 1.6$ 160   **90.** $\frac{n}{23} = 0.1$ 2.3

EQUATIONS/RATIO AND PROPORTION   **253**

Problem Solving and Applications

Batting Average

See the Teacher's Manual for the objectives.
This lesson applies the skills presented in Section 12-2.

When you know a baseball player's batting average and the
number of times at bat, you can find the number of hits.

$$\underbrace{\text{Number of Hits}}_{h} \div \underbrace{\text{Number of times at Bat}}_{t} = \underbrace{\text{Batting Average}}_{a}$$

EXAMPLE Anna's batting average is .280. She has
been at bat 100 times. Find the number of
hits.

Solution: $h \div t = a$ ◀ **Replace t with 100 and a with .280.**

$h \div 100 = .280,$ or

$\dfrac{h}{100} = .280$

$\dfrac{h}{100} \times 100 = .280 \times 100$

$h = 28$ Anna has **28 hits.**

The check is left for you.

Exercises

Note that Exercises 1–8 non-verbal.

For Exercises 1–10, use the formula $\dfrac{h}{t} = a$.

	Times at Bat	Batting Average	Number of Hits
1.	250	.200	? 50
2.	100	.300	? 30
3.	150	.260	? 39
4.	225	.280	? 63

	Times at Bat	Batting Average	Number of Hits
5.	250	.380	? 95
6.	340	.350	? 119
7.	150	.240	? 36
8.	200	.285	? 57

9. Diana Lopez has a batting average
of .250. She has been at bat 104
times. Find her number of hits.
26

10. Nick DeMarco has been at bat 124
times. He has a batting average of
.250. Find his number of hits. 31

Application

Problem Solving and Applica

Driving Range

The **driving range** of a car is how far it can
travel on a full tank of fuel (tank capacity).
When you know the driving range and tank
capacity of a car, you can use this formula to
find how many miles it can travel on one gallon
of gasoline.

Tank Capacity × Miles Per Gallon = Driving Range, or

$$c \times m = r$$

EXAMPLE   The tank capacity of a car is 11.9 gallons. The car travels 297.5
miles on this amount of fuel. How many miles can it travel on one
gallon?

Solution: $c \times m = r$ ◀ **Replace c with 11.9 and r with 297.5.**

$11.9 \times m = 297.5$, or

$11.9m = 297.5$

$\dfrac{11.9m}{11.9} = \dfrac{297.5}{11.9}$

$m = 25$

The car can travel **25 miles** on 1 gallon of fuel.

Exercises

For Exercises 1–8, use the formula $c \times m = r$.

	Tank Capacity	Driving Range	Miles per Gallon
1.	10.6 gal	296.8	? 28
2.	15.8 gal	284.4	? 18
3.	12.5 gal	262.5	? 21
4.	10.6 gal	296.8	? 28
5.	16.1 gal	289.8	? 18
6.	14.4 gal	273.6	? 19
7.	14.4 gal	338.4	? 23.5
8.	11.6 gal	275.5	? 23.75

**Keeping the engine tuned will
increase the driving range.**

Note: The objective of this lesson is not only to teach students how to solve equations, but also to use solving equations as a vehicle for reviewing addition, subtraction, multiplication, and division of whole numbers, decimals, and fractions.

12-3 More on Solving Equations

See the Teacher's Manual for the objectives.

Sometimes you use more than one operation $(+, -, \times, \div)$ to solve an equation.

PROCEDURE To solve an equation:

1. Add or subtract the same number from each side of the equation when necessary.

2. Multiply or divide each side of the equation by the same number (except zero) when necessary.

EXAMPLE 1 Solve and check: $14n + 0.2 = 3$

Solution: $14n + 0.2 = 3$ ◀ **Subtract 0.2 from each side.**

1. $14n + 0.2 - 0.2 = 3 - 0.2$

   $14n = 2.8$ ◀ **Divide each side by 14.**

2. $\dfrac{14n}{14} = \dfrac{2.8}{14}$

   $n = 0.2$

Check: $14n + 0.2 = 3$ ◀ **Replace n with 0.2.**

$14 \times 0.2 + 0.2 \stackrel{?}{=} 3$

$2.8 + 0.2 \stackrel{?}{=} 3$

$3 \stackrel{?}{=} 3$ Yes ✔

After completing Example 1, you may wish to have students do some or all of Exercises 1-6, 9, and 10-27.

When solving equations, it is usually easier to add or subtract first.

EXAMPLE 2 Solve and check: $\dfrac{n}{8} - \dfrac{1}{4} = \dfrac{1}{2}$

Solution: $\dfrac{n}{8} - \dfrac{1}{4} = \dfrac{1}{2}$ ◀ **Add $\frac{1}{4}$ to each side.**

1. $\dfrac{n}{8} - \dfrac{1}{4} + \dfrac{1}{4} = \dfrac{1}{2} + \dfrac{1}{4}$

   $\dfrac{n}{8} = \dfrac{3}{4}$ ◀ **Multiply each side by 8.**

2. $\dfrac{n}{8} \times 8 = \dfrac{3}{4} \times 8$ ◀ $\dfrac{3}{4} \times \dfrac{\overset{2}{8}}{\underset{1}{1}} = 6$

   $n = 6$ The check is left for you.

REVIEW OF RELATED SKILLS
You may wish to use these exercises before teaching the lesson.

Solve and check.   (Pages 248–249)   111

1. $n + 1 = 12$ 11   **2.** $n + 40 = 55$ 15   **3.** $n - 18 = 39$ 57   **4.** $n - 40 = 71$

5. $n + 4 = 13$ 9   **6.** $n - 3 = 6$ 9   **7.** $n - 5 = 11$ 16   **8.** $n + 2 = 108$

106

(Pages 252–253)

9. $12n = 84$ $\quad 7$ **10.** $7n = 63$ $\quad 9$ **11.** $\dfrac{n}{9} = 8$ $\quad 72$ **12.** $\dfrac{n}{7} = 3$ $\quad 21$ **13.** $\dfrac{n}{51} = 2$ $\quad 102$

14. $5n = 215$ $\quad 43$ **15.** $\dfrac{n}{5} = 48$ $\quad 240$ **16.** $\dfrac{n}{6} = 21$ $\quad 126$ **17.** $3n = 186$ $\quad 62$ **18.** $\dfrac{n}{85} = 4$ $\quad 340$

EXERCISES
See the suggested assignment guide in the Teacher's Manual.

In Exercises 1–9, write the first step you would use to solve the equation. Write "Subtract 5 from each side," "Add 3 to each side." and so on.
(Examples 1 and 2, step 1)

Subtract 7 from each side
1. $4n + 7 = 15$

Subtract 18 from each side.
2. $3n + 18 = 21$

Add 2 to each side
3. $5n - 2 = 38$

4. $31n - 29 = 23$ Add 29 to each side **5.** $12n - 0.4 = 2$ Add 0.4 to each side **6.** $27n - 1.8 = 0.36$
Add 1.8 to each side

7. $\dfrac{n}{6} + \dfrac{1}{3} = \dfrac{5}{6}$ Subtract $\dfrac{1}{3}$ from each side **8.** $\dfrac{n}{4} - \dfrac{1}{2} = \dfrac{1}{4}$ Add $\dfrac{1}{2}$ to each side **9.** $31n + 2.1 = 23.8$
Subtract 2.1 from each side

Solve and check. (Example 1)

10. $21n + 6 = 48$ $\quad 2$ **11.** $8n + 25 = 57$ $\quad 4$ **12.** $6n - 3 = 15$ $\quad 3$

13. $8n - 7 = 41$ $\quad 6$ **14.** $12n - 6 = 30$ $\quad 3$ **15.** $4n - 6 = 34$ $\quad 10$

16. $3n + 1 = 19$ $\quad 6$ **17.** $7n + 2 = 51$ $\quad 7$ **18.** $4n + 4 = 40$ $\quad 9$

19. $10n + 3 = 93$ $\quad 9$ **20.** $2n - 1 = 13$ $\quad 7$ **21.** $8n - 12 = 121$

22. $7n + 0.5 = 4$ $\quad 0.5$ **23.** $5n + 0.1 = 2.1$ $\quad 0.4$ **24.** $14n - 1.2 = 1.6$ $\,0.2$

25. $20n - 2.5 = 2.5$ $\quad 0.25$ **26.** $6n + 0.8 = 3.2$ $\quad 0.4$ **27.** $6n + 2 = 9.56$ $\,1.26$

21. 16.625

(Example 2)

28. $\dfrac{n}{6} - 19 = 3$ $\quad 132$ **29.** $\dfrac{n}{5} - 8 = 42$ $\quad 250$ **30.** $\dfrac{n}{3} + 6 = 9$ $\quad 9$ **31.** $\dfrac{n}{9} + 2 = 5$ $\,27$

32. $\dfrac{n}{8} + 1 = 15$ $\quad 112$ **33.** $\dfrac{n}{6} + 1 = 17$ $\quad 96$ **34.** $\dfrac{n}{5} - 4 = 4$ $\quad 40$ **35.** $\dfrac{n}{9} - 1 = 4$ $\,45$

36. $\dfrac{n}{30} + 62 = 65$ $\quad 90$ **37.** $\dfrac{n}{28} + 16 = 25$ $\quad 252$ **38.** $\dfrac{n}{7} - 6 = 21$ $\quad 189$ **39.** $\dfrac{n}{2} - 7 = 12$ $\,38$

40. $\dfrac{n}{9} - 1 = 4$ $\quad 45$ **41.** $\dfrac{n}{6} - 3 = 8$ $\quad 66$ **42.** $\dfrac{n}{4} + 9 = 10$ $\quad 4$ **43.** $\dfrac{n}{6} + 8 = 23$ $\,90$

Mixed Practice The Mixed Practice contains exercises that relate to both Examples 1 and 2.

44. $2n - 27 = 9$ $\quad 18$ **45.** $4n + 13 = 77$ $\quad 16$ **46.** $4n - 2.2 = 1.8$ $\quad 1$

47. $9n + 16 = 81.7$ $\quad 7.3$ **48.** $3n - 1.4 = 8.2$ $\quad 3.2$ **49.** $12n - 1.7 = 13.9$ $\,1.3$

50. $\dfrac{n}{5} + 1 = 3$ $\quad 10$ **51.** $\dfrac{n}{4} - 6 = 1$ $\quad 28$ **52.** $\dfrac{3n}{2} - 5 = 10$ $\quad 10$

53. $\dfrac{2n}{3} + 7 = 11$ $\quad 6$ **54.** $\dfrac{6n}{5} + 8 = 20$ $\quad 10$ **55.** $\dfrac{5n}{4} - 3 = 37$ $\quad 32$

56. $16n + 12 = 20$ $\quad 0.5$ **57.** $4n - 7 = 49$ $\quad 14$ **58.** $0.5n + 1 = 26$ $\quad 50$

59. $0.4n - 1 = 15$ $\quad 40$ **60.** $2n + 1.6 = 9.8$ $\quad 4.1$ **61.** $3n - 1.1 = 4.3$ $\quad 1.8$

62. $\dfrac{n}{5} + 3 = 12$ $\quad 45$ **63.** $\dfrac{n}{7} - 8 = 15$ $\quad 161$ **64.** $\dfrac{n}{4} - 5 = 11$ $\quad 64$

Problem Solving and Applications

Overtime Pay

See the Teacher's Manual for the objectives.
This lesson applies the skills presented in Section 12-3.

Some employees are paid at a regular rate for the first 40 hours worked each week. They receive **time and a half** for all hours worked over 40.

$$\underbrace{\begin{array}{c}\text{Earnings for}\\\text{40 hours}\end{array}}_{40r} + \underbrace{\begin{array}{c}\text{Earnings for}\\\text{Overtime Hours}\end{array}}_{o} = \underbrace{\begin{array}{c}\text{Gross}\\\text{Earnings}\end{array}}_{g}$$

r = rate per hour
o = overtime pay
g = gross earnings

EXAMPLE Last week, Fred's gross earnings were $412.50. Overtime pay amounted to $112.50. What is Fred's rate of pay per hour?

Solution:

$40r + o = g$ ◀ Replace o with $112.50 and g with 412.50.

$40r + 112.50 = 412.50$

$40r + 112.50 - 112.50 = 412.50 - 112.50$

$40r = 300$

$\dfrac{40r}{40} = \dfrac{300}{40}$

$r = 7.50$

MONTH ENDING 3- 31 -   19 81

	MORNING		NOON		NOON		NIGHT		EXTRA		EXTRA
	IN	OUT	IN	OUT	IN	OUT					

Fred's rate of pay is **$7.50** per hour. ◀ The check is left for you.

Exercises

Note that Exercises 1-8 are non-verbal.

For Exercises 1–10, use the formula $40r + o = g$.

	Overtime Pay	Gross Earnings	Rate Per Hour			Overtime Pay	Gross Earnings	Rate Per Hour
1.	$ 93.00	$341.00	? $6.20		5.	$112.50	$352.50	? $6.00
2.	$ 92.25	$256.25	? $4.10		6.	$ 52.50	$332.50	? $7.00
3.	$ 66.00	$268.00	? $5.05		7.	$ 76.50	$416.50	? $8.50
4.	$104.00	$336.40	? $5.81		8.	$131.25	$381.25	? $6.25

9. Jill's gross earnings last week were $182.45. She received $18.45 in overtime pay. What was her rate of pay per hour? $4.10

10. Gregory earned $25.50 in overtime pay one week. His gross earnings for the week were $175.50. What was his rate of pay per hour? $3.75

Application

Problem Solving and Applications

Renting a Car

See the Teacher's Manual for the objectives.
This lesson applies the skills presented in Section 12-3.

When you rent a car, you usually have to pay a charge that depends on the number of days you rent the car and on the number of miles you drive the car.

The formula below shows how the total charges, C, for renting a car for a weekend from the Fine-Line Rental Company and the number of miles, driven, n, are related.

Fine-Line Rentals

$52.50 for 3-Day Weekend
(includes insurance)

Plus 22¢ per mile

$$52.50 + 0.22n = C$$

EXAMPLE Kerry De Angelo rented a car for a weekend from Fine-Line Rentals. The total charges were $272.50. How many miles did she drive?

Solution: Replace C with 272.50.

$$52.50 + 0.22n = C$$

$$52.50 + 0.22n = 272.50$$

$$52.50 - 52.50 + 0.22n = 272.50 - 52.50$$

$$0.22n = 220$$

$$\frac{0.22n}{0.22} = \frac{220}{0.22n}$$

$$n = 1000 \qquad \text{Kerry drove } \textbf{1000 miles.}$$

Exercises

For Exercises 1–8, use the formula $52.50 + 0.22n = C$.

	Total Cost	Miles Driven			Total Cost	Miles Driven
1.	$162.50	? 500		**5.**	$231.80	? 815
2.	$223.00	? 775		**6.**	$441.02	? 1766
3.	$261.50	? 950		**7.**	$329.04	? 1257
4.	$382.50	? 1500		**8.**	$495.80	? 2015

12-4 Ratio   See the Teacher's Manual for the objectives.

A **ratio** is a way to compare numbers. You can write a ratio as a fraction.

TABLE	Ratio	Written as a Fraction
	5 to 11	$\frac{5}{11}$
	9 to 30	$\frac{9}{30}$, or $\frac{3}{10}$ ◀ **Lowest terms**
	80 to 25	$\frac{80}{25}$, or $\frac{16}{5}$

Ratios such as $\frac{9}{30}$ and $\frac{3}{10}$ are **equivalent ratios**. Equivalent ratios are equal.

$$\frac{3}{6} = \frac{1}{2} \quad ◀ \textit{Equivalent ratios}$$

PROCEDURE   To determine whether two ratios are equivalent:

1. Find the cross–product.

2. Compare the cross–products. Equivalent ratios have equal cross–products.

EXAMPLE   Determine whether the ratios are equivalent.

a. $\frac{2}{5}$ and $\frac{14}{35}$ b. $\frac{3}{8}$ and $\frac{9}{16}$

Solutions: a. $\frac{2}{5} \overset{?}{\diagup\!\!\!\diagdown} \frac{14}{35}$ ◀ **The loop shows the cross–product.**

b. $\frac{3}{8} \overset{?}{\diagup\!\!\!\diagdown} \frac{9}{16}$

$2 \times 35 \overset{?}{=} 5 \times 14$ $3 \times 16 \overset{?}{=} 8 \times 9$

$70 \overset{?}{=} 70$ Yes ✔ $48 \overset{?}{=} 72$ No

The cross–products are equal.   The cross–products are not equal.
So the ratios are **equivalent**.   So the ratios are **not equivalent**.

REVIEW OF RELATED SKILLS   You may wish to use the exercises before teaching the lesson.

Write each fraction in lowest terms.   (Pages 182–183) $\frac{2}{11}$

1. $\frac{5}{10}$ $\frac{1}{2}$ 2. $\frac{6}{18}$ $\frac{1}{3}$ 3. $\frac{14}{21}$ $\frac{2}{3}$ 4. $\frac{24}{36}$ $\frac{2}{3}$ 5. $\frac{7}{28}$ $\frac{1}{4}$ 6. $\frac{19}{57}$ $\frac{1}{3}$ 7. $\frac{32}{64}$ $\frac{1}{2}$ 8. $\frac{10}{55}$

9. $\frac{27}{45}$ $\frac{3}{5}$ 10. $\frac{16}{24}$ $\frac{2}{3}$ 11. $\frac{9}{81}$ $\frac{1}{9}$ 12. $\frac{26}{32}$ $\frac{13}{16}$ 13. $\frac{70}{80}$ $\frac{7}{8}$ 14. $\frac{15}{225}$ $\frac{1}{15}$ 15. $\frac{21}{49}$ $\frac{3}{7}$ 16. $\frac{121}{143}$

$\frac{11}{13}$

Multiply.   (Pages 26–27, 32–33)

17. 9×18 162   18. 35×2 70   19. 72×5 360   20. 36×3 108   21. 15×4 60

22. 13×8 104   23. 12×15 180   24. 18×10 180   25. 180×6 1080   26. 251×9

2259

Write a fraction in lowest terms for each ratio. (Table)

1. 3 to 7 $\frac{3}{7}$ **2.** 4 to 20 $\frac{1}{5}$ **3.** 14 to 42 $\frac{1}{3}$ **4.** 16 to 25 $\frac{16}{25}$

5. 7 to 21 $\frac{1}{3}$ **6.** 30 to 80 $\frac{3}{8}$ **7.** 5 to 25 $\frac{1}{5}$ **8.** 15 to 60 $\frac{1}{4}$

9. 16 to 64 $\frac{1}{4}$ **10.** 5 to 9 $\frac{5}{9}$ **11.** 10 to 100 $\frac{1}{10}$ **12.** 4 to 11 $\frac{4}{11}$

13. 36 to 20 $\frac{9}{5}$ **14.** 44 to 11 $\frac{4}{1}$ **15.** 2 to 50 $\frac{1}{25}$ **16.** 17 to 51 $\frac{1}{3}$

17. 9 to 45 $\frac{1}{5}$ **18.** 25 to 75 $\frac{1}{3}$ **19.** 8 to 48 $\frac{1}{6}$ **20.** 2 to 12 $\frac{1}{6}$

21. 8 to 3 $\frac{8}{3}$ **22.** 16 to 5 $\frac{16}{5}$ **23.** 6 to 54 $\frac{1}{9}$ **24.** 7 to 84 $\frac{1}{12}$

Determine whether the ratios are equivalent. Answer <u>Yes</u> or <u>No</u>. (Example)

25. $\frac{3}{4}$ and $\frac{15}{22}$ No   **26.** $\frac{1}{2}$ and $\frac{6}{12}$ Yes   **27.** $\frac{4}{5}$ and $\frac{18}{25}$ No   **28.** $\frac{2}{3}$ and $\frac{14}{21}$ Yes

29. $\frac{2}{7}$ and $\frac{21}{63}$ No   **30.** $\frac{5}{8}$ and $\frac{30}{32}$ No   **31.** $\frac{1}{6}$ and $\frac{10}{72}$ No   **32.** $\frac{1}{4}$ and $\frac{25}{100}$ Yes

33. $\frac{2}{5}$ and $\frac{20}{45}$ No   **34.** $\frac{3}{10}$ and $\frac{22}{80}$ No   **35.** $\frac{5}{7}$ and $\frac{25}{35}$ Yes   **36.** $\frac{2}{15}$ and $\frac{10}{75}$ Yes

37. $\frac{11}{6}$ and $\frac{66}{36}$ Yes   **38.** $\frac{12}{5}$ and $\frac{60}{25}$ Yes   **39.** $\frac{3}{7}$ and $\frac{20}{49}$ No   **40.** $\frac{7}{20}$ and $\frac{40}{120}$ No

41. $\frac{9}{7}$ and $\frac{36}{28}$ Yes   **42.** $\frac{8}{3}$ and $\frac{18}{48}$ No   **43.** $\frac{1}{5}$ and $\frac{4}{20}$ Yes   **44.** $\frac{3}{5}$ and $\frac{21}{35}$ Yes

45. $\frac{4}{1}$ and $\frac{28}{7}$ Yes   **46.** $\frac{12}{1}$ and $\frac{132}{13}$ No   **47.** $\frac{3}{16}$ and $\frac{9}{48}$ Yes   **48.** $\frac{3}{2}$ and $\frac{27}{18}$ Yes

49. $\frac{7}{10}$ and $\frac{54}{80}$ No   **50.** $\frac{7}{12}$ and $\frac{36}{60}$ No   **51.** $\frac{6}{5}$ and $\frac{18}{12}$ No   **52.** $\frac{1}{3}$ and $\frac{16}{51}$ No

53. $\frac{1}{8}$ and $\frac{21}{168}$ Yes   **54.** $\frac{9}{8}$ and $\frac{36}{32}$ Yes   **55.** $\frac{8}{12}$ and $\frac{10}{15}$ Yes   **56.** $\frac{15}{25}$ and $\frac{3}{5}$ Yes

57. $\frac{4}{6}$ and $\frac{20}{24}$ No   **58.** $\frac{5}{8}$ and $\frac{15}{25}$ No   **59.** $\frac{39}{26}$ and $\frac{3}{2}$ Yes   **60.** $\frac{18}{3}$ and $\frac{12}{2}$ Yes

APPLICATIONS: Using Ratios Most students should be able to do these word problems which apply the concept of ratio.

For Exercises 61–64, write your answers in lowest terms.

61. Kiyo won 24 out of 30 games that he pitched. What is the ratio of games won to games played? 4 to 5 or $\frac{4}{5}$

62. To make orange juice, Laura mixed 3 cans of water with 1 can of orange juice concentrate. What is the ratio of water to concentrate? 3 to 1 or $\frac{3}{1}$

63. A recipe for cream sauce calls for one cup of flour for every two cups of milk. What is the ratio of flour to milk? 1 to 2 or $\frac{1}{2}$

64. For every 10 columns of news stories in a newspaper, 4 columns are advertisements. What is the ratio of advertisements to news stories? 2 to 5 or $\frac{2}{5}$

Problem Solving and Applications

Energy Efficiency Ratio

See the Teacher's Manual for the objectives.
This lesson applies the skills presented in Section 12-4.

The **energy efficiency ratio** (abbreviated: EER) of an air conditioner is a number, usually between 7 and 12, that shows how efficiently it uses electricity. The higher the air conditioner's EER, the more efficient and economical it is.

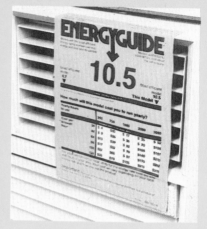

You can use a formula to find the EER of an air conditioner. In the formula, the number of **British thermal units** (abbreviated: Btu) is the amount of power needed for cooling. The number of **watts** is the amount of electricity used.

$$EER = \frac{Number\ of\ Btu}{Number\ of\ watts}$$

EXAMPLE   Find the EER of a 5000 Btu–unit that uses 600 watts.

Solution: $EER = \frac{Number\ of\ Btu}{Number\ of\ watts}$

$EER = \frac{5000}{600}$

$EER = 8.3$ The energy efficiency ratio is **8.3**.

In Exercises 1–3, find the EER of each air conditioner.

1. A 12,000 Btu–unit that uses 2000 watts   6
2. A 12,000 Btu–unit that uses 1500 watts   8
3. A 15,000 Btu–unit that uses 2000 watts   7.5
4. Which is more efficient, the air conditioner in Exercise 1 or the air conditioner in Exercise 2?   Exercise 2
5. Which is more efficient, the air conditioner in Exercise 3 or the air conditioner in Exercise 2?   Exercise 2
6. Which is more efficient, a 14,000 Btu–unit that uses 2000 watts or a 8000 Btu–unit that uses 1000 watts?   The 8000 Btu-unit
7. Which is more efficient, a 6000 Btu–unit that uses 500 watts or a 12,000 Btu–unit that uses 1600 watts?   The 6000 Btu-unit

Application

PHOTOGRAPHY

Career Lessons are optional.
This lesson applies the skills presented in Section 12-4.

In order to obtain the best results, a **photographer** controls the amount of light that hits the film.

Light enters a camera through a small hole called an **aperture.** The size of the aperture is related to numbers on a ring that the photographer turns to change the size. The numbers are called "**f stops.**" The largest f stop has the number 2. Each f stop after f 2 allows $\frac{1}{2}$ **as much light** into the camera as the previous f stop.

Comparative Sizes of f Stops

2   2.8

4   5.6   8   11   16 22

EXAMPLE

Write the ratio of f 8 to f 2.8.

Solution:

1 Count the number of f stops <u>from</u> f 8 <u>to</u> f 2.8.

f 5.6	f 4	f 2.8
1	2	3 ⟶

There are three stops.

2 Since there are three f stops, multiply $\frac{1}{2}$ by itself three times.

$$\frac{1}{2} \times \frac{1}{2} \times \frac{1}{2} = \frac{1}{8}$$

Thus, the ratio of f 8 to f 2.8 is $\frac{1}{8}$.

EXERCISES

Write the ratio of each pair of apertures.

1. f 11 to f 8 $\frac{1}{2}$
2. f 22 to f 11 $\frac{1}{4}$
3. f 22 to f 8 $\frac{1}{8}$
4. f 4 to f 2 $\frac{1}{4}$
5. f 5.6 to f 2.8 $\frac{1}{4}$
6. f 16 to f 2.8 $\frac{1}{32}$
7. f 16 to f 5.6 $\frac{1}{8}$
8. f 11 to f 4 $\frac{1}{8}$
9. f 22 to f 5.6 $\frac{1}{16}$
10. f 16 to f 2 $\frac{1}{64}$

12-5 Proportion

A **proportion** is an equation that shows equivalent ratios. Here are some examples.

$$\frac{n}{16} = \frac{15}{20} \qquad\qquad \frac{9}{5} = \frac{108}{n}$$

PROCEDURE To solve a proportion for n:

□1 Write the cross–products.

□2 Solve the equation for n.

EXAMPLE Solve the proportions shown above for n.

Solutions: **a.** $\dfrac{n}{16} = \dfrac{15}{20}$

□1 $n \times 20 = 16 \times 15$, or

$20n = 240$

□2 $\dfrac{20n}{20} = \dfrac{240}{20}$

$n = 12$

Check: $\dfrac{n}{16} = \dfrac{15}{20}$ ◀ **Replace n with 12.**

$\dfrac{12}{16} \overset{?}{=} \dfrac{15}{20}$

$12 \times 20 \overset{?}{=} 16 \times 15$

$240 \overset{?}{=} 240$ Yes ✔

b. $\dfrac{9}{5} = \dfrac{108}{n}$

□1 $9 \times n = 5 \times 108$, or

$9n = 540$

□2 $\dfrac{9n}{9} = \dfrac{540}{9}$

$n = 60$

Check: $\dfrac{9}{5} = \dfrac{108}{n}$ ◀ **Replace n with 60.**

$\dfrac{9}{5} \overset{?}{=} \dfrac{108}{60}$

$9 \times 60 \overset{?}{=} 5 \times 108$

$540 \overset{?}{=} 540$ Yes ✔

REVIEW OF RELATED SKILLS

Multiply. (Pages 26–27, 32–33)

1. 9×51 459   **2.** 6×48 288   **3.** 5×62 310   **4.** 4×85 340   **5.** 12×13 156

6. 60×10 600   **7.** 25×15 375   **8.** 14×26 364   **9.** 73×41 2993   **10.** 68×29 1972

Divide. (Pages 50–51, 54–55)

11. $35 \div 5$ 7   **12.** $54 \div 3$ 18   **13.** $64 \div 2$ 32   **14.** $215 \div 5$ 43   **15.** $456 \div 8$ 57

16. $504 \div 6$ 84   **17.** $69 \div 23$ 3   **18.** $68 \div 34$ 2   **19.** $475 \div 19$ 25   **20.** $287 \div 41$ 7

Solve for n. (Pages 252–253)

21. $30n = 600$ 20   **22.** $5n = 75$ 15   **23.** $13n = 130$ 10   **24.** $21n = 546$ 26

EXERCISES

See the suggested assignment guide in the Teacher's Manual.

Solve each proportion for n. (Example, a)

1. $\frac{n}{36} = \frac{1}{4}$ 9
2. $\frac{n}{27} = \frac{2}{9}$ 6
3. $\frac{n}{100} = \frac{13}{20}$ 65
4. $\frac{n}{35} = \frac{4}{7}$ 20
5. $\frac{n}{98} = \frac{13}{14}$ 91

6. $\frac{n}{28} = \frac{18}{42}$ 12
7. $\frac{n}{30} = \frac{5}{6}$ 25
8. $\frac{n}{27} = \frac{1}{3}$ 9
9. $\frac{n}{72} = \frac{1}{12}$ 6
10. $\frac{n}{36} = \frac{11}{12}$ 33

11. $\frac{n}{70} = \frac{6}{21}$ 20
12. $\frac{n}{64} = \frac{9}{8}$ 72
13. $\frac{n}{60} = \frac{3}{20}$ 9
14. $\frac{n}{80} = \frac{9}{10}$ 72
15. $\frac{n}{56} = \frac{6}{7}$ 48

16. $\frac{n}{21} = \frac{10}{15}$ 14
17. $\frac{n}{24} = \frac{5}{4}$ 30
18. $\frac{n}{84} = \frac{3}{14}$ 18
19. $\frac{n}{64} = \frac{7}{16}$ 28
20. $\frac{n}{25} = \frac{3}{15}$ 5

(Example, b)

21. $\frac{5}{8} = \frac{15}{n}$ 24
22. $\frac{9}{21} = \frac{3}{n}$ 7
23. $\frac{42}{48} = \frac{7}{n}$ 8
24. $\frac{16}{72} = \frac{2}{n}$ 9
25. $\frac{7}{12} = \frac{21}{n}$ 36

26. $\frac{5}{7} = \frac{10}{n}$ 14
27. $\frac{3}{4} = \frac{9}{n}$ 12
28. $\frac{4}{15} = \frac{16}{n}$ 60
29. $\frac{1}{3} = \frac{20}{n}$ 60
30. $\frac{16}{100} = \frac{4}{n}$ 25

31. $\frac{9}{57} = \frac{3}{n}$ 19
32. $\frac{12}{20} = \frac{3}{n}$ 5
33. $\frac{3}{20} = \frac{9}{n}$ 60
34. $\frac{5}{6} = \frac{25}{n}$ 30
35. $\frac{9}{42} = \frac{3}{n}$ 14

36. $\frac{13}{26} = \frac{5}{n}$ 10
37. $\frac{12}{32} = \frac{3}{n}$ 8
38. $\frac{3}{10} = \frac{6}{n}$ 20
39. $\frac{7}{10} = \frac{35}{n}$ 50
40. $\frac{6}{11} = \frac{18}{n}$ 33

Mixed Practice   The Mixed Practice contains exercises that relate to both problems in the Example.

41. $\frac{n}{25} = \frac{4}{5}$ 20
42. $\frac{2}{25} = \frac{6}{n}$ 75
43. $\frac{n}{10} = \frac{72}{80}$ 9
44. $\frac{n}{9} = \frac{16}{36}$ 4
45. $\frac{9}{16} = \frac{27}{n}$ 48

46. $\frac{57}{95} = \frac{18}{n}$ 30
47. $\frac{2}{n} = \frac{18}{27}$ 3
48. $\frac{3}{15} = \frac{n}{45}$ 9
49. $\frac{n}{5} = \frac{36}{30}$ 6
50. $\frac{7}{n} = \frac{42}{48}$ 8

51. $\frac{64}{n} = \frac{16}{17}$ 68
52. $\frac{11}{12} = \frac{n}{144}$ 132
53. $\frac{2}{5} = \frac{n}{20}$ 8
54. $\frac{n}{13} = \frac{28}{26}$ 14
55. $\frac{n}{64} = \frac{1}{8}$ 8

56. $\frac{64}{100} = \frac{n}{25}$ 16
57. $\frac{35}{100} = \frac{n}{20}$ 7
58. $\frac{1}{4} = \frac{12}{n}$ 48
59. $\frac{1}{n} = \frac{8}{48}$ 6
60. $\frac{6}{n} = \frac{3}{8}$ 16

These word problems may be considered optional for some students.

APPLICATIONS: Using Proportions

61. Sandra's art teacher told her that she could obtain the shade of orange paint she wanted by mixing yellow paint with red in the ratio 4:3. How much yellow paint should she buy to mix with 8 quarts of red paint? $10\frac{2}{3}$ quarts

62. A painter mixed yellow paint with blue in the ratio of 2:3 to obtain a shade of green. How many gallons of blue paint are needed to mix with 12 gallons of yellow paint? 18 gallons

63. A certain shade of paint can be obtained by mixing yellow with red in the ratio of 1:2. How many gallons of red paint are needed to mix with 5 gallons of yellow? 10 gallons

Peggy Kahana, Artist

EQUATIONS/RATIO AND PROPORTION   **265**

Problem Solving and Applications

Scale Drawings

See the Teacher's Manual for the objectives.
This lesson applies the skills presented in Sections 12-4 and 12-5.

On a scale drawing, the scale compares distance on the drawing to actual distance. You can write a ratio for the scale.

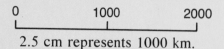

2.5 cm represents 1000 km.

Ratio: $\dfrac{2.5}{1000}$

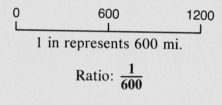

1 in represents 600 mi.

Ratio: $\dfrac{1}{600}$

EXAMPLE

On a map, the distance from San Francisco to Pasadena is 9 centimeters. The scale on the map is shown at the right. Find the actual distance between the cities.

```
0            130           260
├─────────────┼─────────────┤
```

2 cm represents 130 km.

Solution:

1 Write a ratio for the scale. $\dfrac{2}{130}$ ⟵ Map distance ⟵ Actual distance

2 Write a proportion. $\dfrac{2}{130} = \dfrac{9}{n}$ ⟵ Map distance ⟵ Actual distance

3 Solve for n. $2 \times n = 130 \times 9$, or

$$2n = 1170$$
$$\frac{2n}{2} = \frac{1170}{2}$$
$$n = 585$$

The actual distance is **585 kilometers**.

Exercises

For Exercises 1–4, the map distance between two cities in California is given. Use the scale in the Example to find the actual distance between the cities.

	From	To	Map Distance	Actual Distance	
1.	San Francisco	Sacramento	2 cm	?	130 km
2.	Monterey	Santa Barbara	5 cm	?	325 km
3.	Pasadena	San Diego	3 cm	?	195 km
4.	Fresno	Santa Ana	6 cm	?	390 km

DRAFTING

This lesson applies the skills presented in Sections 12-4 and 12-5.

Drafting technicians make drawings to scale. The drawing below shows a plan for a house. The scale of the drawing is:

1 centimeter represents 1.2 meters.

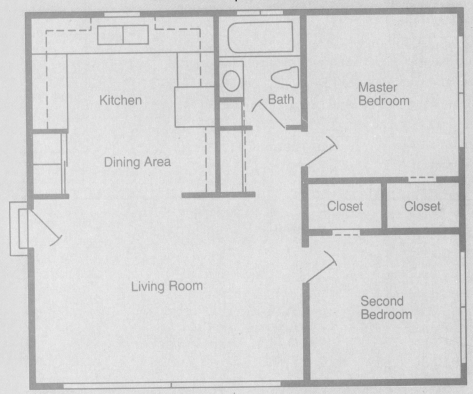

EXERCISES

1. Write a ratio for the scale of the drawing above. $\frac{1}{1.2}$

2. On the drawing, the length of the house is 12 centimeters. Find the actual length. 14.4 meters

3. On the drawing, the length of one closet is 2 centimeters. Find the actual length. 2.4 meters

4. On the drawing, the bedrooms are each about 4 centimeters wide. Find the actual width. 4.8 meters

5. On the drawing, the width of the house is 10 centimeters. Find the actual length. 12 meters

6. On the drawing, the kitchen is 5 centimeters wide. What is its actual width? 6 meters

7. Suppose that the actual length and width of the living room are 9 meters and 6 meters. What will be the length and width on the drawing? 7.5 centimeters and 5 centimeters

8. Suppose that the actual length and width of the kitchen are 3.6 meters and 2.4 meters. What will be the length and width on the drawing? 3 centimeters and 2 centimeters

Chapter Review

Part 1: Vocabulary

For Exercises 1–6, choose from the box at the right the word(s) that completes each statement.

1. An equation such as $n + 6 = 9$ is an __?__ equation. (Page 248)
   addition

2. To solve an addition equation, you __?__ the same number from each side of the equation. (Page 248)
   subtract

3. An equation such as $4n = 8$ is a __?__ equation. (Page 252)
   multiplication

4. You can write a ratio as a __?__. (Page 260)
   fraction

5. Equal ratios are called __?__ ratios. (Page 260)
   equivalent

6. An equation that shows equivalent ratios is called a __?__. (Page 264)
   proportion

addition
equivalent
division
multiplication
proportion
fraction
subtract
add

Part 2: Skills

Solve for n. Check each answer. (Pages 248–249)

7. $n + 5 = 21$ 16
8. $n + 6 = 19$ 13
9. $n + 7 = 30$ 23
10. $n + 3 = 12$ 9

11. $n - 8 = 20$ 28
12. $n - 5 = 16$ 21
13. $n - 4 = 13$ 17
14. $n - 7 = 21$ 28

15. $n + 6.2 = 9.8$ 3.6
16. $n + 7.1 = 8.5$ 1.4
17. $n + 2.9 = 12.3$ 9.4

18. $n + 9.8 = 17.4$ 7.6
19. $n - 3.4 = 5.6$ 9
20. $n - 4.9 = 7.3$ 12.2

21. $n + \frac{1}{2} = \frac{3}{4}$ $\frac{1}{4}$
22. $n + \frac{1}{8} = \frac{1}{2}$ $\frac{3}{8}$
23. $n + \frac{2}{3} = \frac{5}{6}$ $\frac{1}{6}$
24. $n + \frac{1}{5} = \frac{7}{10}$ $\frac{1}{2}$

25. $n - \frac{1}{3} = \frac{1}{4}$ $\frac{7}{12}$
26. $n - \frac{3}{8} = \frac{1}{4}$ $\frac{5}{8}$
27. $n - \frac{5}{6} = \frac{1}{3}$ $1\frac{1}{6}$
28. $n - \frac{4}{9} = \frac{1}{3}$ $\frac{7}{9}$

(Pages 252–253)

29. $3n = 21$ 7
30. $5n = 40$ 8
31. $10n = 90$ 9
32. $20n = 160$ 8

33. $12n = 108$ 9
34. $11n = 132$ 12
35. $1.6n = 4.8$ 3
36. $2.4n = 7.2$ 3

37. $1.8n = 90$ 50
38. $3.6n = 144$ 40
39. $\frac{n}{3} = 7$ 21
40. $\frac{n}{5} = 9$ 45

41. $\frac{n}{6} = 18$ 108
42. $\frac{n}{4} = 13$ 52
43. $\frac{n}{12} = 10$ 120
44. $\frac{n}{13} = 14$ 182

45. $\frac{n}{6} = 2.1$ 12.6
46. $\frac{n}{9} = 1.7$ 15.3
47. $\frac{n}{11} = 6.4$ 70.4
48. $\frac{n}{12} = 3.9$ 46.8

(Pages 256–257)

49. $14n + 9 = 51$ 3
50. $12n + 8 = 32$ 2
51. $5n - 7 = 28$ 7

52. $6n - 4 = 20$ 4
53. $\frac{n}{4} + 6 = 12$ 24
54. $\frac{n}{5} + 8 = 14$ 30

55. $\frac{n}{6} - 7 = 10$ 102
56. $\frac{n}{7} - 9 = 18$ 189
57. $3n + 20 = 41$ 7

58. $4n + 19 = 39$ 5
59. $\frac{n}{5} - 12 = 16$ 140
60. $\frac{n}{4} - 17 = 23$ 160

61. $2n + 1.2 = 4.8$ 1.8
62. $4n + 3.8 = 12.2$ 2.1
63. $0.3n - 5 = 16$ 70

64. $0.4n - 7 = 21$ 70
65. $\frac{3n}{4} + 5 = 20$ 20
66. $\frac{5n}{8} + 2 = 12$ 16

Write a fraction in lowest terms for each ratio. (Pages 260–261)

67. 2 to 4 $\frac{1}{2}$

68. 7 to 14 $\frac{1}{2}$

69. 36 to 9 $\frac{4}{1}$

70. 84 to 36 $\frac{7}{3}$

71. 18 to 45 $\frac{2}{5}$

72. 15 to 45 $\frac{1}{3}$

73. 60 to 48 $\frac{5}{4}$

74. 9 to 6 $\frac{3}{2}$

75. 7 to 4 $\frac{7}{4}$

76. 9 to 2 $\frac{9}{2}$

77. 13 to 39 $\frac{1}{3}$

78. 16 to 48 $\frac{1}{3}$

79. 6 to 5 $\frac{6}{5}$

80. 10 to 7 $\frac{10}{7}$

81. 14 to 32 $\frac{7}{16}$

82. 12 to 44 $\frac{3}{11}$

Determine whether the ratios are equivalent. Answer Yes or No.
(Pages 260–261)

83. $\frac{1}{2}$ and $\frac{4}{6}$ No

84. $\frac{2}{3}$ and $\frac{16}{24}$ Yes

85. $\frac{4}{5}$ and $\frac{8}{20}$ No

86. $\frac{2}{7}$ an $\frac{6}{14}$ No

87. $\frac{5}{7}$ and $\frac{35}{49}$ Yes

88. $\frac{2}{15}$ and $\frac{12}{60}$ No

89. $\frac{8}{3}$ and $\frac{24}{9}$ Yes

90. $\frac{9}{5}$ and $\frac{18}{12}$ No

91. $\frac{4}{3}$ and $\frac{16}{13}$ No

92. $\frac{6}{5}$ and $\frac{12}{10}$ Yes

93. $\frac{5}{12}$ and $\frac{15}{36}$ Yes

94. $\frac{3}{10}$ and $\frac{9}{30}$ Yes

95. $\frac{5}{6}$ and $\frac{10}{18}$ No

96. $\frac{4}{7}$ and $\frac{8}{14}$ Yes

97. $\frac{6}{13}$ and $\frac{18}{39}$ Yes

98. $\frac{4}{5}$ and $\frac{23}{30}$ No

Solve each proportion for n. (Pages 264–265)

99. $\frac{n}{14} = \frac{2}{7}$ 4

100. $\frac{n}{12} = \frac{5}{6}$ 10

101. $\frac{n}{8} = \frac{3}{4}$ 6

102. $\frac{n}{21} = \frac{5}{7}$ 15

103. $\frac{n}{16} = \frac{3}{8}$ 6

104. $\frac{n}{20} = \frac{3}{5}$ 12

105. $\frac{n}{13} = \frac{8}{52}$ 2

106. $\frac{4}{9} = \frac{20}{n}$ 45

107. $\frac{6}{5} = \frac{24}{n}$ 20

108. $\frac{9}{7} = \frac{81}{n}$ 63

109. $\frac{7}{12} = \frac{14}{n}$ 24

110. $\frac{1}{3} = \frac{12}{n}$ 36

111. $\frac{n}{16} = \frac{21}{28}$ 12

112. $\frac{n}{12} = \frac{10}{15}$ 8

113. $\frac{n}{8} = \frac{5}{10}$ 4

114. $\frac{n}{20} = \frac{24}{32}$ 15

115. $\frac{16}{18} = \frac{24}{n}$ 27

116. $\frac{n}{4} = \frac{21}{28}$ 3

117. $\frac{16}{n} = \frac{32}{10}$ 5

118. $\frac{8}{n} = \frac{10}{15}$ 12

Part 3: Applications   The use of these word problems depends on which applications were studied.

119. Hector's gross pay amounted to $289.90. His net pay was $217.00. Use the formula $n + d = g$ to find the total deductions. (Page 250) $72.90

120. Gina made 25 out of 30 foul shots. What is the ratio of shots made to shots attempted? (Pages 260–261) 25 to 30 or $\frac{5}{6}$

121. The tank capacity of a car is 11.2 gallons. The car travels 336 miles on this amount. Use the formula $c \times m = r$ to find the number of miles the car travels on one gallon. (Page 255) 30

122. Maria Hernandez has a batting average of .300. She has been at bat 90 times. Use the formula $h \div t = a$ to find the number of hits. (Page 254) 27

123. A painter mixed blue and red paint in the ratio of 3:4. How many gallons of red paint will be needed to mix with 9 gallons of blue paint? (Page 265) 12

Chapter Test

The Teacher's Resource Book contains two forms of each chapter test.

Solve and check.

1. $n + 7 = 23$ 16   **2.** $n - 8 = 16$ 24   **3.** $2n = 24$ 12   **4.** $\frac{n}{5} = 15$ 75

5. $n + 2.6 = 4.9$ 2.3   **6.** $n - 3.2 = 7.8$ 11   **7.** $1.3n = 2.6$ 2   **8.** $\frac{n}{6} = 12.2$ 73.2

9. $n + \frac{1}{4} = \frac{5}{8}$ $\frac{3}{8}$ **10.** $n - \frac{2}{3} = \frac{3}{4}$ $1\frac{5}{12}$ **11.** $2n + 8 = 14$ 3   **12.** $3n - 9 = 21$

                                                                                           10

Write a fraction in lowest terms for each ratio.

13. 5 to 16 $\frac{5}{16}$ **14.** 27 to 3 $\frac{9}{1}$ **15.** 14 to 49 $\frac{2}{7}$ **16.** 60 to 20 $\frac{3}{1}$

Determine whether the ratios are equivalent. Answer <u>Yes</u> or <u>No</u>.

17. $\frac{2}{3}$ and $\frac{9}{12}$ No   **18.** $\frac{9}{20}$ and $\frac{44}{100}$ No   **19.** $\frac{3}{10}$ and $\frac{27}{90}$ Yes   **20.** $\frac{5}{4}$ and $\frac{25}{20}$ Yes

Solve each proportion.

                                                                                                   70

21. $\frac{2}{3} = \frac{n}{9}$ 6   **22.** $\frac{3}{5} = \frac{9}{n}$ 15   **23.** $\frac{2}{7} = \frac{n}{21}$ 6   **24.** $\frac{3}{8} = \frac{24}{n}$ 64   **25.** $\frac{3}{10} = \frac{21}{n}$

26. $\frac{24}{27} = \frac{n}{9}$ 8   **27.** $\frac{24}{56} = \frac{3}{n}$ 7   **28.** $\frac{9}{20} = \frac{n}{100}$ 45   **29.** $\frac{3}{5} = \frac{18}{n}$ 30   **30.** $\frac{15}{1} = \frac{n}{2}$

                                                                                                            30

Solve. The use of these word problems depends on which applications were studied.

31. A recipe for cookies calls for 3 grams of salt for every 2 grams of baking powder. What is the ratio of salt to baking powder? 3 to 2 or $\frac{3}{2}$

32. Joshua Levitz has been at bat 125 times. His batting average is .280. Use the formula $h \div t = a$ to find his number of hits. 35

33. A certain shade of paint can be obtained by mixing yellow with blue in the ratio 2:3. How many gallons of blue paint are needed to mix with 6 gallons of yellow paint? 9

Additional Practice

You may wish to use some or all of these exercises depending on how well students performed on the formal chapter test.

Skills

Solve and check. (Pages 248–249)

1. $n + 8 = 12$ ₄

2. $n - 2.1 = 3.2$ 5.3

3. $n - 5 = 17$ 22

4. $n - 9 = 26$ 35

5. $n - 6.9 = 4.8$ 11.7

6. $n + 3.8 = 9.6$ 5.8

7. $n + 4.3 = 7.1$ 2.8

8. $n - 14 = 23$ 37

9. $n - \frac{5}{6} = \frac{7}{8}$ $1\frac{17}{24}$

10. $n + \frac{1}{3} = \frac{4}{5}$ $\frac{7}{15}$

11. $n + \frac{3}{8} = \frac{7}{9}$ $\frac{29}{72}$

12. $n - \frac{2}{3} = \frac{1}{4}$ $\frac{11}{12}$

(Pages 252–253)

13. $4n = 48$ 12

14. $2.6n = 5.2$ 2

15. $\frac{n}{6} = 8$ 48

16. $\frac{n}{3.1} = 2.8$ 8.68

17. $16n = 64$ 4

18. $\frac{n}{7} = 92$ 644

19. $2.8n = 14$ 5

20. $15n = 900$ 60

21. $\frac{n}{2.6} = 4.9$ 12.74

22. $25n = 350$ 14

23. $4.3n = 129$ 30

24. $0.38n = 76$ 200

(Pages 256–257)

25. $3n + 7 = 25$ 6

26. $\frac{n}{4} - 5 = 8$ 52

27. $1.2n - 4.6 = 0.2$ 4

28. $\frac{4n}{3} + 7 = 19$ 9

29. $5n - 2 = 38$ 8

30. $\frac{n}{2} + 6 = 12$ 12

31. $6.3n + 8.1 = 64.8$ 9

32. $\frac{2n}{6} - 3 = 4$ 21

Write a fraction in lowest terms for each ratio. (Pages 260–261)

33. 4 to 8 $\frac{1}{2}$

34. 7 to 56 $\frac{1}{8}$

35. 12 to 18 $\frac{2}{3}$

36. 16 to 20 $\frac{4}{5}$

37. 14 to 7 $\frac{2}{1}$

38. 36 to 24 $\frac{3}{2}$

39. 5 to 25 $\frac{1}{5}$

40. 18 to 30 $\frac{3}{5}$

Determine whether the ratios are equivalent. Answer <u>Yes</u> *or* <u>No</u>.
(Pages 260–261)

41. $\frac{3}{4}$ and $\frac{6}{9}$ No

42. $\frac{5}{8}$ and $\frac{25}{40}$ Yes

43. $\frac{14}{21}$ and $\frac{8}{12}$ Yes

44. $\frac{4}{20}$ and $\frac{6}{36}$ No

Solve each proportion. (Pages 264–265)

45. $\frac{1}{2} = \frac{n}{6}$ 3

46. $\frac{2}{3} = \frac{n}{12}$ 8

47. $\frac{2}{3} = \frac{12}{n}$ 18

48. $\frac{3}{5} = \frac{9}{n}$ 15

49. $\frac{3}{n} = \frac{15}{20}$ 4

50. $\frac{9}{n} = \frac{90}{100}$ 10

51. $\frac{n}{9} = \frac{12}{18}$ 6

52. $\frac{n}{7} = \frac{56}{49}$ 8

53. $\frac{4}{9} = \frac{24}{n}$ 54

54. $\frac{5}{8} = \frac{35}{n}$ 56

55. $\frac{5}{9} = \frac{n}{99}$ 55

56. $\frac{1}{3} = \frac{n}{36}$ 12

57. $\frac{4}{n} = \frac{28}{56}$ 8

58. $\frac{3}{n} = \frac{27}{36}$ 4

59. $\frac{n}{16} = \frac{24}{48}$ 8

60. $\frac{n}{9} = \frac{56}{63}$ 8

61. $\frac{7}{8} = \frac{n}{48}$ 42

62. $\frac{5}{6} = \frac{n}{72}$ 60

63. $\frac{7}{10} = \frac{35}{n}$ 50

64. $\frac{8}{13} = \frac{24}{n}$ 39

Applications
The use of these word problems depends on which applications were studied.

65. Kuni's gross pay amounted to $256.00. The net pay was $218.40. Use the formula $n + d = g$ to find the total deductions. (Page 250) $37.60

66. Jack has a batting average of .275. He has been at bat 86 times. Use the formula $h \div t = a$ to find the number of hits. (Page 254) $23.65

Additional Practice

REVIEW OF RELATED SKILLS FOR CHAPTER 13

We suggest that some or all of this page be reviewed before proceeding with the chapter.

Give the place value of the underlined digit.   (Pages 90–91)

1. 32.6̱4   tenths   **2.** 4̱9.83   tens   **3.** 64.8̱9   hundredths   **4.** 1̱2.75   ones   **5.** 1.46̱3   thousandths   **6.** 7.89̱2   hundredths

Add.   (Pages 94–95)

7. 1300 + 16.50   1316.50   **8.** 9.85 + 46   55.85   **9.** 752.50 + 19.95   772.45   **10.** 62.21 + 0.87   63.08

Multiply.   (Pages 98–99)

11. 642 × 0.13   83.46   **12.** 729 × 0.04   29.16   **13.** 1600 × 0.06   96   **14.** 2400 × 0.15   360

Multiply each number by 100.   (Pages 102–103)

15. 0.41   41   **16.** 0.62   62   **17.** 0.814   81.4   **18.** 0.927   92.7   **19.** 0.004   0.4   **20.** 0.008   0.8

Multiply each number by .01.   (Pages 102–103)

21. 16   0.16   **22.** 23   0.23   **23.** 4   0.04   **24.** 2   0.02   **25.** 1.7   0.017   **26.** 6.9   0.069

Divide. Carry the division to two decimal places.   (Pages 122–123)

27. $7\overline{)6}$ $0.85\frac{5}{7}$ **28.** $8\overline{)5}$ $0.62\frac{1}{2}$ **29.** $6\overline{)5}$ $0.83\frac{1}{3}$ **30.** $9\overline{)5}$ $0.55\frac{5}{9}$ **31.** $12\overline{)11}$ $0.91\frac{2}{3}$ **32.** $20\overline{)13}$ 0.65

Round each number as indicated.   (Pages 120–121)

33. 42.61; to the nearest whole number   43   **34.** 39.73; to the nearest tenth   39.7

35. 16.752; to the nearest hundredth   16.75   **36.** 8.637; to the nearest hundredth   8.64

37. 0.0575; to the nearest thousandth   0.058   **38.** 0.05; to the nearest tenth   0.1

39. 1.0002; to the nearest thousandth   1.000   **40.** 17.01; to the nearest whole number   17

Write in lowest terms.   (Pages 182–183)

41. $\frac{16}{100}$ $\frac{4}{25}$ **42.** $\frac{29}{100}$ $\frac{29}{100}$ **43.** $\frac{48}{100}$ $\frac{12}{25}$ **44.** $\frac{55}{100}$ $\frac{11}{20}$ **45.** $\frac{34}{100}$ $\frac{17}{50}$ **46.** $\frac{12}{100}$ $\frac{3}{25}$

Multiply. Write each answer in lowest terms.   (Pages 204–205)

47. $\frac{3}{8} \times \frac{1}{100}$ $\frac{3}{800}$ **48.** $\frac{5}{9} \times \frac{1}{100}$ $\frac{1}{180}$ **49.** $1400 \times \frac{3}{4}$ 1050   **50.** $2300 \times \frac{4}{5}$ 1840

Write a fraction for each mixed number.   (Pages 208–209)

51. $1\frac{3}{4}$ $\frac{7}{4}$ **52.** $4\frac{1}{2}$ $\frac{9}{2}$ **53.** $15\frac{1}{4}$ $\frac{61}{4}$ **54.** $14\frac{2}{7}$ $\frac{100}{7}$ **55.** $21\frac{5}{6}$ $\frac{131}{6}$ **56.** $66\frac{2}{3}$ $\frac{200}{3}$

Divide. Write each answer in lowest terms.   (Pages 212–213)

57. $\frac{3}{8} \div 100$ $\frac{3}{800}$ **58.** $\frac{3}{5} \div 100$ $\frac{3}{500}$ **59.** $\frac{1}{4} \div 100$ $\frac{1}{400}$ **60.** $\frac{5}{9} \div 100$ $\frac{1}{180}$ **61.** $\frac{7}{10} \div 100$ $\frac{7}{1000}$

Write a fraction in lowest terms for each ratio.   (Pages 260–261)

62. 6 to 100 $\frac{3}{50}$ **63.** 8 to 100 $\frac{2}{25}$ **64.** 25 to 100 $\frac{1}{4}$ **65.** 30 to 100 $\frac{3}{10}$ **66.** 50 to 100 $\frac{1}{2}$

67. 12 to 100 $\frac{3}{25}$ **68.** 20 to 100 $\frac{1}{5}$ **69.** 98 to 100 $\frac{49}{50}$ **70.** 66 to 100 $\frac{33}{50}$ **71.** 2 to 100 $\frac{1}{50}$

CHAPTER
13 PER CENT

SKILLS

13-1   Meaning of Per Cent
13-2   Per Cents and Decimals
13-3   Writing Fractions for Per Cents
13-4   Writing Per Cents for Fractions
13-5   Finding a Per Cent of a Number
13-6   Interest
13-7   Rounding and Estimation

APPLICATIONS

Discount
Commission

CAREER

Banking

13-1 Meaning of Per Cent

See the Teacher's Manual for the objectives.

Per cent means **per hundred** or **hundredths.** You can write a per cent for a fraction with a denominator of 100.

EXAMPLE 1 Write a per cent for $\frac{10}{100}$.

Solution: *Ten hundredths* ▶ $\frac{10}{100} = 10\%$ ◀ *Ten per cent*

After completing Example 1, you may wish to have students do some or all of Exercises 1-18.

Since **per cent** means **hundredths,** you can write a per cent for a two–place decimal.

EXAMPLE 2 Write a per cent for 0.25.

Solution: *Twenty–five hundredths* ▶ $0.25 = 25\%$ ◀ *Twenty–five per cent*

The tables below show how fractions with a denominator of 100, two-place decimals, and per cents are related.

Fraction	Two–Place Decimal	Per Cent	Fraction	Two–Place Decimal	Per Cent
$\frac{1}{100}$	0.01	1%	$\frac{43}{100}$	0.43	43%
$\frac{5}{100}$	0.05	5%	$\frac{97}{100}$	0.97	97%
$\frac{20}{100}$	0.20	20%	$\frac{100}{100}$	1.00	100%

REVIEW OF RELATED SKILLS
You may wish to use these exercises before teaching the lesson.

Write a fraction in lowest terms for each ratio.   (Pages 260–261)

1. 5 to 100 $\frac{1}{20}$ **2.** 7 to 100 $\frac{7}{100}$ **3.** 10 to 100 $\frac{1}{10}$ **4.** 21 to 100 $\frac{21}{100}$ **5.** 9 to 100 $\frac{9}{100}$

Give the place value of the underlined digit in each number.   (Pages 90–91)

6. 13.5<u>1</u>   **7.** 0.0<u>1</u>   **8.** <u>1</u>4.63   **9.** 27.6<u>3</u>   **10.** 9.80<u>5</u>   **11.** 2.0<u>0</u>7

tenths   hundredths   tens   hundredths   thousandths   hundredths

EXERCISES
See the suggested assignment guide in the Teacher's Manual.

Write a per cent for each fraction.   (Example 1)

1. $\frac{30}{100}$ 30% **2.** $\frac{40}{100}$ 40% **3.** $\frac{16}{100}$ 16% **4.** $\frac{21}{100}$ 21% **5.** $\frac{19}{100}$ 19% **6.** $\frac{12}{100}$ 12%

7. $\frac{9}{100}$ 9% **8.** $\frac{7}{100}$ 7% **9.** $\frac{5}{100}$ 5% **10.** $\frac{3}{100}$ 3% **11.** $\frac{8}{100}$ 8% **12.** $\frac{1}{100}$ 1%

13. $\frac{51}{100}$ 51% **14.** $\frac{83}{100}$ 83% **15.** $\frac{90}{100}$ 90% **16.** $\frac{77}{100}$ 77% **17.** $\frac{6}{100}$ 6% **18.** $\frac{45}{100}$ 45%

Write a per cent for each decimal.   (Example 2)

19. 0.15 15% **20.** 0.35 35% **21.** 0.71 71% **22.** 0.83 83% **23.** 0.33 33% **24.** 0.16 16%

25. 0.09 9% **26.** 0.02 2% **27.** 0.07 7% **28.** 0.05 5% **29.** 0.02 2% **30.** 0.08 8%

31. 0.40 40% **32.** 0.90 90% **33.** 0.30 30% **34.** 0.50 50% **35.** 0.70 70% **36.** 0.10 10%

Write a two-place decimal and a per cent for each fraction.   (Table)

	Two-Place Decimal	Per Cent		Two-Place Decimal	Per Cent		Two-Place Decimal	Per Cent
37. $\frac{19}{100}$	?0.19	?19%	**43.** $\frac{25}{100}$	? 0.25	?25%	**49.** $\frac{2}{100}$	? 0.02	? 2%
38. $\frac{11}{100}$	?0.11	?11%	**44.** $\frac{75}{100}$	? 0.75	?75%	**50.** $\frac{4}{100}$	? 0.04	? 4%
39. $\frac{6}{100}$	?0.06	? 6%	**45.** $\frac{42}{100}$	? 0.42	?42%	**51.** $\frac{56}{100}$	? 0.56	? 56%
40. $\frac{9}{100}$	?0.09	? 9%	**46.** $\frac{83}{100}$	? 0.83	?83%	**52.** $\frac{37}{100}$	? 0.37	? 37%
41. $\frac{20}{100}$	?0.20	?20%	**47.** $\frac{29}{100}$	? 0.29	?29%	**53.** $\frac{60}{100}$	? 0.60	? 60%
42. $\frac{80}{100}$	?0.80	?80%	**48.** $\frac{13}{100}$	? 0.13	?13%	**54.** $\frac{50}{100}$	? 0.50	? 50%

APPLICATIONS: From Words to Per Cent   These are two-step problems that most students should be able to handle.

For Exercises 55–57, write a fraction for the underlined expression.
Then write a per cent for the fraction.

55. In 1970, <u>40 out of every 100</u> persons in the United States were under age 21. $\frac{40}{100}$, 40%

56. By 1990, <u>32 out of every 100</u> persons in the United States will be under age 21. $\frac{32}{100}$, 32%

57. In 1978, <u>11 out of every 100</u> persons in the United States were over 65 years of age. $\frac{11}{100}$, 11%

58. By 1990, 12 out of every 100 persons in the United States will be 65 years old or older. What per cent will be <u>under</u> 65 years of age? $\frac{88}{100}$, 88%

59. By 1990, 38 out of every 100 persons in the United States will be 40 years old or older. What per cent will be <u>under</u> 40 years of age? $\frac{62}{100}$, 62%

13-2 Per Cents and Decimals See the Teacher's Manual for the objectives.

Since per cent means **hundredths,** you can write a decimal for a per cent.

PROCEDURE To write a decimal for a per cent:

1 Move the decimal point <u>two</u> places to the left.

2 Drop the per cent symbol.

EXAMPLE 1 Write a decimal for each per cent.
   a. 16%   **b.** 123%   **c.** 12.5%

Solutions: **a.**   **b.**   **c.**

1        $16\% = 16\%$ $123\% = 1\,23\%$ $12.5\% = 12.5$

2             $= .16,$ or **0.16** $= 1.23$ $= .125,$ or **0.125**

Sometimes you may have to insert zeros.

After completing Example 1, you may wish to have students do some or all of Exercises 1-20.

EXAMPLE 2 Write a decimal for each per cent.
   a. 5%   **b.** 1.5%   **c.** 0.5%

Solutions:

   a.   **b.**   **c.**

1 $5\% = 05\%$ ◀ **Insert one zero.** $1.5\% = 01.5\%$ $0.5\% = 00.5\%$ ◀ **Insert one zero.**

2    $= .05,$ or **0.05** $= .015,$ or **0.015** $= .005,$ or **0.005**

After completing Example 2, you may wish to have students do some or all of Exercises 21-40.

You can write a per cent for a decimal by moving the decimal point <u>two</u> places to the <u>right</u>.

PROCEDURE To write a per cent for a decimal:

1 Move the decimal point <u>two</u> places to the <u>right</u>.

2 Write the per cent symbol.

EXAMPLE 3 Write a per cent for each decimal.
   a. 0.25   **b.** 0.09   **c.** 0.675   **d.** 0.008

Solutions:

      a.   **b.**   **c.**   **d.**

1 $0.25 = 0.25$ $0.09 = 0.09$ $0.675 = 0.67\,5$ $0.008 = 0.00\,8$

2    $= 25\%$ $= 9\%$ $= 67.5\%$ $= 0.8\%$

Multiply each number by 0.01.   (Pages 102–103)

1. 18 0.18   2. 21 0.21   3. 5 0.05   4. 3 0.03   5. 19.5 0.195   6. 50.15 0.5015

7. 119 1.19   8. 154 1.54   9. 0.5 0.005   10. 0.8 0.008   11. 1.56 0.0156   12. 7.83 0.0783

Multiply each number by 100.   (Pages 102–103)

13. 0.35 35   14. 0.71 71   15. 0.08 8   16. 0.04 4   17. 0.875 87.5   18. 0.165 16.5

19. 1.45 145   20. 1.97 197   21. 0.005 0.5   22. 0.008 0.8   23. $0.33\frac{1}{3}$ $33\frac{1}{3}$ 24. $0.66\frac{2}{3}$ $66\frac{2}{3}$

EXERCISES
See the suggested assignment guide in the Teacher's Manual.

Write a decimal for each per cent.   (Example 1)

1. 13% 0.13   2. 29% 0.29   3. 65% 0.65   4. 75% 0.75   5. 70% 0.70

6. 10% 0.10   7. 112% 1.12   8. 139% 1.39   9. 375% 3.75   10. 106% 1.06

11. 208% 2.08   12. 301% 3.01   13. 37.5% 0.375   14. 87.5% 0.875   15. 16.8% 0.168

16. 52.3% 0.523   17. 91.7% 0.917   18. 72.6% 0.726   19. 13.9% 0.139   20. 12.9% 0.129

(Example 2)

21. 9% 0.09   22. 7% 0.07   23. 8% 0.08   24. 6% 0.06   25. 1% 0.01

26. 3% 0.03   27. 2.5% 0.025   28. 8.5% 0.085   29. 5.8% 0.058   30. 3.2% 0.032

31. 6.9% 0.069   32. 1.3% 0.013   33. 0.3% 0.003   34. 0.7% 0.007   35. 0.9% 0.009

36. 0.1% 0.001   37. 0.8% 0.008   38. 0.4% 0.004   39. 0.6% 0.006   40. 0.2% 0.002

Write a per cent for each decimal.   (Example 3)

41. 0.35 35%   42. 0.27 27%   43. 0.39 39%   44. 0.93 93%   45. 0.47 47%

46. 0.21 21%   47. 0.05 5%   48. 0.01 1%   49. 0.07 7%   50. 0.02 2%

51. 0.08 8%   52. 0.04 4%   53. 0.575 57.5%   54. 0.815 81.5%   55. 0.375 37.5%

56. 0.875 87.5%   57. 0.038 3.8%   58. 0.047 4.7%   59. 0.015 1.5%   60. 0.055 5.5%

61. 0.041 4.1%   62. 0.074 7.4%   63. 0.045 4.5%   64. 0.095 9.5%   65. 0.005 0.5%

66. 0.001 0.1%   67. 0.006 0.6%   68. 0.004 0.4%   69. 0.002 0.2%   70. 0.009 0.9%

APPLICATIONS: From Per Cents to Decimals Most students should be able to handle these
word problems which apply the skills presented in the lesson.
Write a decimal for each per cent.

71. In a recent year. the United States imported about 40% of its oil from abroad. 0.40

72. In that year, Canada supplied the United States with 5.7% of its total oil imports. 0.057

73. In that year, Mexico supplied the United States with 3.6% of its total oil imports. 0.036

13-3 Writing Fractions for Per Cents

See the Teacher's Manual for the objectives.

You can write a fraction for a per cent.

9% means 9 per hundred, or $\frac{9}{100}$.

PROCEDURE To write a fraction for a per cent:

$\boxed{1}$ Write a fraction with a denominator of 100 for the per cent.

$\boxed{2}$ Write the fraction in lowest terms.

EXAMPLE 1 Write a fraction for each per cent. **a.** 11% **b.** 5%

Solutions: $\boxed{1}$ **a.** $11\% = \frac{11}{100}$ **b.** $5\% = \frac{5}{100}$ ◀ **Write in lowest terms.**

$\boxed{2}$ $= \frac{1}{20}$

EXAMPLE 2 Write a fraction for each per cent. **a.** $\frac{1}{4}\%$ **b.** $66\frac{2}{3}\%$

Solutions: Recall that dividing by 100 is the same as multiplying by $\frac{1}{100}$.

a. $\frac{1}{4}\% = \frac{\frac{1}{4}}{100}$, or $\frac{1}{4} \div 100$

$= \frac{1}{4} \times \frac{1}{100}$

$= \frac{1}{400}$

b. $66\frac{2}{3}\% = \frac{66\frac{2}{3}}{100}$, or $66\frac{2}{3} \div 100$

$= 66\frac{2}{3} \times \frac{1}{100}$ ◀ **Write a fraction for $66\frac{2}{3}$.**

$= \frac{\overset{2}{\cancel{200}}}{3} \times \frac{1}{\underset{1}{\cancel{100}}}$

$= \frac{2}{3}$

REVIEW OF RELATED SKILLS

You may wish to use the exercises before teaching the lesson.

Write in lowest terms. (Pages 182–183)

1. $\frac{8}{100}$ $\frac{2}{25}$ 2. $\frac{4}{100}$ $\frac{1}{25}$ 3. $\frac{25}{100}$ $\frac{1}{4}$ 4. $\frac{50}{100}$ $\frac{1}{2}$ 5. $\frac{635}{1000}$ $\frac{127}{200}$ 6. $\frac{380}{1000}$ $\frac{19}{50}$

Multiply. Write each answer in lowest terms. (Pages 204–205)

7. $\frac{1}{2} \times \frac{1}{100}$ $\frac{1}{200}$ 8. $\frac{1}{8} \times \frac{1}{100}$ $\frac{1}{800}$ 9. $\frac{5}{6} \times \frac{1}{100}$ $\frac{1}{120}$ 10. $\frac{2}{3} \times \frac{1}{100}$ $\frac{1}{150}$

Divide. Write each answer in lowest terms. (Pages 212–213)

11. $\frac{1}{3} \div 100$ $\frac{1}{300}$ 12. $\frac{7}{8} \div 100$ $\frac{7}{800}$ 13. $\frac{2}{5} \div 100$ $\frac{1}{250}$ 14. $\frac{2}{3} \div 100$ $\frac{1}{150}$

Write a fraction for each mixed number. (Pages 208–209)

15. $1\frac{1}{2}$ $\frac{3}{2}$ 16. $7\frac{1}{8}$ $\frac{57}{8}$ 17. $33\frac{1}{3}$ $\frac{100}{3}$ 18. $18\frac{1}{2}$ $\frac{37}{2}$ 19. $16\frac{2}{3}$ $\frac{50}{3}$ 20. $62\frac{1}{2}$ $\frac{125}{2}$

278 CHAPTER 13

EXERCISES

See the suggested assignment guide in the Teacher's Manual.

Write a fraction in lowest terms for each per cent. (Example 1)

1. 12% $\frac{3}{25}$ **2.** 19% $\frac{19}{100}$ **3.** 26% $\frac{13}{50}$ **4.** 91% $\frac{91}{100}$ **5.** 9% $\frac{9}{100}$ **6.** 7% $\frac{7}{100}$

7. 8% $\frac{2}{25}$ **8.** 6% $\frac{3}{50}$ **9.** 20% $\frac{1}{5}$ **10.** 90% $\frac{9}{10}$ **11.** 40% $\frac{2}{5}$ **12.** 50% $\frac{1}{2}$

13. 75% $\frac{3}{4}$ **14.** 25% $\frac{1}{4}$ **15.** 35% $\frac{7}{20}$ **16.** 15% $\frac{3}{20}$ **17.** 44% $\frac{11}{25}$ **18.** 66% $\frac{33}{50}$

9. 98% $\frac{49}{50}$ **20.** 87% $\frac{87}{100}$ **21.** 39% $\frac{39}{100}$ **22.** 72% $\frac{18}{25}$ **23.** 61% $\frac{61}{100}$ **24.** 43%

$\frac{43}{100}$.

(Example 2)

25. $\frac{1}{2}\%$ $\frac{1}{200}$ **26.** $\frac{1}{3}\%$ $\frac{1}{300}$ **27.** $\frac{3}{4}\%$ $\frac{3}{400}$ **28.** $\frac{5}{8}\%$ $\frac{1}{160}$ **29.** $\frac{2}{3}\%$ $\frac{1}{150}$ **30.** $\frac{1}{5}\%$ $\frac{1}{500}$

31. $\frac{4}{5}\%$ $\frac{1}{125}$ **32.** $\frac{3}{8}\%$ $\frac{3}{800}$ **33.** $\frac{1}{10}\%$ $\frac{1}{1000}$ **34.** $\frac{9}{10}\%$ $\frac{9}{1000}$ **35.** $\frac{1}{6}\%$ $\frac{1}{600}$ **36.** $\frac{5}{6}\%$ $\frac{1}{120}$

37. $12\frac{1}{2}\%$ $\frac{1}{8}$ **38.** $37\frac{1}{2}\%$ $\frac{3}{8}$ **39.** $33\frac{1}{3}\%$ $\frac{1}{3}$ **40.** $83\frac{1}{3}\%$ $\frac{5}{6}$ **41.** $62\frac{1}{2}\%$ $\frac{5}{8}$ **42.** $18\frac{1}{2}\%$ $\frac{37}{200}$

43. $16\frac{1}{4}\%$ $\frac{13}{80}$ **44.** $12\frac{3}{4}\%$ $\frac{51}{400}$ **45.** $8\frac{1}{5}\%$ $\frac{41}{500}$ **46.** $7\frac{1}{4}\%$ $\frac{29}{400}$ **47.** $20\frac{2}{5}\%$ $\frac{51}{250}$ **48.** $25\frac{3}{5}\%$

$\frac{32}{125}$

Mixed Practice   The Mixed Practice contains exercises that relate to both Examples 1 and 2.

49. 80% $\frac{4}{5}$ **50.** 76% $\frac{19}{25}$ **51.** 3% $\frac{3}{100}$ **52.** 1% $\frac{1}{100}$ **53.** $\frac{2}{5}\%$ $\frac{1}{250}$ **54.** $\frac{7}{8}\%$ $\frac{7}{800}$

55. $17\frac{1}{5}\%$ $\frac{43}{250}$ **56.** $6\frac{1}{4}\%$ $\frac{1}{16}$ **57.** $2\frac{3}{4}\%$ $\frac{11}{400}$ **58.** $8\frac{1}{10}\%$ $\frac{81}{1000}$ **59.** $\frac{9}{10}\%$ $\frac{9}{1000}$ **60.** $\frac{3}{5}\%$ $\frac{3}{500}$

61. 91% $\frac{91}{100}$ **62.** 67% $\frac{67}{100}$ **63.** 48% $\frac{12}{25}$ **64.** 52% $\frac{13}{25}$ **65.** $11\frac{2}{3}\%$ $\frac{7}{60}$ **66.** $20\frac{1}{3}\%$ $\frac{61}{300}$

67. $14\frac{2}{7}\%$ $\frac{1}{7}$ **68.** $11\frac{1}{9}\%$ $\frac{1}{9}$ **69.** $\frac{1}{7}\%$ $\frac{1}{700}$ **70.** $\frac{1}{8}\%$ $\frac{1}{800}$ **71.** 2% $\frac{1}{50}$ **72.** 4% $\frac{1}{25}$

73. $2\frac{1}{2}\%$ $\frac{1}{40}$ **74.** $7\frac{1}{2}\%$ $\frac{3}{40}$ **75.** 62% $\frac{31}{50}$ **76.** 18% $\frac{9}{50}$ **77.** $\frac{3}{10}\%$ $\frac{3}{1000}$ **78.** $\frac{4}{9}\%$ $\frac{1}{225}$

APPLICATIONS: From Per Cents to Fractions

Most students should be able to do these word problems which apply the skills presented in the lesson.

Write a fraction in lowest terms for each per cent.

79. Over a period of 6 years, the population of Miami, Florida increased by 6%. $\frac{3}{50}$

80. Over a period of 6 years, the population of Omaha, Nebraska increased by $3\frac{1}{2}\%$. $\frac{7}{200}$

81. Over a period of 8 years, the population of Nevada increased by 35%. $\frac{7}{20}$

82. Over a period of 8 years, the population of Florida increased by $26\frac{1}{2}\%$. $\frac{53}{200}$

83. Over a period of 8 years, the population of Michigan increased by $5\frac{1}{2}\%$. $\frac{11}{200}$

The population of the Sun Belt states is increasing steadily.

13-4 Writing Per Cents for Fractions

See the Teacher's Manual for the objectives.

You can write a per cent for a fraction.

PROCEDURE To write a per cent for a fraction:

1. Divide the numerator of the fraction by the denominator. Carry the division to two decimal places.

2. Write a per cent for the decimal.

EXAMPLE 1 Write a per cent for each number: **a.** $\frac{3}{5}$ **b.** $1\frac{1}{4}$

Solutions: **a.** $\frac{3}{5}$ means $3 \div 5$ **b.** $1\frac{1}{4} = \frac{5}{4}$ ◀ $\frac{5}{4}$ *means* $5 \div 4$.

$$\begin{array}{r} .60 = 0.60 \\ \boxed{1}\ 5\overline{)3.00} \end{array} \qquad \begin{array}{r} 1.25 \\ 4\overline{)5.00} \end{array}$$

$\boxed{2}$ $0.60 = 60\%$ $\qquad\qquad$ $1.25 = 125\%$

After completing Example 1, you may wish to have students do some or all of Exercises 1-30.

Sometimes you do not have a zero remainder when you divide.

EXAMPLE 2 Write a per cent for each fraction: **a.** $\frac{2}{3}$ **b.** $\frac{7}{8}$

Solutions: **a.** $\frac{2}{3}$ means $2 \div 3$. **b.** $\frac{7}{8}$ means $7 \div 8$.

$$\begin{array}{r} .66\frac{2}{3} = 0.66\frac{2}{3} \\ \boxed{1}\ 3\overline{)2.00} \\ \underline{1\ 8} \\ 20 \\ \underline{18} \\ 2 \end{array} \qquad \begin{array}{r} .87\frac{4}{8} = 0.87\frac{1}{2} \\ 8\overline{)7.00} \\ \underline{6\ 4} \\ 60 \\ \underline{56} \\ 4 \end{array}$$

$\boxed{2}$ $0.66\frac{2}{3} = 66\frac{2}{3}\%$ $\qquad\qquad$ $0.87\frac{1}{2} = 87\frac{1}{2}\%$

REVIEW OF RELATED SKILLS

You may wish to use these exercises before teaching the lesson.

Divide. Carry the division to two decimal places. (Pages 122–123)

1. $5\overline{)4}$ 0.80 **2.** $10\overline{)1}$ 0.10 **3.** $2\overline{)1}$ 0.50 **4.** $4\overline{)3}$ 0.75 **5.** $20\overline{)17}$ 0.85 **6.** $50\overline{)13}$ 0.26

7. $40\overline{)15}$ 0.37$\frac{1}{2}$ **8.** $30\overline{)14}$ 0.46$\frac{2}{3}$ **9.** $5\overline{)3}$ 0.60 **10.** $7\overline{)6}$ 0.85$\frac{5}{7}$ **11.** $60\overline{)13}$ 0.21$\frac{2}{3}$ **12.** $20\overline{)19}$ 0.95

Write a per cent for each decimal. (Pages 276–277)

13. 0.28 28% **14.** 0.39 39% **15.** 0.06 6% **16.** 0.01 1% **17.** 0.125 12.5% **18.** 0.615 61.5%

19. 1.6 160% **20.** 5.4 540% **21.** 0.9 90% **22.** 0.8 80% **23.** 0.12$\frac{1}{2}$ 12$\frac{1}{2}$% **24.** 0.16$\frac{1}{3}$ 16$\frac{1}{3}$%

EXERCISES

Write a per cent for each fraction or mixed number. (Example 1)

1. $\frac{1}{2}$ 50%
2. $\frac{1}{4}$ 25%
3. $\frac{1}{5}$ 20%
4. $\frac{1}{10}$ 10%
5. $\frac{1}{20}$ 5%
6. $\frac{1}{25}$ 4%

7. $\frac{1}{50}$ 2%
8. $\frac{3}{4}$ 75%
9. $\frac{3}{20}$ 15%
10. $\frac{4}{5}$ 80%
11. $\frac{29}{50}$ 58%
12. $\frac{4}{25}$ 16%

13. $\frac{11}{20}$ 55%
14. $\frac{37}{50}$ 74%
15. $\frac{9}{25}$ 36%
16. $\frac{49}{50}$ 98%
17. $\frac{17}{20}$ 85%
18. $\frac{3}{25}$ 12%

19. $1\frac{3}{4}$ 175%
20. $2\frac{1}{5}$ 220%
21. $6\frac{1}{10}$ 610%
22. $5\frac{1}{25}$ 504%
23. $3\frac{2}{5}$ 340%
24. $9\frac{3}{20}$ 915%

25. $12\frac{1}{2}$ 1250%
26. $37\frac{1}{2}$ 3750%
27. $8\frac{4}{5}$ 880%
28. $1\frac{1}{50}$ 102%
29. $11\frac{9}{10}$ 1190%
30. $8\frac{7}{20}$ 835%

(Example 2)

31. $\frac{1}{3}$ $33\frac{1}{3}$%
32. $\frac{3}{8}$ $37\frac{1}{2}$%
33. $\frac{5}{8}$ $62\frac{1}{2}$%
34. $\frac{1}{12}$ $8\frac{1}{3}$%
35. $\frac{5}{12}$ $41\frac{2}{3}$%
36. $\frac{7}{12}$ $58\frac{1}{3}$%

37. $\frac{11}{12}$ $91\frac{2}{3}$%
38. $\frac{1}{40}$ $2\frac{1}{2}$%
39. $\frac{9}{40}$ $22\frac{1}{2}$%
40. $\frac{1}{6}$ $16\frac{2}{3}$%
41. $\frac{5}{6}$ $83\frac{1}{3}$%
42. $\frac{1}{16}$ $6\frac{1}{4}$%

43. $\frac{3}{16}$ $18\frac{3}{4}$%
44. $\frac{5}{16}$ $31\frac{1}{4}$%
45. $\frac{1}{7}$ $14\frac{2}{7}$%
46. $\frac{5}{7}$ $71\frac{3}{7}$%
47. $\frac{1}{9}$ $11\frac{1}{9}$%
48. $\frac{8}{9}$ $88\frac{8}{9}$%

49. $\frac{3}{7}$ $42\frac{6}{7}$%
50. $\frac{7}{8}$ $87\frac{1}{2}$%
51. $\frac{2}{9}$ $22\frac{2}{9}$%
52. $\frac{4}{7}$ $57\frac{1}{7}$%
53. $\frac{9}{11}$ $81\frac{9}{11}$%
54. $\frac{7}{11}$ $63\frac{7}{11}$%

55. $\frac{13}{40}$ $32\frac{1}{2}$%
56. $\frac{5}{9}$ $55\frac{5}{9}$%
57. $1\frac{1}{3}$ $133\frac{1}{3}$%
58. $2\frac{1}{12}$ $208\frac{1}{3}$%
59. $3\frac{1}{7}$ $314\frac{2}{7}$%
60. $1\frac{3}{8}$ $137\frac{1}{2}$%

WRITING PER CENTS

You can use a calculator to write a per cent for a mixed number.

EXAMPLE: Write a per cent for $1\frac{1}{8}$.

Solution:
[1] Write a fraction for $1\frac{1}{8}$. $1\frac{1}{8} = \frac{9}{8}$

[2] Write a per cent for $\frac{9}{8}$. $9 \div 8 \times 100$

$\boxed{9}\;\boxed{\div}\;\boxed{8}\;\boxed{\times}\;\boxed{1}\;\boxed{0}\;\boxed{0}\;\boxed{=}$ $\boxed{112.5}$

Thus, $1\frac{1}{8} = 112.5\%$.

EXERCISES

Write a per cent for each mixed number.   118.75%

1. $1\frac{5}{8}$ 162.5%
2. $5\frac{7}{8}$ 587.5%
3. $3\frac{1}{8}$ 312.5%
4. $6\frac{1}{5}$ 620%
5. $9\frac{3}{4}$ 975%
6. $1\frac{3}{16}$

7. $1\frac{1}{40}$ 102.5%
8. $3\frac{1}{50}$ 302%
9. $2\frac{1}{25}$ 204%
10. $3\frac{1}{20}$ 305%
11. $1\frac{1}{16}$ 106.25%
12. $6\frac{7}{10}$ 670%

13-5 Finding a Per Cent of a Number

See the Teacher's Manual for the objectives.

To find a per cent of a number, you write a decimal or a fraction for the per cent.

PROCEDURE To find a per cent of a number:

$\boxed{1}$ Write a decimal or a fraction for the per cent.

$\boxed{2}$ Multiply.

EXAMPLE 1 Find 8% of 1200.

Solution: 8% of 1200 means 8% × 1200.

$\boxed{1}$ 8% × 1200 = 0.08 × 1200 ◀ **8% = 0.08**

$\boxed{2}$ = 96

Thus, 8% of 1200 is **96**.

After completing Example 1, you may wish to have students do some or all of Exercises 1-20.

Sometimes it is easier to use a fraction for the per cent. The tab can help you.

You should memorize the equivalent fractions and per cents in the table.

TABLE

EQUIVALENT FRACTIONS AND PER CENTS			
$\frac{1}{4} = 25\%$	$\frac{1}{2} = 50\%$	$\frac{3}{4} = 75\%$	
$\frac{1}{5} = 20\%$	$\frac{2}{5} = 40\%$	$\frac{3}{5} = 60\%$	$\frac{4}{5} = 80\%$
$\frac{1}{6} = 16\frac{2}{3}\%$	$\frac{1}{3} = 33\frac{1}{3}\%$	$\frac{2}{3} = 66\frac{2}{3}\%$	$\frac{5}{6} = 83\frac{1}{3}\%$
$\frac{1}{8} = 12\frac{1}{2}\%$	$\frac{3}{8} = 37\frac{1}{2}\%$	$\frac{5}{8} = 62\frac{1}{2}\%$	$\frac{7}{8} = 87\frac{1}{2}\%$

EXAMPLE 2 Find $83\frac{1}{3}\%$ of 1200.

Solution: $\boxed{1}$ $83\frac{1}{3}\% = \frac{5}{6}$ ◀ *From the table.*

$\boxed{2}$ $83\frac{1}{3}\%$ of $1200 = \frac{5}{6} \times 1200$ ◀ $\frac{5}{\cancel{6}_1} \times \frac{\cancel{1200}^{200}}{1}$

     $= 5 \times 200$

     $= 1000$

Thus, $83\frac{1}{3}\%$ of 1200 is **1000**.

Write a decimal for each per cent. (Pages 276–277)

1. 21% 0.21 2. 35% 0.35 3. 5% 0.05 4. 4% 0.04 5. 12.5% 0.125 6. 8.5% 0.085

Multiply. (Pages 98–99)

7. 800 × 0.15 120 8. 912 × 0.38 346.56 9. 461 × 0.03 13.83 10. 72 × 0.09 6.48 11. 53 × 0.21 11.13

(Pages 204–205)

12. $920 \times \frac{7}{8}$ 805 13. $618 \times \frac{2}{3}$ 412 14. $804 \times \frac{5}{6}$ 670 15. $340 \times \frac{1}{2}$ 170 16. $276 \times \frac{11}{12}$ 253

EXERCISES
See the suggested assignment guide in the Teacher's Manual.

Find each answer. Write a decimal for the per cent. (Example 1)

1. 12% of 900 108 2. 65% of 500 325 3. 8% of 80 6.4 4. 7% of 160 11.2
5. 28% of 75 21 6. 36% of 85 30.6 7. 3% of 27 0.81 8. 1% of 69 0.69
9. 95% of 188 178.6 10. 36% of 25 9 11. 18% of 215 38.7 12. 81% of 52 42.12
13. 16% of 200 32 14. 35% of 246 86.1 15. 19% of 400 76 16. 27% of 1500 405
17. 37.5% of 500 187.5 18. 16.5% of 300 49.5 19. 87.5% of 912 798 20. 62.5% of 480 300

Find each answer. Write a fraction for the per cent. (Example 2)

21. 25% of 16 4 22. 75% of 20 15 23. 80% of 60 48 24. 40% of 35 14
25. $37\frac{1}{2}$% of 56 21 26. $12\frac{1}{2}$% of 24 3 27. $16\frac{2}{3}$% of 42 7 28. $33\frac{1}{3}$% of 990 330
29. $66\frac{2}{3}$% of 720 480 30. $83\frac{1}{3}$% of 120 100 31. 10% of 516 51.6 32. 30% of 505 151.5
33. 60% of 325 195 34. 50% of 812 406 35. 40% of 324 129.6 36. 70% of 910 637

Mixed Practice The Mixed Practice contains exercises that relate to both Examples 1 and 2.

37. 25% of 160 40 38. 75% of 200 150 39. 1% of 27 0.27 40. 8% of 56 4.48
41. $37\frac{1}{2}$% of 64 24 42. $12\frac{1}{2}$% of 96 12 43. 30% of 60 18 44. 40% of 18 7.2
45. $16\frac{2}{3}$% of 420 70 46. $33\frac{1}{3}$% of 521 $173\frac{2}{3}$ 47. $62\frac{1}{2}$% of 568 355 48. $83\frac{1}{3}$% of 186 155
49. 2% of 90 1.8 50. 7% of 20 1.4 51. 50% of 456 228 52. 80% of 900 720
53. $87\frac{1}{2}$% of 464 406 54. $66\frac{2}{3}$% of 840 560 55. 35% of 200 70 56. 90% of 82 73.8
57. 77% of 350 269.5 58. 30% of 27 8.1 59. 60% of 92 55.2 60. 20% of 412 82.4

These are one-step problems which most students should be able to handle.

APPLICATIONS: Using Per Cents

61. In 1970, the price of eggs was 76% of the price in 1980. In 1980, eggs were 81¢ a dozen. Find the cost in 1970. 62¢

62. In 1970, the price of bacon was 62% of the price in 1980. In 1980, bacon was $1.56 per pound. Find the cost in 1970. 97¢

Discount

See the Teacher's Manual for the objectives.
This lesson applies the skills presented in Section 13-5.

one day only
thursday. dec. 11

44% off
14k gold jewelry

selection includes
chains. bracelets.
earrings. charms and
charmholders

all sales final

The **discount** is the amount the customer saves when the regular price of an item is reduced.

The **selling price** is the amount the customer actually pays. To find the selling price, first answer the question:

"What is the amount of discount?"

This is the <u>hidden question</u> in the problem. Then you can find the selling price.

SALE!

20% OFF ◀ Rate of Discount

REGULARLY
$117.50 ◀ Regular Price

EXAMPLE Find the selling price of the bicycle in the advertisement.

Solution: ☐1 Find the discount.

20% of 117.50 = 0.20 × 117.50 ◀ Rate of Discount × Regular Price = Discount

= 23.50   The discount is $23.50.

☐2 Find the selling price.

117.50 − 23.50 = 94.00 ◀ Regular Price − Discount = Selling Price

The selling price is $94.00.

Application

Exercises

Note that Exercises 1-10 are one-step problems.
Exercises 11-12 are two-step problems.

For Exercises 1–6, find the discount on each item.
(Example, step 1)

1. $51.74

CAMERAS
MINICA
SL-101

26% OFF

REGULARLY
$199

2. $15.58

SALE!
40% Off

Tennis
Racquet

ORIGINALLY
$38.95

3. $17.37

CLOSE-OUT
warm–up
suits

ORIGINALLY $28.95
NOW
60% Off

4. $5.94

SAVE
BLUE-JEANS

33 % OFF

REGULARLY
$18

5. $42.50

Final Sale!
GAZEBO
DRESSES

50% OFF
REGULARLY $85

6. $27.30

SALE
SALE   SALE

35% OFF!
CHAINS
14-KARAT GOLD
REGULARLY $78

Find the selling price of each item. Use the advertisements for Exercises 1–6.
(Example, step 2)

7. Tennis racquet $23.37   **8.** Camera $147.26   **9.** Warm-up suit $11.58   **10.** Blue jeans $12.00

11. The regular price of a ticket at the Carlyle Theatre is $4.50. The student discount is 10% off the regular price. Find the cost of a student ticket. $4.05

12. Senior citizens receive a special discount of 15% off at Ortega's Pharmacy. The regular price of a prescription is $12.40. Find the cost for a senior citizen. $10.54

Problem Solving and Applications

Commission

See the Teacher's Manual for the objectives.
This lesson applies the skills presented in Section 13-5.

Some salespersons are paid a **commission** based on their total amount of sales. You can use this rule to find the commission.

Commission = Amount of Sales × Rate

EXAMPLE 1 Janice is paid a 5% commission on all sales. Last week, her total sales amounted to $2800. How much was her commission?

Solution: Commission = Amount of sales × Rate

$$= \qquad 2800 \qquad × 0.05 \qquad \blacktriangleleft \text{5\% = 0.05}$$

$$= 140.00 \qquad \text{Janice's commission was } \$140.00.$$

Some salespersons are paid a base salary <u>and</u> a commission on sales. To find the total salary, first answer the question:

"What is the commission?"

This is the <u>hidden question</u> in the problem. Then you find the total salary.

EXAMPLE 2 Luis Hernandez works in a department store. He is paid a base salary of $125 per week and a 1% commission on sales. What is his total salary for a week in which he sells $13,128 worth of merchandise?

Solution: 1 Find the commission.

$$13,128 × 0.01 = 131.28 \qquad \blacktriangleleft \text{Amount of Sales} × \text{Rate} = \text{Commission}$$

2 Find the total salary.

$$125.00 + 131.28 = 256.28 \qquad \blacktriangleleft \text{Base Salary} + \text{Commission} = \text{Total Salary}$$

Luis' total salary for the week is **$256.28.**

Exercises

Note that Exercises 1-12 are one-step problems.
Exercises 13-15 are two-step problems.

For Exercises 1–8, find the commission.

	Amount of Sales	Rate of Commission	Commission		Amount of Sales	Rate of Commission	Commission
1.	$25,000	4%	? $1000	**5.**	$78,000	7%	? $5460
2.	$35,000	5%	? $1750	**6.**	$ 5,000	2%	? $100
3.	$27,500	3%	? $825	**7.**	$ 8,760	$5\frac{1}{2}$%	? $481.80
4.	$10,000	6%	? $600	**8.**	$100,000	10%	? $10,000

Application

AUCTION

9. An auctioneer sold goods amounting to $125,000. The rate of commission was 8%. What was the auctioneer's commission? $10,000

10. A real estate agent received a 7% commission on $112,000. How much did the agent receive? $7840

11. A lawyer was paid a 15% commission for collecting a debt of $25,000 for a client. How much did the lawyer receive for collecting the debt? $3750

12. An auto mechanic is paid a commission of $33\frac{1}{3}\%$ of the service income brought in each week. What is the commission for a mechanic who brings in $1860 in service income? $620

13. A broker is paid a yearly salary of $25,000 plus a commission of 6% on total sales of $1,984,000. Compute the broker's total earnings. $144,040

14. Madelyn Lee is a sales representative. She earns a salary of $560 a month plus a 6% commission on all sales. What is her total salary for a month in which her sales total $8000? $1040

15. A salesperson for Dobbs Clothiers is paid a salary of $3.80 an hour plus a 3.25% commission on all sales. Find the sales person's total earnings for a week in which he worked 40 hours and had total sales of $8100. $415.25

13-6 Interest

See the Teacher's Manual for the objectives.

Money deposited in a savings account earns **interest**. The amount deposited is called the **principal.**

PROCEDURE To find the amount of interest, multiply the principal, the rate of interest, and the time in years.

$$i = p \times r \times t \quad \begin{cases} i = interest;\ p = principal \\ r = rate;\ t = time\ in\ years. \end{cases}$$

EXAMPLE How much interest will $700 earn in 6 months? The rate of interest is 6%.

Solution:
$$i = p \times r \times t \quad \begin{cases} p = 700;\ r = 6\% = 0.06 \\ t = 6\ months = \frac{1}{2}\ year \end{cases}$$

$$i = 700 \times 0.06 \times \frac{1}{2}$$

$$i = 21.00 \quad \text{The interest is \$21.00.}$$

After completing the Example, you may wish to have students do some or all of Exercises 1-10.

Interest is often paid at the end of a quarter (every 3 months or $\frac{1}{4}$ year). Both the original deposit <u>and</u> the interest earned are left on deposit during the next quarter and earn interest. This is **compound interest** paid quarterly.

Compound interest may be considered optional for some students.

TABLE	Quarter	Interest (to nearest cent)	New Balance
	First	$1200 \times .06 \times \frac{1}{4} = \$18.00$	$\$1200 + \$18.00 = \$1218.00$
	Second	$1218 \times .06 \times \frac{1}{4} = \$18.27$	$\$1218 + \$18.27 = \$1236.27$
	Third	$1236.27 \times .06 \times \frac{1}{4} = \$18.54$	$\$1236.27 + \$18.54 = \$1254.81$
	Fourth	$1254.81 \times .06 \times \frac{1}{4} = \$18.82$	$\$1254.81 + \$18.82 = \$1273.63$

REVIEW OF RELATED SKILLS

You may wish to use these exercises before teaching the lesson.

Write a decimal for each per cent. (Pages 276–277)

1. 6% 0.06 **2.** 9% 0.09 **3.** 3% 0.03 **4.** 5% 0.05 **5.** 12% 0.12 **6.** 25% 0.25 **7.** 20% 0.20 **8.** 10% 0.10

Multiply. (Pages 98–99)

9. 900×0.07 63 **10.** 2500×0.07 175 **11.** 2000×0.06 120 **12.** 700×0.08 56

(Pages 204–205)

13. $1896 \times \frac{1}{2}$ 948 **14.** $4200 \times \frac{1}{3}$ 1400 **15.** $20,000 \times \frac{1}{4}$ 5000 **16.** $1900 \times \frac{3}{4}$ 1425 **17.** $2500 \times \frac{1}{8}$ 312.5

Add.   (Pages 94–95)

18. $1200 + 18.50$ 1218.50 **19.** $7.70 + 55$ 62.70   **20.** $675.50 + 18.55$ 694.05 **21.** $25.92 + 0.71$
26.63

Round to the nearest hundredth.   (Pages 120–121)

82.90
22. 8.157 8.16   **23.** 19.555 19.56   **24.** 110.782 110.78   **25.** 73.481 73.48   **26.** 82.903

27. 0.733 0.73   **28.** 7.205 7.21   **29.** 15.368 15.37   **30.** 34.281 34.28   **31.** 0.423

0.42
32. 0.308 0.31   **33.** 10.379 10.38   **34.** 15.061 15.06   **35.** 8.302 8.30   **36.** 18.222

18.22
37. $\$0.268$ $0.27   **38.** $\$0.590$ $0.59   **39.** $\$6.752$ $6.75   **40.** $\$14.995$ $15.00 **41.** $\$7.214$
$7.21

EXERCISES

See the suggested assignment guide in the Teacher's Manual.

For Exercises 1–10, find the interest.   (Example)

	Principal	Rate	Time	
1.	$800	5%	4 months	$13.33
2.	$1500	6%	9 months	$67.50
3.	$2500	5%	6 months	$62.50
4.	$3200	8%	3 months	$64.00
5.	$5000	6%	8 months	$200.00

	Principal	Rate	Time	
6.	$7200	5%	10 months	
7.	$1200	8%	3 months	$300.00
8.	$10,000	8%	7 months	$24.00
9.	$15,000	6%	4 months	$466.67
10.	$25,000	7%	6 months	$300.00
				$875.00

Find the interest earned on $2000 at 6% compounded quarterly.   (Table)

11. 30; 30; $2030

12. $2030 × .06 × $\frac{1}{4}$ = $30.45; $2030 + 30.45 = $2060.45

	Quarter	Interest (to nearest cent)	New Balance
11.	First	$2000 × .06 × $\frac{1}{4}$ = ?	$2000 + ? = ?
12.	Second	?	?
13.	Third	?	?
See below. **14.**	Fourth	?	?

Find the interest earned on $1200 at 8% compounded quarterly.

	Quarter	Interest (to nearest cent)	New Balance
15.	First	$1200 × .08 × $\frac{1}{4}$ = ?	$1200 + ? = ?
16.	Second	?	?
17.	Third	?	?
18.	Fourth	?	?

24; 24; $1224

$1224 × .08 × $\frac{1}{4}$ = $24.48; $1224 + 24.48 = $1248.48

$1248.48 × .08 × $\frac{1}{4}$ = $24.97; $1248.48 + 24.97 = $1273.45

$1273.45 × .08 × $\frac{1}{4}$ = $25.47; $1273.45 + 25.47 = $1298.92

13. $2060.45 × .06 × $\frac{1}{4}$ = $30.91; $2060.45 + 30.91 = $2091.36

14. $2091.36 × .06 × $\frac{1}{4}$ = $31.37; $2091.36 + 31.37 = $2122.73

career

BANKING

Compound interest is computed on the principal and on the interest previously earned. You can use a table to compute compound interest.

EXAMPLE

A bank offers 6% interest compounded quarterly (every three months). Find how much $750 will amount to (new balance) after 6 months.

Solution:

1. Find the quarterly rate.
   6% ÷ 4 = **1.5%.**

2. Find the number of quarters.
   6 months = **2 quarters**

3. Use the table to find how much $1.00 will amount to at a rate of 1.5% for 2 quarters: **1.0302**

4. Multiply 750 and 1.0302.
   750 × 1.0302 = **772.65**
   The new balance is **$772.65.**

Compound Interest for $1.00			
Quarters	1%	1.25%	1.5%
1	1.0100	1.0125	1.0150
2	1.0201	1.0252	1.0302
3	1.0303	1.0380	1.0457
4	1.0406	1.0509	1.0614
5	1.0510	1.0641	1.0773
6	1.0615	1.0774	1.0934
7	1.0721	1.0909	1.1098

EXERCISES   Note that Exercises 1-5 are non-verbal.

Find the new balance. The interest is compounded quarterly.

	Present Balance	Annual Rate	Quarterly Rate	Time	Number of Quarters	New Balance
1.	$ 500	6%	1.5% ?	6 months	? 2	? $515.10
2.	$1000	6%	1.5% ?	1 year	? 4	? $1061.40
3.	$ 850	5%	1.25% ?	6 months	? 2	? $871.42
4.	$ 900	5%	1.25% ?	1½ years	? 6	? $969.66
5.	$1500	4%	1% ?	1 year	? 4	? $1560.90

6. Mayumi has a balance of $1600 in her savings account. Interest is compounded quarterly at 6%. Find the new balance after six months. $1648.32

7. A bank offers 5% interest compounded quarterly. Find how much $1250 will amount to after one year. $1313.63

13-7 Rounding and Estimation

See the Teacher's Manual for the objectives.

This lesson may be considered optional for some students.

To estimate a per cent of a number, you can sometimes round the number only.

EXAMPLE 1 Estimate the discount on the handbag.

Solutions:
1. $20\% = \frac{1}{5}$
2. Round to a <u>convenient price</u>; that is, to a price that is easy to multiply by $\frac{1}{5}$.

   59.95 is about 60.
3. $\frac{1}{5} \times 60 = 12$ **Estimated discount: $12.**

After completing Example 1, you may wish to have students do some or all of Exercisees 1-10.

Sometimes you can round to a convenient per cent.

EXAMPLE 2 Estimate the discount on the running shoes.

Solution:
1. Round to a <u>convenient per cent</u>; that is, to a per cent close to 26% <u>and</u> easy to multiply by 40.

   26% is about 25%. $25\% = \frac{1}{4}$
2. $\frac{1}{4} \times 40 = 10$ **Estimated Discount: $10**

REVIEW OF RELATED SKILLS
You may wish to use these exercises before teaching the lesson.

Round to the nearest whole number.   (Pages 120–121)

1. 58.75 59   2. 16.50 17   3. 11.21 11   4. 32.95 33   5. 70.55 71   6. 83.05 83

7. 43.8 44   8. 5.499 5   9. 6.3 6   10. 19.5 20   11. 2.09 2   12. 69.5 70

13. 399.90 400   14. 151.62 152   15. 100.91 101   16. 100.31 100   17. 68.55 69   18. 42.48 42

Round to the nearest ten.   (Pages 120–121)

19. 58.75 60   20. 16.50 20   21. 11.21 10   22. 32.95 30   23. 70.55 70   24. 83.05 80

25. 39.5 40   26. 46.81 50   27. 50.05 50   28. 86.91 90   29. 70.62 70   30. 78.62 80

Multiply.   (Pages 204–205)

31. $\frac{1}{10} \times 900$ 90   32. $\frac{1}{8} \times 512$ 64   33. $\frac{1}{6} \times 426$ 71   34. $\frac{1}{12} \times 1560$ 130   35. $\frac{2}{5} \times 75$ 30

36. $\frac{2}{3} \times 960$ 640   37. $\frac{1}{4} \times 188$ 47   38. $\frac{5}{8} \times 200$ 125   39. $\frac{3}{10} \times 900$ 270   40. $\frac{5}{6} \times 900$ 750

PER CENT   **291**

EXERCISES

Choose the best estimate. Choose a, b, or c. (Example 1)

1. 10% of $29.95 c **a.** 10% of $20   **b.** 10% of $25   **c.** 10% of $30
2. 50% of $91.30 a **a.** 50% of $90   **b.** 50% of $95   **c.** 50% of $100
3. 20% of $34.75 b **a.** 20% of $30   **b.** 20% of $35   **c.** 20% of $40
4. 30% of $10.06 a **a.** 30% of $10   **b.** 30% of $15   **c.** 30% of $20
5. 60% of $73.90 a **a.** 60% of $70   **b.** 60% of $90   **c.** 60% of $80
6. 50% of $121.90 a **a.** $60   **b.** $62.50   **c.** $65
7. 20% of $98.50 b **a.** $18   **b.** $20   **c.** $25
8. 40% of $179.55 c **a.** $68   **b.** $70   **c.** $72
9. 25% of $20.98 a **a.** $5   **b.** $6   **c.** $7
10. 75% of $101.17 a **a.** $75   **b.** $90   **c.** $60

Choose the best estimate. Choose a, b, or c. (Example 2)

11. 21% of $150 c **a.** 30% of $150   **b.** 25% of $150   **c.** 20% of $150
12. 9.5% of $700 b **a.** 5% of $700   **b.** 10% of $700   **c.** 20% of $700
13. 26% of $100 b **a.** 20% of $100   **b.** 25% of $100   **c.** 30% of $100
14. 33% of $90 b **a.** 30% of $90   **b.** $33\frac{1}{3}$% of $90   **c.** 40% of $90
15. 12% of $24 a **a.** $12\frac{1}{2}$% of $24   **b.** $16\frac{2}{3}$% of $24   **c.** 20% of $24
16. 19% of $80 b **a.** $8   **b.** $16   **c.** $20
17. 8.5% of $40 a **a.** $4   **b.** $2   **c.** $8
18. 41% of $1600 c **a.** $800   **b.** $480   **c.** $640
19. 37.5% of $800 b **a.** $240   **b.** $320   **c.** $400
20. 10.5% of $1200 a **a.** $120   **b.** $60   **c.** $240

Mixed Practice   The Mixed Practice contains exercises that relate to both Examples 1 and 2.

Choose the best estimate for each discount. Choose a, b, or c.

21.
a

a. $4 **b.** $15 **c.** $20

22.
c

a. $18 **b.** $24 **c.** $20

23.
c

a. $16 **b.** $18 **c.** $20

24.
a

Sale!
SnowTires
9% OFF
REGULARLY $39.95

a. $4   **b.** $5   **c.** $6

25.
c

Sale
19% OFF
Tape Deck
REGULARLY $50

a. $1   **b.** $5   **c.** $10

26.
b

SALE
RAIN COAT
58% OFF
REGULARLY $91.20

a. $48   **b.** $54   **c.** $60

Calculator exercises are optional.

FINDING DISCOUNT

Before using a calculator to find the amount of discount:

1 Estimate the answer.

2 Use the calculator to find the exact answer.

3 Compare the exact answer with the estimate to see whether the exact answer is reasonable.

EXAMPLE: Regular Price: $200.00   Rate of Discount: 9.5%   Discount: __?__

Solution: Estimated Discount: $\frac{1}{10} \times \$200 = \$20$ ◀ **9.5% is about 10%.**

Exact Discount: $200 \times 9.5\%$

[2] [0] [0] [×] [9] [·] [5] [%] | 19. |

Since the estimate is $20, **$19** is a reasonable answer.

EXERCISES

First estimate the discount. Then find the exact discount.

	Regular Price	Rate of Discount	Estimated Discount	Exact Discount
1.	$800.00	26%	? $200	? $208
2.	$401.50	20%	? $80	? $80.30
3.	$ 87.90	25%	? $22	? $21.98
4.	$996.85	30%	? $300	? $299.06
5.	$ 25.00	8.5%	? $2	? $2.13

Calculator

PER CENT   **293**

Chapter Review

These exercises review the vocabulary, skills, and applications presented in the chapter as a preparation for the chapter test.

Part 1: Vocabulary

For Exercises 1–5, choose from the box at the right the word(s) that completes each statement.

1. Per cent means per hundred or __?__. (Page 274) hundredths
2. To write a decimal for a per cent, move the decimal point __?__ places to the left. (Page 276) two
3. To write a per cent for a decimal, move the decimal point two places to the __?__. (Page 276) right
4. To write a fraction for a per cent, write a fraction with a __?__ of 100 for the per cent. (Page 278) denominator
5. To write a per cent for a fraction, first __?__ the numerator of the fraction by the denominator. (Page 280) divide

> right
> numerator
> hundredths
> left
> denominator
> two
> divide
> multiply

Part 2: Skills

Write a per cent for each fraction. (Pages 274–275)

6. $\frac{2}{100}$ 2% 7. $\frac{4}{100}$ 4% 8. $\frac{17}{100}$ 17% 9. $\frac{35}{100}$ 35% 10. $\frac{60}{100}$ 60% 11. $\frac{18}{100}$ 18%

12. $\frac{42}{100}$ 42% 13. $\frac{80}{100}$ 80% 14. $\frac{27}{100}$ 27% 15. $\frac{43}{100}$ 43% 16. $\frac{57}{100}$ 57% 17. $\frac{79}{100}$ 79%

Write a decimal for each per cent. (Pages 276–277)

18. 43% 0.43 19. 54% 0.54 20. 321% 3.21 21. 280% 2.80 22. 61.2% 0.612 23. 17.9% 0.179

24. 5% 0.05 25. 3% 0.03 26. 2.1% 0.021 27. 7.9% 0.079 28. 0.8% 0.008 29. 0.5% 0.005

Write a per cent for each decimal. (Pages 276–277)

30. 0.26 26% 31. 0.31 31% 32. 0.73 73% 33. 0.46 46% 34. 0.09 9% 35. 0.06 6%

36. 0.431 43.1% 37. 0.792 79.2% 38. 0.068 6.8% 39. 0.071 7.1% 40. 0.007 0.7% 41. 0.003 0.3%

Write a fraction in lowest terms for each per cent. (Pages 278–279)

42. 16% $\frac{4}{25}$ 43. 24% $\frac{6}{25}$ 44. 5% $\frac{1}{20}$ 45. 4% $\frac{1}{25}$ 46. $\frac{7}{8}$% $\frac{7}{800}$ 47. $\frac{5}{7}$% $\frac{1}{140}$

48. $\frac{7}{9}$% $\frac{7}{900}$ 49. $\frac{5}{9}$% $\frac{1}{180}$ 50. $6\frac{1}{2}$% $\frac{13}{200}$ 51. $5\frac{3}{4}$% $\frac{23}{400}$ 52. $12\frac{2}{3}$% $\frac{19}{150}$ 53. $15\frac{1}{2}$% $\frac{31}{200}$

Write a per cent for each fraction or mixed number. (Pages 280–281)

54. $\frac{3}{5}$ 60% 55. $\frac{7}{10}$ 70% 56. $\frac{9}{20}$ 45% 57. $\frac{7}{25}$ 28% 58. $\frac{6}{7}$ $85\frac{5}{7}$% 59. $\frac{7}{9}$ $77\frac{7}{9}$%

60. $2\frac{1}{2}$ 250% 61. $3\frac{1}{4}$ 325% 62. $2\frac{2}{5}$ 240% 63. $4\frac{3}{4}$ 475% 64. $1\frac{3}{11}$ $127\frac{3}{11}$ 65. $6\frac{1}{12}$ $608\frac{1}{3}$%

Find each answer. Write a decimal for the per cent. (Pages 282–283)

66. 15% of 300 45 67. 23% of 200 46 68. 9% of 700 63 69. 7% of 210 14.7

70. 3% of 65 1.95 71. 1% of 82 0.82 72. 43% of 221 95.03 73. 51% of 145 73.95

Find each answer. Write a fraction for the per cent.   (Pages 282–283)

74. 25% of 20 ₅   **75.** 50% of 14 ₇   **76.** $37\frac{1}{2}$% of 64 ₂₄   **77.** $66\frac{2}{3}$% of 39 ₂₆

78. 40% of 55 ₂₂   **79.** 75% of 28 ₂₁   **80.** $33\frac{1}{3}$% of 120 ₄₀   **81.** $12\frac{1}{2}$% of 72 ₉

For Exercises 82–89, find the interest.   (Pages 288–289)

	Principal	Rate	Time			Principal	Rate	Time
82.	$500	5%	4 months $8.33		**86.**	$1800	6%	10 months $90.00
83.	$900	6%	9 months $40.50		**87.**	$3200	8%	3 months $64.00
84.	$1200	5%	6 months $30.00		**88.**	$10,000	5%	7 months $291.67
85.	$1400	8%	3 months $28.00		**89.**	$15,000	8%	4 months $400.00

Find the interest earned on $3000 at 8% compounded quarterly.
(Pages 288–289)

	Quarter	Interest (to nearest cent)	New Balance
90.	First	$3000 \times .08 \times \frac{1}{4} = \underline{\ ?\ }$ $60	$3000 + \underline{\ ?\ } = \underline{\ ?\ }$ $60 $3060
91.	Second	?	$3060 + $61.20 ? = $3121.20
92.	Third	?	? $3120 + 62.42 = $3183.62
93.	Fourth	?	?

$3183.62 \times 0.08 \times \frac{1}{4} = 63.67 $3183.62 + $63.67 = 3247.29

Choose the best estimate. Choose a, b, c, or d.   (Pages 291–293)

94. 10% of $49.95 ᵦ   **a.** $4   **b.** $5   **c.** $6   **d.** $10

95. 50% of $81.50   ᵈ   **a.** $50   **b.** $45   **c.** $60   **d.** $40

96. 9.6% of $100 ₐ   **a.** $10   **b.** $9   **c.** $8   **d.** $7

97. 19% of $500 ᵦ   **a.** $90   **b.** $100   **c.** $110   **d.** $120

91. $3060 \times 0.08 \times \frac{1}{4} = 61.20 92. $3121.20 \times 0.08 \times \frac{1}{4} = 62.42

Part 3: Applications   The use of these word problems depends on which applications were studied.

98. In 1970, the price of chicken was 58% of the price in 1980. In 1980, chicken cost $0.67 a pound. Find the cost in 1970. $0.39 (Pages 282–283)

99. The regular price of a hardwood table at Mason's Furniture is $300. Display models are sold at 40% off. Find the new price. $180 (Pages 284–285)

100. An appliance repairmen is paid a $12\frac{1}{2}$% commission on all the repairs he makes in a week. One week his repairs totaled $640. What was his commission? $80 (Pages 286–287)

101. A box of ping pong balls regularly sells for $2.98. They are on sale at 50% off. Choose the best estimate for the discount. c (Pages 291–292)

    a. $2   **b.** $2.50   **c.** $1.50

Chapter Test
The Teacher's Resource Book contains two forms of each chapter test.

Write a decimal for each per cent.

1. 25% ₀.₂₅ **2.** 63% 0.63 **3.** 181% 1.81 **4.** 4% 0.04 **5.** 3% 0.03 **6.** 6.2%
0.062

Write a per cent for each decimal.

7. 0.32 32% **8.** 0.41 41% **9.** 0.58 58% **10.** 0.046 4.6% **11.** 0.073 7.3% **12.** 0.007
0.7%

Write a fraction in lowest terms for each per cent.

13. 23% $\frac{23}{100}$ **14.** 44% $\frac{11}{25}$ **15.** 5% $\frac{1}{20}$ **16.** 6% $\frac{3}{50}$ **17.** $\frac{5}{6}$% $\frac{1}{120}$ **18.** $3\frac{1}{2}$%
$\frac{7}{200}$

Write a per cent for each fraction or mixed number.

19. $\frac{4}{5}$ 80% **20.** $\frac{3}{4}$ 75% **21.** $\frac{7}{20}$ 35% **22.** $\frac{5}{7}$ $71\frac{3}{7}$% **23.** $\frac{8}{9}$ $88\frac{8}{9}$% **24.** $1\frac{1}{4}$
125%

Find each answer.

25. 10% of 40 4 **26.** $12\frac{1}{2}$% of 24 3 **27.** 23% of 60 13.8 **28.** 1% of 810
8.10

For Exercises 29–30, find the interest. The use of these word problems depends on which applications were studied.

29. Principal: $600;   Rate: 6%;
Time: 3 months $9.00

30. Principal: $10,000;   Rate: 8%;
Time: 9 months $600.00

31. In 1970, the price of gasoline
was 28% of the price in 1980. In
1980, gasoline cost $1.33 per
gallon. Find the price in 1970. 37¢

32. The regular price of soccer balls
at Friedman's Sports is $8.95. They
are on sale at 10% off. Find the
sale price. $8.06

33. Choose the best estimate for the
discount. Choose *a*, *b*, or *c*. a

REGULARLY $24.88
25% OFF

a. $6   **b.** $7   **c.** $8

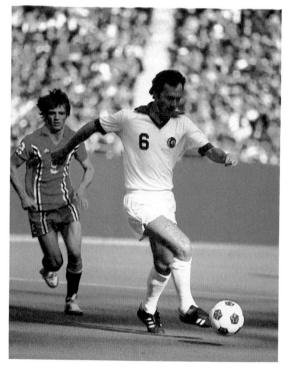

Additional Practice

You may wish to use some or all of these exercises depending on how well students performed on the formal chapter test.

Skills

Write a decimal for each per cent.   (Pages 276–277)

1. 24% 0.24   2. 46% 0.46   3. 7% 0.07   4. 3% 0.03   5. 246% 2.46   6. 382% 3.82

7. 34.2% 0.342   8. 21.3% 0.213   9. 2.8% 0.028   10. 6.4% 0.064   11. 0.7% 0.007   12. 0.9% 0.009

Write a per cent for each decimal.   (Pages 276–277)

13. 0.25 25%   14. 0.47 47%   15. 0.58 58%   16. 0.63 63%   17. 0.04 4%   18. 0.02 2%

19. 0.273 27.3%   20. 0.452 45.2%   21. 0.003 0.3%   22. 0.009 0.9%   23. 0.027 2.7%   24. 0.051 5.1%

Write a fraction in lowest terms for each per cent.
(Pages 278–279)

25. 10% $\frac{1}{10}$ 26. 26% $\frac{13}{50}$ 27. 34% $\frac{17}{50}$ 28. 3% $\frac{3}{100}$ 29. 6% $\frac{3}{50}$ 30. 28% $\frac{7}{25}$

31. $\frac{5}{8}$% $\frac{1}{160}$ 32. $\frac{1}{2}$% $\frac{1}{200}$ 33. $3\frac{2}{3}$% $\frac{11}{300}$ 34. $6\frac{1}{4}$% $\frac{1}{16}$ 35. $5\frac{3}{4}$% $\frac{23}{400}$ 36. $12\frac{1}{2}$% $\frac{1}{8}$

Write a per cent for each fraction or mixed number.
(Pages 280–281)

37. $\frac{1}{2}$ 50%   38. $\frac{3}{10}$ 30%   39. $\frac{4}{11}$ $36\frac{4}{11}$%   40. $\frac{2}{7}$ $28\frac{4}{7}$%   41. $\frac{4}{25}$ 16%   42. $\frac{3}{50}$ 6%

43. $3\frac{1}{5}$ 320%   44. $2\frac{4}{5}$ 280%   45. $4\frac{2}{7}$ $428\frac{4}{7}$%   46. $5\frac{1}{3}$ $533\frac{1}{3}$%   47. $6\frac{1}{8}$ $612\frac{1}{2}$%   48. $7\frac{2}{3}$ $766\frac{2}{3}$%

Find each answer. Write a decimal for the per cent.   (Pages 282–283)

49. 21% of 86 18.06   50. 14% of 22 3.08   51. 9% of 45 4.05   52. 5% of 16 0.8

53. 51% of 73 37.23   54. 42% of 34 14.28   55. 56% of 26 14.56   56. 26% of 33 8.58

Find each answer. Write a fraction for the per cent.   (Pages 282–283)

57. 25% of 80 20   58. 20% of 65 13   59. 40% of 30 12   60. 50% of 48 24

61. $33\frac{1}{3}$% of 66 22   62. $37\frac{1}{2}$% of 64 24   63. $12\frac{1}{2}$% of 48 6   64. $66\frac{2}{3}$% of 96 64

For Exercises 65–68, find the interest.   (Pages 288–289)

	Principal	Rate	Time
65.	$600	4%	4 months $8
66.	$800	7%	6 months $28

	Principal	Rate	Time
67.	$2500	6%	8 months $100
68.	$10,000	8%	3 months $200

Applications   The use of these word problems depends on which applications were studied.

69. The regular price of a desk at Thompson's Furniture Mart is is $388. Display models are sold at 35% off. Find the new price. (Pages 284–285) $252.20

70. A sales clerk in a jewelry store is paid a 3% commission on weekly sales. One week the clerk's sales were $1400. Find the commission. (Pages 286–287) $42

REVIEW OF RELATED SKILLS FOR CHAPTER 14

Chapter 14 may be considered optional for some students.
We suggested that some or all of this page be reviewed before proceeding with the chapter.

Subtract.　　(Pages 10–11, 14–15)

1. 1600 − 1200 _400_　　**2.** 4500 − 2800 _1700_　　**3.** 6300 − 5400 _900_　　**4.** 2100 − 1900 _200_

Multiply.　　(Pages 98–99)

5. 1600 × 0.34 _544_　　**6.** 2400 × 0.16 _384_　　**7.** 850 × 0.05 _42.5_　　**8.** 961 × 0.04 _38.44_

Divide.　　(Pages 112–113)

9. 26 ÷ 0.5 _52_　　**10.** 132 ÷ 0.11 _1200_　　**11.** $0.08\overline{)64}$ _800_　　**12.** $0.25\overline{)1.25}$ _5_

Round each decimal to the nearest whole number.　　(Pages 120–121)

13. 3.05 _3_　　**14.** 12.9 _13_　　**15.** 8.62 _9_　　**16.** 13.2 _13_　　**17.** 19.55 _20_　　**18.** 4.67 _5_

Write each fraction in lowest terms.　　(Pages 182–183)

19. $\frac{1400}{2400}$ _$\frac{7}{12}$_　　**20.** $\frac{3200}{3600}$ _$\frac{8}{9}$_　　**21.** $\frac{1600}{4800}$ _$\frac{1}{3}$_　　**22.** $\frac{1200}{6000}$ _$\frac{1}{5}$_　　**23.** $\frac{1500}{4500}$ _$\frac{1}{3}$_　　**24.** $\frac{4200}{8000}$ _$\frac{21}{40}$_

Solve each equation.　　(Pages 252–253)

25. $6n = 84$ _14_　　**26.** $0.5n = 80$ _160_　　**27.** $\frac{n}{7} = 25$ _175_　　**28.** $\frac{n}{5} = 6.2$ _31_

Solve each proportion.　　(Pages 264–265)

29. $\frac{n}{4} = \frac{15}{20}$ _3_　　**30.** $\frac{20}{100} = \frac{n}{35}$ _7_　　**31.** $\frac{16}{48} = \frac{1}{n}$ _3_　　**32.** $\frac{14}{n} = \frac{42}{57}$ _19_

Write a decimal for each per cent.　　(Pages 276–277)

33. 16% _0.16_　　**34.** 45% _0.45_　　**35.** 6% _0.06_　　**36.** 9% _0.09_　　**37.** $12\frac{1}{2}\%$ _$0.12\frac{1}{2}$_　　**38.** $33\frac{1}{3}\%$ _$0.33\frac{1}{3}$_

Write a per cent for each decimal.　　(Pages 276–277)

39. 0.63 _63%_　　**40.** 0.56 _56%_　　**41.** 0.05 _5%_　　**42.** 0.03 _3%_　　**43.** $0.14\frac{2}{7}$ _$14\frac{2}{7}\%$_　　**44.** $0.37\frac{1}{2}$ _$37\frac{1}{2}\%$_

Write a fraction for each per cent.　　(Pages 278–279)

45. 40% _$\frac{2}{5}$_　　**46.** 55% _$\frac{11}{20}$_　　**47.** 37% _$\frac{37}{100}$_　　**48.** 21% _$\frac{21}{100}$_　　**49.** $66\frac{2}{3}\%$ _$\frac{2}{3}$_　　**50.** $62\frac{1}{2}\%$ _$\frac{5}{8}$_

Write a two-place decimal for each fraction. Then write a per cent for each decimal.　　(Pages 280–281)

51. $\frac{3}{4}$　　**52.** $\frac{2}{5}$　　**53.** $\frac{1}{2}$　　**54.** $\frac{1}{4}$　　**55.** $\frac{3}{8}$　　**56.** $\frac{5}{9}$　　**57.** $\frac{25}{125}$　　**58.** $\frac{16}{56}$

_0.75 = 75%_　_0.40 = 40%_　_0.50 = 50%_　_0.25 = 25%_　_$0.37\frac{1}{2} = 37\frac{1}{2}\%$_　_$0.55\frac{5}{9} = 55\frac{5}{9}\%$_　_0.20 = 20%_　_$0.28\frac{4}{7} = 28\frac{4}{7}\%$_

Divide. Carry the division to two decimal places.　　(Pages 280–281)

59. 1 ÷ 4 _0.25_　　**60.** 3 ÷ 5 _0.60_　　**61.** 6 ÷ 10 _0.60_　　**62.** 4 ÷ 5 _0.80_　　**63.** 7 ÷ 9 _$0.77\frac{7}{9}$_　　**64.** 5 ÷ 6 _$0.83\frac{1}{3}$_

65. 1 ÷ 25 _0.04_　　**66.** 1 ÷ 20 _0.05_　　**67.** 2 ÷ 4 _0.5_　　**68.** 9 ÷ 12 _0.75_　　**69.** 7 ÷ 20 _0.35_　　**70.** 6 ÷ 8 _0.75_

71. 9 ÷ 50 _0.18_　　**72.** 6 ÷ 30 _0.2_　　**73.** 8 ÷ 20 _0.4_　　**74.** 7 ÷ 50 _0.14_　　**75.** 1 ÷ 50 _0.02_　　**76.** 2 ÷ 9 _$0.22\frac{2}{9}$_

14 MORE ON PER CENT

SKILLS

14-1   Finding What Per Cent a Number is of Another

14-2   Per Cent of Increase or Decrease

14-3   Finding a Number Given a Per Cent

14-4   Review of Per Cent

14-5   Review of Word Problems with Per Cent

APPLICATIONS

Interest Rate
Sports
Markup and Selling Price
Energy Costs
Minimum Wage

CAREER

Health

14-1 Finding What Per Cent A Number is Of Another

See the Teacher's Manual for the objectives.

PROCEDURE To find what per cent a number is of another:

    $\boxed{1}$ Write an equation.

    $\boxed{2}$ Solve the equation for n.

    $\boxed{3}$ Write a per cent for n.

EXAMPLE 1 What per cent of 85 is 17?

Solution: $\boxed{1}$ Write an equation. $\boxed{2}$ Solve the equation.

What per cent of 85 is 17?

$$n \qquad \times 85 = 17, \quad \text{or}$$

$$85n = 17$$

$$85n = 17$$

$$\frac{85n}{85} = \frac{17}{85}$$

$$n = \frac{17}{85}$$

$\boxed{3}$ Write a per cent for $\frac{17}{85}$.

$\frac{17}{85}$ means $17 \div 85$. $\blacktriangleleft$ $85)\overline{17.0}^{\,0.2\,=\,0.20}$

$0.20 = \mathbf{20\%}$ Thus, 17 is **20% of 85**.

After completing Example 1, you may wish to have students do some or all of Exercises 1-4, and 7-22.
In step $\boxed{3}$ of Example 1, you could write $\frac{17}{85}$ in lowest terms.

$$\frac{\overset{1}{\cancel{17}}}{\underset{5}{\cancel{85}}} = \frac{1}{5} \quad \text{and} \quad \frac{1}{5} = \mathbf{20\%}$$

Sometimes the per cent problem is written in another way.

EXAMPLE 2 9 is what per cent of 6?

Solution: $\boxed{1}$ 9 is what per cent of 6? $\boxed{2}$ $6n = 9$ $\blacktriangleleft$ *9 = 6n is the same as 6n = 9.*

$$9 = n \qquad \times 6, \quad \text{or}$$

$$9 = 6n$$

$$\frac{6n}{6} = \frac{9}{6}$$

$\boxed{3}$ $\frac{3}{2} \longrightarrow 2)\overline{3.0}^{\,1.5}$ $\blacktriangleleft$ *1.5 = 1.50*

$n = \frac{9}{6}$, or $\frac{3}{2}$ $\blacktriangleleft$ **Lowest terms**

$1.50 = 150\%$

Thus, 9 is **150% of 6**.

Solve each equation for n.   (Pages 252–253)

1. $20n = 80$ 4   **2.** $15n = 75$ 5   **3.** $7n = 98$ 14   **4.** $5n = 125$ 25   **5.** $16n = 144$ 9

6. $12n = 384$ 32   **7.** $14n = 70$ 5   **8.** $20n = 280$ 14   **9.** $10n = 120$ 12   **10.** $19n = 171$ 9

Write a per cent for each fraction.   (Pages 280–281)

11. $\frac{12}{48}$ 25% **12.** $\frac{15}{75}$ 20% **13.** $\frac{9}{180}$ 5% **14.** $\frac{8}{240}$ $3\frac{1}{3}$% **15.** $\frac{21}{56}$ $37\frac{1}{2}$% **16.** $\frac{63}{72}$ $87\frac{1}{2}$% **17.** $\frac{30}{48}$ $62\frac{1}{2}$% **18.** $\frac{72}{96}$

75%

EXERCISES

See the suggested assignment guide in the Teacher's Manual.

Write an equation for each exercise.   (Example 1, step 1)

1. What per cent of 20 is 15? $n \times 20 = 15$ **2.** What per cent of 60 is 20? $n \times 60 = 20$

3. What per cent of 80 is 60? $n \times 80 = 60$ **4.** What per cent of 64 is 56? $n \times 64 = 56$

5. 30 is what per cent of 66? $30 = n \times 66$ **6.** 2 is what per cent of 50? $2 = n \times 50$

Solve.   (Example 1)

7. What per cent of 80 is 20? 25%   **8.** What per cent of 25 is 16? 64%

9. What per cent of 15 is 3? 20%   **10.** What per cent of 15 is 12? 80%

11. What per cent of 48 is 16? $33\frac{1}{3}$%   **12.** What per cent of 72 is 36? 50%

13. What per cent of 90 is 9? 10%   **14.** What per cent of 120 is 30? 25%

15. What per cent of 70 is 14? 20%   **16.** What per cent of 96 is 72? 75%

17. What per cent of 80 is 24? 30%   **18.** What per cent of 50 is 5? 10%

19. What per cent of 45 is 9? 20%   **20.** What per cent of 64 is 16? 25%

21. What per cent of 30 is 25? $83\frac{1}{3}$%   **22.** What per cent of 4 is 12? 300%

(Example 2)

23. 3 is what per cent of 4? 75%   **24.** 2 is what per cent of 5? 40%

25. 7 is what per cent of 8? $87\frac{1}{2}$%   **26.** 1 is what per cent of 4? 25%

27. 5 is what per cent of 20? 25%   **28.** 10 is what per cent of 10? 100%

29. 24 is what per cent of 8? 300%   **30.** 54 is what per cent of 27? 200%

31. 9 is what per cent of 12? 75%   **32.** 25 is what per cent of 30? $83\frac{1}{3}$%

33. 20 is what per cent of 16? 125%   **34.** 90 is what per cent of 18? 500%

Mixed Practice The Mixed Practice contains exercises that relate to both Examples 1 and 2.

35. What per cent of 60 is 50? $83\frac{1}{3}$%   **36.** What per cent of 180 is 30? $16\frac{2}{3}$%

37. 350 is what per cent of 200? 175%   **38.** 63 is what per cent of 70? 90%

39. 75 is what per cent of 200? $37\frac{1}{2}$%   **40.** 25 is what per cent of 125? 20%

41. What per cent of 32 is 4? $12\frac{1}{2}$%   **42.** What per cent of 120 is 18? 15%

Problem Solving and Applications

Interest Rate

See the Teacher's Manual for the objectives.
This lesson applies the skills presented in Section 14-1.

When you borrow money, you pay a fee, or **interest,** for the use of the money. When you know the **principal** (amount of the loan), the amount of interest, and the time, you can find the yearly interest rate for the loan.

Interest rate = Interest ÷ (Principal × Time), or

$$r \quad = \quad i \quad ÷ (\quad p \quad × \quad t \quad)$$

EXAMPLE   Susan Knight borrowed $650.00 for 3 months. She agreed to pay $29.25 in interest on the loan. What is the yearly interest rate?

Solution: $r = i ÷ (p × t)$ ◀   *i = $29.25; p = $650.00*
t = 3 months = $\frac{1}{4}$ year

$r = 29.95 ÷ (650.00 × \frac{1}{4})$

$r = 29.25 ÷ 162.5$ ◀   **Carry the division to 3 decimal places.**

$r = 0.180$ 0.18 0 = **18%**   The yearly interest rate is **18%**.

Exercises

Find the yearly interest rate for each loan. Round your answers to the nearest whole per cent. Note that Exercises 1-6 are nonverbal.

	Principal	Time	Interest			Principal	Time	Interest
1.	$560	3 months	$16.80 12%		**4.**	$450	3 months	$20.81 18%
2.	$463	9 months	$27.78 8%		**5.**	$450	4 months	$27.00 18%
3.	$1450	9 months	$66.70 6%		**6.**	$3450	24 months	$741.75 11%

7. Bob borrows $670 to install a solar hot water heating system. He agrees to repay the loan and $20.10 in interest in 3 months. What is the yearly interest rate? 12%

8. Rosa borrows $690 to repair the roof of her house. She agrees to repay the loan in 6 months and pay $44.85 in interest. What is the yearly rate of interest? 13%

14-2 Per Cent of Increase or Decrease See the Teacher's Manual for the objectives.

The **per cent of increase** is the ratio of the amount of increase to the original amount.

PROCEDURE To find the per cent of increase:

[1] Find the amount of increase.

[2] Write the ratio: $\dfrac{\text{Amount of Increase}}{\text{Original Amount}}$

[3] Write a per cent for the ratio.

EXAMPLE 1 In 1978, the cost for the first 3 ounces of first–class mail was 15¢. In 1981, the cost rose to 18¢. Find the per cent of increase.

Solution:

[1] Amount of increase: $18 - 15 = 3$

[2] $\dfrac{\text{Amount of increase}}{\text{Original amount}} = \dfrac{3}{15}$ ◀ **Write in lowest terms.**

$= \dfrac{1}{5}$

[3] Per cent of increase: **20%**

After completing Example 1, you may wish to have students do some or all of Exercises 1-6.

You follow the same procedure to find the **per cent of decrease.**

PROCEDURE To find the per cent of decrease:

[1] Find the amount of decrease.

[2] Write the ratio: $\dfrac{\text{Amount of Decrease}}{\text{Original Amount}}$

[3] Write a per cent for the ratio.

EXAMPLE 2 Last month, the Gadbois family paid $90 for heating. By lowering the thermostat setting, they reduced this month's bill to $85. Find the per cent of decrease. Round your answer to the nearest whole per cent.

Solution:

[1] Amount of decrease: $90 - 85 = 5$

[2] $\dfrac{\text{Amount of decrease}}{\text{Original amount}} = \dfrac{5}{90} = \dfrac{1}{18} = 0.055$

[3] Per cent of decrease: $0.06 = 6\%$ ◀ **Nearest whole per cent**

REVIEW OF RELATED SKILLS
You may wish to use these exercises before teaching the lesson.

Subtract. (Pages 10–11, 14–15)

1. $2500 - 1900$ ₆₀₀ **2.** $3600 - 2800$ ₈₀₀ **3.** $2600 - 1200$ ₁₄₀₀ **4.** $4200 - 2500$
₁₇₀₀

Write each fraction in lowest terms. (Pages 182–183)

5. $\frac{2500}{4000}$ $\frac{5}{8}$ **6.** $\frac{2700}{3600}$ $\frac{3}{4}$ **7.** $\frac{1400}{4800}$ $\frac{7}{24}$ **8.** $\frac{1200}{6400}$ $\frac{3}{16}$ **9.** $\frac{5000}{5800}$ $\frac{25}{29}$ **10.** $\frac{3200}{8000}$
$\frac{2}{5}$

Write a per cent for each fraction. (Pages 280–281)

11. $\frac{1}{4}$ 25% **12.** $\frac{1}{3}$ 33⅓% **13.** $\frac{1}{5}$ 20% **14.** $\frac{1}{6}$ 16⅔% **15.** $\frac{1}{8}$ 12½% **16.** $\frac{1}{10}$ 10% **17.** $\frac{1}{20}$ 5% **18.** $\frac{1}{25}$ 4%

19. $\frac{3}{4}$ 75% **20.** $\frac{3}{5}$ 60% **21.** $\frac{2}{3}$ 66⅔% **22.** $\frac{5}{8}$ 62½% **23.** $\frac{5}{6}$ 83⅓% **24.** $\frac{7}{8}$ 87½% **25.** $\frac{7}{10}$ 70% **26.** $\frac{13}{20}$ 65%

Round each decimal to the nearest whole number. (Pages 120–121)

27. 6.05 6 **28.** 11.9 12 **29.** 7.28 7 **30.** 25.1 25 **31.** 18.55 19 **32.** 9.05 9

EXERCISES
See the suggested assignment guide in the Teacher's Manual.

For Exercises 1–6, find the per cent of increase. (Example 1)

Item	Original Value	Present Value		Item	Original Value	Present Value
1. Bicycle	$100	$125 25%	**4.**	Ring	$45	$85 89⅘%
2. Sports Car	$6000	$8000 33⅓%	**5.**	Stamp Album	$1200	$1800 50%
3. House	$40,000	$65,000 62½%	**6.**	Antique Chair	$25	$40 60%

For Exercises 7–12, find the per cent of decrease. (Example 2)

Item	Original Value	Present Value		Item	Original Value	Present Value
7. Bicycle	$125	$90 28%	**10.**	Motorcycle	$2400	$1500 37½%
8. Car	$8000	$6000 25%	**11.**	Typewriter	$325	$260 20%
9. Boat	$18,000	$15,000 16⅔%	**12.**	Watch	$45	$30 33⅓%

APPLICATIONS: Using Per Cent of Increase or Decrease
Most students should be able to solve these word problems.

13. In 1976, the value of an early comic book was $5000. In 1980, the value was $8500. What was the per cent of increase? 70%

14. In 1972, a pocket calculator cost $40. In 1981, the same type of pocket calculator cost $10. Find the per cent of decrease. 75%

15. In May, the depth of water in a reservoir was 30 feet. In August, the depth was 18 feet. Find the percent of decrease. 40%

16. Train fare by coach from Chicago to New Orleans cost $45 in 1970. By 1980, the fare had increased to $75. Find the per cent of increase. 66⅔%

Problem Solving and Applications

Sports

See the Teacher's Manual for the objectives.
This lesson applies the skills presented in Section 14-2.

Sports reporters use estimation to report the per cent of increase or decrease in attendance at games.

EXAMPLE Estimate the per cent of increase in attendance from 1979 to 1980.

Cleveland Indians	1979	1980
Attendance	800,584	1,011,444

Solution:

1 Round each attendance to the nearest hundred thousands.

1979: 800,000   1980: 1,000,000

2 Find the amount of increase.

$1,000,000 - 800,000 = 200,000$

3 $\dfrac{\text{Amount of increase}}{\text{Original amount}} = \dfrac{200,000}{800,000} = \dfrac{1}{4}$

4 Write the per cent. $\dfrac{1}{4} = 0.25 = 25\%$

The per cent of increase was **25%**.

Exercises

Complete the table. Round the per cent of increase or decrease to the nearest whole per cent.

		Major League Attendance		Estimated Increase or Decrease	Per Cent
	Team	1979	1980		
1.	Pittsburgh Pirates	1,025,945	1,237,359	200,000 increase	? 20%
2.	New York Yankees	1,012,434	2,103,092	1,100,000 ? increase	? 110%
3.	Oakland A's	780,593	495,578	300,000 ? decrease	? 38%
4.	Philadelphia Phillies	2,480,150	2,700,020	200,000 ? increase	? 8%
5.	San Francisco Giants	626,868	703,851	100,000 ? increase	? 17%
6.	Texas Rangers	1,164,982	1,250,691	100,000 ? increase	? 8%

14-3 Finding a Number Given a Per Cent

See the Teacher's Manual for the objectives.

You can use an equation to find a number when you know a per cent of the number.

PROCEDURE To find a number when a per cent of it is known:

1. Write an equation.
2. Solve the equation.

EXAMPLE 1   20 is 80% of <u>what number?</u>

Solution: 1. $20 = 80\% \times \qquad n$

$0.80n = 20$ ◀ **20 = 0.80n is the same as 0.80n = 20.**

2. $\dfrac{0.80n}{0.80} = \dfrac{20}{0.80}$

$n = 25$ 20 is 80% of **25.**

After completing Example 1, you may wish to have students do some or all of Exercises 1-24.

Sometimes it is convenient to write a fraction for the per cent.

EXAMPLE 2   50 is $33\frac{1}{3}\%$ of <u>what number?</u>

Solution: 1. $50 = \dfrac{1}{3} \times \qquad n$, or $50 = \dfrac{1}{3}n$ ◀ $33\frac{1}{3}\% = \frac{1}{3}$

$\dfrac{n}{3} = 50$ ◀ $\frac{1}{3}n = \frac{n}{3}$

2. $\dfrac{n}{3} \times \dfrac{3}{1} = 50 \times 3$

$n = 150$ 50 is $33\frac{1}{3}\%$ of **150.**

REVIEW OF RELATED SKILLS

You may wish to use these exercises before teaching the lesson.

Write a decimal for each per cent.   (Pages 276–277)

0.92

1. 70% 0.70 **2.** 50% 0.50 **3.** 7% 0.07 **4.** 4% 0.04 **5.** 1% 0.01 **6.** 9% 0.09 **7.** 18% 0.18 **8.** 92%

Divide.   (Pages 112–113)

240

9. $24 \div 0.2$ 120 **10.** $14 \div 0.5$ 28 **11.** $84 \div 0.12$ 700 **12.** $96 \div 0.32$ 300 **13.** $144 \div 0.6$

14. $0.09\overline{)63}$ 700 **15.** $0.05\overline{)65}$ 1300 **16.** $0.04\overline{)148}$ 3700 **17.** $0.12\overline{)1.68}$ 14 **18.** $0.25\overline{)6.25}$

25

Solve each equation.   (Pages 252–253)

19. $0.5n = 90$ ·180   **20.** $0.7n = 2.1$ 3   **21.** $0.3n = 111$ 370   **22.** $0.75n = 18$ 24

Write a fraction for each per cent.   (Pages 278–279)

23. 20% $\frac{1}{5}$ **24.** 30% $\frac{3}{10}$ **25.** 25% $\frac{1}{4}$ **26.** 50% $\frac{1}{2}$ **27.** $33\frac{1}{3}\%$ $\frac{1}{3}$ **28.** $12\frac{1}{2}\%$ $\frac{1}{8}$

Solve each equation.   (Pages 252–253)

29. $\frac{n}{9} = 12$ 108   **30.** $\frac{n}{6} = 2$ 12   **31.** $\frac{n}{8} = 3$ 24   **32.** $\frac{n}{12} = 1$ 12   **33.** $\frac{n}{18} = 7$ 126   **34.** $\frac{n}{25} = 4$ 100

EXERCISES

Write an equation for each exercise.   (Example, step 1) $9 = 30\% \times n$

1. 50 is 20% of what number? $50 = 20\% \times n$ **2.** 9 is 30% of what number?

3. 18 is 75% of what number? $18 = 75\% \times n$ **4.** 4 is 20% of what number?

5. 25 is 50% of what number? $25 = 50\% \times n$ **6.** 21 is 7% of what number?

4. $4 = 20\% \times n$
6. $21 = 7\% \times n$

Solve.   (Example 1)

7. 18 is 20% of what number? 90   **8.** 6 is 15% of what number? 40

9. 14 is 5% of what number? 280   **10.** 84 is 50% of what number? 168

11. 9 is 2% of what number? 450   **12.** 93 is 10% of what number? 930

13. 15 is 1% of what number? 1500   **14.** 18 is 60% of what number? 30

15. 5 is 25% of what number? 20   **16.** 52 is 80% of what number? 65

17. 14 is 70% of what number? 20   **18.** 12 is 30% of what number? 40

19. 24 is 15% of what number? 160   **20.** 81 is 27% of what number? 300

21. 7 is 20% of what number? 35   **22.** 4 is 2% of what number? 200

23. 16 is 80% of what number? 20   **24.** 60 is 75% of what number? 80

Solve. Write a fraction for the per cent.   (Example 2)

25. 18 is 10% of what number? 180   **26.** 16 is 20% of what number? 80

27. 23 is 50% of what number? 46   **28.** 42 is 25% of what number? 168

29. 6 is $12\frac{1}{2}\%$ of what number? 48   **30.** 10 is $16\frac{2}{3}\%$ of what number? 60

31. 27 is $33\frac{1}{3}\%$ of what number? 81   **32.** 12 is $66\frac{2}{3}\%$ of what number? 18

33. 80 is $12\frac{1}{2}\%$ of what number? 640   **34.** 64 is $16\frac{2}{3}\%$ of what number? 384

APPLICATIONS: Using Per Cent   These word problems may be considered optional for some students.

35. Juan made 15 baskets in a basketball game. This was 75% of his free throws. How many free throws did Juan make? 20

36. Nora spent four vacation days at the beach. This was 20% of her total number of vacation days. How long was her vacation? 20

Problem Solving and Applications

Markup and Selling Price

See the Teacher's Manual for the objectives.
This lesson applies the skills presented in Section 14-3.

Retailers sell directly to the public. In order to pay for expenses and to make a profit, retailers add an amount called the **markup** to the cost price. The sum of the cost price and the markup is the **selling price.**

EXAMPLE   Mr. Roper sells Hold–Fast bowling shoes for $40 a pair. The markup is 60%. How much do the shoes cost Mr. Roper?

Solution:

1. Write a per cent for the selling price.

$$100\% + 60\% = 160\% \quad \blacktriangleleft \quad \textbf{Cost} + \textbf{Markup} = \textbf{Selling Price}$$

2. Write an equation.   40 is 160% of what number?

$$40 = 160\% \times \qquad n \quad \blacktriangleleft \quad \textbf{40} = \textbf{1.60n}$$

3. Solve the equation.

$$1.6n = 40$$
$$\frac{1.6n}{1.6} = \frac{40}{1.6}$$
$$n = 25$$

Thus, the cost of the shoes to Mr. Roper is **$25.**

Exercises

Note that Exercises 1-8 are nonverbal.

For Exercises 1–8, find the cost.

	Selling Price	Markup	Cost			Selling Price	Markup	Cost
1.	$24	60%	? $15	**5.**		$240	60%	? $150
2.	$55	20%	? $45.83	**6.**		$ 37.35	50%	? $24.90
3.	$75	38%	? $54.35	**7.**		$695.10	40%	? $496.50
4.	$75	28%	? $58.59	**8.**		$ 74.75	25%	? $59.80

9. A video cassette recorder sells for $880. The markup is 35%. What did the recorder cost the retailer? $651.85

10. The markup on a wristwatch is 40%. The watch sells for $121.10. Find the cost to the retailer. $86.50

Application

Career lessons are optional.

The **RDA,** or **recommended daily allowance,** indicates the total amount of vitamins, minerals, and so on, that should be included in a daily diet. The table below shows the per cent of RDA for two vitamins, one mineral, and the protein provided by one serving of a certain cereal.

The Four Basic Food Groups

	Amount	Per Cent of RDA
Calcium	280 milligrams	20%
Niacin	5 milligrams	25%
Phosphorus	252 milligrams	18%.
Protein	12 grams	20%

EXERCISES
These word problems combine the skill of reading a table with the skills presented in Section 14-3.

1. Find the total RDA for calcium.
   (HINT: 280 milligrams are 20% of ?
   1400 milligrams

2. Find the total RDA for protein.
   (HINT: 12 grams are 20% of ? 60 grams

3. Find the total RDA for niacin.
   20 milligrams

4. Find the total RDA for phosphorus.
   1400 milligrams

The table at the right shows the amounts of vitamin D, iron, magnesium and riboflavin in 120 milliliters of milk poured over the cereal and the per cent of RDA for each. Use this information for Exercises 5–8.

	Amount	Per Cent of RDA
Vitamin D	18 grams	25%
Iron	1.8 grams	4%
Magnesium	2.88 grams	10%
Riboflavin	9.8 grams	35%

72 grams
5. Find the total RDA for vitamin D.

7. Find the total RDA for magnesium.
   28.8 grams

6. Find the total RDA for iron. 45 grams

8. Find the total RDA for riboflavin.
   28 grams

9. One orange (medium size) provides 74 units of vitamin C. This is 164% of the total RDA for vitamin C. Find the total RDA. 45 units

10. One baked potato provides 20 units of vitamin A. This is 0.5% of the total RDA for vitamin A. Find the total RDA. 4000 units

14-4 Review of Per Cent

See the Teacher's Manual for the objectives.

You have studied the three types of per cent problems. Each type involves three numbers. In a per cent problem, two of these numbers are known. The third number is the one you have to find.

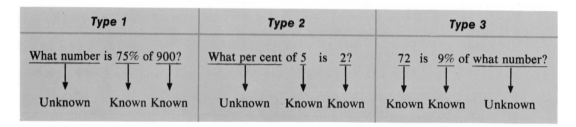

Type 1	Type 2	Type 3
What number is 75% of 900?	What per cent of 5 is 2?	72 is 9% of what number?
Unknown Known Known	Unknown Known Known	Known Known Unknown

PROCEDURE   To solve a per cent problem:

1 Write an equation for the problem.

2 Solve the equation.

EXAMPLE 1   What number is 75% of 900?

Solution: 1 $n = 75\% \times 900$

2 $n = 0.75 \times 900$

$n = 675$

75% of 900 is **675**.

Example 2 shows how you use the same procedure to solve the other two types of per cent problems.

EXAMPLE 2   **a.** What per cent of 5 is 2?   **b.** 72 is 9% of what number?

Solutions:

1 $n \times 5 = 2$ $72 = 0.09 \times n$

2 $5n = 2$ $0.09n = 72$

$\dfrac{5n}{5} = \dfrac{2}{5}$ $\dfrac{0.09n}{0.09} = \dfrac{72}{0.09}$

$n = \dfrac{2}{5}$ $n = 800$

$n = 40\%$

Thus, **40%** of 5 is 2.   Thus, 72 is 9% of **800**.

Write a decimal for each per cent.

1. 15% $^{0.15}$ **2.** 37% $^{0.37}$ **3.** 5% $^{0.05}$ **4.** 8% $^{0.08}$ **5.** 90% $^{0.90}$ **6.** $12\frac{1}{2}$%
$^{0.12\frac{1}{2} \text{ or } 0.125}$

Write a fraction for each per cent.   (Pages 278–279)

7. 20% $^{\frac{1}{5}}$ **8.** 10% $^{\frac{1}{10}}$ **9.** 25% $^{\frac{1}{4}}$ **10.** $87\frac{1}{2}$% $^{\frac{7}{8}}$ **11.** $33\frac{1}{3}$% $^{\frac{1}{3}}$ **12.** $16\frac{2}{3}$% $^{\frac{1}{6}}$

Multiply.   (Pages 98–99)

$^{398.56}$

13. 1200×0.28 ^{336} **14.** 750×0.04 ^{30} **15.** 255×0.10 $^{25.5}$ **16.** 752×0.53

17. 670×0.17 $^{113.9}$ **18.** 349×0.20 $^{69.8}$ **19.** 483×0.64 $^{309.12}$ **20.** 2300×0.15
^{345}

Divide. Carry the division to two decimal places.   (Pages 280–281)

$^{0.75}$

21. $1 \div 2$ $^{0.50}$ **22.** $1 \div 5$ $^{0.20}$ **23.** $1 \div 4$ $^{0.25}$ **24.** $1 \div 8$ $^{0.12\frac{1}{2}}$ **25.** $2 \div 5$ $^{0.40}$ **26.** $3 \div 4$

27. $5 \div 8$ $^{0.62\frac{1}{2}}$ **28.** $4 \div 5$ $^{0.80}$ **29.** $7 \div 8$ $^{0.87\frac{1}{2}}$ **30.** $3 \div 5$ $^{0.60}$ **31.** $3 \div 8$ $^{0.37\frac{1}{2}}$ **32.** $9 \div 10$
$^{0.90}$

Write a per cent for each decimal.   (Pages 276–277)

33. 0.72 $^{72\%}$ **34.** 0.81 $^{81\%}$ **35.** 0.02 $^{2\%}$ **36.** 0.09 $^{9\%}$ **37.** $0.33\frac{1}{3}$ $^{33\frac{1}{3}\%}$ **38.** $0.87\frac{1}{2}$
$^{87\frac{1}{2}\%}$

EXERCISES

See the suggested assignment guide in the Teacher's Manual.

For Exercises 1–8, choose the correct equation.   (Examples 1 and 2, step 1)

1. What per cent of 65 is 15? ᵃ
   a. $n \times 65 = 15$
   b. $n \times 15 = 65$
   c. $n = 15 \times 65$

2. What is 30% of 87? ᶜ
   a. $n \times 0.30 = 87$
   b. $n \times 87 = 0.30$
   c. $n = 0.30 \times 87$

3. 8 is 10% of what number? ᵇ
   a. $8 \times n = 0.10$
   b. $8 = 0.10 \times n$
   c. $8 \times 0.10 = n$

4. 16 *is* 15% of what number? ᵃ
   a. $16 = 0.15 \times n$
   b. $16 \times n = 0.15$
   c. $16 \times 0.15 = n$

5. What per cent of 10 is 3? ᵇ
   a. $n \times 3 = 10$
   b. $n \times 10 = 3$
   c. $n = 10 \times 3$

6. What is 3% of 24? ᶜ
   a. $n \times 0.03 = 24$
   b. $n \times 24 = 0.03$
   c. $n = 0.03 \times 24$

7. 14 is 5% of what number? ᵇ
   a. $14 \times n = 0.05$
   b. $14 = 0.05 \times n$
   c. $14 \times 0.5 = n$

8. 36 is 9% of what number? ᶜ
   a. $36 \times 0.09 = n$
   b. $36 \times n = 0.09$
   c. $36 = 0.09 \times n$

Match each question with the correct equation. (Examples 1 and 2, Step 1)

Problem	Equations
9. What is 30% of 50? c	**a.** $n \times 50 = 30$
10. 50 is 30% of what number? b	**b.** $50 = 0.30 \times n$
11. What per cent of 50 is 30? a	**c.** $n = 0.30 \times 50$
12. What per cent of 72 is 18? e	**d.** $18 = 0.72 \times n$
13. What is 72% of 18? f	**e.** $n \times 72 = 18$
14. 18 is 72% of what number? d	**f.** $n = 0.72 \times 18$
15. 36 is 12% of what number? i	**g.** $n = 0.12 \times 36$
16. What per cent of 36 is 12? h	**h.** $n \times 36 = 12$
17. What is 12% of 36? g	**i.** $36 = 0.12 \times n$
18. What is 25% of 90? l	**j.** $90 = 0.25 \times n$
19. What per cent of 90 is 25? k	**k.** $n \times 90 = 25$
20. 90 is 25% of what number? j	**l.** $n = 0.25 \times 90$
21. What per cent of 55 is 45? n	**m.** $55 = 0.45 \times n$
22. What is 45% of 55? o	**n.** $n \times 55 = 45$
23. 55 is 45% of what number? m	**o.** $n = 0.45 \times 55$
24. What per cent of 36 is 24? r	**p.** $36 = 0.24 \times n$
25. 36 is 24% of what number? p	**q.** $n = 0.24 \times 36$
26. What is 24% of 36? q	**r.** $n \times 36 = 24$
27. 8 is what per cent of 32? t	**s.** $n = 0.32 \times 8$
28. What is 32% of 8? s	**t.** $8 = 32 \times n$
29. 32 is 8% of what number? u	**u.** $32 = 0.08 \times n$

Mixed Practice The Mixed Practice contains exercises that relate to both Examples 1 and 2.

30. What per cent of 20 is 12? 60%

31. What is 45% of 120? 54

32. 16 is 90% of what number? $17\frac{7}{9}$

33. What is 18% of 150? 27

34. 50 is 50% of what number? 100

35. What per cent of 84 is 63? 75%

36. What per cent of 72 is 60? $83\frac{1}{3}$%

37. 72 is 9% of what number? 800

38. 2 is 8% of what number? 25

39. What is 15% of 40? 6

40. What is 4% of 7.8? 0.312

41. What per cent of 1.5 is 1.2? 80%

42. What is 65% of 100? 65

43. 48.6 is 90% of what number? 54

44. What per cent of 39 is 13? $33\frac{1}{3}$%

45. What is 24% of 36.1? 8.664

46. 28 is what per cent of 70? 40%

47. What is 0.4% of 1200? 4.8

48. 16.1 is 3.5% of what number? 460

49. 20 is 125% of what number? 16

Problem Solving and Applications

Energy Costs

See the Teacher's Manual for the objectives.
This lesson combines the skill of reading a graph with finding a percent of a number.

You can save on the cost of energy during the warmer months of the year by keeping the thermostat of your air conditioner set at about 80°F. The figure at the right shows the per cent of increase in energy costs when the thermostat of the air conditioner is set at 79° F, 78° F, 77° F, 76° F, and 75° F.

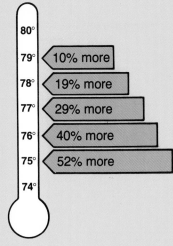

EXAMPLE Suppose that it costs a family $550 to operate an air conditioner with the thermostat set at 80° F during the summer months. What would be the increase in cost for a thermostat setting of 77°?

Solution: Use paper and pencil or use a calculator.

Per cent increase for 77°: **29%** ◀ **From the figure above**

The increase would be **$159.50.**

Exercises

The table below shows different costs for operating an air conditioner with the thermostat set at 80° during the months of June, July and August. Use this information and the figure at the right above to calculate the increase in cost for each thermostat setting.

	Cost for Thermostat Setting of 80°	Increase in Cost for Lower Thermostat Setting				
		79°	78°	77°	76°	75°
1.	$ 400	? $40	? $76	? $116	? $160	? $208
2.	$ 600	? $60	? $114	? $174	? $240	? $312
3.	$ 725	? $72.50	? $137.75	? $210.25	? $290	? $377
4.	$ 850	? $85	? $161.50	? $246.50	? $340	? $442
5.	$1000	? $100	? $190	? $290	? $400	? $520
6.	$2500	? $250	? $475	? $725	? $1000	? $1300

Application

MORE ON PER CENT **313**

14-5 Review of Word Problems with Per Cent

See the Teacher's Manual for the objectives.

You have studied the three types of word problems involving per cents in the Applications lessons of Chapters 13 and 14. Now you will review the three types in this lesson.

PROCEDURE To solve word problems involving per cents:

1. Use the given information to restate the problem.

2. Write an equation for the question.

3. Solve the equation.

EXAMPLE 1 In the 1980 presidential elections, about 52% of the registered voters voted. There were 161,000,000 registered voters in 1980. How many voted? Round your answer to the nearest million.

Solution:

1. Restate the problem.
2. Write an equation.
3. Solve the equation.

What is 52% of 161,000,000?

$n = 0.52 \times 161,000,000$

$n = \textbf{83,720,000}$ ◀ *Round to the nearest million.*

About **84,000,000** voters voted.

Example 2 shows the second type of per cent problem.

EXAMPLE 2 A real estate agent received a commission of $36,000 on sales of $1,200,000. What was the agent's rate of commission?

1. What per cent of 1,200,000 is 36,000?

2. $n \times 1,200,000 = 36,000$, or $1,200,000n = 36,000$

3. $$\frac{1,200,000n}{1,200,000} = \frac{36,000}{1,200,000}$$

$$n = \frac{36}{1200} = \frac{3}{100} \quad \blacktriangleleft \; \tfrac{3}{100} = 0.03$$

$$n = 0.03 = 3\%$$

The agent's rate of commission was **3%**.

The **cost price** is the price that a store owner pays for goods. The **selling price** is the amount the consumer pays.

EXAMPLE 3 The cost price of an electronic football game is $16.50. This is 55% of the selling price. What is the selling price?

Solution: 1. 16.50 is 55% of what number?

2. $16.50 = 0.55 \times n$, or $0.55n = 16.50$

3. $\dfrac{0.55n}{0.55} = \dfrac{16.50}{0.55}$

$n = 30$ The selling price is **$30.**

REVIEW OF RELATED SKILLS

You may wish to use these exercises before teaching the lesson.

Write an equation for each question. (Pages 310–312)

1. What per cent of 200 is 175? $n \times 200 = 175$ **2.** What is 25% of 200? $n = 25\% \times 200$

3. 900 is 2% of what number? $900 = 2\% \times n$ **4.** What per cent of 9 is 3? $n \times 9 = 3$

Write a two-place decimal for each fraction. (Pages 280–281)

5. $\dfrac{1}{2}$ 0.50   **6.** $\dfrac{4}{5}$ 0.80   **7.** $\dfrac{9}{10}$ 0.90   **8.** $\dfrac{1}{4}$ 0.25   **9.** $\dfrac{7}{20}$ 0.35   **10.** $\dfrac{9}{50}$ 0.18   **11.** $\dfrac{3}{25}$ 0.12   **12.** $\dfrac{3}{8}$ 0.37$\frac{1}{2}$

Solve each equation. Write a decimal for your answer. (Pages 252–253)

13. $80n = 400$ 5   **14.** $175 \times n = 200$ 1.143   **15.** $30 = 27 \times n$ 1.11   **16.** $456n = 48$ 0.105

Write a per cent for each fraction. (Pages 280–281)

17. $\dfrac{1}{4}$ 25%   **18.** $\dfrac{3}{5}$ 60%   **19.** $\dfrac{7}{10}$ 70%   **20.** $\dfrac{13}{20}$ 65%   **21.** $\dfrac{8}{25}$ 32%   **22.** $\dfrac{1}{3}$ 33$\frac{1}{3}$%   **23.** $\dfrac{1}{8}$ 12$\frac{1}{2}$%   **24.** $\dfrac{5}{6}$ 83$\frac{1}{3}$%

EXERCISES

See the suggested assignment guide in the Teacher's Manual.

For Exercises 1–5, choose the correct question for each problem.
Choose a, b, or c. (Examples 1 and 2, step 1)

1. One hundred seventy-five students voted. a
There are 200 students.
What per cent voted?

  a. What per cent of 200 is 175?
  b. What is 175% of 200?
  c. 200 is 175% of what number?

2. Four per cent of the students are absent. b
There are 900 students.
How many are absent?

  a. What per cent of 900 is 4%?
  b. What is 4% of 900?
  c. 900 is 4% of what number?

3. One hundred fifty students took the test. a
This is 60% of the students.
How many students are there?

  a. 150 is 60% of what number?
  b. What is 60% of 150?
  c. What per cent of 150 is 60?

4. Five students live on North Street. There are 600 students in all. What per cent live on North Street? b

    a. What is 5% of 600?
    b. What per cent of 600 is 5?
    c. 600 is 5% of what number?

5. Four hundred students participated. This is 80% of the students. How many students are there? c

    a. What per cent of 400 is 80?
    b. What is 80% of 400?
    c. 400 is 80% of what number?

Solve each problem. (Example 1)

6. A family budgets 25% of take–home pay for food. The family's monthly take-home pay is $910. How much is budgeted for food each month?
$227.50

7. A real estate agent gets a 3% commission on sales. How much commission does the agent receive on a house that sells for $110,000?
$3,300

(Example 2)

8. A waiter in a restaurant received a tip of $2.25 from a customer. The customer's bill for the meal was $15.00. What per cent of the bill was the tip? 15%

9. The cruising range of a car is 432 miles for city driving and 675 miles for highway driving. What per cent of the highway driving range is the city driving range? 64%

(Example 3)

10. One season, a softball player got a hit 30% of her times at bat. She had 25 hits in all. How many times was she at bat? 83

11. John paid a sales tax of $1.10 on a pair of gloves. The rate of sales tax in his state is 5%. How much did John pay for the gloves? $22

Mixed Practice The Mixed Practice contains exercises that relate to Examples 1, 2, and 3.

12. A worker who earns $5.40 an hour receives a raise for $0.65 an hour What is the per cent of increase? Round your answer to the nearest whole per cent. 12%

13. A certain automobile lost 14% of its original value in a year. When new, the car cost $7800. How much did the value of the car decrease in one year? $1092

14. The Corlaer Basketball team lost 28% of the games it played this year. They lost 7 games in all. How many games did the team play this year? 25

15. Ten years ago, the population of a city was 3,500,000. The latest census shows a population decrease of 490,000. What per cent of its population did the city lose? 14%

Problem Solving and Applications

Minimum Wage
See the Teacher's Manual for the objectives.
This lesson applies the skills presented in Section 14-2 and the skill of reading a bar graph.

Some per cents that occur in everyday situations are greater than 100%. The graph below shows that the Federal minimum wage has increased 1240% since 1938.

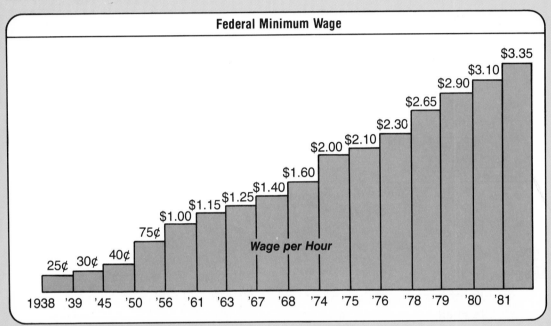

Federal Minimum Wage

$3.35
$3.10
$2.90
$2.65
$2.30
$2.10
$2.00
$1.60
$1.40
$1.25
$1.15
$1.00
75¢
40¢
30¢
25¢

Wage per Hour

1938 '39 '45 '50 '56 '61 '63 '67 '68 '74 '75 '76 '78 '79 '80 '81

EXAMPLE Find the per cent of increase in the Federal minimum wage from 1946 to 1981.

Solution:
[1] Find the amount of increase. ◀ *From the graph*
$3.35 − $0.40 = $2.95

[2] $\dfrac{\text{Amount of increase}}{\text{Original amount}} = \dfrac{2.95}{0.40}$

$= 7.375$ ◀ *Write a per cent for 7.375.*

$7.375 = 737.5\%$ The per cent of increase was **737.5%**.

Exercises
Note that these exercises involve some per cents that are greater than 100%.

Find the per cent of increase in the Federal minimum wage for these years.

$33\frac{1}{3}\%$

1. From 1938 to 1939 20%   **2.** From 1945 to 1956 150%   **3.** From 1950 to 1956

15%
4. From 1956 to 1963 25%   **5.** From 1963 to 1967 12%   **6.** From 1974 to 1976

7. From 1974 to 1981 $67\frac{1}{2}\%$ **8.** From 1956 to 1981 235%   **9.** From 1938 to 1981

1240%

Application   MORE ON PER CENT   **317**

Chapter Review

These exercises review the vocabulary, skills, and applications presented in the chapter as a preparation for the chapter test.

Part 1: Vocabulary

For Exercises 1–4, choose from the box at the right the word(s) that completes each statement.

number
decrease
selling price
equation
markup
increase

1. The per cent of increase is the ratio of the amount of __?__ to the original amount.   (Page 303)   *increase*

2. The ratio of the amount of decrease to the original amount is the per cent of __?__ .   (Page 303)   *decrease*

3. The amount of money a retailer adds to the cost price in order to pay expenses and make a profit is called the __?__ .   *markup* (Page 308)

4. The sum of the cost price and the markup is the __?__ .   (Page 308)   *selling price*

Part 2: Skills

For Exercises 5–14, first write an equation. Then solve the equation.   (Pages 300–301)

5. What per cent of 6 is 4? $n \times 6{=}4; n{=}66\frac{2}{3}\%$

6. 7 is what per cent of 49? $7{=}n \times 49; n{=}14\frac{2}{7}\%$

7. What per cent of 25 is 5? $n \times 25{=}5; n{=}20\%$

8. 20 is what per cent of 70? $20{=}n \times 70; n{=}28\frac{4}{7}\%$

9. 9 is what per cent of 15? $9{=}n \times 15; n{=}60\%$

10. 81 is what per cent of 90? $81{=}n \times 90; n{=}90\%$

11. 12 is what per cent of 30? $12{=}n \times 30; n{=}40\%$

12. What per cent of 30 is 27? $n \times 30{=}27; n{=}90\%$

13. 25 is what per cent of 5? $25{=}n \times 5; n{=}500\%$

14. What per cent of 8 is 24? $n \times 8{=}24; n{=}300\%$

For Exercises 15–22, find the per cent of increase or decrease. Identify each answer as a per cent of increase or decrease.   (Pages 303–304)

	Item	Original Value	Present Value		Item	Original Value	Present Value
15.	Car	$4000	$5000 25% increase	19.	Ring	$100	$120 20% increase
16.	House	$50,000	$56,000 12% increase	20.	Watch	$150	$175 See below
17.	Boat	$12,000	$10,000 $16\frac{2}{3}$% decrease	21.	Radio	$60	$50 below
18.	Blouse	$30	$25 $16\frac{2}{3}$% decrease	22.	Typewriter	$800	$640 20% decrease

20. $16\frac{2}{3}$% increase

21. $16\frac{2}{3}$% decrease

For Exercises 23–32, first write an equation. Then solve the equation.   (Pages 306–307)

23. 15 is 50% of what number? $15{=}50\% \times n; n{=}30$

24. 75 is 75% of what number? $75{=}75\% \times n; n{=}100$

25. 5 is 10% of what number? $5{=}10\% \times n; n{=}50$

26. 6 is 25% of what number? $6{=}25\% \times n; n{=}24$

27. 25 is 20% of what number? $25{=}20\% \times n; n{=}125$

28. 50 is 1% of what number? $50{=}1\% \times n; n{=}5000$

29. 72 is 30% of what number? $72{=}30\% \times n; n{=}240$

30. 65 is 13% of what number? $65{=}13\% \times n; n{=}500$

31. 3 is $33\frac{1}{3}$% of what number? $3{=}33\frac{1}{3}\% \times n; n{=}9$

32. 24 is $37\frac{1}{2}$% of what number? $24{=}37\frac{1}{2}\% \times n; n{=}64$

For Exercises 33–38, choose the correct equation.
(Pages 310–312)

33. What is 16% of 18? b
    a. $0.16 \times n = 18$
    b. $n = 0.16 \times 18$
    c. $18 \times n = 0.16$

34. 21 is 30% of what number? a
    a. $21 = 0.30 \times n$
    b. $21 \times 0.30 = n$
    c. $21 \times n = 0.30$

35. 20 is what per cent of 500? b
    a. $n = 20 \times 500$
    b. $20 = n \times 500$
    c. $20 \times n = 500$

36. What is 40% of 72? c
    a. $0.40 \times n = 72$
    b. $n \times 72 = 0.40$
    c. $n = 0.40 \times 72$

37. 15 is 75% of what number? c
    a. $n = 0.75 \times 15$
    b. $0.75 = 15 \times n$
    c. $15 = 0.75 \times n$

38. 16 is what per cent of 75? a
    a. $16 = n \times 75$
    b. $n = 16 \times 75$
    c. $75 = 16 \times n$

For Exercises 39–52, first write an equation. Then solve the equation. (Pages 306–307, 311–313)

39. What is 5% of 60? n=5% × 60; n=3

40. What is 7% of 20? n=7% × 20; n=1.4

41. What is $33\frac{1}{3}$% of 75? n=33$\frac{1}{3}$% × 75; n=25

42. What is 23% of 45? n=23% × 45; n=10.35

43. What is 90% of 200? n=90% × 200; n=180

44. What is $66\frac{2}{3}$% of 60? n=66$\frac{2}{3}$% × 60; n=40

45. 26 is 20% of what number? 26=20% × n; n=130

46. What per cent of 16 is 32? n × 16=32; n=200%

47. What per cent of 48 is 64? See below

48. What is 55% of 23? n=55% × 23; n=12.65

49. What is 16% of 71? n=16% × 71; n=11.36

50. 14 is 40% of what number? 14=40% × n; n=35

51. 16 is what per cent of 80? 16=n × 80; n=20%

52. 20 is what per cent of 35? 20=n × 35; n=57$\frac{1}{7}$%

47. n × 48=64; n=133$\frac{1}{3}$%

Part 3: Applications The use of these word problems depends on which applications were studied.

53. In 1970, eggs cost $0.60 a dozen. In 1980, they cost $0.80 a dozen. Find the per cent of increase. (Pages 303–304) 33$\frac{1}{3}$%

54. Warren made 25 errors on his first typing test and 20 errors on his second test. Find the per cent of decrease. (Pages 303–304) 20%

55. A living room couch sells for $260.00. The markup is 30%. What did the couch cost the retailer? (Pages 306–307, 314–316) $200

56. A real estate agent receives a 7% commission on sales. How much commission does the agent receive on an acre of land that sells for $20,000? (Pages 310–312) $1400

Chapter Test

The Teacher's Resource Book contains two forms of each chapter test.

For Exercises 1–4, choose the correct equation.

1. 60 is what per cent of 150? a
   a. $60 = n \times 150$
   b. $n = 60 \times 150$
   c. $60 \times n = 150$

2. 40 is 20% of what number? c
   a. $n = 40 \times 0.20$
   b. $40 \times n = 0.20$
   c. $40 = 0.20 \times n$

3. What is 45% of 600? a
   a. $n = 0.45 \times 600$
   b. $0.45 = n \times 600$
   c. $600 = 0.45 \times n$

4. What per cent of 200 is 100? b
   a. $n \times 100 = 200$
   b. $n \times 200 = 100$
   c. $100 \times 200 = n$

For Exercises 5–16, first write an equation. Then solve the equation.

5. What is 60% of 300? $n=60\% \times 300; n=180$

6. 200 is what per cent of 500? $200=n \times 500; n=40\%$

7. 16 is what per cent of 64? $16=n \times 64; n=25\%$

8. 64 is 25% of what number? $64=25\% \times n; n=256$

9. 75 is 30% of what number? $75=30\% \times n; n=250$

10. What is 16% of 80? $n=16\% \times 80; n=12.8$

11. 20 is what per cent of 200? $20=n \times 200; n=10\%$

12. 35 is what per cent of 50? $35=n \times 50; n=70\%$

13. What is 25% of 40? $n=25\% \times 40; n=10$

14. 70 is 50% of what number? $70=50\% \times n; n=140$

15. 81 is 90% of what number? $81=90\% \times n; n=90$

16. What is 40% of 600? $n=40\% \times 600; n=240$

Solve each problem. The use of these word problems depends on which applications were studied.

17. Jenna made 10 baskets in one basketball game and 12 baskets in the next game. What was the per cent of increase? 20%

18. The Thomas family spends 35% of total income on food each month. Last month they spent $500 on food. What was the total income? $1428.57

19. A gold watch costs $300. The markup is 50%. What did the watch cost the retailer? $200

20. An appliance salesman receives a 30% commission on sales. What is the commission on sales of $1500? $450

Additional Practice

You may wish to use some or all of these exercises depending on how well students performed on the formal chapter test.

Skills

For Exercises 1–8, first write an equation. Then solve the equation.
(Pages 300–301, 306–307, 311–312)   2. n × 4=3; n=75%   4. 24=n × 12; n=200%

1. What per cent of 12 is 6? n × 12=6; n=50%   **2.** What per cent of 4 is 3?

3. 6 is what per cent of 10? 6=n × 10; n=60%   **4.** 24 is what per cent of 12?

5. 9 is what per cent of 15? 9=n × 15; n=60%   **6.** What per cent of 5 is 4?

7. What per cent of 18 is 10? n × 18=10; n=55$\frac{5}{9}$% **8.** 12 is what per cent of 40?

9. 30 is what per cent of 6? 30=n × 6; n=500%   **10.** 7 is what per cent of 28?
   6. n × 5=4; n=80%   8. 12=n × 40; n=30%   7=n × 28; n=25%

For Exercises 11–18, find the per cent of increase or decrease.
(Pages 303–304)

	Item	Original Value	Present Value		Item	Original Value	Present Value
11.	Television	$320	$360 12$\frac{1}{2}$% increase	**15.**	Basketball	$50	$45
12.	Bed	$200	$180 10% decrease	**16.**	Cruise	$580	$609 See below
13.	Sailboat	$4000	$4400 10% increase	**17.**	Bicycle	$210	$140
14.	Camera	$200	$150 25% decrease	**18.**	Suit	$120	$150

15. 10% decrease   16. 5% increase   17. 33$\frac{1}{3}$% decrease   18. 25% increase

For Exercises 19–38, first write an equation. Then solve the equation.
(Pages 307–308)   20. 18=36% × n; n=50   22. 14=66$\frac{2}{3}$% × n; n=21   24. 44=55% × n; n=80

19. 24 is 12% of what number? 24=12% × n; n=200   **20.** 18 is 36% of what number?

21. 20 is 20% of what number? 20=20% × n; n=100   **22.** 14 is 66$\frac{2}{3}$% of what number? See above

23. 90 is 45% of what number? 90=45% × n; n=200   **24.** 44 is 55% of what number?

25. 9 is 15% of what number? 9=15% × n; n=60   **26.** 17 is 85% of what number? See below

27. 70 is 87$\frac{1}{2}$% of what number? 70=87$\frac{1}{2}$% × n; n=80 **28.** 65 is 65% of what number?

(Pages 310–312)   26. 17=85% × n; n=20   28. 65=65% × n; n=100

29. What is 5% of 200? n=5% × 200; n=10   **30.** What is 6% of 650? n=6% × 650; n=39

31. What is 25% of 32? n=25% × 32, n=8   **32.** What is 20% of 75? n=20% × 75; n=15

33. What is 12$\frac{1}{2}$% of 800? n=12$\frac{1}{2}$% × 800; n=100 **34.** What is 33$\frac{1}{3}$% of 768? n=33$\frac{1}{3}$% × 768; n=256

35. 42 is 20% of what number? 42=20% × n; n=210   **36.** 10 is what per cent of 40? See below

37. 11 is what per cent of 66? 11=n × 66; n=16$\frac{2}{3}$% **38.** 56 is 25% of what number?
   36. 10=n × 40; n=25%   38. 56=25% × n; n=224

Applications   The use of these word problems depends on which applications were studied.

39. Luis earned $30.00 on Monday. This was 20% of his weekly earnings. What does he earn per week? (Pages 306–307) $150.00

40. A gold watch sells for $150.00 The markup is 50%. What did the watch cost the retailer? (Page 308) $100.00

Cumulative Review: Chapters 12–14

You may also wish to use at this time the cumulative review on page 448 titled Review of Skills that reviews only the skills presented in Chapters 1-14.

Choose the correct answer. Choose a, b, c, or d.

1. Solve for n. c

$$n + 6 = 27$$

a. 33   b. $3\frac{1}{3}$ c. 21   d. $4\frac{1}{2}$

2. Write a fraction in lowest terms for $62\frac{1}{2}\%$. b

a. $62\frac{1}{2}$ b. $\frac{5}{8}$ c. $\frac{5}{6}$ d. $\frac{2}{3}$

3. Solve the proportion for n. b

$$\frac{6}{7} = \frac{36}{n}$$

a. 6   b. 42   c. $5\frac{1}{5}$ d. 49

4. Find 20% of 72. c

a. 144   b. 1440   c. 14.4   d. 1.44

5. Solve for n. b

$$2n + 1.5 = 7.7$$

a. 4.6   b. 3.1   c. 2.35   d. 5.35

6. Find $16\frac{2}{3}\%$ of 78. a

a. 13   b. 68   c. 52   d. 12

7. Write a per cent for $\frac{3}{8}$. a

a. 37.5%   b. 3.75%   c. $\frac{3}{8}\%$ d. 38%

8. 18 is 20% of what number? b

a. 660   b. 90   c. 0.66   d. 9.6

9. Solve the proportion for n. c

$$\frac{41}{20} = \frac{n}{100}$$

a. 25   b. 250   c. 205   d. 82

10. Write a fraction for the ratio 17 to 25. c

a. $\frac{17}{42}$ b. $\frac{25}{17}$ c. $\frac{17}{25}$ d. $\frac{8}{25}$

11. Write a decimal for 5.5%. a

a. 0.055   b. 5.5
c. 0.55   d. $0.5\frac{1}{2}$

12. Write a per cent for 0.57. d

a. 0.57%   b. 0.057%
c. 5.7%   d. 57%

13. Write a per cent for $\frac{17}{100}$. b

a. 170%   b. 17%
c. 1.7%   d. 0.17%

14. 48 is 16% of what number? d

a. 30   b. 3   c. 3000   d. 300

15. What per cent of 20 is 4? a

a. 20   b. 200   c. 12   d. 28

16. What number is 25% of 60? c

a. 5.88   b. 1.5   c. 15   d. 7.5

17. Solve for n: $\frac{n}{2.3} = 4.6$ d

a. 2   b. 0.2   c. 1.058   d. 10.58

18. Which ratios are equivalent? d

a. $\frac{25}{50}$ and $\frac{2}{3}$ b. $\frac{4}{5}$ and $\frac{16}{25}$

c. $\frac{3}{16}$ and $\frac{3}{4}$ d. $\frac{3}{12}$ and $\frac{9}{36}$

19. What per cent of 85 is 34? a

   a. 40   **b.** 35   **c.** 50   **d.** 28

20. Mike's vacuum cleaner sales totaled $2500. He earns a 25% commission. How much did he earn? b

   a. $62.50   **b.** $625

   c. $500   **d.** $50

21. A car cost $3500 in 1978. Three years later it cost $4900. Find the per cent of increase. c

   a. $16\frac{2}{3}\%$ **b.** 25% **c.** 40% **d.** 60%

22. Marie spent $17.50 on clothes. She paid a 7% sales tax. How much was the sales tax? a

   a. $1.23   **b.** $16.28

   c. $17.57   **d.** $18.73

23. The directions for making fruit juice say to mix water with concentrate in a ratio of 5:1. How many cans of water are needed with 8 cans of concentrate? b

   a. 20   **b.** 40   **c.** 10   **d.** 13

24. Bill spent $400 on food in one month. This was 20% of his monthly income. What was Bill's monthly income? c

   a. $1500   **b.** $1000

   c. $2000   **d.** $2500

25. Solve for n. $\frac{n}{2}+4=37$ d

   a. $22\frac{1}{2}$ **b.** $14\frac{1}{2}$ **c.** $20\frac{1}{2}$ **d.** 66

26. The scale on a map is: 1 cm represents 250 km. On this map, the distance between two cities is 4.5 centimeters. Find the actual distance in kilometers. a

   a. 1125   **b.** 55.55

   c. 1000   **d.** 1050

27. A jacket is selling for 25% off its regular price of $22.00. Find the new selling price. b

   a. $26.50   **b.** $16.50

   c. $5.50   **d.** $16.00

28. Find the interest on $500 at 11% for 6 months. Use this formula: d

$$i = p \times r \times t \ (t \text{ is in years})$$

   a. $330   **b.** $9.17

   c. $110   **d.** $27.50

29. The net pay for a store detective was $285.60. The detective's gross pay was $371. Find the total deductions. Use this formula: c

$$n + d = g$$

   a. $100   **b.** $50.76

   c. $85.40   **d.** $95.60

30. A television regularly sells for $298.95. It is now selling at a $33\frac{1}{3}\%$ discount. Choose the best estimate for the discount. d

   a. $150   **b.** $50

   c. $200   **d.** $100

Sample Competency Test: Chapters 1–14

Choose the correct answer. Choose a, b, c, or d.

1. Add: 642
b 3591
+ 46

  a. 4379 **b.** 4279
  c. 4281 **d.** 3280

2. Divide: $13\overline{)4667}$
a
  a. 359 **b.** 349 **c.** 360 **d.** 35

3. Subtract: 4006
d − 548

  a. 4458 **b.** 3442
  c. 4442 **d.** 3458

4. This bar graph shows Billy's
b earnings for four months. During
which month did he earn between
$30 and $40?

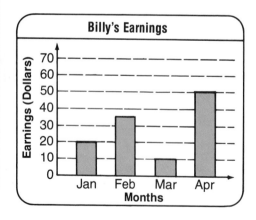

Billy's Earnings

  a. January **b.** February
  c. March **d.** April

5. Add: $1\frac{2}{9} + 3\frac{4}{9}$
b
  a. $3\frac{1}{3}$ **b.** $4\frac{2}{3}$ **c.** $4\frac{7}{9}$ **d.** $3\frac{5}{9}$

6. Multiply: 604
c × 83

  a. 49,132 **b.** 50,387
  c. 50,132 **d.** 49,032

7. How many centimeters long is this
a pin?

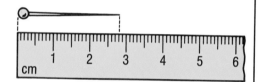

  a. 2.8 **b.** 3.8 **c.** 2.9 **d.** 3.4

8. Which decimal has the smallest
c value?

  a. 0.270 **b.** 0.207
  c. 0.0027 **d.** 2.7

9. Write a mixed number for $\frac{65}{11}$.
a
  a. $5\frac{10}{11}$ **b.** $6\frac{1}{11}$ **c.** $6\frac{5}{11}$ **d.** $5\frac{5}{11}$

10. Subtract: $5\frac{7}{9}$
b $-2\frac{4}{9}$

  a. $3\frac{2}{3}$ **b.** $3\frac{1}{3}$ **c.** $2\frac{1}{3}$ **d.** $2\frac{2}{3}$

11. Multiply: $1\frac{3}{5} \times 1\frac{7}{8}$
d

    a. 1   **b.** 2   **c.** $3\frac{1}{2}$ **d.** 3

12. Which is equal to 55%?
b

    a. $\frac{55}{60}$ **b.** $\frac{11}{20}$ **c.** $\frac{1}{5}$ **d.** $\frac{1}{2}$

13. Add: 3.26
d
               14.3
               7.481
        +926.2

    a. 941.232   **b.** 950.241
    c. 951.242   **d.** 951.241

14. Multiply 0.36 by 0.04.
a
    a. 0.0144   **b.** 0.144
    c. 1.44   **d.** 14.4

15. Subtract: $\frac{7}{9} - \frac{1}{3}$
c

    a. $\frac{2}{3}$ **b.** $\frac{5}{9}$ **c.** $\frac{4}{9}$ **d.** $\frac{5}{9}$

16. Divide: $9\overline{)4.86}$
a
    a. 0.54   **b.** 54   **c.** 5.4   **d.** 0.054

17. What is 34% of 40?
b
    a. 136   **b.** 13.6
    c. 1.36   **d.** 0.136

18. What is $\frac{48}{64}$ in lowest terms?
b
    a. $\frac{2}{3}$ **b.** $\frac{3}{4}$ **c.** $\frac{5}{6}$ **d.** $\frac{8}{9}$

19. Which of these represents eleven and forty–two thousandths?
c

    a. 11.42   **b.** 11,042
    c. 11.042   **d.** 42,000

20. 30% of what number is 93?
c
    a. 31   **b.** 3.1   **c.** 310   **d.** 0.31

21. What temperature is shown on the Celsius thermometer at the right?
c
    a. 10°
    b. 15°
    c. 5°
    d. 13°

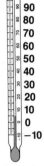

22. What per cent of 48 is 12?
b
    a. 4   **b.** 25   **c.** 50   **d.** 30

23. Divide: $2.4\overline{)9.648}$
b
    a. 4.2   **b.** 4.02   **c.** 42   **d.** 40.2

24. In lowest terms, the ratio of 6 to 48 is
b
    a. $\frac{1}{9}$ **b.** $\frac{1}{8}$ **c.** $\frac{2}{3}$ **d.** $\frac{1}{3}$

25. Solve for n: $\frac{2}{3} = \frac{n}{21}$
c
    a. 8   **b.** 7   **c.** 14   **d.** 12

26. Written in words, 3.07 is

    c

    a. three hundred seven.

    b. three and seven tenths.

    c. three and seven hundredths.

    d. thirty–seven hundredths.

27. Add: 48 + 329 + 4648

    d

    a. 6025   **b.** 5125

    c. 5026   **d.** 5025

28. Multiply: $\frac{2}{3} \times \frac{4}{5}$

    a

    a. $\frac{8}{15}$ **b.** $\frac{4}{5}$ **c.** $\frac{2}{3}$ **d.** $\frac{2}{5}$

29. Subtract: 34.006 − 8.95

    d

    a. 25.146   **b.** 24.056

    c. 24.046   **d.** 25.056

30. Each banana below represents

    c   50,000 bananas grown.
    What is the total number of
    bananas grown?

    a. 20,000   **b.** 2,000,000

    c. 200,000   **d.** 2,000

31. At which price will one peach cost

    d   the least?

    a. 4 for 60¢   **b.** 5 for 65¢

    c. 3 for 40¢   **d.** 6 for 70¢

32. What is the area in square meters

    c   of this rectangular yard?

    a. 7

    b. 14   3 m

    c. 12

    d. 18

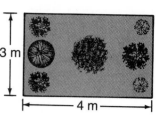

    4 m

33. Which fraction has the largest

    b   value?

    a. $\frac{3}{5}$ **b.** $\frac{7}{8}$ **c.** $\frac{3}{4}$ **d.** $\frac{2}{3}$

34. June earns $4 per hour. How much

    a   does she earn by working $3\frac{1}{2}$ hours?

    a. $14   **b.** $12   **c.** $15   **d.** $20

35. Using the formula $A = \pi \times r \times r$,

    a   find the area of a circle whose
    radius is 5 (Use $\pi = 3.14$).

    a. 78.5   **b.** 79.5   **c.** 78   **d.** 79

36. Soap is selling at 4 bars for $1.20.

    a   What does one bar cost?

    a. 30¢   **b.** 20¢   **c.** 40¢   **d.** 50¢

37. Find the discount.

    b

    a. $35

    b. $15

    c. $20

    d. $30

Sale 30% OFF REGULARLY $50

38. Divide: $46\overline{)170.2}$

^d   **a.** 42   **b.** 37   **c.** 4.2   **d.** 3.7

39. Divide: $32 \div \frac{1}{8}$

^b   **a.** 4   **b.** 256   **c.** 16   **d.** 240

40. On Monday, Jim worked from 8:30
^a A.M. until 1:00 P.M. How many hours did he work?

   a. $4\frac{1}{2}$ **b.** $4\frac{3}{4}$ **c.** $3\frac{1}{2}$ **d.** $\frac{1}{2}$

41. What is the perimeter in meters of
^c this rectangular court?

   a. 500
   b. 400
   c. 90
   d. 45

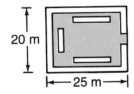

42. A football team won 8 of the 10
^b games it played. What per cent of its games did the team win?

   a. 40   **b.** 80   **c.** 50   **d.** 60

43. Julio paid $4.80 for lunch. A 15%
^b tip is closest to

   a. 60¢   **b.** 70¢   **c.** 80¢   **d.** 90¢

44. A recipe that serves 6 people calls
^c for 2 pounds of meat. How many pounds of meat are needed to serve 18 people?

   a. 2   **b.** 4   **c.** 6   **d.** 8

45. Which decimal is equal to 42%?
^b   **a.** 0.042   **b.** 0.42   **c.** 4.2   **d.** 42

46. Subtract: $12\frac{1}{4} - 8\frac{3}{4}$

^a   **a.** $3\frac{1}{2}$ **b.** $4\frac{1}{2}$ **c.** $4\frac{1}{4}$ **d.** $3\frac{1}{4}$

47. What is the volume in cubic
^a centimeters of this box?

   a. 1800
   b. 2000
   c. 1500
   d. 41

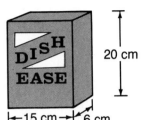

48. Amy bought a blouse at 20% off
^a the regular price of $25. How much did she pay for it?

   a. $20   **b.** $15   **c.** $5   **d.** $23

49. Juan's bill for sporting goods was
^b $15.64. He paid with a twenty-dollar bill. How much change should he receive?

   a. $4.40   **b.** $4.36
   c. $4.50   **d.** $4.46

50. On a map, 1 centimeter represents
^d 50 kilometers. What is the real distance in kilometers between two towns that are 6 centimeters apart on the map?

   a. 56   **b.** 60   **c.** 200   **d.** 300

REVIEW OF RELATED SKILLS FOR CHAPTER 15

We suggest that some or all of this page be reviewed before proceeding with the chapter.

Add. (Pages 6–7)

1. 612 + 413 + 927 + 462 ₂₄₁₄ **2.** 361 + 425 + 980 + 602 ₂₃₆₈ **3.** 407 + 519 + 223 + 645 ₁₇₉₄

4. 733 + 981 + 496 + 500 ₂₇₁₀ **5.** 386 + 777 + 435 + 911 ₂₅₀₉ **6.** 588 + 230 + 476 + 743 ₂₀₃₇

Divide. (Pages 50–51, 110–111)

7. 385 ÷ 7 ₅₅ **8.** 644 ÷ 4 ₁₆₁ **9.** 924 ÷ 6 ₁₅₄ **10.** 850 ÷ 5 ₁₇₀ **11.** 464 ÷ 2 ₂₃₂

12. 596 ÷ 4 ₁₄₉ **13.** 73.8 ÷ 6 _{12.3} **14.** 41 ÷ 5 _{8.2} **15.** 31.5 ÷ 9 _{3.5} **16.** 76.8 ÷ 8 _{9.6}

The bar graph at the right shows the total sales for the Benson Automobile Agency for March through July in a recent year. Use this graph for Exercises 17–19. (Pages 74–75)

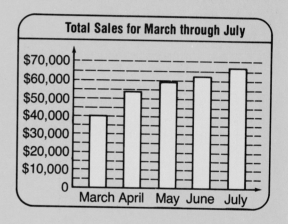

Total Sales for March through July

17. During which month did the agency have the least sales? _{March}

18. During which month did the agency have the most sales? _{July}

19. Between which two consecutive months was the increase in sales the greatest? _{March-April}

Replace the ● with <, =, or >. (Pages 90–91)

20. 17.8 ● 17.80 ₌ **21.** 16.3 ● 16.2 _> **22.** 21.05 ● 21.15 _<

23. 46.3 ● 47.3 _< **24.** 23.4 ● 23.3 _> **25.** 17.6 ● 17.5 _>

Round to the nearest whole number. (Pages 120–121)

26. 14.2 ₁₄ **27.** 25.1 ₂₅ **28.** 16.9 ₁₇ **29.** 19.8 ₂₀ **30.** 321.4 ₃₂₁ **31.** 686.3 ₆₈₆

32. 75.5 ₇₆ **33.** 68.5 ₆₉ **34.** 21.2 ₂₁ **35.** 37.3 ₃₇ **36.** 96.7 ₉₇ **37.** 101.6 ₁₀₂

Write a decimal for each per cent. (Pages 276–277)

38. 65% _{0.65} **39.** 42% _{0.42} **40.** 3% _{0.03} **41.** 6% _{0.06} **42.** $14\frac{2}{7}\%$ _{$0.14\frac{2}{7}$} **43.** $66\frac{2}{3}\%$ _{$0.66\frac{2}{3}$}

Use a protractor to find the measure of each angle to the nearest degree.
(Pages 228–229)

44. _{80°} **45.** _{115°} **46.** _{90°} **47.** _{30°}

SKILLS/APPLICATIONS

15-1 The Mean and the Mode with Applications

15-2 The Median with Applications

15-3 Listing Data

15-4 The Histogram with Applications

15-5 Circle Graphs

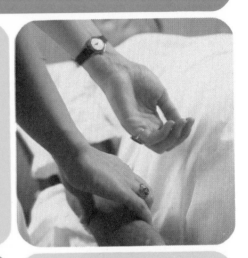

CAREER

Business

15-1 The Mean and the Mode with Applications

See the Teacher's Manual for the objectives.

Recall that the term **mean** is another word for average.

PROCEDURE To find the mean, divide the sum of the measures by the number of measures.

$$\text{Mean} = \frac{\textbf{Sum of Measures}}{\textbf{Number of Measures}}$$

EXAMPLE 1 This table shows the home run records of five famous baseball players. Find the mean number of home runs for the five players.

Home Run Records	
Player	**Number**
Hank Aaron	755
Babe Ruth	714
Willie Mays	660
Harmon Killebrew	573
Mickey Mantle	536

Solution:

$$\text{Mean} = \frac{\text{Sum of Measures}}{\text{Number of Measures}}$$

$$= \frac{755 + 714 + 660 + 573 + 536}{5}$$

$$= 647.6 \quad \text{The mean number of home runs is } \textbf{647.6.}$$

After completing Example 1, you may wish to have students do some or all of Exercises 1-6.

The **mode** is the measure that occurs most often in a set of data.

EXAMPLE 2 This table shows the traffic count at an intersection from 7 A.M. to 12 noon.

a. During which hour would a traffic policeman be needed most?

b. What hour is the mode for this data?

Traffic at Charles and North	
Time (A.M.)	**Count**
7-8	650
8-9	1350
9-10	550
10-11	510
11-12	405

Solutions: a. Since the highest traffic count occurs **between 8 and 9,** a traffic policeman would be needed most during this hour.

b. The mode is **8-9.**

When the highest count occurs <u>more than once</u>, there is more than one mode.

REVIEW OF RELATED SKILLS
You may wish to use these exercises before teaching the lesson.

Add. (Pages 6–7)

1715
1. $215 + 913 + 211 + 376$

1758
2. $417 + 911 + 325 + 105$

1495
3. $206 + 132 + 763 + 394$

4. $392 + 111 + 776 + 111$
1390

5. $119 + 369 + 129 + 999$
1616

6. $876 + 543 + 210 + 123$
1752

Divide. (Pages 50–51, 110–111)

1498
7. $729 \div 9$ 81   **8.** $846 \div 6$ 141   **9.** $861 \div 3$ 287   **10.** $684 \div 12$ 57   **11.** $7490 \div 5$

12. $59.5 \div 7$ 8.5   **13.** $15.6 \div 6$ 2.6   **14.** $219.2 \div 8$ 27.4   **15.** $284.7 \div 13$ 21.9   **16.** $9.28 \div 4$

2.32

EXERCISES
See the suggested assignment guide in the Teacher's Manual.

For Exercises 1–6, find the mean. (Example 1)

1. 28

Number of Pages in Eight Newspapers

20	16	12	52
22	34	18	50

2. 21.5

Miles Per Gallon for Twelve Cars

22	30	18	16	26	16
25	32	15	18	21	19

3. 22.7

Number of Hit Records Sold in Ten Days

16	13	26	32	18
21	26	18	30	27

4. 3.4

Number of Inches of Rainfall for Newfane Over Six Months

3.6	5.5	4.3
3.2	2.9	0.9

5. 6.15

Earnings Per Hour for Eight Workers

$6.50	$5.75	$5.25	$4.95
$6.25	$5.00	$8.15	$7.35

6. 7.2

Number of Hours of Sleep for Ten Adults

8	6	$6\frac{1}{2}$	$8\frac{1}{2}$	7
$7\frac{1}{2}$	7	8	$5\frac{1}{2}$	8

For Exercises 7–8, find the mode. (Example 2)

7. **Survey of Favorite Sports**

Sport	Count
Bowling	18
Tennis	12
Swimming	25
Softball	25
Basketball	19
Football	15

Swimming and Softball

8. **Grades of Thirty Students on a Math Test**

Grade	Count
70-74	1
75-79	3
80-84	8
85-89	9
90-94	7
95-100	2

85-89

15-2 The Median with Applications

See the Teacher's Manual for the objectives.

In a listing of data, the **median** is the middle measure or score.

PROCEDURE To find the median:

1 Arrange the data in order.

2 **a.** For an **odd** number of items, the median is the middle measure listed.

b. For an **even** number of items, the median is the average of the two middle measures.

EXAMPLE 1 This table shows the prices of five different cars. What is the median price?

Car	Price
A	$6,212
B	$5,659
C	$6,365
D	$5,719
E	$7,140

Solution: 1 Arrange the prices in order. Start with the least.

5,659   5,719   6,212
        6,365   7,140

2 Since there is an odd number of items (5), choose the middle number. ⟶ **6,212**

The median price is **$6,212.**

After completing Example 1, you may wish to have students do some or all of Exercises 1, 2, 4, and 6.

Sometimes a listing has two middle numbers.

EXAMPLE 2 This table shows the income tax rate in a recent year for eight cities in the United States. Find the median income tax rate.

City Income Tax Rate

City	Per Cent
Columbus, OH	1.5
Detroit, MI	2.0
Kansas City, MO	1.0
New York, NY	4.0
Pittsburgh, PA	1.0
St. Louis, MO	1.0

Solution: 1 Arrange the rates in order.

1.0   1.0   **1.0**

1.5   2.0   4.0

2 Find the average of the middle numbers.

$$\frac{1.0 + 1.5}{2} = \frac{2.5}{2} = 1.25$$

The median rate is **1.25%.**

REVIEW OF RELATED SKILLS

You may wish to use these exercises before teaching the lesson.

Replace the ● *with* <, >, *or* =.   (Pages 90–91)

1. 18.7 ● 18.6 >   **2.** 20.1 ● 20.01 >   **3.** 17.3 ● 17.31 <   **4.** 1.45 ● 1.51 <

5. 67.3 ● 67.34 <   **6.** 0.04 ● 0.040 =   **7.** 9.2 ● 9.02 >   **8.** 3.8 ● 3.80 =

EXERCISES

See the suggested assignment guide in the Teacher's Manual.

Find the median.   (Examples 1 and 2)

1. **Renell High School Enrollment** 1075

Year	Number of Students
1976	1032
1977	1021
1978	1095
1979	1098
1980	1075

2. **Number of Characters in Five Plays** 26

Play	Number of Characters
Julius Caeser	34
Hamlet	26
Romeo and Juliet	28
The Tempest	16
Twelfth Night	12

3. **Years in Office** 5.5

President	Years in Office
F. Roosevelt	14
H. Truman	7
D. Eisenhower	8
J. Kennedy	3
L. Johnson	5
R. Nixon	6
G. Ford	2
J. Carter	4

4. **Share of U.S. Exports in 1980** 10.0

World Area	Per Cent of U.S. Exports
Eastern Europe	20.9
Western Europe	35.6
Latin America	17.2
Middle East	9.8
Southeast Asia	10.0
South Asia	1.9
Other	4.3

5. **Coal Exports From the U.S. in 1980** 1.765

Country	Thousands of Tons
Belgium	1.15
Britain	1.97
Canada	9.90
Denmark	1.24
France	2.82
Holland	1.56

6. **Oil Stockpiles in 1980** 242

Country	Millions of Barrels
Britain	161
Canada	169
France	242
Germany	330
Italy	183
Japan	469
United States	1319

BUSINESS

People in many different kinds of businesses and careers use the mean, median, and mode to help in planning and to give information to consumers. In some situations, one of these may provide more useful information than the others.

INFORMATION

EXERCISES

A store manager recorded the number of customers entering the store from 9 A.M. to 6 P.M. on an average day. Use this information for Exercises 1–5.

Hours	Customers
9:00 – 10:00	10
10:00 – 11:00	21
11:00 – 12:00	25
12:00 – 1:00	27
1:00 – 2:00	30
2:00 – 3:00	40
3:00 – 4:00	35
4:00 – 5:00	45
5:00 – 6:00	53

1. Over what 5-hour period does the store have the greatest number of customers? 1:00 – 6:00

2. During what hour does the mode occur? 5:00 – 6:00

3. Suppose that the manager decides to hire part-time help from 4:00 P.M. to 6:00 P.M. Why is this a reasonable decision? The greatest number of customers are in the store at this time.

4. What is the mean number of customers per hour coming into the store? Round your answer to the nearest whole number. 32

5. Is the answer to Exercise 4 helpful to the manager in deciding when to hire part-time help? Explain. No. It doesn't indicate when the most help is needed.

The table at the right shows yearly salaries for six persons who work at the Torvale Car Rental Agency. Use this table for Exercises 6–10.

Yearly Salaries	
Manager	$40,000
Assistant	$25,000
Clerk	$12,500
Clerk	$12,000
Clerk	$11,500
Clerk	$10,000

6. What is the mean yearly salary? $18,500

7. Is the mean yearly salary greater or less than most of the salaries? greater than

8. What is the median yearly salary? $12,250

9. Are most of the salaries closer to the mean yearly salary or the median yearly salary? median yearly salary

10. Which average—the mean yearly salary or the median yearly salary—best represents most of the yearly salaries? median yearly salary

This table shows the number of centimeters of rain that fell in Barrow, Alaska in a recent year. Use this table for Exercises 11–14.

Rainfall in Barrow			
Jan.	0.5 cm	July	2 cm
Feb.	0.5 cm	Aug.	3 cm
March	0.5 cm	Sept.	2 cm
April	0.5 cm	Oct.	2 cm
May	0.5 cm	Nov.	1 cm
June	1 cm	Dec.	0.5 cm

Rain Gauge

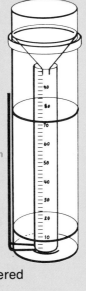

Roberto Tiraldo, weather reporter

11. What is the mean monthly rainfall? Round your answer to the nearest whole number. 1 cm

12. What is the median monthly rainfall? 0.75 cm

13. What is the mode for this data? 0.5 cm

14. Meteorologists and weather reporters use the mean to give average monthly rainfall. Why do you think that the mean is considered the best average in this case?

The mean is the one number that is closest to all the numbers.

15-3 Listing Data

See the Teacher's Manual for the objectives.

You can make information or **data** easier to read by listing the data in a table. Using equal intervals makes the table shorter.

PROCEDURE To make data easier to read:

1 Count how many times each measure occurs.

2 List the data in equal intervals in a table.

EXAMPLE The prices of twelve different brands of tennis rackets are listed at the right. Show the data in a table.

Prices of Tennis Rackets

$32.99	$32.99	$75.99	$29.99
$75.99	$29.99	$32.99	$64.99
$32.99	$29.99	$32.99	$45.99

Solution:

Prices	Tally	Count
$21-$40	⊞ |||	8
$41-$60			1
$61-$80	|||	3

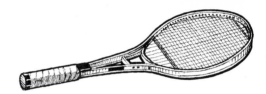

REVIEW OF RELATED SKILLS

You may wish to use these exercises before teaching the lesson.

Replace the ● *with <, =, or >.* (Pages 90–91)

1. 11.6 ● 11.7 <   **2.** 11.5 ● 11.4 >   **3.** 11.6 ● 11.60 =   **4.** 11.70 ● 11.8 <

5. 12.4 ● 12.35 >   **6.** 12.9 ● 12.19 >   **7.** 12.25 ● 12.2 >   **8.** 12.1 ● 12.05 >

EXERCISES

See the suggested assignment guide in the Teacher's Manual.

For Exercises 1–6, use the given information to complete the table.

1. Tour Earnings of Twelve Women Golfers in a Recent Year

$20,000	$11,000	$7,000
$16,000	$11,000	$6,000
$13,000	$ 7,000	$6,000
$19,000	$ 7,000	$9,000

Earnings	Tally	Count
$ 6,000–$10,000	? ⊞|	? 6
$11,000–$15,000	? |||	? 3
$16,000–$20,000	? |||	? 3

2.

Lengths in Feet of Sixteen U.S. Suspension Bridges

4260	2800	2190	1850
4200	2778	2150	1800
3800	2310	2150	1750
3500	2300	2000	1632

Length in Feet	Tally	Count
1601–2500	? ‖‖‖ ‖‖‖	? 10
2501–3400	? ‖	? 2
3401–4300	? ‖‖‖	? 4

3.

Monthly Rainfall in Millimeters for Chicago, Illinois in a Recent Year

50.8	81.9	70.2
50.8	82.6	60.0
65.5	88.9	63.5
56.2	70.2	50.8

Millimeters of Rainfall	Tally	Count
50–58	? ‖‖‖	? 4
59–67	? ‖‖	? 3
68–76	? ‖	? 2
77–85	? ‖	? 2
86–94	? ‖	? 1

4.

Life Spans in Days of 12 Fruit Flies

16	15	14	16
$15\frac{1}{2}$	8	16	16
14	14	$15\frac{1}{2}$	14

Days	Tally	Count
8–10	? ‖	? 1
11–13	?	? 0
14–16	? ‖‖‖ ‖‖‖ ‖	? 11

5.

Capacity of 16 College Football Stadiums

59,000	61,000	30,000	70,000
70,000	48,000	77,000	54,000
57,000	32,000	21,000	59,000
43,500	23,000	26,000	71,000

Capacity	Tally	Count
21,000–35,000	? ‖‖‖	? 5
36,000–50,000	? ‖	? 2
51,000–65,000	? ‖‖‖	? 5
66,000–80,000	? ‖‖‖	? 4

6.

Times in Seconds for the 100-Yard Dash

11.6	11.2	11.5	12.0	12.0
11.2	11.5	11.6	11.8	11.4
12.0	11.4	11.2	11.6	11.4

Times	Tally	Count
11.2–11.4	? ‖‖‖ ‖	? 6
11.5–11.7	? ‖‖‖	? 5
11.8–12.0	? ‖‖‖	? 4

15-4 The Histogram with Applications

See the Teacher's Manual for the objectives.

A **histogram** is a special kind of bar graph.

PROCEDURE   To draw a histogram:

1. List the data by intervals.

2. Draw a rectangle to represent the count for each interval.

EXAMPLE   Pulse rates for 60 people are listed below. Draw a histogram to show the data.

Pulse Rates of 60 People					
68	70	82	72	74	81
77	73	78	73	77	72
72	75	74	73	76	80
77	74	73	72	84	73
75	79	79	81	69	77
79	69	70	71	84	85
69	74	75	79	75	70
69	70	76	76	75	73
79	81	74	72	76	78
79	71	80	77	79	80

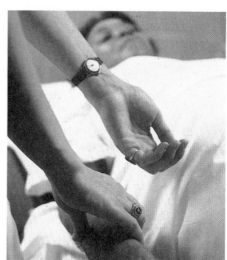

Solution:

1. List the data by intervals.   2. Draw a rectangle for each interval.

Pulse Rates	Count
65–69	5
70–74	22
75–79	23
80–84	9
85–89	1

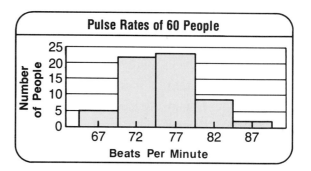

Note that the middle number in each interval is at the center of the base of its corresponding bar in the graph. For example, 67 is the middle number in the interval 65–69. It is also the center of the base of the first bar.

The bar graph at the right shows personal income for Americans in the first six months of a recent year. Use this graph for Exercises 1–3. (Pages 74–75)

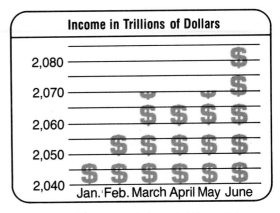

1. Between which two months was there the greatest increase in personal income? *May and June*

2. Between which two months was there the least increase in personal income? *April and May*

3. For which month was total personal income about 2.056 trillion dollars? *February*

EXERCISES

See the suggested assignment guide in the Teacher's Manual.

For Exercises 1–2, use the given information to complete the table. Then make a histogram to show the data.

1.

Average Class Size in Twenty Schools

19	32	28	38	24
25	39	20	35	37
29	26	25	33	38
32	34	22	18	31

Class Size	Count
15–20	? 3
21–25	? 4
26–30	? 3
31–35	? 6
36–40	? 4

2.

Price of One Ounce of Gold Over One Year

$625	$600	$500
$525	$540	$610
$630	$600	$660
$630	$615	$595

Prices	Count
$500–$539	? 2
$540–$579	? 1
$580–$619	? 5
$620–$659	? 3
$640–$679	? 1

For Exercises 3–4, make a histogram to show the data.

3. Diameters of 50 Trees

Centimeters	Count
17–23	9
24–30	23
31–37	14
38–44	4

4. Bowling Scores for One Week

Scores	Count
121–140	2
141–160	14
161–180	10
181–200	1

15-5 Circle Graphs See the Teacher's Manual for the objectives.

You can also use a circle graph to show data. There are 360° in a circle.

PROCEDURE To draw a circle graph:

1. Write a decimal for each per cent.

2. Multiply the decimal by 360°. Round your answer to the nearest degree.

3. Use a protractor to draw the graph.

EXAMPLE This table shows the per cent of each of four kinds of tissue in the human body. Make a circle graph to show the data.

Body Tissue

Type	Per Cent
Muscle	47%
Supporting	33%
Blood	7%
Surface	13%

Solution:

1. Write a decimal for each per cent.

    $47\% = 0.47$ $33\% = 0.33$

    $13\% = 0.13$ $7\% = 0.07$

2. Multiply each per cent by 360°. Round to the nearest degree.

    $0.47 \times 360° = 169.2$, or **169°** $0.13 \times 360° = 46.8$, or **47°**

    $0.33 \times 360° = 118.8$, or **119°** $0.07 \times 360° = 25.2$, or **25°**

3. Draw the graph.

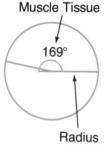

Muscle Tissue   New Radius   Radius   Supporting Tissue

169°   119°

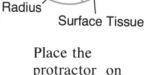

New Radius   47°   Surface Tissue

Body Tissue

Muscle 47%   Supporting 33%   13%   Blood 7%   Surface

Draw a radius. Place the protractor on the radius. Draw the angle for muscle tissue.

Place the protractor on the "new" radius. Draw the angle for supporting tissue.

Place the protractor on the "new" radius. Draw the angle for surface tissue.

The remaining angle represents the blood tissue.

Write a decimal for each per cent. (Pages 276–277)

1. 38% 0.38   **2.** 25% 0.25   **3.** 9% 0.09   **4.** 3% 0.03   **5.** 16.5% 0.165   **6.** $37\frac{1}{2}$%

$0.37\frac{1}{2}$

Round to the nearest whole number. (Pages 120-121)

7. 17.3 17   **8.** 89.2 89   **9.** 46.5 47   **10.** 316.1 316   **11.** 41.9 42   **12.** 136.5

137

Use a protractor to find the measure of each angle to the nearest degree.
(Pages 228–229)

13. 145°   **14.** 90°   **15.** 65°   **16.** 85°

EXERCISES

See the suggested assignment guide in the Teacher's Manual.

For Exercises 1–6, make a circle graph to show the data.

1. Composition of the Earth's Crust

Element	Per Cent	
Oxygen	47%	169°
Silicon	28%	101°
Aluminum	8%	29°
Iron	5%	18°
Other	12%	43°

2. Area of World's Oceans

Ocean	Per Cent	
Pacific	46%	166°
Atlantic	23%	83°
Indian	20%	72°
Arctic	4%	14°
Other	7%	25°

3. Per Cent of Vote in Election

Candidate	Per Cent	
R. Arico	40%	144°
A. Jones	30%	108°
D. Sanchez	16%	58°
S. Yoto	14%	50°

4. Vehicles Passing a Toll Booth

Vehicle	Per Cent	
Automobiles	47%	169°
Motorcycles	10%	36°
Trucks	25%	90°
Vans	18%	65°

5. Immigration to U.S. Since 1820

From	Per Cent	
Asia	5%	18°
Europe	75%	270°
North and South America	18%	65°
Other	2%	7°

6. Personal Budget

Item	Per Cent	
Clothing	4%	14°
Food	25%	90°
Housing	28%	101°
Other	43%	155°

Chapter Review

These exercises review the vocabulary, skills, and applications presented in the chapter as a preparation for the chapter test.

Part 1: Vocabulary

For Exercises 1–4, choose from the box at the right the word(s) that completes each statement.

<table>
<tr><td>

1. The sum of a group of measures divided by the number of measures is called the __?__. (Page 330) *mean*

2. The measure that occurs most often in a set of data is the __?__. (Page 330) *mode*

3. In a listing of data, the middle measure or score is the __?__. (Page 332) *median*

4. A special kind of bar graph that shows the data in equal intervals is called a __?__. (Page 338) *histogram*

</td><td>

mode

histogram

median

mean

</td></tr>
</table>

Part 2: Skills and Applications

For Exercises 5–6, find the mean.   (Pages 330–331)

5. $0.99 **Cost of Cantaloupe at Eight Stores**

$1.20	$1.00	$0.72	$1.00
$1.05	$0.95	$0.80	$1.20

6. $241.75 **Kilometers Driven Per Day on a Vacation Trip**

248	310	162	248
225	286	230	225

For Exercises 7–8, find the mode.   (Pages 330–331)

7. 201-210 **Car Output Per Day for 24 Factories**

Cars	Count
161–170	5
171–180	4
181–190	3
191–200	3
201–210	6
211–220	3

8. 15.0 – 15.9 **Distance in Meters for Shot-Put**

Distance	Count
12.0–12.9	2
13.0–13.9	4
14.0–14.9	5
15.0–15.9	7
16.0–16.9	5
17.0–17.9	1

For Exercises 9–10, find the median.   (Pages 332–333)

9. 56 **Age on Taking Oath of Office of Some Recent Presidents**

President	LBJ	RN	GF	JC	RR
Age	55	56	61	52	69

10. 21 **Number of Baskets Scored by a Basketball Team**

Game	1	2	3	4	5
Baskets	22	17	26	19	21

For Exercises 11–12, use the given information to complete the table. (Pages 336–337)

11. Number of Commuters on 20 Trains

372	392	300	494
511	458	616	333
489	529	650	369
501	603	575	347
307	579	425	481

Commuters	Tally	Count
300–399	卌 II ?	? 7
400–499	卌I ?	? 5
500–599	卌 ?	? 5
600–699	III ?	? 3

12. Prices of 1 Record Album

$13.97	$15.25	$14.32	$10.98
$ 8.86	$ 5.57	$ 5.17	$11.75
$ 6.37	$ 7.23	$12.99	$ 7.29
$ 9.99	$ 8.01	$ 7.57	$ 8.05

Prices	Tally	Count
$ 5.00–$ 7.99	卌 I?	? 6
$ 8.00–$10.99	卌 ?	? 5
$11.00–$13.99	III ?	? 3
$14.00–$16.99	II ?	? 2

For Exercises 13–14, make a histogram to show the data. (Pages 338–339)

13. Number of Passengers on 100 Buses

Passengers	Count
0–10	2
11–20	20
21–30	18
31–40	22
41–50	38

14. Water Reservoir Levels (Per Cent Full) for 12 Months

Per Cent Full	Count
28.0–31.9	2
32.0–35.9	6
36.0–39.9	3
40.0–43.9	1

For Exercises 15–16, make a circle graph to show the data. (Pages 340–341)

15. Books in a Library

Type of Book	Per Cent	
Fiction	45%	162°
History	25%	90°
Science	10%	36°
Reference	8%	29°
Others	12%	43°

16. U.S. Energy Sources

Source	Per Cent	
Oil	49%	176°
Natural Gas	25%	90°
Coal	20%	72°
Nuclear	3%	11°
Water	3%	11°

Chapter Test

The Teacher's Resource Book contains two forms of each chapter test.

For Exercises 1–2, find the mean.

1. **Number of Weeks on the Chart for the Top Ten Records**
9.1

14	6	8	14	15
9	8	3	7	7

2. **Number of Customers Per Hour at National Consumer Bank**
16.6

15	18	15	16	12
12	25	18	15	20

For Exercises 3–4, find the mode.

3. 71-75 **Scores for 18 Holes of Golf**

Scores	Count
66–70	1
71–75	5
76–80	3
81–85	3

4. **Heights in Centimeters of 20 Students**

Heights	Count
151–155	1
156–160	2
161–165	4
166–170	7

166-170

For Exercises 5–6, find the median.

5. 18.5 **Number of Hit Records Sold**

Day	Mon.	Tues.	Wed.	Thurs.
Number	16	21	13	26

6. 11 **Fish Caught Per Person**

Person	Bill	Jose	Ann	Sue	Tim
Number	16	11	14	9	8

For Exercises 7, use the given information to complete the table.

7. **Heights in Meters of Fifteen Trees**

23	14	17	22	16
23	19	12	15	11
18	23	16	11	19

Heights	Tally	Count
11–14	? ||||	? 4
15–18	? ⊦⊦⊦⊦	? 5
19–22	? |||	? 3
23–26	? |||	? 3

8. Make a histogram for the data in Exercise 7.

For Exercises 9–10, make a circle graph to show the data.

9. **Uses of Paper**

Uses	Per Cent
Packaging	48% 173°
Writing Paper	29% 104°
Tissues	7% 25°
Other	16% 58°

10. **Population of a City by Age**

Age	Per Cent
65 and over	11% 40°
45–64	20% 72°
20–44	35% 126°
19 and under	34% 122°

Additional Practice

You may wish to use some or all of these exercises depending on how well students performed on the formal chapter test.

For Exercises 1–2, find the mean.   (Pages 330–331)

1. **Scores for 10 Basketball Games**

82	87	76	91	68
96	83	75	56	70

78.4

2. **High Temperatures for 8 Weeks**

23°	35°	32°	41°
14°	28°	30°	40°

30.375

For Exercises 3–4, find the mode.   (Pages 330–331)

3. **Times for the 100-Meter Dash**

Time in Seconds	Count
9–9.99	1
10–10.99	3
11–11.99	5
12–12.99	6

12-12.99

4. **Population by Age in a City**

Age	Count
10 and under	25,321
11–39	66,756
40–69	62,283
70 and over	16,346

11-39

For Exercises 5–6, find the median.   (Pages 332–333)

5. **Weekly Salaries for Five Clerks**

Clerk	1	2	3	4	5
Salary	$150	$250	$100	$225	$300

$225

6. **Points Scored by a Football Team**

Game	1	2	3	4	5	6
Points	21	48	3	14	28	31

24.5

For Exercise 7, use the given information to complete the table.
(Pages 336–337)

7. **Heights in Meters of 16 Buildings**

237	216	206	183
225	244	229	188
181	219	204	203
210	224	223	238

Heights	Tally	Count
180–199	?|||	? 3
200–219	?⧚TI	? 6
220–239	?⧚TI	? 6
240–259	?|	? 1

8. Make a histogram for the data in Exercise 7.   (Pages 338–339)

For Exercises 9–10, make a circle graph to show the data.
(Pages 340–341)

9. **Vacation Expenditures**

Expenditures	Per Cent
Transportation	15% 54°
Meals	20% 72°
Lodging	28% 101°
Recreation	17% 61°
Other	20% 72°

10. **Land Use in a Town**

Use	Per Cent
Roads	25% 90°
Railroad	3% 11°
Public Use	12% 43°
Farm	8% 29°
Housing	52% 187°

Additional Practice   STATISTICS   **345**

REVIEW OF RELATED SKILLS FOR CHAPTER 16

We suggest that some or all of this page be reviewed before proceeding with the chapter.

Write each fraction in lowest terms.   (Pages 182–183)

1. $\frac{2}{4}$ $\frac{1}{2}$ 2. $\frac{5}{15}$ $\frac{1}{3}$ 3. $\frac{6}{20}$ $\frac{3}{10}$ 4. $\frac{7}{35}$ $\frac{1}{5}$ 5. $\frac{6}{36}$ $\frac{1}{6}$ 6. $\frac{8}{32}$ $\frac{1}{4}$

7. $\frac{10}{15}$ $\frac{2}{3}$ 8. $\frac{6}{9}$ $\frac{2}{3}$ 9. $\frac{12}{18}$ $\frac{2}{3}$ 10. $\frac{8}{12}$ $\frac{2}{3}$ 11. $\frac{14}{21}$ $\frac{2}{3}$ 12. $\frac{18}{24}$ $\frac{3}{4}$

13. $\frac{25}{30}$ $\frac{5}{6}$ 14. $\frac{30}{36}$ $\frac{5}{6}$ 15. $\frac{9}{36}$ $\frac{1}{4}$ 16. $\frac{8}{40}$ $\frac{1}{5}$ 17. $\frac{12}{100}$ $\frac{3}{25}$ 18. $\frac{12}{144}$ $\frac{1}{12}$

19. $\frac{16}{48}$ $\frac{1}{3}$ 20. $\frac{50}{75}$ $\frac{2}{3}$ 21. $\frac{75}{100}$ $\frac{3}{4}$ 22. $\frac{36}{90}$ $\frac{2}{5}$ 23. $\frac{14}{63}$ $\frac{2}{9}$ 24. $\frac{15}{25}$ $\frac{3}{5}$

25. $\frac{46}{92}$ $\frac{1}{2}$ 26. $\frac{71}{142}$ $\frac{1}{2}$ 27. $\frac{96}{128}$ $\frac{3}{4}$ 28. $\frac{63}{81}$ $\frac{7}{9}$ 29. $\frac{50}{72}$ $\frac{25}{36}$ 30. $\frac{24}{72}$ $\frac{1}{3}$

Add. Write your answers in lowest terms.   (Pages 186–187)

31. $\frac{1}{5}$ $+\frac{2}{5}$ $\frac{3}{5}$ 32. $\frac{3}{7}$ $+\frac{1}{7}$ $\frac{4}{7}$ 33. $\frac{1}{4}$ $+\frac{3}{4}$ 1 34. $\frac{5}{8}$ $+\frac{3}{8}$ 1 35. $\frac{5}{36}$ $+\frac{7}{36}$ $\frac{1}{3}$ 36. $\frac{8}{36}$ $+\frac{12}{36}$ $\frac{5}{9}$

37. $\frac{5}{24}$ $+\frac{7}{24}$ $\frac{1}{2}$ 38. $\frac{7}{15}$ $+\frac{8}{15}$ 1 39. $\frac{9}{17}$ $+\frac{8}{17}$ 1 40. $\frac{7}{12}$ $+\frac{5}{12}$ 1 41. $\frac{4}{13}$ $+\frac{8}{13}$ $\frac{12}{13}$ 42. $\frac{11}{24}$ $+\frac{7}{24}$ $\frac{3}{4}$

43. $\frac{1}{4}+\frac{1}{4}$ $\frac{1}{2}$ 44. $\frac{1}{8}+\frac{3}{8}$ $\frac{1}{2}$ 45. $\frac{13}{36}+\frac{13}{36}$ $\frac{13}{18}$ 46. $\frac{4}{9}+\frac{1}{9}$ $\frac{5}{9}$ 47. $\frac{1}{6}+\frac{1}{6}$ $\frac{1}{3}$

48. $\frac{3}{8}+\frac{3}{8}$ $\frac{3}{4}$ 49. $\frac{7}{9}+\frac{0}{9}$ $\frac{7}{9}$ 50. $\frac{5}{36}+\frac{5}{36}$ $\frac{5}{18}$ 51. $\frac{1}{2}+\frac{1}{2}$ 1 52. $\frac{3}{10}+\frac{3}{10}$ $\frac{3}{5}$

Write a fraction in lowest terms for each ratio.   (Pages 260–261)

53. 3 to 5 $\frac{3}{5}$ 54. 7 to 10 $\frac{7}{10}$ 55. 12 to 36 $\frac{1}{3}$ 56. 14 to 36 $\frac{7}{18}$

57. 5 to 9 $\frac{5}{9}$ 58. 8 to 12 $\frac{2}{3}$ 59. 4 to 16 $\frac{1}{4}$ 60. 12 to 16 $\frac{3}{4}$

61. 10 to 25 $\frac{2}{5}$ 62. 12 to 24 $\frac{1}{2}$ 63. 18 to 36 $\frac{1}{2}$ 64. 14 to 21 $\frac{2}{3}$

65. 25 to 75 $\frac{1}{3}$ 66. 16 to 128 $\frac{1}{8}$ 67. 20 to 32 $\frac{5}{8}$ 68. 9 to 36 $\frac{1}{4}$

69. 10 to 15 $\frac{2}{3}$ 70. 15 to 45 $\frac{1}{3}$ 71. 20 to 48 $\frac{5}{12}$ 72. 30 to 36 $\frac{5}{6}$

73. 6 to 12 $\frac{1}{2}$ 74. 21 to 56 $\frac{3}{8}$ 75. 72 to 120 $\frac{3}{5}$ 76. 55 to 100 $\frac{11}{20}$

Write a per cent for each fraction.   (Pages 274–275, 281–282)

77. $\frac{1}{2}$ 50%   78. $\frac{2}{10}$ 20%   79. $\frac{3}{5}$ 60%   80. $\frac{4}{8}$ 50%   81. $\frac{7}{10}$ 70%   82. $\frac{2}{5}$ 40%

83. $\frac{7}{20}$ 35%   84. $\frac{15}{20}$ 75%   85. $\frac{12}{48}$ 25%   86. $\frac{7}{50}$ 14%   87. $\frac{8}{25}$ 32%   88. $\frac{7}{100}$ 7%

89. $\frac{19}{100}$ 19%   90. $\frac{18}{18}$ 100%   91. $\frac{36}{36}$ 100%   92. $\frac{0}{10}$ 0%   93. $\frac{0}{12}$ 0%   94. $\frac{7}{40}$ $17\frac{1}{2}$%

95. $\frac{19}{50}$ 38%   96. $\frac{21}{40}$ $52\frac{1}{2}$%   97. $\frac{5}{8}$ $62\frac{1}{2}$%   98. $\frac{5}{6}$ $83\frac{1}{3}$%   99. $\frac{1}{9}$ $11\frac{1}{9}$%   100. $\frac{1}{12}$ $8\frac{1}{3}$%

101. $\frac{1}{8}$ $12\frac{1}{2}$%   102. $\frac{7}{8}$ $87\frac{1}{2}$%   103. $\frac{12}{28}$ $42\frac{6}{7}$%   104. $\frac{14}{21}$ $66\frac{2}{3}$%   105. $\frac{8}{12}$ $66\frac{2}{3}$%   106. $\frac{6}{36}$ $16\frac{2}{3}$%

16

PROBABILITY

SKILLS

16-1   Probability
16-2   Probability and Tables
16-3   Tree Diagrams

APPLICATION

Chances and Choices

CAREER

Quality Control

16-1 Probability

Probability is a number between 0 and 1 that tells you how likely it is that a certain event will happen. You can write a fraction or a per cent for a probability.

PROCEDURE   To find the probability of an event, use this ratio.

$$\text{Probability (abbreviated: P)} = \frac{\textbf{Number of Successful Ways}}{\textbf{Number of Possible Ways}}$$

EXAMPLE   These three cards are shuffled and placed face down. Then one card is drawn. Find each probability.

a. Drawing the five hearts

b. Drawing a heart   **c.** Drawing a club   **d.** Drawing a red card

Solutions: a. One of the 3 cards is the five of hearts. So

$$\frac{\text{Number of Successful Ways}}{\text{Number of Possible Ways}} = \frac{1}{3}$$

$P = \frac{1}{3}$, or $33\frac{1}{3}$ %.

b. Two of the 3 cards are hearts. So

$$\frac{\text{Number of Successful Ways}}{\text{Number of Possible Ways}} = \frac{2}{3}$$

$P = \frac{2}{3}$, or $66\frac{2}{3}$ %.

c. None of the 3 cards is a club. So,

$$\frac{\text{Number of Successful Ways}}{\text{Number of Possible Ways}} = \frac{0}{3}$$

$P = 0$, or **0%.**

d. All 3 cards are red. So,

$$\frac{\text{Number of Successful Ways}}{\text{Number of Possible Ways}} = \frac{3}{3}$$

$P = 1$, or **100%.**

As the Example shows, the <u>probability of an event that cannot happen</u> is **0.** The <u>probability of an event that is certain to happen is 1.</u>

REVIEW OF RELATED SKILLS

Write each fraction in lowest terms.   (Pages 182–183)

1. $\frac{4}{6}$ $\frac{2}{3}$ **2.** $\frac{20}{24}$ $\frac{5}{6}$ **3.** $\frac{6}{18}$ $\frac{1}{3}$ **4.** $\frac{54}{60}$ $\frac{9}{10}$ **5.** $\frac{15}{40}$ $\frac{3}{8}$ **6.** $\frac{15}{30}$ $\frac{1}{2}$ **7.** $\frac{21}{36}$ $\frac{7}{12}$ **8.** $\frac{48}{128}$ $\frac{3}{8}$

Write a fraction in lowest terms for each ratio.   (Pages 260–261)

9. 5 to 11 $\frac{5}{11}$ **10.** 6 to 15 $\frac{2}{5}$ **11.** 27 to 100 $\frac{27}{100}$ **12.** 16 to 80 $\frac{1}{5}$ **13.** 9 to 30 $\frac{3}{10}$

Write a per cent for each fraction.   (Pages 274–275, 281–282)

14. $\frac{1}{4}$ 25%   **15.** $\frac{1}{10}$ 10%   **16.** $\frac{3}{4}$ 75%   **17.** $\frac{4}{5}$ 80%   **18.** $\frac{37}{50}$ 74%   **19.** $\frac{9}{20}$ 45%   **20.** $\frac{2}{2}$ 100%   **21.** $\frac{3}{8}$
                                                                                                                                                              $37\frac{1}{2}$%

EXERCISES

See the assignment guide in the Teacher's Manual.

These four cards were shuffled and placed face down. One card is drawn. Find each probability.

1. Drawing the ace of clubs. $\frac{1}{4}$, or 25%

2. Drawing the 10 of clubs $\frac{1}{4}$, or 25%

3. Drawing a club $\frac{1}{2}$, or 50%

4. Drawing a black card $\frac{3}{4}$, or 75%

5. Drawing the 4 of diamonds $\frac{1}{4}$, or 25%   **6.** Drawing a red card $\frac{1}{4}$, or 25%

7. Drawing a heart 0, or 0%   **8.** Drawing a queen 0, or 0%

9. Drawing an ace $\frac{1}{2}$, or 50%   **10.** Not drawing an ace $\frac{1}{2}$, or 50%

A coin purse contains two pennies, a nickel, a dime, and a quarter. One coin is drawn. Find each probability.

11. Drawing a dime $\frac{1}{5}$, or 20%

12. Drawing a penny $\frac{2}{5}$, or 40%

13. Drawing a quarter $\frac{1}{5}$, or 20%

14. Drawing a nickel $\frac{1}{5}$, or 20%

15. Drawing a coin worth more than 1¢ $\frac{3}{5}$, or 60%

16. Drawing a coin worth more than 5¢

17. Drawing a coin worth less than 5¢

18. Drawing a coin worth more than 25¢

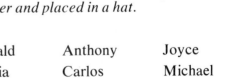

16. $\frac{2}{5}$, or 40%   17. $\frac{2}{5}$, or 40%   18. 0, or 0%

These ten names are written on slips of paper and placed in a hat. One name is drawn. Find each probability.

| Alice | Jennifer | Ronald | Anthony | Joyce |
| Philip | Anna | Sylvia | Carlos | Michael |

19. What is the probability that the name drawn begins with the letter "A"? $\frac{3}{10}$, or 30%

20. What is the probability that the name drawn begins with the letter "J"? $\frac{1}{5}$, or 20%

21. What is the probability of drawing a girl's name? $\frac{1}{2}$, or 50%

22. What is the probability of drawing a boy's name? $\frac{1}{2}$, or 50%

23. What is the probability of drawing a boy's name that begins with "J"? 0, or 0%

24. What is the probability of drawing a girl's name that begins with "J"? $\frac{1}{5}$, or 20%

PROBABILITY   **349**

16-2 Probability and Tables See the Teacher's Manual for the objectives.

This table shows the 36 possible ways for a pair of dice to land.

Second Die

First Die

This table shows the <u>sum</u> for each of the ways shown in Table 1.

Second Die

+	1	2	3	4	5	6
1	2	3	4	5	6	7
2	3	4	5	6	7	8
3	4	5	6	7	8	⑨
4	5	6	7	8	⑨	10
5	6	7	8	⑨	10	11
6	7	8	⑨	10	11	12

First Die

TABLE 1   **TABLE 2**

Table 2 shows that you can get certain sums in more than one way. For example, there are <u>4 ways </u>to get a sum of 9.

    6 and 3   5 and 4   4 and 5   3 and 6

PROCEDURE To find a probability:

    1 Make a table that shows all the possible ways.

    2 Use the table to find the probability.

EXAMPLE 1 A pair of dice is tossed. Use Table 2 to find the probability that the sum is 9. Write a fraction for the probability.

Solution: There are 4 ways to get a sum of 9.

$$P = \frac{\text{Number of Successful Ways}}{\text{Number of Possible Ways}}$$

$$= \frac{4}{36}, \text{ or } \frac{1}{9}$$

Thus, the probability that the sum is 9 is $\frac{1}{9}$.

Always write your answer in lowest terms.

EXAMPLE 2 A pair of dice is tossed. Use Table 2 to find the probability that the sum is 7 _or_ 11. Write a fraction for the probability.

Solution: There are six ways to get a 7, and two ways to get an 11.

$$P = \frac{\text{Number of Successful Ways}}{\text{Number of Possible Ways}}$$

$$= \frac{6}{36} + \frac{2}{36}$$

$$= \frac{8}{36}, \text{ or } \frac{2}{9}$$ ◀ **Probability that the sum is 7 or 11.**

REVIEW OF RELATED SKILLS
You may wish to use these exercises before teaching the lesson.

Write each fraction in lowest terms. (Pages 182-183)

1. $\frac{10}{14}$ $\frac{5}{7}$ **2.** $\frac{6}{10}$ $\frac{3}{5}$ **3.** $\frac{13}{26}$ $\frac{1}{2}$ **4.** $\frac{11}{33}$ $\frac{1}{3}$ **5.** $\frac{15}{45}$ $\frac{1}{3}$ **6.** $\frac{36}{48}$ $\frac{3}{4}$ **7.** $\frac{63}{72}$ $\frac{7}{8}$ **8.** $\frac{18}{54}$ $\frac{1}{3}$

Add. (Pages 186-187)

9. $\frac{1}{3} + \frac{1}{3}$ $\frac{2}{3}$ **10.** $\frac{2}{5} + \frac{2}{5}$ $\frac{4}{5}$ **11.** $\frac{3}{7} + \frac{2}{7}$ $\frac{5}{7}$ **12.** $\frac{5}{36} + \frac{2}{36}$ $\frac{7}{36}$ **13.** $\frac{2}{15} + \frac{6}{15}$ $\frac{8}{15}$

EXERCISES
See the suggested assignment guide in the Teacher's Manual.

A pair of dice is tossed. Use Table 2 on page 350 to find each probability. Write each answer as a fraction in lowest terms. (Example 1)

1. Getting a sum of 5 $\frac{1}{9}$ **2.** Getting a sum of 3 $\frac{1}{18}$ **3.** Getting a sum of 7 $\frac{1}{6}$

4. Getting a sum of 11 $\frac{1}{18}$ **5.** Getting a sum of 2 $\frac{1}{36}$ **6.** Getting a sum of 1 $\frac{0}{36}$

(Example 2)

7. Getting a sum of 2 _or_ 3 $\frac{1}{12}$ **8.** Getting a sum of 5 _or_ 6 $\frac{1}{4}$

9. Getting a sum of 6 _or_ 9 $\frac{1}{4}$ **10.** Getting a sum of 1 _or_ 13 $\frac{0}{36}$

11. Getting a sum of 4 _or_ 5 $\frac{7}{36}$ **12.** Getting a sum of 5 _or_ 12 $\frac{5}{36}$

13. Getting a sum _less than_ 5 $\frac{1}{6}$ **14.** Getting a sum _greater than_ 12 $\frac{0}{36}$

These word problems apply the concept of probability. Most students should be able to do these exercises.

APPLICATIONS: Using Probability

15. A weather forecaster says that there is an 80% chance of rain tomorrow. Write this probability as a fraction. $\frac{4}{5}$

16. A weather forecaster says there is an 85% chance of snow. Is it more likely to snow than not to snow? Yes

17. The probability of rain tomorrow is 80%. What is the probability that it will _not_ rain? Write a fraction for your answer. (HINT: 100% − 80% = ___?___) $\frac{1}{5}$

18. There is an 85% chance for snow during the night. What is the probability that it will _not_ snow? 15%

QUALITY CONTROL

Career lessons are optional.
This lesson combines the concept of probability with the skill of finding a per cent of a number.

To find how many defective light bulbs there might be in a large shipment, a quality control technician inspects and tests a certain number of bulbs. The number of bulbs tested is called a **sample.**

EXAMPLE

A technician found that 2 out of every 100 light bulbs tested were defective. Find the probable number of defective bulbs in a shipment of 120,000.

Solution:

1. Find the per cent of defective bulbs in the sample.

   2 out of $100 = \frac{2}{100} = 0.02$

   $= 2\%$ ◀ *0.02 = 2%*

2. Since 2% of the light bulbs in the sample are defective, it is probable that 2% of the bulbs in the shipment are also defective. Find 2% of 120,000.

   2% of $120,000 = 0.02 \times 120,000$

   $= 2400$ The probable number of defective bulbs is **2400.**

EXERCISES Note that Exercises 1-4 are nonverbal.

For Exercises 1–4, complete the table.

Product	Defective Items in the Sample	Per Cent of Defective Items in the Sample	Total Number of Items in a Shipment	Probable Number of Defective Items in a Shipment
1. Brite Ovens	7 out of 100	7%	600	? 42
2. Affordo Watches	5 out of 100	? 5%	12,000	? 600
3. Pix TV's	4 out of 100	? 4%	500	? 20
4. Curleze Hair Dryer	1 out of 20	5%	1,000	? 50

5. A sample of 800 toasters contains 40 that are defective. Find the probable number of defective toasters in a shipment of 36,000. 1800

6. In a shipment of 800 typewriters, the probability that any one typewriter is defective is 2%. Find the probable number of defective typewriters in the shipment. 16

Career

16-3 Tree Diagrams

See the Teacher's Manual for the objectives.

This lesson may be considered optional for some students.

When you toss two coins, they can land in four possible ways. You can draw a **tree diagram** to show the ways.

TOSSING TWO COINS

First Toss	Second Toss	Possible Ways of Landing
H	H	H H
	T	H T
T	H	T H
	T	T T

PROCEDURE   To find the probability of an event:

1. Draw a tree diagram that shows all the possible ways the event can happen.

2. Use the tree diagram to find the probability.

EXAMPLE   Two coins are tossed. Use the tree diagram above to find the probability of getting one head and one tail.

Solution: There are two ways of getting one head and one tail: HT and TH

$$P = \frac{\text{Number of Successful Ways}}{\text{Number of Possible Ways}}$$

$$= \frac{2}{4}, \text{ or } \frac{1}{2}$$

The probability is $\frac{1}{2}$, or **50%**.

REVIEW OF RELATED SKILLS

You may wish to use these exercises before teaching the lesson.

Write each fraction in lowest terms.   (Pages 182–183)

1. $\frac{4}{36}$ $\frac{1}{9}$ **2.** $\frac{12}{16}$ $\frac{3}{4}$ **3.** $\frac{24}{60}$ $\frac{2}{5}$ **4.** $\frac{18}{64}$ $\frac{9}{32}$ **5.** $\frac{18}{32}$ $\frac{9}{16}$ **6.** $\frac{15}{20}$ $\frac{3}{4}$ **7.** $\frac{6}{27}$ $\frac{2}{9}$ **8.** $\frac{10}{15}$ $\frac{2}{5}$

Write a per cent for each fraction.   (Pages 274–275, 281–282)

9. $\frac{3}{5}$ 60% **10.** $\frac{1}{4}$ 25% **11.** $\frac{4}{5}$ 80% **12.** $\frac{2}{3}$ $66\frac{2}{3}$% **13.** $\frac{1}{6}$ $16\frac{2}{3}$% **14.** $\frac{7}{8}$ $87\frac{1}{2}$% **15.** $\frac{9}{10}$ 90% **16.** $\frac{9}{20}$ 45%

17. $\frac{3}{25}$ 12% **18.** $\frac{13}{50}$ 26% **19.** $\frac{5}{40}$ $12\frac{1}{2}$% **20.** $\frac{8}{40}$ 20% **21.** $\frac{1}{12}$ $8\frac{1}{3}$% **22.** $\frac{8}{8}$ 100% **23.** $\frac{0}{9}$ 0% **24.** $\frac{17}{25}$ 68%

EXERCISES

Two coins are tossed. Use the tree diagram on page 353 to find each probability. Write a fraction and a per cent for each probability.

1. Getting two heads $\frac{1}{4}$, or 25%

2. Getting two tails $\frac{1}{4}$, or 25%

3. Getting a head on the first coin $\frac{1}{2}$, or 50%

4. Getting a head on the second coin

5. Getting two heads <u>or</u> two tails $\frac{1}{2}$, or 50%

6. Getting no heads $\frac{1}{4}$, or 25% $\frac{1}{2}$, or 50%

Three coins are tossed. This tree diagram shows all the possible ways the coins can land.

TOSSING THREE COINS

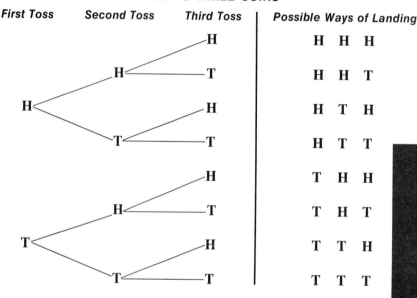

First Toss	Second Toss	Third Toss	Possible Ways of Landing

For Exercises 7–14, use the tree diagram above to find each probability. Write a fraction and a per cent for each probability.

7. Getting two tails and a head $\frac{3}{8}$, or $37\frac{1}{2}$%

8. Getting a head on the first coin $\frac{1}{2}$, or 50%

9. Getting a head on the first and second coins $\frac{1}{4}$, or 25%

10. Getting tails on the second and third coins $\frac{1}{4}$, or 25%

11. Getting three heads $\frac{1}{8}$, or $12\frac{1}{2}$%

12. Getting three tails $\frac{1}{8}$, or $12\frac{1}{2}$%

13. Getting more than one head $\frac{1}{2}$, or 50%

14. Getting <u>exactly</u> one head $\frac{3}{8}$, or $37\frac{1}{2}$%

Problem Solving and Applications

Chances and Choices

See the Teacher's Manual for the objectives.
This lesson applies the skills presented in Sections 16-1, 16-2, and 16-3.

Sometimes you multiply probabilities.

EXAMPLE Roger has 8 pairs of socks. One pair is red, 4 are blue and 3 are green. He also has 6 shirts. Three are white, 2 are blue and 1 is green. What is the probability of picking a pair of blue socks <u>and</u> a blue shirt?

Solution:

1 Find the probability of picking a pair of blue socks.

$P = \frac{4}{8}$, or $\frac{1}{2}$

2 Find the probability of picking a blue shirt.

$P = \frac{2}{6}$, or $\frac{1}{3}$

3 Multiply to find the probability of picking a pair of blue socks <u>and</u> a blue shirt.

$P = \frac{1}{2} \times \frac{1}{3}$

$= \frac{1}{6}$ ◀ **Probability of picking blue socks <u>and</u> a blue shirt.**

The table below shows that Roger had 48 ways of picking socks and shirts.

SOCKS								
	B	**B**	**B**	**B**	**R**	**G**	**G**	**G**
W	BW	BW	BW	BW	RW	GW	GW	GW
W	BW	BW	BW	BW	RW	GW	GW	GW
W	BW	BW	BW	BW	RW	GW	GW	GW
B	BB	BB	BB	BB	RB	GB	GB	GB
B	BB	BB	BB	BB	RB	GB	GB	GB
G	BG	BG	BG	BG	RG	GG	GG	GG

SHIRTS

Using the table, you can see that the probability of getting blue socks <u>and</u> a blue shirt is $\frac{8}{48}$, and

$$\frac{8}{48} = \frac{1}{6}.$$

This is the same probability as in the Example.

Exercises

Use the information in the Example for Exercises 1–4.

1. What is the probability of picking a white shirt and a pair of green socks? $\frac{9}{48} = \frac{3}{16}$

2. What is the probability of picking a green shirt and a pair of green socks? $\frac{3}{48} = \frac{1}{16}$

3. What is the probability of picking a pair of red socks and a white shirt? $\frac{3}{48} = \frac{1}{16}$

4. What is the probability of picking a pair of blue socks and a green shirt? $\frac{4}{48} = \frac{1}{12}$

A menu in a restaurant offers a choice of five main courses and four vegetables. Andrew chooses one of the main courses and one vegetable.

5. What is the probability of choosing roast turkey <u>and</u> glazed carrots? $\frac{1}{20}$

6. What is the probability of choosing broiled salmon <u>and</u> a baked potato? $\frac{1}{20}$

7. What is the probability of choosing one of the meat main courses <u>and</u> a salad? $\frac{1}{5}$

8. What is the probability of choosing one of the meat main courses <u>and</u> any vegetable except a salad? $\frac{3}{5}$

Menu

Main Courses
Roast Beef
Duckling a l'Orange
Roast Turkey • Lamb Chops
Broiled Salmon

Vegetables
Baked Potato • Glazed Carrots
Salad • Spinach Souffle

Application

Chapter Review

These exercises review the vocabulary, skills, and applications presented in the chapter as a preparation for the chapter test.

Part 1: Vocabulary

For Exercises 1–3, choose from the box at the right the word(s) or number(s) that completes each statement.

1. A number between 0 and 1 that tells how likely it is that a certain event will happen is called the __?__ of the event. (Page 348)
   probability

2. The probability of an event that cannot happen is __?__. 0 (Page 348)

3. The probability of an event that is certain to happen is __?__. 1 (Page 348)

4. To show all the possible ways that an event can happen, you can make a table or draw a __?__. (Page 353) tree diagram

probability
1
possible
0
tree diagram
$\frac{1}{2}$

Part 2: Skills and Applications

The names of the seven days of the week are written on slips of paper and placed in a hat. One slip of paper is drawn. Find each probability. Write each answer as a fraction in lowest terms. (Pages 348–349)

5. What is the probability of drawing "Sunday"? $\frac{1}{7}$

6. What is the probability of drawing "Friday"? $\frac{1}{7}$

7. What is the probability of drawing a day that begins with "T"? $\frac{2}{7}$

8. What is the probability of drawing a day that begins with "M"? $\frac{1}{7}$

9. What is the probability of drawing a day that begins with "H"? $\frac{0}{7}$

10. What is the probability of drawing a day that begins with "S"? $\frac{2}{7}$

A bag contains four green marbles, six white marbles, and ten red marbles. One marble is picked from the bag. Find each probability. Write a fraction in lowest terms for each answer. (Pages 350–351)

11. What is the probability of picking a green marble? $\frac{1}{5}$

12. What is the probability of picking a red marble? $\frac{1}{2}$

13. What is the probability of picking a white marble? $\frac{3}{10}$

14. What is the probability of picking a red <u>or</u> a white marble? $\frac{4}{5}$

15. What is the probability of picking a white <u>or</u> a green marble? $\frac{1}{2}$

16. What is the probability of picking a green <u>or</u> a red marble? $\frac{7}{10}$

A test contains three True–False questions. The tree diagram below shows all the possible ways to answer the questions.

First Question	Second Question	Third Question	Possible Ways
		T	T T T
	T	F	T T F
		T	T F T
T	F	F	T F F
		T	F T T
	T	F	F T F
		T	F F T
F	F	F	F F F

For Exercises 17–24, use the tree diagram to find each probability. Write a fraction in lowest terms and a per cent for each probability.
(Pages 353–354)

17. Answering two questions true and one false $\frac{3}{8}$; $37\frac{1}{2}$%

18. Answering all three questions false $\frac{1}{8}$; $12\frac{1}{2}$%

19. Answering the first question true $\frac{1}{2}$; 50%

20. Answering the last question false $\frac{1}{2}$; 50%

21. Answering <u>exactly one</u> question true $\frac{3}{8}$; $37\frac{1}{2}$%

22. Answering no question false $\frac{1}{8}$; $12\frac{1}{2}$%

23. Answering more than one question false $\frac{1}{2}$; 50%

24. Answering more than one question true $\frac{1}{2}$; 50%

The use of these word problems depends on which applications were studied.

Sue has six pairs of socks. One pair is red, three are navy blue and two are brown. She also has five scarves. Two are red, one is blue and two are green. She chooses a pair of socks and a scarf. Use this information for Exercises 25–30. Write a fraction in lowest terms for each answer.   (Pages 355–356)

25. What is the probability of picking a pair of blue socks? $\frac{1}{2}$

26. What is the probability of picking a blue scarf? $\frac{1}{5}$

27. What is the probability of picking blue socks <u>and</u> a blue scarf? $\frac{1}{10}$

28. What is the probability of picking a pair of red socks? $\frac{1}{6}$

29. What is the probability of picking a green scarf? $\frac{2}{5}$

30. What is the probability of picking red socks <u>and</u> a green scarf? $\frac{1}{15}$

Chapter Test

The names of the twelve months of the year are written on slips of paper and placed in a hat. One name is drawn. Find each probability. Write each answer as a fraction in lowest terms.

1. What is the probability of drawing "January"? $\frac{1}{12}$

2. What is the probability of drawing "August"? $\frac{1}{12}$

3. What is the probability of drawing a month that begins with "J"? $\frac{1}{4}$

4. What is the probability of drawing a month that begins with "A"? $\frac{1}{6}$

5. What is the probability of drawing a month that begins with "O"? $\frac{1}{12}$

6. What is the probability of drawing a month that begins with "T"? 0

A bag contains 2 green marbles, 4 red marbles and 4 blue marbles. One marble is picked. Find each probability. Write each answer as a fraction in lowest terms.

7. Picking a green marble $\frac{1}{5}$

8. Picking a red marble $\frac{2}{5}$

9. Picking a blue marble $\frac{2}{5}$

10. Picking a green <u>or</u> a red marble $\frac{3}{5}$

11. Picking a blue or a green marble $\frac{3}{5}$

12. Picking a blue <u>or</u> a red marble $\frac{4}{5}$

Jane has four skirts. Two skirts are gray, one is blue, and one is red. She also has ten blouses. Four are white, two are red, and four are prints. On a certain day, Jane wants to wear one of her skirts and one of her blouses. Find each probability. Write each answer as a fraction in lowest terms and as a per cent.

13. Picking a gray skirt $\frac{1}{2}$, or 50%

14. Picking a red blouse $\frac{1}{5}$, or 20%

15. Picking a red skirt $\frac{1}{4}$, or 25%

16. Picking a white blouse $\frac{2}{5}$, or 40%

17. Picking a gray skirt <u>and</u> a white blouse $\frac{1}{5}$, or 20%

18. Picking a red skirt <u>and</u> a white blouse $\frac{1}{10}$, or 10%

19. Picking a blue skirt <u>and</u> a print blouse $\frac{1}{10}$, or 10%

20. Picking a gray skirt <u>and</u> a print blouse $\frac{1}{5}$, or 20%

The use of Exercises 17-20 depends on which applications were studied.

Additional Practice

You may wish to use some or all of these exercises depending on how well students performed on the formal chapter test.

These ten names are written on slips of paper and placed in a hat. One name is drawn. Find each probability. Write a fraction in lowest terms for each answer. (Pages 348–349)

Monica	Jim	Ellen	Kim	Maria
Juan	Anne	Raoul	Elaine	Marcus

1. Picking a name that begins with "M" $\frac{3}{10}$

2. Picking a name that begins with "E" $\frac{1}{5}$

3. Picking a boy's name $\frac{2}{5}$

4. Picking a girl's name $\frac{3}{5}$

5. Picking a name that begins with "A" $\frac{1}{10}$

6. Picking a name that begins with "R" $\frac{1}{10}$

A bag contains eight green marbles, twelve white marbles, and four red marbles. One marble is picked from the bag. Find each probability. Write a fraction in lowest terms for each answer. (Pages 350–351)

7. Picking a red marble $\frac{1}{6}$

8. Picking a green marble $\frac{1}{3}$

9. Picking a red <u>or</u> a green marble $\frac{1}{2}$

10. Picking a white <u>or</u> a red marble $\frac{2}{3}$

A game uses the spinner shown at the right below. Two spins make a turn. The score is the sum of the two spins. The table at the left shows the possible sums you can get in the game. Use the table for Exercises 11–20. Write each probability as a fraction in lowest terms. (Pages 350–351)

Second Spin

+	3	6	9	12	15
3	6	9	12	15	18
6	9	12	15	18	21
9	12	15	18	21	24
12	15	18	21	24	27
15	18	21	24	27	30

First Spin

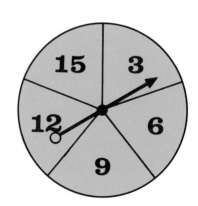

11. How many possible sums are shown in the table? 25

12. How many ways are there to get a score of 21? 4

13. What is the probability of scoring a 21? $\frac{4}{25}$

14. What is the probability of scoring an 18? $\frac{1}{5}$

15. What is the probability of scoring a 6? $\frac{1}{25}$

16. What is the probability of scoring a 30? $\frac{1}{25}$

17. What is the probability of scoring a 12 <u>or</u> a 15? $\frac{7}{25}$

18. What is the probability of scoring a 9 <u>or</u> a 30? $\frac{3}{25}$

19. What is the probability of scoring <u>less than</u> 15? $\frac{6}{25}$

20. What is the probability of scoring <u>more than</u> 18? $\frac{2}{5}$

There are three seats left on a bus. Six people, three men and three women, get on the bus. The tree diagram below shows all the possible ways for the people to occupy the three seats.

First Seat	Second Seat	Third Seat	Possible Ways
		M	M M M
	M	W	M M W
M		M	M W M
	W	W	M W W
		M	W M M
	M	W	W M W
W		M	W W M
	W	W	W W W

For Exercises 21–26, use the tree diagram to find each probability. Write a fraction in lowest terms and a per cent for each probability. (Pages 353–354)

21. A man in the first seat and women in the other two seats $\frac{1}{8}$; $12\frac{1}{2}$%

22. A woman in the second seat and men in the other two seats $\frac{1}{8}$; $12\frac{1}{2}$%

23. Two women and a man sitting $\frac{3}{8}$; $37\frac{1}{2}$%

24. Two men and a woman sitting $\frac{3}{8}$; $37\frac{1}{2}$%

25. A man in the third seat $\frac{1}{2}$; 50%

26. Women in all three seats $\frac{1}{8}$; $12\frac{1}{2}$%

The use of these word problems depends on which applications were studied.

Juanita has six scarves. Three are prints, one is blue, and two are white. She also has ten blouses. Three are blue, two are yellow, and five are prints. She chooses a scarf and a blouse. Use this information to find the probabilities in Exercises 27–32. Write a fraction in lowest terms for each answer. (Pages 355–356)

27. Picking a blue scarf $\frac{1}{6}$

28. Picking a white scarf $\frac{1}{3}$

29. Picking a yellow blouse $\frac{1}{5}$

30. Picking a print blouse $\frac{1}{2}$

31. Picking a white scarf <u>and</u> a print blouse $\frac{1}{6}$

32. Picking a blue scarf <u>and</u> a yellow blouse $\frac{1}{30}$

Cumulative Review: Chapters 15–16

You may also wish to use at this time the cumulative review on page 449 titled <u>Review of Skills</u> that reviews only the skills presented in chapters 1-16.

Choose the correct answer. Choose a, b, c, or d.

1. What is the probability of getting a 4 on one spin of the pointer? a

a. $\frac{1}{4}$ b. $\frac{1}{2}$ c. $\frac{1}{3}$ d. 1

2. Find the mean of the following five numbers. d

18   21   23   22   31

a. 30   b. 22   c. 21   d. 23

3. A bag contains two red marbles and 5 green marbles. One marble is drawn. What is the probability that it is red? d

a. $\frac{2}{5}$ b. $\frac{1}{4}$ c. $\frac{5}{7}$ d. $\frac{2}{7}$

4. The ages of six people are given below. Find the median age. b

16   18   13   19   15   19

a. 16   b. 17   c. 18   d. 19

5. Jesse is making a circle graph. How many degrees should he use to d represent a section marked "40%"?

a. 20°   b. 180°   c. 90°   d. 144°

6. There is an 80% chance of snow. What is the probability that it will <u>not</u> snow? b

a. $\frac{4}{5}$ b. $\frac{1}{5}$ c. $\frac{3}{4}$ d. $\frac{1}{4}$

7. In the circle graph below, how many degrees represent the section "Over $10,000"? c

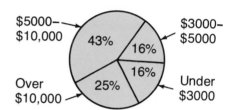

a. 25°   b. 80°   c. 90°   d. 100°

8. Find the median price of these five radios. a

$21.95 $28.50 $27.80
$19.85 $31.55

a. $27.80   b. $25.94
c. $28.50   d. $28.15

9. Find the mode of these numbers. c

18   20   24   36   20
32   13   18   20   36
44   20   58   76   36

a. 36   b. 18   c. 20   d. 22

10. What is the probability of rolling a 2 <u>or</u> a 4 on one roll of a single die? a

a. $\frac{1}{3}$ b. $\frac{1}{2}$ c. $\frac{1}{6}$ d. $\frac{1}{4}$

11. Two pennies, 3 nickels and a dime are placed in a box. One coin is drawn. What is the probability that it is a nickel? d

a. $\frac{1}{3}$ b. $\frac{3}{4}$ c. $\frac{1}{6}$ d. $\frac{1}{2}$

12. The table below shows the results of a survey of favorite games. Find the mode. b

Game	Count
Monopoly	29
Scrabble	40
Checkers	40
Chess	36
Backgammon	40
Bridge	17

a. 29　　**b.** 40　　**c.** 36　　**d.** 17

13. The following golf scores were recorded in the first round of a tournament. Find the mode of the scores. c

69　70　73　72　74
72　74　78　74　76

a. 69　　**b.** 72　　**c.** 74　　**d.** 76

14. In the circle graph below, how many degrees represent the section titled "Reserved Seat Sales"? c

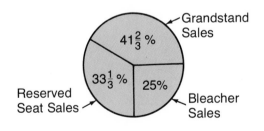

Grandstand Sales
$41\frac{2}{3}\%$
$33\frac{1}{3}\%$　25%
Reserved Seat Sales
Bleacher Sales

a. 90°　　**b.** 100°　　**c.** 120°　　**d.** 150°

15. What is the probability of rolling a number less than 5 on a single roll of one die? c

a. 0　　**b.** $\frac{1}{3}$　　**c.** $\frac{2}{3}$　　**d.** 1

16. Jane recorded the temperatures below at 10:00 A.M. on seven consecutive days. Find the mean temperature. c

65°　72°　56°　76°
58°　72°　63°

a. 72°　　**b.** 76°　　**c.** 66°　　**d.** 56°

17. There are 4 red marbles and 3 yellow marbles in a bag. One marble is drawn. What is the probability that it is red? a

Marbles

a. $\frac{4}{7}$　　**b.** $\frac{3}{7}$　　**c.** $\frac{3}{4}$　　**d.** $\frac{1}{4}$

18. Ken wrote the names of the days of the week on 7 slips of paper and put them in a hat. He chose one slip. What is the probability that the word on the slip was Monday? b

a. 1　　**b.** $\frac{1}{7}$　　**c.** $\frac{2}{7}$　　**d.** $\frac{5}{7}$

19. Sue has a yellow sweater and an orange sweater. She also has a gray skirt, a green skirt, and a brown skirt. She picks one sweater and one skirt. What is the probability that she will choose a yellow sweater and a brown skirt? b

a. 0　　**b.** $\frac{1}{6}$　　**c.** $\frac{1}{3}$　　**d.** 1

20. What is the probability of rolling a 3 <u>or</u> a 5 on a single roll of one die? c

a. 0　　**b.** $\frac{1}{6}$　　**c.** $\frac{1}{3}$　　**d.** 1

REVIEW OF RELATED SKILLS FOR CHAPTER 17

We suggest that some or all of this page be reviewed before proceeding with the chapter.

Multiply.   (Pages 32–33)

1. 12×12 144   **2.** 14×14 196   **3.** 8×8 64   **4.** 16×16 256   **5.** 23×23 529

6. 7×7 49   **7.** 56×56 3136   **8.** 30×30 900   **9.** 47×47 2209 **10.** 61×61 3721

Round each decimal to the nearest whole number.   (Pages 120–121)

11. 38.3 38   **12.** 27.5 28   **13.** 42.1 42   **14.** 16.9 17   **15.** 72.8 73   **16.** 24.6 25

17. 6.27 6   **18.** 18.39 18   **19.** 74.09 74   **20.** 9.06 9   **21.** 67.33 67   **22.** 58.97 59

23. 99.23 99   **24.** 101.48 101   **25.** 2.307 2   **26.** 79.5 80   **27.** 123.72 124   **28.** 8.099 8

Round each decimal to the nearest tenth.   (Pages 120–121)

29. 43.24 43.2 **30.** 16.91 16.9 **31.** 27.83 27.8 **32.** 14.01 14.0 **33.** 82.87 82.9 **34.** 93.14 93.1

35. 12.52 12.5 **36.** 39.76 39.8 **37.** 55.54 55.5 **38.** 68.33 68.3 **39.** 10.89 10.9 **40.** 50.11 50.1

41. 97.19 97.2 **42.** 64.46 64.5 **43.** 80.23 80.2 **44.** 77.77 77.8 **45.** 37.08 37.1 **46.** 45.75 45.8

Write a two-place decimal for each fraction.
(Pages 110–111, 122–123, 280–281)

47. $\frac{4}{5}$ 0.80 **48.** $\frac{3}{4}$ 0.75 **49.** $\frac{1}{2}$ 0.50 **50.** $\frac{7}{10}$ 0.70 **51.** $\frac{5}{4}$ 1.25 **52.** $\frac{29}{25}$ 1.16 **53.** $\frac{3}{2}$ 1.50 **54.** $\frac{1}{5}$ 0.20

55. $\frac{3}{10}$ 0.30 **56.** $\frac{11}{25}$ 0.44 **57.** $\frac{9}{20}$ 0.45 **58.** $\frac{13}{4}$ 3.25 **59.** $\frac{3}{25}$ 0.12 **60.** $\frac{1}{20}$ 0.05 **61.** $\frac{7}{5}$ 1.40 **62.** $\frac{18}{25}$ 0.72

Solve and check.   (Pages 248–249)

63. $n + 14 = 20$ 6   **64.** $n + 3 = 11$ 8   **65.** $n + 16 = 16$ 0   **66.** $n + 2.1 = 3.6$ 1.5

67. $n + 4.1 = 10.3$ 6.2 **68.** $n + \frac{1}{3} = \frac{1}{2}$ $\frac{1}{6}$ **69.** $n + \frac{1}{4} = \frac{7}{8}$ $\frac{5}{8}$ **70.** $n + 26 = 45$ 19

(Pages 252–253)

71. $2n = 24$ 12 **72.** $6n = 36$ 6 **73.** $11n = 77$ 7 **74.** $15n = 60$ 4 **75.** $0.3n = 2.7$ 9

76. $1.3n = 2.6$ 2 **77.** $4n = 108$ 27 **78.** $0.5n = 22$ 44 **79.** $2.5n = 1.7$ 0.68 **80.** $30n = 960$ 32

81. $\frac{n}{3} = 6$ 18 **82.** $\frac{n}{100} = 1.32$ 132 **83.** $\frac{n}{7} = 15$ 105 **84.** $11 = \frac{n}{14}$ 154 **85.** $\frac{n}{20} = 6.3$ 126

86. $\frac{n}{9} = 12$ 108 **87.** $0.6 = \frac{n}{15}$ 9 **88.** $\frac{n}{8} = 3$ 24 **89.** $\frac{n}{5} = 26$ 130 **90.** $\frac{n}{4} = 25$ 100

Solve each proportion for n.   (Pages 264–265)

91. $\frac{n}{18} = \frac{2}{3}$ 12 **92.** $\frac{n}{6} = \frac{1}{2}$ 3 **93.** $\frac{10}{3} = \frac{n}{27}$ 90 **94.** $\frac{5}{12} = \frac{n}{36}$ 15 **95.** $\frac{36}{n} = \frac{12}{1}$ 3

96. $\frac{21}{n} = \frac{7}{2}$ 6 **97.** $\frac{5}{16} = \frac{25}{n}$ 80 **98.** $\frac{3}{8} = \frac{24}{n}$ 64 **99.** $\frac{n}{48} = \frac{7}{8}$ 42 **100.** $\frac{n}{2} = \frac{15}{1}$ 30

101. $\frac{3}{4} = \frac{n}{8}$ 6 **102.** $\frac{9}{5} = \frac{n}{20}$ 36 **103.** $\frac{3}{8} = \frac{15}{n}$ 40 **104.** $\frac{4}{n} = \frac{7}{28}$ 16 **105.** $\frac{3}{n} = \frac{6}{14}$ 7

CHAPTER

17 SQUARES AND SQUARE ROOTS

SKILLS/APPLICATIONS

17-1   Squares and Square Roots

17-2   Using a Table of Squares and Square Roots

17-3   Right Triangle Rule and Applications

17-4   Similar Triangles and Applications

17-5   Tangent Ratios and Applications

CAREER

Traffic Officer

17-1 Squares and Square Roots See the Teacher's Manual for the objectives.

The **square** of a number is the product of a number and itself. Thus,

Read: "9 squared". $\quad 9^2 = 9 \times 9 = 81$ **The "2" in 9^2 is an exponent.**

PROCEDURE To square a number, multiply the number by itself.

EXAMPLE 1 Find each answer. **a.** 7^2 **b.** 21^2

Solutions: **a.** $7^2 = 7 \times 7$ **b.** $21^2 = 21 \times 21$

$\qquad 7^2 = 49$ **49 is the square of 7.** $\qquad$ **b.** $21^2 = 441$ **441 is the square of 21.**

After completing Example 1, you may wish to have students do some or all of Exercises 1-24.

Finding one of the two equal factors of a number is called finding its **square root**. The symbol for square root is $\sqrt{}$.

Since $4 \times 4 = 16$, $\sqrt{16} = 4$. **Read: "The square root of 16 is 4."**

Since $12 \times 12 = 144$, $\sqrt{144} = 12$.

PROCEDURE To find the square root of a number, find one of the two equal factors of the number.

EXAMPLE 2 Find each answer. **a.** $\sqrt{25}$ **b.** $\sqrt{121}$

Solutions: **a. Think:** $25 = 5 \times 5$. So $\sqrt{25} = 5$,

b. Think: $121 = 11 \times 11$. So $\sqrt{121} = 11$.

REVIEW OF RELATED SKILLS *You may wish to use these exercises before teaching the lesson.*

Multiply. (Pages 26–27, 32–33)

1. 10×10 100   **2.** 6×6 36   **3.** 8×8 64   **4.** 12×12 144   **5.** 3×3 9

6. 7×7 49   **7.** 1×1 1   **8.** 9×9 81   **9.** 4×4 16   **10.** 2×2 4

11. 5×5 25   **12.** 20×20 400   **13.** 23×23 529   **14.** 30×30 900   **15.** 31×31 961

16. 14×14 196   **17.** 16×16 256   **18.** 11×11 121   **19.** 15×15 225   **20.** 45×45 2025

EXERCISES

See the suggested assignment guide in the Teacher's Manual.

Find each answer. (Example 1)

1. 2^2 4   **2.** 3^2 9   **3.** 6^2 36   **4.** 9^2 81   **5.** 10^2 100   **6.** 1^2 1

7. 4^2 16   **8.** 11^2 121   **9.** 15^2 225   **10.** 25^2 625   **11.** 30^2 900   **12.** 40^2 1600

13. 21^2 441 **14.** 51^2 2601 **15.** 13^2 169 **16.** 19^2 361 **17.** 18^2 324 **18.** 14^2 196

19. 60^2 3600 **20.** 80^2 6400 **21.** 24^2 576 **22.** 36^2 1296 **23.** 100^2 10,000 **24.** 200^2 40,000

(Example 2)

25. $\sqrt{4}$ 2 **26.** $\sqrt{1}$ 1 **27.** $\sqrt{49}$ 7 **28.** $\sqrt{64}$ 8 **29.** $\sqrt{9}$ 3 **30.** $\sqrt{81}$ 9

31. $\sqrt{36}$ 6 **32.** $\sqrt{16}$ 4 **33.** $\sqrt{100}$ 10 **34.** $\sqrt{400}$ 20 **35.** $\sqrt{169}$ 13 **36.** $\sqrt{225}$ 15

37. $\sqrt{144}$ 12 **38.** $\sqrt{900}$ 30 **39.** $\sqrt{256}$ 16 **40.** $\sqrt{289}$ 17 **41.** $\sqrt{625}$ 25 **42.** $\sqrt{441}$ 21

43. $\sqrt{196}$ 14 **44.** $\sqrt{484}$ 22 **45.** $\sqrt{1600}$ 40 **46.** $\sqrt{2500}$ 50 **47.** $\sqrt{3600}$ 60 **48.** $\sqrt{4900}$ 70

These word problems combine the skill of using a formula with the skills presented in the lesson.

APPLICATIONS: Using Squares and Square Roots

You can use the following formula to find the distance in feet that an object will fall in t seconds.

$$d = 16t^2 \quad \begin{matrix} d = distance \\ t = time \end{matrix}$$

49. How far will an object fall in 2 seconds? 64 feet

(HINT: $d = 16 \times 2^2 = \underline{\quad?\quad}$)

50. How far will an object fall in 5 seconds? 400 feet

51. How far will an object fall in $\frac{1}{2}$ second? 4 feet

52. How far will an object fall in $\frac{1}{4}$ second? 1 foot

53. How long will it take an object to fall 64 feet? 2 seconds

(HINT: $64 = 16t^2$; $t = \underline{\quad?\quad}$)

Skydivers fall freely at speeds of more than 160 kilometers per hour.

54. How long will it take an object to fall 256 feet? 4 seconds

More Challenging Problems The More Challenging Problems are optional.

Find each answer.

55. $(\frac{1}{2})^2$ $\frac{1}{4}$ **56.** $(\frac{1}{4})^2$ $\frac{1}{16}$ **57.** $(\frac{1}{5})^2$ $\frac{1}{25}$ **58.** $(\frac{1}{6})^2$ $\frac{1}{36}$ **59.** $(\frac{3}{4})^2$ $\frac{9}{36}$ **60.** $(\frac{2}{5})^2$ $\frac{4}{25}$

61. $(\frac{2}{3})^2$ $\frac{4}{9}$ **62.** $(\frac{5}{6})^2$ $\frac{25}{36}$ **63.** $(\frac{3}{8})^2$ $\frac{9}{64}$ **64.** $(\frac{2}{9})^2$ $\frac{4}{81}$ **65.** $(\frac{3}{10})^2$ $\frac{9}{100}$ **66.** $(\frac{5}{12})^2$ $\frac{25}{144}$

67. $(1.2)^2$ 1.44 **68.** $(1.1)^2$ 1.21 **69.** $(1.3)^2$ 1.69 **70.** $(1.4)^2$ 1.96 **71.** $(0.1)^2$ 0.01 **72.** $(0.2)^2$ 0.04

73. $(0.3)^2$ 0.09 **74.** $(0.5)^2$ 0.25 **75.** $(2.5)^2$ 6.25 **76.** $(2.1)^2$ 4.41 **77.** $(1.8)^2$ 3.24 **78.** $(1.6)^2$ 2.56

79. $\dfrac{\sqrt{1}}{\sqrt{25}}$ $\frac{1}{5}$ **80.** $\dfrac{\sqrt{4}}{\sqrt{81}}$ $\frac{2}{9}$ **81.** $\dfrac{\sqrt{25}}{\sqrt{81}}$ $\frac{5}{9}$ **82.** $\dfrac{\sqrt{16}}{\sqrt{25}}$ $\frac{4}{5}$ **83.** $\dfrac{\sqrt{4}}{\sqrt{144}}$ $\frac{2}{12}$ **84.** $\dfrac{\sqrt{9}}{\sqrt{169}}$ $\frac{3}{13}$

85. $\sqrt{0.81}$ 0.9 **86.** $\sqrt{0.25}$ 0.5 **87.** $\sqrt{0.16}$ 0.4 **88.** $\sqrt{0.64}$ 0.8 **89.** $\sqrt{0.01}$ 0.1 **90.** $\sqrt{0.09}$ 0.3

91. $\sqrt{1.96}$ 1.4 **92.** $\sqrt{1.21}$ 1.1 **93.** $\sqrt{1.44}$ 1.2 **94.** $\sqrt{1.69}$ 1.3 **95.** $\sqrt{2.25}$ 1.5 **96.** $\sqrt{6.25}$ 2.5

17-2 Using a Table of Squares and Square Roots

See the Teacher's Manual for the objectives.

You can use the table on page 369 to find the squares and square roots of numbers from 1 to 150.

PROCEDURE   To use a square and square root table:

1. Find the number in the NUMBER column.

2. Look directly to the right.

     a. Read the square of the number in the SQUARE column.

     b. Read the square root of the number in the SQUARE ROOT column.

EXAMPLE 1   Find each answer.

     a. 24^2 **b.** $\sqrt{23}$

Solutions: **a.** $24^2 = 576$ **b.** $\sqrt{23} = 4.796$

To check your answer in **b,** multiply 4.796 by 4.796. The product is 23.001616. Thus, $\sqrt{23}$ is about 4.796.

Number	Square	Square Root
21	441	4.583
22	484	4.690
23	529	4.796
24	576	4.899
25	625	5.000

After completing Example 1, you may wish to have students do some or all of Exercises 1-49.

Note that most numbers in the SQUARE ROOT column in the table are approximations correct to thousandths. Thus, when you find the square root of a number in the table, you may be asked to round your answer to the nearest tenth, to the nearest hundredth, and so on.

You can use the table to find the square roots of some numbers greater than 150. First, find the number in the SQUARE column. Then read the square root in the NUMBER column.

EXAMPLE 2 $\sqrt{4761} = \underline{\quad ? \quad}$

Solution:

1. Find 4761 in the SQUARE column.

2. Look directly to the left.

     Read the number.   ⟶   **69**

     $\sqrt{4761} = 69$

Number	Square
66	4356
67	4489
68	4624
69	4761
70	4900

Table of Squares and Square Roots

Number	Square	Square Root	Number	Square	Square Root	Number	Square	Square Root
1	1	1.000	51	2601	7.141	101	10,201	10.050
2	4	1.414	52	2704	7.211	102	10,404	10.100
3	9	1.732	53	2809	7.280	103	10,609	10.149
4	16	2.000	54	2916	7.348	104	10,816	10.198
5	25	2.236	55	3025	7.416	105	11,025	10.247
6	36	2.449	56	3136	7.483	106	11,236	10.296
7	49	2.646	57	3249	7.550	107	11,449	10.344
8	64	2.828	58	3364	7.616	108	11,664	10.392
9	81	3.000	59	3481	7.681	109	11,881	10.440
10	100	3.162	60	3600	7.746	110	12,100	10.488
11	121	3.317	61	3721	7.810	111	12,321	10.536
12	144	3.464	62	3844	7.874	112	12,544	10.583
13	169	3.606	63	3969	7.937	113	12,769	10.630
14	196	3.742	64	4096	8.000	114	12,996	10.677
15	225	3.873	65	4225	8.062	115	13,225	10.724
16	256	4.000	66	4356	8.124	116	13,456	10.770
17	289	4.123	67	4489	8.185	117	13,689	10.817
18	324	4.243	68	4624	8.246	118	13,924	10.863
19	361	4.359	69	4761	8.307	119	14,161	10.909
20	400	4.472	70	4900	8.367	120	14,400	10.954
21	441	4.583	71	5041	8.426	121	14,641	11.000
22	484	4.690	72	5184	8.485	122	14,884	11.045
23	529	4.796	73	5329	8.544	123	15,129	11.091
24	576	4.899	74	5476	8.602	124	15,376	11.136
25	625	5.000	75	5625	8.660	125	15,625	11.180
26	676	5.099	76	5776	8.718	126	15,876	11.225
27	729	5.196	77	5929	8.775	127	16,129	11.269
28	784	5.292	78	6084	8.832	128	16,384	11.314
29	841	5.385	79	6241	8.888	129	16,641	11.358
30	900	5.477	80	6400	8.944	130	16,900	11.402
31	961	5.568	81	6561	9.000	131	17,161	11.446
32	1024	5.657	82	6724	9.055	132	17,424	11.489
33	1089	5.745	83	6889	9.110	133	17,689	11.533
34	1156	5.831	84	7056	9.165	134	17,956	11.576
35	1225	5.916	85	7225	9.220	135	18,225	11.619
36	1296	6.000	86	7396	9.274	136	18,496	11.662
37	1369	6.083	87	7569	9.327	137	18,769	11.705
38	1444	6.164	88	7744	9.381	138	19,044	11.747
39	1521	6.245	89	7921	9.434	139	19,321	11.790
40	1600	6.325	90	8100	9.487	140	19,600	11.832
41	1681	6.403	91	8281	9.539	141	19,881	11.874
42	1764	6.481	92	8464	9.592	142	20,164	11.916
43	1849	6.557	93	8649	9.644	143	20,449	11.958
44	1936	6.633	94	8836	9.695	144	20,736	12.000
45	2025	6.708	95	9025	9.747	145	21,025	12.042
46	2116	6.782	96	9216	9.798	146	21,316	12.083
47	2209	6.856	97	9409	9.849	147	21,609	12.124
48	2304	6.928	98	9604	9.899	148	21,904	12.166
49	2401	7.000	99	9801	9.950	149	22,201	12.207
50	2500	7.071	100	10,000	10.000	150	22,500	12.247

EXERCISES

Use the table on page 369 to find each answer. (Example 1)

1. 33^2 1089 **2.** 19^2 361 **3.** 52^2 2704 **4.** 36^2 1296 **5.** 21^2 441 **6.** 35^2 1225 **7.** 71^2 5041

8. 45^2 2025 **9.** 73^2 5329 **10.** 80^2 6400 **11.** 115^2 13225 **12.** 121^2 14641 **13.** 62^2 3844 **14.** 99^2 9801

15. 125^2 15625 **16.** 110^2 12100 **17.** 148^2 21904 **18.** 135^2 18225 **19.** 66^2 4356 **20.** 91^2 8281 **21.** 82^2 6724

22. $\sqrt{70}$ 8.367 **23.** $\sqrt{18}$ 4.243 **24.** $\sqrt{141}$ 6.325 **25.** $\sqrt{118}$ 11.225 **26.** $\sqrt{105}$ 12.166 **27.** $\sqrt{125}$ 9.487 **28.** $\sqrt{81}$ 9

29. $\sqrt{63}$ 7.937 **30.** $\sqrt{40}$ **31.** $\sqrt{126}$ **32.** $\sqrt{148}$ **33.** $\sqrt{90}$ **34.** $\sqrt{5}$ 2.236 **35.** $\sqrt{7}$ 2.646

36. $\sqrt{3}$ 1.732 **37.** $\sqrt{11}$ 3.317 **38.** $\sqrt{49}$ 7 **39.** $\sqrt{57}$ 7.550 **40.** $\sqrt{84}$ 9.165 **41.** $\sqrt{98}$ 9.899 **42.** $\sqrt{69}$ 8.307

43. $\sqrt{113}$ 10.630 **44.** $\sqrt{127}$ 11.269 **45.** $\sqrt{101}$ 10.050 **46.** $\sqrt{76}$ 8.718 **47.** $\sqrt{32}$ 5.657 **48.** $\sqrt{4}$ 2 **49.** $\sqrt{9}$ 3

(Example 2)

50. $\sqrt{324}$ 18 **51.** $\sqrt{900}$ 30 **52.** $\sqrt{676}$ 26 **53.** $\sqrt{529}$ 23 **54.** $\sqrt{1600}$ 40 **55.** $\sqrt{196}$ 14

56. $\sqrt{484}$ 22 **57.** $\sqrt{729}$ 27 **58.** $\sqrt{9801}$ 99 **59.** $\sqrt{9216}$ 96 **60.** $\sqrt{19,881}$ 141 **61.** $\sqrt{14,884}$ 122

62. $\sqrt{841}$ 29 **63.** $\sqrt{2209}$ 47 **64.** $\sqrt{1681}$ 41 **65.** $\sqrt{5776}$ 76 **66.** $\sqrt{13,689}$ 117 **67.** $\sqrt{10,816}$ 104

68. $\sqrt{5041}$ 71 **69.** $\sqrt{7396}$ 86 **70.** $\sqrt{1849}$ 43 **71.** $\sqrt{5329}$ 73 **72.** $\sqrt{3136}$ 56 **73.** $\sqrt{8836}$ 94

74. $\sqrt{7225}$ 85 **75.** $\sqrt{8649}$ 93 **76.** $\sqrt{2116}$ 46 **77.** $\sqrt{1849}$ 43 **78.** $\sqrt{21,025}$ 145 **79.** $\sqrt{17,956}$ 134

APPLICATIONS: Using the Table of Squares and Square Roots

Most students should be able to do these word problems which combine the skill of using a formula with the skills presented in the lesson.

You can use the following formula to find the distance in miles from a viewer to the horizon.

$$D = 1.2 \times \sqrt{H}$$

⟨ H: number of feet from the ground

NOTE: *D* is in miles.

Use this formula for Exercises 80–83. Round each answer to the nearest whole number.

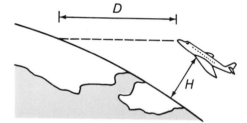

80. Find the distance to the horizon from a plane. The plane is 3025 feet above the ground. 66 mi

81. Find the distance to the horizon from a plane flying at an altitude (height) of 22,500 feet. 180 mi

82. The height of a plane above the ground is 20,736 feet. Find the distance to the horizon. 173 mi

83. A plane is flying at a height of 16,900 feet above the ground. Find the distance to the horizon. 156 mi

Solving horizon problems in outer space is a concern of engineers like Ruben Ramos who works for NASA.

Right Triangle Rule and Applications

A **right triangle** is a triangle with one right angle (90°).

When you know the lengths of two sides of a right triangle, you can use the Rule of Pythagoras to find the length of the other side.

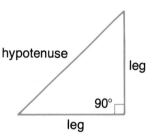

Rule of Pythagoras: $\underbrace{(\text{Hypotenuse})^2}_{c^2} = \underbrace{(\text{leg})^2}_{a^2} + \underbrace{(\text{leg})^2}_{b^2}$, or

PROCEDURE To find the measure of a side of a right triangle:

1 Draw a right triangle. Label the sides with the given measures.

2 Write the rule of Pythagoras. Replace two letters in the rule by the corresponding given measures.

3 Solve for the third measure.

EXAMPLE 1 The sail on this boat is 4 meters high and 2 meters wide. Find the length of the third side. Round your answer to the nearest tenth. 1

Solution: Use the Rule of Pythagoras to find c, the side opposite the right angle. This is the hypotenuse.

2 $c^2 = a^2 + b^2$ ◀ **Replace a with 4 and b with 2.**

$c^2 = 4^2 + 2^2$

3 $c^2 = 16 + 4$

$c^2 = 20$

$c = \sqrt{20}$ ◀ **Use the table on page 369 to find $\sqrt{20}$.**

$c = 4.472$

The length is about **4.5 meters.**

After completing Example 1, you may wish to have students do some or all of Exercises 1-5.

When you know the lengths of the hypotenuse and one leg of a right triangle, you can use the Rule of Pythagoras to find the length of the other leg.

SQUARES AND SQUARE ROOTS **371**

EXAMPLE 2 The top of a 6–meter ladder reaches 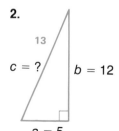 a window ledge. The ledge is 5 meters above the ground. How far from the house is the foot of the ladder? Round your answer to the nearest tenth.

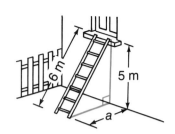

Solution: Use the Rule of Pythagoras to find a, the length of one leg of the right triangle.

2

$$c^2 = a^2 + b^2 \qquad \text{Replace } c \text{ with 6 and } b \text{ with 5.}$$
$$6^2 = a^2 + 5^2$$

3

$$36 = a^2 + 25 \qquad \text{Subtract 25 from each side.}$$
$$36 - 25 = a^2 + 25 - 25$$
$$11 = a^2$$
$$\sqrt{11} = a \qquad \text{Use the table on page 369 to find } \sqrt{11}.$$
$$3.317 = a$$

The ladder is about **3.3** meters from the house.

REVIEW OF RELATED SKILLS
You may wish to use these exercises before teaching the lesson.

Solve and check. (Pages 248–249)

1. $n + 6 = 10$ 4   **2.** $n + 17 = 30$ 13   **3.** $n + 3 = 12$ 9   **4.** $n + 17 = 17$ 0

Round each number to the nearest tenth. (Pages 120–121)

5. 12.35 12.4   **6.** 21.72 21.7   **7.** 18.09 18.1   **8.** 32.15 32.2   **9.** 49.53 49.5   **10.** 62.43 62.4

EXERCISES
See the suggested assignment guide in the Teacher's Manual.

In Exercises 1–3, find the length of the hypotenuse of each right triangle. Use the Table of Squares and Square Roots on page 369.
(Example 1)

1.
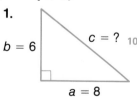
$b = 6$ $c = ?$ 10 $a = 8$

2.
13   $c = ?$ $b = 12$ $a = 5$

3.
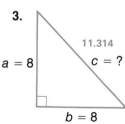
$a = 8$ 11.314 $c = ?$ $b = 8$

4. In the figure below, a wire supports a pole that is 5 meters high. The distance from the foot of the pole to the point where the wire is fastened to a stake in the ground is 7 meters. How long is the wire? Round your answer to the nearest tenth. $c = 8.6$ m

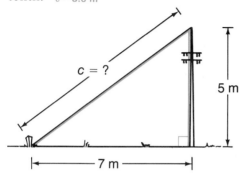

$c = ?$

5 m

7 m

5. The figure below shows the escalator between two floors of a department store. How many meters are you carried as you travel on the escalator from one floor to the next? Round your answer to the nearest tenth. $c = 12.0$

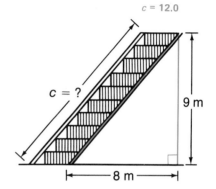

$c = ?$

9 m

8 m

In Exercises 6–8, find the length of the unknown side of each right triangle. Use the Table of Squares and Square Roots on page 369. (Example 2)

6.

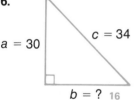

$a = 30$

$c = 34$

$b = ?$ 16

7.

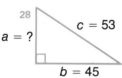

28

$a = ?$

$c = 53$

$b = 45$

8.

$c = 91$

$a = 84$

$b = ?$ 35

9. A ladder is placed against the side of the house as shown in the figure at the right. Find the length of the ladder. Round your answer to the nearest tenth. $c = 5.4$

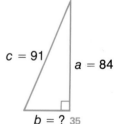

5 m

$c = ?$

2 m

10. The distance from first base to second base is 90 feet and the distance from second base to third base is 90 feet. What is the shortest distance from first base to third base? Round your answer to the nearest tenth. (HINT: $\sqrt{16,200}$ is about 127.28) $c = 127.3$

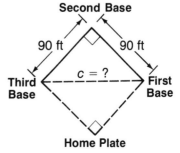

Second Base

90 ft

90 ft

$c = ?$

Third Base

First Base

Home Plate

17-4 Similar Triangles and Applications See the Teacher's Manual for the objectives.

Similar triangles are triangles that have the same shape.

In similar triangles, angles that correspond have equal measures.
In similar triangles, sides that correspond are opposite equal angles.
Sides that correspond have <u>equivalent ratios</u>.

Equivalent Ratios	
Triangle 1	**Triangle 2**
$\frac{4}{8}$	$=$ $\frac{7}{14}$
$\frac{4}{10}$	$=$ $\frac{7}{17.5}$
$\frac{8}{10}$	$=$ $\frac{14}{17.5}$

Triangle 1: 50°, 10 cm, 22°, 4 cm, 108°, 8 cm
Triangle 2: 17.5 cm, 50°, 7 cm, 22°, 108°, 14 cm

TABLE

When you know that triangles are similar, you can write a
proportion to find the length of an unknown side.

PROCEDURE

1. Use the unknown side and a known side in one triangle to write a ratio.

2. Use sides that correspond in the second triangle to write another ratio.

3. Use the two ratios to write a proportion.

4. Solve the proportion.

EXAMPLE   Jill is 1.8 meters tall. On a sunny day, she found that her shadow
was 2 meters long at the same time that the shadow of a water
tower was 40 meters long. Find the height of the tower.

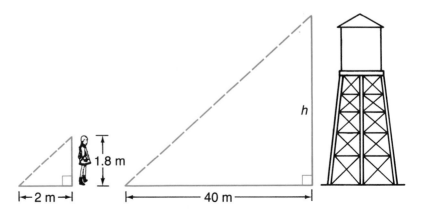

Solution: ☐1 Use the triangle with the unknown side to write a ratio.

$\dfrac{h}{40}$ ←— *Tower's height*
←— *Shadow length*

☐2 Use sides that correspond in the second triangle to write another ratio.

$\dfrac{1.8}{2}$ ←— *Jill's height*
←— *Shadow length*

☐3 Use the ratios to write a proportion.

$\dfrac{h}{40} = \dfrac{1.8}{2}$

☐4 Solve the proportion.

$h \times 2 = 40 \times 1.8$

$2h = 72$

$\dfrac{2h}{2} = \dfrac{72}{2}$

$h = 36$ ◀ *The tower is 36 meters high.*

REVIEW OF RELATED SKILLS

You may wish to use these exercises before teaching the lesson.

Solve and check.   (Pages 252–253)

1. $3n = 21$ 7   **2.** $7n = 42$ 6   **3.** $14n = 28$ 2   **4.** $0.8n = 2.5$ 3.125   **5.** $0.4n = 1.9$
  4.75

Solve each proportion for n.   (Pages 264–265)

6. $\dfrac{n}{18} = \dfrac{15}{20}$ **7.** $\dfrac{10}{9} = \dfrac{40}{n}$ **8.** $\dfrac{16}{n} = \dfrac{4}{2}$ **9.** $\dfrac{n}{12} = \dfrac{2}{1}$ **10.** $\dfrac{11}{8} = \dfrac{n}{24}$ **11.** $\dfrac{25}{n} = \dfrac{5}{3}$
  13.5   36   8   24   33   15

Round each decimal to the nearest tenth.   (Pages 120–121)

12. 9.83 9.8   **13.** 11.88 11.9 **14.** 11.58 11.6 **15.** 11.85 11.9 **16.** 11.05 11.1 **17.** 11.51 11.5

EXERCISES

See the suggested assignment guide in the Teacher's Manual.

For Exercises 1–6, each pair of triangles is similar. Complete the proportion.   (Table)

1.

$\dfrac{n}{10} = \dfrac{?}{20}$ 17

2.

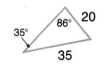

$\dfrac{n}{56} = \dfrac{20}{?}$ 35

3.

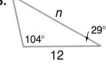

$\dfrac{n}{12} = \dfrac{20}{?}$ 15

4.

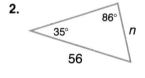

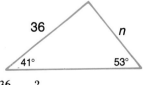

$\dfrac{36}{n} = \dfrac{?}{9}$ 24

SQUARES AND SQUARE ROOTS   **375**

5.

$$\frac{n}{30} = \frac{?}{?} \quad \frac{20}{24}$$

6.

$$\frac{n}{14} = \frac{?}{?} \quad \frac{5}{7}$$

(Example)

7. Norman is 1.8 meters tall. On a sunny day, Patty measured Norman's shadow and the shadow of the school. Use the similar triangles shown below to find the height of the school. Round your answer to the nearest tenth of a meter.

$$\frac{h}{5} = \frac{?}{?} \quad \frac{1.8}{1.4}; h = 6.4$$

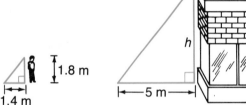

8. On the same sunny day, the shadow of a tree was 12 meters long. Use the similar triangles below to find the height of the tree. Round your answer to the nearest tenth of a meter.

$$\frac{?}{?} = \frac{1.8}{1.4} \quad \frac{h}{12}; h = 15.4$$

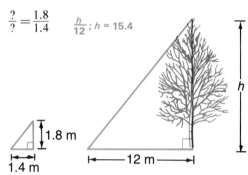

9. Jaimie found the height of a street lamp by placing a mirror on the sidewalk. Then he walked backwards until he saw the top of the streetlight in the mirror. The figure below shows how he formed similar triangles. Find the height of of the street lamp. Round your answer to the nearest tenth of a meter.

$$\frac{?}{?} = \frac{1.5}{2.4}$$

$$\frac{h}{6}; h = 3.8$$

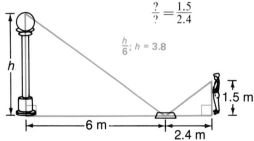

10. Find the distance across this lake. Round your answer to the nearest tenth of a meter.

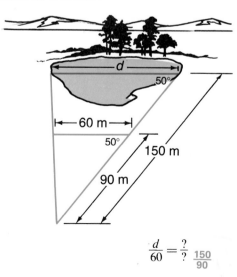

$$\frac{d}{60} = \frac{?}{?} \quad \frac{150}{90}$$

$$d = 100$$

TRAFFIC OFFICER

Career lessons are optional.
This lesson combines the skills of using a formula, reading a table, finding square roots, and multiplication of decimals.

The speed of a car just before the driver brakes to come to a quick stop can be estimated from the length of the skid marks and from the coefficient of friction. The table at the right gives the coefficient of friction for four road surfaces and for dry and wet driving conditions.

Surface	Coefficient of Friction	
	Dry Road	Wet Road
Asphalt	0.85	0.65
Concrete	0.90	0.60
Gravel	0.65	0.65
Packed Snow	0.45	0.45

You can use the formula below to estimate the speed of a car just before braking.

$S = 5.5 \times \sqrt{d \times f}$

◄ S = speed in miles per hour
d = length of skid marks in feet
f = coefficient of friction

EXAMPLE   A car leaves skid marks of 150 feet on wet asphalt. Estimate the speed of the car before braking. Round your answer to the nearest mile.

Solution: Use paper and pencil or use a calculator.

$S = 5.5 \times \sqrt{d \times f}$ ◄ Use the table to find
$f = 0.65$ (wet asphalt).

$S = 5.5 \times \sqrt{150 \times 0.65}$

$\boxed{1}\ \boxed{5}\ \boxed{0}\ \boxed{\times}\ \boxed{\cdot}\ \boxed{6}\ \boxed{5}\ \boxed{=}\ \boxed{\sqrt{\ }}$ $\boxed{9.8742088}$

$\boxed{\times}\ \boxed{5}\ \boxed{\cdot}\ \boxed{5}\ \boxed{=}$ $\boxed{54.308148}$

The car was traveling at about **54 miles per hour.**

EXERCISES

Estimate the speed of an automobile for the given length of skid marks and the given road surface. Round each answer to the nearest mile.

	Length of Skid marks	Road Surface			Length of Skid marks	Road Surface
1.	90 feet	Dry concrete 50		**4.**	60 feet	Packed snow 29
2.	100 feet	Wet asphalt 44		**5.**	150 feet	Dry gravel 54
3.	120 feet	Wet gravel 49		**6.**	110 feet	Wet concrete 45

7. A car leaves skid marks 175 feet long on a wet gravel road. What is the speed of the car before braking? 59

8. A car leaves skid marks of 100 feet on a dry asphalt road. What was the speed of the car before braking? 51

17-5 Tangent Ratios and Applications

See the Teacher's Manual for the objectives.

You can also use the **tangent ratio** to find the lengths of the legs of a right triangle.

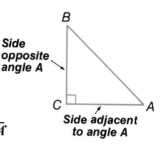

Side opposite angle A

Side adjacent to angle A

The abbreviation for the "tangent of angle A" is "tan A."

$$\tan A = \frac{\text{length of side opposite angle } A}{\text{length of side adjacent to angle } A}$$

EXAMPLE 1 Find tan A. Use this right triangle.

Solution:

$$\tan A = \frac{\text{length of side opposite angle } A}{\text{length of side adjacent to angle } A}$$

$$\tan A = \frac{3}{4}$$

$$\tan A = 0.75$$

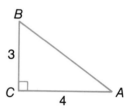

After completing Example 1, you may wish to have students do some or all of Exercises 1-8.

When you know the measure of an acute angle of a right triangle such as angle A or angle B, you can use a table to find tan A.

TANGENT TABLE

Angles	Tangents	Angles	Tangents
5°	0.087	50°	1.19
10°	0.176	55°	1.43
15°	0.268	60°	1.73
20°	0.364	65°	2.14
25°	0.466	70°	2.75
30°	0.577	75°	3.73
35°	0.700	80°	5.67
40°	0.839	85°	11.43
45°	1.00		

Thus, $\tan 65° = 2.14$ and $\tan 80° = 5.67$.

When you know the measure of angle A and the length of one leg of a right triangle, you can use the table and the definition of tan A to find the length of the other leg.

After explaining the use of the Tangent Table, you may wish to have students do Exercises 9-13.

PROCEDURE To use the tangent ratio to find a leg of a right triangle:

[1] Draw and label a right triangle.

[2] Use the known angle, the known leg, and the unknown leg to write the tangent ratio.

[3] Solve for the unknown leg.

EXAMPLE 2 Find the height of this flagpole. Round your answer to the nearest meter.

Solution: Use the tangent ratio and the tangent table.

$$\tan A = \frac{\text{length of side opposite angle } A}{\text{length of side adjacent to angle } A}$$

$$\tan 50° = \frac{h}{12}$$ ◀ *Find tan 50° in the Tangent Table.*

$$1.19 = \frac{h}{12}$$ ◀ *Multiply each side by 12.*

$$1.19 \times 12 = \frac{h}{12} \times \frac{12}{1}$$

$$14.28 = h$$

The flagpole is about **14** meters high.

REVIEW OF RELATED SKILLS

You may wish to use these exercises before teaching the lesson.

Write a two–place decimal for each fraction.   (Pages 110–111, 122–123, 280–281)

1. $\frac{1}{2}$ 0.50   **2.** $\frac{9}{10}$ 0.90   **3.** $\frac{5}{2}$ 2.50   **4.** $\frac{6}{5}$ 1.20   **5.** $\frac{9}{4}$ 2.25   **6.** $\frac{7}{20}$ 0.35   **7.** $\frac{2}{5}$ 0.40   **8.** $\frac{8}{25}$ 0.32

Round to the nearest whole number.   (Pages 120–121)

9. 12.1 $_{12}$ **10.** 18.7 $_{19}$ **11.** 26.5 $_{27}$ **12.** 90.3 $_{90}$ **13.** 60.7 $_{61}$ **14.** 18.08 $_{18}$

15. 37.32 $_{37}$ **16.** 75.8 $_{76}$ **17.** 100.49 $_{100}$ **18.** 5.98 $_{6}$ **19.** 46.4 $_{46}$ **20.** 2.18 $_{2}$

Solve and check.   (Pages 252–253)

21. $\frac{n}{10} = 7$ $_{70}$ **22.** $\frac{n}{8} = 4$ $_{32}$ **23.** $15 = \frac{n}{100}$ $_{1500}$ **24.** $9 = \frac{n}{72}$ $_{648}$ **25.** $2 = \frac{n}{50}$ $_{100}$

26. $5 = \frac{n}{25}$ $_{125}$ **27.** $\frac{n}{14} = 7$ $_{98}$ **28.** $\frac{n}{9} = 13$ $_{117}$ **29.** $\frac{n}{10} = 1.5$ $_{15}$ **30.** $\frac{n}{7} = 6.8$ $_{47.6}$

31. $\frac{n}{6} = 1.5$ $_{9}$ **32.** $\frac{n}{9} = 0.2$ $_{1.8}$ **33.** $5 = \frac{n}{5}$ $_{25}$ **34.** $8 = \frac{n}{7}$ $_{56}$ **35.** $1 = \frac{n}{20}$ $_{20}$

36. $27 = \frac{n}{4}$ $_{108}$ **37.** $10 = \frac{n}{10}$ $_{100}$ **38.** $\frac{n}{3} = 4.6$ $_{13.8}$ **39.** $\frac{n}{13} = 1$ $_{13}$ **40.** $0.9 = \frac{n}{9}$ $_{8.1}$

SQUARES AND SQUARE ROOTS   **379**

EXERCISES

In Exercises 1–8, find tan A. Write a two-place decimal for your answer. (Example 1)

1. *B* tan A = 1

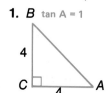

2. tan A = 3.33

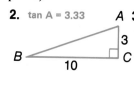

A **3.** tan A = 0.67 *A*

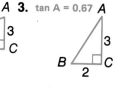

4. *B* tan A = 0.80

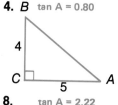

5. tan A = 0.67 *A*

6. tan A = 0.42

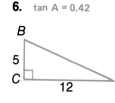

7. *B* tan A = 0.32

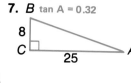

8. tan A = 2.22

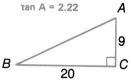

In Exercises 9–13, use the Table of Tangents to find each of the following. (Table)

9. tan 10° 0.176 **10.** tan 85° 11.43 **11.** tan 25° 0.466 **12.** tan 60° 1.73 **13.** tan 45° 1.00

In Exercises 14–17, use the tangent ratio and the Table of Tangents to solve each problem. Round each answer to the nearest whole number. (Example 2)

14. Find the distance, *d*, across the widest point of Sweet Moss Lake below. (HINT: $\tan 40° = \frac{d}{?}$) 67

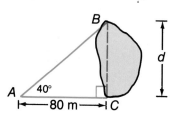

15. Find the width, *w*, of Lake Unknown. (HINT: $\tan 40° = \frac{?}{240}$) 201

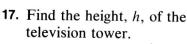

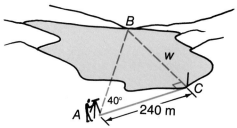

16. Find the height, *h*, of the plane above the ground. (HINT: $\tan 15° = \frac{h}{?}$) 8

17. Find the height, *h*, of the television tower. (HINT: $\tan \underline{\ ?\ } = \frac{h}{40}$) 57

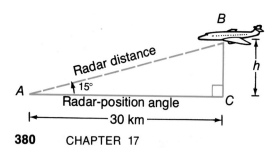

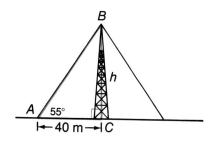

Chapter Review

These exercises review the vocabulary, skills, and applications presented in the chapter as a preparation for the chapter test.

Part 1: Vocabulary

For Exercises 1–5, choose from the box at the right the word(s) that completes each statement.

square root
hypotenuse
square
identical
right
similar

1. The product of a number and itself is the _?_ of the number. (Page 366)
   square

2. One of the two equal factors of a number is the _?_ of the number. (Page 366)
   square root

3. A triangle with one right angle is called a _?_ triangle. (Page 371)
   right

4. In a right triangle, the side opposite the right angle is the _?_. (Page 371)
   hypotenuse

5. Triangles that have the same shape are _?_ triangles. (Page 374)
   similar

Part 2: Skills

Find each answer. (Pages 366–367)

6. 4^2 16
7. 9^2 81
8. 15^2 225
9. 21^2 441
10. 13^2 169
11. 20^2 400
12. $\sqrt{16}$ 4
13. $\sqrt{25}$ 5
14. $\sqrt{81}$ 9
15. $\sqrt{100}$ 10
16. $\sqrt{225}$ 15
17. $\sqrt{144}$ 12

For Exercises 18–49, find each answer. Use the Table of Squares and Square Roots on page 369. (Pages 368–370)

18. 18^2 324
19. 37^2 1369
20. 74^2 5476
21. 92^2 8464
22. 134^2 17956
23. 147^2 21609
24. 27^2 729
25. 56^2 3136
26. 89^2 7921
27. 43^2 1849
28. 112^2 12544
29. 131^2 17161
30. $\sqrt{75}$ 8.660
31. $\sqrt{103}$ 10.149
32. $\sqrt{114}$ 10.677
33. $\sqrt{62}$ 7.874
34. $\sqrt{95}$ 9.747
35. $\sqrt{28}$ 5.292
36. $\sqrt{3481}$ 59
37. $\sqrt{961}$ 31
38. $\sqrt{9025}$ 95
39. $\sqrt{19,044}$ 138
40. $\sqrt{11,236}$ 106
41. $\sqrt{729}$ 27

For Exercises 42–45, find the length of the hypotenuse of each right triangle. Round each answer to the nearest tenth. (Pages 371–373)

42. $a = 3$, $c = ?$, $b = 4$
 $c = 5$

43. $a = 5$, $c = ?$, $b = 7$
 $c = 8.6$

44. $c = ?$, $b = 7$, $a = 7$
 $c = 9.9$

45. $c = ?$, $b = 3$, $a = 9$
 $c = 9.5$

For Exercises 46–49, find the length of the unknown side of each right triangle. Round each answer to the nearest tenth. (Pages 371–373)

46. $c = 17$, $b = 15$, $a = ?$
 $a = 8$

47. $c = 53$, $b = 28$, $a = ?$
 $a = 45$

48. $a = 24$, $c = 26$, $b = ?$
 $b = 10$

49. $c = 41$, $a = ?$, $b = 40$
 $a = 9$

For Exercises 50–51, each pair of triangles is similar. Complete the proportion.   (Pages 374–376)

50.

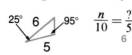

$\dfrac{n}{10} = \dfrac{?}{5}$

51.

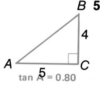

$\dfrac{n}{3} = \dfrac{?}{?}$

$\dfrac{6}{9}$

For Exercises 52–55, find tan A. Write a two–place decimal for your answer.   (Pages 378–380)

52. B

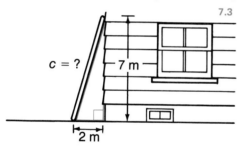

tan A = 1.00

53. A

6

C ⌐ B
   3

tan A = 0.50

54.

B **55.** A

4   4

A ⌐ C   C ⌐ B
  5   9

tan A = 0.80   tan A = 2.25

Part 3: Applications

56. A ladder is placed against the side of a house as shown below. Find the length of the ladder. Use the Table of Squares and Square Roots on page 369. Round your answer to the nearest tenth.   (Pages 371–373)

7.3

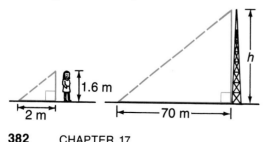

c = ?   ⌐ 7 m ⌐

2 m

57. The roof of a house is 10 meters long as shown below. It is 3 meters from the edge of the roof to the middle of the door. Find the height of the house. Use the table on page 369. Round your answer to the nearest tenth.   (Pages 371–373)

9.5

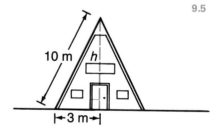

10 m h

|←3 m→|

58. Sue is 1.6 meters tall. On a sunny day, her shadow is 2 meters long at the same time as the shadow of a TV tower is 70 meters long. Find the height of the tower. 56
(Pages 374–376)

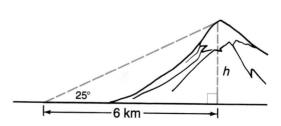

1.6 m

2 m |←——70 m——→|

h

59. Find the height, h, of the mountain below. Use the Table of Tangents on page 378. Round your answer to the nearest whole number. (HINT: $\tan 25° = \dfrac{h}{?}$)
(Pages 378–380)   3

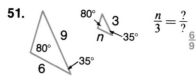

h

25°
|←——————6 km——————→|

Chapter Test

The Teacher's Resource Book contains two forms of each chapter test.

Find each answer.

1. 5^2 25   **2.** 9^2 81   **3.** 7^2 49   **4.** $\sqrt{36}$ 6   **5.** $\sqrt{144}$ 12   **6.** $\sqrt{9}$ 3

For Exercises 7–12, use the Table of Squares and Square Roots on page 369.

7. 64^2 4096   **8.** 37^2 1369   **9.** $\sqrt{95}$ 9.747   **10.** $\sqrt{102}$ 10.1   **11.** $\sqrt{4356}$ 66   **12.** $\sqrt{1521}$ 39

For Exercises 13–16, use the Table of Squares and Square Roots on page 369 to help you find the missing side of each right triangle. Round each answer to the nearest tenth.

13.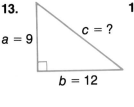
$a = 9$
$c = ?$
$b = 12$
$c = 15$

14.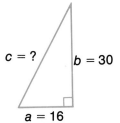
$c = ?$
$b = 30$
$a = 16$
$c = 34$

15.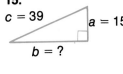
$c = 39$ $a = 15$
$b = ?$
$b = 36$

16.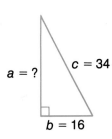
$c = 34$
$a = ?$
$b = 16$
$a = 30$

For Exercises 17–18, each pair of triangles is similar. Complete the proportion.

17.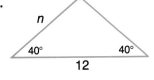
n
$40°$ $40°$
12

$40°$ $40°$
2
3

$$\frac{n}{12} = \frac{?}{3} \quad 2$$

18.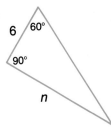
6 $60°$
$90°$
n

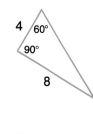
4 $60°$
$90°$
8

$$\frac{6}{n} = \frac{4}{?} \quad 8$$

19. A ramp to a bridge is 12 meters long and 5 meters high as shown below. Find the length of the ramp. Use the Table of Squares and Square Roots on page 369.

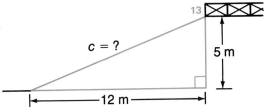
13
$c = ?$
5 m
12 m

20. Find the height of the building shown below.
(HINT: $\tan 28° = \dfrac{?}{42}$; $\tan 28° = .531$)

22.3

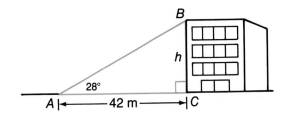
B
h
$28°$
A 42 m C

Additional Practice

You may wish to use some or all of these exercises depending on how well students performed on the formal chapter test.

Skills

Find each answer. (Pages 366–367)

1. 12^2 144 **2.** 10^2 100 **3.** 14^2 196 **4.** 17^2 289 **5.** 19^2 361 **6.** 6^2 36

7. $\sqrt{121}$ 11 **8.** $\sqrt{64}$ 8 **9.** $\sqrt{169}$ 13 **10.** $\sqrt{256}$ 16 **11.** $\sqrt{25}$ 5 **12.** $\sqrt{49}$ 7

For Exercises 13–52, use the Table of Squares and Square Roots on page 369. (Pages 368–370)

13. 26^2 676 **14.** 77^2 5929 **15.** 71^2 5041 **16.** 59^2 3481 **17.** 42^2 1764 **18.** 31^2 961

19. 142^2 20164 **20.** 126^2 15876 **21.** 111^2 12321 **22.** 98^2 9604 **23.** 54^2 2916 **24.** 49^2 2401

25. $\sqrt{68}$ 8.246 **26.** $\sqrt{125}$ 11.180 **27.** $\sqrt{142}$ 11.916 **28.** $\sqrt{43}$ 6.557 **29.** $\sqrt{122}$ 11.045 **30.** $\sqrt{107}$ 10.344

31. $\sqrt{9409}$ 97 **32.** $\sqrt{1296}$ 36 **33.** $\sqrt{3844}$ 62 **34.** $\sqrt{2916}$ 54 **35.** $\sqrt{11,236}$ 106 **36.** $\sqrt{19,321}$ 139

For Exercises 37–44, find the length of the hypotenuse of each right triangle. Round each answer to the nearest tenth. (Pages 371–373)

37. 15 $c = ?$ $a = 9$ $b = 12$

38. $c = ?$ 26 $a = 10$ $b = 24$

39. 25 $c = ?$ $a = 7$ $b = 24$

40. $c = 9.2?$ $a = 6$ $b = 7$

41. 11.2 $c = ?$ $a = 5$ $b = 10$

42. $c = 6.7?$ $a = 3$ $b = 6$

43. 61 $c = ?$ $a = 60$ $b = 11$

44. 20 $c = ?$ $a = 12$ $b = 16$

For Exercises 45–52, find the length of the unknown side of each right triangle. Round each answer to the nearest tenth. (Pages 371–373)

45. $c = 17$ $a = 8$ $b = ?$ 15

46. $a = ?$ 27 $c = 45$ $b = 36$

47. 40 $a = ?$ $c = 41$ $b = 9$

48. $c = 25$ $a = 7$ $b = ?$ 24

49. 5.7 $a = ?$ $c = 17$ $b = 16$

50. 10.2 $a = ?$ $c = 27$ $b = 25$

51. 39 $a = ?$ $c = 89$ $b = 80$

52. $c = 50$ $a = 40$ $b = ?$ 30

For Exercises 53–56, each pair of triangles is similar. Complete the proportion. (Pages 374–376)

53.

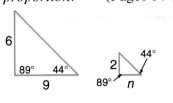

$$\frac{6}{?} = \frac{2}{n}$$

54.

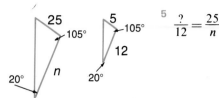

$$\frac{?}{12} = \frac{25}{n}$$

55.

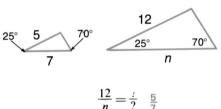

$$\frac{12}{n} = \frac{?}{?} \quad \frac{5}{7}$$

56.

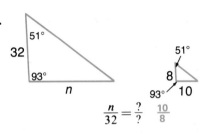

$$\frac{n}{32} = \frac{?}{?} \quad \frac{10}{8}$$

For Exercises 57–64, find tan A. Write a two-place decimal for your answer. (Pages 378–380)

57. tan A = 1.00

58. tan A = 1.75

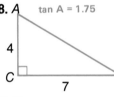

59. tan A = 0.50

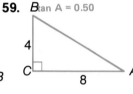

60. tan A = 1.20

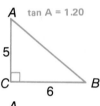

61. tan A = 0.78

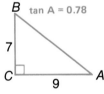

62. tan A = 1.00

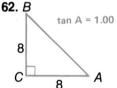

63. tan A = 2.33

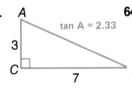

64. tan A = 2.33

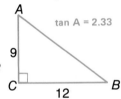

Applications

65. Jim is 1.8 meters tall. On a sunny day his shadow is 1.5 meters long at the same time as the shadow of a building is 12 meters long. Find the height of the building. 14.4 (Pages 374–376)

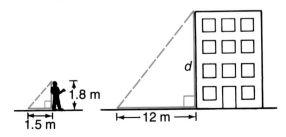

66. A ladder is placed against a shed as shown below. Find the length of the ladder. Use the Table of Squares and Square Roots on page 369. Round your answer to the nearest tenth. (Pages 371–373) 6.3

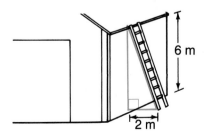

REVIEW OF RELATED SKILLS FOR CHAPTER 18

We suggest that some or all of this page be reviewed before proceeding with the chapter.

Add.   (Pages 2–3, 6–7)

1. 21 +36 = 57	**2.** 26 +48 = 74	**3.** 72 +93 = 165	**4.** 41 +97 = 138	**5.** 16 +71 = 87	**6.** 69 +11 = 80
7. 95 +15 = 110	**8.** 57 +52 = 109	**9.** 76 +28 = 104	**10.** 68 +87 = 155	**11.** 82 +76 = 158	**12.** 29 +65 = 94

13. 12 / 97 / +37 = 146 **14.** 92 / 68 / +38 = 198 **15.** 34 / 54 / +18 = 106 **16.** 83 / 26 / +99 = 208 **17.** 35 / 91 / +76 = 202 **18.** 71 / 38 / +92 = 201

19. 126 / 814 / 429 / +843 = 2212 **20.** 474 / 347 / 483 / +546 = 1850 **21.** 292 / 381 / 725 / +114 = 1512 **22.** 173 / 291 / 764 / +467 = 1695 **23.** 472 / 863 / 109 / +763 = 2207 **24.** 442 / 721 / 180 / +263 = 1606

25. 16 / 381 / + 9 = 406 **26.** 480 / 47 / +822 = 1349 **27.** 5674 / 981 / + 3 = 6658 **28.** 2743 / 321 / + 46 = 3110 **29.** 632 / 38 / +426 = 1096 **30.** 25 / 862 / +1096 = 1983

31. 7 + 621 + 96 + 438   1162
32. 13 + 705 + 96 + 2   816
33. 4864 + 283 + 17   5164
34. 19 + 385 + 472 + 5   881
35. 210 + 604 + 96 + 8   918
36. 5693 + 27 + 328   6048
37. 65 + 986 + 27 + 321   1399
38. 375 + 486 + 99 + 17   977
39. 8726 + 490 + 16   9232
40. 46 + 365 + 416 + 2   829
41. 127 + 84 + 919 + 66   1196
42. 5236 + 891 + 16   6143
43. 292 + 81 + 425 + 14   812
44. 567 + 801 + 64 + 73   1505
45. 3717 + 825 + 74   4616
46. 85 + 104 + 761 + 5   955
47. 226 + 72 + 189 + 27   514
48. 2761 + 843 + 42   3646

Replace each ___?___ with <, =, or >.   (Pages 90–91)

49. 8.5 _?_ 8.6 <
50. 3.6 _?_ 3.06 >
51. 4.2 _?_ 4.20 =

52. 5.1 _?_ 5.11 <
53. 3.7 _?_ 3.77 <
54. 7.8 _?_ 7.80 =

55. 8.2 _?_ 8.1 >
56. 6.9 _?_ 6.91 <
57. 7.6 _?_ 7.63 <

58. 9.8 _?_ 9.7 >
59. 3.5 _?_ 4.5 <
60. 7.4 _?_ 8.4 <

61. 6.4 _?_ 6.04 >
62. 3.9 _?_ 3.8 >
63. 4.7 _?_ 4.6 >

64. 2.9 _?_ 2.91 <
65. 0.30 _?_ 0.31 <
66. 0.03 _?_ 0.01 >

67. 0.04 _?_ 0.004 >
68. 0.05 _?_ 0.057 <
69. 0.020 _?_ 0.02 =

70. 0.005 _?_ 0.05 <
71. 0.07 _?_ 0.007 >
72. 0.06 _?_ 0.060 =

73. 0.37 _?_ 0.47 <
74. 0.56 _?_ 0.55 >
75. 0.42 _?_ 0.41 >

18 INTEGERS ADDITION/SUBTRACTION

SKILLS

18-1 Positive and Negative Numbers
18-2 Comparing Integers
18-3 Adding Integers: Like Signs
18-4 Adding Integers: Unlike Signs
18-5 Subtracting Integers

APPLICATION

Wind Chill

CAREER

Automobile Maintenance

18-1 Positive and Negative Numbers

See the Teacher's Manual for the objectives.

Positive and negative numbers are used to represent temperatures above and below zero. Positive and negative numbers can be used to describe many other situations.

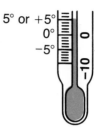

5° or +5°
0°
−5°

EXAMPLE 1 Write a positive or negative number to represent each word description.

Word Description	Number Description
a. 95 meters below sea level	−95
b. 10 hours before rocket lift-off	−10
c. A gain of 15 yards	15
d. A gain of 3% in humidity	3
e. A loss of 1500 feet in altitude	−1500

After completing Example 1, you may wish to have students do some or all of Exercises 1-18.

Numbers such as the positive and negative numbers in Example 1 and zero are called **integers.** You can show the integers on a number line.

EXAMPLE 2 Write the integer represented by each letter on the number line.

Solution: Start at 0. Numbers to the right of 0 are positive. Numbers to the left of 0 are negative.

A: 1   B: 2   C: 5   D: −1   E: −5

The number 0 is <u>neither positive nor negative.</u>

EXERCISES   See the suggested assignment guide in the Teacher's Manual.

Write a positive or negative number to represent each word description. (Example 1)

1. A rise of 8° in temperature   8

2. A pay raise of $0.65 per hour   .65

3. A loss of 2000 feet in altitude   −2000

4. 150 meters above sea level   150

5. Three years ago   −3

6. Ten years from now   10

7. One second before rocket lift-off. −1   **8.** Nine seconds after rocket lift-off 9

9. A weight gain of 1 kilogram 1   **10.** A weight loss of 3 kilograms −3

11. Water level in a reservoir that is 40% below normal −40   **12.** Water level in a reservoir that is 5% above normal 5

13. A business profit of $2500 2500   **14.** A business loss of $4000 −4000

15. A team penalty of 15 yards −15   **16.** A paycheck deduction of $3.65 −3.65

17. A deposit of $50 in a savings account 50   **18.** A forward speed of 60 kilometers per hour 60

For Exercises 19–24, use this number line to write the integer represented by each letter. (Example 2)

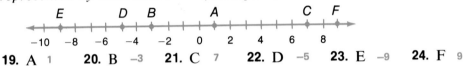

19. A 1   **20.** B −3   **21.** C 7   **22.** D −5   **23.** E −9   **24.** F 9

For Exercises 25–30, write the integer represented by each letter.

25. A 1   **26.** B −1   **27.** E −7   **28.** F 8   **29.** C −5   **30.** D 4

APPLICATIONS: Using Integers   Most students should be able to do these word problems which apply the concept of positive and negative numbers presented in the lesson.

Write an integer to represent each height or depth. Write a positive integer, a negative integer, or zero.

31. The highest point in North America is in Alaska at the top of Mt. McKinley. This point is 20,320 feet above sea level. 20,320

32. The lowest point in North America is Death Valley, California, which is 282 feet below sea level. −282

Mount Mansfield in Vermont

33. The highest point in the state of Vermont is at the top of Mount Mansfield. This point is 1318 meters above sea level. 1318

34. The lowest point in Vermont is Lake Champlain which is 29 meters above sea level. 29

35. The highest point in the state of Louisiana is at the top of Driskill Mountain. This point is 535 feet above sea level. 535

36. The lowest point in Louisiana is the city of New Orleans which is 5 feet below sea level. −5

18-2 Comparing Integers · See the Teacher's Manual for the objectives.

The integers 5 and −5 are each 5 units from 0.

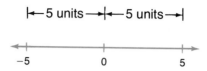

The integers 5 and −5 are on <u>opposite sides</u> of 0 on the number line. 5 and −5 are **opposites.** <u>The number 0 is its own opposite.</u>

PROCEDURE To write the opposite of a number, identify the number that is the same distance from 0 on the number line <u>and</u> in the opposite direction from 0.

EXAMPLE 1 Write the opposite of each integer.

Integer:	−2	0	7	−248
Opposite:	2	0	−7	248

After completing Example 1, you may wish to have students do some or all of Exercises 1-14.

Numbers become larger as you move <u>from left to right</u> on the number line. You can use the number line and the symbols < (less than), and > (greater than) to compare integers.

EXAMPLE 2 Replace each __?__ with < or >. Refer to this number line.

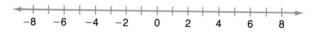

Problem	Think	Solution
a. 2 __?__ −3	2 is to the <u>right</u> of −3.	2 > −3
b. −5 __?__ 0	−5 is to the <u>left</u> of 0.	−5 < 0
c. −3 __?__ −5	−3 is to the <u>right</u> of −5.	−3 > −5

REVIEW OF RELATED SKILLS · You may wish to use these exercises before teaching the lesson.

Replace each __?__ with <, =, or >. (Pages 90–91)

1. 3.7 __?__ 3.6 >   **2.** 3.7 __?__ 3.8 <   **3.** 9.6 __?__ 9.1 >   **4.** 8.3 __?__ 8.35 <

5. 0.01 __?__ 0.001 >   **6.** 0.5 __?__ 0.50 =   **7.** 0.92 __?__ 0.91 >   **8.** 0.56 __?__ 0.55 >

9. 0.36 __?__ 0.4 <   **10.** 0.036 __?__ 0.36 <   **11.** 4.8 __?__ 5 <   **12.** 0.087 __?__ 0.07 >

EXERCISES

See the suggested assignment guide in the Teacher's Manual.

Write the opposite of each integer.　　(Example 1)

1. 12　−12 **2.** −15　15　　**3.** 0　0　　**4.** 156　−156 **5.** −511　511　　**6.** −77　77　　**7.** 91　−91

8. 75　−75 **9.** −56　56　　**10.** 18　−18　**11.** 311　−311 **12.** −212　212　**13.** −8000　8000 **14.** 900　−900

Replace each ___?___ with < or >.　　(Example 2)

15. 0 __?__ 4　<　　　　**16.** 0 __?__ −4　>　　　**17.** 2 __?__ −2　>　　　**18.** −5 __?__ 3　<

19. −5 __?__ −4　<　　　**20.** 4 __?__ 0　>　　　　**21.** −3 __?__ 3　<　　　**22.** 3 __?__ −3　>

23. −1 __?__ −2　>　　　**24.** 1 __?__ −2　>　　　**25.** −2 __?__ −1　<　　　**26.** 5 __?__ −2　>

27. −5 __?__ 2　<　　　　**28.** −5 __?__ −2　<　　　**29.** −7 __?__ −6　<　　　**30.** 0 __?__ −1　>

31. 18 __?__ −18　>　　　**32.** −20 __?__ 0　<　　　**33.** 0 __?__ −8　>　　　**34.** −7 __?__ −6　<

35. −9 __?__ 9　<　　　　**36.** 6 __?__ −1　>　　　**37.** −1 __?__ 0　<　　　**38.** −3 __?__ −4　>

APPLICATIONS: Using Integers

These one-step problems apply the skills presented in the lesson.

Replace each ___?___ with < or >. Temperatures are given in Fahrenheit degrees.

A beach in Hawaii

39. The lowest temperature ever recorded in Hawaii was 18°. The lowest temperature ever recorded in Delaware was −17°.

Complete:　−17° __?__ 18°　<

40. The lowest temperature ever recorded in Florida was −2°. The lowest temperature ever recorded in South Carolina was −13°.

Complete:　−2° __?__ −13°　>

41. The lowest temperature ever recorded in Wisconsin was −54°. The lowest temperature ever recorded in Tennessee was −32°.

Complete:　−54° __?__ −32°　<

Pinkham Notch, New Hampshire

42. The lowest temperature ever recorded in New Hampshire was −46°. The lowest temperature ever recorded in Illinois was −35°.

Complete:　−35° __?__ −46°　>

43. The lowest temperature ever recorded in Louisiana was −16°. The lowest temperature ever recorded in Georgia was −15°.

Complete:　−15° __?__ −16°　>

18-3 Adding Integers: Like Signs See the Teacher's Manual for the objectives.

You can use a number line to find the sum of two integers.

PROCEDURE: To add two integers on the number line:

[1] Start at the point that represents the first integer.

[2] Draw an arrow to represent the second integer.

    a. Move to the <u>right</u> if the second integer is <u>positive</u>.
    b. Move to the <u>left</u> if the second integer is <u>negative</u>.

[3] Read the answer at the tip of the arrow.

EXAMPLE 1 $5 + 3 = \underline{\ ?\ }$

Solution: Start at 5. Move 3 units to the <u>right</u>.

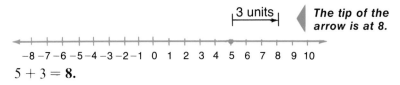

$5 + 3 = \mathbf{8}.$

After completing Example 1, you may wish to have students do some or all of Exercises 1-15.

RULE *The sum of two positive integers is a positive integer.*

EXAMPLE 2 $-2 + (-3) ; \underline{\ ?\ }$

Solution: Start at -2. Move 3 units to the <u>left</u>.

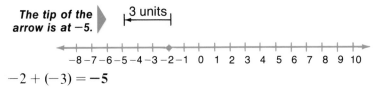

$-2 + (-3) = \mathbf{-5}$

RULE *The sum of two negative integers is a negative integer.*

REVIEW OF RELATED SKILLS You may wish to use these exercises before teaching the lesson.

Add.   (Pages 6–7)

1. $102 + 76$ 178   **2.** $318 + 91$ 409   **3.** $11 + 716$ 727   **4.** $1012 + 5$ 1017   **5.** $172 + 89$ ²⁶¹

6. $6 + 21 + 48 + 278$ 353   **7.** $412 + 903 + 72 + 5$ 1392   **8.** $6545 + 45 + 901$

9. $30 + 927 + 21 + 8$ 986   **10.** $396 + 558 + 800 + 9$ 1763   **11.** $9046 + 703 + 34$

8. 7491   9783

EXERCISES

Use a number line to add. (Example 1)

1. $1 + 3$ 4
2. $4 + 4$ 8
3. $8 + 2$ 10
4. $7 + 3$ 10
5. $0 + 4$ 4
6. $9 + 3$ 12
7. $4 + 2$ 6
8. $6 + 4$ 10
9. $7 + 1$ 8
10. $10 + 0$ 10
11. $3 + 3$ 6
12. $6 + 3$ 9
13. $3 + 9$ 12
14. $6 + 3$ 9
15. $6 + 2$ 8

(Example 2)

16. $-1 + (-1)$ −2
17. $-3 + (-4)$ −7
18. $-4 + (-3)$ −7
19. $-3 + (-2)$ −5
20. $-2 + (-2)$ −4
21. $-1 + 0$ −1
22. $0 + (-7)$ −7
23. $-5 + (-2)$ −7
24. $0 + (-4)$ −4
25. $-7 + (-1)$ −8
26. $-6 + (-3)$ −9
27. $-1 + (-5)$ −6
28. $-5 + (-3)$ −8
29. $-4 + (-5)$ −9
30. $-2 + (-5)$ −7
31. $-8 + 0$ −8
32. $-3 + (-5)$ −8
33. $-1 + (-2)$ −3
34. $-9 + (-8)$ −17
35. $-8 + (-3)$ −11
36. $-2 + (-9)$ −11
37. $-1 + (-8)$ −9
38. $-8 + (-1)$ −9
39. $-4 + (-5)$ −9
40. $-7 + (-2)$ −9
41. $-2 + (-7)$ −9
42. $-8 + (-8)$ −16
43. $-1 + (-3)$ −4

Mixed Practice

44. $4 + 7$ 11
45. $-4 + (-7)$ −11
46. $-4 + (-6)$ −10
47. $4 + 6$ 10
48. $-1 + 0$ −1
49. $0 + (-1)$ −1
50. $5 + 5$ 10
51. $-5 + (-5)$ −10
52. $4 + 4$ 8
53. $-4 + (-4)$ −8
54. $-3 + (-4)$ −7
55. $3 + 4$ 7
56. $11 + 1$ 12
57. $-1 + (-11)$ −12
58. $9 + 2$ 11
59. $-2 + (-9)$ −11
60. $-3 + (-6)$ −9
61. $6 + 3$ 9
62. $0 + 12$ 12
63. $0 + (-12)$ −12
64. $-5 + (-5)$ −10
65. $-1 + (-1)$ −2
66. $(-13) + 0$ −13
67. $8 + 4$ 12

APPLICATIONS: Using Addition of Integers These word problems apply the skills presented in the lesso

Represent each problem by the sum of two integers. Then use a number line to find the sum.

$-3 + (-2) = -5$

68. The temperature at 7 P.M. was 0°C. Two hours later, the temperature was 3 degrees below zero. How much did the temperature fall?

$0 + (-3) = -3$

69. Albert's team lost 3 penalty points the first quarter. The team lost 2 penalty points the next quarter. Find the total number of points lost.

70. Raoul had to write checks for $4 and $7 to pay some bills. By how much did he decrease his checking account? $-4 + (-7) = -11$

71. Susan lost 8 pounds last month. This month she lost 7 pounds. How much did she lose in all? $-8 + (-7) = -15$

INTEGERS: ADDITION/SUBTRACTION **393**

18-4 Adding Integers: Unlike Signs

See the Teacher's Manual for the objectives.

You can also use a number line to add integers with unlike signs.

Like Signs	Unlike Signs
$7 + 5$	$8 + -4$
$-6 + -8$	$-9 + 5$

The steps for adding integers that have unlike signs are the same as those for adding integers that have like signs.

PROCEDURE   To add integers with unlike signs:

1. Start at the point that represents the first integer.
2. Draw an arrow to represent the second integer.
   - **a.** Move to the <u>right</u> if the second integer is <u>positive</u>.
   - **b.** Move to the <u>left</u> if the second integer is <u>negative</u>.
3. Read the answer at the tip of the arrow.

EXAMPLE 1 $-9 + 5 = \underline{\ \ ?\ \ }$

Solution: Start at -9. Move 5 units to the <u>right</u>.

├─5 units──┤ *The tip of the arrow is at -4.*

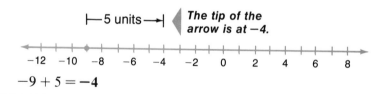

$-9 + 5 = \mathbf{-4}$

After completing Example 1, you may wish to have students do some or all of Exercises 1-20.

In Example 2, the first addend is a positive integer.

EXAMPLE 2   **a.** $8 + -4 = \underline{\ \ ?\ \ }$ **b.** $3 + -3 = \underline{\ \ ?\ \ }$

Solutions:

a.   *The tip of the arrow is at 4.*   ├─4 units─┤

$8 + -4 = \mathbf{4}$

b.   *The tip of the arrow is at 0.*   ├─3 units─┤

$3 + -3 = \mathbf{0}$

RULE   *The sum of an integer and its opposite is 0.*

REVIEW OF RELATED SKILLS
You may wish to use these exercises before teaching the lesson.

Add.   (Pages 2–3, 6–7)

1. $16 + 70$ 86   **2.** $23 + 17$ 40   **3.** $4 + 13$ 17   **4.** $14 + 9$ 23   **5.** $11 + 12$ 23

6. $28 + 13$ 41   **7.** $11 + 17$ 28   **8.** $22 + 47$ 69   **9.** $212 + 0$ 212   **10.** $0 + 615$ 615

EXERCISES
See the suggested assignment guide in the Teacher's Manual.

Use a number line to add.   (Example 1)

1. $-6 + 1$ _5   **2.** $-4 + 9$ 5   **3.** $-11 + 2$ _9   **4.** $-5 + 8$ 3   **5.** $-7 + 9$ 2

6. $-8 + 4$ _4   **7.** $-9 + 6$ _3   **8.** $-3 + 5$ 2   **9.** $-2 + 10$ 8   **10.** $-7 + 8$ 1

11. $-11 + 4$ _7   **12.** $-6 + 10$ 4   **13.** $-1 + 8$ 7   **14.** $-6 + 3$ _3   **15.** $-15 + 2$ _13

16. $-10 + 1$ _9   **17.** $-4 + 8$ 4   **18.** $-6 + 3$ _3   **19.** $-6 + 8$ 2   **20.** $-6 + 6$ 0

(Example 2)

21. $7 + (-3)$ 4   **22.** $3 + (-7)$ _4   **23.** $1 + (-6)$ _5   **24.** $6 + (-1)$ 5

25. $4 + (-5)$ _1   **26.** $5 + (-4)$ 1   **27.** $8 + (-8)$ 0   **28.** $5 + (-5)$ 0

29. $5 + (-3)$ 2   **30.** $3 + (-2)$ 1   **31.** $2 + (-1)$ 1   **32.** $6 + (-6)$ 0

33. $9 + (-9)$ 0   **34.** $7 + (-4)$ 3   **35.** $4 + (-8)$ _4   **36.** $6 + (-12)$ _6

37. $9 + (-3)$ 6   **38.** $11 + (-8)$ 3   **39.** $7 + (-6)$ 1   **40.** $4 + (-3)$ 1

Mixed Practice   The Mixed Practice contains exercises that relate to both Examples 1 and 2.

41. $-3 + 11$ 8   **42.** $-9 + 11$ 2   **43.** $11 + (-9)$ 2   **44.** $11 + (-3)$ 8

45. $10 + (-8)$ 2   **46.** $-8 + 10$ 2   **47.** $-8 + 8$ 0   **48.** $8 + (-8)$ 0

49. $2 + (-7)$ _5   **50.** $-7 + 2$ _5   **51.** $-9 + 5$ _4   **52.** $5 + (-9)$ _4

53. $-9 + 9$ 0   **54.** $9 + (-9)$ 0   **55.** $-15 + 10$ _5   **56.** $10 + (-15)$ _5

57. $-10 + 10$ 0   **58.** $10 + (-10)$ 0   **59.** $-6 + 12$ 6   **60.** $12 + (-6)$ 6

APPLICATIONS: Using Addition of Integers   These are one-step problems that most students should be able to handle.

Represent each change in temperature by the sum of two integers. Then use the thermometer scale at the right to find the sum.

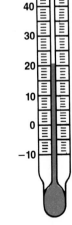

61. The temperature was 21°C and rose 9 degrees. Find the new temperature. 21 + 9 = 30

62. The temperature was 0°C and dropped 3 degrees. Find the new temperature. 0 + (−3) = −3

63. The temperature was 0°C and rose 10 degrees. Find the new temperature. 0 + 10 = 10

64. The temperature was −4°C and rose 4 degrees. Find the new temperature. −4 + 4 = 0

65. The temperature was −5°C and rose 7 degrees. Find the new temperature. −5 + 7 = 2

18-5 Subtracting Integers See the Teacher's Manual for the objectives.

Subtracting an integer is the same as <u>adding its opposite</u>.

Subtraction	Related Addition	Solution

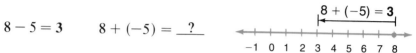

$$8 - 5 = 3 \qquad 8 + (-5) = \underline{\ ?\ }$$

$8 + (-5) = 3$

$-1\ 0\ 1\ 2\ 3\ 4\ 5\ 6\ 7\ 8$

PROCEDURE To write an addition problem for a subtraction problem, add the opposite of the number you are subtracting.

EXAMPLE 1 Write an addition problem for each subtraction problem.

Subtraction Problem	Think	Addition Problem
a. $10 - 4$	The opposite of 4 is -4.	$10 + (-4)$
b. $8 - (-6)$	The opposite of (-6) is 6.	$8 + 6$
c. $-5 - 3$	The opposite of 3 is -3.	$-5 + (-3)$
d. $-7 - (-1)$	The opposite of (-1) is 1.	$-7 + 1$

After completing Example 1, you may wish to have students do some or all of Exercises 1-12.

You use opposites to subtract two integers.

PROCEDURE To subtract two integers:

1 Write an addition problem for the subtraction problem.

2 Add.

EXAMPLE 2 **a.** $5 - 8 = \underline{\ ?\ }$ **b.** $-1 - (-3) = \underline{\ ?\ }$

Solutions: First write an addition problem for the subtraction problem.

1 **a.** $5 - 8 = 5 + (-8)$ **b.** $-1 - (-3) = -1 + 3$

$5 - 8 = -3$

$-1 - (-3) = 2$

2

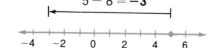

$-4 \quad -2 \quad 0 \quad 2 \quad 4 \quad 6$ $\qquad -4 \quad -2 \quad 0 \quad 2 \quad 4 \quad 6$

The tip of the arrow is at -3. So, $5 - 8 = -3$.

The tip of the arrow is at 2. So, $-1 - (-3) = 2$.

Use a number line to add.   (Pages 392–395)

1. $6 + 5$ 11   **2.** $-6 + 8$ 2   **3.** $-5 + 7$ 2   **4.** $4 + 8$ 12   **5.** $-2 + (-7)$ -9

6. $(-8) + (-1)$ -9   **7.** $12 + (-3)$ 9   **8.** $14 + (-4)$ 10   **9.** $-6 + 10$ 4   **10.** $-8 + 11$ 3

Write the opposite of each integer.   (Pages 390–391)

11. -3 3   **12.** 5 -5   **13.** 19 -19   **14.** -10 10   **15.** 0 0   **16.** -20 20   **17.** 80 -80   **18.** -87 87

EXERCISES
See the suggested assignment guide in the Teacher's Manual.

Write an addition problem for each subtraction problem.   (Example 1)   12 + 9

1. $11 - 3$ 11 + (-3)   **2.** $14 - 2$ 14 + (-2)   **3.** $14 - (-6)$ 14 + 6   **4.** $12 - (-9)$

5. $-6 - 1$ -6 + (-1)   **6.** $-9 - 7$ -9 + (-7)   **7.** $-8 - (-5)$ -8 + 5   **8.** $-12 - (-1)$ -12 + 1

9. $-7 - 7$ -7 + (-7)   **10.** $-8 - 8$ -8 + (-8)   **11.** $19 - 4$ 19 + (-4)   **12.** $12 - 11$ 12 + (-11)

Use a number line to subtract.   (Example 2)

13. $3 - 5$ -2   **14.** $4 - 5$ -1   **15.** $-1 - (-2)$ 1   **16.** $-3 - (-6)$ 3

17. $-5 - 1$ -6   **18.** $-10 - 9$ -19   **19.** $12 - 8$ 4   **20.** $8 - 12$ -4

21. $-3 - 7$ -10   **22.** $-7 - 3$ -10   **23.** $-14 - (-8)$ -6   **24.** $-8 - (-14)$ 6

25. $0 - 8$ -8   **26.** $0 - 7$ -7   **27.** $0 - (-5)$ 5   **28.** $0 - (-12)$ 12

29. $-3 - (-7)$ 4   **30.** $-2 - (-11)$ 9   **31.** $6 - (-2)$ 8   **32.** $7 - (-11)$ 18

33. $13 - 8$ 5   **34.** $13 - 11$ 2   **35.** $10 - (-8)$ 18   **36.** $9 - (-4)$ 13

37. $-6 - 10$ -16   **38.** $-9 - 5$ -14   **39.** $-1 - (-8)$ 7   **40.** $-4 - (-1)$ -3

41. $-3 - 0$ -3   **42.** $-9 - 0$ -9   **43.** $-7 - (-5)$ -2   **44.** $-5 - (-7)$ 2

More Challenging Problems More Challenging Problems are optional.

Add without using a number line.

45. $-1 + (-2)$ -3   **46.** $-6 + (-2)$ -8   **47.** $-8 + (-7)$ -15   **48.** $-5 + (-20)$ -25

49. $-8 + 9$ 1   **50.** $-4 + 7$ 3   **51.** $-12 + 21$ 9   **52.** $-18 + 30$ 12

53. $12 + (-9)$ 3   **54.** $9 + (-5)$ 4   **55.** $16 + (-8)$ 8   **56.** $27 + (-7)$ 20

57. $-6 + 5$ -1   **58.** $-10 + 7$ -3   **59.** $-30 + 15$ -15   **60.** $-17 + 4$ -13

61. $9 + (-11)$ -2   **62.** $6 + (-9)$ -3   **63.** $4 + (-9)$ -5   **64.** $13 + (-8)$ 5

Write an addition problem for each subtraction problem. Then find each answer without using a number line.

65. $6 - 5$ 1   **66.** $9 - 8$ 1   **67.** $-3 - (-1)$ -2   **68.** $-4 - (-2)$ -2

69. $-1 - (-6)$ 5   **70.** $-3 - (-9)$ 6   **71.** $-12 - (-3)$ -9   **72.** $-11 - (-9)$ -2

73. $-8 - (-1)$ -7   **74.** $-6 - (-5)$ -1   **75.** $-15 - 5$ -20   **76.** $-16 - 10$ -26

Problem Solving and Applications

Wind Chill

See the Teacher's Manual for the objectives.
This lesson combines the skill of reading a table with the skills presented
in Section 18-5.

A combination of cold temperatures and high winds can make a person feel colder than the actual temperature. This is called **wind chill**.

Winds in MPH	Temperatures in °F																
	35	30	25	20	15	10	5	0	−5	−10	−15	−20	−25	−30	−35	−40	−45
5	33	27	21	19	12	7	0	−5	−10	−15	−21	−26	−31	−36	−42	−47	−52
10	22	16	10	3	−3	−9	−15	−22	−27	−34	−40	−46	−52	−58	−64	−71	−77
15	16	9	2	−5	−11	−18	−25	−31	−38	−45	−51	−58	−65	−72	−78	−85	−92
20	12	4	3	−10	−17	−24	−31	−39	−46	−53	−60	−67	−74	−81	−88	−95	−103
25	8	1	7	−15	−22	−29	−36	−44	−51	−59	−66	−74	−81	−88	−96	−103	−110
30	6	−2	−10	−18	−25	−33	−41	−49	−56	−64	−71	−79	−86	−93	−101	−109	−116
35	4	−4	−12	−20	−27	−35	−43	−52	−58	−67	−74	−82	−89	−97	−105	−113	−120
40	3	−5	−13	−21	−29	−37	−45	−53	−60	−69	−76	−84	−92	−100	−107	−115	−123
45	2	−6	−14	−22	−30	−38	−46	−54	−62	−70	−78	−85	−93	−102	−109	−117	−125

EXAMPLE 1 Find the wind chill when winds are blowing at 25 miles per hour and the temperature is 20°F.

Solution: 1 Find 25 in the "MPH" column. Look directly right to the number under the "20" column.

2 Read the number: −15. The wind chill is **−15°F**.

The answer to Example 1 means that the 25 mile-per-hour wind makes the temperature of 20°F feel like −15°F.

EXAMPLE 2 In Example 1, how many degrees colder does the wind chill make it feel?

Solution: Subtract the actual temperature <u>from</u> the wind chill temperature.
$$-15° − 20° = −15° + (−20°) = −35°.$$
The wind chill makes it feel **35° colder**.

Exercises

In Exercises 1–4, find the wind chill. (Example 1)

	Winds in MPH	Temperature	Wind Chill
1.	10	0°F	? −22°
2.	20	20°F	? −10°

	Winds in MPH	Temperature	Wind Chill
3.	40	25°F	? −13°
4.	20	10°F	? −24°

For each exercise, how many degrees colder does the wind chill make it feel? (Example 2)

5. Exercise 1 −22°   **6.** Exercise 2 −30°   **7.** Exercise 3 −38°   **8.** Exercise 4 −34°

Application

AUTOMOBILE MAINTENANCE

Career lessons are optional.
This lesson combines the skill of reading a graph with the concept of positive and negative numbers.

Auto mechanics know the importance of oil in keeping an automobile engine running smoothly. Some oils work well over a wide range of temperatures. These oils have code names such as SW–20 or 10W–40.

The chart below shows the temperature ranges for which four different oils work well.

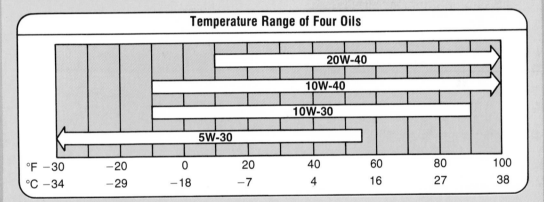

Temperature Range of Four Oils

	20W-40
	10W-40
	10W-30
5W-30	

°F	−30	−20	0	20	40	60	80	100
°C	−34	−29	−18	−7	4	16	27	38

EXAMPLE

Which oils can be used for temperatures between 0°F and 70°F?

Solution:

Look at the chart. Find the bars that extend between 0°F and 70°F.

Either **10W–40** or **10W–30** will work.

EXERCISES

1. Which oil can be used only with temperatures above 10°F?   20W–40

2. Which oil can be used only in winter temperatures?   5W–30

3. Which oil can be used with temperatures below −29°C?   5W–30

4. Which oil can be used in temperatures from −10°F to over 100°F?   10W–40

5. How many degrees Fahrenheit are there between the highest and lowest temperatures in which Oil 10W-30 can be used?   100°

6. How many degrees Celsius are there between the highest and lowest temperatures in which Oil 10W–30 can be used?   56°

Chapter Review

These exercises review the vocabulary, skills and applications presented in the chapter as a preparation for the chapter test.

Part 1: Vocabulary

For Exercises 1–4, choose from the box at the right the word(s) that completes each statement.

1. Numbers to the right of 0 on a number line are __?__ numbers. (Page 388) *positive*

2. Numbers to the left of 0 on a number line are __?__ numbers. (Page 388) *negative*

3. The sum of two negative integers is a __?__ integer. (Page 392) *negative*

4. The sum of a number and its __?__ is zero. (Page 394) *opposite*

negative
positive
integers
opposite

Part 2: Skills

Write a positive or negative number to represent each word description. (Pages 388–389)

5. A rise of 5° in temperature 5

6. 250 feet below sea level −250

7. Six hours ago −6

8. Eight hours from now 8

9. A business loss of $400 −400

10. Fifteen seconds before rocket lift–off −15

For Exercises 11–16, use the number line to write the integer represented by each letter. (Pages 388–389)

11. A −3   12. B 2   13. C −9   14. D 6   15. E −1   16. F −7

Write the opposite of each integer. (Pages 390–391)

17. 6 −6   18. 200 −200   19. −56 56   20. −81 81   21. 72 −72   22. −31 31   23. 408 −408

24. −14 14   25. −650 650   26. 85 −85   27. −75 75   28. 325 −325   29. 64 −64   30. 750 −750

Replace the __?__ with < or >. (Pages 390–391)

31. 6 __?__ −2 >   32. −3 __?__ 3 <   33. −10 __?__ −8 <   34. −2 __?__ −12 >

35. −13 __?__ 4 <   36. −15 __?__ −9 <   37. 5 __?__ −16 >   38. 12 __?__ −7 >

39. −4 __?__ −15 >   40. −18 __?__ 3 <   41. −12 __?__ 12 <   42. 8 __?__ −21 >

Use a number line to add. (Pages 392–393)

43. 6 + 8 14   44. −6 + (−8) −14   45. 0 + (−4) −4   46. 7 + 10 17

47. 21 + 3 24   48. −12 + (−14) −26   49. −2 + (−5) −7   50. 13 + 9 22

51. −7 + (−10) −17   52. −3 + 0 −3   53. 3 + 9 12   54. −8 + (−4) −12

(Pages 394–395)

55. $3 + (-7)$ _-4_   **56.** $-4 + 8$ _4_   **57.** $10 + (-4)$ _6_   **58.** $-6 + 2$ _-4_

59. $-10 + 6$ _-4_   **60.** $4 + (-9)$ _-5_   **61.** $8 + (-10)$ _-2_   **62.** $-9 + 3$ _-6_

63. $-10 + 12$ _2_   **64.** $5 + (-10)$ _-5_   **65.** $-8 + 3$ _-5_   **66.** $12 + (-5)$ _7_

Write an addition problem for each subtraction problem.
(Pages 396–397)

67. $12 - 4$ _12 + (-4)_   **68.** $18 - 5$ _18 + (-5)_   **69.** $13 - (-3)$ _13 + 3_   **70.** $16 - (-8)$ _16 + 8_

71. $-5 - 7$ _-5 + (-7)_   **72.** $-3 - 9$ _-3 + (-9)_   **73.** $-4 - (-8)$ _-4 + 8_   **74.** $-12 - (-7)$ _-12 + 7_

Use a number line to substract.   (Pages 396–397)

75. $8 - 9$ _-1_   **76.** $3 - 7$ _-4_   **77.** $2 - (-6)$ _8_   **78.** $4 - (-5)$ _9_

79. $-6 - 4$ _-10_   **80.** $-8 - 10$ _-18_   **81.** $-5 - (-12)$ _7_   **82.** $-3 - (-10)$ _7_

83. $0 - 10$ _-10_   **84.** $0 - 8$ _-8_   **85.** $-8 - 0$ _-8_   **86.** $4 - 0$ _4_

87. $-3 - (-9)$ _6_   **88.** $-5 - (-13)$ _8_   **89.** $10 - (-3)$ _13_   **90.** $12 - (-4)$ _16_

Part 3: Applications

For Exercises 91–92, write an integer to represent each height or depth. Write a positive integer, a negative integer or zero.   (Pages 388–389)

91. The highest point in Texas is at the top of Guadalupe Peak. This point is 2,667 meters above sea level. _2667_

92. The greatest known depth of the Atlantic Ocean is in the Puerto Rico Trench. This point is 8,648 meters below the surface. _-8648_

For Exercises 93–94, replace each ___?___ with < or >.   (Pages 390–391)

Guadalupe Peak in Texas

93. The lowest temperature ever recorded in Nebraska was $-47°F$. The lowest temperature ever recorded in Nevada was $-50°F$.

Complete: $-47°$ ___?___ $-50°$ >

94. The lowest temperature ever recorded in West Virginia was $-37°F$. The lowest temperature recorded in Wyoming was $-63°F$.

Complete: $-63°$ ___?___ $-37°$ <

For Exercises 95–96, represent each change in temperature by the sum of two integers. Then use a number line to find the sum.   (Pages 394–395)

95. The temperature was 6°C and rose 4°. Find the new temperature.

_6 + 4 = 10_

96. The temperature was $-2°C$ and rose 8°. Find the new temperature.

_-2 + 8 = 6_

Chapter Test

The Teacher's Resource Book contains two forms of each chapter test.

For Exercises 1–6, use this number line to write the integer represented by each letter.

1. A –3   **2.** B 2   **3.** C –9   **4.** D 6   **5.** E –1   **6.** F
                                                                                                      –7

Replace the __?__ with < or >.

7. $4 \underline{\ ?\ } -8$ >   **8.** $-6 \underline{\ ?\ } -2$ <   **9.** $-12 \underline{\ ?\ } -8$ <   **10.** $-8 \underline{\ ?\ } 3$ <

Use a number line to add.

11. $4+7$ 11   **12.** $-3+(-5)$ –8   **13.** $-2+(-1)$ –3   **14.** $7+6$ 13

15. $-5+4$ –1   **16.** $-6+8$ 2   **17.** $5+(-9)$ –4   **18.** $10+(-4)$
                                                                                              6

Use a number line to subtract.

19. $2-6$ –4   **20.** $4-10$ –6   **21.** $-3-9$ –12   **22.** $-7-3$ –10

23. $3-(-5)$ 8   **24.** $6-(-10)$ 16   **25.** $-4-(-2)$ –2   **26.** $-5-(-8)$ 3

For Exercises 27–30, represent each change in temperature by the sum of two integers. Then use the thermometer scale to find the sum.

27. The temperature was 3°C and rose 7 degrees. Find the new temperature.
$3 + 7 = 10$

28. The temperature was −2°C and rose 4 degrees. Find the new temperature. $-2 + 4 = 2$

29. The temperature was −5°C and fell 3 degrees. Find the new temperature.
$-5 + (-3) = -8$

30. The temperature was 6°C and fell 10°. Find the new temperature. $6 + (-10) = -4$

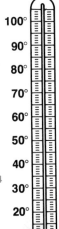

100°
90°
80°
70°
60°
50°
40°
30°
20°
10°
0°
−10°

Celsius Scale Thermometer

Additional Practice

You may wish to use some or all of these exercises depending on how well students performed on the formal chapter test.

Skills

For Exercises 1–6, write a positive or negative number to represent each word description. (Pages 388–389)

1. A weight loss of 2 kilograms −2

2. A profit of $20.00 20

3. Five hours ago −5

4. Three weeks from now 3

5. Ten seconds before lift-off −10

6. A drop of 10° in temperature −10

For Exercises 7–12, use the number line to write the integer represented by each letter. (Pages 388–389)

7. *A* 2 **8.** *B* −7 **9.** *C* −4 **10.** *D* 4 **11.** *E* −1 **12.** *F* −5

Write the opposite of each integer. (Pages 390–391)

13. 5 −5 **14.** 42 −42 **15.** −300 300 **16.** 8 −8 **17.** −62 62 **18.** 55 −55 **19.** 87 −87

20. −450 450 **21.** −13 13 **22.** 46 −46 **23.** 73 −73 **24.** −95 95 **25.** −64 64 **26.** −48 48

Replace the __?__ with < or >. (Pages 390–391)

27. −5 __?__ −4 < **28.** 6 __?__ −9 > **29.** 12 __?__ −3 > **30.** −2 __?__ 1 <

31. −7 __?__ −1 < **32.** −4 __?__ 2 < **33.** 3 __?__ −1 > **34.** −3 __?__ −6 >

Use a number line to add. (Pages 392–393)

35. 4 + 3 7 **36.** −5 + (−9) −14 **37.** −2 + 0 −2 **38.** 9 + 5 14

39. −8 + (−7) −15 **40.** −6 + 0 −6 **41.** −7 + (−2) −9 **42.** −2 + (−4) −6

(Pages 394–395)

43. 6 + (−7) −1 **44.** −4 + 2 −2 **45.** 5 + (−3) 2 **46.** −7 + 10 3

47. −8 + 6 −2 **48.** 8 + (−3) 5 **49.** −4 + 6 2 **50.** 12 + (−8) 4

Use a number line to subtract. (Pages 396–397)

51. 4 − 5 −1 **52.** 3 − (−4) 7 **53.** −2 − 7 −9 **54.** −12 − 9 −21

55. 6 − (−3) 9 **56.** −10 − (−6) −4 **57.** −12 − (−4) −8 **58.** 6 − 8 −2

Applications

For Exercises 59–60, represent each change in temperature by the sum of two integers. Then use a number line to find the sum. (Pages 394–395)

59. The temperature was 2°C and fell 5 degrees. 2 + (−5) = −3

60. The temperature was −3°C and rose 7 degrees. −3 + 7 = 4

REVIEW OF RELATED SKILLS FOR CHAPTER 19

We suggest that some or all of this page be reviewed before proceeding with the chapter.

Multiply.   (Pages 26–27, 32–33)

1. 12×5 60   **2.** 13×8 104   **3.** 22×3 66   **4.** 14×9 126   **5.** 63×4 252

6. 71×3 213   **7.** 53×2 106   **8.** 72×9 648   **9.** 64×8 512   **10.** 92×4 368

11. 84×12 1008   **12.** 73×23 1679   **13.** 91×49 4459   **14.** 72×48 3456   **15.** 53×31 1643

16. 41×23 943   **17.** 32×94 3008   **18.** 74×15 1110   **19.** 25×58 1450   **20.** 57×33 1881

21. 25×59 1475   **22.** 61×92 5612   **23.** 76×52 3952   **24.** 82×26 2132   **25.** 53×11 583

26. 86×37 3182   **27.** 45×19 855   **28.** 58×91 5278   **29.** 38×36 1368   **30.** 46×22 1012

Divide.   (Pages 50–51, 54–55)

31. $21 \div 7$ 3   **32.** $48 \div 3$ 16   **33.** $64 \div 4$ 16   **34.** $90 \div 5$ 18   **35.** $168 \div 8$ 21

36. $80 \div 16$ 5   **37.** $128 \div 4$ 32   **38.** $192 \div 12$ 16   **39.** $338 \div 13$ 26   **40.** $360 \div 15$ 24

41. $9\overline{)1134}$ 126   **42.** $8\overline{)2016}$ 252   **43.** $3\overline{)1689}$ 563   **44.** $4\overline{)1872}$ 468   **45.** $6\overline{)2580}$ 430

46. $3\overline{)2343}$ 781   **47.** $5\overline{)3210}$ 642   **48.** $2\overline{)1624}$ 812   **49.** $7\overline{)6671}$ 953   **50.** $4\overline{)2092}$ 523

51. $11\overline{)3575}$ 325   **52.** $14\overline{)3234}$ 231   **53.** $25\overline{)9225}$ 369   **54.** $13\overline{)8554}$ 658   **55.** $24\overline{)6024}$ 251

56. $23\overline{)14,352}$ 624   **57.** $21\overline{)16,422}$ 782   **58.** $23\overline{)21,942}$ 954   **59.** $52\overline{)18,148}$ 349   **60.** $51\overline{)19,941}$ 391

Complete.   (Pages 54–55)

61. $12 \times 14 = 168$ **62.** $23 \times 22 = 506$ **63.** $13 \times 25 = 325$

  $168 \div 12 = \underline{\ ?\ }$ 14 $506 \div 23 = \underline{\ ?\ }$ 22 $325 \div 13 = \underline{\ ?\ }$ 25

  $168 \div 14 = \underline{\ ?\ }$ 12 $506 \div 22 = \underline{\ ?\ }$ 23 $325 \div 25 = \underline{\ ?\ }$ 13

64. $18 \times 16 = 288$ **65.** $21 \times 19 = 399$ **66.** $17 \times 11 = 187$

  $288 \div 18 = \underline{\ ?\ }$ 16 $399 \div 21 = \underline{\ ?\ }$ 19 $187 \div 17 = \underline{\ ?\ }$ 11

  $288 \div 16 = \underline{\ ?\ }$ 18 $399 \div 19 = \underline{\ ?\ }$ 21 $187 \div 11 = \underline{\ ?\ }$ 17

Write a fraction for each mixed number.   (Pages 208–209)

67. $1\frac{3}{4}$ $\frac{7}{4}$ **68.** $8\frac{1}{8}$ $\frac{65}{8}$ **69.** $9\frac{1}{3}$ $\frac{28}{3}$ **70.** $7\frac{3}{5}$ $\frac{38}{5}$ **71.** $3\frac{1}{6}$ $\frac{19}{6}$ **72.** $3\frac{1}{2}$ $\frac{7}{2}$

73. $4\frac{1}{3}$ $\frac{13}{3}$ **74.** $6\frac{1}{2}$ $\frac{13}{2}$ **75.** $8\frac{2}{3}$ $\frac{26}{3}$ **76.** $5\frac{1}{4}$ $\frac{21}{4}$ **77.** $3\frac{1}{8}$ $\frac{25}{8}$ **78.** $1\frac{1}{4}$ $\frac{5}{4}$

79. $2\frac{4}{5}$ $\frac{14}{5}$ **80.** $7\frac{2}{3}$ $\frac{23}{3}$ **81.** $9\frac{3}{4}$ $\frac{39}{4}$ **82.** $6\frac{5}{8}$ $\frac{53}{8}$ **83.** $5\frac{1}{2}$ $\frac{11}{2}$ **84.** $2\frac{5}{6}$ $\frac{17}{6}$

Write the integer represented by each letter. Use the number line.
(Pages 388–389)

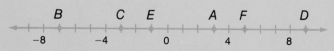

85. A 3   **86.** B -7   **87.** C -3   **88.** D 9   **89.** E -1   **90.** F 5

19

INTEGERS
MULTIPLICATION/DIVISION

SKILLS

19-1   Multiplying Integers:
Unlike Signs

19-2   Multiplying Integers:
Like Signs

19-3   Dividing Integers

19-4   Rational Numbers

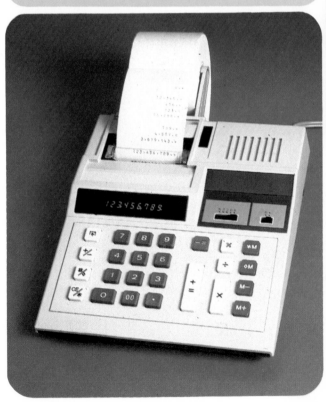

APPLICATION

Conserving Energy

CAREER

Business

19-1 Multiplying Integers: Unlike Signs

See the Teacher's Manual for the objectives.

Study the patterns in each column.

TABLE

Column 1

$$3 \times 2 = 6$$
$$3 \times 1 = 3$$
$$3 \times 0 = 0$$
$$3 \times (-1) = -3$$
$$3 \times (-2) = -6$$
$$3 \times (-3) = -9$$

The products are decreasing by 3.

Column 2

$$2 \times 4 = 8$$
$$1 \times 4 = 4$$
$$0 \times 4 = 0$$
$$-1 \times 4 = -4$$
$$-2 \times 4 = -8$$
$$-3 \times 4 = -12$$

The products are decreasing by 4.

RULE   *The product of two integers having unlike signs is negative.*

PROCEDURE   To multiply two integers with <u>unlike</u> signs:

1 Multiply as with whole numbers.

2 Insert a negative sign before the product.

EXAMPLE   Find each product.

  a. $8 \times (-4)$ **b.** -9×3 **c.** $0 \times (-10)$

Solutions: **a.** $8 \times (-4) = -32$ **b.** $-9 \times 3 = -27$ **c.** $0 \times (-10) = 0$

When you <u>multiply by zero</u>, the <u>product is zero</u>. Recall that zero is neither positive nor negative.

REVIEW OF RELATED SKILLS

You may wish to use these exercises before teaching the lesson.

Multiply.   (Pages 26–27, 32–33)

1. 3×8 24   **2.** 9×6 54   **3.** 1×11 11   **4.** 7×5 35   **5.** 10×4 40

6. 0×17 0   **7.** 28×6 168   **8.** 3×45 135   **9.** 21×10 210   **10.** 20×100
2000

EXERCISES

See the suggested assignment guide in the Teacher's Manual.

In Exercises 1–8, study each pattern. Then write the missing product(s).   (Table)

1. $9 \times 1 = 9$
$9 \times 0 = 0$
$9 \times (-1) = -9$
$9 \times (-2) = \underline{\ ?\ }$ −18

2. $2 \times 5 = 10$
$1 \times 5 = 5$
$0 \times 5 = 0$
$-1 \times 5 = \underline{\ ?\ }$ −5

3. $0 \times 7 = 0$
$-1 \times 7 = -7$
$-2 \times 7 = -14$
$-3 \times 7 = \underline{\ ?\ }$ −21

4. $6 \times 1 = 6$
$6 \times 0 = 0$
$6 \times (-1) = -6$
$6 \times (-2) = \underline{\ ?\ }$ −12

5. $12 \times 1 = 12$ **6.** $-1 \times 10 = -10$ **7.** $-2 \times 6 = -12$ **8.** $16 \times 1 = 16$
$\;12 \times 0 = 0$ $\;-2 \times 10 = -20$ $\;-3 \times 6 = -18$ $\;16 \times 0 = 0$
$\;12 \times (-1) = \underline{\;?\;}\,_{-12}$ $\;-3 \times 10 = \underline{\;?\;}\,_{-30}$ $\;-4 \times 6 = \underline{\;?\;}\,_{-24}$ $\;16 \times (-1) = \underline{\;?\;}\,^{-16}$
$\;12 \times (-2) = \underline{\;?\;}\,_{-24}$ $\;-4 \times 10 = \underline{\;?\;}\,_{-40}$ $\;-5 \times 6 = \underline{\;?\;}\,_{-30}$ $\;16 \times (-2) = \underline{\;?\;}\,_{-32}$

Multiply. (Example)

9. $5 \times (-2)$ –10 **10.** $7 \times (-1)$ –7   **11.** -3×12 –36 **12.** -10×10 –100 **13.** -7×0 0

14. $0 \times (-8)$ 0 **15.** -8×12 –96   **16.** -9×6 –54   **17.** $11 \times (-4)$ –44 **18.** $11 \times (-9)$ –99

19. -7×18 –126 **20.** -9×11 –99   **21.** -4×3 –12   **22.** -12×13 –156 **23.** $0 \times (-16)$ 0

24. -100×0 0 **25.** $6 \times (-5)$ –30   **26.** $4 \times (-21)$ –84 **27.** $8 \times (-10)$ –80 **28.** $20 \times (-9)$ –180

29. -16×3 –48 **30.** -18×5 –90   **31.** -100×7 –700 **32.** -1000×9 –9000 **33.** $8 \times (-5)$ –40

34. $7 \times (-13)$ –91 **35.** $41 \times (-7)$ –287 **36.** $83 \times (-9)$ –747 **37.** -25×4 –100 **38.** -75×2 –150

39. -12×12 –144 **40.** -13×13 –169 **41.** $72 \times (-5)$ –360 **42.** $83 \times (-6)$ –498 **43.** -9×19 –171

44. -6×90 –540 **45.** $100 \times (-31)$ –3100 **46.** $100 \times (-50)$ –5000 **47.** -238×0 0 **48.** -1×0 0

APPLICATIONS: Using Multiplication With Integers

49. $3 \times (-5) = -15$ 52. $2 \times (-200) = -400$

Use positive and negative integers to represent each situation by a multiplication problem. Then find the product.

49. Three penalties of 5 yards each

50. Five times a debt of $100 $5 \times (-100) = -500$

51. Six times a depth of 15 meters below sea level $6 \times (-15) = -90$

52. Twice a loss of 200 feet in altitude

53. Four times a temperature drop of 6 degrees $4 \times (-6) = -24$

54. Three times a loss of 4 yards in rushing $3 \times (-4) = -12$

55. Two debts of $78 each $2 \times (-78) = -156$

56. Twice a drop in temperature of one degree $2 \times (-1) = -2$

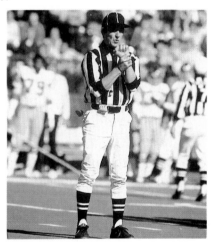

More Challenging Problems   More Challenging Problems are optional.

Find each answer.

57. $4 \times (-29) + 8 \times (-3)$ –140   **58.** $2 \times (-1) + 7 \times (-2)$ –16

59. $9 \times (-2) + 3 \times (-22)$ –84   **60.** $-7 \times 10 + (-5) \times 3$ –85

61. $-5 \times (-3 + 4)$ –5   **62.** $9 \times (-8 + 2)$ –54   **63.** $10 \times (-20 + 5)$ –150

64. $-2 \times (-8 + 9)$ –2   **65.** $-8 \times (-6 + 14)$ –64   **66.** $-9 \times (-2 + 5)$ –27

67. $12 \times (-21 + 19) + (-3)$ –27   **68.** $8 + (-3) \times (-6 + 12)$ –10

69. $-6 \times 3 + 4 + (-9)$ –23   **70.** $7 + (-6) + 3 \times (-1)$ –2

19-2 Multiplying Integers: Like Signs

See the Teacher's Manual for the objectives.

You know that the product of two positive integers is positive. Study the pattern in each column to find the product of two negative integers.

TABLE

Column 1

$2 \times (-5) = -10$
$1 \times (-5) = -5$
$0 \times (-5) = 0$
$-1 \times (-5) = 5$
$-2 \times (-5) = 10$
$-3 \times (-5) = 15$

The products are increasing by 5.

Column 2

$-10 \times 2 = -20$
$-10 \times 1 = -10$
$-10 \times 0 = 0$
$-10 \times -1 = 10$
$-10 \times -2 = 20$
$-10 \times -3 = 30$

The products are increasing by 10.

RULE *The product of two integers having like signs is positive.*

PROCEDURE To multiply two integers with like signs, multiply as with whole numbers. The product is a positive integer.

EXAMPLE Find each product.

a. $-3 \times (-8)$ **b.** $-9 \times (-1)$ **c.** 6×5

Solutions: **a.** $-3 \times (-8) = 24$ **b.** $-9 \times (-1) = 9$ **c.** $6 \times 5 = 30$

REVIEW OF RELATED SKILLS

You may wish to use these exercises before teaching the lesson.

Multiply.   (Pages 26–27, 32–33)

1. 9×8 72   **2.** 7×6 42   **3.** 5×4 20   **4.** 8×12 96   **5.** 21×7 147

6. 80×10 800   **7.** 19×5 95   **8.** 37×8 296   **9.** 46×5 230   **10.** 92×3 276

EXERCISES

See the suggested assignment guide in the Teacher's Manual.

In Exercises 1–8, study each pattern. Then write the missing product(s).   (Table)

1.
$2 \times (-6) = -12$
$1 \times (-6) = -6$
$0 \times (-6) = 0$
$-1 \times (-6) = 6$
$-2 \times (-6) = \underline{\quad}$? 12

2.
$-8 \times 2 = -16$
$-8 \times 1 = -8$
$-8 \times 0 = 0$
$-8 \times (-1) = 8$
$-8 \times (-2) = \underline{\quad}$? 16

3.
$-2 \times 2 = -4$
$-2 \times 1 = -2$
$-2 \times 0 = 0$
$-2 \times (-1) = 2$
$-2 \times (-2) = \underline{\quad}$? 4

4.
$2 \times (-3) = -6$
$1 \times (-3) = -3$
$0 \times (-3) = 0$
$-1 \times (-3) = 3$
$-2 \times (-3) = \underline{\quad}$? 6

5. $-9 \times \quad 2 = -18$ **6.** $2 \times (-7) = -14$ **7.** $2 \times (-6) = -12$ **8.** $-11 \times \quad 2 = -22$
$-9 \times \quad 1 = \quad -9 \qquad 1 \times (-7) = \quad -7 \qquad 1 \times (-6) = \quad -6 \qquad -11 \times \quad 1 = -11$
$-9 \times \quad 0 = \quad 0 \qquad 0 \times (-7) = \quad 0 \qquad 0 \times (-6) = \quad 0 \qquad -11 \times \quad 0 = \quad 0$
$-9 \times (-1) = \underline{\quad ?\quad}_{9} \quad -1 \times (-7) = \underline{\quad ?\quad}_{7} \quad -1 \times (-6) = \underline{\quad ?\quad}_{6} \quad -11 \times (-1) = \underline{^{11}\ ?\ }$
$-9 \times (-2) = \underline{\quad ?\quad}^{18} -2 \times (-7) = \underline{\quad ?\ }^{14} -2 \times (-6) = \underline{\quad ?\ }^{12} -11 \times (-2) = \underline{^{22}\ ?\ }$

Multiply. (Example)

9. $-5 \times (-3)$ ₁₅ **10.** 5×3 15 **11.** $-9 \times (-2)$ 18 **12.** 9×2 18

13. $-7 \times (-7)$ 49 **14.** 8×10 80 **15.** $-8 \times (-11)$ 88 **16.** $-6 \times (-6)$ 36

17. $-7 \times (-12)$ 84 **18.** $-8 \times (-16)$ 128 **19.** $-17 \times (-5)$ 85 **20.** $-17 \times (-7)$ 119

21. $-9 \times (-7)$ 63 **22.** $-5 \times (-12)$ 60 **23.** $-11 \times (-11)$ 121 **24.** $-2 \times (-21)$ 42

25. $-4 \times (-2)$ 8 **26.** $-3 \times (-10)$ 30 **27.** $-10 \times (-21)$ 210 **28.** $-4 \times (-32)$ 128

29. $-43 \times (-9)$ 387 **30.** $-6 \times (-7)$ 42 **31.** $-4 \times (-9)$ 36 **32.** $-3 \times (-12)$ 36

33. $-18 \times (-9)$ 162 **34.** $-95 \times (-74)$ 7030 **35.** $-32 \times (-41)$ 1312 **36.** $-63 \times (-27)$ 1701

37. $-35 \times (-15)$ 525 **38.** $-32 \times (-100)$ 3200 **39.** -10×-72 720 **40.** $-45 \times (-22)$ 990

41. $-8 \times (-45)$ 360 **42.** $-14 \times (-11)$ 154 **43.** 18×36 648 **44.** 40×16 640

45. $-16 \times (-200)$ 3200 **46.** $-18 \times (-100)$ 1800 **47.** $-13 \times (-27)$ 351 **48.** $-202 \times (-68)$ 13736

More Challenging Problems More Challenging Problems are optional.

Find each answer.

EXAMPLE: $(-9)^2 = -9 \times (-9) = 81$

49. $(-2)^2$ 4 **50.** $(-3)^2$ 9 **51.** $(-8)^2$ 64 **52.** $(-12)^2$ 144 **53.** $(-20)^2$ 400

54. $(-1.1)^2$ 1.21 **55.** $(-1.2)^2$ 1.44 **56.** $(-0.4)^2$ 0.16 **57.** $(-0.1)^2$ 0.01 **58.** $(-1.5)^2$ 2.25

59. $(-1)^2 + 12 \times (-13 + 10)$ −35

60. $-8 \times (-8 + 2) + (-2)^2$ 52

61. $(-9 + 6) \times (-12)$ 36

62. $(-21 + 7) \times (-3)$ 42

63. $(-1)^2 \times (-1) \times (-1)$ 1

64. $(-12 + 10) \times (-11)$ 22

65. $(-2)^2 \times (-2)^2$ 16

66. $-5 \times (-5) \times (-5)$ 125

CHECKING MULTIPLICATION

Use a calculator to check each answer. Be sure to check whether the product is a positive or negative number.

1. $324 \times (-13) = 3888$ −4212

2. $-64 \times 1234 = -78976$

3. $-314 \times (-416) = -130624$ 130624

4. $-825 \times (-917) = -756525$ 756525

5. $-2879 \times 175 = -503822$ −503825

6. $308 \times (-3089) = -941412$

7. $-21.9 \times (-21.9) = -479.61$ 479.61

8. $-12.5 \times 1.25 = 15.625$ −15.625

9. $8.10 \times 4.06 = 32.886$

10. $24.8 \times (-12.4) = -317.52$ −307.52

19-3 Dividing Integers See the Teacher's Manual for the objectives.

A multiplication problem has two related division problems.

Multiplication	Related Division
$4 \times 8 = 32$	$32 \div 8 = 4$ and $32 \div 4 = 8$

You can use this fact to find the pattern for dividing a positive integer by a negative integer.

Multiplication	Related Division
$-3 \times (-8) = 24$	$24 \div (-3) = -8$ and $24 \div (-8) = -3$
$-2 \times (-7) = 14$	$14 \div (-2) = -7$ and $14 \div (-7) = -2$

RULE *The quotient of a positive integer and a negative integer is negative.*

Now study these patterns.

Multiplication	Related Division
$-5 \times 3 = -15$	$-15 \div (-5) = 3$ and $-15 \div 3 = -5$
$-9 \times 6 = -54$	$-54 \div (-6) = 9$ and $-54 \div 9 = -6$

RULE *The quotient of two negative integers is positive.*

RULE *The quotient of a negative integer and a positive integer is negative.*

You can use these patterns to divide integers.

PROCEDURE To divide two integers:

1. Divide as with whole numbers.

2. **a.** When the two integers have like signs, the quotient is positive.

   b. When the two integers have unlike signs, the quotient is negative.

EXAMPLE Find each quotient.

a. $-36 \div (-4)$ **b.** $-27 \div 9$ **c.** $12 \div (-2)$

Solutions: **a.** $-36 \div (-4) = 9$ ◀ *Procedure 2a*   **b.** $-27 \div 9 = -3$ ◀ *Procedure 2b*

c. $12 \div (-2) = -6$ ◀ *Procedure 2b*

Divide.   (Pages 50–51, 54–55)

1. $12 \div 3$ 4   **2.** $16 \div 2$ 8   **3.** $81 \div 9$ 9   **4.** $72 \div 12$ 6   **5.** $7\overline{)567}$ 81

6. $5\overline{)215}$ 43   **7.** $9\overline{)756}$ 84   **8.** $8\overline{)744}$ 93   **9.** $6\overline{)3168}$ 528   **10.** $4\overline{)1900}$ 475

Complete.   (Pages 54–55)

11. $12 \times 13 = 156$
$156 \div 12 = \underline{\ ?\ }$ 13
$156 \div 13 = \underline{\ ?\ }$ 12

12. $14 \times 15 = 210$
$210 \div 14 = \underline{\ ?\ }$ 15
$210 \div 15 = \underline{\ ?\ }$ 14

13. $21 \times 18 = 378$
$378 \div 21 = \underline{\ ?\ }$ 18
$378 \div 18 = \underline{\ ?\ }$ 21

EXERCISES
See the suggested assignment guide in the Teacher's Manual.

Complete.   (Table)

1. $-7 \times (-9) = 63$
$63 \div (-7) = \underline{\ ?\ }$ −9
$63 \div (-9) = \underline{\ ?\ }$ −7

2. $-18 \times (-5) = 90$
$90 \div (-18) = \underline{\ ?\ }$ −5
$90 \div (-5) = \underline{\ ?\ }$ −18

3. $-11 \times 12 = -132$
$-132 \div (-11) = \underline{\ ?\ }$ 12
$-132 \div 12 = \underline{\ ?\ }$ −11

Divide.   (Example)

4. $-36 \div (-12)$ 3   **5.** $-30 \div (-6)$ 5   **6.** $-63 \div (-9)$ 7   **7.** $-35 \div (-5)$ 7

8. $21 \div (-7)$ −3   **9.** $81 \div (-9)$ −9   **10.** $49 \div (-7)$ −7   **11.** $36 \div (-4)$ −9

12. $-39 \div 13$ −3   **13.** $-45 \div 15$ −3   **14.** $-138 \div 6$ −23   **15.** $-154 \div 77$ −2

16. $-100 \div 5$ −20   **17.** $-200 \div 40$ −5   **18.** $-300 \div (-75)$ 4   **19.** $-200 \div (-8)$ 25

20. $-756 \div (-28)$ 27   **21.** $-442 \div (-17)$ 26   **22.** $72 \div (-12)$ −6   **23.** $55 \div (-11)$ −5

24. $-98 \div 14$ −7   **25.** $-133 \div 19$ −7   **26.** $504 \div (-14)$ −36   **27.** $756 \div (-28)$ −27

28. $-345 \div (-15)$ 23   **29.** $-176 \div (-11)$ 16   **30.** $-902 \div 82$ −11   **31.** $-455 \div 13$ −35

Calculator exercises are optional.

CHECKING DIVISION

Use a calculator to check each answer. Be sure to check whether the quotient is a positive or negative number.

1. $-4536 \div (-21) = -216$

2. $795 \div (-53) = -15$

3. $-4992 \div 48 = -104$

4. $-2489 \div (-19) = -131$ 131

5. $56088 \div (-123) = -455$ −456

6. $-18334 \div (-89) = -206$ 206

7. $-30.12 \div (-1.2) = -25.1$ 25.1

8. $304.85 \div (-0.13) = -234.5$ −2345

9. $136.17 \div (-0.17) = 8.01$ −801

10. $-2044.5 \div (-2.9) = 7050$ 705

19-4 Rational Numbers See the Teacher's Manual for the objectives.

Numbers such as these are **positive rational numbers.**

$$\frac{1}{4} \quad 1 \quad \frac{7}{3} \quad 3\frac{2}{3} \quad 15$$

Numbers such as these are **negative rational numbers.**

$$-\frac{1}{5} \quad -1 \quad -\frac{9}{5} \quad -8\frac{1}{6} \quad -27$$

Any rational number can be written as a fraction.

EXAMPLE 1 Write a fraction for each rational number.

    a. 9   **b.** $-6\frac{1}{5}$ **c.** 0

Solutions: **a.** $9 = \frac{9}{1}$ **b.** $-6\frac{1}{5} = -\frac{31}{5}$ **c.** $0 = \frac{0}{8}$

After completing Example 1, you may wish to have students do some or all of Exercises 1-32.

In c of Example 1, you could have written any number except 0 in the denominator. Thus,

$$0 = \frac{0}{8} = \frac{0}{11} = \frac{0}{25} = \frac{0}{100}, \text{ and so on.}$$

You can show the rational numbers on a number line.

EXAMPLE 2 Write the rational number represented by each letter.

Solutions: A: $\frac{1}{2}$ B: $2\frac{1}{4}$ C: $-1\frac{1}{2}$ D: $-1\frac{3}{4}$

You can use the number line to arrange numbers in order. A number is greater than a second number if it is to the right of the second number on the number line. Thus, the rational numbers in Example 2 arranged in order from least to greatest are

$$-1\frac{3}{4} \quad -1\frac{1}{2} \quad \frac{1}{2} \quad 2\frac{1}{4}.$$

REVIEW OF RELATED SKILLS   You may wish to use these exercises before teaching the lesson.

Write a fraction for each mixed number.   (Pages 208–209)

1. $2\frac{1}{5}$ $\frac{11}{5}$ **2.** $5\frac{2}{3}$ $\frac{17}{3}$ **3.** $8\frac{7}{9}$ $\frac{79}{9}$ **4.** $3\frac{1}{6}$ $\frac{19}{6}$ **5.** $10\frac{1}{2}$ $\frac{21}{2}$ **6.** $1\frac{11}{12}$ $\frac{23}{12}$

Write the integer represented by each letter. Use the number line.
(Pages 388–389)

7. A ⁹ **8.** B ⁻³ **9.** C ⁻¹ **10.** D ¹ **11.** E ⁷ **12.** F ⁵

EXERCISES
See the suggested assignment guide in the Teacher's Manual.

Write a fraction for each rational number. (Example 1) $-\frac{43}{6}$

1. 8 $\frac{8}{1}$ **2.** 12 $\frac{12}{1}$ **3.** -10 $-\frac{10}{1}$ **4.** -9 $-\frac{9}{1}$ **5.** $2\frac{1}{4}$ $\frac{9}{4}$ **6.** $1\frac{1}{3}$ $\frac{4}{3}$ **7.** $-8\frac{1}{5}$ $-\frac{41}{5}$ **8.** $-7\frac{1}{6}$

9. -7 $-\frac{7}{1}$ **10.** -5 $-\frac{5}{1}$ **11.** $-3\frac{1}{3}$ $-\frac{10}{3}$ **12.** $-1\frac{1}{12}$ $-\frac{13}{12}$ **13.** 17 $\frac{17}{1}$ **14.** 52 $\frac{52}{1}$ **15.** 0 $\frac{0}{1}$ **16.** 26 $\frac{26}{1}$

17. $-1\frac{4}{5}$ $-\frac{9}{5}$ **18.** $-3\frac{1}{8}$ $-\frac{25}{8}$ **19.** -6 $-\frac{6}{1}$ **20.** -9 $-\frac{9}{1}$ **21.** $5\frac{1}{10}$ $\frac{51}{10}$ **22.** $9\frac{5}{12}$ $\frac{113}{12}$ **23.** $-7\frac{1}{2}$ $-\frac{15}{2}$ **24.** $-2\frac{4}{5}$ $-\frac{14}{5}$

25. 1 $\frac{1}{1}$ **26.** $7\frac{1}{2}$ $\frac{15}{2}$ **27.** $8\frac{1}{6}$ $\frac{49}{6}$ **28.** $-3\frac{1}{4}$ $-\frac{13}{4}$ **29.** 3 $\frac{3}{1}$ **30.** 8 $\frac{8}{1}$ **31.** $-2\frac{4}{5}$ $-\frac{14}{5}$ **32.** $-1\frac{3}{8}$ $-\frac{11}{8}$

Write the rational number represented by each letter. (Example 2)

33. A $-\frac{1}{2}$ **34.** B $1\frac{1}{2}$ **35.** C -4 **36.** D $-5\frac{1}{2}$ **37.** E $-8\frac{1}{2}$ **38.** F 0

39. Arrange the rational numbers in Exercises 33–38 in order from least to greatest. $-8\frac{1}{2}, -5\frac{1}{2}, -4, -\frac{1}{2}, 0, 1\frac{1}{2}$

Write the rational number represented by each letter.

40. G $-2\frac{1}{2}$ **41.** K $-2\frac{3}{4}$ **42.** M $\frac{1}{4}$ **43.** H $-\frac{1}{2}$ **44.** P $-\frac{1}{4}$ **45.** R $-\frac{3}{4}$

46. Arrange the rational numbers in Exercises 40–45 in order from least to greatest. $-2\frac{3}{4}, -2\frac{1}{2}, -\frac{3}{4}, -\frac{1}{2}, -\frac{1}{4}, \frac{1}{4}$

For Exercises 47–54, arrange these numbers in order. Begin with the least.   **50.** $-3\frac{1}{5}, -2\frac{3}{4}, -\frac{2}{3}, 0, \frac{2}{3}, 1\frac{1}{2}$ **52.** $-2, -1, -\frac{7}{8}, \frac{8}{9}, \frac{15}{16}, 1$ $-8, -7\frac{1}{2}, -\frac{2}{5}, 0, 2, 4\frac{1}{3}$

47. $1; \frac{1}{4}; -2\frac{1}{5}; 3\frac{1}{3}; -5\frac{1}{5}; -\frac{1}{4}$ $-5\frac{1}{5}, -2\frac{1}{5}, -\frac{1}{4}, \frac{1}{4}, 1, 3\frac{1}{3}$ **48.** $-8; 0; 4\frac{1}{3}; -7\frac{1}{2}; -\frac{2}{5}; 2$

49. $2; -\frac{3}{4}; 1; -\frac{2}{3}; \frac{4}{5}; -1\frac{1}{2}$ $-1\frac{1}{2}, -\frac{3}{4}, -\frac{2}{3}, \frac{4}{5}, 1, 2$ **50.** $0; -\frac{2}{3}; 1\frac{1}{2}; -2\frac{3}{4}; \frac{2}{3}; -3\frac{1}{5}$

51. $2\frac{1}{4}; -1\frac{5}{6}; -1\frac{7}{8}; 1\frac{1}{2}; 0; -\frac{11}{16}$ $-1\frac{7}{8}, -1\frac{5}{6}, -\frac{11}{16}, 0,$ **52.** $-\frac{7}{8}; 1; -2; \frac{15}{16}; -1; \frac{8}{9}$

53. $-1\frac{1}{8}; -3; -2\frac{1}{2}; -1; -\frac{1}{4}, -2\frac{7}{8}$ $1\frac{1}{2}, 2\frac{1}{4}$ **54.** $\frac{1}{5}; 0; -\frac{1}{4}; 1\frac{1}{2}; -2\frac{7}{10}; -5$ $-5, -2\frac{7}{10}, -\frac{1}{4}, 0, \frac{1}{5}, 1\frac{1}{2}$

$-3, -2\frac{7}{8}, -2\frac{1}{2}, -1\frac{1}{8}, -1, -\frac{1}{4}$

INTEGERS: MULTIPLICATION/DIVISION **413**

Problem Solving and Applications
Conserving Energy

See the Teacher's Manual for the objectives.
This lesson combines the technique of using a formula to solve
problems with the use of negative numbers.

In warm weather, the temperature outside is
higher than the temperature inside. The
following formula and the table at the right can
be used to estimate the rate at which heat
passes from the outside through the walls or
windows of a house. This is called **heat
transfer**. Heat transfer is measured in Btu's
per hour.

Surface	Value of U
Concrete, 6 inches thick	0.58
Glass, single pane	1.13
Brick, 8 inches thick	0.41
Wood, 2 inches thick	0.43

Heat transfer $= a \times U(i - o)$

a: surface area in square feet
U: heat transfer number from the table
i: inside temperature in °F
o: outside temperature in °F

EXAMPLE Estimate the rate at which heat is passing through a concrete wall
(6 inches thick) when the inside temperature is 72°F and the outside
temperature is 90°F. The area of the wall is 200 square feet.

Solution: Replace a with 200, U with 0.58 (see the table), i with 72, and a
with 90.

Heat transfer $= a \times U(i - o)$
Heat transfer $= 200 \times 0.58(72 - 90)$
Heat transfer $= 200 \times 0.58(-18)$ ◀ **Use paper and pencil or
use a calculator.**
Heat transfer $= 116 \times -18$
Heat transfer $= -2088$ ◀ **The negative number means
that heat is lost.**

Thus, heat is being lost at the rate of **2088 Btu's per hour.**

Exercises

*In Exercises 1–4, use the heat transfer formula and the table
above to find the rate of heat transfer.*

1. Surface: glass
   Area: 40 square feet loss of 994.4 Btu's per hour
   Temperature: $i = 70°F$; $o = 92°F$

2. Surface: brick
   Area: 300 square feet loss of 1845 Btu's per hour
   Temperature: $i = 75°F$; $o = 90°F$

3. Surface: wood
   Area: 400 square feet loss of 3440 Btu's per hour
   Temperature: $i = 73°F$; $o = 93°F$

4. Surface: concrete
   Area: 350 square feet loss of 3045 Btu's per hour
   Temperature: $i = 72°F$; $o = 87°F$

Application

BUSINESS   career

Owning shares of stock means that you own part of a business or corporation.

The table at the right shows the net change (abbreviated: Net Chg) for six stocks at the end of the day's trading on April 19. **Net change** is the difference between the final sale price of a stock and the final sale price on the previous day. Net change is given in fractions of a dollar.

Stock	Net Chg
Es Kod	$+\frac{5}{8}$
Eaton	$-\frac{1}{4}$
Edis Br	$+\frac{3}{4}$
Edcon Cp	$-\frac{1}{8}$
Eng MC	$+\frac{1}{2}$
Epsor	-1

This lesson combines the concept of positive and negative numbers with the skills presented in Sections 19-1 and 19-2.

EXAMPLE Give the meaning of each net change.

　　　　a. $+\frac{1}{4}$　　　　　b. $-\frac{1}{8}$

Solution:　a. $+\frac{1}{4}$ means up $\frac{1}{4}$ of a dollar per share.

$$4\overline{)1.00} \quad \frac{.25}{} = \textbf{0.25}$$

Thus, $+\frac{1}{4}$ means the price of the stock **rose $0.25** per share.

b. $-\frac{1}{8}$ means down $\frac{1}{8}$ of a dollar per share.

$$8\overline{)1.000} \quad \frac{.125}{} = \textbf{0.125}$$

Thus, $-\frac{1}{8}$ means the price of the stock **fell $0.125** per share.

EXERCISES   Note that Exercises 1-4 are nonverbal.

For Exercises 1–4, complete the table. Use the table of stocks above.

Stock	Net Chg	Meaning		Stock	Net Chg	Meaning
1. Eng MC	$?+\frac{1}{2}$	rose ? $0.50 per share ?	**3.** Edis Br	$?+\frac{3}{4}$	? rose $0.75 per share
2. Eaton	$?-\frac{1}{4}$	share ? fell $0.25 per share	**4.** Edcon Cp.	$?-\frac{1}{8}$	? fell $0.125 per share

5. Jaime Garcia owns 100 shares of Edcon Cp. How much more or less were these 100 shares worth at the end of the trading day on April 19? (HINT: $100 \times (-\frac{1}{8}) = \underline{?}$)
   $12.50 less

6. Karen Lightfoot owns 60 shares of Edis Br. How much more or less were these 60 shares worth at the end of the trading day on April 19?
   $45.00 more

Chapter Review

These exercises review the vocabulary, skills, and applications presented in the chapter as a preparation for the chapter test.

Part 1: Vocabulary

For Exercises 1–4, choose from the box at the right the word(s) that completes each statement.

<table>
<tr><td>zero</td></tr>
<tr><td>negative</td></tr>
<tr><td>fraction</td></tr>
<tr><td>positive</td></tr>
<tr><td>one</td></tr>
</table>

1. The product of two integers having unlike signs is __?__. (Page 406) negative

2. When you multiply by zero, the product is __?__. (Page 406) zero

3. The quotient of two negative integers is __?__. (Page 410) positive

4. Any rational number can be written as a __?__. (Page 412) fraction

Part 2: Skills

Multiply. (Pages 406–407)

5. -4×5 −20
6. -9×8 −72
7. $7 \times (-6)$ −42
8. $5 \times (-9)$ −45

9. -8×4 −32
10. $11 \times (-12)$ −132
11. -10×6 −60
12. -4×11 −44

13. $6 \times (-15)$ −90
14. -9×7 −63
15. -14×3 −42
16. $21 \times (-4)$ −84

17. -5×16 −80
18. -8×25 −200
19. -12×7 −84
20. $26 \times (-2)$ −52

21. -48×4 −192
22. $6 \times (-19)$ −114
23. $5 \times (-21)$ −105
24. $8 \times (-17)$ −136

25. $24 \times (-3)$ −72
26. -10×9 −90
27. $100 \times (-3)$ −300
28. 0×6 0

29. $14 \times (-1000)$ −14000
30. -17×22 −374
31. $18 \times (-13)$ −234
32. $12 \times (-10)$ −120

(Pages 408–409)

33. 8×6 48
34. 9×5 45
35. 12×6 72
36. 7×5 35

37. $-3 \times (-7)$ 21
38. $-5 \times (-4)$ 20
39. $-3 \times (-6)$ 18
40. $-2 \times (-9)$ 18

41. $-4 \times (-8)$ 32
42. $-7 \times (-2)$ 14
43. $-12 \times (-9)$ 108
44. $-8 \times (-13)$ 104

45. $-9 \times (-10)$ 90
46. $-6 \times (-21)$ 126
47. $-8 \times (-15)$ 120
48. $-7 \times (-14)$ 98

49. $-23 \times (-9)$ 207
50. $-31 \times (-4)$ 124
51. $-46 \times (-8)$ 368
52. $-20 \times (-13)$ 260

53. $-14 \times (-25)$ 350
54. $-16 \times (-18)$ 288
55. $-36 \times (-12)$ 432
56. $-10 \times (-21)$ 210

57. $-46 \times (-10)$ 460
58. $-12 \times (-11)$ 132
59. $-10 \times (-34)$ 340
60. $-15 \times (-23)$ 345

Divide. (Pages 410–411)

61. $-25 \div 5$ −5
62. $36 \div (-9)$ −4
63. $-60 \div 12$ −5
64. $-48 \div (-16)$ 3

65. $320 \div (-10)$ −32
66. $-400 \div (-20)$ 20
67. $65 \div (-13)$ −5
68. $-284 \div 4$ −71

69. $-600 \div (-25)$ 24
70. $624 \div (-12)$ −52
71. $-957 \div (-3)$ 319
72. $-338 \div 13$ −26

73. $768 \div (-12)$ −64
74. $-720 \div 15$ −48
75. $460 \div (-10)$ −46
76. $-979 \div (-11)$ 89

77. $-252 \div 21$ −12
78. $-736 \div (-16)$ 46
79. $-588 \div (-12)$ 49
80. $868 \div (-14)$ −62

81. $-672 \div (-21)$ 32
82. $368 \div (-23)$ −16
83. $-475 \div 25$ −19
84. $-456 \div (-19)$ 24

85. $-493 \div (-17)$ 29
86. $-580 \div 10$ −58
87. $-570 \div (-15)$ 38
88. $-810 \div (-18)$ 45

Write a fraction for each rational number. (Pages 412–413)

89. 4 $\frac{4}{1}$ **90.** 12 $\frac{12}{1}$ **91.** -8 $-\frac{8}{1}$ **92.** -21 $-\frac{21}{1}$ **93.** $-3\frac{1}{2}$ $-\frac{7}{2}$ **94.** $4\frac{1}{6}$ $\frac{25}{6}$

95. $3\frac{5}{6}$ $\frac{23}{6}$ **96.** $-7\frac{1}{4}$ $-\frac{29}{4}$ **97.** $6\frac{3}{8}$ $\frac{51}{8}$ **98.** $1\frac{1}{2}$ $\frac{3}{2}$ **99.** $-9\frac{4}{5}$ $-\frac{49}{5}$ **100.** $-7\frac{2}{3}$ $-\frac{23}{3}$

101. $5\frac{7}{10}$ $\frac{57}{10}$ **102.** -17 $-\frac{17}{1}$ **103.** $2\frac{3}{4}$ $\frac{11}{4}$ **104.** $-3\frac{3}{5}$ $-\frac{18}{5}$ **105.** 26 $\frac{26}{1}$ **106.** $6\frac{7}{8}$ $\frac{55}{8}$

107. 30 $\frac{30}{1}$ **108.** $6\frac{1}{4}$ $\frac{25}{4}$ **109.** $-8\frac{1}{8}$ $-\frac{65}{8}$ **110.** -5 $-\frac{5}{1}$ **111.** $-4\frac{5}{9}$ $-\frac{41}{9}$ **112.** $-9\frac{1}{2}$ $-\frac{19}{2}$

Write the rational number represented by each letter.
(Pages 412–413)

113. A $-1\frac{1}{2}$ **114.** B $1\frac{1}{2}$ **115.** C $-2\frac{3}{4}$ **116.** D $\frac{3}{4}$ **117.** E $-5\frac{1}{2}$ **118.** F $-3\frac{1}{4}$

119. Arrange the rational numbers in Exercises 113–118 in order from least to greatest. (Pages 412–413) $-5\frac{1}{2}, -3\frac{1}{4}, -2\frac{3}{4}, -1\frac{1}{2}, \frac{3}{4}, 1\frac{1}{2}$

Write the rational number represented by each letter.
(Pages 412–413)

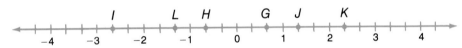

120. G $\frac{2}{3}$ **121.** H $-\frac{2}{3}$ **122.** I $-2\frac{2}{3}$ **123.** J $1\frac{1}{3}$ **124.** K $2\frac{1}{3}$ **125.** L $-1\frac{1}{3}$

126. Arrange the rational numbers in Exercises 120–125 in order from least to greatest. (Pages 412–413) $-2\frac{2}{3}, -1\frac{1}{3}, -\frac{2}{3}, \frac{2}{3}, 1\frac{1}{3}, 2\frac{1}{3}$

For Exercises 131–142, arrange these numbers in order. Begin with the least. (Pages 412–413)

127. $6\frac{1}{2}; -3\frac{1}{4}; 3\frac{1}{5}; 1; -2\frac{1}{2}; 0$ $-3\frac{1}{4}, -2\frac{1}{2}, 0, 1, 3\frac{1}{5}, 6\frac{1}{2}$ **128.** $\frac{1}{2}; -\frac{1}{2}; 1; -2; \frac{1}{4}; -\frac{1}{4}$ $-2, -\frac{1}{2}, -\frac{1}{4}, \frac{1}{4}, \frac{1}{2}, 1$

129. $-3; -4\frac{1}{2}; 2; 4\frac{1}{4}; 0; -1$ $-4\frac{1}{2}, -3, -1, 0, 2, 4\frac{1}{4}$ **130.** $\frac{6}{7}; -\frac{5}{7}; \frac{5}{6}; -\frac{5}{6}; -\frac{6}{7}; \frac{5}{7}$ $-\frac{6}{7}, -\frac{5}{6}, -\frac{5}{7}, \frac{5}{7}, \frac{5}{6}, \frac{6}{7}$

131. $-2\frac{3}{8}; -3\frac{3}{7}; 4\frac{1}{3}; 2; -\frac{7}{16}; -1$ See below   **132.** $-3\frac{1}{2}; -4\frac{2}{3}; 4; -6; 0; \frac{1}{2}$ $-6, -4\frac{2}{3}, -3\frac{1}{2}, 0, \frac{1}{2}, 4$

133. $-1\frac{1}{9}; -4\frac{2}{3}; 5\frac{1}{2}; -3; 6; 0$ $-4\frac{2}{3}, -3, -1\frac{1}{9}, 0, 5\frac{1}{2}, 6$ **134.** $-2\frac{1}{2}; 4\frac{1}{5}; -3; 1; 5\frac{1}{6}; -3\frac{1}{4}$ $-3\frac{1}{4}, -3, -2\frac{1}{2}, 1, 4\frac{1}{5}, 5\frac{1}{6}$

131. $-3\frac{3}{7}, -2\frac{3}{8}, -1, -\frac{7}{16}, 2, 4\frac{1}{3}$

Part 3: Applications

Use positive and negative integers to represent each situation by a multiplication problem. Then find the product. (Pages 406–407) $4 \times (-6) = -24$

135. Two penalties of 10 yards each   See below   **136.** Four times a loss of 6 pounds

137. Three times a depth of 200 feet below sea level $3 \times (-200) = -600$ **138.** Seven times a loss of 3 yards rushing $7 \times (-3) = -21$

139. Twice a temperature drop of 5 degrees $2 \times (-5) = -10$ **140.** Six times a debt of \$50 $6 \times (-50) = -300$

135. $2 \times (-10) = -20$

Chapter Test

The Teacher's Resource Book contains two forms of each chapter test.

Multiply.

1. 2×9 ₁₈ **2.** $-5 \times (-10)$ ₅₀ **3.** $6 \times (-4)$ ₋₂₄ **4.** -8×9 ₋₇₂ **5.** $-12 \times (-7)$ ⁸⁴

6. 10×15 ₁₅₀ **7.** -13×21 ₋₂₇₃ **8.** $14 \times (-17)$ ₋₂₃₈ **9.** -16×21 ₋₃₃₆ **10.** $11 \times (-13)$ ₋₁₄₃

Divide.

11. $-48 \div (-6)$ ₈ **12.** $-96 \div 6$ ₋₁₆ **13.** $80 \div (-16)$ ₋₅ **14.** $-24 \div (-12)$ ²

15. $-735 \div 15$ ₋₄₉ **16.** $-351 \div (-13)$ ₂₇ **17.** $391 \div (-23)$ ₋₁₇ **18.** $510 \div (-17)$ ₋₃₀

Write a fraction for each rational number.

19. -3 $-\frac{3}{1}$ **20.** $4\frac{1}{3}$ $\frac{13}{3}$ **21.** $5\frac{1}{2}$ $\frac{11}{2}$ **22.** $-1\frac{1}{4}$ $-\frac{5}{4}$ **23.** 14 $\frac{14}{1}$ **24.** $-6\frac{1}{2}$ $-\frac{13}{2}$

Write the rational number represented by each letter.

25. A $2\frac{1}{2}$ **26.** B $-\frac{1}{2}$ **27.** C $-4\frac{1}{2}$ **28.** D $\frac{3}{4}$ **29.** E $3\frac{1}{2}$ **30.** F $-1\frac{1}{2}$

31. Arrange the rational numbers in Exercises 25–30 in order from least to greatest. $-4\frac{1}{2}; -1\frac{1}{2}; -\frac{1}{2}; \frac{3}{4}; 2\frac{1}{2}; 3\frac{1}{2}$

For Exercises 32–33, use positive and negative integers to represent each situation by a multiplication problem. Then find the product.

32. Five times a debt of $25

$5 \times (-25) = -125$

33. Twice a temperature drop of 4 degrees $2 \times (-4) = -8$

Additional Practice

You may wish to use some or all of these exercises depending on how well students performed on the formal chapter test.

1. -7×28 _−196_ **2.** $9 \times (-28)$ _−252_ **3.** -16×8 _−128_ **4.** $46 \times (-3)$ _−138_

5. $6 \times (-36)$ _−216_ **6.** -10×31 _−310_ **7.** $54 \times (-2)$ _−108_ **8.** -17×3 _−51_

9. -100×4 _−400_ **10.** $68 \times (-8)$ _−544_ **11.** -8×48 _−384_ **12.** -100×46 _−4600_

13. $71 \times (-3)$ _−213_ **14.** -10×81 _−810_ **15.** -1000×16 _−16000_ **16.** -9×34 _−306_

(Pages 408–409)

17. $-10 \times (-16)$ _160_ **18.** $-100 \times (-21)$ _2100_ **19.** $-100 \times (-46)$ _4600_ **20.** $-10 \times (-92)$ _920_

21. $-21 \times (-21)$ _441_ **22.** $-36 \times (-12)$ _432_ **23.** $-46 \times (-25)$ _1150_ **24.** $-72 \times (-81)$ _5832_

25. $-38 \times (-42)$ _1596_ **26.** $-41 \times (-27)$ _1107_ **27.** $-53 \times (-16)$ _848_ **28.** $-87 \times (-29)$ _2523_

Divide.   (Pages 410–411)

29. $-345 \div 23$ _−15_ **30.** $765 \div (-17)$ _−45_ **31.** $957 \div (-11)$ _−87_ **32.** $-352 \div (-16)$ _22_

33. $-510 \div (-15)$ _34_ **34.** $-672 \div 16$ _−42_ **35.** $882 \div (-14)$ _−63_ **36.** $-860 \div (-43)$ _20_

37. $-714 \div 51$ _−14_ **38.** $-832 \div (-26)$ _32_ **39.** $-612 \div 18$ _−34_ **40.** $483 \div (-21)$ _−23_

41. $-726 \div (-22)$ _33_ **42.** $-693 \div 33$ _−21_ **43.** $874 \div (-1)$ _−874_ **44.** $-684 \div 36$ _−19_

Write a fraction for each rational number.   (Pages 412–413)

45. 7 _$\frac{7}{1}$_ **46.** 15 _$\frac{15}{1}$_ **47.** -9 _$-\frac{9}{1}$_ **48.** -36 _$-\frac{36}{1}$_ **49.** $-2\frac{1}{8}$ _$-\frac{17}{8}$_ **50.** $-7\frac{1}{6}$ _$-\frac{43}{6}$_

51. $3\frac{1}{2}$ _$\frac{7}{2}$_ **52.** $-5\frac{3}{5}$ _$-\frac{28}{5}$_ **53.** -32 _$-\frac{32}{1}$_ **54.** 42 _$\frac{42}{1}$_ **55.** $-17\frac{2}{5}$ _$-\frac{87}{5}$_ **56.** $-18\frac{1}{9}$ _$-\frac{163}{9}$_

57. $-4\frac{1}{7}$ _$-\frac{29}{7}$_ **58.** $4\frac{2}{3}$ _$\frac{14}{3}$_ **59.** $-6\frac{3}{8}$ _$-\frac{51}{8}$_ **60.** -48 _$-\frac{48}{1}$_ **61.** 74 _$\frac{74}{1}$_ **62.** -160 _$-\frac{160}{1}$_

Write the rational number represented by each letter.   (Pages 412–413)

63. A _$-3\frac{2}{3}$_ **64.** B _$\frac{1}{3}$_ **65.** C _$1\frac{2}{3}$_ **66.** D _$-\frac{2}{3}$_ **67.** E _$-2\frac{2}{3}$_ **68.** F _$2\frac{1}{3}$_

69. Arrange the rational numbers in Exercises 63–68 in order form least to greatest. (Pages 412–413) _$-3\frac{2}{3}; -2\frac{2}{3}; -\frac{2}{3}; \frac{1}{3}; 1\frac{2}{3}; 2\frac{1}{3}$_

Applications

Use positive and negative integers to represent each situation by a multiplication problem. Then find the product.   (Page 407)

70. Three times a loss of 4 pounds _$3 \times (-4) = -12$_

71. Twice a debt of $15.00 _$2 \times (-15) = -30$_

72. Five penalties of 15 yards each _See below_

73. Six times a loss of $20.00 _$6 \times (-20) = -120$_

74. Six times a gain of $25 _$6 \times 25 = 150$_

75. Eight times a loss of 3 meters _$8 \times (-3) = -24$_

72. $5 \times (-15) = -75$

REVIEW OF RELATED SKILLS FOR CHAPTER 20

We suggest that some or all of this page be reviewed before proceeding with the chapter.

Solve and check.   (Pages 248–249)

1. $n + 8 = 14$ 6
2. $n + 9 = 21$ 12
3. $n + 3 = 46$ 43
4. $n + 7 = 29$ 22

5. $n + 12 = 38$ 26
6. $n + 14 = 42$ 28
7. $n + 16 = 54$ 38
8. $n + 20 = 31$ 11

9. $n - 9 = 40$ 49
10. $n - 5 = 63$ 68
11. $n - 8 = 42$ 50
12. $n - 10 = 21$ 31

13. $n - 13 = 82$ 95
14. $n - 14 = 29$ 43
15. $n - 17 = 37$ 54
16. $n - 24 = 46$ 70

(Pages 252–253)

17. $3n = 51$ 17
18. $4n = 76$ 19
19. $5n = 80$ 16
20. $8n = 96$ 12

21. $12n = 144$ 12
22. $13n = 39$ 3
23. $25n = 400$ 16
24. $30n = 960$ 32

25. $\frac{n}{4} = 16$ 64
26. $\frac{n}{5} = 90$ 450
27. $\frac{n}{8} = 32$ 256
28. $\frac{n}{7} = 41$ 287

29. $\frac{n}{10} = 18$ 180
30. $\frac{n}{12} = 17$ 204
31. $\frac{n}{21} = 12$ 252
32. $\frac{n}{25} = 16$ 400

Add.   (Pages 392–393, 394–395)

33. $-7 + 9$ 2
34. $4 + (-8)$ -4
35. $-5 + (-13)$ -18
36. $3 + (-12)$ -9
37. $-14 + 2$ -12

38. $-5 + (-18)$ -23
39. $9 + (-12)$ -3
40. $-11 + 2$ -9
41. $3 + (-16)$ -13
42. $-25 + 1$ -24

Subtract.   (Pages 396–397)

43. $4 - (-6)$ 10
44. $-3 - 9$ -12
45. $-12 - (-7)$ -5
46. $5 - 18$ -13
47. $-3 - 1$ -4

48. $-12 - (-5)$ -7
49. $6 - 28$ -22
50. $10 - (-4)$ 14
51. $0 - 6$ -6
52. $0 - (-6)$ 6

Multiply.   (Pages 406–407; 408–409)

53. $-3 \times (-6)$ 18
54. -4×12 -48
55. $-13 \times (-5)$ 65
56. $21 \times (-2)$ -42

57. $16 \times (-4)$ -64
58. $-20 \times (-5)$ 100
59. -100×4 -400
60. $-10 \times (-6)$ 60

Divide.   (Pages 410–411)

61. $24 \div (-6)$ -4
62. $-49 \div (-7)$ 7
63. $-54 \div 9$ -6
64. $-108 \div (-12)$ 9

65. $-90 \div (-3)$ 30
66. $28 \div (-4)$ -7
67. $-72 \div (-3)$ 24
68. $-46 \div 2$ -23

69. $-30 \div 15$ -2
70. $56 \div (-2)$ -28
71. $-80 \div (-5)$ 16
72. $-132 \div 12$ -11

Write the rational numbers represented by each letter. Use the number line below.   (Pages 412–413)

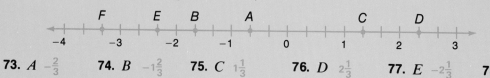

73. A $-\frac{2}{3}$
74. B $-1\frac{2}{3}$
75. C $1\frac{1}{3}$
76. D $2\frac{1}{3}$
77. E $-2\frac{1}{3}$
78. F $-3\frac{1}{3}$

SKILLS

20-1   Graphing Ordered Pairs

20-2   Graphing Equations

20-3   Equations and Integers:
       Addition/Subtraction

20-4   Equations and Integers:
       Multiplication/Division

20-5   Equations and Integers:
       Two Operations

APPLICATION

Latitude and Longitude

CAREER

Travel Planning

20-1 Graphing Ordered Pairs

You can use an **ordered pair** of numbers to give the location of Building A at the corner of 2nd Avenue and 1st Street.

A(2nd Avenue, 1st Street)

You can also use ordered pairs to locate points in a **coordinate plane.** First, you draw a horizontal number line, the *x* **axis.** Then draw a vertical number line, the *y* **axis.** They meet at a point called the **origin.**

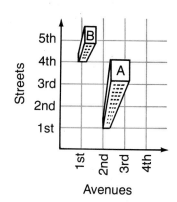

In the figure at the right, the ordered pair (3, 2) gives the location of point A. The <u>first</u> number, 3, is the *x* **coordinate;** the <u>second</u> number, 2, is the *y* **coordinate.**

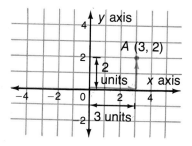

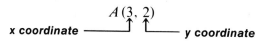

Cordinate Plane

PROCEDURE To locate a point:

1 Start at the origin. Count the number of units to the right (positive number) or to the left (negative number). This is the *x* coordinate.

2 Count the number of units up (positive number) or down (negative number). This is the *y* coordinate.

3 Write the ordered pair, (*x*, *y*).

EXAMPLE 1 Use the graph at the right to give the coordinates (ordered pair) for each point.

a. Q **b.** R **c.** S

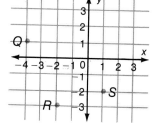

Solutions: Start at the origin.

a. Point Q is 4 units to the <u>left</u> and 1 unit <u>up</u>.
Ordered pair: $(-4, 1)$

b. Point R is 2 units to the <u>left</u> and 3 units <u>down</u>.
Ordered pair: $(-2, -3)$

c. Point S is 1 unit to the <u>right</u> and 2 units <u>down</u>.
Ordered pair: $(1, -2)$

You can follow steps 1 and 2 of the Procedure to graph points.

EXAMPLE 2 Graph each point.

  a. $P(4, -2)$ **b.** $Q(-1, 3)$

Solutions: **a.** Start at the origin. Move 4 units to the <u>right</u>. Then move 2 units <u>down</u>. Label the point P.

  b. Start at the origin. Move 1 unit to the <u>left</u>. Then move 3 units <u>up</u>. Label the point Q.

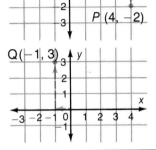

REVIEW OF RELATED SKILLS You may wish to use these exercises before teaching the lesson.

Write the rational number represented by each letter. Use the number line below.   (Pages 412–413)

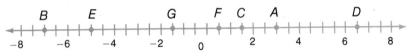

1. A 3   **2.** B –7   **3.** C $1\frac{1}{2}$ **4.** D $6\frac{1}{2}$ **5.** E –5   **6.** F $\frac{1}{2}$ **7.** G $-1\frac{1}{2}$

EXERCISES ———— See the suggested assignment guide in the Teacher's Manual.

For Exercises 1–12, give the coordinates (ordered pair) for the points graphed at the right.
(Example 1)

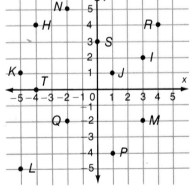

1. L (−5, −5)   **2.** N (−2, 5)   **3.** P (1, −4)

4. J (1, 1)   **5.** K (−5, 1)   **6.** Q (−2, −2)

7. M (3, −2)   **8.** I (3, 2)   **9.** R (4, 4)

10. S (0, 3)   **11.** H (−4, 4)   **12.** T (−4, 0)

For Exercises 13–17, draw and label a pair of axes. Then graph the point for each ordered pair. Label each point.   (Example 2)

14. 4 units up   15. 4 units to the left; 3 units up
13. $A(4, 2)$ **14.** $B(0, 4)$ **15.** $C(-4, 3)$ **16.** $D(-3, -2)$ **17.** $E(3, -3)$
13. 4 units to the right; 2 units up   16. 3 units to the left; 2 units down   17. 3 units to the right; 3 units down
18. Connect the points in Exercises 13–17 in this order.

  Start at E. Then go to B, to D, to A, to C, and back to E.
  What kind of figure have you drawn?   A star

Problem Solving and Applications

Latitude and Longitude

See the Teacher's Manual for the objectives.
This lesson applies the skills presented in Section 20-1.

You can locate points on a globe or map by using the ordered pair **(longitude, latitude)**. **Latitudes** measure distance in degrees north (N) or south (S) of the equator. **Longitudes** measure distance in degrees east (E) or west (W) of the **prime meridian**. The origin, or 0°, is the point where a longitude called the **prime meridian** crosses the equator.

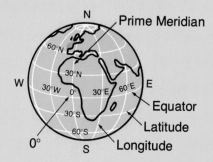

EXAMPLE Give the location of point *R* on the map. Use the ordered pair (latitude, longitude).

Solution:
1 Start at 0°.
2 Point *R* is one unit to the right (1° east) and two units up (2° north).
3 Write the ordered pair.

The location of point *R* is **(1°E, 2°N)**.

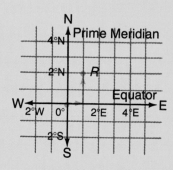

Exercises

In Exercises 1–6, complete the ordered pair that gives the location of each point. Use the map at the right.

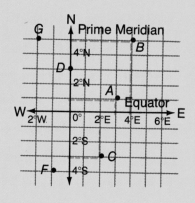

	Point	(Longitude, Latitude)	
1.	*A*	(3°E, ?)	1°N
2.	*B*	4°E (? , 5°N)	
3.	*C*	2°E (? , 3°S)	
4.	*D*	(? , ?)	(0°, 3°N)
5.	*F*	(? , ?)	(1°W, 4°S)
6.	*G*	(? , ?)	(2°W, 5°N)

In Exercises 7–11, give the location of each city.

	City	Location (Longitude, Latitude)	
7.	Cairo	(?, ?)	(30°E, 30°N)
8.	Folgares	(?, ?)	(15°E, 15°S)
9.	St. Louis	(?, ?)	(15°W, 15°N)
10.	Mogadishu	(?, ?)	(45°E, 0°)
11.	El Obeid	(?, ?)	(30°E, 15°N)

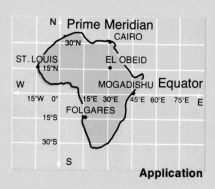

Application

TRAVEL PLANNING

Career lessons are optional.
This lesson applies the skills presented in Section 20-1.

Travel advisors help to plan travel routes. Some maps that they use are marked off in squares. Each square can be identified by a letter and a number (letter–number).

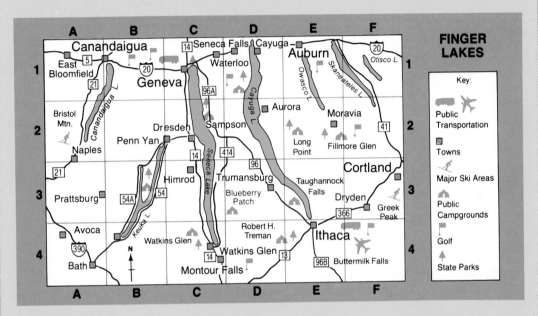

EXAMPLE What town is located in D–2?

Solution:

1 Locate the letter D either above or below the map.

2 Move down or up to the square opposite the number 2 at the right or left.

3 Find the ■ mark. ◀ From the key:
■ means town.

The town in D–2 is **Aurora.**

EXERCISES

For Exercises 1–6, use the map and the key above.

1. What town in located in E–2? Moravia
2. What lake is located in D–1? Cayuga Lake
3. What town is located in A–3? Prattsburg
4. Give the location of Otisco Lake. F 1
5. What lake is almost entirely located in B–3? Keuka Lake
6. Give the location of Bristol Mountain (MTN). A 2

Give the location of these public camp grounds.

7. Blueberry Patch D 3
8. Long Point E 2
9. Taughannock Falls E 3

20-2 Graphing Equations See the Teacher's Manual for the objectives.

An equation such as

$$d = 80t \quad \begin{cases} d = \text{number of kilometers} \\ t = \text{number of hours} \end{cases}$$

describes the relation between distance and time for a car traveling at a speed of 80 kilometers per hour. You can use this equation to make a table of ordered pairs.

EXAMPLE 1 Make a table of ordered pairs for the equation $d = 80t$.

Solution: **1** Choose at least   **2** Find d.   **3** Make a table.

3 values for t.

$d = 80t$

Let $t = 0$. $d = 80 \times 0 = 0$

Let $t = 2$. $d = 80 \times 2 = 160$

Let $t = 4$. $d = 80 \times 4 = 320$

t	d
0	0
2	160
4	320

You can use the table of ordered pairs to graph the equation.

PROCEDURE To graph an equation:

1 Make a table of ordered pairs.

2 Graph the ordered pairs. Draw a straight line connecting them.

EXAMPLE 2 Graph the equation $d = 80 \times t$. Use the table of ordered pairs from Example 1.

Solution: **1**

t	d
1	80
3	240
5	400

2

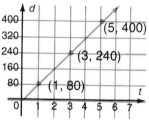

After completing Example 2, you may wish to have students do some or all of Exercises 1-4.

You follow a similar procedure to graph an equation such as $y = 2x + 3$.

EXAMPLE 3 Graph the equation $y = 2x + 3$.

Solution: **1** Make a table.

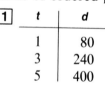

$y = 2x + 3$

x	$2x + 3$
-2	$2 \times (-2) + 3 = -1$
0	$2 \times 0 + 3 = 3$
1	$2 \times 1 + 3 = 5$

x	y
-2	-1
0	3
1	5

2

426   CHAPTER 20

Add.   (Pages 392–393, 394–395)

1. $9 + (-1)$ 8   **2.** $8 + (-10)$ −2   **3.** $-1 + 4$ 3   **4.** $-12 + 9$ −3   **5.** $-7 + (-4)$ ^{−11}

6. $-3 + (-6)$ −9   **7.** $-5 + 1$ −4   **8.** $-4 + 9$ 5   **9.** $6 + (-7)$ −1   **10.** $12 + (-4)$ ₈

Subtract.   (Pages 396–397)

11. $0 - 7$ −7   **12.** $9 - 11$ −2   **13.** $-1 - 5$ −6   **14.** $-7 - 3$ −10   **15.** $21 - (-8)$ ²⁹

16. $13 - (-4)$ 17   **17.** $-2 - (-1)$ −1   **18.** $-4 - (-7)$ 3   **19.** $0 - (-7)$ 7   **20.** $5 - (-6)$ ₁₁

Multiply.   (Pages 406–407, 408–409)

21. $6 \times (-8)$ −48   **22.** $5 \times (-15)$ −75   **23.** $-18 \times (-3)$ 54   **24.** $-91 \times (-10)$ ⁹¹⁰

25. -18×12 −216   **26.** -17×21 −357   **27.** $0 \times (-100)$ 0   **28.** $-100 \times (-21)$ ₂₁₀₀

Divide.   (Pages 410–411)

29. $18 \div -6$ −3   **30.** $-516 \div 4$ −129   **31.** $-144 \div (-8)$ 18   **32.** $-196 \div -14$ ₁₄

Graph each point on a coordinate plane. Use the same pair of x and y axes.   (Pages 422–423)

33. $P(4, 6)$ **34.** $Q(-3, 2)$ **35.** $R(-1, -6)$ **36.** $T(5, -4)$ **37.** $V(-7, 5)$

4 units to the right;   3 units to the left;   1 unit to the left;   5 units to the right;   7 units to the left;
6 units up   2 units up   6 units down   4 units down   5 units up

EXERCISES
See the suggested assignment guide in the Teacher's Manual.

For each equation in Exercises 1–4, copy the table and the coordinate axes. Then complete the table and draw the graph. (Examples 1 and 2)

1. The equation $d = 50t$ relates distance in miles and time in hours for a car traveling at the rate of 50 miles per hour.
The graph is the line joining the points.

$d = 50t$

t	d	
0	?	0
2	?	100
4	?	200

2. There are 16 tablespoons in a cup. The equation $T = 16C$ describes this relation.
The graph is the line joining the points.

$T = 16C$

C	T	
1	?	16
3	?	48
5	?	80

3. On a math test, 5 points are subtracted for each incorrect answer. The equation $s = 100 - 5c$ describes this relation.

The graph is the line joining the points.

$$s = 100 - 5c$$

c	s	
0	?	100
2	?	90
4	?	80

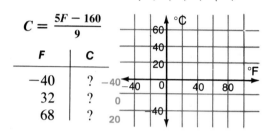

4. The equation $C = \dfrac{5F - 160}{9}$ relates temperature in degrees Fahrenheit to temperature in degrees Celsius.

The graph is the line joining the points.

$$C = \frac{5F - 160}{9}$$

F	C	
-40	?	-40
32	?	0
68	?	20

Copy and complete the table of ordered pairs for each equation. (Example 3, step 1)

5. $y = x - 1$

x	y	
2	?	1
0	?	-1
-2	?	-3

6. $y = x - 5$

x	y	
5	?	0
0	?	-5
-3	?	-8

7. $y = x + 2$

x	y	
1	?	3
-1	?	1
-3	?	-1

8. $y = x + 1$

x	y	
2	?	3
-2	?	-1
-4	?	-3

9. $y = x$

x	y	
1	?	1
0	?	0
-2	?	-2

10. $y = -x$

x	y	
1	?	-1
0	?	0
-2	?	2

11. $y = 3x$

x	y	
2	?	6
0	?	0
-2	?	-6

12. $y = -3x$

x	y	
1	?	-3
0	?	0
-1	?	3

Graph these equations. Use the corresponding tables from Exercises 5–12. (Example 3, step 2) The graph is the line joining the sample points given in the tables above.

13. $y = x - 1$ **14.** $y = x - 5$ **15.** $y = x + 2$ **16.** $y = x + 1$

17. $y = x$ **18.** $y = -x$ **19.** $y = 3x$ **20.** $y = -3x$

Graph each equation. (Example 3) The graph is the line joining the given sample points.

21. $y = 3x - 1$ **22.** $y = 2x + 5$ **23.** $y = 4x - 3$ **24.** $y = 3x - 2$

25. $y = -2x + 4$ **26.** $y = -3x + 6$ **27.** $y = 2x - 3$ **28.** $y = 3x - 4$

29. $y = -x + 1$ **30.** $y = -x - 1$ **31.** $y = 2x$ **32.** $y = -2x$

33. $y = -2x - 1$ **34.** $y = -2x + 1$ **35.** $y = \frac{1}{2}x$ **36.** $y = -\frac{1}{2}x - 1$

21. (0, −1); (1, 2); (2, 5)
25. (1, 2); (0, 4); (2, 0)
29. (0, 1); (1, 0); (2, −1)
22. (−2, 1); (0,5); (1, 7)
26. (0, 6); (1, 3); (2, 0)
30. (−1, 0); (0, −1); (1, −2)
33. (0, −1); (1, −3); (2, −5)
36. (−2, 0); (0, −1); (2, −2)
23. (0, −3); (1, 1); (2, 5)
27. (−1, −5); (0, −3); (1, −1)
31. (−1, −2); (0, 0); (1, 2)
34. (0, 1); (1, −1); (2, −3)
24. (−1, −5); (0, −2); (1, 1)
28. (0, −4); (1, −1); (2, 2)
32. (−1, 2); (0, 0); (1, −2)
35. (−2, −1), (0, 0); (2, 1)

20-3 Equations and Integers: Addition/Subtraction

See the Teacher's Manual for the objectives.

You can use the positive and negative integers to solve equations. Recall that to <u>solve an equation for n means to get n alone on one side of the equation.</u>

PROCEDURE To solve an addition equation such as $n + 5 = -3$, add -5 to each side of the equation.

EXAMPLE 1 Solve and check: $n + 5 = -3$

Solution: $n + 5 = -3$ ◀ *Add -5 to each side.*

$n + 5 + (-5) = -3 + (-5)$

$n = -8$ ◀ *n is alone.*

The solution is -8.

Check: $n + 5 = -3$ ◀ *Replace n with -8.*

$-8 + 5 \overset{?}{=} -3$

$-3 \overset{?}{=} -3$ Yes ✔

After completing Example 1, you may wish to have students do some or all of Exercises 1-20.

You can use any letter to represent the unknown in an equation.

PROCEDURE To solve a subtraction equation such as $s - 3 = -9$, add 3 to each side of the equation.

EXAMPLE 2 Solve and check: $s - 3 = -9$

Solution: $s - 3 = -9$ ◀ *Add 3 to each side.*

$s - 3 + 3 = -9 + 3$

$s = -6$

The solution is -6.

Check: $s - 3 = -9$ ◀ *Replace s with -6.*

$-6 - 3 \overset{?}{=} -9$

$-9 \overset{?}{=} -9$ Yes ✔

REVIEW OF RELATED SKILLS

You may wish to use these exercises before teaching the lesson.

Add. (Pages 394–395)

1. $9 + (-5)$ 4 **2.** $6 + (-12)$ −6 **3.** $11 + (-15)$ −4 **4.** $7 + (-4)$ 3 **5.** $5 + (-5)$ 0

6. $-11 + 11$ 0 **7.** $-9 + 5$ −4 **8.** $-7 + 14$ 7 **9.** $-8 + 10$ 2 **10.** $-8 + 6$ −2

Solve and check. (Pages 248–249)

11. $n + 6 = 21$ 15 **12.** $n + 1 = 12$ 11 **13.** $n + 16 = 21$ 5 **14.** $n + 26 = 50$ 24

15. $n - 8 = 13$ 21 **16.** $n - 5 = 25$ 30 **17.** $n - 7 = 30$ 37 **18.** $n - 9 = 41$ 50

19. $n - 21 = 40$ 61 **20.** $n + 13 = 27$ 14 **21.** $n + 9 = 46$ 37 **22.** $n - 43 = 96$ 139

Solve and check. **(Example 1)**

1. $n+1=-4$ $\quad$ -5 $\qquad$ **2.** $n+3=-8$ $\quad$ -11 $\qquad$ **3.** $n+7=-1$ $\quad$ -8 $\qquad$ **4.** $n+6=-5$ -11

5. $x+3=-7$ $\quad$ -10 $\qquad$ **6.** $x+10=-4$ $\quad$ -14 $\qquad$ **7.** $r+12=-3$ $\quad$ -15 $\qquad$ **8.** $r+7=-2$ -9

9. $s+13=2$ $\quad$ -11 $\qquad$ **10.** $s+11=5$ $\quad$ -6 $\qquad$ **11.** $t+10=4$ $\quad$ -6 $\qquad$ **12.** $t+1=0$ $\quad$ -1

13. $y+7=8$ $\quad$ 1 $\qquad$ **14.** $y+9=12$ $\quad$ 3 $\qquad$ **15.** $p+5=19$ $\quad$ 14 $\qquad$ **16.** $p+4=8$ $\quad$ 4

17. $a+1=-1$ $\quad$ -2 $\qquad$ **18.** $b+3=-3$ $\quad$ -6 $\qquad$ **19.** $d+7=0$ $\quad$ -7 $\qquad$ **20.** $f+8=-5$ $\quad$ -13

(Example 2)

21. $s-4=-3$ $\quad$ 1 $\qquad$ **22.** $s-2=-1$ $\quad$ 1 $\qquad$ **23.** $t-8=-8$ $\quad$ 0 $\qquad$ **24.** $t-5=-5$ $\quad$ 0

25. $q-8=-20$ $\quad$ -12 $\qquad$ **26.** $q-9=-18$ $\quad$ -9 $\qquad$ **27.** $r-11=12$ $\quad$ 23 $\qquad$ **28.** $r-7=9$ $\quad$ 16

29. $t-3=2$ $\quad$ 5 $\qquad$ **30.** $t-7=5$ $\quad$ 12 $\qquad$ **31.** $q-8=0$ $\quad$ 8 $\qquad$ **32.** $q-10=0$ $\quad$ 10

33. $y-15=0$ $\quad$ 15 $\qquad$ **34.** $y-30=0$ $\quad$ 30 $\qquad$ **35.** $x-1=1$ $\quad$ 2 $\qquad$ **36.** $x-6=6$ $\quad$ 12

37. $m-1=1$ $\quad$ 2 $\qquad$ **38.** $m-14=-14$ $\quad$ 0 $\qquad$ **39.** $a-9=1$ $\quad$ 10 $\qquad$ **40.** $b-5=3$ $\quad$ 8

Mixed Practice
The Mixed Practice contains exercises that relate to both Examples 1 and 2.

41. $z-4=4$ $\quad$ 8 $\qquad$ **42.** $t+9=0$ $\quad$ -9 $\qquad$ **43.** $r-47=-1$ $\quad$ 46 $\qquad$ **44.** $q+20=-10$ $\quad$ -30

45. $x+8=5$ $\quad$ -3 $\qquad$ **46.** $q-8=20$ $\quad$ 28 $\qquad$ **47.** $t-9=11$ $\quad$ 20 $\qquad$ **48.** $h+11=-11$ $\quad$ -22

49. $n+8=-2$ $\quad$ -10 $\qquad$ **50.** $y+16=0$ $\quad$ -16 $\qquad$ **51.** $a+12=-15$ $\quad$ -27 $\qquad$ **52.** $x-30=22$ $\quad$ 52

53. $t-8=-40$ $\quad$ -32 $\qquad$ **54.** $b-14=-7$ $\quad$ 7 $\qquad$ **55.** $c+5=-3$ $\quad$ -8 $\qquad$ **56.** $x-3=-9$ $\quad$ -6

57. $x+2=-1$ $\quad$ -3 $\qquad$ **58.** $y+9=7$ $\quad$ -2 $\qquad$ **59.** $z+28=5$ $\quad$ -23 $\qquad$ **60.** $t+14=6$ $\quad$ -8

61. $m-9=5$ $\quad$ 14 $\qquad$ **62.** $q-15=13$ $\quad$ 28 $\qquad$ **63.** $m+1=0$ $\quad$ -1 $\qquad$ **64.** $t-19=0$ $\quad$ 19

65. $y-3=-27$ $\quad$ -24 $\qquad$ **66.** $n-8=14$ $\quad$ 22 $\qquad$ **67.** $t+100=-1$ $\quad$ -101 $\qquad$ **68.** $s-100=5$ $\quad$ 105

69. $c+12=9$ $\quad$ -3 $\qquad$ **70.** $p-21=-13$ $\quad$ 8 $\qquad$ **71.** $a-17=9$ $\quad$ 26 $\qquad$ **72.** $r+22=-6$ $\quad$ -28

More Challenging Problems
More Challenging Problems are optional.

73. $t+11.2=3.7$ $\quad$ -7.5 $\qquad$ **74.** $r+5.6=7.1$ $\quad$ 1.5 $\qquad$ **75.** $s-\frac{1}{2}=\frac{1}{2}$ $\quad$ 1 $\qquad$ **76.** $q+\frac{3}{4}=\frac{1}{4}$ $\quad$ $-\frac{1}{2}$

77. $m+4\frac{1}{2}=7$ $\quad$ $2\frac{1}{2}$ $\qquad$ **78.** $a-7\frac{2}{3}=9$ $\quad$ $16\frac{2}{3}$ $\qquad$ **79.** $q+\frac{1}{2}=\frac{5}{6}$ $\quad$ $\frac{2}{6}$ or $\frac{1}{3}$ $\qquad$ **80.** $z-\frac{2}{3}=\frac{1}{15}$ $\quad$ $\frac{11}{15}$

81. $a-0.9=1.5$ $\quad$ 2.4 $\qquad$ **82.** $c+1.7=-3.4$ $\quad$ -5.1 $\qquad$ **83.** $x-5.8=-1$ $\quad$ 4.8 $\qquad$ **84.** $y+9.7=-10$ $\quad$ -19.7

85. $n+1.1=0$ $\quad$ -1.1 $\qquad$ **86.** $q-5.4=0$ $\quad$ 5.4 $\qquad$ **87.** $t-\frac{1}{5}=-\frac{1}{4}$ $\quad$ $-\frac{1}{20}$ $\qquad$ **88.** $r+\frac{1}{8}=-\frac{3}{4}$ $\quad$ $-\frac{7}{8}$

89. $25=x+5$ $\quad$ 20 $\qquad$ **90.** $-1=y-4$ $\quad$ 3 $\qquad$ **91.** $-11=z+1$ $\quad$ -12 $\qquad$ **92.** $13=a-40$ $\quad$ 53

93. $5+d=21$ $\quad$ 16 $\qquad$ **94.** $-8+r=7$ $\quad$ 15 $\qquad$ **95.** $12+a=-90$ $\quad$ -102 $\qquad$ **96.** $-15+t=-50$ $\quad$ -35

97. $-9+m=-5$ $\quad$ 4 $\qquad$ **98.** $-11+y=-1$ $\quad$ 10 $\qquad$ **99.** $17+t=0$ $\quad$ -17 $\qquad$ **100.** $-8+q=0$ $\quad$ 8

101. $b+\frac{4}{5}=-\frac{1}{2}$ $\quad$ $-1\frac{3}{10}$ $\qquad$ **102.** $c-\frac{1}{3}=\frac{3}{4}$ $\quad$ $1\frac{1}{12}$ $\qquad$ **103.** $z-12=-4$ $\quad$ 8 $\qquad$ **104.** $g+8=19$ $\quad$ 11

105. $f-0.9=2.0$ $\quad$ 2.9 $\qquad$ **106.** $m+1.4=-0.8$ $\quad$ -2.2 $\qquad$ **107.** $v+\frac{5}{8}=-\frac{7}{8}$ $\quad$ $-1\frac{1}{2}$ $\qquad$ **108.** $n-\frac{1}{6}=-\frac{2}{3}$ $\quad$ $-\frac{1}{2}$

20-4 Equations and Integers: Multiplication/Division

See the Teacher's Manual for the objectives.

You can also use positive and negative integers to solve multiplication and division equations.

PROCEDURE To solve a multiplication equation such as $-6y = 42$, divide each side of the equation by -6.

EXAMPLE 1 Solve and check: $-6y = 42$ ◀ $-6y$ means $-6 \times y$.

Solution: $-6y = 42$ ◀ **Divide each side by −6.**

$$\frac{-6y}{-6} = \frac{42}{-6}$$

$$y = -7$$ ◀ **y is alone.**

The solution is −7.

Check: $-6y = 42$ ◀ **Replace y with (−7).**

$$-6 \times (-7) \overset{?}{=} 42$$

$$42 \overset{?}{=} 42 \quad \text{Yes} ✔$$

After completing Example 1, you may wish to have students do some or all of Exercises 1-20.

PROCEDURE To solve a division equation such as $\frac{r}{-3} = -18$, multiply each side of the equation by -3.

EXAMPLE 2 Solve and check: $\frac{r}{-3} = -18$

Solution: $\frac{r}{-3} = -18$ ◀ **Multiply each side by −3.**

$$\frac{r}{-3} \times \frac{-3}{1} = -18 \times -3$$ ◀ $\frac{r}{-3} \times \frac{-3}{1} = r$

$$r = 54$$

The solution is **54**.

Check: $\frac{r}{-3} = -18$ ◀ **Replace r with 54.**

$$\frac{54}{-3} \overset{?}{=} -18$$

$$-18 \overset{?}{=} -18 \quad \text{Yes} ✔$$

REVIEW OF RELATED SKILLS

You may wish to use these exercises before teaching the lesson.

Multiply. (Pages 406–409)

1. $2 \times (-16)$ −32 **2.** -21×5 −105 **3.** $-1 \times (-6)$ 6 **4.** $-80 \times (-1)$ 80 **5.** $-7 \times (-18)$ 126

6. $-18 \times (-10)$ 180 **7.** -9×85 −765 **8.** -11×12 −132 **9.** -100×0 0 **10.** $0 \times (-75)$ 0

Divide. (Pages 410–411)

11. $24 \div (-6)$ −4 **12.** $-225 \div 15$ −15 **13.** $-120 \div (-20)$ 6 **14.** $-144 \div (-6)$ 24

15. $-169 \div 13$ −13 **16.** $625 \div (-25)$ −25 **17.** $0 \div (-8)$ 0 **18.** $-500 \div (-10)$ 50

19. $144 \div (-4)$ −36 **20.** $-180 \div 15$ −12 **21.** $-56 \div (-14)$ 4 **22.** $100 \div (-10)$ −10

GRAPHING AND EQUATIONS **431**

Solve and check.   (Pages 252–253)

23. $9n = 45$ ₅

24. $13n = 52$ ₄

25. $23n = 460$ ₂₀

26. $30n = 900$ ₃₀

Solve and check.   (Pages 252–253)

27. $\frac{n}{6} = 15$ ₉₀

28. $\frac{n}{2} = 13$ ₂₆

29. $\frac{n}{7} = 84$ ₅₈₈

30. $\frac{n}{90} = 3$ ₂₇₀

EXERCISES
See the suggested assignment guide in the Teacher's Manual.

Solve and check.   (Example 1)

1. $-4n = 32$ ₋₈

2. $-6x = 36$ ₋₆

3. $-7x = 21$ ₋₃

4. $-5x = 15$ ₋₃

5. $17t = -34$ ₋₂

6. $18t = -54$ ₋₃

7. $10r = -90$ ₋₉

8. $15r = -75$ ₋₅

9. $-2q = -6$ ₃

10. $-8t = -64$ ₈

11. $-18r = -288$ ₁₆

12. $-25r = -625$ ₂₅

13. $-4a = 144$ ₋₃₆

14. $-12z = 132$ ₋₁₁

15. $-17y = -85$ ₅

16. $-20t = -800$ ₄₀

17. $11q = -143$ ₋₁₃

18. $72s = -360$ ₋₅

19. $-18u = 0$ ₀

20. $-18u = 90$ ₋₅

(Example 2)

21. $\frac{r}{-2} = -9$ ₁₈

22. $\frac{r}{-3} = -2$ ₆

23. $\frac{t}{-7} = 1$ ₋₇

24. $\frac{s}{-5} = 1$ ₋₅

25. $\frac{x}{-3} = -8$ ₂₄

26. $\frac{w}{-5} = -20$ ₁₀₀

27. $\frac{w}{4} = -9$ ₋₃₆

28. $\frac{p}{6} = -12$ ₋₇₂

29. $\frac{m}{-5} = 0$ ₀

30. $\frac{t}{-6} = -1$ ₆

31. $\frac{y}{6} = -30$ ₋₁₈₀

32. $\frac{z}{19} = -2$ ₋₃₈

33. $\frac{t}{-24} = 32$ ₋₇₆₈

34. $\frac{s}{-12} = 50$ ₋₆₀₀

35. $\frac{x}{-9} = -7$ ₆₃

36. $\frac{z}{-15} = -10$ ₁₅₀

37. $\frac{y}{-2} = -24$ ₄₈

38. $\frac{q}{-6} = -120$ ₇₂₀

39. $\frac{w}{10} = -9$ ₋₉₀

40. $\frac{z}{90} = -1$ ₋₉₀

Mixed Practice The Mixed Practice contains exercises that relate to both Examples 1 and 2.

41. $13t = 52$ ₄

42. $-15y = 60$ ₋₄

43. $\frac{r}{-2} = 700$ ₋₁₄₀₀

44. $\frac{r}{-4} = -80$ ₃₂₀

45. $\frac{w}{6} = -90$ ₋₅₄₀

46. $\frac{t}{-5} = -35$ ₁₇₅

47. $-5y = 0$ ₀

48. $18y = 0$ ₀

49. $-96w = -288$ ₃

50. $-70t = -210$ ₃

51. $\frac{a}{24} = -5$ ₋₁₂₀

52. $\frac{c}{-2} = -130$ ₂₆₀

53. $13m = -65$ ₋₅

54. $-43t = 86$ ₋₂

55. $\frac{r}{12} = -8$ ₋₉₆

56. $\frac{z}{-11} = -1$ ₁₁

57. $\frac{d}{-3} = -9$ ₂₇

58. $11w = -110$ ₋₁₀

59. $-7b = 133$ ₋₁₉

60. $\frac{k}{13} = -8$ ₋₁₀₄

More Challenging Problems More Challenging Problems are optional.

61. $78 = -2m$ ₋₃₉

62. $-36 = -18m$ ₂

63. $-14 = \frac{w}{7}$ ₋₉₈

64. $-40 = \frac{t}{20}$ ₋₈₀₀

65. $-14q = 7$ $-\frac{1}{2}$

66. $30s = -15$ $-\frac{1}{2}$

67. $-144 = 1.2x$ ₋₁₂₀

68. $-1.25 = 2.5y$ ₋₀.₅

69. $-9 = \frac{t}{-4}$ ₃₆

70. $-1 = \frac{m}{-100}$ ₁₀₀

71. $\frac{y}{-2} = \frac{1}{4}$ $-\frac{1}{2}$

72. $\frac{s}{-3} = -1\frac{1}{3}$

432   CHAPTER 20

4

20-5 Equations and Integers: Two Operations

See the Teacher's Manual for the objectives.

Sometimes you have to use more than one operation to solve an equation.

PROCEDURE To solve an equation:

1. Add the same positive or negative number to each side.
2. Multiply or divide each side by the same number.

EXAMPLE 1 Solve and check: $3y - 10 = -19$

Solution: $3y - 10 = -19$ ◀ *Add 10 to each side.*

1. $3y - 10 + 10 = -19 + 10$

   $3y = -9$ ◀ *Divide each side by 3.*
2. $\frac{3y}{3} = \frac{-9}{3}$

   $y = -3$

The solution is **-3**.

Check: $3y - 10 = -19$ ◀ *Replace y with -3.*

$3 \times (-3) - 10 \overset{?}{=} -19$

$-9 - 10 \overset{?}{=} -19$

$-19 \overset{?}{=} -19$ Yes ✔

After completing Example 1, you may wish to have students do some or all of Exercises 1-20.

Be sure to check your answer in the original equation.

EXAMPLE 2 Solve and check: $\frac{n}{-2} + 1 = -3$

Solution: $\frac{n}{-2} + 1 = -3$ ◀ *Add -1 to each side.*

1. $\frac{n}{-2} + 1 + (-1) = -3 + (-1)$

   $\frac{n}{-2} = -4$ ◀ *Multiply each side by -2.*
2. $\frac{n}{-2} \times \frac{-2}{1} = -4 \times (-2)$

   $n = 8$

The solution is **8**.

Check: $\frac{n}{-2} + 1 = -3$ ◀ *Replace n with 8.*

$\frac{8}{-2} + 1 \overset{?}{=} -3$

$-4 + 1 \overset{?}{=} -3$

$-3 \overset{?}{=} -3$ Yes ✔

REVIEW OF RELATED SKILLS

You may wish to use these exercises before teaching the lesson.

Add. (Pages 392–395)

1. $-12 + 6$ -6
2. $-9 + 8$ -1
3. $7 + (-16)$ -9
4. $9 + (-21)$ -12
5. $-1 + (-5)$ -6
6. $-16 + (-16)$ -32
7. $41 + (-28)$ 13
8. $32 + (-18)$ 14
9. $-54 + 27$ -27
10. $-22 + 30$ 8

Multiply.   (Pages 406–409)

11. -6×3 –18 **12.** -18×9 –162 **13.** $12 \times (-8)$ –96 **14.** $40 \times (-4)$ ⁻¹⁶⁰ **15.** $-8 \times (-1)$ 8

16. $-1 \times (-18)$ 18 **17.** $-14 \times (-6)$ 84 **18.** $-42 \times (-8)$ 336 **19.** -70×0 0   **20.** $0 \times (-1)$ 0

Divide.   (Pages 410–411)

21. $16 \div -2$ –8 **22.** $-120 \div 15$ –8 **23.** $600 \div -15$ ⁻⁴⁰ **24.** $189 \div -3$ –63

25. $-72 \div (-36)$ 2 **26.** $-56 \div (-14)$ 4 **27.** $0 \div -7$ 0 **28.** $30 \div (-6)$ –5

Solve and check.   (Pages 429–430)

29. $y + 30 = 22$ –8 **30.** $x + 13 = -31$ –44 **31.** $t - 9 = -11$ –2 **32.** $h + 11 = 11$ 0

(Pages 431–432)

33. $-6r = 24$ –4 **34.** $7t = -21$ –3 **35.** $-3w = -36$ 12 **36.** $-8m = -32$ 4

37. $\frac{z}{-3} = 5$ –15 **38.** $\frac{p}{-8} = 1$ –8 **39.** $\frac{s}{-5} = -20$ 100 **40.** $\frac{w}{-6} = -30$ 180

EXERCISES

See the suggested assignment guide in the Teacher's Manual.

Solve and check.   (Example 1)

1. $2x + 7 = -5$ –6 **2.** $3a - 17 = 13$ 10 **3.** $3b + 6 = -12$ –6 **4.** $-4m + 9 = -49$ $14\frac{1}{2}$

5. $2y + 6 = 22$ 8 **6.** $8t - 15 = 17$ 4 **7.** $-5m - 12 = 3$ –3 **8.** $11s + 10 = 120$ 10

9. $16a + 12 = 20$ $\frac{1}{2}$ **10.** $2w + 5 = 73$ 34 **11.** $5r + 3 = 33$ 6 **12.** $5t - 3 = 17$ 4

13. $-5w - 9 = -19$ 2 **14.** $-3t + 17 = 5$ 4 **15.** $4q + 17 = 53$ 9 **16.** $3n - 17 = 4$ 7

17. $-8a - 7 = 41$ –6 **18.** $-3p - 4 = 17$ –7 **19.** $-6b + 1 = 27$ $-4\frac{1}{3}$ **20.** $-2x + 5 = 15$ –5

(Example 2)

21. $\frac{f}{5} - 7 = 13$ 100 **22.** $\frac{r}{10} + 6 = 36$ 300 **23.** $\frac{x}{5} + 3 = -9$ –60 **24.** $\frac{t}{8} - 1 = -7$ –48

25. $\frac{w}{8} + 1 = 9$ 64 **26.** $\frac{m}{6} - 3 = 11$ 84 **27.** $\frac{z}{-2} + 7 = 8$ –2 **28.** $\frac{y}{-4} - 9 = 2$ –48

29. $\frac{x}{-3} + 8 = -7$ 45 **30.** $\frac{r}{8} + 9 = -12$ –168 **31.** $\frac{t}{-4} + 7 = 1$ 24 **32.** $\frac{m}{-10} + 6 = 5$ 10

33. $\frac{q}{4} + 1 = 0$ –4 **34.** $\frac{s}{9} - 1 = 0$ 9 **35.** $\frac{t}{-35} = 0$ 0 **36.** $\frac{p}{-10} + 6 = 6$ 0

37. $\frac{n}{9} - 20 = -18$ 18 **38.** $\frac{w}{12} - 15 = -3$ 144 **39.** $\frac{r}{-4} + 7 = 11$ –16 **40.** $\frac{x}{-7} + 9 = -5$ 98

Mixed Practice

41. $4y + 9 = -15$ –6 **42.** $-3m + 9 = -60$ 23 **43.** $-14d + 32 = 39$ $-\frac{1}{2}$ **44.** $4y - 12 = -16$ –1

45. $\frac{z}{-3} + 7 = -9$ 48 **46.** $\frac{s}{-6} + 1 = -2$ 18 **47.** $\frac{w}{8} - 9 = -10$ –8 **48.** $\frac{t}{4} - 3 = -6$ –12

49. $5t - 12 = 8$ 4 **50.** $\frac{k}{-6} + 9 = -11$ 120 **51.** $\frac{p}{6} - 4 = 13$ 102 **52.** $-11c + 3 = -41$ 4

Chapter Review

These exercises review the vocabulary, skills, and applications presented in the chapter as a preparation for the chapter test.

Part 1: Vocabulary

For Exercises 1–5, choose from the box at the right the word(s) that completes each statement.

1. In a coordinate plane, the horizontal number line is called the __?__. (Page 422) *x axis*

2. In a coordinate plane, the vertical number line is called the __?__. (Page 422) *y axis*

3. The *x* axis and the *y* axis meet at a point called the __?__. (Page 422) *origin*

4. The first number in an ordered pair is the __?__. (Page 422) *x coordinate*

5. The second number in an ordered pair is the __?__. (Page 422) *y coordinate*

Part 2: Skills

For Exercises 6–17, give the coordinates (ordered pair) for the points graphed at the right. (Pages 422–423)

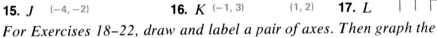

6. *A* (0, 4)　　　7. *B* (1, −1)　　(3, −2)　**8.** *C*

9. *D* (−4, 2)　　**10.** *E* (−1, −3)　(4, 3)　**11.** *F*

12. *G* (−3, 4)　　**13.** *H* (2, 1)　　(−2, 0)　**14.** *I*

15. *J* (−4, −2)　　**16.** *K* (−1, 3)　(1, 2)　**17.** *L*

For Exercises 18–22, draw and label a pair of axes. Then graph the point for each ordered pair. Label each point. (Pages 422–423)

18. (−3, 2)　　**19.** (4, −4)　　**20.** (1, 2)　　**21.** (3, −2)　　**22.** (0, −3)

18. 3 units to the left; 2 units up
19. 4 units to the right; 4 units down
20. 1 unit to the right; 2 units up
21. 3 units to the right; 2 units down
22. 3 units down

For each equation in Exercises 23–24, copy the table and the coordinate axes. Then complete the table and draw the graph. (Pages 426–428)

23. The equation $d = 40t$ relates distance in miles and time in hours for a car traveling at the rate of 40 miles per hour.

   The graph is the line containing the points.

$d = 40t$

t	d
0	? 0
2	? 80
4	? 160

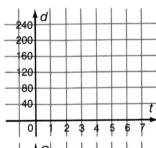

24. There are 4 quarts in a gallon. The equation $Q = 4G$ describes this relation.

   The graph is the line containing the points.

$Q = 4G$

G	Q
1	? 4
3	? 12
5	? 20

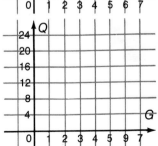

Copy and complete the table of ordered pairs for each equation.
(Pages 426–428)

25. $y = x + 2$

x	y
2	?	4
0	?	2
−2	?	0

26. $y = x - 3$

x	y
5	?	2
3	?	0
1	?	−2

27. $y = 2x$

x	y
2	?	4
0	?	0
−2	?	−4

28. $y = -2x$

x	y
2	?	−4
0	?	0
−2	?	4

Graph these equations. Use the corresponding tables from Exercises 25–28. (Pages 426–428)

Each graph is a straight line connecting the points.

29. $y = x + 2$ **30.** $y = x - 3$ **31.** $y = 2x$ **32.** $y = -2x$

Graph each equation. (Pages 426–428)

Each graph is a straight line connecting the given sample points.

33. $y = 2x - 1$
$(-1, -3); (0, -1); (1, 1)$

34. $y = 3x + 2$
$(-1, -1); (0, 2); (1, 5)$

35. $y = -3x - 1$
$(-1, 2); (0, -1); (1, -4)$

36. $y = -2x + 2$
$(0, 2); (1, 0); (2, -2)$

Solve and check. (Pages 429–430)

37. $n + 5 = 12$ 7 **38.** $p - 7 = 3$ 10 **39.** $q + 9 = 15$ 6 **40.** $r - 3 = 7$ 10

41. $s - 6 = 4$ 10 **42.** $t + 10 = 14$ 4 **43.** $a - 12 = -15$ −3 **44.** $d - 9 = -12$
−3

(Pages 431–432)

45. $\frac{n}{-6} = -7$ 42 **46.** $-5x = -30$ 6 **47.** $6y = -48$ −8 **48.** $\frac{b}{5} = -6$ −30

49. $-4c = -20$ 5 **50.** $\frac{w}{-2} = -9$ 18 **51.** $9t = -27$ −3 **52.** $\frac{t}{-3} = 7$ −21

(Pages 433–434)

53. $-3x + 5 = -4$ 3 **54.** $6a - 10 = -16$ −1 **55.** $-5d - 3 = -13$ 2 **56.** $8f + 11 = 35$ 3

57. $4y + 16 = 8$ −2 **58.** $-11b - 9 = 2$ −1 **59.** $3t + 4 = 16$ 4 **60.** $-9s - 16 = -34$
2

Part 3: Applications The use of these exercises depends on which applications were taught.

In Exercises 61–66, give the location of each city. Use the ordered pair (longitude, latitude). (Page 424)

City	Location (Longitude, Latitude)
61. Kankan	(?, ?) (10°W, 10°N)
62. Bauchi	(?, ?) (10°E, 10°N)
63. Libreville	(?, ?) (10°E, 0°)
64. Kampala	(?, ?) (30°E, 0°)
65. Kasama	(?, ?) (30°E, 10°S)
66. Lindi	(?, ?) (40°E, 10°S)

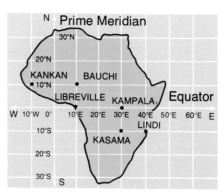

Chapter Test

The Teacher's Resource Book contains two forms of each chapter test.

For Exercises 1–9, give the coordinates (ordered pair) for the points graphed at the right.

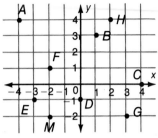

1. A $(-4, 4)$ **2.** B $(1, 3)$ **3.** C $(4, 0)$

4. E $(-3, -1)$ **5.** F $(-2, 1)$ **6.** G $(3, -2)$

7. D $(0, -1)$ **8.** H $(2, 4)$ **9.** M $(-2, -2)$

For Exercises 10–13, draw and label a pair of axes. Then graph the point for each ordered pair. Label each point.

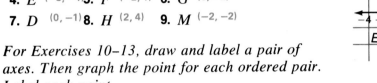

	11. 2 units up	**12.** 1 unit to the left	**13.** 5 units to the left; 4 units down

10. $(4, -2)$ **11.** $(0, 2)$ **12.** $(-1, 0)$ **13.** $(-5, -4)$

10. 4 units to the right; 2 units down

For Exercises 14–17, graph each equation.   Each graph is a straight line connecting the given sample points.

14. $y = 3x + 4$ **15.** $y = 2x - 5$ **16.** $y = -2x + 3$ **17.** $y = -x - 4$
$(-1, 1); (0, 4); (1, 7)$ $(0, -5); (1, -3); (3, 1)$ $(0, 3); (1, 1); (2, -1)$ $(-2, -2); (0, -4); (1, -5)$

Solve and check.

18. $a + 7 = -2$ -9 **19.** $b - 6 = 9$ 15 **20.** $s - 8 = 12$ 20 **21.** $t + 6 = 14$ 8

22. $6d = -24$ -4 **23.** $-3s = 36$ -12 **24.** $\frac{y}{-4} = -6$ 24 **25.** $\frac{x}{-2} = -4$ 8

26. $2b - 3 = 7$ 5 **27.** $-4a + 3 = -13$ 4 **28.** $9t + 4 = -14$ -2 **29.** $-5q - 9 = 11$ -4

30. $-3d + 2 = 8$ -2 **31.** $6c - 4 = -40$ -6 **32.** $-8s - 5 = -29$ 3 **33.** $7g + 7 = 28$ 3

Additional Practice

You may wish to use some or all of these exercises depending on how well students performed on the formal chapter test.

For Exercises 1–12, give the coordinates (ordered pair) for the points graphed at the right.
(Pages 422–423)

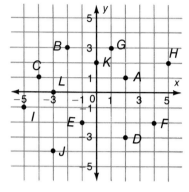

1. A (2, 1)
2. B (−2, 3)
3. C (−4, 1)
4. D (2, −3)
5. E (−1, −2)
6. F (4, −2)
7. G (1, 3)
8. H (5, 2)
9. I (−5, −1)
10. J (−3, −4)
11. K (0, 2)
12. L (−3, 0)

For Exercises 13–17, draw and label a pair of axes. Then graph the point for each ordered pair. Label each point. (Pages 422–423)

14. 6 units to the left; 7 units up   16. 3 units to the right

13. (2, 3)
13. 2 units to the right; 3 units up
14. (−6, 7)
15. (−4, −3)
15. 4 units to the left; 3 units down
16. (0, 3)
17. (5, −2)
17. 5 units to the right; 2 units down

Graph each equation.   (Pages 426–428) In Exercises 18-29, each graph is a straight line connecting the given sample points.

18. $y = x + 1$
(−1, 0), (0, 1), (1, 2)
19. $y = x − 5$
(0, −5), (1, −4), (2, −3)
20. $y = 3x$
(−1, −3), (0, 0), (2, 6)
21. $y = −2x$
(−2, 4), (0, 0), (2, −4)
22. $y = x − 3$
(−1, −4), (0, −3), (3, 0)
23. $y = x + 4$
(−4, 0), (−2, 2), (0, 4)
24. $y = −5x$
(−1, 5), (0, 0), (1, −5)
25. $y = 4x$
(−1, −4), (0, 0), (1, 4)
26. $y = 2x − 2$
(0, −2); (1, 0); (2, 2)
27. $y = −3x + 3$
(0, 3); (1, 0); (2, −3)
28. $y = −2x + 6$
(0, 6); (1, 4); (2, 2)
29. $y = 3x − 1$
(0, −1); (1, 2); (2, 5)

Solve and check.   (Pages 429–430)

30. $n + 6 = 13$ 7
31. $s − 2 = 5$ 7
32. $p + 4 = −2$ −6
33. $c − 8 = −2$ 6
34. $a − 3 = 9$ 12
35. $p + 3 = 12$ 9
36. $b − 10 = −4$ 6
37. $n + 6 = −5$ −11
38. $x − 6 = −8$ −2
39. $t + 7 = −10$ −17
40. $q + 6 = 4$ −2
41. $d − 3 = 7$ 10
42. $y + 3 = −8$ −11
43. $x − 4 = −6$ −2
44. $b − 4 = 5$ 9
45. $t + 9 = 6$ −3

(Pages 431–432)

46. $−2c = 10$ −5
47. $−3a = −27$ 9
48. $4x = −32$ −8
49. $−8t = −104$ 13
50. $−6b = −96$ 16
51. $−5d = 25$ −5
52. $−2c = −28$ 14
53. $6d = −48$ −8
54. $\frac{x}{−4} = −7$ 28
55. $\frac{s}{2} = −21$ −42
56. $\frac{n}{−3} = 18$ −54
57. $\frac{a}{−7} = −14$ 98
58. $\frac{t}{5} = −16$ −80
59. $\frac{b}{−4} = −3$ 12
60. $\frac{y}{−9} = −7$ 63
61. $\frac{c}{−4} = 13$ −52

(Pages 433–434)

62. $2x + 2 = 16$ 7
63. $−2a − 5 = 17$ −11
64. $4b + 6 = −14$ −5
65. $−8d − 3 = −35$ 4
66. $−3y − 4 = 14$ −6
67. $3p + 5 = 26$ 7
68. $−6t − 7 = −31$ 4
69. $5c + 9 = −21$ −6
70. $\frac{b}{3} + 6 = 12$ 18
71. $\frac{q}{−2} − 6 = −5$ −2
72. $\frac{p}{−5} + 9 = 4$ 25
73. $\frac{d}{7} − 6 = 12$ 126
74. $\frac{h}{−4} − 7 = −3$ −16
75. $\frac{d}{2} + 8 = 4$ −8
76. $\frac{f}{4} − 8 = 7$ 60
77. $\frac{q}{−6} + 3 = 15$ −72

Cumulative Review: Chapters 17–20

You may also wish to use at this time the cumulative review on page 450 titled Review of Skills that reviews only the skills presented in Chapters 1-20.

Choose the correct answer. Choose a, b, c, or d.

1. $21^2 =$ __?__ . c

   a. 121   **b.** 42   **c.** 441   **d.** 2100

2. Add: $-17 + (-23)$ c

   a. -6 **b.** 6   **c.** -40 **d.** 40

3. Which point on the number line below represents the opposite of *A*? d

   a. *E*   **b.** *B*   **c.** *C*   **d.** *D*

4. Which statement below is true? c

   a. $3 > 5$ **b.** $3 < -5$

   c. $3 > -5$ **d.** $3 = 5$

5. Divide: $-27 \div 3$ a

   a. -9 **b.** 9   **c.** $-\frac{1}{9}$ **d.** $\frac{1}{9}$

6. What rational number is represented by point *X* on the number line? d

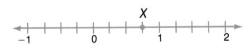

   a. $\frac{1}{3}$ **b.** $\frac{2}{3}$ **c.** $\frac{1}{4}$ **d.** $\frac{3}{4}$

7. Subtract: $-21 - 33$ b

   a. -12 **b.** -54 **c.** 54   **d.** 12

8. Solve for *n*. b

$$n - 7 = -16$$

   a. $n = -23$ **b.** $n = -9$

   c. $n = 23$ **d.** $n = 9$

9. $\sqrt{36} =$ __?__ . b

   a. $\frac{1}{6}$ **b.** 6   **c.** 1296   **d.** 9

10. Multiply: -8×50 a

   a. -400 **b.** 400   **c.** -58 **d.** 42

11. Use the table below to find $\sqrt{103}$. b

Table of Squares and Square Roots

Number	Square	Square Root
101	10,201	10,050
102	10,404	10,100
103	10,609	10,149
104	10,816	10,198
105	11,025	10,247

   a. 10,609   **b.** 10.149

   c. 10.100   **d.** 10,816

12. Use the Rule of Pythagoras,

$$c^2 = a^2 + b^2$$

to find *c* when $a = 3$ and $b = 4$. b

   a. a. 13   **b.** 5   **c.** 25   **d.** 7

13. Subtract: $-21 - (-17)$ a

   a. -4 **b.** 4   **c.** -38 **d.** 38

14. Find the height in feet of this tower. (Hint: $\tan 25° = .466$) c

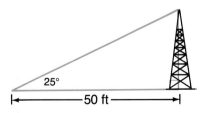

   a. 233   **b.** 107.3

   c. 23.3   **d.** 1250

15. Choose the correct formula for tangent A. d

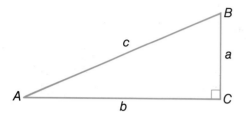

a. $\tan A = \frac{b}{c}$ **b.** $\tan A = \frac{c}{a}$

c. $\tan A = \frac{c}{b}$ **d.** $\tan A = \frac{a}{b}$

16. Find the distance a, in feet across this lake. Use the Rule of Pythagoras,

$$c^2 = a^2 + b^2.$$ b

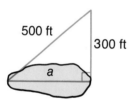

a. 100   **b.** 400   **c.** 600   **d.** 700

17. Name the coordinates of point P. c

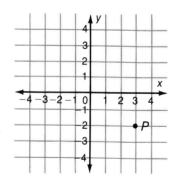

a. $(3, 2)$ **b.** $(-2, 3)$

c. $(3, -2)$ **d.** $(2, 3)$

18. Give the location in longitude and latitude of point N. a

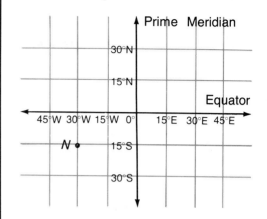

a. $(30°\,W, 15°\,S)$ **b.** $(30°\,S, 15°\,N)$

c. $(15°\,W, 30°\,N)$ **d.** $(15°\,N, 30°\,W)$

19. Triangle ABC is similar to triangle DEF. Which proportion would you use to find side d? c

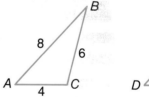

a. $\frac{4}{8} = \frac{6}{d}$ **b.** $\frac{4}{6} = \frac{d}{2}$

c. $\frac{4}{6} = \frac{2}{d}$ **d.** $\frac{4}{8} = \frac{d}{2}$

20. How many feet long is the ladder? Use $c^2 = a^2 + b^2$. b

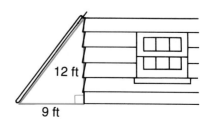

a. 12   **b.** 15   **c.** 8   **d.** 6

Sample Competency Test: Chapters 1–20

Choose the correct answer. Choose a, b, c, or d.

1. Add: 65 a
3421
+ 946

    a. 4432   **b.** 4532

    c. 4431   **d.** 4442

2. Subtract 758 from 3523.   d

    a. 3235   **b.** 4281

    c. 4280   **d.** 2765

3. Multiply: 407 b
× 96

    a. 39,082   **b.** 39,072

    c. 39,172   **d.** 39,182

4. Which decimal has the smallest value? b

    a. 3.6   **b.** 0.036

    c. 0.36   **d.** 0.136

5. Which equals 35%?   d

    a. 3.5   **b.** $\frac{7}{10}$ **c.** $\frac{35}{50}$ **d.** $\frac{7}{20}$

6. Which equals $\frac{1}{4}$?   a

    a. 25%   **b.** 2.5   **c.** 0.05   **d.** 0.04

7. The scale on a road map is:

1 centimeter represents 50 kilometers.

Two towns are 4 centimeters apart on the map. What is the real distance in kilometers between the towns? c

    a. 100   **b.** 150   **c.** 200   **d.** 250

8. This spinner has six equal areas labeled as shown. What is the probability that the pointer will stop in Area 3 on the next spin?   c

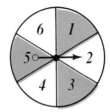

    a. $\frac{1}{3}$ **b.** $\frac{1}{2}$ **c.** $\frac{1}{6}$ **d.** 0

9. What is 55% of 75?   c

    a. 41.05   **b.** 412.5

    c. 41.25   **d.** 4.125

10. Divide: $34\overline{)714}$ b

    a. 20   **b.** 21   **c.** 24   **d.** 26

11. Add: 3.61 c
44.2
0.987
+ 1.8

    a. 50.598   **b.** 505.98

    c. 50.597   **d.** 505.97

12. Which of these represents twelve and thirty-five thousandths? c

    a. 12.35   **b.** 12,035

    c. 12.035   **d.** 1235

13. Subtract: $5\frac{2}{9}$ a
$-3\frac{7}{9}$

    a. $1\frac{4}{9}$ **b.** $2\frac{5}{9}$ **c.** $1\frac{5}{9}$ **d.** $2\frac{4}{9}$

14. Multiply: $\frac{3}{4} \times \frac{5}{7}$ a

  a. $\frac{15}{28}$ **b.** $\frac{15}{24}$ **c.** $\frac{21}{20}$ **d.** $\frac{20}{21}$

15. Multiply 15 by -9. b

  a. 135   **b.** -135 **c.** 125   **d.** -125

16. Solve for a: $\frac{3}{8} = \frac{21}{a}$ c

  a. 24   **b.** 48   **c.** 56   **d.** 30

17. Add: $17 + (-21)$ d

  a. 38   **b.** 4   **c.** -38 **d.** -4

18. Written in words, 4.003 is c

  a. four thousand three.
  b. four and three hundredths.
  c. four and three thousandths.
  d. four hundred three.

19. Using $C = 2 \times \pi \times r$, find the circumference of a circle whose radius is 4. (Use $\pi = 3.14$) a

  a. 25.12   **b.** 26.12
  c. 28.04   **d.** 31.14

20. Each pear below represents 100,000 pears. What is the total number of pears represented? b

  a. 100,000   **b.** 500,000
  c. 400,000   **d.** 300,000

21. Which number of degrees represents the measure of an acute angle? a

  a. 25   **b.** 90   **c.** 106   **d.** 180

22. Divide: $1\frac{1}{2} \div 3\frac{3}{5}$ d

  a. $\frac{4}{5}$ **b.** $\frac{54}{10}$ **c.** $\frac{5}{18}$ **d.** $\frac{5}{12}$

23. Add: $\frac{2}{3} + \frac{3}{8}$ b

  a. $\frac{23}{24}$ **b.** $1\frac{1}{24}$ **c.** $\frac{5}{24}$ **d.** $\frac{6}{24}$

24. Divide: $0.01 \overline{)3}$ c

  a. 3   **b.** 30   **c.** 300   **d.** 0.3

25. Solve for n: $\frac{n}{4} = -20$ c

  a. 80   **b.** 5   **c.** -80 **d.** -5

26. Use $c^2 = a^2 + b^2$ to find the length of the hypotenuse of a right triangle whose legs are 5 and 12. b

  a. 6   **b.** 13   **c.** 21   **d.** 14

27. How many square meters of carpet are needed to cover a rectangular floor 2 meters in length and 3 meters in width? c

  a. 5   **b.** 10   **c.** 6   **d.** 7

28. What is the volume in cubic inches of this suitcase? d

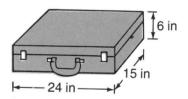

  a. 45   **b.** 2000
  c. 2060   **d.** 2160

29. Ed Lewis earns $14.50 per hour. How much does he earn for $7\frac{1}{2}$ hours of work? a

  a. $108.75   **b.** $110
  c. $2.25   **d.** $100

30. Subtract: $17 - (-21)$ a

   a. 38   **b.** 4   **c.** -38 **d.** 4

31. Which is equal to $\frac{25}{3}$?   c

   a. $2\frac{5}{3}$ **b.** $7\frac{1}{3}$ **c.** $8\frac{1}{3}$ **d.** $6\frac{1}{3}$

32. What per cent of 36 is 9?   c

   a. 20% **b.** 50% **c.** 25% **d.** 30%

33. Written as a per cent, $\frac{3}{4}$ is   b

   a. $\frac{3}{4}$% **b.** 75% **c.** 34% **d.** 7.5%

34. Which has the largest value?   d

   a. $\frac{1}{8}$ **b.** $\frac{1}{5}$ **c.** $\frac{1}{4}$ **d.** $\frac{1}{3}$

35. Which has the smallest value?   d

   a. 9   **b.** -2 **c.** 3   **d.** -6

36. Raoul bought a coat at 25% off the regular price of $60. How much did Raoul pay for the coat?   c

   a. $15 **b.** $30 **c.** $45 **d.** $50

37. Name the coordinates of point B.   a

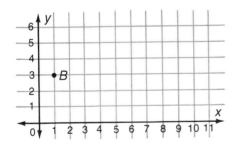

   a. $(1, 3)$ **b.** $(3, 1)$
   c. $(1, -3)$ **d.** $(-3, -1)$

38. Seven gallons of gasoline cost $10.64. What does one gallon cost?   c

   a. $1.33   **b.** $1.40
   c. $1.52   **d.** $1.63

39. Divide: $2.6\overline{)520}$ c

   a. 2   **b.** 20   **c.** 200   **d.** 2000

40. Add: $4.6 + 26.35$ d

   a. 3.095   **b.** 2.681
   c. 26.81   **d.** 30.95

41. Which of these is equal to 4%?   b

   a. 0.4 **b.** 0.04 **c.** 4.0 **d.** 0.004

42. Multiply 8.03 by 3.6.   c

   a. 2.8908   **b.** 289.08
   c. 28.908   **d.** 2890.8

43. Subtract: $36 - 4.781$ b

   a. 31.781   **b.** 31.219
   c. 32.781   **d.** 31.218

44. What is $\frac{2}{3}$ of 18?   d

   a. $\frac{2}{54}$ **b.** 27   **c.** 6   **d.** 12

45. In the last 6 years, a basketball team won 59, 82, 67, 74, 98 and 103 games.
What is the median number of games won?   c

   a. 59   **b.** 103   **c.** 78   **d.** 82

46. This circle graph shows how a city spends its money. For which item is the most money spent?   c

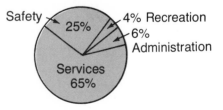

   a. Safety   **b.** Recreation
   c. Services   **d.** Administration

47. Solve for x: $3x + 4 = 13$ c

   a. 1   **b.** 2   **c.** 3   **d.** 4

48. A car costs $7000. The sales tax is 8% of the price. How much money is the sales tax?   b

   a. $420 **b.** $560 **c.** $38 **d.** $56

49. Find the average of 46, 54, and 74.

   a. 58   **b.** 60   **c.** 174   **d.** 180

50. Sue drove at an average rate of 50 miles per hour for $3\frac{1}{2}$ hours. How many miles did she drive?   a

   a. 175   **b.** 160   **c.** 150   **d.** 200

51. The sun rose at 6:30 A.M. and set at 7:00 P.M. How many hours were there between sunrise and sunset?   d

   a. 11   **b.** $10\frac{1}{2}$ **c.** $11\frac{1}{2}$ **d.** $12\frac{1}{2}$

52. Dot Ramirez had $5603 in the bank. She withdrew $395. How much money was left?   c

   a. $5308   **b.** $5402

   c. $5208   **d.** $5252

53. Bill bought a camera. He gave the clerk $20 and made 10 payments of $15 each. What was the total cost of the camera?   c

   a. $150   **b.** $215

   c. $170   **d.** $300

54. A recipe that serves 7 people calls for 2 cups of milk. How many cups of milk are needed for a recipe that serves 28 people?   c

   a. 14   **b.** 10   **c.** 8   **d.** 6

55. Divide: $25 \div (-5)$ d

   a. 5   **b.** 125   **c.** -125 **d.** -5

56. How many centimeters long is this safety pin?   a

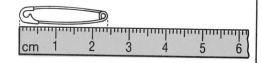

   a. 2.4   **b.** 2.6   **c.** 1.9   **d.** 3.4

57. This bar graph shows the maximum speeds of four animals. Which animal is the fastest?   a

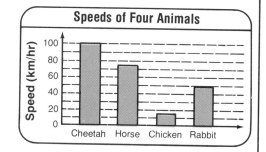

   a. cheetah   **b.** horse

   c. chicken   **d.** rabbit

58. A bag contains 3 red marbles and 6 green marbles. One marble is chosen. What is the probability that it is green?   b

   a. $\frac{1}{3}$ **b.** $\frac{2}{3}$ **c.** 1   **d.** 0

59. How many centimeters are in the perimeter of a square whose sides are each 20 centimeters long?   b

   a. 40   **b.** 80   **c.** 60   **d.** 100

60. A dinner cost $15.50. A 20% tip for the waiter is   d

   a. $2.00.   **b.** $3.00.

   c. $2.50.   **d.** $3.10.

Copy and complete this puzzle.
Write the answers to the exercises
in the boxes of the puzzle.
The answers should check across
and down. Each box holds one digit.

	1 4	7		2 1	2	3 1		4 2
5 9	8		6 4			7 6	8 3	5
9 7	2	10 9	11 9	12 8			2	
	13 5	9		14 1	15 4		16 7	17 5
	18 2	19 4			20 3	21 4	0	0
		3		22 1	0	1		6
23 4		24 7	25 1	0		26 9	27 3	
2		2	8		28 4		29 6	30 2
31 1	32 6	4	33 2	3	5	34 6		4
35 3	2				36 3	6	3	8

ACROSS

1. 19 + 28
2. 11 × 11
5. 7 × 7 × 2
7. 3175 ÷ 5
9. 13,412 − 12,683
11. 7 × 14
13. 177 ÷ 3
14. 13)‾182
16. 3 + 6 × 12
18. In a pictograph, one baseball
     represents 10 hits. How many
     baseballs are needed to represent
     240 hits?
20. Round 3362 to the nearest hundred.
22. 10 × 10 + 1
24. 701 × 10
26. 558 ÷ 6
29. 130 − 68
31. 14 × 21 − 130
33. 62 × 38
35. 20 + 24 ÷ 2
36. 1819 × 2

DOWN

1. 10,000 − 5175
3. 2 × 7 + 16 ÷ 8
4. 5 × 5
5. 8)‾776
6. 25 × 2 − 1
8. 654 × 5
10. 128 + 476 + 218 + 170
12. 432)‾34,992
15. Round 426 to the nearest ten.
17. 319 + 187
19. 5 × 86
21. 1295 − 876
22. 12 − 8 ÷ 4
23. 837 + 642 + 1364 + 1370
24. 4 × 181
25. 3094 ÷ 17
27. 36)‾1296
28. 3 × (76 + 75)
30. 8 × 31
32. 132 + 47 − 117
34. In a pictograph, one light bulb
     represents 6 lamps. How many
     lamps are represented by 11
     light bulbs?

Copy and complete this puzzle.
Write the answers to the exercises
in the boxes of the puzzle.
The answers should check across
and down. Each box holds one digit.

¹9	²4	0		³	1	4	⁴2	⁵7	
⁶5	3		⁷2		7		⁸6	1	⁹4
	¹⁰2	7	4		6		6		8
¹¹2	0		¹²8	¹³7	3			¹⁴	2	9
3				0			¹⁵6	8	6
7		¹⁶1	8	0	6		¹⁷4	3	
¹⁸1	8	6		0		¹⁹7		²⁰5	²¹3
		²²3	6			²³5	²⁴3		5
²⁵4	²⁶1	7		²⁷4		²⁸2	6	²⁹7	0
³⁰3	2		³¹3	5	8			³²8	0

ACROSS

1. Round 936 to the nearest ten.
3. 14.27 × 100
6. 23.47 + 16.24 + 13.29
8. 426.47 + 83.494 + 104.036
10. 0.274 kg = __?__ g
11. The perimeter of a square with each side of 5 is __?__ .
12. 87.3 ÷ 0.1
14. 173 − 144
15. 6.86 × 100
16. 43 × 42
17. 24)‾1032‾
18. 30 × 12.4 ÷ 2
20. 530 ÷ 10
22. The area of a square with each side of 6 cm is __?__ cm².
23. 53000 mL = __?__ L
25. 4.17 ÷ 0.01
28. 89 × 30
30. The perimeter of a rectangle with a length of 9 m and a width of 7 m is __?__ m.
31. 12)‾4296‾
32. 8000 ÷ 100

DOWN

1. 152 ÷ 1.6
2. 43.2 ÷ 0.01
3. 4.1 × 4.3 ÷ 0.01
4. 0.7)‾186.2‾
5. 8 + 9 × 7
7. 0.248 L = __?__ mL
9. 16 × 306
11. Round 2370.6 to the nearest whole number.
13. 7 kg = __?__ g
14. 81 × (40 − 5)
15. 8 × 8
16. 16.37 ÷ 0.01
19. 354 + 436 − 38
21. Round 3486 to the nearest hundred.
24. 36,000 × 0.001
25. 4824 − 4781
26. 0.382)‾4.584‾
27. 4 × 5 + 50 ÷ 2
29. 156 × 0.5

Copy and complete this puzzle.
Write the answers to the exercises
in the boxes of the puzzle.
The answers should check across
and down. Each box holds one digit.

ACROSS

1. $7\frac{3}{8} + 6\frac{5}{8}$
3. $\frac{3}{8} \times 56$
5. 21×23
6. $1175 \times \frac{1}{5}$
8. $6 \times 4 - 14 \div 2$
9. $18 \times \frac{5}{9}$
10. 64 quarts = __?__ gallons
12. $\frac{1}{8}$ mile = __?__ feet
13. $168 \times \frac{1}{4}$
14. 2.7×100
16. $3\frac{1}{8} + 8\frac{5}{6} - 1\frac{23}{24}$
17. $7 \times 2\frac{3}{4} \times \frac{8}{11}$
18. 6×73
20. The least common denominator
    for $\frac{1}{3}, \frac{2}{5}, \frac{7}{9}$ is __?__.
21. $2009 \div 7$
24. $2\frac{2}{3} \times 22\frac{1}{2}$
25. $5\frac{2}{3} \div \frac{1}{6}$
27. $36 \times \frac{3}{4}$
28. 16×54
30. 720×0.2
32. $3 \times 3 \times 3$
33. $11,000 \times 0.002$

DOWN

1. $24\frac{2}{3} - 6\frac{2}{3}$
2. $2\frac{2}{5} \times 180$
3. The circumference of a circle with a
   radius of 35 cm is __?__ cm. (π is $\frac{22}{7}$)
4. $4\frac{3}{4} + 8\frac{1}{4}$
5. Round 476.43 to the nearest
   whole number.
7. 11×47
8. $9 \times 3 - (5 + 6)$
9. 6 pints = __?__ cups
11. $0.6 \div 0.01$
14. $1\frac{1}{2} \div \frac{3}{40}$
15. $5\frac{1}{3} \times 8\frac{1}{4}$
16. $6 + 3 \times 4$
17. $2\frac{2}{5} \times 7\frac{1}{2}$
18. $22.37 + 32.65 - 9.02$
19. $4 \times 7 \times 11$
20. $0.25 \overline{)11}$
22. $15,367 - 14,543$
23. $99 \div 1\frac{2}{7}$
25. $231 + 478 - 362$
26. $0.612 \div 0.001$
29. $31 \div 0.5$
31. $168 \times \frac{1}{4}$

Copy and complete this puzzle.
Write the answers to the exercises
in the boxes of the puzzle.
The answers should check across
and down. Each box holds one digit.

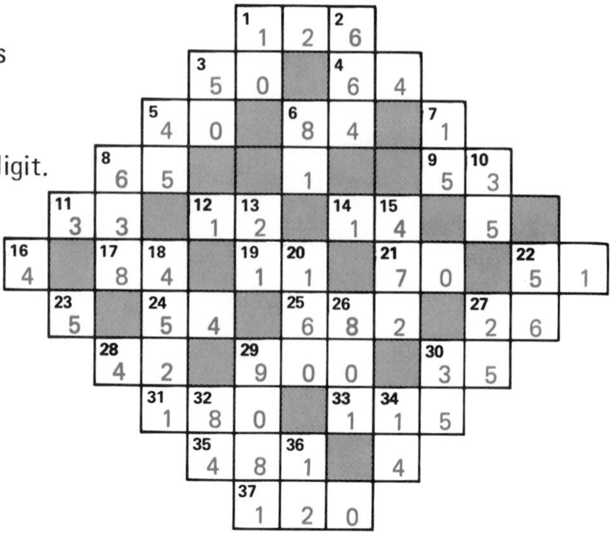

Puzzle grid (filled digits):

1:1	2	2:6		
3:5	0	4:6	4	
5:4	0	6:8	4	7:1
8:6	5	1	9:5	10:3
11:3	3	12:1	13:2	14:1	15:4	5
16:4	17:8	18:4	19:1	20:1	21:7	0	22:5	1
23:5	24:5	4	25:6	26:8	2	27:2	6
28:4	2	29:9	0	0	30:3	5
31:1	32:8	0	33:1	34:1	5
35:4	8	1	36:4
37:1	2	0

ACROSS

1. 20% of 630
3. 60% $\times$ n = 30
4. $66\frac{2}{3}$% of 96
5. $20n$ = 800
6. $\frac{n}{4}$ = 21, n = ___?___
8. 5% of 1300 = ___?___
9. 2356 − 2303
11. $\frac{18}{n}$ = $\frac{6}{11}$, n = ___?___
12. 5.79 + 8.73 − 2.52
14. 476)6664
16. $12\frac{2}{3} \div 3\frac{1}{6}$
17. $3n$ = 252, n = ___?___
19. $16\frac{2}{3}$% of 66 = ___?___
21. 80% of ___?___ = 56
22. $12 \times 4\frac{1}{4}$
23. $83\frac{1}{3}$% of 6 = ___?___
24. $45 \times 1\frac{1}{5}$
25. 40.92 ÷ .06
27. 7.44 + 9.8 + 8.76
28. 5.25 $\times$ 8
29. 15% of ___?___ = 135
30. $7.2n + 16.4$ = 268.4, n = ___?___
31. $5 \times 3 \times 3 \times 4$
33. 2.9)333.5
35. 2392 − 1911
37. $12\frac{1}{2}$% of 960 = ___?___

DOWN

1. $\frac{3}{5}$ = $\frac{6}{n}$, n = ___?___
2. 1574 − 910
3. 60% $\times$ ___?___ = 30
5. 20% $\times$ ___?___ = 9
6. $9 \div \frac{1}{9}$
7. $2n + 6$ = 36, n = ___?___
8. $\frac{n}{2}$ = 319, n = ___?___
10. $4n − 8$ = 132, n = ___?___
13. 1848 ÷ 88
15. 8 $\times$ 59
18. 137 $\times$ 33
20. 80% of 200 = ___?___
22. $\frac{7}{8}$ = $\frac{n}{64}$, n = ___?___
26. $\frac{n}{3}$ + 3 = 270, n = ___?___
27. $\frac{1}{4}$ = ___?___ %
29. 2024 + 1746 + 895 + 4416
30. ___?___ is 50% of 70
32. $\frac{n}{28}$ = 3, n = ___?___
34. $3\frac{3}{8} + 6\frac{7}{24} + 4\frac{1}{3}$
36. $18n$ = 216, n = ___?___

Copy and complete this puzzle.
Write the answers to the exercises
in the boxes of the puzzle.
The answers should check across
and down. Each box holds one digit.

Number puzzle grid (each cell shows its clue number, where present, and its digit; ■ = shaded cell):

1:5	2:7	3:8	4:4	■	5:2	6:2	■	7:1	0
■	8:4	5	0	■	9:3	7	8	■	■
■	0	10:5	11:5	4	4	■	■	12:9	13:2
14:7	3	15:5	2	■	■	16:4	0	5	■
2	0	■	■	17:6	18:9	7	■	■	6
19:3	20:8	■	21:6	■	22:2	0	0	■	■
■	8	■	23:3	8	7	■	■	24:2	25:1
26:3	0	■	4	■	■	27:6	28:2	1	6
8	■	■	29:2	30:8	31:8	■	4	■	4
32:2	5	6	■	33:6	3	4	2	■	3

ACROSS

1. $874 + 1125 + 2146 + 1639$
5. $4\frac{1}{6} + 8\frac{7}{12} + 9\frac{1}{4}$
7. If the numbers 1 to 10 are put in a hat, the probability of drawing a 5 is ? %.
8. $\frac{9}{2} = $? %
9. $\frac{2}{5} \times 945$
10. 12×462
12. $4n + 12 = 380, n = $?
14. $4.2\overline{)3087}$
16. $6075 \div 15$
17. $2 \times 21 + 5 \times 131$
19. $12.037 + 9.49 + 16.473$
22.   ? % of $45 = 90$
23. $3n = 1161, n = $?
24. The mean of 16, 21, 34, and 13 is ? .
26. 120 quarts = ? gallons
27. 56×111
29. $\frac{n}{16} + 3 = 21, n = $?
32. 8×32
33. $\frac{n}{6} = 1057, n = $?

DOWN

2. $14{,}386 - 6{,}983$
3. $5 + 8 \times 10$
4. $3n - 5 = 1210, n = $?
6. $0.61\overline{)142.74}$
7. $386 + 231 + 462 + 811$
11. $6n = 312, n = $?
13. The perimeter of a square with each side of length 64 yd is ? yd.
14. The mean of 968, 739, and 462 is ? .
15. When tossing a coin, the probability that it will turn up heads is ? %.
16. Round 469.8 to the nearest whole number.
17. $3\frac{2}{3} \times 171$
18. $\frac{90}{100} = $? %
20. 40% of ? $= 352$
21. 42×151
24. 0.021×1000
25. $1.643 \div 0.001$
26. $16 \div 8 + 10 \times 38$
28. $2 \times 11 \times 11$
30. $\frac{2}{9} \times 387$
31. $83{,}000 \text{ mL} = $? L

Copy and complete this puzzle.
Write the answers to the exercises
in the boxes of the puzzle.
The answers should check across
and down. Each box holds one digit.

¹2	²7	³6	1		⁴1	⁵9	6	⁶7
	⁷6	8		⁸1	0	8		⁹2	3
¹⁰6	4	8		¹¹2	4		¹²3	0
6		¹³9	¹⁴3	8		¹⁵3	¹⁶7	2
	¹⁷1		4			¹⁸5	2		¹⁹5
²⁰4	3	2	0		²¹6	4		²²6	6
²³3	2		²⁴2	8	9		²⁵4	9
6		²⁶4		²⁷1	6	²⁸8		²⁹4
³⁰8	³¹4	7		³²2		³³3	³⁴1	2
	³⁵2	0	6	1	3		³⁶7	6	4

ACROSS

1. 2416 + 283 + 62
4. 14^2
7. 14 − (−54)
8. −18 × (−6)
9. $4.6n = 105.8, n = \underline{\ ?\ }$
10. 54 × 12
11. $\frac{n}{-3} - 6 = -14, n = \underline{\ ?\ }$
12. $\frac{n}{4} = \frac{15}{2}, n = \underline{\ ?\ }$
13. $2n - 546 = 1330, n = \underline{\ ?\ }$
15. 80% of 465 = $\underline{\ ?\ }$
18. 39 ÷ .75
20. Round 4324 to the nearest ten.
21. $120 - 2n = 240 - 248$
22. The mean of 41, 83, 72, and 68 is $\underline{\ ?\ }$.
23. $5\frac{1}{3} \div \frac{1}{6}$
24. The area of a square with side 17 is $\underline{\ ?\ }$ square units.
25. $n - 16.4 = 32.6, n = \underline{\ ?\ }$
27. The least common denominator of $\frac{1}{8}, \frac{4}{7}, \frac{2}{3}$ is $\underline{\ ?\ }$.
30. 463 − 232 + 981 − 365
33. $\frac{n}{10} = 31.2, n = \underline{\ ?\ }$
35. 206.13 ÷ .01
36. 7.64 = $\underline{\ ?\ }$ %

DOWN

2. 14,680 − 13,916
3. 83^2
4. $16\overline{)1664}$
5. $\sqrt{49} \cdot \sqrt{196}$
6. −6n = −4380
8. $\frac{n}{-4} + 12 = -20, n = \underline{\ ?\ }$
9. $\frac{n}{16} = \frac{58}{4}, n = \underline{\ ?\ }$
10. $66\frac{2}{3}$% of 99 = $\underline{\ ?\ }$
14. 12,416 − 9,014
15. $0.3n = 106.2, n = \underline{\ ?\ }$
16. $\sqrt{5184}$
17. 150 − 6 × 3
19. $\sqrt{3136}$
20. Round 4367.6 to the nearest whole number.
21. $84\overline{)58044}$
22. 46 − (−23)
25. $n - 4837 = 0, n = \underline{\ ?\ }$
26. 6 × 120 − 10 × 25
29. $\underline{\ ?\ }$ is 25% of 1696
31. $4\frac{1}{5} = \frac{n}{10}, n = \underline{\ ?\ }$
32. $\sqrt{441}$
34. 4^2

TABLES OF MEASUREMENT

METRIC SYSTEM OF MEASURES

Length

10 millimeters (mm) = 1 centimeter (cm)
10 centimeters = 1 decimeter (dm)
100 millimeters = 1 decimeter (dm)
10 decimeters = 1 meter (m)
100 centimeters = 1 meter (m)
1000 meters = 1 kilometer (km)

Area

100 sq millimeters (mm^2) = 1 sq centimeter (cm^2)
10,000 sq centimeters = 1 sq meter (m^2)
100 sq meters = 1 are (a)
10,000 sq meters = 1 hectare (ha)

Volume

1000 cu millimeters (mm^3) = 1 cu centimeter (cm^3)
1000 cu centimeters = 1 cu decimeter (dm^3)
1,000,000 cu centimeters = 1 cu meter (m^3)

Mass

1000 milligram (mg) = 1 gram (g)
1000 grams = 1 kilogram (kg)
1000 kilograms = 1 metric ton (t)

Capacity

1000 milliliters (mL) = 1 liter (L)
1000 liters = 1 kiloliter (kL)

Temperature

Water freezes at 0° Celsius (°C).
Water boils at 100° Celsius.
Normal body temperature is 37° Celsius.

CUSTOMARY SYSTEM OF MEASURES

Length

12 inches (in) = 1 foot (ft)
3 feet = 1 yard (yd)
36 inches = 1 yard (yd)
1760 yards = 1 mile (mi)
5280 feet = 1 mile (mi)
6076 feet = 1 nautical mile

Area

144 sq inches (sq in) = 1 sq foot (sq ft)
9 sq feet = 1 sq yard (sq yd)
4840 sq yards = 1 acre (A)

Volume

1728 cu inches (cu in) = 1 cu foot (cu ft)
27 cu feet = 1 cu yard (cu yd)

Weight

16 ounces (oz) = 1 pound (lb)
2000 pounds = 1 ton (T)

Capacity

8 fluid ounces (fl oz) = 1 cup (c)
2 cups = 1 pint (pt)
2 pints = 1 quart (qt)
4 quarts = 1 gallon (gal)

Temperature

Water freezes at 32° Fahrenheit (°F).
Water boils at 212° Fahrenheit.
Normal body temperature is 98.6° Fahrenheit.

ANSWERS TO REVIEW OF RELATED SKILLS

Chapter 1   Whole Numbers: Addition/Subtraction

Page VIII   1. 15   2. 14   3. 14   4. 5   5. 13   6. 6   7. 8   8. 12   9. 7   10. 4   11. 10
12. 12   13. 5   14. 9   15. 7   16. 6   17. 10   18. 10   19. 9   20. 6   21. 11   22. 8
23. 14   24. 18   25. 7   26. 8   27. 8   28. 8   29. 17   30. 13   31. 7   32. 10
33. 14   34. 10   35. 16   36. 21   37. 22   38. 170   39. 110   40. 2100   41. 1600
42. 280   43. 210   44. 1000   45. 1800   46. 2300   47. 1600   48. 7 tens + 3 ones
49. 6 hundreds + 7 tens + 2 ones   50. 9 tens + 4 ones   51. 8 hundreds + 3 tens + 6 ones
52. 4 tens + 5 ones   53. 6 hundreds + 1 ten + 2 ones   54. 8   55. 3   56. 5   57. 9   58. 0
59. 9   60. 7   61. 3   62. 4   63. 7   64. 8   65. 4   66. 7   67. 7   68. 9   69. 9
70. 3   71. 6   72. 2   73. 6   74. 0   75. 5   76. 0   77. 7   78. 7   79. 4   80. 0
81. 7

Page 2   1. 7   2. 13   3. 11   4. 9   5. 17   6. 10   7. 10   8. 9   9. 5   10. 11   11. 11
12. 15   13. 12   14. 13

Page 7   1. 16   2. 22   3. 22   4. 19   5. 17   6. 15   7. 210   8. 160   9. 180   10. 2900
11. 2700   12. 2200

Page 10   1. 2   2. 4   3. 6   4. 5   5. 6   6. 8   7. 9   8. 6   9. 8   10. 8   11. 6   12. 2
13. 4   14. 8   15. 1 ten + 8 ones   16. 5 tens + 9 ones   17. 4 tens + 3 ones   18. 7
hundreds + 5 tens + 4 ones

Page 14   1. 10   2. 7   3. 3   4. 12   5. 7   6. 5   7. 5   8. 10   9. 4   10. 6   11. 14   12. 6
13. 8   14. 9
15. 7 tens + 0 ones   16. 2 tens + 18 ones   17. 7 hundreds + 0 tens + 1 ones   18. 3 hundreds
+ 0 tens + 0 ones   19. 5 tens + 15 ones   20. 2 tens + 19 ones   21. 8 tens + 16 ones
22. 3 tens + 15 ones

Page 17   1. 680   2. 1200   3. 410   4. 8900   5. 11,500   6. 620   7. 540   8. 240   9. 3500
10. 3900

Chapter 2   Whole Numbers: Multiplication

Page 24   1. 8   2. 12   3. 9   4. 81   5. 18   6. 28   7. 72   8. 24   9. 40   10. 27   11. 9
12. 0   13. 21   14. 14   15. 9   16. 6   17. 48   18. 63   19. 3   20. 36   21. 6
22. 36   23. 30   24. 0   25. 45   26. 42   27. 0   28. 28   29. 0   30. 24   31. 12
32. 0   33. 18   34. 18   35. 0   36. 54   37. 72   38. 40   39. 32   40. 7   41. 49
42. 24   43. 8   44. 2   45. 0   46. 63   47. 4   48. 0   49. 8   50. 4   51. 56   52. 1
53. 32   54. 0   55. 56   56. 27   57. 18   58. 0   59. 7   60. 25   61. 6   62. 0
63. 24   64. 45   65. 64   66. 21   67. 42   68. 2   69. 35   70. 5   71. 6335
72. 10,064   73. 5632   74. 7855   75. 6105   76. 7284   77. 9303   78. 5411
79. 3579   80. 10,234   81. 12,252   82. 10,835   83. 3770   84. 10,543   85. 12,795
86. 14,592   87. 11,318   88. 13,773   89. 13,944   90. 22,120

Page 26   1. 27   2. 49   3. 21   4. 45   5. 0   6. 40   7. 24   8. 0   9. 24   10. 32   11. 42
12. 30   13. 27   14. 72   15. 32   16. 35   17. 40   18. 0   19. 36   20. 64   21. 28
22. 1   23. 42   24. 72   25. 28   26. 36   27. 0   28. 18   29. 56   30. 0   31. 54
32. 0   33. 45   34. 21   35. 81   36. 56   37. 63   38. 0   39. 24   40. 48   41. 14
42. 9   43. 4   44. 25   45. 18   46. 12   47. 63   48. 9   49. 12

Page 32   1. 120   2. 279   3. 230   4. 426   5. 64   6. 340   7. 448   8. 4615   9. 4326
10. 3825   11. 1284   12. 1179   13. 4104   14. 10,256   15. 3048   16. 4735

17. 15,737   18. 6922   19. 12,353   20. 13,461   21. 12,022   22. 5704   23. 8889
24. 10,234

Page 36   1. 0   2. 728   3. 0   4. 1484   5. 18,520   6. 10,410   7. 2418   8. 4183   9. 44,462
10. 15,147   11. 367,380   12. 210,542

Page 40   1. 500   2. 900   3. 1200   4. 2400   5. 1800   6. 700   7. 1600   8. 3000   9. 700
10. 1000   11. 3600   12. 1200

Chapter 3   Whole Numbers: Division

Page 46   1. 8   2. 6   3. 11   4. 6   5. 16   6. 22   7. 15   8. 12   9. 15   10. 121   11. 24
12. 43   13. 84   14. 55   15. 100   16. 428   17. 149   18. 181   19. 1237   20. 5686
21. 1512   22. 10   23. 40   24. 790   25. 720   26. 50   27. 10   28. 900   29. 100
30. 600   31. 6800   32. 3600   33. 200   34. 5000   35. 2000   36. 18,000   37. 29,000
38. 1000   39. 1000   40. 417   41. 1240   42. 984   43. 1650   44. 2401   45. 392
46. 1100   47. 570   48. 872   49. 1472   50. 3370   51. 4338   52. 1638   53. 1887
54. 3066   55. 744   56. 1085   57. 3976   58. 5   59. 4   60. 6   61. 4   62. 4
63. 3   64. 4   65. 5   66. 3   67. 5   68. 7   69. 9   70. 9   71. 7   72. 3   73. 9
74. 4   75. 8   76. 9   77. 10   78. 9   79. 6   80. 8   81. 6   82. 7   83. 9   84. 8
85. 8   86. 2   87. 6   88. 7   89. 7   90. 9   91. 5   92. 2   93. 8   94. 5   95. 7
96. 8   97. 3   98. 10   99. 3

Page 49   1. 11   2. 11   3. 10   4. 12   5. 10   6. 17   7. 13   8. 14   9. 8   10. 30

Page 51   1. 4   2. 15   3. 18   4. 15   5. 189   6. 3001   7. 9   8. 4   9. 6   10. 9   11. 4
12. 2   13. 9   14. 7   15. 8   16. 5   17. 6   18. 9   19. 3   20. 9   21. 9   22. 6
23. 8   24. 0   25. 8   26. 7   27. 4   28. 7   29. 6   30. 3   31. 5   32. 7   33. 3
34. 3   35. 9   36. 8   37. 6   38. 8   39. 8   40. 7   41. 5   42. 2   43. 4   44. 7
45. 4   46. 7   47. 0   48. 2

Page 58   1. 10   2. 20   3. 10   4. 80   5. 50   6. 30   7. 80   8. 10   9. 10   10. 10   11. 60
12. 90   13. 60   14. 30   15. 100   16. 100   17. 400   18. 900   19. 600   20. 400
21. 100   22. 500   23. 100   24. 700   25. 200   26. 200   27. 900   28. 100   29. 678
30. 2155   31. 8505   32. 2889   33. 3512   34. 3738   35. over the 9   36. over the 0
37. over the 6   38. over the 6   39. over the 7

Page 63   1. 102   2. 60   3. 15   4. 46   5. 276   6. 3240   7. 5   8. 3   9. 28   10. 27

Page 64   1. 10   2. 20   3. 70   4. 640   5. 170   6. 430   7. 570   8. 100   9. 400   10. 400
11. 300   12. 400   13. 200   14. 300   15. 5000   16. 2000   17. 1000   18. 4000
19. 4000   20. 17,000

Chapter 4   Graphs and Applications

Page 70   1. 800   2. 19,000   3. 3,210,000   4. 42,000   5. 80,000   6. 34,670   7. 283,000
8. 46,240   9. 68,900   10. 731,000   11. 3300   12. 4,860,000   13. 28,310   14. 4600
15. 74,000   16. 70,000   17. 60   18. 10   19. 60   20. 90   21. 100   22. 60   23. 70
24. 900   25. 160   26. 120   27. 260   28. 800   29. 350   30. 740   31. 400   32. 300
33. 500   34. 400   35. 600   36. 200   37. 4500   38. 6000   39. 5000   40. 3400
41. 2200   42. 5900   43. 9000   44. 3000   45. 7000   46. 10,000   47. 4000   48. 63,000
49. 73,000   50. 82,000   51. 44,000   52. 40,000   53. 30,000   54. 40,000   55. 60,000
56. 40,000   57. 60,000   58. 160,000   59. 290,000   60. 400,000   61. 480,000
62. 680,000   63. 5,000,000   64. 10,000,000   65. 21,000,000   66. 43,000,000   67. 49
68. 55   69. 66   70. 75   71. 46   72. 19   73. 39   74. 9   75. 36   76. 18   77. 8

78. 25   79. 60   80. 30   81. 25   82. 4   83. 29   84. 29   85. 6045   86. 7910
87. 5917   88. 2224   89. 7011   90. 5724   91. 4186   92. 1502   93. 3166   94. 1039
95. 3362   96. 4453

Page 72   1. 700   2. 9800   3. 41,600   4. 131,900   5. 9,182,000   6. 62,000   7. 58,900
8. 25,700   9. 60,000   10. 8,620,000   11. 70,000   12. 120,000   13. 9000   14. 6000
15. 21,000   16. 10,000   17. 2100   18. 315,000   19. 700   20. 91,000   21. 1000
22. 10,000   23. 100,000   24. 1,000,000

Page 74   1. 60   2. 60   3. 90   4. 100   5. 350   6. 800   7. 180   8. 8000   9. 3000   10. 4000
11. 7000   12. 9000   13. 7000   14. 51,000   15. 78,000   16. 43,000   17. 16,000
18. 13,000   19. 25,000   20. 100,000   21. 80,000   22. 60,000   23. 120,000
24. 150,000

Page 76   1. 11   2. 15   3. 25   4. 24   5. 19   6. 26   7. 68   8. 59   9. 74   10. 46   11. 79
12. 67   13. 16   14. 27   15. 72   16. 49   17. 70   18. 56

Page 78   1. 2500   2. 1850   3. 4925   4. 3425   5. 3025   6. 19,000,000   7. 22,000,000
8. 4,000,000   9. 4,000,000   10. 13,000,000   11. 12,000,000   12. 17,000,000
13. 7,000,000

Chapter 5   Decimals: Addition/Subtraction/Multiplication

Page 88   1. 4   2. 9   3. 7   4. 6   5. 90   6. 50   7. 30   8. 40   9. 6   10. 7   11. 2   12. 3
13. 40   14. 90   15. 50   16. 7   17. 10   18. 30   19. 9   20. 6   21. 5   22. 363
23. 765   24. 252   25. 397   26. 451   27. 355   28. 839   29. 878   30. 5642
31. 10,699   32. 67,513   33. 75,122   34. 113,914   35. 116,695   36. 54,728
37. 65,073   38. 12   39. 219   40. 805   41. 3753   42. 1318   43. 717   44. 256
45. 569   46. 342   47. 3027   48. 441   49. 145   50. 754   51. 1738   52. 88,596
53. 209,664   54. 584,528   55. 2916   56. 42,081   57. 1,219,624   58. 504,000
59. 955,253   60. 2678   61. 603,000   62. 66,608   63. 266,500   64. 70   65. 700
66. 7000   67. 70,000   68. 7,150   69. 900   70. 9,000   71. 90,000   72. 9,300
73. **93,000**   74. 6,000   75. 61,000   76. 52,000   77. 10,000   78. 100,000

Page 91   1. 3   2. 9   3. 5   4. 7   5. 6   6. 8   7. 10   8. 50   9. 1   10. 4   11. 3   12. 7
13. 9   14. 2   15. 10   16. 70   17. 1   18. 3   19. 6   20. 8   21. 10   22. 20

Page 94   1. 83,508   2. 104,793   3. 12   4. 36   5. 857   6. 387   7. 752

Page 98   1. 783   2. 325   3. 30,888   4. 55,917   5. 1,794,898   6. 1,356,414

Page 102   1. 50   2. 520   3. 5140   4. 56,960   5. 7830   6. 900   7. 4700   8. 98,300
9. 782,100   10. 2500   11. 3000   12. 83,000   13. 426,000   14. 3,826,000
15. 228,000

Chapter 6   Decimals: Division

Page 108   1. 837   2. 2714   3. 16,842   4. 23,085   5. 302,706   6. 451,612   7. 34   8. 26
9. 68   10. 37   11. 348   12. 228   13. 66   14. 89   15. 524   16. 741   17. 3
18. 9   19. 21.9   20. 62.1   21. 0.13   22. 2.86   23. 31   24. 87   25. 0.17   26. 5.74
27. 48.9   28. 63.8   29. 34   30. 772   31. 376   32. 48.9   33. 430   34. 80   35. 17
36. 29   37. 860.2   38. 690.8   39. 710   40. 890   41. 6809   42. 4393   43. 84,700
44. 68,300   45. 5080   46. 2950   47. 39,960   48. 51,905   49. 2800   50. 16,490
51. 25,031   52. 7300   53. 0.03   54. 0.17   55. 3.61   56. 23.43   57. 0.003
58. 0.045   59. 6.134   60. 0.119   61. 0.0072   62. 0.0003   63. 0.3345   64. 0.0482
65. 60   66. 10   67. 70   68. 20   69. 230   70. 4120   71. 100   72. 100   73. 300
74. 300   75. 8300   76. 7500   77. 9000   78. 1000   79. 6000   80. 5000   81. 2000
82. 9000   83. 6 ones   84. 6 tens   85. 6 tenths   86. 6 hundredths   87. 6 thousandths

88. 6 ten-thousandths   89. 8 tenths   90. 8 hundreds   91. 8 hundredths   92. 8 ones
93. 8 thousandths   94. 8 ten-thousandths

Page 110   1. 546   2. 10,166   3. 15,808   4. 141,174   5. 67,872   6. 13   7. 103   8. 53   9. 46
10. 107

Page 113   1. 5   2. 16.7   3. 204.58   4. 150   5. 0.9   6. 14.05   7. 17   8. 5   9. 730.9
10. 2160   11. 80   12. 466.5   13. 5612   14. 21,009   15. 9730   16. 80   17. 5100
18. 5652

Page 117   1. 0.05   2. 0.13   3. 2.32   4. 15.61   5. 0.005   6. 0.037   7. 3.62   8. 0.755
9. 0.0094   10. 0.0005   11. 0.1248   12. 0.0392

Page 120   1. 20   2. 10   3. 60   4. 150   5. 1610   6. 21,980   7. 100   8. 200   9. 600
10. 2700   11. 5900   12. 50,100   13. 5000   14. 7000   15. 5000   16. 11,000
17. 53,000   18. 196,000   19. 9 ones   20. 9 hundredths   21. 9 thousandths
22. 9 tenths   23. 9 ten-thousandths   24. 9 tens

Page 122   1. 6.7   2. 0.9   3. 3.7   4. 0.7   5. 73.1   6. 109.1   7. 7.33   8. 4.93   9. 11.99
10. 7.50   11. 0.41   12. 5.05

Chapter 7   **Applying Metric Measures I**

Page 132   1. 10   2. 0   3. 20   4. 20   5. 40   6. 60   7. 50   8. 70   9. 40   10. 80   11. 70
12. 100   13. 100   14. 210   15. 470   16. 560   17. 340   18. 680   19. 900
20. 400   21. 230   22. 8   23. 4   24. 10   25. 8   26. 6   27. 9   28. 21   29. 34
30. 17   31. 20   32. 43   33. 59   34. 24   35. 82   36. 65   37. 73   38. 31   39. 29
40. 101   41. 201   42. 322   43. 684   44. 310   45. 411   46. 10   47. 24   48. 72
49. 160   50. 188   51. 140   52. 19.9   53. 18.4   54. 21.5   55. 22.4   56. 57.2
57. 29.7   58. 214.2   59. 88.3   60. 218   61. 181.7   62. 71.9   63. 160.6   64. 42
65. 189   66. 120   67. 153   68. 264   69. 143   70. 336   71. 252   72. 1720
73. 3720   74. 5183   75. 7308   76. 60.68   77. 64.17   78. 16.66   79. 53.95
80. 129.32   81. 189.95   82. 404.92   83. 198.88   84. 405   85. 84   86. 700
87. 240   88. 144   89. 120   90. 7.98   91. 18.88   92. 2.38   93. 7.02   94. 146
95. 226.5   96. 38.16   97. 59.63   98. 81.88   99. 68.355   100. 243.96   101. 525.98

Page 136   1. 10   2. 20   3. 10   4. 20   5. 20   6. 60   7. 80   8. 100   9. 10   10. 50   11. 20
12. 90   13. 160   14. 170   15. 150   16. 230   17. 9   18. 5   19. 47   20. 34
21. 91   22. 69   23. 15   24. 76   25. 100   26. 126   27. 290   28. 305

Page 140   1. 66   2. 360   3. 18   4. 25.8   5. 81.4   6. 169.7

Page 143   1. 136   2. 399   3. 2100   4. 16   5. 490   6. 9.12   7. 97.85   8. 554.32

Page 146   1. 315   2. 387   3. 16.47   4. 101.97   5. 156   6. 136

Page 147   1. 35   2. 135   3. 29.575   4. 10.08   5. 105.885   6. 1075

Chapter 8   **Applying Metric Measures II**

Page 154   1. 3; right   2. 3; left   3. 6000   4. 48,000   5. 716,000   6. 11,800   7. 7000   8. 37,000
9. 293,000   10. 9200   11. 0.0021   12. 0.000986   13. 0.7123   14. 0.091   15. 0.0035
16. 0.00048   17. 0.8441   18. 0.02   19. 27,360   20. 0.00872   21. 0.398270   22. 4200
23. 0.08523   24. 720,300   25. 9872   26. 0.0036   27. 79,380   28. 218.4   29. 0.00021
30. 0.0093   31. 132   32. 448   33. 288   34. 420   35. 336   36. 210   37. 3840

38. 1800   39. 112   40. 672   41. 2952   42. 234   43. 4599   44. 1320   45. 4320
46. 3618   47. 755.2   48. 583.8   49. 117.8   50. 97.6   51. 492.32   52. 14.58
53. 636.5   54. 18.2   55. 747   56. 478.4   57. 938.7   58. 0   59. 75.15   60. 741.32
61. 923.1   62. 95.2   63. 99   64. 20   65. 82   66. 145   67. 22   68. 57   69. 142
70. 93   71. 35   72. 154   73. 975   74. 145   75. 90   76. 65   77. 118   78. 76
79. 38   80. 178   81. 97   82. 44   83. 387   84. 504   85. 56   86. 312   87. 15
88. 20   89. 16   90. 8   91. 6   92. 7.14   93. 20.37   94. 14.5   95. 7.2   96. 0.775
97. 2.852   98. 1.242   99. 4.964   100. 17.952

Page 156   1. 3; right   2. 3; left   3. 6000   4. 65,000   5. 659,000   6. 2800   7. 9.857   8. 0.09857
9. 0.9857   10. 0.009857   11. 985.7   12. 90   13. 0.00009   14. 0.0009857

Page 158   1. 3; right   2. 3; left   3. 3500   4. 350   5. 358   6. 700   7. 0.958   8. 0.095
9. 0.009   10. 0.00009   11. 0.00095   12. 0.000958   13. 50,000   14. 1006

Page 162   1. 109   2. 122   3. 625   4. 98   5. 103   6. 57   7. 81   8. 772   9. 150   10. 56
11. 126   12. 108

Page 164   1. 756   2. 3240   3. 6080   4. 1000   5. 1710   6. 709.5   7. 10074.12   8. 36.4
9. 33.6   10. 1272   11. 905.28   12. 41.85

Page 167   1. 18   2. 126   3. 21   4. 85   5. 18.9   6. 8.8   7. 9.8   8. 18.2   9. 0.135   10. 1.68
11. 5.98   12. 13.92   13. 52   14. 135.88

Chapter 9   Fractions: Addition/Subtraction

Page 176   1. 39   2. 29   3. 38   4. 75   5. 36   6. 42   7. 42   8. 101   9. 100   10. 42   11. 57
12. 33   13. 59   14. 66   15. 82   16. 14   17. 15   18. 15   19. 28   20. 5   21. 17
22. 15   23. 17   24. 9   25. 12   26. 12   27. 37   28. 23   29. 17   30. 3   31. 217
32. 112   33. 132   34. 225   35. 84   36. 64   37. 150   38. 208   39. 279   40. 190
41. 78   42. 108   43. 44   44. 128   45. 216   46. 200   47. 108   48. 63   49. 126
50. 153   51. Yes   52. Yes   53. No   54. No   55. Yes   56. Yes   57. No   58. No
59. Yes   60. Yes   61. No   62. No   63. Yes   64. Yes   65. No   66. 5   67. 14
68. 14   69. 10   70. 16   71. 11   72. 7   73. 12   74. 12   75. 16   76. 8   77. 21
78. 9   79. 15   80. 12   81. 21   82. 12   83. 11   84. 8   85. 9   86. >   87. <
88. <   89. >   90. >   91. <   92. =   93. <   94. >   95. <   96. =   97. <   98. >
99. <   100. <   101. >

Page 179   1. 3   2. 5   3. 1   4. 1   5. 12   6. 20   7. 5   8. 27   9. 19   10. 13   11. <   12. >
13. >   14. <   15. =   16. >   17. >   18. =

Page 182   1. 3   2. 9   3. 3   4. 25   5. 25   6. 14   7. 16   8. 41   9. 14   10. 72   11. 57
12. 11   13. 13   14. 103   15. 27   16. No   17. Yes   18. Yes   19. No   20. Yes
21. Yes   22. Yes   23. No   24. Yes   25. Yes   26. No   27. Yes   28. Yes   29. Yes
30. No   31. No   32. No   33. Yes

Page 186   1. 42   2. 25   3. 35   4. 44   5. 54   6. 19   7. 43   8. 33   9. 53   10. 9   11. $\frac{1}{2}$
12. $\frac{1}{6}$ 13. $2\frac{1}{4}$ 14. $\frac{5}{7}$ 15. $\frac{2}{9}$ 16. $\frac{1}{2}$ 17. $\frac{4}{7}$ 18. $\frac{9}{11}$

Page 189   1. 42   2. 90   3. 75   4. 98   5. 80   6. 160   7. 40   8. 54   9. 36   10. 33   11. 96
12. 112

Page 190   1. 42   2. 90   3. 75   4. 98   5. 95   6. 108   7. 117   8. 80   9. 104   10. 105
11. 102   12. 56   13. 176   14. 225   15. 238   16. 96   17. 72   18. 57   19. $\frac{2}{3}$

20. $1\frac{1}{3}$ 21. $\frac{7}{8}$ 22. $\frac{3}{4}$ 23. $2\frac{1}{2}$ 24. $1\frac{5}{9}$

Page 194   1. 4   2. 3   3. 5   4. 10   5. 400   6. $\frac{2}{5}$ 7. $\frac{1}{9}$ 8. $\frac{7}{12}$ 9. $\frac{2}{5}$ 10. $\frac{3}{4}$ 11. $\frac{4}{15}$ 12. 12

13. 20   14. 15   15. 18   16. 40

Chapter 10   Fractions: Multiplication/Division

Page 202   1. 168   2. 155   3. 69   4. 33   5. 189   6. 76   7. 132   8. 125   9. 182   10. 450
11. 387   12. 270   13. 76   14. 87   15. 280   16. 96   17. 102   18. 144   19. 120
20. 308   21. 28   22. 144   23. 240   24. 344   25. 184   26. 90   27. 84   28. 91
29. 162   30. 180   31. 9, 3   32. 14, 15   33. 6, 7   34. 7, 18   35. 8, 7   36. 5, 8
37. 3, 4   38. 4, 12   39. 7, 13   40. 4, 5   41. 4, 9   42. 2, 3   43. 6, 10   44. 3, 4
45. 2, 3   46. 5, 16   47. 2, 5   48. 13, 16   49. 5, 14   50. 6, 10   51. 5, 11   52. $3\frac{1}{3}$

53. $1\frac{5}{6}$ 54. $4\frac{1}{2}$ 55. $1\frac{7}{9}$ 56. $2\frac{4}{5}$ 57. $1\frac{3}{4}$ 58. $1\frac{5}{7}$ 59. $1\frac{3}{5}$ 60. $3\frac{1}{2}$ 61. $4\frac{1}{3}$ 62. $2\frac{1}{6}$

63. $2\frac{1}{7}$ 64. $2\frac{1}{2}$ 65. $4\frac{1}{4}$ 66. $3\frac{5}{6}$ 67. $2\frac{3}{4}$ 68. $5\frac{1}{2}$ 69. $3\frac{2}{5}$ 70. $5\frac{2}{3}$ 71. $3\frac{4}{7}$ 72. $3\frac{1}{8}$

73. $2\frac{8}{9}$ 74. $4\frac{2}{5}$ 75. $5\frac{7}{8}$ 76. $7\frac{1}{3}$ 77. $2\frac{1}{6}$ 78. $7\frac{1}{2}$ 79. $6\frac{3}{7}$ 80. $9\frac{1}{8}$ 81. $9\frac{2}{3}$ 82. $7\frac{1}{5}$

83. $10\frac{1}{2}$ 84. $5\frac{4}{9}$ 85. $2\frac{1}{9}$ 86. $4\frac{3}{4}$ 87. $\frac{2}{5}$ 88. $\frac{3}{8}$ 89. $\frac{1}{5}$ 90. $\frac{5}{6}$ 91. $\frac{1}{2}$ 92. $\frac{3}{4}$

93. $\frac{1}{4}$ 94. $\frac{1}{3}$ 95. $\frac{1}{4}$ 96. $\frac{1}{3}$ 97. $\frac{1}{3}$ 98. $\frac{1}{3}$ 99. $\frac{2}{3}$ 100. $\frac{2}{3}$ 101. $\frac{2}{3}$ 102. $\frac{2}{15}$

103. $\frac{1}{3}$ 104. $\frac{1}{2}$ 105. $\frac{1}{3}$ 106. $\frac{1}{2}$ 107. $\frac{7}{8}$ 108. $\frac{1}{4}$ 109. $\frac{3}{5}$ 110. $\frac{5}{7}$ 111. $\frac{5}{6}$ 112. $\frac{9}{10}$

113. $\frac{8}{9}$ 114. $\frac{3}{4}$ 115. $\frac{1}{2}$ 116. $\frac{1}{8}$ 117. $\frac{1}{8}$ 118. $\frac{5}{11}$ 119. $\frac{1}{3}$ 120. $\frac{3}{7}$ 121. $\frac{4}{7}$

Page 205   1. $1\frac{3}{7}$ 2. $2\frac{8}{9}$ 3. $5\frac{7}{9}$ 4. $33\frac{1}{3}$ 5. $9\frac{3}{5}$ 6. $12\frac{3}{4}$ 7. $7\frac{7}{12}$ 8. $7\frac{3}{11}$ 9. $\frac{1}{2}$ 10. $\frac{3}{8}$ 11. $\frac{2}{5}$

12. $\frac{9}{16}$ 13. $\frac{3}{4}$ 14. $\frac{1}{2}$ 15. $\frac{1}{4}$ 16. $\frac{2}{3}$

Page 208   1. $4\frac{1}{2}$ 2. $2\frac{1}{5}$ 3. $5\frac{2}{5}$ 4. $9\frac{5}{6}$ 5. $6\frac{4}{7}$ 6. $9\frac{1}{4}$ 7. $4\frac{2}{3}$ 8. $9\frac{1}{8}$ 9. $\frac{2}{3}$ 10. $\frac{1}{3}$ 11. $\frac{1}{3}$

12. $\frac{5}{9}$ 13. $\frac{1}{6}$ 14. $\frac{3}{16}$ 15. $\frac{4}{5}$ 16. $\frac{6}{7}$

Page 212   1. $\frac{11}{12}$ 2. $\frac{5}{9}$ 3. $\frac{3}{5}$ 4. $\frac{1}{5}$ 5. $\frac{1}{3}$ 6. $\frac{3}{10}$ 7. $\frac{2}{3}$ 8. $\frac{8}{25}$ 9. $\frac{7}{10}$ 10. $\frac{5}{7}$ 11. $\frac{9}{10}$ 12. $\frac{2}{3}$

13. $\frac{3}{7}$ 14. $\frac{2}{3}$ 15. $\frac{8}{11}$ 16. $\frac{5}{6}$ 17. 1   18. 1   19. 1   20. 1   21. $\frac{3}{4}$ 22. $\frac{3}{7}$ 23. $2\frac{1}{10}$

24. 49   25. $\frac{1}{4}$ 26. 2   27. $1\frac{3}{4}$ 28. $1\frac{1}{2}$ 29. 12   30. $12\frac{3}{5}$ 31. $\frac{1}{2}$ 32. $\frac{3}{7}$ 33. 3

34. $\frac{1}{12}$

Page 214   1. $\frac{7}{3}$ 2. $\frac{57}{8}$ 3. $\frac{48}{5}$ 4. $\frac{38}{3}$ 5. $\frac{135}{8}$ 6. $\frac{100}{9}$ 7. $\frac{11}{10}$ 8. $\frac{29}{6}$ 9. $\frac{8}{5}$ 10. $\frac{7}{6}$ 11. 15

12. $\frac{1}{21}$ 13. $\frac{50}{41}$ 14. $\frac{1}{18}$ 15. 50   16. $\frac{25}{9}$ 17. $1\frac{7}{8}$ 18. $\frac{3}{10}$ 19. $2\frac{1}{3}$ 20. $\frac{2}{9}$ 21. $2\frac{16}{27}$

22. $4\frac{4}{9}$ 23. $\frac{3}{4}$ 24. $\frac{1}{3}$ 25. $\frac{2}{3}$ 26. $\frac{1}{2}$ 27. 8   28. 3

Chapter 11   Circles and Applications

Page 224   1. Yes   2. Yes   3. No   4. Yes   5. Yes   6. No   7. Yes   8. No   9. No   10. Yes
11. No   12. No   13. Yes   14. Yes   15. 9.42   16. 28.26   17. 37.68   18. 50.24
19. 7.222   20. 21.352   21. 8.478   22. 53.694   23. 37.68   24. 56.52   25. 43.96
26. 25.12   27. 1   28. 2   29. 14   30. 25   31. 47   32. 100   33. 62   34. 25
35. 18   36. 37   37. 86   38. 103   39. 100 cm^3 40. 27 cm^3 41. 168 cm^3

42. 960 cm^3 43. 729 cm^3 44. 12.6 cm^3 45. 62.976 cm^3 46. 13.34 cm^3 47. $\frac{8}{3}$

48. $\frac{9}{8}$ 49. $\frac{39}{4}$ 50. $\frac{13}{2}$ 51. $\frac{99}{8}$ 52. $\frac{89}{6}$ 53. $\frac{64}{3}$ 54. $\frac{53}{16}$ 55. $\frac{33}{2}$ 56. $\frac{213}{10}$
57. $\frac{139}{10}$ 58. $\frac{51}{2}$ 59. 44 60. 66 61. 176 62. 22 63. 176 64. 220 65. 396
66. 484 67. $17\frac{3}{5}$ 68. $29\frac{1}{3}$ 69. 33 70. $13\frac{1}{5}$ 71. 0 72. 1 73. 1 74. 0 75. 3
76. 3 77. 10 78. 9 79. 7 80. 20 81. 21 82. 13

Page 226
1. 6.28 2. 31.4 3. 185.26 4. 5.024 5. 227.65 6. 61.544 7. 59.66 8. 174.584
9. $\frac{22}{7}$ 10. $\frac{7}{4}$ 11. $\frac{21}{4}$ 12. $\frac{87}{8}$ 13. $\frac{77}{3}$ 14. $\frac{197}{16}$ 15. $\frac{113}{6}$ 16. $\frac{504}{5}$ 17. 308
18. 1760 19. 2200 20. $157\frac{1}{7}$ 21. 21 22. 74 23. 55 24. 35 25. 62 26. 41
27. 1 28. 5 29. 24 30. 153 31. 302 32. 28

Page 230
1. 50.24 2. 314 3. 0.0314 4. 19.625 5. $\frac{22}{7}$ 6. $\frac{31}{10}$ 7. $\frac{17}{8}$ 8. $\frac{23}{2}$ 9. $\frac{48}{5}$
10. $\frac{201}{16}$ 11. $\frac{20}{3}$ 12. $\frac{1029}{20}$ 13. 1386 14. $254\frac{4}{7}$ 15. $55\frac{11}{25}$ 16. $31\frac{9}{11}$ 17. 616
18. $63\frac{9}{14}$ 19. $236\frac{4}{63}$ 20. $86\frac{5}{8}$ 21. 1 22. 2 23. 9 24. 30 25. 15 26. 5
27. 22 28. 18 29. 63 30. 85 31. 51 32. 95

Page 233
1. 240 cm³ 2. 64 cm³ 3. 229.5 cm³ 4. 401.8 cm³ 5. 13 6. 36 7. 10 8. 81
9. 116 10. 402 11. 4 12. 9 13. 12 14. 404 15. 1023 16. 5340

Page 236
1. Yes 2. Yes 3. Yes 4. No 5. No 6. Yes 7. Yes 8. 10 9. 17 10. 101
11. 90 12. 67 13. 9 14. 5 15. 18 16. 10 17. 13 18. 17 19. 1 20. 16
21. 0 22. 28.26 23. 84.78 24. 418 25. 110

Chapter 12   Equations/Ratio/Proportion

Page 246
1. 21 2. 37 3. 61 4. 111 5. 44 6. 7 7. 23 8. 25 9. 32 10. 14 11. 180
12. 128 13. 1302 14. 1700 15. 3133 16. 14 17. 23 18. 19 19. 18 20. 22
21. 4.8 22. 14 23. 7.4 24. 16.1 25. 7.5 26. 2.1 27. 1.9 28. 1.6 29. 1.8
30. 37.8 31. 12.3 32. 145.8 33. 14.7 34. 7.2 35. 17.6 36. 34.56 37. 1.83
38. 13.05 39. 62.31 40. 8.01 41. 5 42. 11.6 43. 4.5 44. 1.2 45. 0.24
46. 0.62 47. 0.4 48. 10 49. 10 50. 2.1 51. $\frac{1}{2}$ 52. $\frac{6}{7}$ 53. $\frac{4}{5}$ 54. $\frac{1}{3}$ 55. $\frac{2}{9}$
56. $\frac{7}{9}$ 57. $\frac{8}{9}$ 58. $\frac{6}{11}$ 59. $\frac{5}{6}$ 60. $\frac{37}{40}$ 61. $1\frac{7}{18}$ 62. $1\frac{5}{8}$ 63. $1\frac{4}{21}$ 64. $\frac{19}{28}$ 65. $\frac{2}{3}$
66. $\frac{43}{56}$ 67. $\frac{13}{14}$ 68. $1\frac{5}{24}$ 69. $\frac{5}{14}$ 70. $\frac{27}{40}$ 71. $\frac{1}{12}$ 72. $\frac{3}{8}$ 73. $\frac{1}{2}$ 74. $\frac{2}{9}$ 75. $\frac{1}{10}$
76. $\frac{1}{20}$ 77. $\frac{4}{21}$ 78. $\frac{1}{12}$

Page 249
1. 11 2. 28 3. 0 4. 88 5. 7 6. 5.5 7. 0.9 8. 42.8 9. 16.7 10. 13.83
11. $\frac{1}{4}$ 12. $\frac{3}{8}$ 13. $\frac{1}{6}$ 14. $\frac{7}{24}$ 15. $\frac{11}{20}$ 16. 24 17. 36 18. 52 19. 75 20. 101
21. 8.9 22. 7.7 23. 2.2 24. 14.5 25. 7.7 26. $\frac{23}{24}$ 27. $\frac{5}{6}$ 28. $\frac{11}{12}$ 29. $1\frac{7}{24}$
30. $\frac{17}{18}$

Page 252
1. 1 2. 14 3. 13 4. 29 5. 22 6. 5 7. 16 8. 10 9. 1.5 10. 2 11. 180
12. 120 13. 132 14. 1625 15. 9000 16. 45 17. 109 18. 14.4 19. 8.12
20. 19.44

Page 256
1. 11 2. 15 3. 57 4. 111 5. 9 6. 9 7. 16 8. 106 9. 7 10. 9 11. 72
12. 21 13. 102 14. 43 15. 240 16. 126 17. 62 18. 340

Page 260 1. $\frac{1}{2}$ 2. $\frac{1}{3}$ 3. $\frac{2}{3}$ 4. $\frac{2}{3}$ 5. $\frac{1}{4}$ 6. $\frac{1}{3}$ 7. $\frac{1}{2}$ 8. $\frac{2}{11}$ 9. $\frac{3}{5}$ 10. $\frac{2}{3}$ 11. $\frac{1}{9}$ 12. $\frac{13}{16}$
13. $\frac{7}{8}$ 14. $\frac{1}{15}$ 15. $\frac{3}{7}$ 16. $\frac{11}{13}$ 17. 162 18. 70 19. 360 20. 108 21. 60 22. 104
23. 180 24. 180 25. 1080 26. 2259

Page 264 1. 459 2. 288 3. 310 4. 340 5. 156 6. 600 7. 375 8. 364 9. 2993
10. 1972 11. 7 12. 18 13. 32 14. 43 15. 57 16. 84 17. 3 18. 2 19. 25
20. 7 21. 20 22. 15 23. 10 24. 26

Chapter 13   Per Cent

Page 272 1. tenths 2. tens 3. hundredths 4. ones 5. thousandths 6. hundredths 7. 1316.50
8. 55.85 9. 772.45 10. 63.08 11. 83.46 12. 29.16 13. 96 14. 360 15. 41
16. 62 17. 81.4 18. 92.7 19. 0.4 20. 0.8 21. 0.16 22. 0.23 23. 0.04
24. 0.02 25. 0.017 26. 0.069 27. $0.85\frac{5}{7}$ 28. $0.62\frac{1}{2}$ 29. $0.83\frac{1}{3}$ 30. $0.55\frac{5}{9}$
31. $0.91\frac{2}{3}$ 32. 0.65 33. 43 34. 39.7 35. 16.75 36. 8.64 37. 0.058 38. 0.1
39. 1.000 40. 17 41. $\frac{4}{25}$ 42. $\frac{29}{100}$ 43. $\frac{12}{25}$ 44. $\frac{11}{20}$ 45. $\frac{17}{50}$ 46. $\frac{3}{25}$ 47. $\frac{3}{800}$
48. $\frac{1}{180}$ 49. 1050 50. 1840 51. $\frac{7}{4}$ 52. $\frac{9}{2}$ 53. $\frac{61}{4}$ 54. $\frac{100}{7}$ 55. $\frac{131}{6}$ 56. $\frac{200}{3}$
57. $\frac{3}{800}$ 58. $\frac{3}{500}$ 59. $\frac{1}{400}$ 60. $\frac{1}{180}$ 61. $\frac{7}{1000}$ 62. $\frac{3}{50}$ 63. $\frac{2}{25}$ 64. $\frac{1}{4}$ 65. $\frac{3}{10}$
66. $\frac{1}{2}$ 67. $\frac{3}{25}$ 68. $\frac{1}{5}$ 69. $\frac{49}{50}$ 70. $\frac{33}{50}$ 71. $\frac{1}{50}$

Page 274 1. $\frac{1}{20}$ 2. $\frac{7}{100}$ 3. $\frac{1}{10}$ 4. $\frac{21}{100}$ 5. $\frac{9}{100}$ 6. tenths 7. hundredths 8. tens
9. hundredths 10. thousandths 11. hundredths

Page 277 1. 0.18 2. 0.21 3. 0.05 4. 0.03 5. 0.195 6. 0.5015 7. 1.19 8. 1.54 9. 0.005
10. 0.008 11. 0.0156 12. 0.0783 13. 35 14. 71 15. 8 16. 4 17. 87.5
18. 16.5 19. 145 20. 197 21. 0.5 22. 0.8 23. $33\frac{1}{3}$ 24. $66\frac{2}{3}$

Page 278 1. $\frac{2}{25}$ 2. $\frac{1}{25}$ 3. $\frac{1}{4}$ 4. $\frac{1}{2}$ 5. $\frac{127}{200}$ 6. $\frac{19}{50}$ 7. $\frac{1}{200}$ 8. $\frac{1}{800}$ 9. $\frac{1}{120}$ 10. $\frac{1}{150}$
11. $\frac{1}{300}$ 12. $\frac{7}{800}$ 13. $\frac{1}{250}$ 14. $\frac{1}{150}$ 15. $\frac{3}{2}$ 16. $\frac{57}{8}$ 17. $\frac{100}{3}$ 18. $\frac{37}{2}$ 19. $\frac{50}{3}$
20. $\frac{125}{2}$

Page 280 1. 0.80 2. 0.10 3. 0.50 4. 0.75 5. 0.85 6. 0.26 7. $0.37\frac{1}{2}$ 8. $0.46\frac{2}{3}$ 9. 0.60
10. $0.85\frac{5}{7}$ 11. $0.21\frac{2}{3}$ 12. 0.95 13. 28% 24. 39% 15. 6% 16. 1% 17. 12.5%
18. 61.5% 19. 160% 20. 540% 21. 90% 22. 80% 23. $12\frac{1}{2}$% 24. $16\frac{1}{3}$%

Page 283 1. 0.21 2. 0.35 3. 0.05 4. 0.04 5. 0.125 6. 0.085 7. 120 8. 346.56
9. 13.83 10. 6.48 11. 11.13 12. 805 13. 412 14. 670 15. 170 16. 253

Page 288 1. 0.06 2. 0.09 3. 0.03 4. 0.05 5. 0.12 6. 0.25 7. 0.20 8. 0.10 9. 63
10. 175 11. 120 12. 56 13. 948 14. 1400 15. 5000 16. 1425 17. 312.5
18. 1218.50 19. 62.70 20. 694.05 21. 26.63 22. 8.16 23. 19.56 24. 110.78
25. 73.48 26. 82.90 27. 0.73 28. 7.21 29. 15.37 30. 34.28 31. 0.42 32. 0.31
33. 10.38 34. 15.06 35. 8.30 36. 18.22 37. $0.27 38. $0.59 39. $6.75
40. $15.00 41. $7.21

Page 291 1. 59 2. 17 3. 11 4. 33 5. 71 6. 83 7. 44 8. 5 9. 6 10. 20 11. 2

12. 70   13. 400   14. 152   15. 101   16. 100   17. 69   18. 42   19. 60   20. 20
21. 10   22. 30   23. 70   24. 80   25. 40   26. 50   27. 50   28. 90   29. 70   30. 80
31. 90   32. 64   33. 71   34. 130   35. 30   36. 640   37. 47   38. 125   39. 270
40. 750

Chapter 14   More On Per Cent

Page 298   1. 400   2. 1700   3. 900   4. 200   5. 544   6. 384   7. 42.5   8. 38.44   9. 52
10. 1200   11. 800   12. 5   13. 3   14. 13   15. 9   16. 13   17. 20   18. 5   19. $\frac{7}{12}$
20. $\frac{8}{9}$ 21. $\frac{1}{3}$ 22. $\frac{1}{5}$ 23. $\frac{1}{3}$ 24. $\frac{21}{40}$ 25. 14   26. 160   27. 175   28. 31   29. 3
30. 7   31. 3   32. 19   33. 0.16   34. 0.45   35. 0.06   36. 0.09   37. $0.12\frac{1}{2}$ 38. $0.33\frac{1}{3}$
39. 63%   40. 56%   41. 5%   42. 3%   43. $14\frac{2}{7}\%$ 44. $37\frac{1}{2}\%$ 45. $\frac{2}{5}$ 46. $\frac{11}{20}$ 47. $\frac{37}{100}$
48. $\frac{21}{100}$ 49. $\frac{2}{3}$ 50. $\frac{5}{8}$ 51. 0.75 = 75%   52. 0.40 = 40%   53. 0.50 = 50%   54. 0.25
= 25%   55. $0.37\frac{1}{2} = 37\frac{1}{2}\%$ 56. $0.55\frac{5}{9} = 55\frac{5}{9}\%$ 57. 0.20 = 20%   58. $0.28\frac{4}{7} = 28\frac{4}{7}\%$
59. 0.25   60. 0.60   61. 0.60   62. 0.80   63. $0.77\frac{7}{9}$ 64. $0.83\frac{1}{3}$ 65. 0.04   66. 0.05
67. 0.5   68. 0.75   69. 0.35   70. 0.75   71. 0.18   72. 0.2   73. 0.4   74. 0.14
75. 0.02   76. $0.22\frac{2}{9}$

Page 301   1. 4   2. 5   3. 14   4. 25   5. 9   6. 32   7. 5   8. 14   9. 12   10. 9   11. 25%
12. 20%   13. 5%   14. $3\frac{1}{3}\%$ 15. $37\frac{1}{2}\%$ 16. $87\frac{1}{2}\%$ 17. $62\frac{1}{2}\%$ 18. 75%

Page 304   1. 600   2. 800   3. 1400   4. 1700   5. $\frac{5}{8}$ 6. $\frac{3}{4}$ 7. $\frac{7}{24}$ 8. $\frac{3}{16}$ 9. $\frac{25}{29}$ 10. $\frac{2}{5}$
11. 25%   12. $33\frac{1}{3}\%$ 13. 20%   14. $16\frac{2}{3}\%$ 15. $12\frac{1}{2}\%$ 16. 10%   17. 5%   18. 4%
19. 75%   20. 60%   21. $66\frac{2}{3}\%$ 22. $62\frac{1}{2}\%$ 23. $83\frac{1}{3}\%$ 24. $87\frac{1}{2}\%$ 25. 70%   26. 65%
27. 6   28. 12   29. 7   30. 25   31. 19   32. 9

Page 306   1. 0.70   2. 0.50   3. 0.07   4. 0.04   5. 0.01   6. 0.09   7. 0.18   8. 0.92   9. 120
10. 28   11. 700   12. 300   13. 240   14. 700   15. 1300   16. 3700   17. 14   18. 25
19. 180   20. 3   21. 370   22. 24   23. $\frac{1}{5}$ 24. $\frac{3}{10}$ 25. $\frac{1}{4}$ 26. $\frac{1}{2}$ 27. $\frac{1}{3}$ 28. $\frac{1}{8}$
29. 108   30. 12   31. 24   32. 12   33. 126   34. 100

Page 311   1. 0.15   2. 0.37   3. 0.05   4. 0.08   5. 0.90   6. $0.12\frac{1}{2}$ or 0.125   7. $\frac{1}{5}$ 8. $\frac{1}{10}$ 9. $\frac{1}{4}$
10. $\frac{7}{8}$ 11. $\frac{1}{3}$ 12. $\frac{1}{6}$ 13. 336   14. 30   15. 25.5   16. 398.56   17. 113.9   18. 69.8
19. 309.12   20. 345   21. 0.50   22. 0.20   23. 0.25   24. $0.12\frac{1}{2}$ 25. 0.40
26. 0.75   27. $0.62\frac{1}{2}$ 28. 0.80   29. $0.87\frac{1}{2}$ 30. 0.60   31. $0.37\frac{1}{2}$ 32. 0.90   33. 72%
34. 81%   35. 2%   36. 9%   37. $33\frac{1}{3}\%$ 38. $87\frac{1}{2}\%$

Page 315   1. n × 200 = 175   2. n = 25% × 200   3. 900 = 2% × n   4. n × 9 = 3   5. 0.50   6. 0.80
7. 0.90   8. 0.25   9. 0.35   10. 0.18   11. 0.12   12. $0.37\frac{1}{2}$ 13. 5   14. 1.143
15. 1.11   16. 0.105   17. 25%   18. 60%   19. 70%   20. 65%   21. 32%   22. $33\frac{1}{3}\%$
23. $12\frac{1}{2}\%$ 24. $83\frac{1}{3}\%$

Chapter 15   Statistics

Page 328   1. 2414   2. 2368   3. 1794   4. 2710   5. 2509   6. 2037   7. 55   8. 161   9. 154
10. 170   11. 232   12. 149   13. 12.3   14. 8.2   15. 3.5   16. 9.6   17. March   18. July
19. March and April   20. =   21. >   22. <   23. <   24. >   25. >   26. 14   27. 25
28. 17   29. 20   30. 321   31. 686   32. 76   33. 69   34. 21   35. 37   36. 97

37. 102   38. 0.65   39. 0.42   40. 0.03   41. 0.06   42. $0.14\frac{2}{7}$ 43. $0.66\frac{2}{3}$ 44. 80°
45. 115°   46. 90°   47. 30°

Page 331   1. 1715   2. 1758   3. 1495   4. 1390   5. 1616   6. 1752   7. 81   8. 141   9. 287
10. 57   11. 1498   12. 8.5   13. 2.6   14. 27.4   15. 21.9   16. 2.32

Page 333   1. >   2. >   3. <   4. <   5. <   6. =   7. >   8. =

Page 336   1. <   2. >   3. =   4. <   5. >   6. >   7. >   8. >

Page 339   1. May and June   2. April and May   3. February

Page 341   1. 0.38   2. 0.25   3. 0.09   4. 0.03   5. 0.165   6. $0.37\frac{1}{2}$ 7. 17   8. 89   9. 47

10. 316   11. 42   12. 137   13. 145°   14. 90°   15. 65°   16. 85°

Chapter 16   Probability

Page 346   1. $\frac{1}{2}$ 2. $\frac{1}{3}$ 3. $\frac{3}{10}$ 4. $\frac{1}{5}$ 5. $\frac{1}{6}$ 6. $\frac{1}{4}$ 7. $\frac{2}{3}$ 8. $\frac{2}{3}$ 9. $\frac{2}{3}$ 10. $\frac{2}{3}$ 11. $\frac{2}{3}$ 12. $\frac{3}{4}$

13. $\frac{5}{6}$ 14. $\frac{5}{6}$ 15. $\frac{1}{4}$ 16. $\frac{1}{5}$ 17. $\frac{3}{25}$ 18. $\frac{1}{12}$ 19. $\frac{1}{3}$ 20. $\frac{2}{3}$ 21. $\frac{3}{4}$ 22. $\frac{2}{5}$ 23. $\frac{2}{9}$

24. $\frac{3}{5}$ 25. $\frac{1}{2}$ 26. $\frac{1}{2}$ 27. $\frac{3}{4}$ 28. $\frac{7}{9}$ 29. $\frac{25}{36}$ 30. $\frac{1}{3}$ 31. $\frac{3}{5}$ 32. $\frac{4}{7}$ 33. 1   34. 1

35. $\frac{1}{3}$ 36. $\frac{5}{9}$ 37. $\frac{1}{2}$ 38. 1   39. 1   40. 1   41. $\frac{12}{13}$ 42. $\frac{3}{4}$ 43. $\frac{1}{2}$ 44. $\frac{1}{2}$ 45. $\frac{13}{18}$

46. $\frac{5}{9}$ 47. $\frac{1}{3}$ 48. $\frac{3}{4}$ 49. $\frac{7}{9}$ 50. $\frac{5}{18}$ 51. 1   52. $\frac{3}{5}$ 53. $\frac{3}{5}$ 54. $\frac{7}{10}$ 55. $\frac{1}{3}$ 56. $\frac{7}{18}$

57. $\frac{5}{9}$ 58. $\frac{2}{3}$ 59. $\frac{1}{4}$ 60. $\frac{3}{4}$ 61. $\frac{2}{5}$ 62. $\frac{1}{2}$ 63. $\frac{1}{2}$ 64. $\frac{2}{3}$ 65. $\frac{1}{3}$ 66. $\frac{1}{8}$ 67. $\frac{5}{8}$

68. $\frac{1}{4}$ 69. $\frac{2}{3}$ 70. $\frac{1}{3}$ 71. $\frac{5}{12}$ 72. $\frac{5}{6}$ 73. $\frac{1}{2}$ 74. $\frac{3}{8}$ 75. $\frac{3}{5}$ 76. $\frac{11}{20}$ 77. 50%

78. 20%   79. 60%   80. 50%   81. 70%   82. 40%   83. 35%   84. 75%   85. 25%

86. 14%   87. 32%   88. 7%   89. 19%   90. 100%   91. 100%   92. 0%   93. 0%   94. $17\frac{1}{2}$%

95. 38%   96. $52\frac{1}{2}$%   97. $62\frac{1}{2}$%   98. $83\frac{1}{3}$%   99. $11\frac{1}{9}$%   100. $8\frac{1}{3}$%   101. $12\frac{1}{2}$%

102. $87\frac{1}{2}$%   103. $42\frac{6}{7}$%   104. $66\frac{2}{3}$%   105. $66\frac{2}{3}$%   106. $16\frac{2}{3}$%

Page 348   1. $\frac{2}{3}$ 2. $\frac{5}{6}$ 3. $\frac{1}{3}$ 4. $\frac{9}{10}$ 5. $\frac{3}{8}$ 6. $\frac{1}{2}$ 7. $\frac{7}{12}$ 8. $\frac{3}{8}$ 9. $\frac{5}{11}$ 10. $\frac{2}{5}$ 11. $\frac{27}{100}$ 12. $\frac{1}{5}$

13. $\frac{3}{10}$ 14. 25%   15. 10%   16. 75%   17. 80%   18. 74%   19. 45%   20. 100%

21. $37\frac{1}{2}$%

Page 351   1. $\frac{5}{7}$ 2. $\frac{3}{5}$ 3. $\frac{1}{2}$ 4. $\frac{1}{3}$ 5. $\frac{1}{3}$ 6. $\frac{3}{4}$ 7. $\frac{7}{8}$ 8. $\frac{1}{3}$ 9. $\frac{2}{3}$ 10. $\frac{4}{5}$ 11. $\frac{5}{7}$ 12. $\frac{7}{36}$

13. $\frac{8}{15}$

Page 353   1. $\frac{1}{9}$ 2. $\frac{3}{4}$ 3. $\frac{2}{5}$ 4. $\frac{9}{32}$ 5. $\frac{9}{16}$ 6. $\frac{3}{4}$ 7. $\frac{2}{9}$ 8. $\frac{2}{5}$ 9. 60%   10. 25%   11. 80%

12. $66\frac{2}{3}$%   13. $16\frac{2}{3}$%   14. $87\frac{1}{2}$%   15. 90%   16. 45%   17. 12%   18. 26%   19. $12\frac{1}{2}$%

20. 20%   21. $8\frac{1}{3}$%   22. 100%   23. 0%   24. 68%

Chapter 17   Squares and Square Roots

Page 364   1. 144   2. 196   3. 64   4. 256   5. 529   6. 49   7. 3136   8. 900   9. 2209
10. 3721   11. 38   12. 28   13. 42   14. 17   15. 73   16. 25   17. 6   18. 18   19. 74
20. 9   21. 67   22. 59   23. 99   24. 101   25. 2   26. 80   27. 124   28. 8   29. 43.2
30. 16.9   31. 27.8   32. 14.0   33. 82.9   34. 93.1   35. 12.5   36. 39.8   37. 55.5
38. 68.3   39. 10.9   40. 50.1   41. 97.2   42. 64.5   43. 80.2   44. 77.8   45. 37.1
46. 45.8   47. 0.80   48. 0.75   49. 0.50   50. 0.70   51. 1.25   52. 1.16   53. 1.50
54. 0.20   55. 0.30   56. 0.44   57. 0.45   58. 3.25   59. 0.12   60. 0.05   61. 1.40
62. 0.72   63. 6   64. 8   65. 0   66. 1.5   67. 6.2   68. $\frac{1}{6}$ 69. $\frac{5}{8}$ 70. 19   71. 12
72. 6   73. 7   74. 4   75. 9   76. 2   77. 27   78. 44   79. 0.68   80. 32   81. 18
82. 132   83. 105   84. 154   85. 126   86. 108   87. 9   88. 24   89. 130   90. 100
91. 12   92. 3   93. 90   94. 15   95. 3   96. 6   97. 80   98. 64   99. 42   100. 30
101. 6   102. 36   103. 40   104. 16   105. 7

Page 366   1. 100   2. 36   3. 64   4. 144   5. 9   6. 49   7. 1   8. 81   9. 16   10. 4   11. 25
12. 400   13. 529   14. 900   15. 961   16. 196   17. 256   18. 121   19. 225
20. 2025

Page 372   1. 4   2. 13   3. 9   4. 0   5. 12.4   6. 21.7   7. 18.1   8. 32.2   9. 49.5   10. 62.4

Page 375   1. 7   2. 6   3. 2   4. 3.125   5. 4.75   6. 13.5   7. 36   8. 8   9. 24   10. 33   11. 15
12. 9.8   13. 11.9   14. 11.6   15. 11.9   16. 11.1   17. 11.5

Page 379   1. 0.50   2. 0.90   3. 2.50   4. 1.20   5. 2.25   6. 0.35   7. 0.40   8. 0.32   9. 12
10. 19   11. 27   12. 90   13. 61   14. 18   15. 37   16. 76   17. 100   18. 6   19. 46
20. 2   21. 70   22. 32   23. 1500   24. 648   25. 100   26. 125   27. 98   28. 117
29. 15   30. 47.6   31. 9   32. 1.8   33. 25   34. 56   35. 20   36. 108   37. 100
38. 13.8   39. 13   40. 8.1

Chapter 18   Integers: Addition/Subtraction

Page 386   1. 57   2. 74   3. 165   4. 138   5. 87   6. 80   7. 110   8. 109   9. 104   10. 155
11. 158   12. 94   13. 146   14. 198   15. 106   16. 208   17. 202   18. 201   19. 2212
20. 1850   21. 1512   22. 1695   23. 2207   24. 1606   25. 406   26. 1349   27. 6658
28. 3110   29. 1096   30. 1983   31. 1162   32. 816   33. 5164   34. 881   35. 918
36. 6048   37. 1399   38. 977   39. 9232   40. 829   41. 1196   42. 6143   43. 812
44. 1505   45. 4616   46. 955   47. 514   48. 3646   49. <   50. >   51. =   52. <
53. <   54. =   55. >   56. <   57. <   58. >   59. <   60. <   61. >   62. >
63. >   64. <   65. <   66. >   67. >   68. <   69. =   70. <   71. >   72. =   73. <
74. >   75. >

Page 390   1. >   2. <   3. >   4. <   5. >   6. =   7. >   8. >   9. <   10. <   11. <   12. >

Page 392   1. 178   2. 409   3. 727   4. 1017   5. 261   6. 353   7. 1392   8. 7491   9. 986
10. 1763   11. 9783

Page 395   1. 86   2. 40   3. 17   4. 23   5. 23   6. 41   7. 28   8. 69   9. 212   10. 615

Page 397   1. 11   2. 2   3. 2   4. 12   5. −9   6. −9   7. 9   8. 10   9. 4   10. 3   11. 3
12. −5   13. −19   14. 10   15. 0   16. 20   17. −80   18. 87

Chapter 19   Integers: Multiplication/Division

Page 404   1. 60   2. 104   3. 66   4. 126   5. 252   6. 213   7. 106   8. 648   9. 512   10. 368
11. 1008   12. 1679   13. 4459   14. 3456   15. 1643   16. 943   17. 3008   18. 1110
19. 1450   20. 1881   21. 1475   22. 5612   23. 3952   24. 2132   25. 583   26. 3182
27. 855   28. 5278   29. 1368   30. 1012   31. 3   32. 16   33. 16   34. 18   35. 21
36. 5   37. 32   38. 16   39. 26   40. 24   41. 126   42. 252   43. 563   44. 468
45. 430   46. 781   47. 642   48. 812   49. 953   50. 523   51. 325   52. 231   53. 369
54. 658   55. 251   56. 624   57. 782   58. 954   59. 349   60. 391   61. 14; 12
62. 22; 23   63. 25; 13   64. 16; 18   65. 19; 21   66. 11; 17   67. $\frac{7}{4}$ 68. $\frac{65}{8}$ 69. $\frac{28}{3}$
70. $\frac{38}{5}$ 71. $\frac{19}{6}$ 72. $\frac{7}{2}$ 73. $\frac{13}{3}$ 74. $\frac{13}{2}$ 75. $\frac{26}{3}$ 76. $\frac{21}{4}$ 77. $\frac{25}{8}$ 78. $\frac{5}{4}$ 79. $\frac{14}{5}$
80. $\frac{23}{3}$ 81. $\frac{39}{4}$ 82. $\frac{53}{8}$ 83. $\frac{11}{2}$ 84. $\frac{17}{6}$ 85. 3   86. −7   87. −3   88. 9   89. −1
90. 5

Page 406   1. 24   2. 54   3. 11   4. 35   5. 40   6. 0   7. 168   8. 135   9. 210   10. 2000

Page 408   1. 72   2. 42   3. 20   4. 96   5. 147   6. 800   7. 95   8. 296   9. 230   10. 276

Page 411   1. 4   2. 8   3. 9   4. 6   5. 81   6. 43   7. 84   8. 93   9. 528   10. 475   11. 13;
12   12. 15; 14   13. 18; 21

Page 412   1. $\frac{11}{5}$ 2. $\frac{17}{3}$ 3. $\frac{79}{9}$ 4. $\frac{19}{6}$ 5. $\frac{21}{2}$ 6. $\frac{23}{12}$ 7. 9   8. −3   9. −1   10. 1   11. 7
12. 5

Chapter 20   Graphing and Equations

Page 420   1. 6   2. 12   3. 43   4. 22   5. 26   6. 28   7. 38   8. 11   9. 49   10. 68   11. 50
12. 31   13. 95   14. 43   15. 54   16. 70   17. 17   18. 19   19. 16   20. 12   21. 12
22. 3   23. 16   24. 32   25. 64   26. 450   27. 256   28. 287   29. 180   30. 204
31. 252   32. 400   33. 2   34. −4   35. −18   36. −9   37. −12   38. −23   39. −3
40. −9   41. −13   42. −24   43. 10   44. −12   45. −5   46. −13   47. −4   48. −7
49. −22   50. 14   51. −6   52. 6   53. 18   54. −48   55. 65   56. −42   57. −64
58. 100   59. −400   60. 60   61. −4   62. 7   63. −6   64. 9   65. 30   66. −7

Page 423   1. 3   2. −7   3. $1\frac{1}{2}$ 4. $6\frac{1}{2}$ 5. −5   6. $\frac{1}{2}$ 7. $-1\frac{1}{2}$

Page 427   1. 8   2. −2   3. 3   4. −3   5. −11   6. −9   7. −4   8. 5   9. −1   10. 8   11. −7
12. −2   13. −6   14. −10   15. 29   16. 17   17. −1   18. 3   19. 7   20. 11
21. −48   22. −75   23. 54   24. 910   25. −216   26. −357   27. 0   28. 2100
29. −3   30. −129   31. 18   32. 12.25   33. 4 units to the right; 6 units up   34. 3 units
to the left; 2 units up   35. 1 unit to the left; 6 units down   36. 5 units to the right; 4 units
down   37. 7 units to the left; 5 units up

Page 429   1. 4   2. −6   3. −4   4. 3   5. 0   6. 0   7. −4   8. 7   9. 2   10. −2   11. 15
12. 11   13. 5   14. 24   15. 21   16. 30   17. 37   18. 50   19. 61   20. 14   21. 37
22. 139

Page 431   1. −32   2. −105   3. 6   4. 80   5. 126   6. 180   7. −765   8. −132   9. 0   10. 0
11. −4   12. −15   13. 6   14. 24   15. −13   16. −25   17. 0   18. 50   19. −36

20. 20. −12 21. 4 22. −10 23. 5 24. 4 25. 20 26. 30 27. 90 28. 26
29. 588 30. 270

Page 433 1. −6 2. −1 3. −9 4. −12 5. −6 6. −32 7. 13 8. 14 9. −27 10. 8
11. −18 12. −162 13. −96 14. −160 15. 8 16. 18 17. 84 18. 336 19. 0
20. 0 21. −8 22. −8 23. −40 24. −63 25. 2 26. 4 27. 0 28. −5 29. −8
30. −44 31. −2 32. 0 33. −4 34. −3 35. 12 36. 4 37. −15 38. −8
39. 100 40. 180

GLOSSARY

The following definitions and statements reflect the usage of terms in this textbook.

Acute angle An angle whose measure is less than 90°. (Page 228)

Acute triangle A triangle with three acute angles. (Page 229)

Angle Two rays with the same endpoint. (Page 228)

Area The measure in square units of the amount of surface inside a closed, plane figure. (Page 143)

Average, or **mean**

$$average = \frac{\text{sum of measures}}{\text{number of measures}} \quad \text{(Page 52)}$$

Axis (Plural: axes) A horizontal or vertical number line used to locate points. (Page 76)

Bar graph A *bar graph* uses horizontal or vertical bars to show data. (Page 74)

Celsius scale A scale used to measure temperature. On this scale, the freezing point of water is 0°C and the boiling point is 100°C. (Page 160)

Circle A closed curve in a plane. (Page 226)

Circle graph A graph in the shape of a circle used to show data. The graph uses per cents to show parts of a whole. (Page 340)

Circumference The distance around a circle.
$C = 2 \times \pi \times r$ or $C = \pi \times d$ (Page 226)

Commission An amount, usually a per cent of goods sold, given to a salesperson, real estate agent, and so on, for services. (Page 286)

Cone A space figure such as the one shown below. (Page 236)

Cone

Coordinate plane The surface formed by two number lines which intersect at 0. The horizontal number line is called the *x axis* and the vertical line is called the *y axis*. (See axis) (Page 422)

Cubic centimeter The capacity of this container is 1 *cubic centimeter* (abbreviated: 1 cm³). (Page 164)

Customary measures The system of measurement commonly used in the United States. (Page 196)

Cylinder A space figure such as the one shown on page 233.

Decimal Numbers such as 7.8, 0.03, and 12.0 that are written using a decimal point and place value. (Page 90)

Degree A measure used to describe the size of an angle such as 30°, 90°, and so on. (Page 228)

Denominator In the fraction $\frac{3}{5}$, the *denominator* is 5. (Page 178)

Diameter A line segment through the center of a circle having its endpoints on the circle. (Page 226)

Discount An amount subtracted from the regular (list) price to obtain the sale price or a per cent of the regular price. (Page 207)

Divisible One number is *divisible* by a second number if the second number divides exactly into the first with no remainder. (Page 48)

Equation A mathematical statement that uses "=", such as $x + 6 = 9$. (Page 248)

Equivalent fractions Equal fractions such as $\frac{2}{3}$ and $\frac{4}{6}$. (Page 189)

Equivalent ratios Equal ratios such as $\frac{3}{4}$ and $\frac{12}{16}$. (Page 260)

Estimation The process of calculating with rounded numbers. (Page 17)

Factor In multiplication, the numbers that are multiplied, such as 8 in $8 \times 5 = 40$. (Page 36)

Formula A rule stated in words or in symbols that can be used in solving problems. (Page 140)

Fraction The quotient of two whole numbers written in the form, $\frac{1}{3}, \frac{5}{6}, \frac{12}{7}$, and so on. The denominators cannot be zero. (Page 178)

Gram A commonly used unit of mass in the metric system. *One gram* equals 0.001 kilogram. (Page 158)

Greater than An inequality relation (symbol: $>$) between two numbers, such as $47 > 45$, $1.1 > 0$, $\frac{3}{4} > \frac{1}{2}$. (Page 9)

Histogram A bar graph that lists data by intervals. (Page 338)

Hypotenuse The side opposite the right angle in a right triangle. (Page 371)

Integer The whole numbers and their opposites, such as -162, -51, 0, 36, 210, and so on. (Page 390)

Interest An amount paid for the use of money. *Interest* is usually a per cent of the amount invested, lent, or borrowed. (Page 288)

Kilogram The base unit of mass in the metric system. (Page 158)

Kilowatt-hour A measure of electricity used. *One kilowatt-hour* is 1000 watts of electricity used for 1 hour. (Page 34)

Latitude Unit used to describe the distance in degrees north (N) or south (S) of the equator. (Page 424)

Least Common Denominator (LCD) The smallest denominator exactly divisible by each of two or more denominators. For example, the LCD of $\frac{3}{5}$ and $\frac{5}{6}$ is 30. (Page 188)

Less than An inequality relation (symbol: $<$) between two numbers, such as $6 < 10$, $7.06 < 7.1$; $\frac{7}{10} < \frac{5}{6}$. (Page 91)

Like fractions Fractions having the same denominator, such as $\frac{1}{6}$ and $\frac{5}{6}$. (Page 186)

Liter The base unit of capacity in the metric system. (Page 156)

Line graph A graph that shows the amount of change over a period of time. (Page 76)

Longitude Unit used to describe the distance in degrees east (E) or west (W) of the equator. (Page 424)

Lowest terms A fraction is in *lowest terms* when its numerator and denominator have no common factors other than 1. (Page 182)

Mass The amount of matter an object contains. (Page 158)

Mean Another name for *average*. The *mean* of 2, 5, 6, and 7 is $2 + 5 + 6 + 7 \div 4$, or 5. (Page 330)

Median When a series of numbers are listed in order, the middle number is the *median*. The median of 1.6, 2.9, 3.4, 7.8 and 12.2 is 3.4. (Page 332)

Meter The base unit of length in the metric system. (Page 134)

Milligram A unit of mass in the metric system. *One milligram* equals 0.001 gram. (Page 158)

Milliliter A unit of capacity in the metric system. *One milliliter* equals 0.001 liter. (Page 156)

Millimeter A unit of length in the metric system. *One millimeter* equals 0.001 meter. (Page 134)

Mixed number A number such as $4\frac{2}{3}$, $5\frac{3}{8}$, and so on. (Page 178)

Mode In a series of numbers, the number that occurs most often. (Page 330)

Negative number A number less than zero, such as -19, -100, -238, and so on. (Page 388)

Numerator In the fraction $\frac{9}{10}$, 9 is the *numerator*. (Page 178)

Obtuse angle An angle whose measure is greater than $90°$. (Page 228)

Obtuse triangle A triangle with an obtuse angle. (Page 229)

Ordered pair Two numbers used in a certain order, such as (2, 1). (Page 422)

Order of operations When more than one operation $(+, -, \times, \div)$ is involved, the order in which the operations are performed. (Page 62)

Origin The point (0, 0) in the coordinate plane at which the *x axis* and the *y axis* intersect. (Page 422)

Parallelogram A four-sided polygon whose opposite sides are parallel. (Page 145)

Per cent *Per cent* means per hundred or hundredths. $\frac{7}{100} = 0.07 = 7\%$ (Page 274)

Perimeter The sum of the lengths of the sides of a polygon, such as a rectangle. (Page 140)

π (pi) The ratio of the circumference of a circle to its diameter. The ratio is approximately equal to 3.14. (Page 226)

Pictograph   A graph that uses pictures or symbols to represent data. (Page 72)

Positive number   A number greater than zero, such as 19, 57, 12, 608, and so on. (Page 388)

Probability   A number from 0 to 1 which tells how likely it is that an event will happen. (Page 348)

Proportion   An equation which states that two ratios are equal. (Page 264)

Pyramid   A space figure with one base. The sides of a *pyramid* are triangles. (Page 167)

Quotient   In a division problem such as $102 \div 6 = 17$, the *quotient* is 17. (Page 48)

Radius   A line segment having one end at the center of the circle and the other on the circle. (Page 226)

Ratio   A comparison of two numbers expressed as 2 to 5, or $\frac{2}{5}$, or 2:5. (Page 260)

Rational number   A number which can be written as a fraction. (Page 412)

Reciprocal   Two numbers whose product is 1 are *reciprocals* of each other. Thus, $\frac{3}{4}$ and $\frac{4}{3}$ are *reciprocals*, because $\frac{3}{4} \times \frac{4}{3} = 1$. (Page 212)

Rectangle   A four-sided polygon whose opposite sides are equal and whose angles are right angles. (Page 143)

Rectangular prism   A space figure having two equal rectangles as bases. The bases are parallel. (Page 162)

Right angle   An angle whose measure is 90°. (Page 228)

Right triangle   A triangle having one right angle. (Page 229)

Rule of Pythagoras   In a right triangle, $(\text{hypotenuse})^2 = (\text{leg})^2 + (\text{leg})^2$, or
$$c^2 = a^2 + b^2. \quad \text{(Page 371)}$$

Similar triangles   Triangles that have the same shape. (Page 374)

Sphere   A round space figure shaped like a basketball. (Page 238)

Square   A rectangle with four equal sides. (Page 143)

Square of a number   The product of a number and itself. (Page 366)

Square root   One of two equal factors of a number. The symbol for square root is $\sqrt{}$. (Page 366)

Tangent ratio

$\text{Tangent of angle A} = \dfrac{\text{length of side opposite angle A}}{\text{length of side adjacent to angle A}}$
(Page 378)

Trapezoid   A four-sided polygon with one pair of parallel sides. (Page 147)

Triangle   A polygon with three sides. (Page 145)

Volume   The measure of the amount of space inside a space figure. (Page 164)

Whole number   A number such as 0, 1, 2, 3, 4, and so on. (Page 10)

X coordinate   The first number in an ordered pair. (Page 422)

Y coordinate   The second number in an ordered pair. (Page 422)

INDEX

Boldfaced numerals indicate the pages that contain formal or informal definitions.

Addition
  of decimals, 94-95, 132, 246, 249, 272, 289
  of fractions, 186-187, 190-191, 246, 249, 351
  of integers, 392-395, 397, 420, 427, 429, 433
  of mixed numbers, 186-187, 191, 198-199, 200-201
  of whole numbers, 2-3, 6-7, 24, 33, 132, 140, 176, 186, 246, 249, 328, 331, 386, 392, 395
Angle(s)
  acute, **228**
  measuring, 228-229, 328, 341
  right, **228**
  obtuse, **228**
Algebra (See Pre-Algebra)
Applications (see Problem Solving and Applications)
  addition and subtraction of fractions, 187
  from per cents to decimals, 277
  from per cents to fractions, 279
  from words to per cents, 275
  moving the decimal point, 103
  using addition of integers, 393, 395
  using decimals, 95
  using division, 111, 123
  using estimation, 18, 65, 126-127
  using fractions, 179, 183, 187, 213
  using integers, 389, 391
  using mixed numbers, 209, 215
  using multiplication, 27
  using multiplication of fractions and mixed numbers, 206-207
  using multiplication with integers, 407
  using per cents, 283, 307
  using per cent of increase or decrease, 304
  using probability, 351
  using proportions, 265
  using ratios, 261
  using rounding, 121

  using squares of numbers, 367
  using subtraction, 11
  using the rules for divisibility, 49
  using the Table of Squares and Square Roots, 370
  using units of capacity, 157
  using units of mass, 159
  using volume, 165, 168, 237
Area
  of a circle, **230**-231, 232
  of a parallelogram, **145**-146
  of a rectangle, **143**-144
  of a square, **143**-144
  of a trapezoid, **147**-148
  of a triangle, **145**-146
  surface area
    cylinder, 235
    rectangular prism, 162-163, 172
Automobile Maintenance, 399
Automobile Repair, 41
Average, **52**

Banking, 56, 290
Bar graphs, **74**
Batting average, **254**
Business, 216, 334, 415
Buying a New Car, 8

Calculator Exercises
  average yearly temperature, **161**
  checking addition/subtraction, 11
  checking answers, 99
  checking division, 411
  checking multiplication, 37, 409
  estimation and subtraction, 19
  finding averages, 65
  finding discount, 293
  finding square roots, 377
  multiplying fractions, 219
  order of operations, 63, 127
  per cent of increase, 313
  surface area, 235
  volume of a sphere, 238
  writing per cents, 281
Cans and Cylinders, 235
Carpet Installer, 181

Career(s)
  Automobile Maintenance, 399
  Automobile Repair, 41
  Banking, 56, 290
  Business, 216, 334, 415
  Carpet Installer, 181
  Construction, 217
  Design, 232
  Drafting Technician, 267
  Food Services, 5
  Government Service, 80
  Health, 309
  Industry, 138
  Insurance, 119
  Office Worker, 57
  Photography, 263
  Quality Control, 352
  Retailing, 101
  Traffic Officer, 377
  Transportation, 185
  Travel Planning, 425
  Weather Forecasting, 161
Celsius scale, **160**
Chances and Choices, 355
Circle(s)
  area of, **230**-231, 232
  circumference, **226**-227
Commission, **286**-287
Comparison
  of decimals, **90**-91, 176, 328, 336, 386, 390
  of fractions, **178**-179
  of integers, **390**-391
  of rational numbers, **413**
Comparison Shopping, 124
Compound Interest, **288**-289
Cone(s)
  volume of, **236**-237
Conserving Energy, 414
Construction, 217
Cost of Credit, **100**
Cost of Electricity, 34
Customary measures, 85, 95-96, 111, 123, 129, 130, 142-148, 151, 152, 157, 159, 165, 166, 168, 170, 171, 180, 187, 196-201, 209, 213, 215, 221-222, 235, 237-241, 267-270, 313, 391, 399, 401, 428

Cylinder(s)
    volume of, **233**-234

Decimals
    addition, 94, 95, 132, 246,
        249, 272, 289
    as a fraction, 280-281, 298
    comparing, 90, 91
    division of, 111, 113, 117,
        123, 246, 252, 272, 298,
        306
    multiplication of, 98, 99, 224,
        226, 230, 236, 246, 272,
        283, 288, 298, 311
    place value, 90, 91, 272
    rounding, 120-121, 218-219,
        227, 230, 233, 272, 289,
        292, 298, 304, 328, 341,
        364, 372, 375, 379
    subtraction, 94, 95, 246, 249
Design, 232
Diameter, **226**
Discount, 207, 284, 293
Distance, 114-115, 135, 139, 210
Divisibility rules for, 48
Division,
    of decimals, 111, 113, 117,
        123, 246, 252, 272, 298
    of decimals with remainders,
        123
    of fractions, 212-213, 278
    of integers, 410-411, 420, 427,
        431, 434
    of mixed numbers, 214-215
Drafting Technician, 267
Driving Range, 255

Energy Costs, 313
Energy Efficiency Ratio, **262**
Equation(s)
    graphing, 426-428
    solving, **248**-257, 264, 301,
        307, 315, 364, 372, 375,
        379, 420, 429-434
    solving by addition, 248-249,
        256-257, 429-430
    solving by division, 252-253,
        264, 301, 307, 315, 375,
        431-432
    solving by multiplication,
        252-253, 307, 431-432
    solving by subtraction, 248-249,
        256-257, 429-430
Estimation (see Rounding and
    Estimation)

Fahrenheit scale, 85, 313,
    391, 399, 401, 428
Finance Charges, **56**
Floor Space, 149
Food Services, 5
Formula(s)
    for area of a circle, **230**
    for area of a parallelogram, **145**
    for area of a rectangle, **143**
    for area of a square, **143**
    for area of a trapezoid, **147**
    for area of a triangle, **145**
    for circumference, **226**
    for commission, **286**
    for compound interest, **288**
    for diameter, **226**
    for discount, **284**
    for distance, **114**, 210
    for finding interest, **288**
    for interest rate, **302**
    for mark-up, **308**
    for mean, **330**
    for median, **332**
    for mode, **330**
    for per cent of decrease, **303**
    for per cent of increase, **303**
    for volume of a pyramid, **167**
    for selling price, **284**
    for surface area of a cylinder,
        235
    for surface area of a rectangular
        prism, **162**
    for volume of a cone, **236**
    for volume of a cylinder, **233**
    for volume of a rectangular
        prism, **164**
    for volume of a sphere, **238**
    Rule of Pythagoras, **371**, 372-
        373
Fraction(s)
    addition, 186-187, 190-191,
        246, 249, 346, 351
    as a decimal, 274-275, 280-281,
        298, 315, 364, 379
    as a per cent, 274-275, 280-281,
        298, 301, 304, 307, 315,
        346, 348
    as a ratio, 260-261, 274-275
    definition, **178**
    division of, 212-213, 246, 272,
        278
    equivalent, **183**, 188-189, 194
    in lowest terms, 182-183, 186,
        191, 194, 202, 205, 208,
        212, 246, 260, 272, 278,

298, 304, 346, 348, 351,
    353
    least common denominator,
        188-189, 194, 195
    multiplication of, 204-205,
        208-209, 212, 214, 224,
        227, 236, 246, 272, 278,
        283, 288, 291
    reciprocal(s), **212**, 214
    rounding, 218-219, 230,
        233, 236
    subtraction, 186-187, 190-191,
        194-195, 246, 249
Fuel costs for a Car, 61
Fuel Economy, **60**

Government Service, 80
Graphing
    equations, 426-428
    ordered pairs, **422**-423,
        427
Graphs
    bar graph, **75**, 328, 339
    circle graph, **340**-341
    histogram, **338**-339
    line graph, **77**
    pictograph, **73**
Gross Pay and Net Pay, **38**

Health, 309
Heating Costs, 118
Hidden question, 30-31, 34-35,
    38-39, 44, 56, 57, 61, 67, 68,
    100, 118, 119, 166, 192, 207,
    211, 217, 284, 286-287
Histogram, **338**-339

Inequalities, (see Comparison
    also.) 90-91, 176, 178, 179,
    328, 333, 336, 386, 390
Insurance, 119
Interest, **288**-289, 302
Integer(s)
    addition of, 392-393, 394-395,
        397, 420, 427, 429, 433
    comparison of, 390-391
    definition of, **388**
    division of, 410-411, 420, 427,
        431, 434
    multiplication of, 406-409,
        420, 427, 431, 434
    negative, **388**-389
    on a number line, 388-389,
        397, 404, 413
    opposite, **390**-391, 397

positive, **388**-389
subtraction of, 396-397, 420, 427

Latitude, 424
Line graph, **76**
Listing data, 336-337
Longitude, **424**

Making Change, 4, 97
Markup and Selling Price, **308**
Mean, **330**-331
Measurement
  customary (see Customary Measures.)
  in the metric system, 134-137
  of angles, 228-229, 328, 341
Median, **332**-333
Message Units, **30**
Metric measures
  of capacity, **156**-157
  of length, **134**-137
  of mass, **158**-159
Minimum wage, 317
Mixed number(s)
  addition, 186-187, 191, 198-199, 200-201
  as a fraction, 208-209, 412
  definition, **178**
  division of, 214-215
  multiplication of, 204-205, 208-209, 224, 227
  rounding, 218-219, 230
  subtraction of, 186-187, 191, 194-195, 198-199, 200-201
  writing a fraction for, 208-209, 214, 224, 226, 230, 272, 404
Mode, **330**-331
Mortgage Loan, **251**
Multiplication
  of decimals, 39, 98, 99, 143, 154, 156, 158, 164, 224, 226, 230, 236, 246, 252, 272, 283, 288, 298, 311
  of fractions, 204-205, 208-209, 212, 214, 224, 227, 230, 236, 272, 278, 283, 288, 291
  of integers, 406-409, 420, 427, 431, 434
  of mixed numbers, 208-209, 224, 227, 230
  of whole numbers, 24-27, 32-33, 36-39, 40, 72, 102-103, 108, 110, 113, 143, 154, 156, 158, 164, 176,

189, 190, 202, 246, 252, 260, 364, 366, 404, 406, 408

Net pay, 38, 250
Net price, **207**
Numbers
  negative, **388**, 406, 412
  positive, **388**, 406, 412
  rational, **412**
  whole numbers, 2-7, 24-27, 32-33, 36-40, 50, 51, 54-55, 102-103

Office Worker, 57
Ordered pair, **422**-423
Order of operations, **62**, 63, 132, 146, 147, 154, 162, 164, 167
Ordering by Mail, 28
Overtime pay, **258**

Per cent
  as a decimal, 276-277, 283, 288, 306, 311, 328, 341
  as a fraction, 278-279, 298, 311
  definition, **274**
  solving, 282-283, 300-301, 306-307, 310-312, 314-316
  word problems, 314-316
Perimeter
  of a rectangle, **140**-142
  of a square, **140**-142
Pi, **226**
Pictograph, **72**
Place value, 90, 91, 108, 272, 274
Pre-Algebra, 366-438
Prism, 167-168, 172, 224
Probability, **348**-361
Problem Solving and Applications
  area, 143, 145, 147
  average, **52**
  bar graph, 74
  Batting Average, **254**
  Buying a New Car, 8
  Cans and Cylinders, 235
  Chances and Choices, 355
  Commission, 286-287
  Comparison Shopping, 124
  Conserving Energy, 414
  Cost of Credit, 100
  Cost of Electricity, 34
  Customary Measures, 180, 196
  Discount, 207, 284
  Distance, 139

Distance Formula, 210
Distance on a Map, 135
Driving Range, 255
Energy Costs, 313
Energy Efficiency Ratio, 262
Finance Charge, 56
Floor Space, 149
Fuel Costs for a Car, 61
Fuel Economy, 60
Gross Pay and Net Pay, 38, 250
Heating Costs, 118
hidden question (See Hidden question)
histogram, 338-339
interest rate, 302
Industry, 138
Latitude and Longitude, 424
line graph, 76
Making Change, 4, 97
Markup and Selling Price, 308
mean, 330-331
Measuring Angles, 228
median, 332-333
Message Units, 30
minimum wage, 317
mode, 330-331
Mortgage Loans, 251
Ordering by Mail, 28
Overtime Pay, 258
per cent, 283, 304
perimeter, 140-142
pictograph, 72
proportion, 265
rate, 114
ratio, 261
Reading a Meter, 16
Renting a Car, 259
right triangle rule, 371
Sales Tax, 96
Scale Drawings, 266
Science, 206
similar triangle, 374-375, 376
Sphere, 238
Sports, 305
tangent ratio, 378-380
temperature, 160-161
Time Card(s), 192
Time Zones, 12
tolerance, **138**
Train Schedule, 184
two or more steps (see Two (or more) -step problem.)
using the hidden question, 30-31, 34-35, 38-39, 44, 56, 57, 61, 67, 68, 100, 118,

119, 166, 192, 207, 211, 217, 284, 286
Volume/Capacity/Mass, 166
Wallpapering and Estimation, 211
Word problems (See Problem Solving and Applications.)
Wind Chill, **398**
Writing Checks, 92
Proportion(s)
  definition, **264**
  solving, 264-265, 298, 364, 375
Protractor, 228
Pyramid(s), 167-168, 172
Pythagorean Theorem, **371**-373

Quality Control, 352

Radius, 226
Rate, **114**
Ratio(s)
  definition, **260**
  equivalent, **260**-261
  writing as a fraction, 260-261, 272, 274, 346, 348
Rational number(s)
  comparison of, 413, 423
  definition, **412**
Reading a Meter, 16
Reciprocal(s)
  of a fraction, **212**, 214
  of a mixed number, **214**
Renting a Car, 259
Retailing, **101**
Right Triangle Rule, **371**
Rounding and estimation
  of decimals, 120-122, 126, 132, 136, 224, 227, 230, 233, 236, 272, 292, 298, 304, 328, 341, 364, 372, 375
  of fractions and mixed numbers, 218-219, 224, 227, 230, 233, 236
  of per cents, 291-292
  of whole numbers, 17, 18, 19, 64, 74, 78, 108, 120, 121, 132, 136

Sales Tax, 96
Scale Drawings, 266
Science, 206
Selling Price, 284-285
Semicircle, **228**
Sphere, **238**
Sports, 305
Squares
  using a table, 368-370
Square root, **366**-367
  using a table, 368-370
Statistics, 72-85, 330-345
Subtraction
  of decimals, 94, 95, 246, 249
  of fractions, 186-187, 190-191, 194-195, 246, 249
  of integers, 396-397, 420, 427
  of mixed numbers, 186-187, 191, 194-195, 198, 200-201
  of whole numbers, 10, 11, 14, 15, 76, 176, 186, 246, 249, 298, 303
Surface area
  cylinder, 235
  rectangular prism, 162-163, 172

Table of Squares and Square Roots, 369
Tables of Measurement, 451
Tangent ratio, 378-380
Temperature, 160-161
Time Cards, 192
Time Zones, 12
Traffic Officer, 377
Train Schedules, 184
Transportation, 185
Travel Planning, 425
Tree diagram, 353-354
Triangle
  right, **371**
  similar, **374**-375, 376
Two (or more) -step problems, 28-29, 31, 35, 39, 41, 43, 44, 52-53, 56, 61, 67, 68, 96, 97, 100-101, 105, 106, 138, 184, 192-193, 207, 211, 217, 221-222, 284, 286, 290

Unit Price, 124

Volume
  of a cone, **236**-237
  of a cylinder, **233**, 234
  of a rectangular prism, **164**-165, 172, 224, 233
  of a sphere, 238
Volume/Capacity/Mass, 166

Wallpapering and Estimation, 211
Weather Forecasting, 161
Whole number(s)
  addition of, 2-7, 24, 33, 132, 140, 176, 186, 246, 249, 328, 331, 386, 392, 395
  division of, 46, 50-51, 54-55, 59, 246, 252, 264, 311, 328, 331, 404, 411
  estimating with, 17, 18, 19, 64
  multiplication of, 24-27, 32-33, 36-40, 72, 102-103, 108, 110, 113, 143, 154, 156, 158, 164, 176, 189, 190, 202, 246, 252, 260, 364, 366, 404, 406, 408
  rounding, 17, 18, 19, 64
  subtraction of, 10-11, 14-15, 246, 249, 298, 303
Wind Chill, **398**
Word Problems (See Problem Solving and Applications)
Writing Checks, 92

X axis, 422
X coordinate, **422**

Y axis, 422
Y coordinate, **422**

Zero(s)
  in division, 116, 128, 130
  in multiplication, 36-37, 43, 44
  in a quotient, 58-59, 66, 68

CAREERS

Food Services	5	Design	232
Automobile Repair	41	Photography	263
Office Worker	57	Drafting	267
Government Service	80	Banking	290
Retailing	101	Health	309
Insurance	119	Business	334
Industry	138	Quality Control	352
Weather Forecasting	161	Traffic Officer	377
Carpet Installer	181	Automobile Maintenance	399
Transportation	185	Business	415
Business	216	Travel Planning	425
Construction	217		

APPLICATIONS

Making Change	4	Science	206
Buying a New Car	8	Discount	207
Time Zones	12	Distance Formula	210
Reading a Meter	16	Wallpapering and Estimation	211
Ordering by Mail	28	Measuring Angles	228
Message Units	30	Cans and Cylinders	235
Cost of Electricity	34	Spheres	238
Gross Pay and Net Pay	38	Net Pay	250
Averages	52	Mortgage Loans	251
Finance Charges	56	Batting Average	254
Fuel Economy	60	Driving Range	255
Fuel Costs for a Car	61	Overtime Pay	258
Writing Checks	92	Renting a Car	259
Sales Tax	96	Energy Efficient Ratio	262
Making Change	97	Scale Drawings	266
Cost of Credit	100	Discount	284
Rate	114	Commission	286
Heating Costs	118	Interest Rate	302
Comparison Shopping	124	Sports	305
Distance on a Map	135	Markup and Selling Price	308
Distance	139	Energy Costs	313
Floor Space	149	Minimum Wage	317
Volume/Capacity/Mass	166	Chances and Choices	355
Using Customary Measures	180	Wind Chill	398
Train Schedules	184	Conserving Energy	414
Time Cards	192	Latitude and Longitude	424
Customary Measures	196		